ACCA

STUDY TEXT

Paper 1.2

Financial Information for Management

IN THIS JUNE 2004 EDITION

- Targeted to the syllabus and study guide
- Quizzes and questions to check your understanding
- Clear layout and style designed to save you time
- Plenty of exam-style questions with detailed guidance from BPP
- Chapter Roundups and summaries to help revision

FOR EXAMS IN DECEMBER 2004 AND JUNE 2005

BPP Professional Education
June 2004

First edition February 2001
Fourth edition June 2004

ISBN 0 7517 1661 8 (previous ISBN 0 7517 1151 9)

British Library Cataloguing-in-Publication Data
A catalogue record for this book
is available from the British Library

Published by

BPP Professional Education
Aldine House, Aldine Place
London W12 8AW

www.bpp.com

Printed in Great Britain by W M Print
45-47 Frederick Street
Walsall, West Midlands
WS2 9NE

We are grateful to the Association of Chartered Certified Accountants for permission to reproduce past examination questions and questions from the pilot paper. The answers have been prepared by BPP Professional Education.

Page

THE BPP STUDY TEXT

Aims of this Study Text

To provide you with the knowledge and understanding, skills and application techniques that you need if you are to be successful in your exams

This Study Text has been written around the **Financial Information for Management** syllabus.

- It is **comprehensive**. It covers the syllabus content. No more, no less.
- It is written at the **right level**. Each chapter is written with the ACCA's **study guide** in mind.
- It is targeted to the **exam**. We have taken account of the **pilot paper and all sittings so far**, questions put to the examiners at ACCA conferences and the assessment methodology.

To allow you to study in the way that best suits your learning style and the time you have available, by following your personal Study Plan (see page (vii))

You may be studying at home on your own until the date of the exam, or you may be attending a full-time course. You may like to (and have time to) read every word, or you may prefer to (or only have time to) skim-read and devote the remainder of your time to question practice. Wherever you fall in the spectrum, you will find the BPP Study Text meets your needs in designing and following your personal Study Plan.

To tie in with the other components of the BPP Effective Study Package to ensure you have the best possible chance of passing the exam (see page (v))

Recommended period of use	Elements of the BPP Effective Study Package
From the outset and throughout	**Learning to Learn Accountancy** Read this invaluable book as you begin your studies and refer to it as you work through the various elements of the BPP Effective Study Package. It will help you to acquire knowledge, practise and revise, efficiently and effectively.
Three to twelve months before the exam	**Study Text and i-Learn** Use the Study Text to acquire knowledge, understanding, skills and the ability to apply techniques. Use BPP's **i-Learn** product to reinforce your learning.
Throughout	**Big Picture Posters** Display these where you're studying and give yourself a feel for the overall shape of the paper and the connections between syllabus areas. Examiners have stressed that you will need to be able to link up different areas when you take the exam. The visual stimulation the posters provide will help you remember the key areas of the syllabus.
Throughout	**Virtual Campus** Study, practise, revise and take advantage of other useful resources with BPP's fully interactive e-learning site with comprehensive tutor support.
Throughout	**i-Pass** **i-Pass**, our computer-based testing package, provides objective test questions in a variety of formats and is ideal for self-assessment.
One to six months before the exam	**Practice & Revision Kit** Try the numerous examination-format questions, for which there are realistic suggested solutions prepared by BPP's own authors. Then attempt the two mock exams.
From three months before the exam until the last minute	**Passcards** Work through these short, memorable notes which are focused on what is most likely to come up in the exam you will be sitting.
One to six months before the exam	**Success Tapes and CDs** The tapes and CDs cover the vital elements of your syllabus in less than 90 minutes per subject. They also contains exam hints to help you fine tune your strategy.

HELP YOURSELF STUDY FOR YOUR ACCA EXAMS

Exams for professional bodies such as ACCA are very different from those you have taken at college or university. You will be under **greater time pressure before** the exam – as you may be combining your study with work as well as in the exam room. There are many different ways of learning and so the BPP Study Text offers you a number of different tools to help you through. Here are some hints and tips: they are not plucked out of the air, but **based on research and experience.** (You don't need to know that long-term memory is in the same part of the brain as emotions and feelings – but it's a fact anyway.)

The right approach

1 **The right attitude**

Believe in yourself	Yes, there is a lot to learn. Yes, it is a challenge. But thousands have succeeded before and you can too.
Remember why you're doing it	Studying might seem a grind at times, but you are doing it for a reason: to advance your career.

2 **The right focus**

Read through the Syllabus and Study guide	These tell you what you are expected to know and are supplemented by exam focus points in the text.
Study the Exam Paper section	Past papers are likely to be a reasonable guide of what you should expect in the exam.

3 **The right method**

The whole picture	You need to grasp the detail – but keeping in mind how everything fits into the big picture will help you understand better. • The **Introduction** of each chapter puts the material in context. • The **Syllabus content, Study guide** and **Exam focus points** show you what you need to **grasp.** • BPP's Big Picture Posters will help you see the links here.
In your own words	To absorb the information (and to practise your written communication skills), it helps **put it into your own words.** • **Take notes.** • Answer the **questions** in each chapter. As well as helping you absorb the information you will practise your written communication skills, which become increasingly important as you progress through your ACCA exams. • Draw **mind maps**. We have an example for the whole syllabus. • Try 'teaching' to a colleague or friend.

Give yourself cues to jog your memory	The BPP Study Text uses **bold text** to **highlight key points** and **icons** to identify key features, such as **Exam focus points** and **Key terms.** • Try **colour coding** with a highlighter pen. • Write **key points** on cards.

4 **The right review**

Review, review, review	It is a **fact** that regularly reviewing a topic in summary form can **fix it in your memory**. Because **review** is so important, the BPP Study Text helps you to do so in many ways. • **Chapter roundups** summarise the key points in each chapter. Use them to recap each study session. • The **Quick quiz** is another review technique to ensure that you have grasped the essentials. • Use the **Key term** index as a quiz. • Go through the **Examples** in each chapter a second or third time.

Developing your personal Study Plan

One thing that the BPP Learning to Learn Accountancy book emphasises (see page (iv)) is the need to prepare (and use) a study plan. Planning and sticking to the plan are key elements of learning success.

There are four steps you should work through.

Step 1. How do you learn?

First you need to be aware of your style of learning. The BPP Learning to Learn Accountancy book commits a chapter to this **self-discovery**. What types of intelligence do you display when learning? You might be advised to brush up on certain study skills before launching into this Study Text.

> BPP's **Learning to Learn Accountancy** book helps you to identify what intelligences you show more strongly and then details how you can tailor your study process to your preferences. It also includes handy hints on how to develop intelligences you exhibit less strongly, but which might be needed as you study accountancy.

Are you a **theorist** or are you more **practical**? If you would rather get to grips with a theory before trying to apply it in practice, you should follow the study sequence on page (x). If the reverse is true (you need to know why you are learning theory before you do so), you might be advised to flick through Study Text chapters and look at questions, case studies and examples (Steps 7, 8 and 9 in the **suggested study sequence**) before reading through the detailed theory.

Step 2. How much time do you have?

Work out the time you have available per week, given the following.

- The standard you have set yourself
- The time you need to set aside later for work on the Practice & Revision Kit and Passcards
- The other exam(s) you are sitting
- Very importantly, practical matters such as work, travel, exercise, sleep and social life

		Hours
Note your time available in box A.	A	

Step 3. Allocate your time

• Take the time you have available per week for this Study Text shown in box A, multiply it by the number of weeks available and insert the result in box B.	B	
• Divide the figure in box B by the number of chapters in this text and insert the result in box C.	C	

Remember that this is only a rough guide. Some of the chapters in this book are longer and more complicated than others, and you will find some subjects easier to understand than others.

Step 4. Implement

Set about studying each chapter in the time shown in box C, following the key study steps in the order suggested by your particular learning style.

This is your personal **Study Plan**. You should try and combine it with the study sequence outlined below. You may want to modify the sequence a little (as has been suggested above) to adapt it to your **personal style**.

BPP's *Learning to Learn Accountancy* gives further guidance in developing a study plan and deciding when and where to study.

Suggested study sequence

Tackle the chapters in the order you find them in the Study Text. Taking into account your individual learning style, you could follow this sequence.

Key study steps	Activity
Step 1 **Topic list**	Each numbered topic is a numbered section in the chapter.
Step 2 **Introduction**	This gives you the **big picture** in terms of the **context** of the chapter. The content is referenced to the **Study Guide**, and **Exam Guidance** shows how the topic is likely to be examined. In other words, it sets your **objectives for study.**
Step 3 **Knowledge brought forward boxes**	In these we highlight information and techniques that it is assumed you have 'brought forward' with you from your earlier studies. If there are topics which have changed recently due to legislation for example, these topics are explained in more detail.
Step 4 **Explanations**	Proceed methodically through the chapter, reading each section thoroughly and making sure you understand.
Step 5 **Key terms and Exam focus points**	• **Key terms** can often earn you *easy marks* if you state them clearly and correctly in an appropriate exam answer (and they are indexed at the back of the text). • **Exam focus points** give you a good idea of how we think the examiner intends to examine certain topics.
Step 6 **Note taking**	Take brief notes if you wish, avoiding the temptation to copy out too much.
Step 7 **Examples**	Follow each through to its solution very carefully.
Step 8 **Case examples**	Study each one, and try to add flesh to them from your own experience – they are designed to show how the topics you are studying come alive (and often come unstuck) in the real world.
Step 9 **Questions**	Make a very good attempt at each one.
Step 10 **Answers**	Check yours against ours, and make sure you understand any discrepancies.
Step 11 **Chapter roundup**	Work through it very carefully, to make sure you have grasped the major points it is highlighting.
Step 12 **Quick quiz**	When you are happy that you have covered the chapter, use the **Quick quiz** to check how much you have remembered of the topics covered.
Step 13 **Question(s) in the Question bank**	Either at this point, or later when you are thinking about revising, make a full attempt at the **Question(s)** suggested at the very end of the chapter. You can find these at the end of the Study Text, along with the **Answers** so you can see how you did. We highlight those that are introductory, and those which are of the standard you would expect to find in an exam.

Short of time: *Skim study technique*?

You may find you simply do not have the time available to follow all the key study steps for each chapter, however you adapt them for your particular learning style. If this is the case, follow the **skim study** technique below (the icons in the Study Text will help you to do this).

- Study the chapters in the order you find them in the Study Text.
- For each chapter:
  - Follow the key study steps 1-3, and then skim-read through step 4. Jump to step 11, and then go back to step 5.
  - Follow through steps 7 and 8, and prepare outline answers to questions (steps 9/10).
  - Try the Quick Quiz (step 12), following up any items you can't answer, then do a plan for the Question (step 13), comparing it against our answers.
  - You should probably still follow step 6 (note-taking), although you may decide simply to rely on the BPP Passcards for this.

Moving on...

However you study, when you are ready to embark on the practice and revision phase of the BPP Effective Study Package, you should still refer back to this Study Text, both as a source of **reference** (you should find the list of key terms and the index particularly helpful for this) and as a **refresher** (the Chapter Roundups and Quick Quizzes help you here).

And remember to keep careful hold of this Study Text – you will find it invaluable in your work.

More advice on Study Skills can be found in the BPP **Learning to Learn Accountancy** book

SYLLABUS

Aim

To develop knowledge and understanding of the application of management accounting techniques to support the management processes of planning, control and decision making.

Objectives

On completion of this paper candidates should be able to:

- explain the role of management accounting within an organisation and the requirement for management information
- describe costs by classification and purpose
- identify appropriate material, labour and expense costs
- understand the principles of costing and apply them in straightforward scenarios
- understand and demonstrate the cost factors affecting production and pricing decisions
- understand the basic principles of performance management
- demonstrate the skills expected in Part 1.

Position of the paper in the overall syllabus

No prior knowledge is required before commencing study for Paper 1.2. Some understanding of the accounting principles and practices from Paper 1.1 Preparing Financial Statements and a basic competence in numeracy are assumed.

This paper provides the basic techniques required to enable the candidate to develop the various methods into more complex problems at later parts. Candidates will, therefore, need a sound understanding of the methods and techniques encountered in this paper to ensure that they can take them further in subsequent papers. The methods introduced in this paper are revisited and extended in Paper 2.4 Financial Management and Control and taken yet further in Papers 3.3 Performance Management and 3.7 Strategic Financial Management.

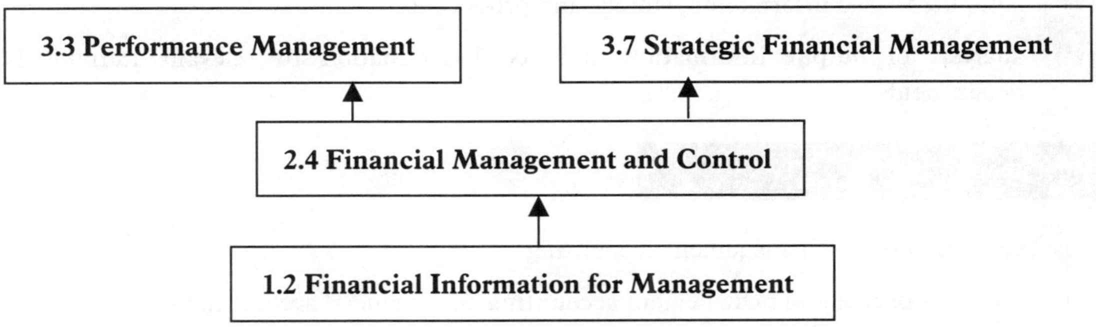

SYLLABUS

1 Accounting for management

(a) The nature, purpose, scope and interrelations of functions carried out by management in relation to resources, costs, operations, performance

- (i) setting objectives (long and short-term, strategic and operational, corporate and personal)
- (ii) planning to meet objectives
- (iii) implementing objectives
- (iv) monitoring and controlling against objectives and plans

(b) Nature of internal reporting

- (i) financial and non-financial information for managers
- (ii) cost centres, revenue centres, profit centres and investment centres and the impact of these on management information

(c) Management information requirements

- (i) importance and definition of good information
- (ii) presentation of information
- (iii) role of accountants and accounting information
- (iv) role of IT

(d) Maintaining and improving an appropriate system

- (i) cost units
- (ii) cost/profit/responsibility centres
- (iii) methods for recording relevant information
- (iv) sources of information and recording/processing information
- (v) computer based information, storage and processing
- (vi) analysis of output information and its dissemination to relevant individuals/ departments

2 Cost accounting

(a) Cost accounting versus management accounting

- (i) purposes of cost and management accounting and financial accounting
- (ii) role of cost accounting in a management information system
- (iii) non-financial information

(b) Nature and purpose of cost classification and definitions

3 Elements of cost

(a) Materials

(i) standard and actual costs for materials including the use of FIFO, LIFO and weighted average for material valuation and the pricing of material issues

(ii) optimal purchase quantities to include discounts

(iii) optimal batch quantities

(iv) reorder levels

(v) material losses

(b) Labour

(i) direct and indirect labour
(ii) different remuneration methods
(iii) labour efficiency
(iv) labour turnover

(c) Overheads

(i) direct and indirect expenses

(ii) principles and processes of overhead cost analysis

(iii) allocation and apportionment of overhead costs including reciprocal service centre situations

(iv) absorption rates

(v) under- and over-absorption

(vi) fixed overhead expenditure and volume variances

(vii) fixed overhead efficiency and capacity variances where appropriate

(viii) changes in the cost structure of a business over time

4 Cost systems

(a) Job, batch and process costing

(i) characteristics

(ii) direct and indirect costs (including waste, scrap and rectification costs)

(iii) valuation of process transfers and work-in-progress using equivalent units of production and based on FIFO and weighted average pricing methods

(iv) process costing, normal losses, abnormal losses and gains

(v) joint and by-products in process costing

(c) Operation/service costing

(i) scope of operation/service costing
(ii) appropriate cost units
(iii) collection, classification and ascertainment of costs

5 Costing methods and techniques

(a) Standard costing

(i) establishment of standard costs
(ii) variance analysis
(iii) explanations of variances and control
(iv) implications for management
(v) operating statements

(b) Marginal and absorption costing

(i) marginal and absorption costing profit and loss accounts
(ii) reconciliation of the profits under the two methods
(iii) contrast of absorption and marginal costing

6 Short-term decision making

(a) Cost behaviour

(i) fixed, variable and semi-variable costs
(ii) cost behaviour using an appropriate graph
(iii) high-low method
(iv) regression analysis

(b) CVP analysis

(i) break-even point and revenue
(ii) margin of safety
(iii) target profit
(iv) profit/volume ratio
(v) break-even chart and profit/volume graph

(c) Limiting factors

(i) optimal production plan given a scarce resource
(ii) linear programming techniques
(iii) other methods for more than two variable problems

(d) Preparation of cost estimates for decision making

(i) relevant costing techniques to include opportunity/sunk, avoidable/unavoidable, fixed/variable applied to such situations as make or buy, shut down and one-off contracts

(e) Pricing of goods and services

(i) price/demand and relationships
(ii) full cost plus pricing
(iii) marginal costing

(f) Price skimming, penetration pricing, premium pricing and price discrimination

Excluded topics

The syllabus content outlines the areas for assessment. No areas of knowledge are specifically excluded from the syllabus.

Key areas of the syllabus

The key topic areas are:

- cost classification and behaviour
- material, labour and overhead costs
- absorption and marginal costing
- process costing
- standard costing
- CVP analysis
- pricing methods.

Paper 1.2

Financial Information for Management
(United Kingdom)

Study Guide

1 INFORMATION FOR MANAGEMENT

Syllabus reference 1c(i), (ii), d (iii), (iv)

- distinguish between 'data' and 'information'
- describe the sources of information
- identify and explain the attributes of good information
- describe the methods of recording and processing information
- describe the ways in which data could be presented to management

2 MANAGEMENT INFORMATION SYSTEMS

Syllabus reference 1b, c(iii), 2a

- explain what is meant by a management information system
- explain the role of accountants and accounting information within a management information system
- describe the purpose and role of cost and management accounting within a management information system
- compare and contrast financial and cost and management accounting
- outline the managerial processes of planning, decision-making and control
- discuss the management of both financial and non-financial information requirements
- describe the various types of responsibility centres and the impact of these on management information

3 OBJECTIVES , STRATEGY AND PLANNING

Syllabus reference 1a (i), (ii), (iii), (iv)

- define the terms 'objectives' and 'strategy'
- describe the different objectives for different types of organisations
- illustrate the links between strategy and organisational structure
- explain how the objectives and strategy of an organisation impact upon its plans
- describe the planning process
- describe the main techniques used in the planning and decision making process for various types of organisation
- explain the difference between strategic, tactical and operational planning
- describe the basic elements of and purpose of a management control system
- illustrate the need for monitoring and evaluation
- describe methods for monitoring and controlling against objectives and plans

4 THE ROLE OF INFORMATION TECHNOLOGY IN MANAGEMENT INFORMATION

Syllabus reference 1c (iv), d (iv), (v), (vi)

- identify the characteristics and different types of computer hardware and software
- evaluate the potential value of computer systems in handling and processing business data
- describe methods of capturing and processing data by computer
- describe how data is grouped, tabulated, stored and output
- explain the role and features of spreadsheet systems
- describe how output could be analysed and used within an organisation

5 COST CLASSIFICATION

Syllabus reference 1b (ii), d (i), (ii), 2b, 6a (i)

- explain and illustrate classifications used in the analysis of product/service costs including by function, direct and indirect, product and period, fixed and variable, avoidable and unavoidable, controllable and uncontrollable
- explain and illustrate the concept of cost objects, cost units, cost centres, revenue centres, profit centres and investment centres
- describe briefly the process of accounting for input costs and relating them to work done
- describe briefly the different methods of costing final outputs and their appropriateness to different types of business organisation/situation
- describe the nature of control achieved through the comparison of actual costs against plan

6 COST BEHAVIOUR - 1

Syllabus reference 6a (i), (ii), (iii)

- explain the importance of cost behaviour in relation to business decision-making
- describe factors which influence cost behaviour
- explain how the terms linear, curvilinear and step functions apply to costs
- identify, describe and illustrate graphically different types of cost behaviour
- explain the structure of linear functions and equations
- provide examples of costs which contain both fixed and variable elements
- use high/low analysis to separate the fixed and variable elements of such costs

7 COST BEHAVIOUR - 2

Syllabus reference 6a (iv)

- construct a scatter graph to establish whether a linear function would be appropriate
- establish a linear function using regression analysis and interpret the results
- calculate and explain the concepts of correlation and coefficient of determination

8 MATERIAL COSTS - 1

Syllabus reference 3a(i), (v)

- describe the different procedures and documents necessary for ordering, receiving and issuing materials from stock
- describe the control procedures used to monitor physical and 'book' stock and to minimise discrepancies and losses
- calculate, explain and evaluate the value of closing stock and material issues using LIFO, FIFO and average methods (weighted and periodic)
- calculate the standard cost of stocks from given information
- prepare ledger entries to record material cost inputs and outputs
- interpret the entries and balances in the material stock account

9 MATERIAL COSTS - 2

Syllabus reference 3a (ii), (iii), (iv)

- explain the reasons for holding stock
- identify and explain the costs of having stocks
- calculate and interpret optimal reorder quantities
- calculate and interpret optimal reorder quantities when discounts apply
- produce and interpret calculations to minimise stock costs when stock is gradually replenished
- describe appropriate methods for establishing reorder levels

10 LABOUR COSTS

Syllabus reference 3b

- explain the difference between, and calculate, direct and indirect labour costs
- explain the methods used to relate input labour costs to work done

- prepare journal and ledger entries to record labour cost inputs and outputs
- describe and illustrate different remuneration methods and incentive schemes
- calculate the level, and analyse the costs and causes of, labour turnover
- describe and illustrate measures of labour efficiency and utilisation
- interpret the entries and balances in the labour account

11 OVERHEADS - 1

Syllabus reference 3c (i), (ii), (iii), (iv)

- explain the difference between the treatment of direct and indirect expenses
- describe and justify the process of apportioning manufacturing overhead costs incurred to production
- allocate and apportion factory overheads using an appropriate basis
- re-apportion service centre costs including the use of the reciprocal method
- comment on the use of blanket, department, cost driver, actual and pre-determined absorption rates
- identify, calculate and discuss the appropriate absorption rates using relevant bases

12 OVERHEADS - 2

Syllabus reference 3c (v), (vi), (vii), (viii)

- prepare journal and ledger entries for manufacturing overheads incurred and absorbed
- calculate, explain and account for under - and over-absorbed overheads
- calculate and explain fixed overhead expenditure, volume and, where appropriate, efficiency and capacity variances
- describe and evaluate methods of attributing non-manufacturing overhead costs to units of output
- perform process and cost accounting transactions for selling, distribution and administration overhead in a given business context
- describe how the cost structure of a business has changed over time and the implication of this with regard to overhead analysis

13 REVISE ALL WORK TO DATE

14 MARGINAL AND ABSORPTION COSTING

Syllabus reference 5b

- explain the concept of contribution
- demonstrate and discuss the impact of absorption and marginal costing on stock valuation and profit measurement
- establish the standard cost per unit from given data under absorption and marginal costing
- produce profit and loss accounts using absorption and marginal costing
- reconcile the profits reported under the two methods
- discuss the advantages and disadvantages of absorption and marginal costing

15 JOB AND BATCH COSTING

Syllabus reference 4a (i), (ii)

- describe the characteristics of job and batch costing
- describe the situations where the use of job or batch costing would be appropriate
- discuss, and illustrate, the treatment of direct, indirect and abnormal costs
- complete cost records and accounts in job and batch cost accounting situations
- estimate job costs from given information

16 PROCESS COSTING - 1

Syllabus reference 4a (i), (ii), (iv)

- describe the characteristics of process costing
- describe situations where the use of process costing is appropriate
- describe the key areas of complexity in process costing

- define 'normal' losses and 'abnormal' gains and losses
- state and justify the treatment of normal losses and abnormal gains and losses in process accounts
- account for process scrap
- calculate the cost per unit of process outputs, and prepare simple process accounts, in absorption and marginal costing systems

17 PROCESS COSTING - 2

Syllabus reference 4a (ii), (iv), (v)

- calculate and explain the concept of equivalent units
- allocate process costs between work remaining in process and transfers out of a process using the weighted average cost and FIFO methods
- prepare process accounts in situations where work remains incomplete
- prepare process accounts in situations where losses and gains are identified at different stages of the process
- distinguish between by-products and joint products
- value by-products and joint-products at the point of separation
- prepare process accounts in situations where by-products and/or joint products occur

18 OPERATION/SERVICE COSTING

Syllabus reference 4b

- describe where the use of operation/service costing is appropriate
- illustrate suitable unit cost measures that may be used in a variety of different operations and services
- carry out service cost analysis in internal service situations
- carry out service cost analysis in service industry situations

19 COST-VOLUME-PROFIT (CVP) ANALYSIS - 1

Syllabus reference 6b (i), (ii), (iii), (iv)

- explain the objective of CVP analysis
- explain the concept of break-even
- calculate and explain the break-even point and revenue, target profit, profit/volume ratio and margin of safety

20 COST-VOLUME-PROFIT (CVP) ANALYSIS - 2

Syllabus reference 6b (v)

- construct break-even, contribution, and profit/volume charts from given data
- apply the CVP model in multi-product situations

21 LIMITING FACTORS

Syllabus reference 6c (i)

- explain and recognise what causes optimisation problems
- identify, formulate and determine the optimal solution when there is a single limiting factor

22 LINEAR PROGRAMMING

Syllabus reference 6c (ii), (iii)

- formulate a linear programming problem involving two variables
- determine the optimal solution to a linear programming problem using a graph
- determine the optimal solution to a linear programming problem using equations
- explain the methods available for dealing with optimisation problems with more than two variables
- formulate, but do not solve, a linear programming problem involving more than two variables
- explain shadow prices (calculations, not examinable)

23 RELEVANT COSTING - 1

Syllabus reference 6d (i)

- explain the concept of relevant costing

- explain the relevance of such terms as opportunity and sunk costs, avoidable and unavoidable costs, fixed and variable costs, historical and replacement costs, controllable and uncontrollable costs, to decision making

24 RELEVANT COSTING - 2

Syllabus reference 6d (i)

- calculate the relevant costs for materials and labour
- calculate and explain the deprival value of an asset
- construct a relevant cost statement and explain the results for such situations as make or buy decisions, shut down decisions and one-off contracts

25 PRICING

Syllabus reference 6e, f

- explain the factors that influence the price of a product
- establish the price/demand relationship of a product
- establish the optimum price/output level when considering profit maximisation and maximisation of revenue
- calculate prices using full cost and marginal cost as the pricing base
- discuss the advantages and disadvantages of these pricing bases
- discuss pricing policy in the context of price skimming, penetration pricing, premium pricing and price discrimination

26 STANDARD COSTING - 1

Syllabus reference 5a (i), (ii), (iii), 3c (vi), (vii)

- explain the purpose of standard costing
- establish the standard cost per unit from given data under absorption and marginal costing
- explain the purpose of the following variances:
  - materials price and usage
  - labour rate, idle time and efficiency
  - variable overhead expenditure and efficiency
  - fixed overhead expenditure, volume and, where appropriate, efficiency and capacity
  - sales volume and price

27 STANDARD COSTING - 2

Syllabus reference 5a (iv), (v)

- calculate and interpret the above variances, using the appropriate costing method
- prepare operating statements to reconcile budgeted to actual profit
- discuss the implications of the results of variance analysis for management

28 REVISE ALL WORK

THE PAPER-BASED EXAMINATION

This examination is a **three hour paper** constructed in **two sections**. Both sections will draw from all parts of the syllabus and will contain both computational and discursive elements.

		Number of Marks
Section A:	25 compulsory multiple choice questions (2 marks each)	50
Section B:	5 compulsory short-form questions (8-12 marks each)	50
		100

Additional information

Formulae as required are included in the formulae sheet given in the exam. This is reproduced at the end of this Text.

Analysis of past papers

The analysis below shows the topics which were examined in the old syllabus and in the pilot paper.

December 2003

Section A

Twenty five multiple choice questions covering various financial information for management topics

Section B

1 Absorption costing
2 CVP analysis
3 Budgeting, variances and variance analysis
4 Stock control
5 Pricing

June 2003

Section A

Twenty five multiple choice questions covering various financial information for management topics

Section B

1 Variance analysis
2 Process costing with joint products and by-products
3 Absorption costing
4 Linear programming
5 Investment appraisal

December 2002

Section A

Twenty five multiple choice questions covering various financial information for management topics

Section B

1 Correlation and regression
2 Decision tree analysis
3 Budgeting
4 The role of information technology in management information

June 2002

Section A

Twenty five multiple choice questions covering various financial information for management topics

Section B

1 Index numbers
2 Relevant costing
3 Information for management
4 Interest and investment appraisal
5 Process costing

December 2001

Section A

Twenty five multiple choice questions covering various financial information for management topics

Section B

1 Pricing
2 Variance analysis
3 CVP analysis
4 Budgeting
5 Marginal costing and absorption costing

Pilot paper

Section A

Twenty five multiple choice questions covering various financial information for management topics

Section B

1 Investment appraisal
2 Absorption costing
3 Linear programming
4 Regression analysis
5 Stock control

EXAMINER'S APPROACH TO THE PAPER-BASED EXAMINATION

The good news for students is that the number of topics on the Paper 1.2 syllabus has been significantly reduced between 2003 and 2004. This is clearly indicated by the removal of seven sessions from the previous Study Guide. However, to maintain the number of study sessions at 28, some of the more important existing sessions have been split into two parts and therefore two study sessions. There are no major additions to the Paper 1.2 syllabus.

Study material

It is recommended that students check that the study material they are using in preparation for 2004 examinations has been revised to remove all the topics that are no longer examinable. This will ensure that students do not waste valuable time. In addition, a number of past examination questions in both Section A and B of Paper 1.2 - some set as recently as in the December 2003 examination – will no longer be relevant under the revised syllabus.

Format of the examination

This is not changing. Section A will continue to consist of 25 multiple-choice questions (MCQ). Each MCQ will be compulsory and will carry two marks. Section B will still comprise five compulsory short form questions.

The opportunity has been taken to allow a little more flexibility in the setting of the Section B questions by stating that each question will carry between eight and 12 marks. This is now consistent with Paper 1.1. However, I can say that for both Paper 1.2 examinations in 2004, each of the Section B questions will carry 10 marks, **any changes could occur from 2005 onwards**.

Question styles

The MCQs in Section A will be in the same style as in recent examinations. The following reminders are given:

- Candidates will have a choice from four answers given to each question (A, B, C or D). Only one answer will be correct.
- There is no negative marking (i.e. there is no deduction of marks for selecting a wrong answer).
- Some questions may be linked by common information provided. Where this occurs the questions will be consecutive.
- Workings are not marked for MCQs.
- Candidates are required to indicate their choices of correct answers on the sheet provided. These sheets are input to be read by optical mark equipment.

In Section B I am making a change in style. In future there will not be one entirely written question containing no numbers or calculations. Most questions set will contain both calculation and written parts. Usually, the written part or parts will carry in total between 2 and 4 marks. Generally, these will test straightforward aspects of syllabus knowledge or require candidates to explain something relating to the calculations performed in the earlier part of the answer. For example, a candidate may have been asked to calculate a standard costing variance and then in the written part may be asked to explain its meaning or to suggest what might have caused it.

Overall effect of the syllabus review

The significant reduction in the number of topics that now need to be studied for Paper 1.2 does mean that students will have more time to study the remaining topics. These are likely to appear more frequently in future examinations. Candidates can expect some slightly more searching questions than have sometimes been set in the past. However, this transition is likely to be very gradual and almost imperceptible.

I think it may be helpful to say something about 'budgeting'. Section 8 of the old syllabus (budgeting) has been completely removed from the revised syllabus. Therefore, no questions will be set which involve candidates being required to prepare budgets, for example. However, candidates can still expect to encounter phrases in questions such as 'budgeted sales are', 'budgeted production is', 'next year's budget'. Careful consideration was given to replacing the word 'budgeted' by 'planned' or 'expected', for example, but on reflection this was thought to be more confusing than helpful to candidates in most cases. Therefore, in standard costing questions, for example, phrases like 'budgeted sales' and 'budgeted fixed overhead costs' are still likely to be found.

Conclusion

It would be appropriate to conclude with some reminders about good examination technique:

- Always read the question carefully.
- Answer the specific question set – this particularly applies to written style parts of questions.
- Start an answer to a completely new question on a new page of your answer book and always clearly indicate the question number and part you are attempting. Different parts of the same question do not need a new page.
- Always show clear workings to calculation type questions in Section B. Marks are awarded for method even if the figures you have calculated are incorrect but the ability to do this often depends on the clarity of your workings.

Finally, I hope that your Paper 1.2 studies will be both successful and rewarding.

David Forster is examiner for Paper 1.2

THE COMPUTER-BASED EXAMINATION

Since the beginning of the year 2002, the ACCA have been offering computer-based examinations (CBE) for Paper 1.2 (in addition to the conventional paper-based examinations).

Computer-based examinations must be taken at ACCA Approved Computer Examination Centres.

How does CBE work?

- Questions are displayed on a monitor
- Candidates enter their answer directly onto the computer
- When the candidate has completed their examination, the computer automatically marks the file containing the candidate's answers
- Candidates are provided with a certificate showing their results before leaving the examination room
- The Approved Assessment Centre returns the test disk to the ACCA (as proof of the candidate's performance)

Paper 1.2 CBE

You will have three hours in which to answer fifty questions which are worth two marks each (Total = 100 marks).

OXFORD BROOKES BSc (Hons) IN APPLIED ACCOUNTING

The standard required of candidates completing Part 2 is that required in the final year of a UK degree. Students completing Parts 1 and 2 will have satisfied the examination requirement for an honours degree in Applied Accounting, awarded by Oxford Brookes University.

To achieve the degree, you must also submit two pieces of work based on a **Research and Analysis Project.**

- A 5,000 word **Report** on your chosen topic, which demonstrates that you have acquired the necessary research, analytical and IT skills.
- A 1,500 word **Key Skills Statement**, indicating how you have developed your interpersonal and communication skills.

BPP was selected by the ACCA and Oxford Brookes University to produce the official text *Success in your Research and Analysis Project* to support students in this task. The book pays particular attention to key skills not covered in the professional examinations.

BPP also offers courses and mentoring services.

THE OXFORD BROOKES PROJECT TEXT CAN BE ORDERED USING THE FORM AT THE END OF THIS STUDY TEXT.

OXFORD INSTITUTE OF INTERNATIONAL FINANCE MBA

The Oxford Institute of International Finance (OXIIF), a joint venture between the ACCA and Oxford Brookes University, offers an MBA for finance professionals.

For this MBA, credits are awarded for your ACCA studies, and entry to the MBA course is available to those who have completed their ACCA professional stage studies. The MBA was launched in 2002 and has attracted participants from all over the world.

The qualification features an introductory module (*Foundations of Management*). Other modules include *Global Business Strategy, Managing Self Development,* and *Organisational Change & Transformation.*

Research Methods are also taught, as they underpin the **research dissertation**.

The MBA programme is delivered through the use of targeted paper study materials, developed by BPP, and taught over the Internet by OXIIF personnel using BPP's virtual campus software.

For further information, please see the Oxford Institute's website: www.oxfordinstitute.org.

CONTINUING PROFESSIONAL DEVELOPMENT

ACCA is introducing a new continuing professional development requirement for members from 1 January 2005. Members will be required to complete and record 40 units of CPD annually, of which 21 units must be verifiable learning or training activity.

BPP has an established professional development department which offers a range of relevant, professional courses to reflect the needs of professionals working in both industry and practice. To find out more, visit the website: www.bpp.com/pd or call the client care team on 0845 226 2422.

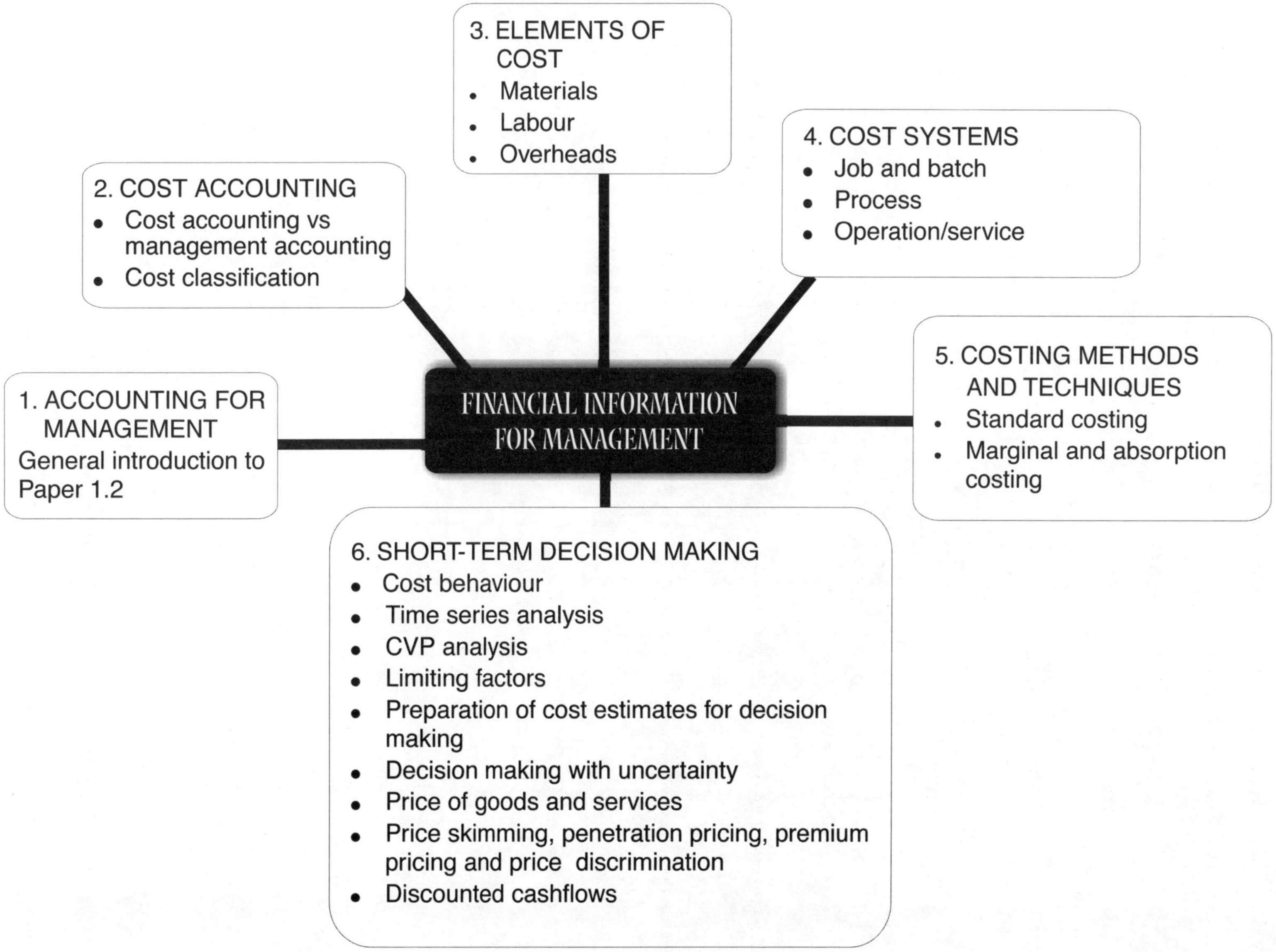
FINANCIAL INFORMATION FOR MANAGEMENT
1. ACCOUNTING FOR MANAGEMENT
General introduction to Paper 1.2
2. COST ACCOUNTING
Cost accounting vs management accounting
Cost classification
3. ELEMENTS OF COST
Materials
Labour
Overheads
4. COST SYSTEMS
Job and batch
Process
Operation/service
5. COSTING METHODS AND TECHNIQUES
Standard costing
Marginal and absorption costing
6. SHORT-TERM DECISION MAKING
Cost behaviour
Time series analysis
CVP analysis
Limiting factors
Preparation of cost estimates for decision making
Decision making with uncertainty
Price of goods and services
Price skimming, penetration pricing, premium pricing and price discrimination
Discounted cashflows

Part A

Introduction to financial information for management

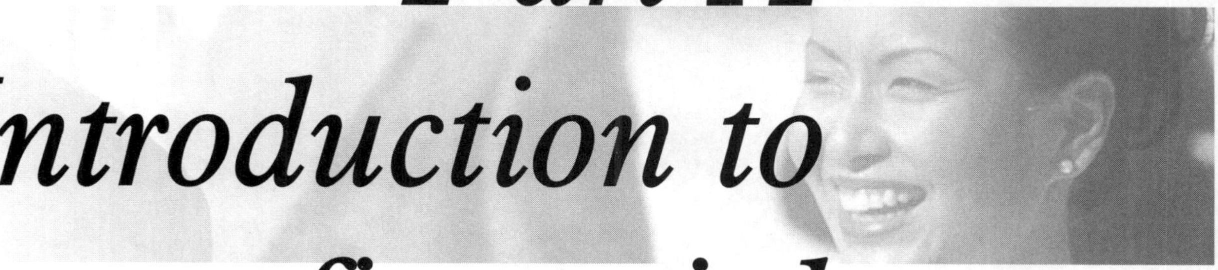

Chapter 1

INFORMATION FOR MANAGEMENT

Topic list		Syllabus reference
1	Information	1, 2(a)
2	Planning, control and decision making	1, 2(a)
3	Information systems and management information systems	1, 2(a)
4	Financial accounting and cost and management accounting	1, 2(a)
5	Presentation of information to management	1, 2(a)

Introduction

Welcome to **Financial Information for Management** – Paper 1.2 of the ACCA's syllabus.

This and the following four chapters provide an introduction to **Financial Information for Management**. This chapter looks at **information** and introduces **cost accounting**. Chapter 2 looks at the role of information technology in management information. Chapters 3-5 provide basic information on how costs are classified and how they behave.

Study guide

Section 1 – Information for management

- Distinguish between 'data' and 'information'
- Describe the sources of information
- Identify and explain the attributes of good information
- Describe the methods of recording and processing information
- Describe the ways in which data could be presented to management

Section 2 – Management information systems

- Explain what is meant by a management information system
- Explain the role of accountants and accounting information within a management information system
- Describe the purpose and role of cost and management accounting within a management information system
- Compare and contrast financial and cost and management accounting
- Outline the managerial processes of planning, decision making and control
- Discuss the management of both financial and non-financial information requirements

Section 3 – Objectives, strategy and planning

- Define the terms 'objectives' and 'strategy'
- Describe the different objectives for different types of organisation
- Illustrate the links between strategy and organisational structure
- Explain how the objectives and strategy of an organisation impact upon its plan

- Describe the planning process
- Describe the main techniques used in the planning and decision making process for various types of organisation
- Explain the difference between strategic, tactical and operational planning
- Describe the basic elements of and purpose of a management control system
- Illustrate the need for monitoring and evaluation
- Describe methods for monitoring and controlling against objectives and plans

Exam guide

The contents of this chapter are mainly to serve as an introduction to the ACCA's **Financial Information for Management** paper. The topics covered here are not classified as key topic areas.

1 INFORMATION

KEY TERMS

- **Data** is the raw material for data processing. Data relates to facts, events and transactions and so forth.
- **Information** is data that has been processed in such a way as to be **meaningful** to the person who receives it. **Information** is anything that is communicated.

1.1 Information is sometimes referred to as **processed data**. The terms 'information' and 'data' are often used interchangeably. It is important to understand the difference between these two terms.

1.2 Researchers who conduct market research surveys might ask members of the public to complete questionnaires about a product or a service. These completed questionnaires are **data**; they are processed and analysed in order to prepare a report on the survey. This resulting report is **information** and may be used by management for decision-making purposes.

1.3 The **qualities of good information** are as follows.

- It should be **relevant** for its purpose.
- It should be **complete** for its purpose.
- It should be sufficiently **accurate** for its purpose.
- It should be **clear** to the user.
- The user should have **confidence** in it.
- It should be **communicated** to the right person.
- Its **volume** should be manageable.
- It should be **timely** - in other words communicated at the most appropriate time.
- It should be communicated by an appropriate **channel** of communication.
- It should be provided at a **cost** which is less than the value of its benefits.

1.4 Let us look at those qualities in more detail.

(a) **Relevance**. Information must be relevant to the purpose for which a manager wants to use it. In practice, far too many reports fail to 'keep to the point' and contain irrelevant paragraphs which only annoy the managers reading them.

(b) **Completeness**. An information user should have all the information he needs to do his job properly. If he does not have a complete picture of the situation, he might well make bad decisions.

(c) **Accuracy**. Information should obviously be accurate because using incorrect information could have serious and damaging consequences. However, information should only be accurate enough for its purpose and there is no need to go into unnecessary detail for pointless accuracy.

(d) **Clarity**. Information must be clear to the user. If the user does not understand it properly he cannot use it properly. Lack of clarity is one of the causes of a breakdown in communication. It is therefore important to choose the most appropriate presentation medium or channel of communication.

(e) **Confidence**. Information must be trusted by the managers who are expected to use it. However not all information is certain. Some information has to be certain, especially operating information, for example, related to a production process. Strategic information, especially relating to the environment, is uncertain. However, if the assumptions underlying it are clearly stated, this might enhance the confidence with which the information is perceived.

(f) **Communication**. Within any organisation, individuals are given the authority to do certain tasks, and they must be given the information they need to do them. An office manager might be made responsible for controlling expenditures in his office, and given a budget expenditure limit for the year. As the year progresses, he might try to keep expenditure in check but unless he is told throughout the year what is his current total expenditure to date, he will find it difficult to judge whether he is keeping within budget or not.

(g) **Volume**. There are physical and mental limitations to what a person can read, absorb and understand properly before taking action. An enormous mountain of information, even if it is all relevant, cannot be handled. Reports to management must therefore be **clear** and **concise** and in many systems, control action works basically on the 'exception' principle.

(h) **Timing**. Information which is not available until after a decision is made will be useful only for comparisons and longer-term control, and may serve no purpose even then. Information prepared too frequently can be a serious disadvantage. If, for example, a decision is taken at a monthly meeting about a certain aspect of a company's operations, information to make the decision is only required once a month, and weekly reports would be a time-consuming waste of effort.

(i) **Channel of communication**. There are occasions when using one particular method of communication will be better than others. For example, job vacancies should be announced in a medium where they will be brought to the attention of the people most likely to be interested. The channel of communication might be the company's in-house journal, a national or local newspaper, a professional magazine, a job centre or school careers office. Some internal memoranda may be better sent by 'electronic mail'. Some information is best communicated informally by telephone or word-of-mouth, whereas other information ought to be formally communicated in writing or figures.

(j) **Cost**. Information should have some value, otherwise it would not be worth the cost of collecting and filing it. The benefits obtainable from the information must also exceed the costs of acquiring it, and whenever management is trying to decide whether or not to produce information for a particular purpose (for example whether to computerise an operation or to build a financial planning model) a cost/benefit study ought to be made.

Question 1

The value of information lies in the action taken as a result of receiving it. What questions might you ask in order to make an assessment of the value of information?

Answer

(a) What information is provided?
(b) What is it used for?
(c) Who uses it?
(d) How often is it used?
(e) Does the frequency with which it is used coincide with the frequency with which it is provided?
(f) What is achieved by using it?
(g) What other relevant information is available which could be used instead?

An assessment of the value of information can be derived in this way, and the cost of obtaining it should then be compared against this value. On the basis of this comparison, it can be decided whether certain items of information are worth having. It should be remembered that there may also be intangible benefits which may be harder to quantify.

Why is information important?

1.5 Consider the following problems and what management needs to solve these problems.

(a) A company wishes to launch a new product. The company's pricing policy is to charge cost plus 20%. What should the price of the product be?

(b) An organisation's widget-making machine has a fault. The organisation has to decide whether to repair the machine, buy a new machine or hire a machine. What does the organisation do if its aim is to control costs?

(c) A firm is considering offering a discount of 2% to those customers who pay an invoice within seven days of the invoice date and a discount of 1% to those customers who pay an invoice within eight to fourteen days of the invoice date. How much will this discount offer cost the firm?

1.6 In solving these and a wide variety of other problems, **management need information**.

(a) In problem (a) of Paragraph 1.5, management would need information about the **cost of the new product**.

(b) Faced with problem (b), management would need information on the **cost of repairing, buying and hiring the machine**.

(c) To calculate the cost of the discount offer described in (c), information would be required about **current sales settlement patterns** and **expected changes to the pattern** if discounts were offered.

1.7 The successful management of *any* organisation depends on information: non-profit making organisations such as charities, clubs and local authorities need information for decision making and for reporting the results of their activities just as multi-nationals do. For example a tennis club needs to know the cost of undertaking its various activities so that it can determine the amount of annual subscription it should charge its members.

Sources of information

1.8 Information may be obtained from either an **internal** source or from an **external** source.

Internal sources of information

1.9 The main internal sources of information within an organisation include the following.

- Financial accounting records
- Personnel records
- Production department records
- Detailed time records (especially in service organisations)

Financial accounting records

1.10 There is no need for us to give a detailed description of the constituents of the financial accounting records. You are probably familiar with the idea of a system of sales ledgers and purchase ledgers, general ledgers, cash books and so on. These records provide a history of an organisation's monetary transactions. Some of this information is of great value outside the accounts department, for example sales information for the marketing function.

1.11 You will also be aware that to maintain the integrity of its financial accounting records, an organisation of any size will have systems for and controls over transactions. These also give rise to valuable information. A stock control system is the classic example. Besides actually recording the monetary value of purchases and stock in hand for external financial reporting purposes, the system will include purchase orders, goods received notes, goods returned notes and so on, and these can be analysed to provide management information about speed of delivery, say, or the quality of supplies.

Other internal sources

1.12 Much of the information that is not strictly part of the financial accounting records is in fact closely tied in to the accounting system.

(a) Information relating to **personnel** will be linked to the **payroll system**. Additional information may be obtained from this source if, say, a project is being costed and it is necessary to ascertain the availability and rate of pay of different levels of staff, or the need for and cost of recruiting staff from outside the organisation.

(b) Much information will be produced by a **production department** about machine capacity, fuel consumption, movement of people, materials, and work in progress, set up times, maintenance requirements and so on. A large part of the traditional work of cost accounting involves ascribing costs to the physical information produced by this source.

(c) Many service businesses - notably accountants and solicitors - need to keep **detailed records of the time** spent on various activities, both to justify fees to clients and to assess the efficiency of operations.

External sources of information

1.13 We hardly need say that an organisation's files are also full of invoices, letters, advertisements and so on received from customers and suppliers. These documents provide information from an external source. There are many occasions when an active search outside the organisation is necessary.

(a) A **primary source** of information is, as the term implies, as close as you can get to the origin of an item of information: the eyewitness to an event, the place in question, the document under scrutiny.

(b) A **secondary source**, again logically enough, provides 'second-hand' information: books, articles, verbal or written reports by someone else.

What type of information is needed?

1.14 Most organisations require the following types of information.

- Financial
- Non-financial
- A combination of financial and non-financial information

1.15 Suppose that the management of ABC Ltd have decided to provide a canteen for their employees.

(a) The **financial information** required by management might include canteen staff costs, costs of subsidising meals, capital costs, costs of heat and light and so on.

(b) The **non-financial information** might include management comment on the effect on employee morale of the provision of canteen facilities, details of the number of meals served each day, meter readings for gas and electricity and attendance records for canteen employees.

1.16 ABC Ltd could now **combine financial and non-financial information** to calculate the **average cost** to the company of each meal served, thereby enabling them to predict total costs depending on the number of employees in the work force.

1.17 Most people probably consider that management accounting is only concerned with financial information and that people do not matter. This is, nowadays, a long way from the truth. For example, managers of business organisations need to know whether employee morale has increased due to introducing a canteen, whether the bread from particular suppliers is fresh and the reason why the canteen staff are demanding a new dishwasher. This type of non-financial information will play its part in **planning, controlling** and **decision making** and is therefore just as important to management as financial information is.

1.18 **Non-financial information** must therefore be **monitored** as carefully, **recorded** as accurately and **taken into account** as fully as financial information. There is little point in a careful and accurate recording of total canteen costs if the recording of the information on the number of meals eaten in the canteen is uncontrolled and therefore produces inaccurate information.

1.19 While management accounting is mainly concerned with the provision of **financial information** to aid planning, control and decision making, the management accountant cannot ignore **non-financial influences** and should qualify the information he provides with non-financial matters as appropriate.

2 PLANNING, CONTROL AND DECISION MAKING

2.1 When we defined the difference between data and information earlier in this chapter, we said that information is data processed into a form meaningful to the person who receives it. In terms of management accounting, the information is most likely to be for **planning**, **control** or **decision making**.

Planning

2.2 An organisation should never be surprised by developments which occur gradually over an extended period of time because the organisation should have **implemented a planning process**. Planning involves the following.

- Establishing objectives
- Selecting appropriate strategies to achieve those objectives

KEY TERMS

- An **objective** is the aim or **goal** of an organisation (or an individual). Note that in practice, the terms objective, goal and aim are often used interchangeably.
- A **strategy** is a possible course of action that might enable an organisation (or an individual) to achieve its objectives.

Planning therefore forces management to think ahead systematically in both the **short term** and the **long term**.

Objectives of organisations

2.3 The two main types of organisation that you are likely to come across in practice are as follows.

- Profit making
- Non-profit making

2.4 The main objective of profit making organisations is to **maximise profits**. A secondary objective of profit making organisations might be to increase output of its goods/services.

2.5 The main objective of non-profit making organisations is usually to **provide goods and services**. A secondary objective of non-profit making organisations might be to minimise the costs involved in providing the goods/services.

2.6 In conclusion, the objectives of an organisation might include one or more of the following.

1 • Maximise profits
2 • Maximise shareholder value
3 • Minimise costs
4 • Maximise revenue
5 • Increase market share

Remember that the type of organisation concerned will have an impact on its objectives.

Strategy and organisational structure

2.7 There are two schools of thought on the link between strategy and organisational structure.

- Structure follows strategy
- Strategy follows structure

2.8 Let's consider the first idea that **structure follows strategy**. What this means is that organisations develop strategies in order that they can cope with changes in the structure of an organisation. Or do they?

2.9 The second school of thought suggests that **strategy follows structure**. This side of the argument suggests that the strategy of an organisation is determined or influenced by the structure of the organisation. The structure of the organisation therefore limits the number of strategies available.

2.10 We could explore these ideas in much more detail, but for the purposes of your **Financial Information for Management** studies, you really just need to be aware that there is a link between **strategy** and the **structure** of an organisation.

Long-term strategic planning

KEY TERM

Long-term planning, also known as **corporate planning**, involves selecting appropriate strategies so as to prepare a long-term plan to attain the objectives.

2.11 The time span covered by a long-term plan depends on the **organisation**, the **industry** in which it operates and the particular **environment** involved. Typical periods are 2, 5, 7 or 10 years although longer periods are frequently encountered.

2.12 **Long-term strategic planning** is a **detailed, lengthy process**, essentially incorporating three stages and ending with a **corporate plan**. The diagram on the next page provides an overview of the process and shows the link between short-term and long-term planning.

Short-term tactical planning

2.13 The **long-term corporate plan** serves as the **long-term framework** for the organisation as a whole but for operational purposes it is necessary to convert the corporate plan into a series of **short-term plans**, usually covering **one year**, which relate to **sections**, **functions** or **departments**. The annual process of short-term planning should be seen as stages in the progressive fulfilment of the corporate plan as each short-term plan steers the organisation towards its long-term objectives. It is therefore vital that, to obtain the maximum advantage from short-term planning, some sort of long-term plan exists.

The planning process

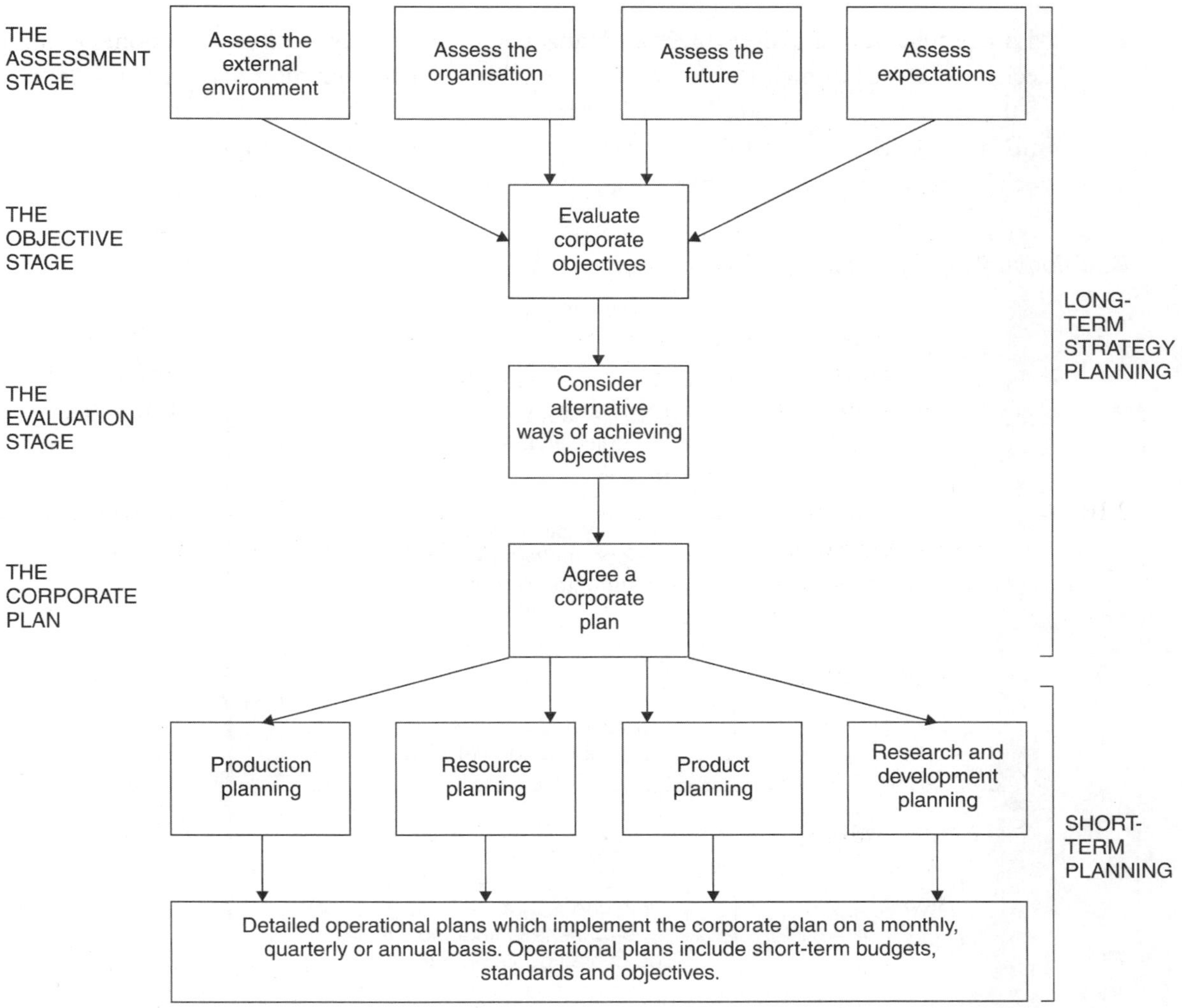

Control

2.14 There are two stages in the **control process**.

(a) The **performance of the organisation** as set out in the detailed operational plans is compared with the actual performance of the organisation on a regular and continuous basis. Any deviations from the plans can then be identified and corrective action taken.

(b) **The corporate plan** is reviewed in the light of the comparisons made and any changes in the parameters on which the plan was based (such as new competitors, government instructions and so on) to assess whether the objectives of the plan can be achieved. The plan is modified as necessary before any serious damage to the organisation's future success occurs.

Effective control is therefore not practical without planning, and planning without control is pointless.

2.15 An established organisation should have a system of management reporting that produces control information in a specified format at regular intervals.

Smaller organisations may rely on informal information flows or ad hoc reports produced as required.

Decision making

2.16 **Management is decision taking**. Managers of all levels within an organisation take decisions. Decision making always involves a **choice between alternatives** and it is the role of the management accountant to provide information so that management can reach an informed decision. It is therefore vital that the management accountant understands the decision making process so that he can supply the appropriate type of information.

Decision making process

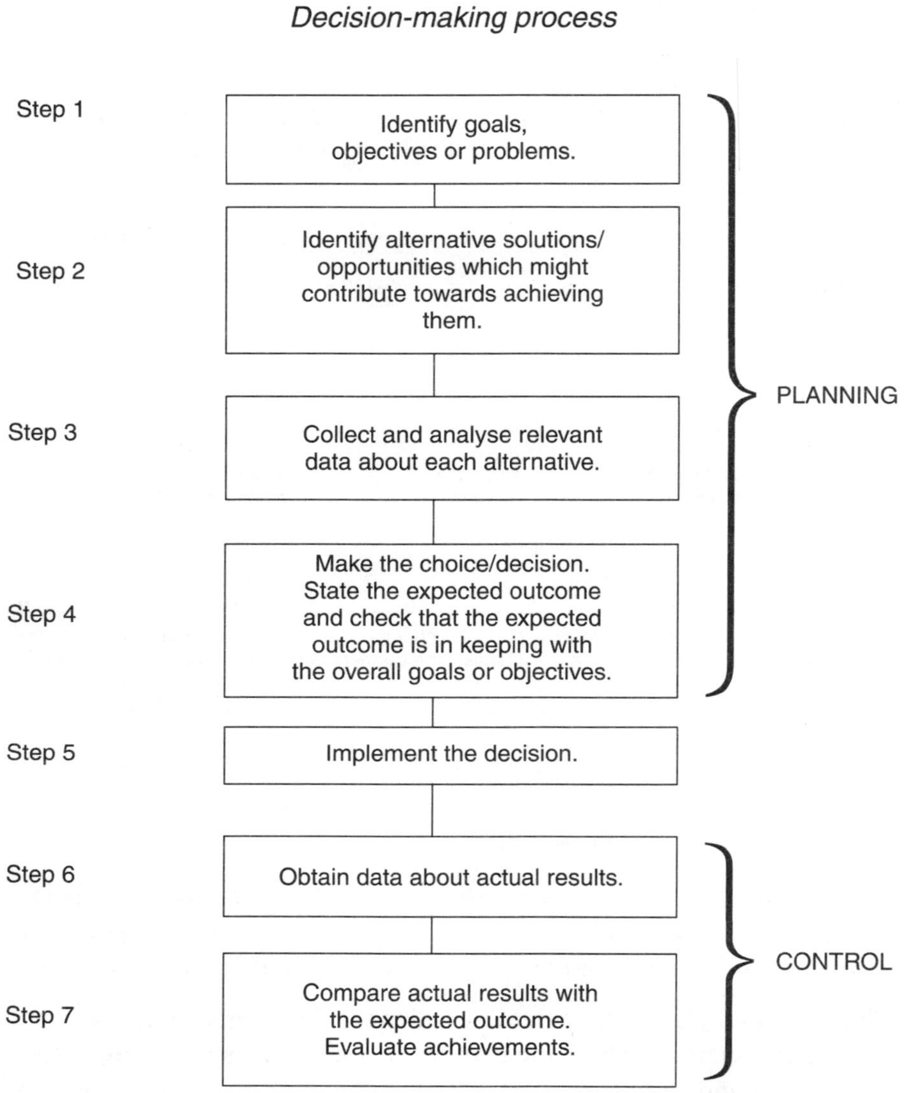

Anthony's view of management activity

2.17 R N Anthony, a leading writer on organisational control, has suggested that the activities of **planning, control and decision making should not be separated** since all managers make planning and control decisions. He has identified three types of management activity.

(a) **Strategic planning:** 'the process of deciding on objectives of the organisation, on changes in these objectives, on the resources used to attain these objectives, and on the policies that are to govern the acquisition, use and disposition of these resources'.

(b) **Management control:** 'the process by which managers assure that resources are obtained and used effectively and efficiently in the accomplishment of the organisation's objectives'.

(c) **Operational control:** 'the process of assuring that specific tasks are carried out effectively and efficiently'.

Strategic planning

2.18 **Strategic plans** are those which **set or change the objectives**, or **strategic targets** of an organisation. They would include such matters as the selection of products and markets, the required levels of company profitability, the purchase and disposal of subsidiary companies or major fixed assets and so on.

Management control

2.19 Whilst strategic planning is concerned with setting objectives and strategic targets, **management control** is concerned with **decisions about the efficient and effective use of an organisation's resources** to achieve these objectives or targets.

(a) **Resources,** often referred to as the **'4 Ms'** (men, materials, machines and money).

(b) **Efficiency** in the use of resources means that optimum **output** is achieved from the **input** resources used. It relates to the combinations of men, land and capital (for example how much production work should be automated) and to the productivity of labour, or material usage.

(c) **Effectiveness** in the use of resources means that the **outputs** obtained are in line with the intended **objectives** or targets.

Operational control

2.20 The third, and lowest tier, in Anthony's hierarchy of decision making, consists of **operational control decisions.** As we have seen, operational control is the task of ensuring that **specific tasks** are carried out effectively and efficiently. Just as 'management control' plans are set within the guidelines of strategic plans, so too are 'operational control' plans set within the guidelines of both strategic planning and management control. Consider the following.

(a) Senior management may decide that the company should increase sales by 5% per annum for at least five years - **a strategic plan.**

(b) The sales director and senior sales managers will make plans to increase sales by 5% in the next year, with some provisional planning for future years. This involves planning direct sales resources, advertising, sales promotion and so on. Sales quotas are assigned to each sales territory - **a tactical plan** (management control).

(c) The manager of a sales territory specifies the weekly sales targets for each sales representative. This is **operational planning:** individuals are given tasks which they are expected to achieve.

Although we have used an example of selling tasks to describe operational control, it is important to remember that this level of planning occurs in all aspects of an organisation's activities, even when the activities cannot be scheduled nor properly estimated because they are non-standard activities (such as repair work, answering customer complaints).

2.21 The scheduling of unexpected or 'ad hoc' work must be done at short notice, which is a feature of much **operational planning.** In the repairs department, for example, routine preventive maintenance can be scheduled, but breakdowns occur unexpectedly and repair work must be scheduled and controlled 'on the spot' by a repairs department supervisor.

Management control systems

> **KEY TERM**
>
> A **management control system** is a system which measures and corrects the performance of activities of subordinates in order to make sure that the objectives of an organisation are being met and the plans devised to attain them are being carried out.

2.22 The management function of control is the measurement and correction of the activities of subordinates in order to make sure that the goals of the organisation, or planning targets are achieved.

2.23 The basic elements of a management control system are as follows.

- **Planning:** deciding what to do and identifying the desired results
- **Recording** the plan which should incorporate standards of efficiency or targets
- **Carrying out** the plan and measuring actual results achieved
- **Comparing** actual results against the plans
- **Evaluating** the comparison, and deciding whether further action is necessary
- Where **corrective action** is necessary, this should be implemented

Types of information

2.24 Information within an organisation can be analysed into the three levels assumed in Anthony's hierarchy.

2.25 **Strategic information is used by senior managers** to plan the objectives of their organisation, and to assess whether the objectives are being met in practice. Such information includes **overall** profitability, the profitability of different segments of the business, capital equipment needs and so on.

Strategic information therefore has the following features.

- It is derived from both **internal** and **external** sources.
- It is summarised at a **high level**.
- It is relevant to the **long term**.
- It deals with the **whole organisation** (although it might go into some detail).
- It is often prepared on an '**ad hoc**' basis.
- It is both **quantitative** and **qualitative** (see below).
- It cannot provide complete certainty, given that the future cannot be predicted.

2.26 **Tactical information is used by middle management** to decide how the resources of the business should be employed, and to monitor how they are being and have been employed. Such information includes **productivity measurements** (output per man hour or per machine hour), **budgetary control** or **variance analysis reports**, and **cash flow forecasts** and so on.

2.27 **Tactical information** therefore has the following features.

- It is primarily generated internally.
- It is summarised at a lower level.
- It is relevant to the short and medium term.
- It describes or analyses activities or departments.

- It is prepared routinely and regularly.
- It is based on quantitative measures.

2.28 **Operational information is used by 'front-line' managers** such as foremen or head clerks to ensure that specific tasks are planned and carried out properly within a factory or office and so on. In the payroll office, for example, information at this level will relate to day-rate labour and will include the hours worked each week by each employee, his rate of pay per hour, details of his deductions, and for the purpose of wages analysis, details of the time each man spent on individual jobs during the week. In this example, the information is required weekly, but more urgent operational information, such as the amount of raw materials being input to a production process, may be required daily, hourly, or in the case of automated production, second by second.

Operational information has the following features.

- It is derived almost entirely from internal sources.
- It is highly detailed, being the processing of raw data.
- It relates to the immediate term.
- It is task-specific.
- It is prepared constantly, or very frequently.
- It is largely quantitative.

3 INFORMATION SYSTEMS AND MANAGEMENT INFORMATION SYSTEMS

3.1 An organisation is made up of a series of **information systems**. It is difficult to define an information system since it is really a series of activities or processes.

- Identification of data requirements
- Collection and transcription of data (data capture)
- Data processing
- Communication of processed data to users
- Use of processed data (as information) by users

3.2 Sometimes there are separate information systems for sales, production, personnel, financial and other matters, sometimes there is integration of these sub-systems.

3.3 Information systems can be divided into two broad categories.

- Transaction (or data) processing systems
- Management information systems

Transaction processing systems

3.4 **Transaction processing systems** could be said to represent the **lowest level** in a company's use of information systems. They are used for routine tasks in which data items or transactions must be recorded and processed so that operations can continue. Handling sales orders, purchase orders and stock records are typical examples.

Management information systems

KEY TERM

A **management information system** (MIS) is defined as 'A collective term for the hardware and software used to drive a database system with the outputs, both to screen and print, being designed to provide easily assimilated information for management'.

(CIMA *Computing Terminology*)

3.5 Management information is by no means confined to accounting information, but until relatively recently accounting information systems have been the most formally-constructed and well-developed part of the overall information system of a business enterprise.

3.6 An alternative definition of a management information system is 'an information system making use of available resources to provide managers at all levels in all functions with the information from all relevant sources to enable them to make timely and effective decisions for planning, directing and controlling the activities for which they are responsible.'

3.7 A management information system is therefore **a system of disseminating information which will enable managers to do their job**. Since managers must have information, there will always be a management information system in any organisation.

3.8 Most management information systems are not designed, but grow up informally, with each manager making sure that he or she gets all the information considered necessary to do the job. It is virtually taken for granted that the necessary information flows to the job, and to a certain extent this is so. Much accounting information, for example, is easily obtained, and managers can often get along with frequent face-to-face contact and co-operation with each other. Such an informal system works best in small organisations.

3.9 However, some information systems are specially designed, often because the introduction of computers has forced management to consider its information needs in detail. This is especially the case in large companies.

3.10 Management should try to develop/implement a management information system for their enterprise with care. If they allow the MIS to develop without any formal planning, it will almost certainly be inefficient because data will be obtained and processed in a random and disorganised way and the communication of information will also be random and hit-and-miss.

(a) Some managers will prefer to keep data in their heads and will not commit information to paper. When the manager is absent from work, or is moved to another job, his stand-in or successor will not know as much as he could and should about the work because no information has been recorded to help him.

(b) The organisation will not collect and process all the information that it should, and so valuable information that ought to be available to management will be missing from neglect.

(c) Information may be available but not disseminated to the managers who are in a position of authority and so ought to be given it. The information would go to waste because it would not be used. In other words, the wrong people would have the information.

(d) Information is communicated late because the need to communicate it earlier is not understood and appreciated by the data processors.

3.11 The consequences of a poor MIS might be dissatisfaction amongst employees who believe they should be told more, a lack of understanding about what the targets for achievement are and a lack of information about how well the work is being done. Whether a management information system is formally or informally constructed, it should therefore have certain essential characteristics.

(a) The functions of individuals and their areas of responsibility in achieving company objectives should be defined.

(b) Areas of control within the company (eg cost centres, investment centres) should also be clearly defined.

(c) Information required for an area of control should flow to the manager who is responsible for it.

Cost accounting systems

3.12 **An organisation's cost accounting system will be part of the overall management information system** and, as we shall see in the next section, it will both provide information to assist management with planning, control and decision making as well as accumulating historical costs to establish stock valuations, profits and balance sheet items.

4 FINANCIAL ACCOUNTING AND COST AND MANAGEMENT ACCOUNTING

Financial accounts and management accounts

4.1 Management information provides a common source from which is drawn information for two groups of people.

(a) **Financial accounts** are prepared for individuals **external** to an organisation: shareholders, customers, suppliers, the Inland Revenue, employees.

(b) **Management accounts** are prepared for **internal** managers of an organisation.

4.2 The data used to prepare financial accounts and management accounts are the same. The differences between the financial accounts and the management accounts arise because the data is analysed differently.

Financial accounts	Management accounts
Financial accounts detail the performance of an organisation over a defined period and the state of affairs at the end of that period.	Management accounts are used to aid management record, plan and control the organisation's activities and to help the decision-making process.
Limited companies must, by law, prepare financial accounts.	There is no legal requirement to prepare management accounts.

Financial accounts	Management accounts
The format of published financial accounts is determined by law (mainly the Companies Acts), by Statements of Standard Accounting Practice and by Financial Reporting Standards. In principle the accounts of different organisations can therefore be easily compared.	The format of management accounts is entirely at management discretion: no strict rules govern the way they are prepared or presented. Each organisation can devise its own management accounting system and format of reports.
Financial accounts concentrate on the business as a whole, aggregating revenues and costs from different operations, and are an end in themselves.	Management accounts can focus on specific areas of an organisation's activities. Information may be produced to aid a decision rather than to be an end product of a decision.
Most financial accounting information is of a monetary nature.	Management accounts incorporate non-monetary measures. Management may need to know, for example, tons of aluminium produced, monthly machine hours, or miles travelled by salesmen.
Financial accounts present an essentially historic picture of past operations.	Management accounts are both an historical record and a future planning tool.

Cost accounts

4.3 Cost accounting and management accounting are terms which are often used interchangeably. It is *not* correct to do so.

Cost accounting is concerned with the following.

- Preparing statements (eg budgets, costing)
- Cost data collection
- Applying costs to inventory, products and services

Management accounting is concerned with the following.

- Using financial data and communicating it as information to users

4.4 **Cost accounting is part of management accounting. Cost accounting provides a bank of data for the management accountant to use.** Cost accounts aim to establish the following.

(a) The **cost** of goods produced or services provided.

(b) The **cost** of a department or work section.

(c) What **revenues** have been.

(d) The **profitability** of a product, a service, a department, or the organisation in total.

(e) **Selling prices** with some regard for the costs of sale.

(f) The **value of stocks of goods** (raw materials, work in progress, finished goods) that are still held in store at the end of a period, thereby aiding the preparation of a balance sheet of the company's assets and liabilities.

(g) **Future costs** of goods and services (costing is an integral part of budgeting (planning) for the future).

(h) **How actual costs compare with budgeted costs.** (If an organisation plans for its revenues and costs to be a certain amount, but they actually turn out differently, the differences can be measured and reported. Management can use these reports as a guide to whether corrective action (or 'control' action) is needed to sort out a problem revealed by these differences between budgeted and actual results. This system of control is often referred to as budgetary control.

(i) **What information management needs** in order to make sensible decisions about profits and costs.

4.5 It would be wrong to suppose that cost accounting systems are restricted to manufacturing operations, although they are probably more fully developed in this area of work. **Service industries, government departments** and **welfare activities** can all make use of cost accounting information. Within a manufacturing organisation, the cost accounting system should be applied not only to **manufacturing** but also to **administration, selling and distribution, research and development** and all other departments.

5 PRESENTATION OF INFORMATION TO MANAGEMENT

5.1 Most information is likely to be presented to management in the form of a **report**. In small organisations it is possible, however, that information will be communicated less formally (orally or using informal reports/memos).

5.2 Throughout this Study Text, you will come across a number of techniques which allow financial information to be collected. Once it has been collected it is usually analysed and reported back to management in the form of a **report**.

5.3 Main features of a report are as follows.

- **TITLE**

  Most reports are usually given a heading to show that it is a report.

- **WHO IS THE REPORT INTENDED FOR?**

  It is vital that the intended recipients of a report are clearly identified. For example, if you are writing a report for Joe Bloggs, it should be clearly stated at the head of the report.

- **WHO IS THE REPORT FROM?**

  If the recipients of the report have any comments or queries, it is important that they know who to contact.

- **DATE**

  We have already mentioned that information should be communicated at the most appropriate **time**. It is also important to show this timeliness by giving your report a date.

- **SUBJECT**

  What is the report about? Managers are likely to receive a great number of reports that they need to review. It is useful to know what a report is about before you read it!

- **APPENDIX**

  In general, information is summarised in a report and the more detailed calculations and data are included in an appendix at the end of the report.

5.4 We recommend that you should use the following format when writing a report in an examination.

REPORT	
To: Board of Directors	
From: Cost Accountant	Date:
Subject: Report Format	
Body of report	
Signed: Cost Accountant	

Exam focus point

When producing reports in an examination, remember that they must include the following.

- **Title** – REPORT
- **To** – Who is the report to?
- **From** – Who is the report from?
- **Date** – What is the date of report?
- **Subject** – What is the subject of the report?

Chapter roundup

- **Data** ('raw material') and **information** (data which has been processed into a form meaningful to the recipient and which is of real or perceived value for the intended purpose) are terms which are often used interchangeably – make sure you are aware of the differences.
- Good information should be **relevant, complete, accurate, clear**, it should **inspire confidence**, it should be **appropriately communicated**, its **volume** should be manageable, it should be **timely** and its **cost** should be less than the benefits it provides.
- Information may be obtained from either an **internal** source or an **external** source.
- **Internal** sources of information include the financial accounting records. **External** sources of information include books, reports and documents.
- An **objective** is the aim or goal of an organisation.
- A **strategy** is a possible course of action that might enable an organisation to achieve its objectives.
- The main objectives of an organisation might include the following.
  - Maximise profits
  - Maximise shareholder value
  - Minimise costs
  - Maximise revenue
  - Increase market share
- Information for management accounting is likely to be used for **planning, control** and **decision making**.
- Anthony divides management activities into **strategic planning, management control** and **operational control**.
- A **management control system** is a system which measures and corrects the performance of activities of subordinates in order to make sure that the objectives of an organisation are being met and the plans devised to attain them are being carried out.
- Information within an organisation can be analysed into the three levels assumed in Anthony's hierarchy: **strategic; tactical**; and **operational**.
- An **MIS** is a system of providing and communicating information which will enable managers to do their jobs and as such an MIS is vital to the role of the cost and management accountant.
- **Financial accounting systems** ensure that the assets and liabilities of a business are properly accounted for, and provide information about profits and so on to shareholders and to other interested parties.
- **Management accounting systems** provide information specifically for the use of managers within the organisation.
- The relationship between cost accounting and management accounting may be summarised as follows: **cost accounting provides a bank of data for the management accountant to use.**
- Data and information are usually presented to management in the form of a report. The main features of a report are as follows.
  - Title
  - To
  - From
  - Date
  - Subject

Quick quiz

1 Define the terms **data** and **information**.

2 The four main qualities of good information are:

- ....
- ....
- ....
- ....

3 Secondary sources of information include documents or reports written for a specific purpose.

True ☐

False ☐

4 In terms of management accounting, information is most likely to be used for (1) ...., (2) .... or (3) ....

5 A strategy is the aim or goal of an organisation.

True ☐

False ☐

6

Organisation	**Objective**
Profit making	
Non-profit making	

7 What are the three types of management activity identified by R N Anthony?

(1) ....
(2) ....
(3) ....

8 A management control system is

A a possible course of action that might enable an organisation to achieve its objectives

B a collective term for the hardware and software used to drive a database system

C a set up that measures and corrects the performance of activities of subordinates in order to make sure that the objectives of an organisation are being met and their associated plans are being carried out

D a system that controls and maximises the profits of an organisation

9 List six differences between financial accounts and management accounts.

10 When preparing reports, what are the five key points to remember?

(1) ....
(2) ....
(3) ....
(4) ....
(5) ....

Answers to quick quiz

1 **Data** is the raw material for data processing. **Information** is data that has been processed in such a way as to be meaningful to the person who receives it. **Information** is anything that is communicated.

2
- Relevance
- Completeness
- Accuracy
- Clarity

3 False. Secondary information sources would include items that have not been prepared for a specific purpose (these would be primary information sources).

4 (1) Planning
(2) Control
(3) Decision making

5 False. This is the definition of an **objective**. A strategy is a possible course of action that might enable an organisation to **achieve** its objectives.

6 Profit making = maximise profits
Non-profit making = provide goods and services

7 (1) Strategic planning
(2) Management control
(3) Operational control

8 C

9 See Paragraph 4.2

10
- Title
- Who is the report to
- Who is the report from
- Date
- Subject

Now try the question below from the Exam Question Bank

Number	Level	Marks	Time
1	MCQ	n/a	n/a

Chapter 2

THE ROLE OF INFORMATION TECHNOLOGY IN MANAGEMENT INFORMATION

Topic list		Syllabus reference
1	The value of computer systems in handling and processing data	1(c), (d)
2	Computer hardware	1(c), (d)
3	Computer software	1(c), (d)
4	Capturing and processing data	1(c), (d)
5	Data output	1(c), (d)
6	Storage devices	1(c), (d)
7	Spreadsheet packages	1(c), (d)
8	Statistical packages	1(c), (d)

Introduction

This Study Text is about financial **information** for management. In the modern business environment the **storage**, **retrieval** and **analysis** of information frequently depends upon **information technology**. In fact, the majority of organisations would cease to function without the support offered by computers since information technology is used for stock control, payroll, sales and purchases, budgeting and a multitude of other tasks. It is therefore vital that you are aware of the terminology used to describe business **information technology**, the elements of a typical business computer system and the principal tasks performed by such a system.

Study guide

Section 4 – The role of information technology in management information

- Identify the characteristics and different types of computer hardware and software
- Evaluate the potential value of computer systems in handling and processing business data
- Describe methods of capturing and processing data by computer
- Describe how data is grouped, tabulated, stored and output
- Explain the role and features of spreadsheet systems
- Describe how output could be analysed and used within an organisation

Exam guide

The role of information technology in management information is not a core syllabus topic in the **Financial Information for Management** syllabus. It is most likely to be examined in the form of objective test questions.

1 THE VALUE OF COMPUTER SYSTEMS IN HANDLING AND PROCESSING DATA

1.1 Here is a very simple example of a data processing model.

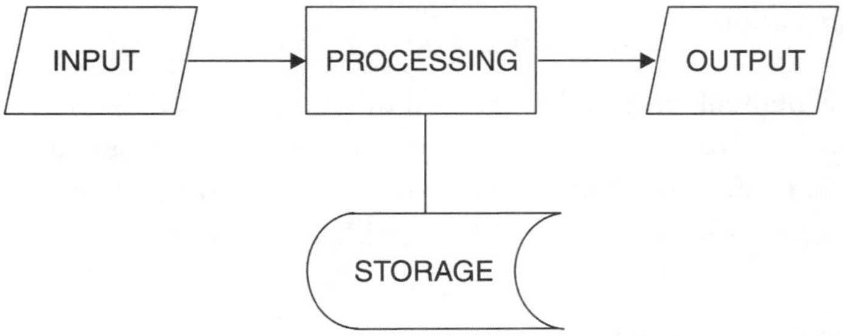

1.2 The processing of business data can be illustrated by a person working at their desk dealing with matters from their in-tray.

(a) A person receives **input from the in-tray**, which must be dealt with.

(b) The person may have a procedures manual or have learned a set of rules which are applied to do the work. Tools such as a calculator or a PC may also be used.

(c) To process data from the in-tray, it may be necessary to refer to other information held on file (either paper or computer-based files).

(d) As a result of doing the work, the person may:

(i) Produce **output**, perhaps a report or a completed routine task.

(ii) Add to the information held on file, or change the information to bring it up to date.

1.3 **Data processing** is essentially the same, no matter whether it is done manually or by computer. The **input**, **process**, **output**, **storage** steps apply to manual and computerised processing.

Advantages of computers

1.4 Computers are widely used for data processing because they have certain advantages over humans.

(a) **Speed**. Computers can process data much more quickly than a human. This means that using a computer to process large volumes of data should be cheaper than doing the work manually. As computer costs have fallen, this cost advantage of the computer has increased.

The ability to process data more quickly means that a computer can produce more timely information, when information is needed as soon as possible.

(b) **Accuracy**. If set-up and programmed correctly, computers are generally accurate, whereas humans are prone to error. Errors in computer processing occur if the people involved inputting data or programming software have made errors, or if faults are present in the computer hardware.

(c) **Volume and complexity**. As businesses grow and become more complex, their data processing requirements increase in volume and complexity too. More managers need better quality information. More transactions have to be processed. The volume of processing required is beyond the capability of even the largest clerical workforce to do manually. Clearing banks, for example, would be unable to function without electronic data processing to ease the demands on their workforce.

(d) **Access to information**. The use of databases and the ability to link a number of users via some form of network improves the distribution of information within and beyond the organisation.

1.5 However, the 'manual' or 'human' method of data processing is more suitable when human judgement is involved in the work. For example, the human brain stores a lifetime of experiences and emotions that influence decisions and it is capable of drawing on them and making connections between them when making decisions.

2 COMPUTER HARDWARE

KEY TERM

A **computer** is 'a **device** which will accept input data, process it according to programmed logical and arithmetic rules, store and output data and/or calculate results. The ability to store programmed instructions and to take decisions which vary the way in which a program executes (although within the defined logic of the program) are the principal distinguishing features of a computer. ...' (CIMA *Computing Terminology*)

2.1 Computer hardware components can be classified by their function.

(a) **Input devices** accept input data for processing.

(b) A **processing device**. The computer has a central processor, which performs the data processing, under the control of the stored program(s), by taking in data from input devices and external storage devices, processing them, and then transferring the processed data (information) to an output device or an external storage device. This processing device is called the **central processing unit** (CPU).

(c) **Storage devices** hold data or information on file until they are needed for processing.

(d) **Output devices** accept output from the processing device and convert it into a usable form. The most common output devices are **printers** (which print the output on paper) and **screens** (which display the output).

The input devices, external storage devices and output devices are collectively known as **peripheral devices**. Any unit connected to a computer is a **peripheral**.

The processor or CPU

KEY TERM

The **processor (CPU)** is 'the collection of circuitry and registers that performs the processing in a particular computer and provides that computer with its specific characteristics. In modern computers the CPU comprises a single chip device, supported by other chips performing specialist functions.' (CIMA *Computing Terminology*)

2.2 The processor (or CPU) is divided into three areas.

- The arithmetic and logic unit

- The control unit
- The main store, or memory

The set of operations that the processor performs is known as the **instruction set**, or **repertoire**, and this determines in part the speed at which processing can be performed.

Computer chips

2.3 In modern computer systems the processing unit may have all its elements - arithmetic and logic unit, control unit, and the input/output interface-on a single 'chip'. A **chip** is a small piece of silicon upon which is etched an integrated circuit, which consists of **transistors** and their interconnecting patterns on an extremely small scale.

2.4 The chip is mounted on a carrier unit which in turn is 'plugged' on to a circuit board - called the **motherboard** - with other chips, each with their own functions.

Arithmetic and logic unit

2.5 The **ALU** is the part of the central processor where the **arithmetic** and **logic** operations are carried out. The **arithmetic** element might be as simple as x + y = z. The **logic** will be something along the lines of '*if* x + y *does not* = z, *then* add 3 to x and try again'.

2.6 The operations are all simple but the significant feature of computer operations is the very rapid speed with which computers can perform vast numbers of simple-step instructions, which combine to represent quite complex processing.

Control unit

2.7 The **control unit** receives program instructions, one at a time, from the main store and decodes them. It then sends out **control signals** to the peripheral devices. The signals are co-ordinated by a clock which sends out a 'pulse' - a sort of tick-tock sequence called a 'cycle' - at regular intervals. The number of cycles produced per second is usually measured in Megahertz (MHz), or Gigahertz (GHz).

1 MHz = one **million** cycles per **second**. 1 GHz = one **billion** cycles per **second**.

2.8 A typical modern PC might have a specification of 750 MHz. Speeds are improving rapidly. A typical business PC with a specification of 1 GHz was available in early 2002 for around £800.

Memory (RAM and ROM)

KEY TERMS

- **RAM** (random access memory) is memory that is **directly available** to the processing unit. It holds the data and programs in current use. Data can be written on to or read from random access memory. RAM can be defined as memory with the ability to access any location in the memory in any order with the same speed.
- **ROM** (read-only memory) is a memory chip into which fixed data is written permanently at the time of its manufacture. New data cannot be written into the memory, and so the data on the memory chip is unchangeable and irremovable.

2.9 Just as humans can work more quickly if they can remember the rules for doing something rather than having to look them up, a computer's processing is much faster if it has the information it needs readily to hand. The computer's memory is also known as **main store, internal store** or **immediate access storage**. This is circuitry which is used to store data within the processing unit whilst the computer is operating.

Bits and bytes

2.10 Each individual storage element in the computer's memory consists of a simple circuit which can be switched on or off. These two states can be conveniently expressed by the numbers 1 and 0 respectively. Any piece of data or instruction must be coded in these symbols before processing can commence.

2.11 Each 1 or 0 is a **bit**. Bits are grouped together in groups of eight to form **bytes**. A byte may be used to represent a character, for example a letter, a number or another symbol. A byte coding system that is commonly used in microcomputers is ASCII.

2.12 The processing capacity of a computer is in part dictated by the capacity of its memory. Memory capacity is calculated in **kilobytes** (1 kilobyte = 2^{10} (1,024) bytes) and **megabytes** (1 megabyte = 2^{20} bytes). These are abbreviated to Kb and Mb.

2.13 Random access is an essential requirement for the main memory of a computer. RAM in microcomputers is '**volatile**' which means that the contents of the memory are erased when the computer's power is switched off.

2.14 The RAM on a typical business PC is likely to have a capacity of 64 to 256 megabytes. The size of the RAM is *extremely* important. A computer with a 1 GHz clock speed but only 64 Mb of RAM will not be as efficient as a 750 MHz PC with 256 Mb of RAM.

2.15 ROM is '**non-volatile**' memory, which means that its contents do not disappear when the computer's power source is switched off. A computer's start-up program, known as a 'bootstrap' program, is always held in the form of a ROM.

2.16 Memory is different to hard disk storage. Hard disks are storage devices that may hold vast amounts of data (eg 20 Gigabytes). Files are stored on storage media such as a hard disk. When files are opened to be referred to or amended, they are stored in RAM. We cover storage devices later in this chapter.

Types of computer

2.17 Computers can be classified as follows, although the differences between these categories are becoming increasingly vague.

- Supercomputers
- Mainframe computers, now sometimes called 'enterprise servers'
- Minicomputers, now often called 'mid-range' computers
- Microcomputers, now commonly called PCs

Supercomputers

2.18 **A supercomputer is used to process very large amounts of data very quickly**. They are particularly useful for occasions where high volumes of calculations need to be performed, for example in meteorological or astronomical applications. Manufacturers of supercomputers include Cray and Fujitsu. They are not used commercially.

Mainframes

2.19 **A mainframe computer system is one that has at its heart a very powerful central computer,** linked by cable or telecommunications to hundreds or thousands of terminals, and capable of accepting simultaneous input from all of them. A mainframe has many times more processing power than a PC and offers extensive data storage facilities.

2.20 Older systems are typically very large in terms of size and very sensitive to fluctuations in temperature and air quality, requiring them to be housed in a controlled environment. However, the main modern examples use the same kind of components that are used in PCs.

2.21 Mainframes are used by organisations such as banks that have very large volumes of processing to perform and have special security needs. Many organisations have now replaced their old mainframes with networked 'client/server' systems of mid-range computers and PCs because this approach (called **downsizing**) is thought to be cheaper and offer more flexibility.

2.22 Nevertheless, mainframes are considered to offer greater reliability, functionality and data security than networked systems. Proponents claim that for organisations with 200 or more users they are cheaper to run in the medium term than other alternatives.

Medium and small business computers

Minicomputers

2.23 **A minicomputer is a computer whose size, speed and capabilities lie somewhere between those of a mainframe and a PC.** The term was originally used before PCs were developed, to describe computers which were cheaper but less well-equipped than mainframe computers (which had until then been the only type of computer available). The advent of more powerful chips now means that some 'superminis', and even PCs linked in a network, can run more powerfully than some older mainframes.

2.24 With the advent of PCs, and with mainframes now being physically smaller than in the past, the definition of a minicomputer has become rather vague. There is really no definition which distinguishes adequately between a PC and a minicomputer. Price, power and number of users supported have been used to identify distinguishing features, but these differences have tended to erode as microchip technology has progressed. Manufacturers of minicomputers include IBM, ICLand DEC.

PCs

2.25 **Personal computers or PCs are now the norm for small to medium-sized business computing and for home computing.** Often they are linked together in a network to enable sharing of information between users.

2.26 A typical PC comprises a keyboard, a screen, a base unit or tower unit (containing the processor and other circuitry, floppy disk drives and CD or DVD drives), a mouse, and sometimes a pair of speakers.

File servers

2.27 A **file server** is more powerful than the average desktop PC and it is dedicated to providing additional services for users of networked PCs.

2.28 A very large network is likely to use a 'mainframe' computer as its server, and indeed mainframes are beginning to be referred to as '**enterprise servers**'.

Portables

2.29 The original portable computers were heavy, weighing around five kilograms, and could only be run from the mains electricity supply. Subsequent developments allow true portability. Many portables are now the size of an A4 pad of paper.

2.30 The **laptop** (or notebook) is powered either from the electricity supply or using a rechargeable battery. It uses 3½" floppy disks, CD-ROMs and DVDs, a liquid crystal or gas plasma screen and is fully compatible with desktop PCs.

2.31 The **handheld computer** or palmtop, may or may not be compatible with true PCs. They range from machines which are little more than electronic diaries to relatively powerful processors with PC compatibility and communications features.

2.32 While portable PCs are becoming extremely popular (even in the office, as they save precious space on crowded desks), they have some **disadvantages**, in particular the following.

(a) Keyboard **ergonomics** (ie keys which are too small, or too close together, for easy, quick typing).

(b) **Battery power** (although manufacturers are trying to reduce power consumption).

Question 1

Which of the following is **not** hardware?

A Printer
B CPU
C Word for Windows
D Keyboard

Answer

C Word for Windows is a word processing software.

3 COMPUTER SOFTWARE

3.1 **Software refers to computer programs.** Hardware cannot operate without software and software is needed to make the hardware process data in the ways required.

3.2 **Software has to be 'written' by a programmer, and program writing is a labour-intensive operation,** so that although hardware costs have fallen in recent years with the development of integrated circuit technology, the costs of software have tended to rise (because salaries and wages have risen). Software costs can now be much higher than the costs of the hardware for a computer system. The two main categories of software are as follows.

- Operating software
- Application software

KEY TERM

Operating software is software that controls the basic operation of a computer system. It is software that makes the hardware perform its functions, such as bringing data input into store and outputting information to an output device.

3.3 An operating system will typically perform the following tasks.

- Initial set-up of the computer, when it is switched on.
- Checking that the hardware (including printers) is functioning properly.
- Calling up of program files and data files from external storage into memory.
- Opening and closing of files, checking of file labels etc.
- Maintenance of directories in external storage.
- Controlling input and output devices, including the interaction with the user.
- Controlling system security (for example monitoring the use of passwords).
- Handling of interruptions (for example program abnormalities or machine failure).
- Managing multi-tasking.

3.4 **Multi-tasking** means doing lots of tasks at once, eg printing out a document you have just finished while working on the next one.

3.5 The best-known operating system is Microsoft Windows – which is available in a range of versions.

KEY TERM

Applications are ready made programs written to perform a particular job for the user rather than operate the computer. The job will be common to many potential users, so that the package could be adopted by all of them for their data processing operations.

3.6 Examples of **applications** for commercial users which are available in software packages include the following.

- Payroll
- Production control
- Sales accounting (sales ledger system)
- Purchase accounting (purchase ledger system)
- Nominal ledger system and cost book system
- General bookkeeping system
- Audit packages (for internal and external audit use)
- Network analysis (or critical path analysis) programs

3.7 A distinction is sometimes made between application packages and more general purpose packages. A **general purpose package** is an off-the-shelf program that can be used for processing of a general type, but the computer user can apply the package to a variety of specific uses of his own choice.

3.8 Examples of general purpose packages are as follows.

(a) **Database systems**. This is a package of programs that allows the user to work with a large collection of data held on file (that is, a data base). With most commercial database packages, the user will key the data on to file to create the database records, but with some packages the database is already provided. The data on file can then be extracted and processed in different ways, according to the nature of the information that the user wants to obtain.

(b) **Expert systems**. This is an advanced software package which holds a large amount of specialised data, eg legal, engineering or medical information. The user keys in certain facts, and the program uses data and processing rules to produce a decision about something on which an expert's decision would normally be required. For example, a user without a legal background could obtain guidance on the law without having to consult a solicitor; or a user could obtain a medical diagnosis without having to consult a doctor.

(c) **Word processing packages**. These give the user the facility of altering and re-organising large blocks of text on a terminal screen (correcting errors, inserting extra text and so on), and keeping files of standard text for repetitive use.

(d) **Spreadsheet packages**. These are used extensively to manipulate numbers. Applications include financial planning, forecasting and other financial modelling.

Integrated software

3.9 **Integrated software** refers to programs, or packages of programs, that perform a variety of different processing operations, using data which is compatible with whatever operation is being carried out. Microsoft Office software allows data to be used within all Office programs, eg an Excel worksheet can be inserted into a Word document.

3.10 Accounts packages often consist of program 'modules' that can be integrated into a larger accounting system. There will be a module each for the sales ledger, the purchase ledger, the nominal ledger, and so on. Output from one 'module' can be used as input to another. The master file in one module can also be used in another module. For example the purchase ledger and sales ledger files could be used to provide input to the nominal ledger system.

4 CAPTURING AND PROCESSING DATA

4.1 The collection of data and its subsequent input to the computer can be a time-consuming and costly task. The computer will only accept data which is in machine-sensible form, data held on a source document must be manually input to produce a computer file.

4.2 **The stages of data input are as follows.**

(a) **Origination** of data (transactions giving rise to data which needs to be recorded and processed).

(b) **Transcription** of data onto a paper document suitable for operators to refer to while keying in data.

(c) Data **input**.

4.3 The ideal methods of data collection and input are those which:

(a) Minimise the time needed to record the original data, and transmit, prepare and input the data to the computer.

(b) Minimise costs.

(c) Minimise errors.

Direct data entry with a keyboard

4.4 The principal method of direct data entry is by means of a keyboard.

Keyboard layout and functions

4.5 A basic keyboard includes the following.

- **Ordinary typing keys** used to enter data or text.
- A **numeric key pad** for use with the built-in calculator.
- **Cursor control keys** (basically up/down/left/right keys to move the cursor).
- A number of **function keys** for use by the system and application software.

4.6 In addition to the function keys, there are special keys that are used to communicate with the operating programs, to let the computer know that you have finished entering a command, that you wish to correct a command and so on. Nothing appears at the cursor point when these keys are used, but they affect operations on screen.

The VDU

4.7 A **VDU** (or monitor) **displays text** and **graphics** and serves a number of purposes.

- It allows the operator to carry out a visual check on what he or she has keyed in.
- It helps the operator to input data by providing 'forms' on the screen for filling in.
- It displays output such as answers to file enquiries.
- It gives messages to the operator.

Character-based systems

4.8 Older systems offer two ways of using a keyboard with VDU to input data. Screen displays typically show white characters on a black background.

(a) **By selecting options from a menu.** A menu is a display of a series of options, and the operator selects which option he or she wants by keying in an appropriate letter or number. A VDU screen might list a number of different options, from which the computer user must choose what he or she wants to do next. For example, a main menu for purchase and sales ledger functions might include:

A - Define codes
B - Set up standing orders
C - Purchase ledger entries
D - Sales ledger entries
E - Supplier details
F - Client details

By selecting D, the operator will be specifying that he or she wants to do some processing of sales ledger entries. When D has been keyed in, another menu may be displayed, calling for the operator to narrow down still further the specification of what he or she wants to do next. A menu-system is thus a hierarchical list of options.

(b) **Using commands**. Command codes or instructions are keyed in, to indicate to the program what it should do with the data that follow. The data are then keyed in and processed by the program.

Graphical user interfaces

4.9 Modern systems are more user-friendly than character-based ones, especially for people who have little experience of using computers and/or who have difficulty using a keyboard. They are based on divisions of the screen into sections and coloured images of various kinds: hence the name graphical user interface (**GUI**).

4.10 **Graphical user interfaces** have become the principal means by which humans communicate with machines. Features include the following.

(a) **Windows**. This basically means that the screen can be divided into sections or 'windows' of flexible size which can be opened and closed. This enables two or more documents to be viewed and edited together, and sections of one to be inserted into another. This is particularly useful for word processed documents and spreadsheets, which are too large for the VDU screen.

(b) **Icons**. An icon is an image of an object used to represent an abstract idea or process. In software design, icons may be used instead of numbers, letters or words to identify and describe the various functions available for selection, or files to access. A common icon is a waste paper bin to indicate the deletion of a document.

(c) **Mouse**. This is a device used with on-screen graphics and sometimes as an alternative to using the keyboard to input instructions. It can be used to pick out the appropriate icon (or other option), to mark out the area of a new window, mark the beginning and end of a block for deletion/insertion and so on. It also has a button to execute the current command.

(d) **Pull-down menu**. An initial menu (or 'menu-bar') will be shown across the top of the VDU screen. Using the mouse to move the pointer to the required item in the menu, the pointer 'pulls down' a subsidiary menu, somewhat similar to pulling down a window blind in a room of a house. The pointer and mouse can then be used to select the required item on the pulled-down menu.

(e) Many GUIs (such as Microsoft Windows) also display dialogue boxes, buttons, sliders, check boxes, and a plethora of other graphical widgets that let you tell the computer what to do and how to do it.

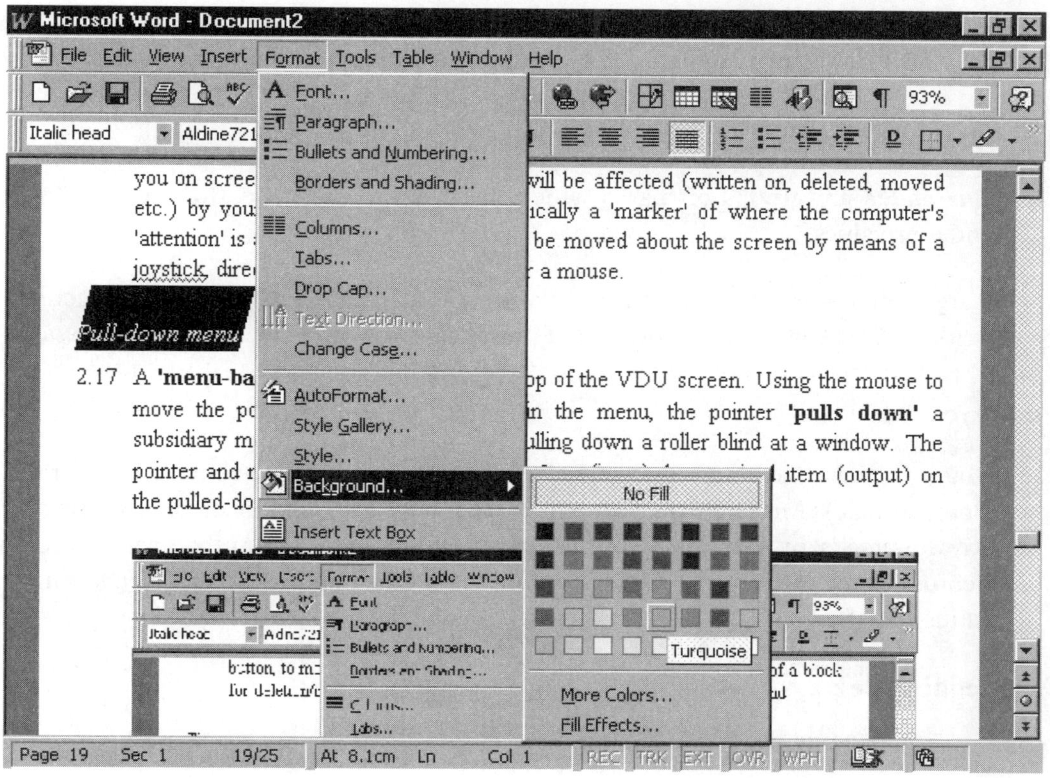

Automatic input devices

4.11 In the following paragraphs we explain some of the most common document reading methods. Document reading methods reduce the manual work involved in data input. This **saves time and money** and also **reduces errors.**

Magnetic ink character recognition (MICR)

4.12 Magnetic ink character recognition **(MICR)** involves the recognition by a machine of special formatted characters printed in magnetic ink. The characters are read using a specialised reading device. The main advantage of MICR is its speed and accuracy, but MICR documents are expensive to produce. The main commercial application of MICR is in the banking industry – on cheques and deposit slips.

Optical mark reading (OMR)

4.13 **Optical mark reading** involves the marking of a pre-printed form with a ballpoint pen or typed line or cross in an appropriate box. The card is then read by an OMR device which senses the mark in each box using an electric current and translates it into machine code. Applications in which OMR is used include **Lotto** entry forms, and answer sheets for multiple choice questions.

Scanners and Optical Character Recognition (OCR)

4.14 A scanner is device that can **read text or illustrations printed on paper** and translate the information into a **form the computer can use**. A scanner works by digitising an image, the resulting matrix of bits is called a **bit map.**

4.15 To edit text read by an optical scanner, you need **optical character recognition (OCR)** software to translate the image into text. Most optical scanners sold today come with OCR packages. Businesses may use a scanner and OCR to obtain 'digital' versions of documents they have only paper copies of. For good results the copy must be of good quality.

Bar coding and EPOS

4.16 **Bar codes** are groups of marks which, by their spacing and thickness, indicate specific codes or values.

4.17 Large retail stores have Electronic Point of Sale (EPOS) devices, which include bar code readers. This enables the provision of immediate sales and stock level information.

EFTPOS

4.18 Many retailers have now introduced EFTPOS systems (Electronic Funds Transfer at the Point of Sale). An EFTPOS terminal is used with a customers credit card or debit card to pay for goods or services. The customer's credit card account or bank account will be debited automatically. EFTPOS systems combine point of sale systems with electronic funds transfer.

Card reading devices

Magnetic stripe cards

4.19 The standard magnetic stripe card contains machine-sensible data on a thin strip of magnetic recording tape stuck to the back of the card. The magnetic card reader converts this information into directly computer-sensible form. The widest application of magnetic stripe cards is as bank credit or service cards.

Smart cards

4.20 A smart card is a plastic card in which is embedded **a microprocessor chip**. A smart card would typically contain a **memory** and a **processing capability**. The information held on smart cards can therefore be updated (eg using a PC and a special device).

Touch screens

4.21 A touch screen is a display screen that enables users to make selections by touching areas of the screen. Sensors, built into the screen surround, detect which area has been touched. These devices are widely used in vending situations, such as the selling of train tickets.

Voice recognition

4.22 Computer software has been developed that can convert speech into computer-sensible form via a microphone. Users are required to speak clearly and reasonably slowly.

Question 2

As we have seen, there is a wide range of input methods, each one having its own advantages and disadvantages. From the descriptions given in this chapter you should be able to formulate your own ideas on the advantages and disadvantages of each method and you may be required in your examination to select the most suitable data input method in a particular situation. What factors should you consider in selecting an input method?

Answer

(a) **Suitability** for the application
(b) The **timing requirements** of the system (response times required)
(c) The **volume** of data
(d) The **accuracy** required
(e) The **cost** of the method chosen as compared with the benefits to be derived
(f) The use of **turnround** documents for data capture and the benefit of OCR methods

---

Question 3

Which of the following is an input device?

A Screen
B Keyboard
C Printer
D CPU

Answer

B The keyboard is an input device. The screen and the printer are output devices, while the CPU performs the processing function.

---

5 DATA OUTPUT

Printers

5.1 A **line printer** prints a complete line in a single operation, usually printing between 600 and 1,000 lines per minutes. They offer the operational speeds necessary for the **bulk printing requirements** of many systems.

5.2 **Character printers** print a single character at a time. Examples include daisy-wheel printers, dot matrix printers.

(a) Daisy wheel printers are **slow and noisy**, but produce print of a **high quality**. Companies are unlikely to buy new daisy wheel printers today because other types of printers are more versatile.

(b) Dot matrix printers are quite widely used in accounting departments. Their main drawback is the **low-resolution** of their printed characters, which is unsuitable for many forms of printed output. They are also relatively **slow** and rather **noisy.** Prices start at under £100.

5.3 **Bubblejet** and **inkjet** printers are small and prices start at under £100, making them popular where a 'private' output device is required, for example in a director's office. They work by sending a jet of ink on to the paper to produce the required characters. They are fairly **quiet and fast**, but they may produce **smudged** output if the paper is not handled carefully.

5.4 **Laser printers** print a whole page at a time, rather than line by line. Unlike daisywheel and dot matrix printers, they print on to individual **sheets of paper** (in the same way as photocopiers do) and so they do not user 'tractor fed' continuous computer stationery.

5.5 The resolution of printed characters and diagrams with laser printers is **very high** - up to 600 dots per inch - and this high-quality resolution makes laser printing output good enough to be used for commercial printing.

5.6 Typically, a desk-top laser printer will print about 4 to 24 A4 pages per minute. **High speed** lasers print up to 500 pages per minute. Laser printers are a microprocessor in their own right, with **RAM memory for storing data prior to printing.**

5.7 Laser printers are **more expensive** than other types - a good one will cost about £700 - but it is quite possible that several users will be able to **share** a single laser printer.

The choice of output medium

5.8 As with choosing an input medium, choosing a suitable output medium depends on a number of factors, which you should bear in mind when we go on to consider each type of output in turn. These factors are as follows.

(a) **Is a 'hard' copy of the output required**; in other words, is a printed version of the output needed? If so, what quality must the output be?

(i) If the output includes documents that are going to be used as OCR turnround documents, the quality of printing must be good.

(ii) If the information will be used as a working document with a short life or limited use (eg a copy of text for type-checking) then a low quality output on a dot matrix printer might be sufficient.

(b) **The volume of information produced.** For example, a VDU screen can hold a certain amount of data, but it becomes more difficult to read when information goes 'off-screen' and can only be read a bit at a time.

(c) **The speed at which output is required.** For example, to print a large volume of data, a high speed printer might be most suitable to finish the work more quickly (and release the CPU for other jobs).

(d) **The suitability of the output medium to the application** - ie the purpose for which the output is needed.

(i) A VDU is well-suited to interactive processing with a computer.

(ii) A graph plotter would be well-suited to output in the form of graphs.

(iii) Output on to a magnetic disk or tape would be well-suited if the data is for further processing.

(iv) Large volumes of reference data for human users to hold in a library might be held on microfilm or microfiche, and so output in these forms would be appropriate.

(e) **Cost**: some output devices would not be worth having because their advantages would not justify their cost, and so another output medium should be chosen as 'second best'.

6 STORAGE DEVICES

Disks

6.1 **Disks** are the predominant form of backing storage medium nowadays because they offer direct access to data, an extremely important feature.

6.2 **Disks are covered on both sides with a magnetic material.** Data is held on a number of circular, concentric tracks on the surfaces of the disk, and is read or written by rotating the disk past read/write heads, which can write data from the CPU's memory on to disk, or can read data from the disk for input to the CPU's memory. The mechanism that causes the disk to rotate is called a **disk drive**. The data on a disk is located by its sector, as each track and sector has a unique identification number.

Hard disks

6.3 A modern business PC invariably has an **internal hard disk**, but external disks may be used too. External disks sit alongside the computer in an extra 'box', with its own power supply and plug socket. Internal disks are incorporated inside the microcomputer itself. At the time of writing the average new PC has a hard disk size of around 4 Gigabytes, but 20 Gb disks are not uncommon. The standard size has increased dramatically over recent years as ever more Windows-based software which is hungry for hard disk space is released.

6.4 In larger computer systems **removable disk packs** are commonly used. Several flat disks are mounted on a spindle. There is one read/write head for each surface, and the heads are moved in a synchronised manner across the disk surfaces.

Floppy disks

KEY TERM

A **floppy disk** is an exchangeable circular, flexible disk (typically $3^1/2$ inches in diameter) which is held permanently in a plastic case. The case can bear an identification label for recognising the disk. A $3^1/2$" disk can hold up to 1.44 Mb of data.

6.5 Almost all PCs will have a **floppy disk** drive. The floppy disk provides an easy way to store and transport small amounts of data.

6.6 **Floppy disks** are subject to physical wear, because the read/write head actually comes into contact with the disk surface during operation. This is not the case with other types of disk. Because they can be left lying around an office, they are also prone to physical damage, such as having cups of coffee spilled over them. As the disks tend to be less reliable than hard disks administrative procedures should be instituted to protect them (for example the use of steel filing cabinets and careful handling).

Tape storage

6.7 Like an audio or video cassette, data has to be recorded **along the length** of a computer tape, making it more difficult to access data held within the tape.

6.8 It follows that magnetic tape as a file storage medium is only practical when every record on the file will be processed in turn. For example, tapes are often used to back-up the contents of a system at the end of the business day.

6.9 Tape cartridges have a **larger capacity** than floppy disks and are still widely used as a **backing storage** medium.

CD-ROM

6.10 **Optical disks**, which use similar technology to the laser-based compact disc audio system, are being used increasingly for data storage. Optical disks have very high capacity compared with floppy disks supplied with a **CD-ROM** drive, and most software is issued on CD.

6.11 The initials **ROM** stand for **read-only memory**. This means that all data is implanted onto the disc when it is made, and subsequent users can only retrieve information, they cannot alter or overwrite or delete what is already on the disk. The **speed** of a CD-ROM drive is relevant to how fast data can be retrieved: an **eight speed** drive is quicker than a **four speed** drive.

6.12 **CD recorders** are available for general business use with blank CDs (CD-R). **Rewritable disks** (CD-RW) are also available. A CD-R can hold up to **650 Mb** of data.

DVD-ROM

6.13 The CD format has started to be superseded by DVD. CD-ROMs hold 650 megabytes of data, which only a few years ago was considered enough for any application. However, the advent of Multimedia files with video graphics and sound encouraged the development of a new storage technology.

6.14 **Digital Versatile Disk (DVD)** ROM technology can store almost 5 gigabytes of data. Access speed is improved as is sound and video quality.

6.15 DVD is some times referred to as **Digital Video Disk**. Many commentators believe DVD will not only replace CD-ROMs, but also VHS cassettes, audio CDs and laser discs.

7 SPREADSHEET PACKAGES

Exam focus point

Section 4 of the study guide for Paper 1.2 states 'explain the role and features of spreadsheet systems'. Remember that you can also draw on your own practical experience at work when answering examination questions.

7.1 As you may already have realised, a large amount of accounting work entails drawing up tables and adding up rows and columns of numbers. A **spreadsheet** is a software package designed to do just that.

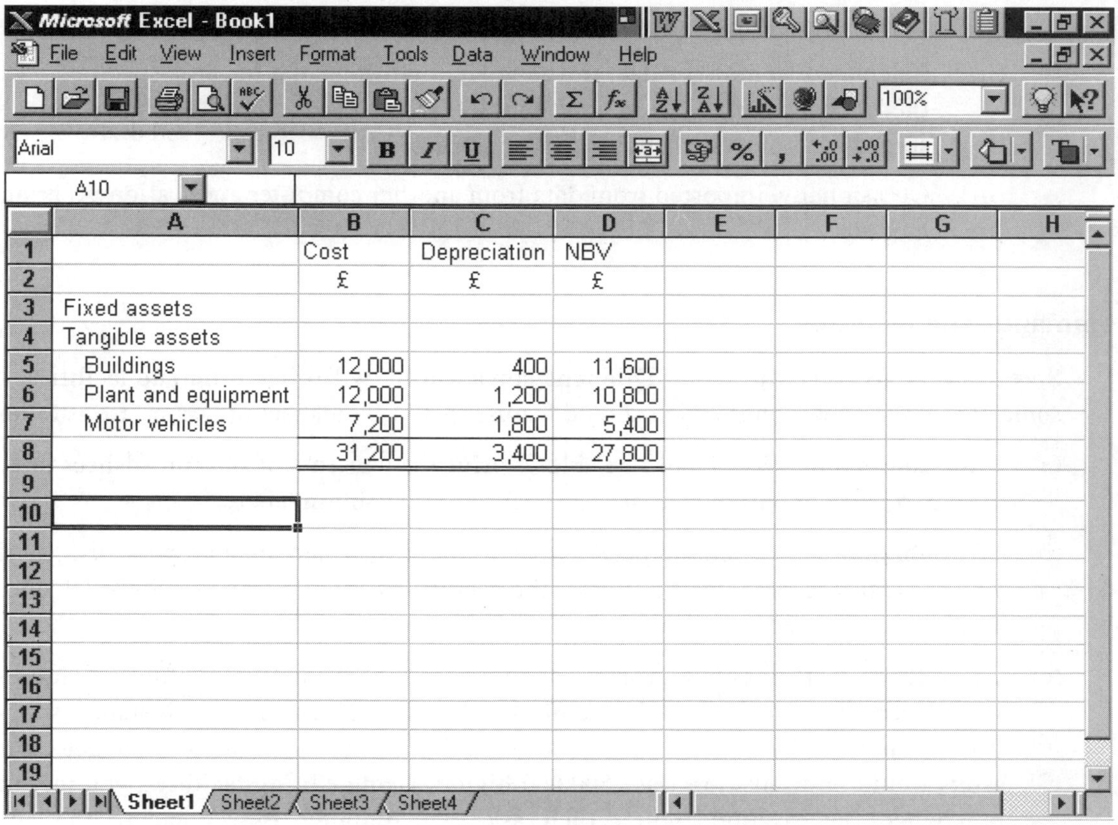

	A	B	C	D
1		Cost	Depreciation	NBV
2		£	£	£
3	Fixed assets			
4	Tangible assets			
5	Buildings	12,000	400	11,600
6	Plant and equipment	12,000	1,200	10,800
7	Motor vehicles	7,200	1,800	5,400
8		31,200	3,400	27,800

7.2 A **spreadsheet** consists of a large number of **boxes** or **cells,** each identified by a reference such as A4, D16, AA20 etc. AA20 is immediately to the right of Z20 and to the left of AB20. The screen cursor will highlight any particular cell - in the example above, it is placed over cell A10. At the top or bottom of the screen, the spreadsheet program will give you such information as:

(a) The **reference** of the cell where the cursor lies
(b) The **width** of the column where the cursor lies
(c) The **contents** of the cell where the cursor lies, if there is anything there

7.3 The contents of the cell can be any one of the following.

(a) **Text.** Text contains words or numbers not used in computation.

(b) **Values.** A value is a number used in a computation, or a formula.

(c) **Formulae.** These refer to other cells in the spreadsheet and perform computations with them.

(d) **Automated commands** or **macros.**

How is a spreadsheet used?

7.4 The idea behind a spreadsheet is that the model builder should construct a model, in rows and columns format as follows.

(a) Identifying what data goes into each row and column, by inserting text - eg column headings and row identifications.

(b) Specifying how the numerical data in the model should be derived. Numerical data might be treated as follows.

(i) Inserted into the model via keyboard input.

(ii) Calculated from other data in the model by means of a formula specified within the model itself. The model builder must insert these formulae into the spreadsheet model when it is first constructed.

(iii) Occasionally, imported from data from another computer application program or module.

Commands and facilities

7.5 Spreadsheets are versatile tools. Different spreadsheets will offer different facilities, but some of the more basic ones which should feature in all spreadsheet programs are as follows.

(a) **Print commands**. You should be able to print the contents of the spreadsheet in total or in part, with or without the spreadsheet row and column labels.

(b) **File commands**. You should be able to save the spreadsheet data on your disk, so that you can use the data again, and so the facility to save data is an essential one. A spreadsheet is saved as a file of data.

(c) **Cell editing facilities**. The program should allow alteration of anything shown on the spreadsheet. This is particularly useful for 'what if?' calculations. For instance, suppose you had prepared a forecast balance sheet and you wanted to know what net current assets would be if taxation was £500,000 higher. Using editing facilities, you just have to change the taxation figure, then ask the computer to recalculate the entire spreadsheet on the basis of the new figures. This 'what if' manipulation of data is probably the most important facility in a spreadsheet package, and we shall return to it again later.

(d) **Facilities to rearrange the spreadsheet**. You can **insert** a column or row at a desired spot. The insert command facilitates this, and the formulae in the spreadsheet are adjusted automatically. You can **move** or **copy** a cell, row or column (or range of cells) elsewhere. You can **delete** a cell row or column.

(e) **Format**. This command controls the way in which headings and data are shown, for example by altering column widths, 'justifying' text and numbers (to indent or have a right-hand justification, etc), changing the number of decimal places displayed etc. You can format the whole spreadsheet, or, in certain cases, a specified **range** of cells.

(f) **Copy a formula**. For example, suppose you wanted to have a cumulative list of numbers as follows.

	A	B	C
1	*Operation*	*Cost per operation*	*Cumulative cost*
2	*No.*	£	£
3	1	9.00	9.00
4	2	10.00	19.00
5	3	14.00	33.00
6	4	3.00	36.00
7	5	86.00	122.00
8	6	9.00	131.00
9		131.00	

The cumulative numbers in the C column are calculated as follows.

	A	B	C
1	Operation	Cost per operation	Cumulative cost
2	No.	£	£
3	1	9	=B3
4	2	10	=C3+B4
5	3	14	=C4+B5
6	4	3	=C5+B6
7	5	86	=C6+B7
8	6	9	=C7+B8
9		=SUM(B3:B8)	

To save time it is possible to input = C3+B4 in the C4 cell and then to copy the formula down the column. The spreadsheet package will generate all the other formulae needed automatically, making the necessary changes each time. It is possible to 'replicate' formulae in this way, downwards or sideways throughout the spreadsheet.

(g) **Database** facility. A spreadsheet package will usually provide a facility for sorting data (alphabetically or numerically).

(h) Most spreadsheets also contain a **graphics** facility which enables the presentation of data as graphs or flowcharts for example.

(i) Some spreadsheets offer a **search and replace** facility to highlight and alter individual formulae.

(j) **Macros**. Many spreadsheet commands are provided as **options** in a menu. Some procedures require a number of commands to be executed. This is often time consuming. For example, if you wish to 'print' some or all of your spreadsheet, you will first execute the print command. You may then see a menu which asks you to specify:

(i) What **range** of the spreadsheet you wish to print.

(ii) What **print 'options'** you wish to use. This will lead to a submenu, which will ask you to specify the length of the pages you are using in the printer, what you wish the size of the margins to be and so forth.

Several commands must be executed before the spreadsheet is printed, and you will have to repeat them each time you wish to print your spreadsheet. Many spreadsheets provide a macro facility. This allows the user to automate a sequence of commands, executing them with the depression of two keys.

(k) Some spreadsheets offer a **'protect' facility** to ensure that the contents of a specified range of cells (for example the text titles, or a column of base data) cannot be tampered with.

Using spreadsheet models: sensitivity analysis

7.6 Whenever a forecast or budget is made, management should consider asking **'what if'** questions, and so carry out a form of **sensitivity analysis.** Suppose a forecast profit and loss account has been prepared using a spreadsheet. The accountant might ask a number of questions about it such as the following.

- What if sales were higher?
- What if administrative expenses were reduced by 25%?
- What if closing stock was reduced by £1 million?

7.7 Using the spreadsheet model, the answers to these questions, and others like them, can be obtained simply and quickly, using the editing facility in the program. A great number of such 'what if' questions can be asked and answered quickly, such as what if sales growth per month is nil, ½%, 1%, 1½%, 2½% or minus 1% etc? The information obtained should provide management with a better understanding of what the cash flow position in the future might be, and what factors are critical to ensuring that the cash position remains reasonable.

8 STATISTICAL PACKAGES

8.1 Before the widespread use of computers and microcomputers, accountants wishing to use certain statistical and mathematical techniques had to be arithmetic wizards. Often endless calculations had to be performed and then re-performed before a conclusion could be reached.

8.2 Fortunately computers have changed that. **Computers will perform any necessary calculations speedily and accurately**, leaving the accountant free to analyse and conclude. Familiarity with computers is therefore vital for any accountant wishing to use mathematical and statistical techniques.

8.3 Accountants could, of course, write their own programs each time they wished to use a mathematical or statistical technique. There are, however, a number of suitable packages on the market which, if used, leave the accountant free to analyse and conclude instead of being involved in computer technicalities.

Spreadsheets and statistics

8.4 Modern spreadsheet packages such as **Microsoft Excel** and **Lotus 1-2-3** include statistical functions that probably go well beyond the need of most accountants.

8.5 Besides financial maths techniques like Discounted Cash Flow and statistical techniques like Normal distributions, spreadsheets can calculate medians, modes, and so on, perform tests such as chi-squared tests, do linear programming, regression and so on. All of the techniques, in fact, that you will learn to do **manually** for Paper 1.2, and in your later studies, can be done easily with a spreadsheet.

Statistical software packages

8.6 There are also a variety of packages available that are dedicated to statistical work. Some of these are specially designed to make the work easy for people who are not adept at the techniques. Here are just two examples.

SPSS

8.7 SPSS is the market leader in statistical software for desktop computers. It offers an extensive set of statistics, graphs and reports and a user-friendly interface that enables the user to enter data in a spreadsheet like format (or import data directly from an existing spreadsheet, accounting package or database) and perform a large number of statistical tests. The results can then be exported into packages such as Word or Excel and incorporated into reports

8.8 It is designed to help with tasks like market research, sales forecasting, process control. It does so by identifying patterns in data, and visualising them in the form of bar charts, scattergraphs and so on. Over 60 statistical functions are offered: far more than you will learn about in this book.

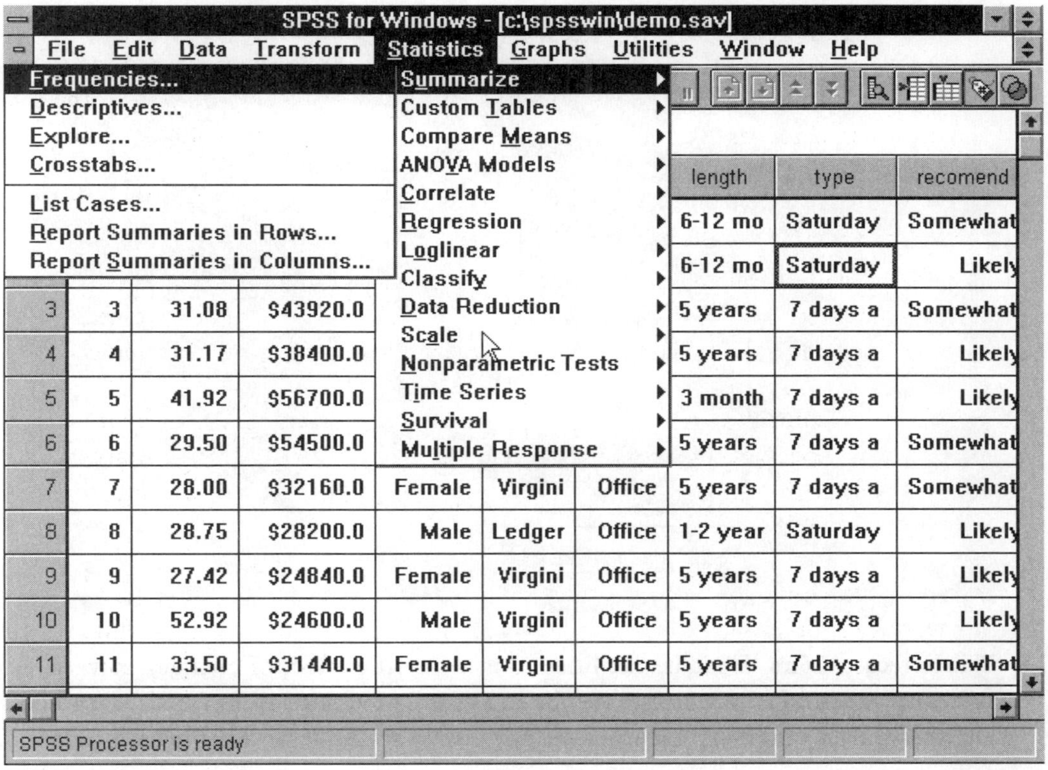

8.9 The **advantage** of statistical software packages is that they take all the agony out of analysing figures. Instead of hours of number-crunching an analysis can be obtained at the click of a button by selecting the rows and columns of data you want to analyse.

8.10 The **disadvantage** is that it is too easy: if users do not understand what the statistic calculated actually means in the first place, they will not be able to draw any conclusions from the results produced. Worse, they may set up the data wrongly and then draw incorrect conclusions because they cannot see that the results do not make sense.

WinForecast

8.11 In practice, more advanced statistical techniques are relatively little used by many businesses, not least because accountants that should be using them do not feel confident about them. More familiar will be simple management accounting techniques such as cash flow forecasting, and projected profit and loss accounts.

8.12 WinForecast is a package designed to help with this sort of work. Its manufacturer claims that it is 5 to 10 times faster than using a spreadsheet to produce a variety of familiar management accounting reports, because it is designed to remove as much of the mechanics of producing projections as possible.

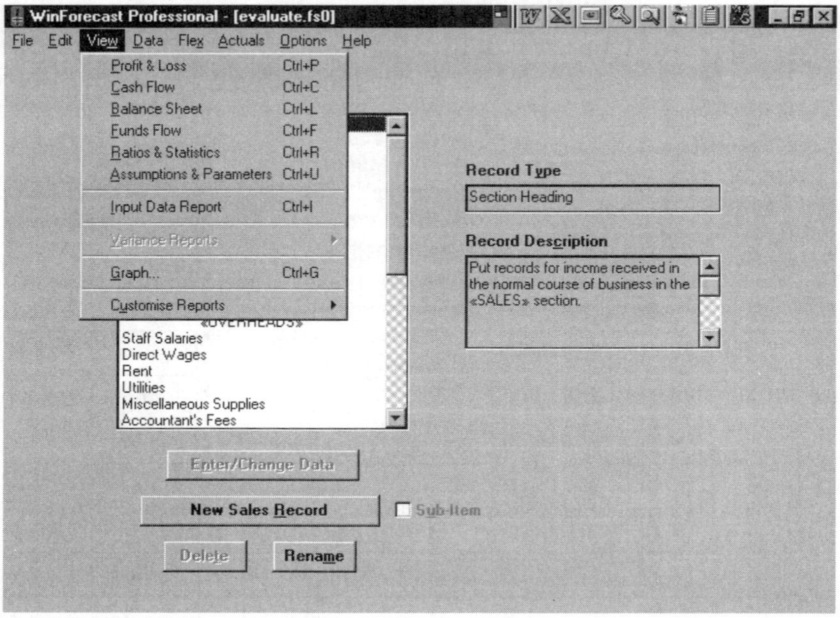

8.13 WinForecast offers What If? facilities to evaluate the effect of changes in variables such as price or demand. It can generate graphs and charts of various types for visual presentation and analysis of data, and it can incorporate formulae to manipulate or compare different scenarios.

Exam focus point

Remember that the contents of this chapter are not one of the key areas of the syllabus and are therefore most likely to be examined in the form of objective test questions in the paper-based exam.

Chapter roundup

- Manual and electronic data processing are essentially the same. When compared with human beings, however, computers can process data much more **quickly**, are generally **accurate** (whereas human beings are prone to error) and can process both **larger volumes of data** and **more complex data.**
- Computers can be classified as mainframe computers, minicomputers or PCs.
- **Hardware** means the physical devices and components that make up a computer system, such as the CPU, disk drives, VDUs and so on. **Software** refers to the computer programs.
- **Operating software** controls the basic operation of a computer system. **Applications software** enables a computer to do the data processing for the various processing applications the user wishes to computerise (such as a sales ledger system or a payroll system).
- The principal method of direct data input to the computer is by means of a terminal comprising a **VDU** and **keyboard**.
- Instead of direct data entry, data may be copied from source documents and be written on to a magnetic disk or a magnetic tape from a keyboard or terminal. This process is called **encoding**.
- **Document reading methods** of data collection involve the use of a source document that both human beings and computers can read. Such methods include **MICR**, **OCR**, **OMR**, **mark sensing**, **bar coding** and **turnround documents**.
- Data can also be collected by **card reading devices**, **magnetic stripe cards** and **EPOS devices**.
- **Output devices** include the **VDU** and **printers** such as **dot matrix** printers and **laser** printers. The choice of output medium will depend on factors such as the volume of information produced, whether a hard copy is required and the speed at which output is required.
- **External storage devices** are used to store data in computer-sensible form. The most commonly used backing storage medium is **magnetic disk**. Other storage media include **magnetic tape** and **CDs**.
- A **spreadsheet** is a software application which allows you to define a problem logically in terms of text, data and formulae, and then lets the computer bear the brunt of the complicated and tedious calculations. It can be used whenever the problem can be set out in logical stages. Spreadsheets are one of the principal means by which computers are used in cost accounting.
- **Statistical packages** are available to carry out a huge range of techniques. Modern spreadsheets incorporate a wider range of statistical functions than most accountants would ever need.

Quick quiz

1 What are the advantages of computerised data processing over manual data processing?

2 What is a CPU?

3 What are the disadvantages of portable PCs?

4 What is an application?

5 Explain the following terms.

MICR, OCR, OMR

6 Which gives better quality output: a dot matrix printer or a laser printer?

7 What is the disadvantage of tape storage?

8 List five features of a spreadsheet package.

9 What are the disadvantages of statistical packages?

Answers to quick quiz

1
- Speed
- Accuracy
- Volume and complexity
- Access to information

2 The **CPU** is the collection of circuitry and registers that performs the processing in a particular computer and provides that computer with its specific characteristics. It is divided into three areas.

- The arithmetic and logic unit
- The control unit
- The main store, or memory

3
- Keyboard ergonomics
- Battery power
- Relative expense

4 An **application** is a ready-made program written to perform a particular job for the user rather than operate the computer.

5 **MICR** (magnetic ink character recognition) is the recognition of characters by a machine that reads special formatted characters printed in magnetic ink.

OCR (optical character recognition) is a method of input which involves a machine that is able to read characters by optical detection of the shape of those characters.

OMR (optical mark reading). Values are denoted by a line or cross in an appropriate box on a pre-printed source document. The document is then read by a device which senses the mark in each box and translates it into machine code. Eg, you use OMR when you do multiple choice questions in an exam.

6 Laser printer.

7 It is only practical when every record on the file will be processed in turn.

8
- Print commands
- File commands
- Cell editing facilities
- Facilities to rearrange the spreadsheet
- Copy a formula

(see paragraph 7.5 for full listing)

9
- Users must understand what the calculated statistics mean before they can draw any conclusions from the results calculated.
- As it is easy to use, data must be set up incorrectly and therefore the wrong conclusions may be drawn.

Now try the question below from the Exam Question Bank

Number	Level	Marks	Time
2	MCQ	n/a	n/a

Chapter 3

COST CLASSIFICATION

Topic list		Syllabus reference
1	Total product/service costs	1(b), (d)
2	Direct costs and indirect costs	1(b), (d), 3(b), (c)
3	Functional costs	1(b), (d)
4	Fixed costs and variable costs	1(b), (d)
5	Product costs and period costs	1(b), (d)
6	Other cost classifications	1(b), (d)
7	Cost units, cost objects and responsibility centres	1(b), (d)

Introduction

The **classification of costs** as either **direct** or **indirect**, for example, is essential in the costing method used by an organisation to determine the cost of a unit of product or service.

The **fixed** and **variable cost classifications**, on the other hand, are important in **absorption** and **marginal costing**, **cost behaviour** and **cost-volume-profit analysis**. You will meet all of these topics as we progress through the Study Text.

This chapter therefore acts as a foundation stone for a number of other chapters in the text and hence an understanding of the concepts covered in it is vital before you move on.

Study guide

Section 2 – Management information systems

- Describe the various types of responsibility centres and the impact of these on management information

Section 5 – Cost classification

- Explain and illustrate classifications used in the analysis of product/service costs including by function, direct and indirect, product and period, fixed and variable, avoidable and unavoidable, controllable and uncontrollable
- Explain and illustrate the concept of cost objects, cost units, cost centres, revenue centres, profit centres and investment centres
- Describe briefly the process of accounting for input costs and relating them to work done

Exam guide

Cost classification is one of the key areas of the syllabus and you can therefore expect to see it in the exam that you will be facing.

1 TOTAL PRODUCT/SERVICE COSTS

1.1 The total cost of making a product or providing a service consists of the following.

(a) Cost of **materials**

(b) Cost of the **wages** and **salaries** (labour costs)

(c) Cost of **other expenses**

- Rent and rates
- Electricity and gas bills
- Depreciation

2 DIRECT COSTS AND INDIRECT COSTS

2.1 Materials, labour costs and other expenses can be classified as either **direct costs** or **indirect costs**.

KEY TERMS

- A **direct cost** is a cost that can be traced in full to the product, service, or department that is being costed.
- An **indirect cost** or **overhead** is a cost that is incurred in the course of making a product, providing a service or running a department, but which cannot be traced directly and in full to the product, service or department.

2.2 (a) **Direct material costs** are the costs of materials that are known to have been used in making and selling a product (or even providing a service).

(b) **Direct labour costs** are the specific costs of the workforce used to make a product or provide a service. Direct labour costs are established by measuring the time taken for a job, or the time taken in 'direct production work'.

(c) **Other direct expenses** are those expenses that have been incurred in full as a direct consequence of making a product, or providing a service, or running a department.

2.3 Examples of indirect costs include supervisors' wages, cleaning materials and buildings insurance.

2.4 Total expenditure may therefore be analysed as follows.

Materials	=	Direct materials	+	Indirect materials
+		+		+
Labour	=	Direct labour	+	Indirect labour
+		+		+
Expenses	=	Direct expenses	+	Indirect expenses
Total cost	=	Direct cost	+	Overhead

Direct material

KEY TERM

Direct material is all material becoming part of the product (unless used in negligible amounts and/or having negligible cost).

2.5 Direct material costs are charged to the product as part of the **prime cost**. Examples of direct material are as follows.

(a) **Component parts,** specially purchased for a particular job, order or process.

(b) **Part-finished work** which is transferred from department 1 to department 2 becomes finished work of department 1 and a direct material cost in department 2.

(c) **Primary packing materials** like cartons and boxes.

Direct labour

KEY TERM

Direct wages are all wages paid for labour (either as basic hours or as overtime) expended on work on the product itself.

2.6 **Direct wages** costs are charged to the product as part of the **prime cost**.

Examples of groups of labour receiving payment as direct wages are as follows.

(a) Workers engaged in **altering** the condition or composition of the product.
(b) Inspectors, analysts and testers **specifically required** for such production.
(c) Foremen, shop clerks and anyone else whose wages are **specifically identified.**

2.7 Two **trends** may be identified in **direct labour costs.**

- The ratio of direct labour costs to total product cost is falling as the use of machinery increases, and hence depreciation charges increase.
- Skilled labour costs and sub-contractors' costs are increasing as direct labour costs decrease.

Question 1

Classify the following labour costs as either direct or indirect.

(a) The basic pay of direct workers (cash paid, tax and other deductions)
(b) The basic pay of indirect workers
(c) Overtime premium
(d) Bonus payments
(e) Employer's National Insurance contributions
(f) Idle time of direct workers
(g) Work on installation of equipment

Answer

(a) The basic pay of direct workers is a direct cost to the unit, job or process.

(b) The basic pay of indirect workers is an indirect cost, unless a customer asks for an order to be carried out which involves the dedicated use of indirect workers' time, when the cost of this time would be a direct labour cost of the order.

(c) Overtime premium paid to both direct and indirect workers is an indirect cost, except in two particular circumstances.

(i) If overtime is worked at the specific request of a customer to get his order completed, the overtime premium paid is a direct cost of the order.

(ii) If overtime is worked regularly by a production department in the normal course of operations, the overtime premium paid to direct workers could be incorporated into the (average) direct labour hourly rate.

(d) Bonus payments are generally an indirect cost.

(e) Employer's National Insurance contributions (which are added to employees' total pay as a wages cost) are normally treated as an indirect labour cost.

(f) Idle time is an overhead cost, that is an indirect labour cost.

(g) The cost of work on capital equipment is incorporated into the capital cost of the equipment.

Direct expenses

KEY TERM

Direct expenses are any expenses which are incurred on a specific product other than direct material cost and direct wages

2.8 **Direct expenses** are charged to the product as part of the **prime** cost. Examples of direct expenses are as follows.

- The **hire of tools** or equipment for a particular job
- **Maintenance costs** of tools, fixtures and so on

Direct expenses are also referred to as **chargeable expenses.**

Production overhead

KEY TERM

Production (or factory) overhead includes all indirect material costs, indirect wages and indirect expenses incurred in the factory from receipt of the order until its completion.

2.9 Production overhead includes the following.

(a) **Indirect materials** which cannot be traced in the finished product.

- Consumable stores, eg material used in negligible amounts

(b) **Indirect wages,** meaning all wages not charged directly to a product.

- Wages of non-productive personnel in the production department, eg foremen

(c) **Indirect expenses** (other than material and labour) not charged directly to production.

- Rent, rates and insurance of a factory
- Depreciation, fuel, power, maintenance of plant, machinery and buildings

Administration overhead

> **KEY TERM**
>
> **Administration overhead** is all indirect material costs, wages and expenses incurred in the direction, control and administration of an undertaking.

2.10 Examples of administration overhead are as follows.

- **Depreciation** of office buildings and equipment.
- **Office salaries**, including salaries of directors, secretaries and accountants.
- Rent, rates, insurance, lighting, cleaning, telephone charges and so on.

Selling overhead

> **KEY TERM**
>
> **Selling overhead** is all indirect materials costs, wages and expenses incurred in promoting sales and retaining customers.

2.11 Examples of selling overhead are as follows.

- **Printing** and **stationery**, such as catalogues and price lists.
- **Salaries** and **commission** of salesmen, representatives and sales department staff.
- **Advertising** and **sales promotion**, market research.
- Rent, rates and insurance of sales offices and showrooms, bad debts and so on.

Distribution overhead

> **KEY TERM**
>
> **Distribution overhead** is all indirect material costs, wages and expenses incurred in making the packed product ready for despatch and delivering it to the customer.

2.12 Examples of distribution overhead are as follows.

- Cost of packing cases.
- Wages of packers, drivers and despatch clerks.
- Insurance charges, rent, rates, depreciation of warehouses and so on.

Question 2

A direct labour employee's wage in week 5 consists of the following.

		£
(a)	Basic pay for normal hours worked, 36 hours at £4 per hour =	144
(b)	Pay at the basic rate for overtime, 6 hours at £4 per hour =	24
(c)	Overtime shift premium, with overtime paid at time-and-a-quarter ¼ × 6 hours × £4 per hour =	6
(d)	A bonus payment under a group bonus (or 'incentive') scheme - bonus for the month =	30
	Total gross wages in week 5 for 42 hours of work	204

What is the direct labour cost for this employee in week 5?

A £144   B £168   C £198   D £204

Answer

Let's start by considering a general approach to answering multiple choice questions (MCQs). In a numerical question like this, the best way to begin is to ignore the available options and work out your own answer from the available data. If your solution corresponds to one of the four options then mark this as your chosen answer and move on. Don't waste time working out whether any of the other options might be correct. If your answer does not appear among the available options then check your workings. If it still does not correspond to any of the options then you need to take a calculated guess.

Do not make the common error of simply selecting the answer which is closest to yours. The best thing to do is to first eliminate any answers which you know or suspect are incorrect. For example you could eliminate C and D because you know that group bonus schemes are usually indirect costs. You are then left with a choice between A and B, and at least you have now improved your chances if you really are guessing.

The correct answer is B because the basic rate for overtime is a part of direct wages cost. It is only the overtime premium that is usually regarded as an overhead or indirect cost.

3 FUNCTIONAL COSTS

Classification by function

3.1 In a 'traditional' costing system for a manufacturing organisation, costs are classified as follows.

(a) **Production** or **manufacturing costs.** These are costs associated with the factory.

(b) **Administration costs.** These are costs associated with general office departments.

(c) **Marketing,** or **selling** and **distribution costs.** These are costs associated with sales, marketing, warehousing and transport departments.

Classification in this way is known as **classification by function**. Expenses that do not fall fully into one of these classifications might be categorised as **general overheads** or even listed as a classification on their own (for example research and development costs).

3.2 In costing a small product made by a manufacturing organisation, direct costs are usually restricted to some of the production costs. A commonly found build-up of costs is therefore as follows.

	£
Production costs	
Direct materials	A
Direct wages	B
Direct expenses	C
Prime cost	A+B+C
Production overheads	D
Full factory cost	A+B+C+D
Administration costs	E
Selling and distribution costs	F
Full cost of sales	A+B+C+D+E+F

3.3 Functional costs include the following.

(a) **Production costs** are the costs which are incurred by the sequence of operations beginning with the supply of raw materials, and ending with the completion of the product ready for warehousing as a finished goods item. Packaging costs are production costs where they relate to 'primary' packing (boxes, wrappers and so on).

(b) **Administration costs** are the costs of managing an organisation, that is, planning and controlling its operations, but only insofar as such administration costs are not related to the production, sales, distribution or research and development functions.

(c) **Selling costs**, sometimes known as marketing costs, are the costs of creating demand for products and securing firm orders from customers.

(d) **Distribution costs** are the costs of the sequence of operations with the receipt of finished goods from the production department and making them ready for despatch and ending with the reconditioning for reuse of empty containers.

(e) **Research costs** are the costs of searching for new or improved products, whereas **development costs** are the costs incurred between the decision to produce a new or improved product and the commencement of full manufacture of the product.

(f) **Financing costs** are costs incurred to finance the business such as loan interest.

Question 3

Within the costing system of a manufacturing company the following types of expense are incurred.

Reference number	
1	Cost of oils used to lubricate production machinery
2	Motor vehicle licences for lorries
3	Depreciation of factory plant and equipment
4	Cost of chemicals used in the laboratory
5	Commission paid to sales representatives
6	Salary of the secretary to the finance director
7	Trade discount given to customers
8	Holiday pay of machine operatives
9	Salary of security guard in raw material warehouse
10	Fees to advertising agency
11	Rent of finished goods warehouse
12	Salary of scientist in laboratory
13	Insurance of the company's premises
14	Salary of supervisor working in the factory
15	Cost of typewriter ribbons in the general office
16	Protective clothing for machine operatives

Required

Complete the following table by placing each expense in the correct cost classification.

Cost classification	Reference number					
Production costs						
Selling and distribution costs						
Administration costs						
Research and development costs						

Each type of expense should appear only once in your answer. You may use the reference numbers in your answer.

Answer

Cost classification	Reference number					
Production costs	1	3	8	9	14	16
Selling and distribution costs	2	5	7	10	11	
Administration costs	6	13	15			
Research and development costs	4	12				

4 FIXED COSTS AND VARIABLE COSTS

4.1 A different way of analysing and classifying costs is into **fixed costs** and **variable costs.** Some items of expenditure are part-fixed and part-variable or 'semi-fixed' costs but, in cost accounting, **semi-fixed** or **semi-variable costs** are divided into their fixed and variable elements.

KEY TERMS

- A **fixed cost** is a cost which is incurred for a particular period of time and which, within certain activity levels, is unaffected by changes in the level of activity.
- A **variable cost** is a cost which tends to vary with the level of activity.

4.2 Examples of fixed and variable costs are as follows.

(a) Direct material costs are **variable costs** because they rise as more units of a product are manufactured.

(b) Sales commission is often a fixed percentage of sales turnover, and so is a **variable cost** that varies with the level of sales.

(c) Telephone call charges are likely to increase if the volume of business expands, but there is also a fixed element of line rental, and so they are a **semi-fixed** or **semi-variable overhead cost.**

(d) The rental cost of business premises is a constant amount, at least within a stated time period, and so it is a **fixed cost.**

5 PRODUCT COSTS AND PERIOD COSTS

KEY TERMS

- **Product costs** are costs identified with a finished product. Such costs are initially identified as part of the value of stock. They become expenses (in the form of cost of goods sold) only when the stock is sold.

- **Period costs** are costs that are deducted as expenses during the current period without ever being included in the value of stock held.

5.1 When preparing financial statements (a profit and loss account and balance sheet), accountants frequently distinguish between **product costs** and **period costs.**

6 OTHER COST CLASSIFICATIONS

KEY TERMS

- **Avoidable costs** are specific costs of an activity or business which would be avoided if the activity or business did not exist.
- **Unavoidable costs** are costs which would be incurred whether or not an activity or sector existed.
- A **controllable cost** is a cost which can be influenced by management decisions and actions.
- An **uncontrollable cost** is any cost that cannot be affected by management within a given time span.
- **Discretionary costs** are costs which are likely to arise from decisions made during the budgeting process. They are likely to be fixed amounts of money over fixed periods of time.

6.1 Examples of discretionary costs are as follows.

- Advertising
- Research and Development
- Training

7 COST UNITS, COST OBJECTS AND RESPONSIBILITY CENTRES

Allocation of costs to cost centres

7.1 Costs consist of the costs of the following.

- Direct materials
- Direct labour
- Direct expenses
- Production overheads
- Administration overheads
- General overheads

7.2 When costs are incurred, they are generally allocated to a **cost centre.** A cost centre acts as a **collecting place** for certain costs before they are analysed further. Cost centres may include the following.

- A department
- A machine, or group of machines
- A project (eg the installation of a new computer system)

- Overhead costs eg rent, rates, electricity (which may then be allocated to departments or projects)

7.3 Cost centres are an essential 'building block' of a costing system. They are the starting point for the following.

(a) The classification of actual costs incurred.
(b) The preparation of budgets of planned costs.
(c) The comparison of actual costs and budgeted costs (management control).

Cost units

7.4 Once costs have been traced to cost centres, they can be further analysed in order to establish a **cost per cost unit**. Alternatively, some items of cost may be charged directly to a cost unit, for example direct materials and direct labour costs.

> **KEY TERM**
>
> A **cost unit** is a unit of product or service to which costs can be related. The cost unit is the basic control unit for costing purposes.

7.5 Examples of cost units include the following.

- Patient episode (in a hospital)
- Barrel (in the brewing industry)
- Room (in a hotel)

Question 4

Suggest suitable cost units which could be used to aid control within the following organisations.

(a) A hotel with 50 double rooms and 10 single rooms
(b) A hospital
(c) A road haulage business

Answer

(a)
- Guest/night
- Bed occupied/night
- Meal supplied

(b)
- Patient/night
- Operation
- Outpatient visit

(c)
- Tonne/mile
- Mile

Cost objects

> **KEY TERM**
>
> A **cost object (or objective)** is any activity for which a separate measurement of costs is desired.

7.6 If the users of management information wish to know the cost of something, this something is called a **cost object**. Examples include the following.

- The cost of a product
- The cost of a service
- The cost of operating a department

Profit centres

7.7 We have seen that a cost centre is where costs are collected. Some organisations, however, work on a profit centre basis. A **profit centre** is similar to a cost centre but is accountable for **costs** *and* **revenues**.

7.8 Profit centre managers should normally have control over how revenue is raised and how costs are incurred. Often, several cost centres will comprise one profit centre.

Revenue centres

7.9 A **revenue centre** is similar to a cost centre and a profit centre but is accountable for **revenues only**.

7.10 Revenue centre managers should normally have control over how revenues are raised.

Investment centres

KEY TERM

An **investment centre** is 'A profit centre with additional responsibilities for capital investment and possibly for financing, and whose performance is measured by its return on investment'. (CIMA *Official Terminology*)

Responsibility centres

7.11 Cost centres, revenue centres, profit centres and investment centres are also known as **responsibility centres**.

KEY TERM

A **responsibility centre** is a department or organisational function whose performance is the direct responsibility of a specific manager.

Exam focus point

This chapter has introduced a number of new terms and definitions. The topics covered in this chapter are key areas of the syllabus and are likely to be tested in the **Financial Information for Management** examination that you will be facing.

Chapter roundup

- A **direct cost** is a cost that can be traced in full to the product, service or department being costed. An **indirect cost** (or overhead) is a cost that is incurred in the course of making a product, providing a service or running a department, but which cannot be traced directly and in full to the product, service or department.
- **Classification by function** involves classifying costs as production/manufacturing costs, administration costs or marketing/selling and distribution costs.
- A different way of analysing and classifying costs is into **fixed costs** and **variable costs**. Many items of expenditure are part-fixed and part-variable and hence are termed **semi-fixed** or **semi-variable**.
- For the preparation of financial statements, costs are often classified as **product costs** and **period costs**. Product costs are costs identified with goods produced or purchased for resale. Period costs are costs deducted as expenses during the current period.
- **Cost centres** are collecting places for costs before they are further analysed. Costs are further analysed into cost units once they have been traced to cost centres.
- A **cost unit** is a unit of product or service to which costs can be related.
- A **cost object** is any activity for which a separate measure of costs is desired.
- **Profit centres** are similar to cost centres but are accountable for both costs and revenues.
- **Revenue centres** are similar to cost centres and profit centres but are accountable for revenues only.
- An **investment centre** is a profit centre with additional responsibilities for capital investment and possibly financing.
- A **responsibility centre** is a department or organisational function whose performance is the direct responsibility of a specific manager.

Quick quiz

1. Give two examples of direct expenses.
2. Give an example of an administration overhead, a selling overhead and a distribution overhead.
3. What are functional costs?
4. What is the distinction between fixed and variable costs?
5. What are product costs and period costs?
6. What is a cost centre?
7. What is a cost unit?
8. What is a profit centre?
9. What is an investment centre?

Answers to quick quiz

1
- The hire of tools or equipment for a particular job
- Maintenance costs of tools, fixtures and so on

2
- **Administration overhead** = Depreciation of office buildings and equipment
- **Selling overhead** = Printing and stationery (catalogues, price lists)
- **Distribution overhead** = Wages of packers, drivers and despatch clerks

3 Functional costs are classified as follows.

- **Production** or **manufacturing costs**
- **Administration costs**
- **Marketing** or **selling and distribution costs**

4 A **fixed cost** is a cost which is incurred for a particular period of time and which, within certain activity levels, is unaffected by changes in the level of activity.

A **variable cost** is a cost which tends to vary with the level of activity.

5 **Product costs** are costs identified with a finished product. Such costs are initially identified as part of the value of stock. They become expenses only when the stock is sold.

Period costs are costs that are deducted as expenses during the current period without ever being included in the value of stock held.

6 A **cost centre** acts as a collecting place for certain costs before they are analysed further.

7 A **cost unit** is a unit of product or service to which costs can be related. The cost unit is the basic control unit for costing purposes.

8 A **profit centre** is similar to a cost centre but is accountable for **costs** and **revenues**.

9 An **investment centre** is a profit centre with additional responsibilities for capital investment and possibly financing.

Now try the question below from the Exam Question Bank

Number	Level	Marks	Time
3	MCQ	n/a	n/a

Chapter 4

COST BEHAVIOUR

Topic list		Syllabus reference
1	Introduction to cost behaviour	6(a)
2	Cost behaviour patterns	6(a)
3	Determining the fixed and variable elements of semi-variable costs	6(a)

Introduction

So far in this text we have introduced you to the subject of management information and explained in general terms what it is and what it does. In Chapter 3 we considered the principal methods of classifying costs. In particular, we introduced the concept of the division of costs into those that vary directly with changes in activity levels (**variable costs**) and those that do not (**fixed costs**). This chapter examines further this two-way split of **cost behaviour** and explains one method of splitting semi-variable costs into these two elements, the **high-low** method.

Study guide

Section 6 – Cost behaviour 1

- Explain the importance of cost behaviour in relation to business decision making
- Describe factors which influence cost behaviour
- Explain how the terms linear, curvilinear and step functions apply to costs
- Identify, describe and illustrate graphically different types of cost behaviour
- Provide examples of costs which contain both fixed and variable elements
- Use high/low analysis to separate the fixed and variable elements of such costs

Exam guide

Cost behaviour is a key area of the **Financial Information for Management** syllabus and could be examined in detail either in Section A or Section B of the paper-based examination.

1 INTRODUCTION TO COST BEHAVIOUR

Cost behaviour and decision making

KEY TERM

Cost behaviour is the way in which costs are affected by changes in the volume of output.

1.1 Management decisions will often be based on how costs and revenues vary at different activity levels. Examples of such decisions are as follows.

- What should the **planned activity level** be for the next period?
- Should the **selling price** be reduced in order to sell more units?
- Should a particular component be **manufactured internally** or **bought in**?
- Should a **contract** be undertaken?

Cost behaviour and cost control

1.2 If the accountant does not know the level of costs which should have been incurred as a result of an organisation's activities, how can he or she hope to control costs?

Cost behaviour and budgeting

1.3 Knowledge of cost behaviour is obviously essential for the tasks of **budgeting, decision making** and **control accounting**.

Exam focus point
Remember that the behavioural analysis of costs is important for planning, control and decision-making.

Cost behaviour and levels of activity

1.4 There are many factors which may influence costs. The major influence is **volume of output**, or the **level of activity**. The level of activity may refer to one of the following.

- Number of units produced
- Value of items sold
- Number of items sold
- Number of invoices issued
- Number of units of electricity consumed

Cost behaviour principles

1.5 The basic principle of cost behaviour is that **as the level of activity rises, costs will usually rise**. It will cost more to produce 2,000 units of output than it will cost to produce 1,000 units.

1.6 This principle is common sense. The problem for the accountant, however, is to determine, for each item of cost, the way in which costs rise and by how much as the level of activity increases. For our purposes here, the level of activity for measuring cost will generally be taken to be the **volume of production**.

1.7 EXAMPLE: COST BEHAVIOUR AND ACTIVITY LEVEL

Hans Bratch Ltd has a fleet of company cars for sales representatives. Running costs have been estimated as follows.

(a) Cars cost £12,000 when new, and have a guaranteed trade-in value of £6,000 at the end of two years. Depreciation is charged on a straight-line basis.

(b) Petrol and oil cost 15 pence per mile.

(c) Tyres cost £300 per set to replace; replacement occurs after 30,000 miles.

(d) Routine maintenance costs £200 per car (on average) in the first year and £450 in the second year.

(e) Repairs average £400 per car over two years and are thought to vary with mileage. The average car travels 25,000 miles per annum.

(f) Tax, insurance, membership of motoring organisations and so on cost £400 per annum per car.

Required

Calculate the average cost per annum of cars which travel 20,000 miles per annum and 30,000 miles per annum.

1.8 SOLUTION

Costs may be analysed into fixed, variable and stepped cost items, a stepped cost being a cost which is fixed in nature but only within certain levels of activity.

(a) **Fixed costs**

	£ per annum
Depreciation £(12,000 – 6,000) ÷ 2	3,000
Routine maintenance £(200 + 450) ÷ 2	325
Tax, insurance etc	400
	3,725

(b) **Variable costs**

	Pence per mile
Petrol and oil	15.0
Repairs (£400 ÷ 50,000 miles)	0.8
	15.8

(c) Step costs are tyre replacement costs, which are £300 at the end of every 30,000 miles.

(i) If the car travels less than or exactly 30,000 miles in two years, the tyres will not be changed. Average cost of tyres per annum = £0.

(ii) If a car travels more than 30,000 miles and up to (and including) 60,000 miles in two years, there will be one change of tyres in the period. Average cost of tyres per annum = £150 (£300 ÷ 2).

(iii) If a car exceeds 60,000 miles in two years (up to 90,000 miles) there will be two tyre changes. Average cost of tyres per annum = £300. (£600 ÷ 2).

The estimated costs per annum of cars travelling 20,000 miles per annum and 30,000 miles per annum would therefore be as follows.

	20,000 miles per annum £	*30,000 miles per annum* £
Fixed costs	3,725	3,725
Variable costs (15.8p per mile)	3,160	4,740
Tyres	–	150
Cost per annum	6,885	8,615

2 COST BEHAVIOUR PATTERNS

Fixed costs

KEY TERM

A **fixed cost** is a cost which tends to be unaffected by increases or decreases in the volume of output.

2.1 Fixed costs are a **period charge**, in that they relate to a span of time; as the time span increases, so too will the fixed costs (which are sometimes referred to as period costs for this reason). It is important to understand that **fixed costs always have a variable element,** since an increase or decrease in production may also bring about an increase or decrease in fixed costs.

2.2 A sketch graph of a fixed cost would look like this.

Graph of fixed cost

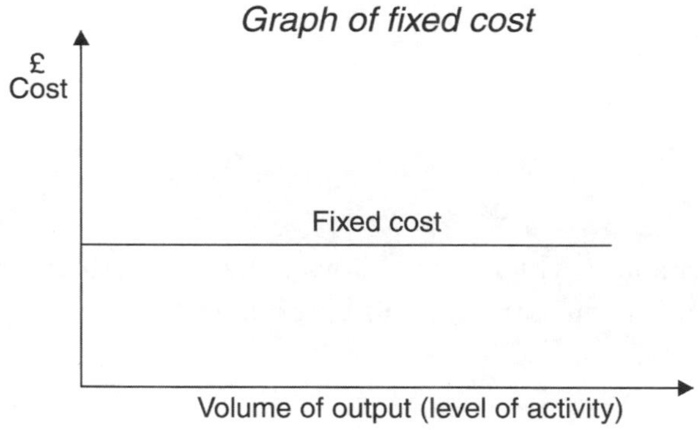

Examples of a fixed cost would be as follows.

- The salary of the managing director (per month or per annum)
- The rent of a single factory building (per month or per annum)
- Straight line depreciation of a single machine (per month or per annum)

Step costs

KEY TERM

A **step cost** is a cost which is fixed in nature but only within certain levels of activity.

2.3 Consider the depreciation of a machine which may be fixed if production remains below 1,000 units per month. If production exceeds 1,000 units, a second machine may be required, and the cost of depreciation (on two machines) would go up a step. A sketch graph of a step cost could look like this.

Graph of step cost

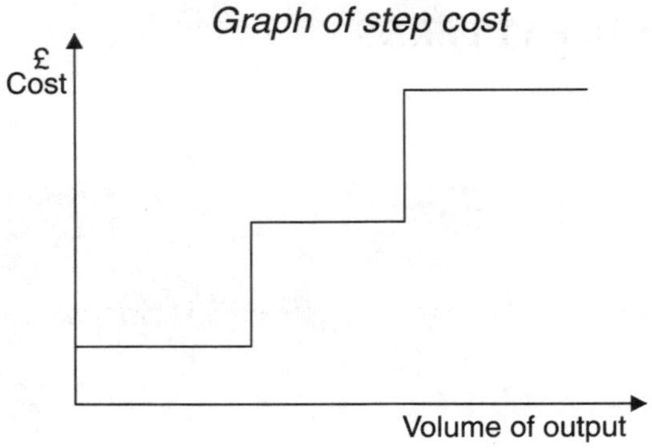

Other examples of step costs are as follows.

(a) Rent is a step cost in situations where accommodation requirements increase as output levels get higher.

(b) Basic pay of employees is nowadays usually fixed, but as output rises, more employees (direct workers, supervisors, managers and so on) are required.

(c) Royalties.

Variable costs

KEY TERM

A **variable cost** is a cost which tends to vary directly with the volume of output. The variable cost per unit is the same amount for each unit produced.

2.4

Graph of variable cost (1)

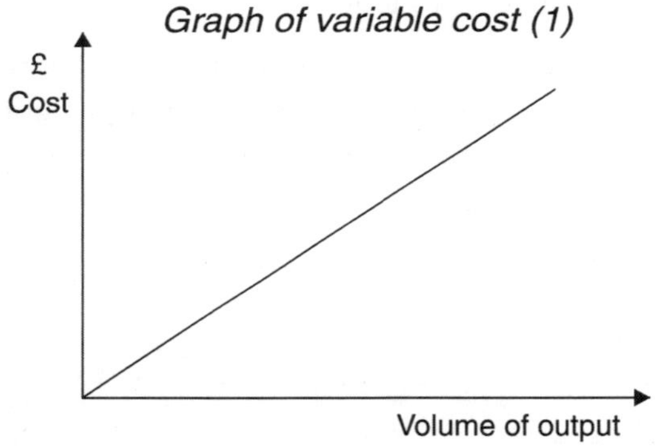

2.5 A constant variable cost per unit implies that the price per unit of say, material purchased is constant, and that the rate of material usage is also constant.

(a) The most important variable cost is the **cost of raw materials** (where there is no discount for bulk purchasing since bulk purchase discounts reduce the cost of purchases).

(b) **Direct labour costs** are, for very important reasons, classed as a variable cost even though basic wages are usually fixed.

(c) **Sales commission** is variable in relation to the volume or value of sales.

(d) **Bonus payments** for productivity to employees might be variable once a certain level of output is achieved, as the following diagram illustrates.

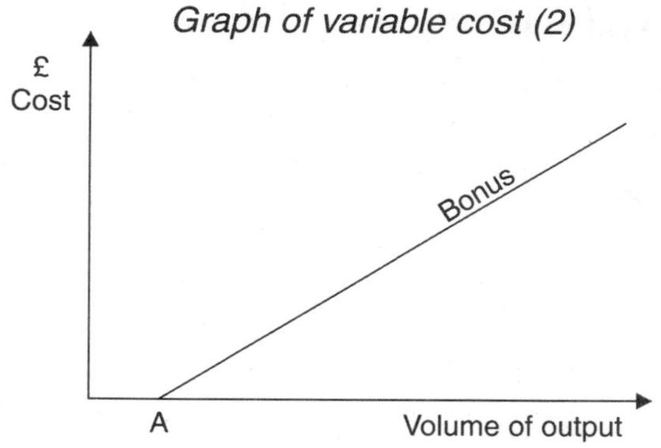

Up to output A, no bonus is earned.

Non-linear or curvilinear variable costs

> **KEY TERM**
>
> If the relationship between total variable cost and volume of output can be shown as a curved line on a graph, the relationship is said to be **curvilinear**.

2.6 Two typical relationships are as follows.

(a)

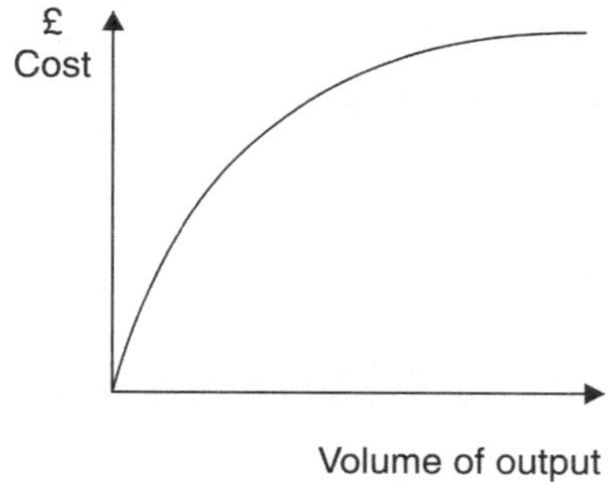

(b)

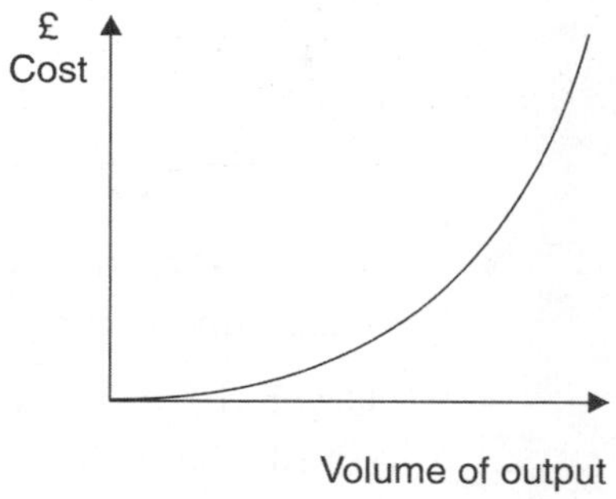

Each extra unit of output in graph (a) causes a **less than proportionate** increase in cost whereas in graph (b), each extra unit of output causes **a more than proportionate** increase in cost.

2.7 The cost of a piecework scheme for individual workers with differential rates could behave in a **curvilinear** fashion if the rates increase by small amounts at progressively higher output levels.

Semi-variable costs (or semi-fixed costs or mixed costs)

> **KEY TERM**
>
> A **semi-variable/semi-fixed/mixed cost** is a cost which contains both fixed and variable components and so is partly affected by changes in the level of activity.

2.8 Examples of these costs include the following.

(a) **Electricity and gas bills**

- Fixed cost = standing charge
- Variable cost = charge per unit of electricity used

(b) **Salesman's salary**

- Fixed cost = basic salary
- Variable cost = commission on sales made

(c) **Costs of running a car**

- Fixed cost = road tax, insurance
- Variable costs = petrol, oil, repairs (which vary with miles travelled)

Other cost behaviour patterns

2.9 Other cost behaviour patterns may be appropriate to certain cost items. Examples of two other cost behaviour patterns are shown below.

(a) *Cost behaviour pattern (1)*

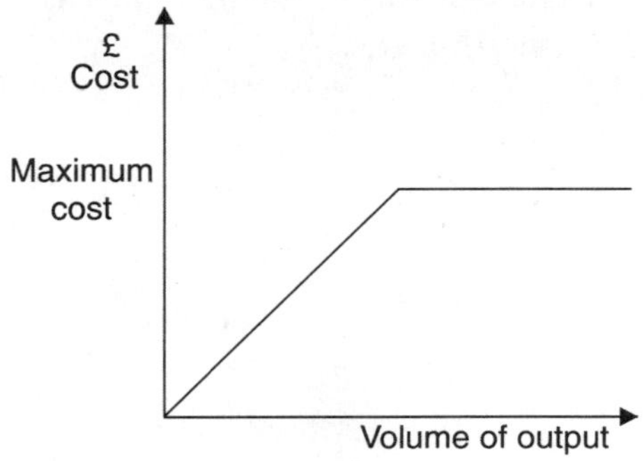

(b) *Cost behaviour pattern (2)*

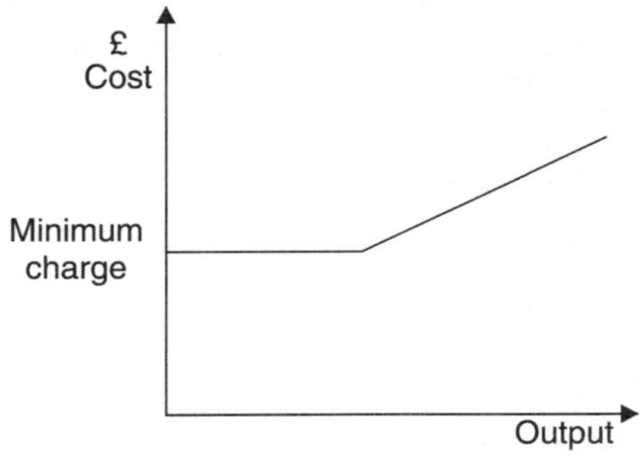

- Graph (a) represents an item of cost which is variable with output up to a certain maximum level of cost.
- Graph (b) represents a cost which is variable with output, subject to a minimum (fixed) charge.

Cost behaviour and total and unit costs

2.10 The following table relates to different levels of production of the zed. The variable cost of producing a zed is £5. Fixed costs are £5,000.

	1 zed £	10 zeds £	50 zeds £
Total variable cost	5	50	250
Variable cost per unit	5	5	5
Total fixed cost	5,000	5,000	5,000
Fixed cost per unit	5,000	500	100
Total cost (fixed and variable)	5,005	5,050	5,250
Total cost per unit	5,005	505	105

What happens when activity levels rise can be summarised as follows.

- The variable cost per unit remains constant
- The fixed cost per unit falls
- The total cost per unit falls

This may be illustrated graphically as follows.

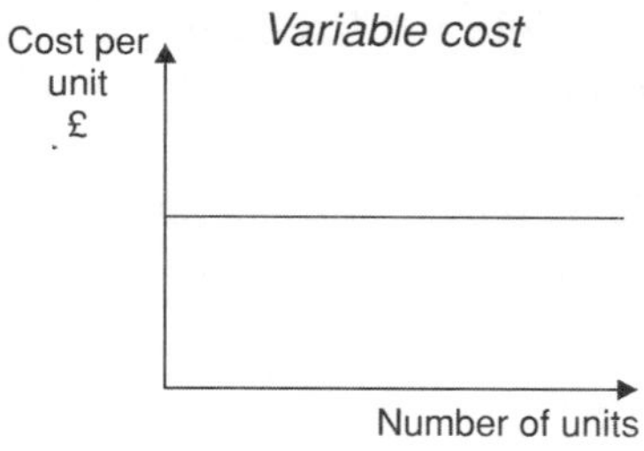

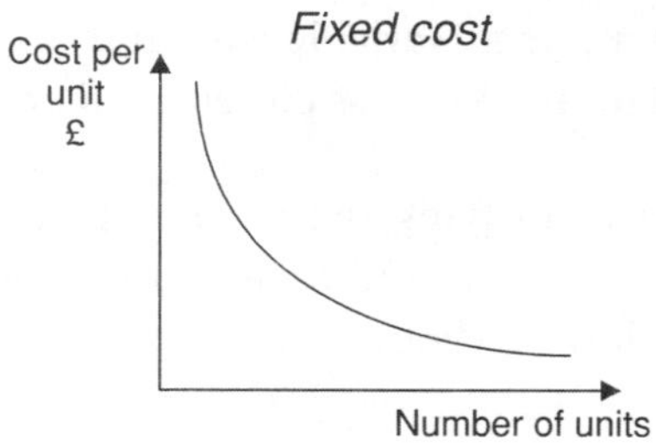

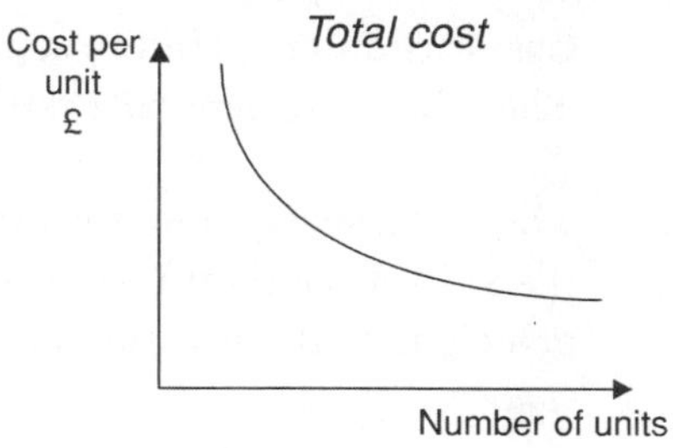

Question 1

Are the following likely to be fixed, variable or mixed costs?

(a) Telephone bill
(b) Annual salary of the chief accountant
(c) The management accountant's annual membership fee to CIMA (paid by the company)
(d) Cost of materials used to pack 20 units of product X into a box
(e) Wages of warehousemen

Answer

(a) Mixed
(b) Fixed
(c) Fixed
(d) Variable
(e) Variable

Exam focus point

Remember that you can pick up easy marks in the paper-based examination for drawing graphs neatly. Always use a ruler, label your axes and use an appropriate scale.

Assumptions about cost behaviour

2.11 Assumptions about cost behaviour include the following.

(a) Within the normal or **relevant range** of output, costs are often assumed to be either **fixed, variable** or **semi-variable** (mixed).

(b) Departmental costs within an organisation are assumed to be **mixed costs,** with a **fixed** and a **variable** element.

(c) Departmental costs are assumed to rise in a straight line as the volume of activity increases. In other words, these costs are said to be **linear.**

2.12 The **high-low method** of determining fixed and variable elements of mixed costs relies on the assumption that mixed costs are linear. We shall now go on to look at this method of cost determination.

3 DETERMINING THE FIXED AND VARIABLE ELEMENTS OF SEMI-VARIABLE COSTS

3.1 It is generally assumed that costs are one of the following.

- Variable
- Fixed
- Semi-variable

Cost accountants tend to separate semi-variable costs into their variable and fixed elements. They therefore generally tend to treat costs as either **fixed** or **variable**.

3.2 There are several methods for identifying the fixed and variable elements of semi-variable costs. Each method is only an estimate, and each will produce different results. One of the principal methods is the **high-low method.**

High-low method

3.3 Follow the steps below to estimate the fixed and variable elements of semi-variable costs.

Step 1. Review records of costs in previous periods.

- Select the period with the **highest** activity level.
- Select the period with the **lowest** activity level.

Step 2. Determine the following.

- Total cost at high activity level
- Total costs at low activity level
- Total units at high activity level
- Total units at low activity level

Step 3. Calculate the following.

$$\frac{\text{Total cost at high activity level} - \text{total cost at low activity level}}{\text{Total units at high activity level} - \text{total units at low activity level}}$$

= variable cost per unit (v)

Step 4. The fixed costs can be determined as follows. (Total cost at high activity level) –(total units at high activity level × variable cost per unit)

3.4 The following graph demonstrates the high-low method.

Demonstration of high-low method

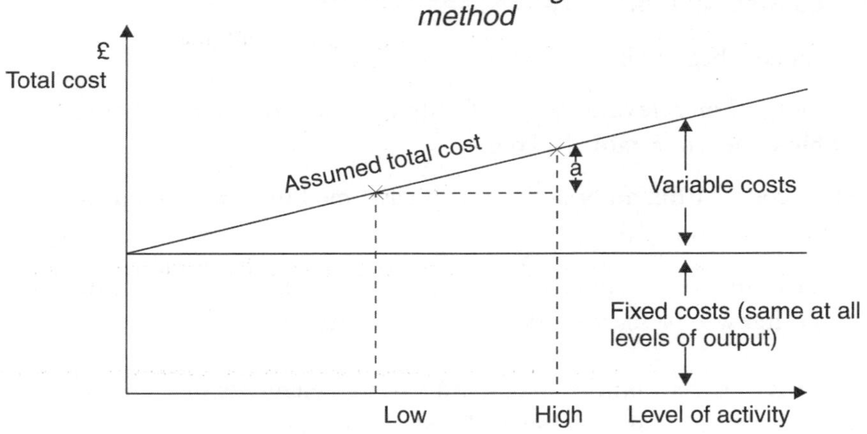

3.5 EXAMPLE: THE HIGH-LOW METHOD

DG Ltd has recorded the following total costs during the last five years.

Year	*Output volume*	*Total cost*
	Units	£
20X0	65,000	145,000
20X1	80,000	162,000
20X2	90,000	170,000
20X3	60,000	140,000
20X4	75,000	160,000

Required

Calculate the total cost that should be expected in 20X5 if output is 85,000 units.

3.6 SOLUTION

Step 1.

- Period with highest activity = 20X2
- Period with lowest activity = 20X3

Step2.

- Total cost at high activity level = 170,000
- Total cost at low activity level = 140,000
- Total units at high activity level = 90,000
- Total units at low activity level = 60,000

Step 3. Variable cost per unit

$$= \frac{\text{total cost at high activity level} - \text{total cost at low activity level}}{\text{total units at high activity level} - \text{total units at low activity level}}$$

$$= \frac{170{,}000 - 140{,}000}{90{,}000 - 60{,}000} = \frac{30{,}000}{30{,}000} = £1 \text{ per unit}$$

Step 4. Fixed costs = (total cost at high activity level) – (total units at high activity level × variable cost per unit)

= 170,000 – (90,000 × 1) = 170,000 – 90,000 = £80,000

Therefore the costs in 20X5 for output of 85,000 units are as follows.

		£
Variable costs =	85,000 × £1 =	85,000
Fixed costs =		80,000
		165,000

3.7 The step-by-step guide has been covered in order that you fully understand the process involved.

Question 2

The Valuation Department of a large firm of surveyors wishes to develop a method of predicting its total costs in a period. The following past costs have been recorded at two activity levels.

	Number of valuations	*Total cost*
	(V)	*(TC)*
Period 1	420	82,200
Period 2	515	90,275

The total cost model for a period could be represented as follows.

A TC = £46,500 + 85V
B TC = £42,000 + 95V
C TC = £46,500 – 85V
D TC = £51,500 – 95V

Answer

Although we only have two activity levels in this question we can still apply the high-low method.

	Valuations	*Total cost*
	V	£
Period 2	515	90,275
Period 1	420	82,200
Change due to variable cost	95	8,075

∴ Variable cost per valuation = £8,075/95 = £85.

Period 2: fixed cost = £90,275 – (515 × £85)

= £46,500

Using good MCQ technique, you should have managed to eliminate C and D as incorrect options straightaway. The variable cost must be added to the fixed cost, rather than subtracted from it. Once you had calculated the variable cost as £85 per valuation (as shown above), you should have been able to select option A without going on to calculate the fixed cost (we have shown this calculation above for completeness).

Chapter roundup

- Costs which are not affected by the level of activity are **fixed** costs or **period** costs.
- Even though fixed costs in total remain constant over a range of activity, the cost per unit will tend to reduce as the level of activity rises because the same fixed cost is being spread over a greater number of units.
- **Step costs** are fixed within a certain range of activity.
- **Variable costs** increase or decrease with the level of activity, and although they can behave in a **curvilinear** fashion, it is usually assumed that there is a linear relationship between cost and activity.
- **Semi-fixed**, **semi-variable** or **mixed costs** are costs which are part fixed and part variable.
- It is often possible to assume that, within the normal range of output, costs are either variable, fixed or semi-variable.
- The fixed and variable elements of semi-variable costs can be determined by the **high-low method**.

Quick quiz

1 Cost behaviour is ....

2 The basic principle of cost behaviour is that as the level of activity rises, costs will usually rise/fall.

3 Fill in the gaps for each of the graph titles below.

(a)

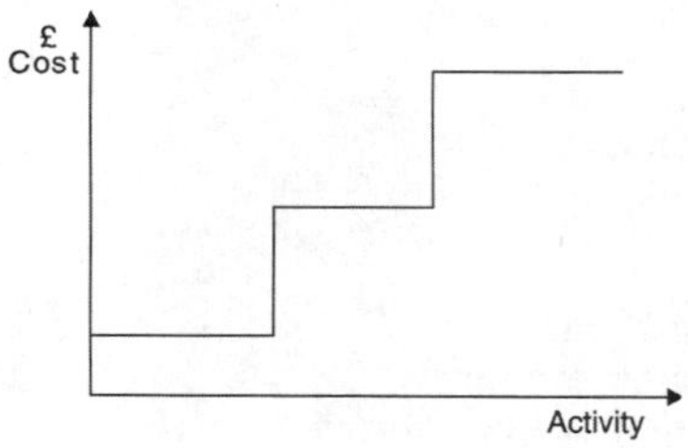

Graph of a ....cost

Example:

(b)

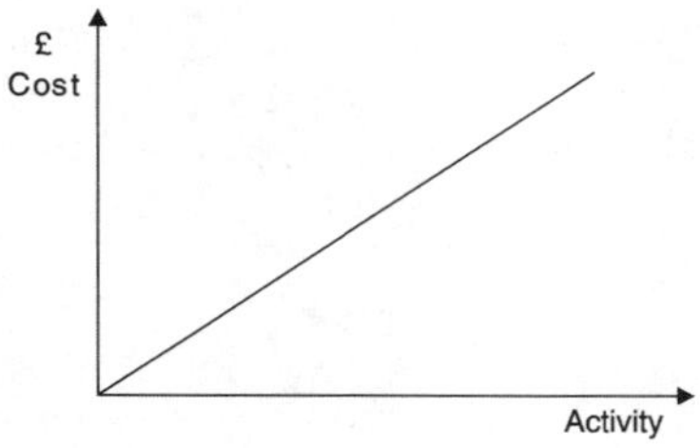

Graph of a ....cost

Example:

(c)

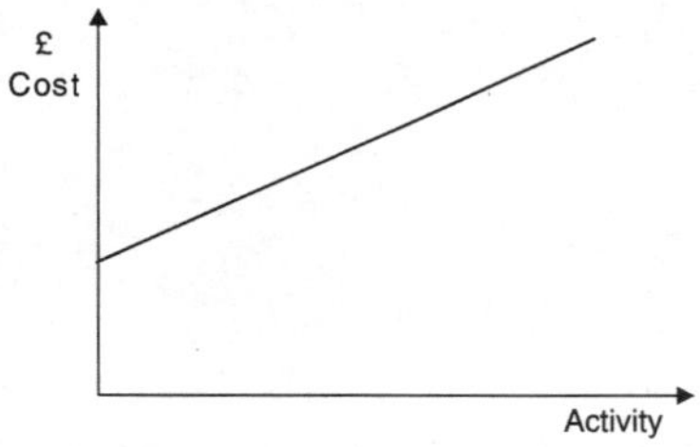

Graph of a ....cost

Example:

(d)

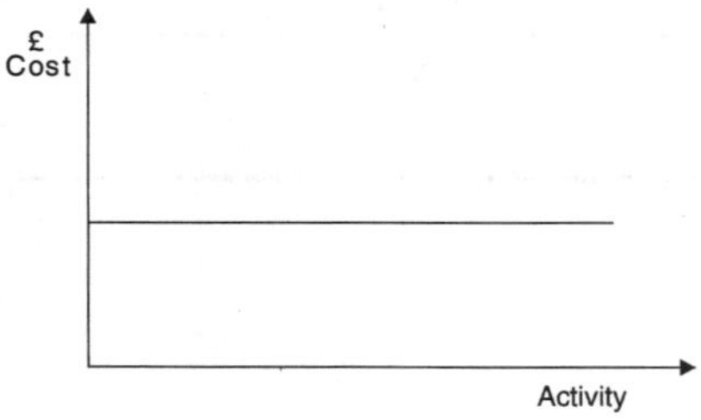

Graph of a ....cost

Example:

4 Costs are assumed to be either fixed, variable or semi-variable within the normal or relevant range of output.

True ☐

False ☐

5 The costs of operating the canteen at 'Eat a lot Company' for the past three months is as follows.

Month	*Cost*	*Employees*
	£	
1	72,500	1,250
2	75,000	1,300
3	68,750	1,175

Variable cost (per employee per month) =
Fixed cost per month =

Answers to quick quiz

1 The variability of input costs with activity undertaken.

2 Rise

3 (a) Step cost. Example: rent, supervisors' salaries
(b) Variable cost. Example: raw materials, direct labour
(c) Semi-variable cost. Example: electricity and telephone
(d) Fixed. Example: rent, depreciation (straight-line)

4 True

5 Variable cost = £50 per employee per month
Fixed costs = £10,000 per month

	Activity	*Cost*
		£
High	1,300	75,000
Low	1,175	68,750
	125	6,250

Variable cost per employee = £6,250/125 = £50

For 1,175 employees, total cost = £68,750

Total cost = variable cost + fixed cost
£68,750 = (1,175 × £50) + fixed cost
∴ Fixed cost = £68,750 – £58,750
= £10,000

Now try the questions below from the Exam Question Bank

Number	Level	Marks	Time
4	MCQ	n/a	n/a
5	Examination	10	18 mins

Chapter 5

CORRELATION AND REGRESSION

Topic list		Syllabus reference
1	Correlation	6(a)
2	The correlation coefficient and the coefficient of determination	6(a)
3	Lines of best fit	6(a)
4	The scattergraph method	6(a)
5	Least squares method of linear regression analysis	6(a)
6	The reliability of regression analysis forecasts	6(a)

Introduction

In chapter 4, we looked at how costs behave and how total costs can be split into fixed and variable costs using the **high-low method**. In this chapter, we shall be looking at another method which is used to split total costs, the **scattergraph method** (line of best fit). This method is used to determine whether there is a linear relationship between two variables. If a **linear function** is considered to be appropriate, **regression analysis** is used to establish the equation (this equation can then be used to make forecasts or predictions).

Study guide

Section 6 – Cost behaviour 1

- Explain the structure of linear functions and equations

Section 7 – Cost behaviour 2

- Construct a scattergraph to establish whether a linear function would be appropriate
- Establish a linear function using regression analysis and interpret the results
- Calculate and explain the concepts of correlation and coefficient of determination

Exam guide

This is a very important topic (forming part of the cost behaviour section of the syllabus) and it is vital that you are able to establish linear equations using regression analysis.

1 CORRELATION

KEY TERM

Two variables are said to be correlated if a change in the value of one variable is accompanied by a change in the value of another variable. This is what is meant by **correlation.**

1.1 Examples of variables which might be correlated are as follows.

- A person's height and weight
- The distance of a journey and the time it takes to make it

1.2 One way of showing the correlation between two related variables is on a **scattergraph** or **scatter diagram,** plotting a number of pairs of data on the graph. For example, a scattergraph showing monthly selling costs against the volume of sales for a 12-month period might be as follows.

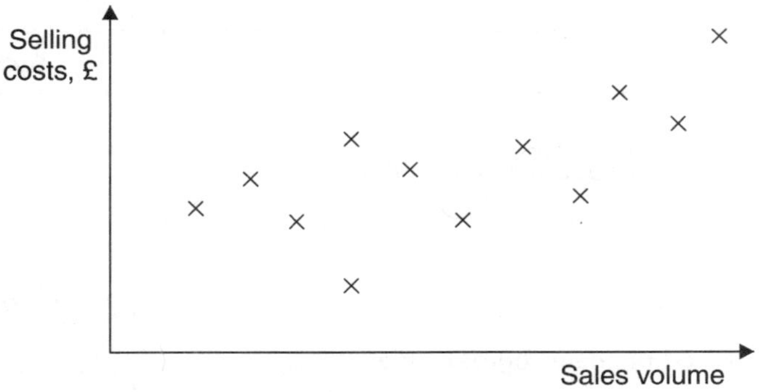

This scattergraph suggests that there is some correlation between selling costs and sales volume, so that as sales volume rises, selling costs tend to rise as well.

Degrees of correlation

1.3 Two variables can be one of the following.

- Perfectly correlated
- Partly correlated
- Uncorrelated

These differing degrees of correlation can be illustrated by scatter diagrams.

Perfect correlation

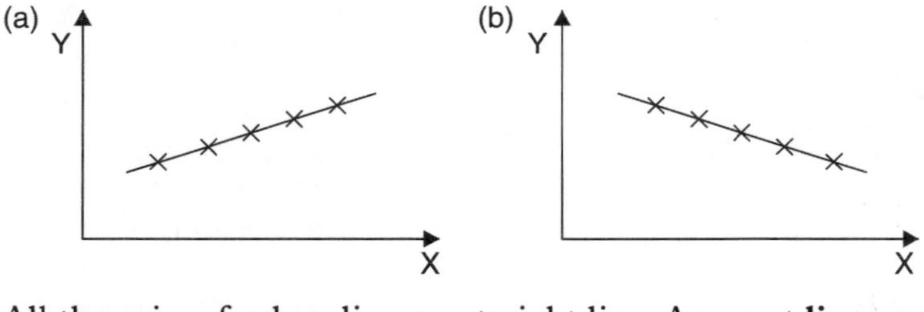

All the pairs of values lie on a straight line. An exact **linear relationship** exists between the two variables.

Partial correlation

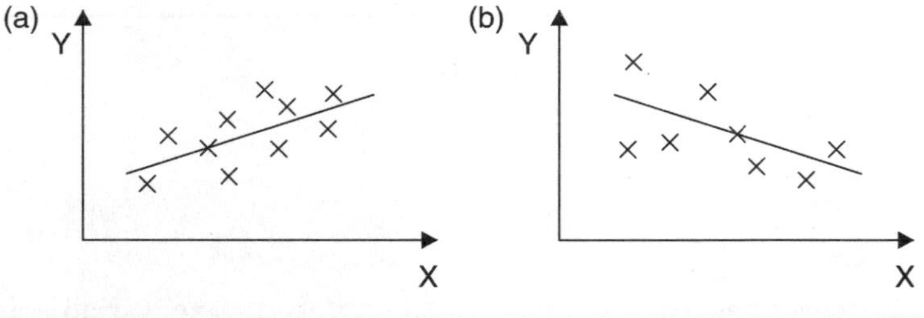

In (a), although there is no exact relationship, low values of X tend to be associated with low values of Y, and high values of X with high values of Y.

In (b) again, there is no exact relationship, but low values of X tend to be associated with high values of Y and vice versa.

No correlation

(c)

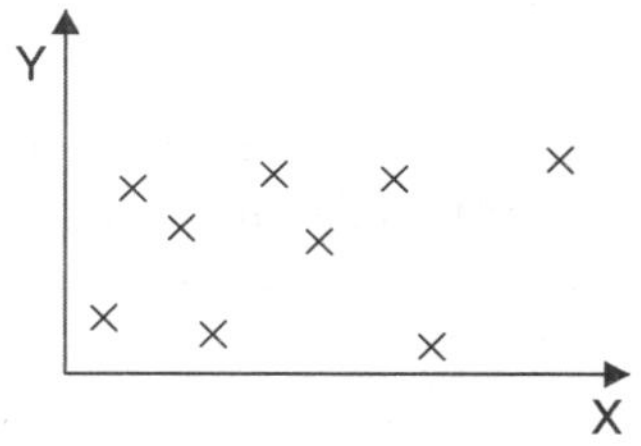

The values of these two variables are not correlated with each other.

Positive and negative correlation

1.4 Correlation, whether perfect or partial, can be **positive** or **negative**.

KEY TERMS

- **Positive correlation** means that low values of one variable are associated with low values of the other, and high values of one variable are associated with high values of the other.
- **Negative correlation** means that low values of one variable are associated with high values of the other, and high values of one variable with low values of the other.

2 THE CORRELATION COEFFICIENT AND THE COEFFICIENT OF DETERMINATION

The correlation coefficient

2.1 The degree of correlation between two variables can be measured, and we can decide, using actual results in the form of pairs of data, whether two variables are perfectly or partially correlated, and if they are partially correlated, whether there is a **high** or **low degree of partial correlation.**

2.2 This degree of correlation is measured by the **Pearsonian correlation coefficient** (the coefficient of correlation), r (also called the 'product moment correlation coefficient').

EXAM FORMULA

Correlation coefficient, $r = \dfrac{n\Sigma XY - \Sigma X \Sigma Y}{\sqrt{[n\Sigma X^2 - (\Sigma X)^2][n\Sigma Y^2 - (\Sigma Y)^2]}}$

where X and Y represent pairs of data for two variables X and Y

n = the number of pairs of data used in the analysis

2.3 The correlation coefficient, r must always fall between –1 and +1. If you get a value outside this range you have made a mistake.

- **r = +1** means that the variables are **perfectly positively correlated**
- **r = –1** means that the variables are **perfectly negatively correlated**
- **r = 0** means that the variables are **uncorrelated**

2.4 EXAMPLE: THE CORRELATION COEFFICIENT

The cost of output at a factory is thought to depend on the number of units produced. Data have been collected for the number of units produced each month in the last six months, and the associated costs, as follows.

Month	*Output* '000s of units *X*	*Cost* £'000 *Y*
1	2	9
2	3	11
3	1	7
4	4	13
5	3	11
6	5	15

Required

Assess whether there is there any correlation between output and cost.

2.5 SOLUTION

$$r = \frac{n\Sigma XY - \Sigma X\Sigma Y}{\sqrt{[n\Sigma X^2 - (\Sigma X)^2][n\Sigma Y^2 - (\Sigma Y)^2]}}$$

We need to find the values for the following.

(a) ΣXY Multiply each value of X by its corresponding Y value, so that there are six values for XY. Add up the six values to get the total.

(b) ΣX Add up the six values of X to get a total. $(\Sigma X)^2$ will be the square of this total.

(c) ΣY Add up the six values of Y to get a total. $(\Sigma Y)^2$ will be the square of this total.

(d) ΣX^2 Find the square of each value of X, so that there are six values for X^2. Add up these values to get a total.

(e) ΣY^2 Find the square of each value of Y, so that there are six values for Y^2. Add up these values to get a total.

Workings

X	*Y*	*XY*	*X^2*	*Y^2*
2	9	18	4	81
3	11	33	9	121
1	7	7	1	49
4	13	52	16	169
3	11	33	9	121
5	15	75	25	225
$\Sigma X =$ 18	$\Sigma Y =$ 66	$\Sigma XY =$ 218	$\Sigma X^2 =$ 64	$\Sigma Y^2 =$ 766

$(\Sigma X)^2 = 18^2 = 324$ $(\Sigma Y)^2 = 66^2 = 4{,}356$

$n = 6$

$$r = \frac{(6 \times 218) - (18 \times 66)}{\sqrt{(6 \times 64 - 324) \times (6 \times 766 - 4{,}356)}}$$

$$= \frac{1{,}308 - 1{,}188}{\sqrt{(384 - 324) \times (4{,}596 - 4{,}356)}}$$

$$= \frac{120}{\sqrt{60 \times 240}} = \frac{120}{\sqrt{14{,}400}} = \frac{120}{120} = 1$$

2.6 There is **perfect positive correlation** between the volume of output at the factory and costs which means that there is a perfect linear relationship between output and costs.

Correlation in a time series

2.7 Correlation exists in a time series if there is a relationship between the period of time and the recorded value for that period of time. The correlation coefficient is calculated with time as the X variable although it is convenient to use simplified values for X instead of year numbers.

For example, instead of having a series of years 20X1 to 20X5, we could have values for X from 0 (20X1) to 4 (20X5).

Note that whatever starting value you use for X (be it 0, 1, 2 ... 721, ... 953), the value of r will always be the same.

Question 1

Sales of product A between 20X7 and 20Y1 were as follows.

Year	*Units sold ('000s)*
20X7	20
20X8	18
20X9	15
20Y0	14
20Y1	11

Required

Determine whether there is a trend in sales. In other words, decide whether there is any correlation between the year and the number of units sold.

Answer

Workings

Let 20X7 to 20Y1 be years 0 to 4.

	X		*Y*		*XY*		*X²*		*Y²*
	0		20		0		0		400
	1		18		18		1		324
	2		15		30		4		225
	3		14		42		9		196
	4		11		44		16		121
$\Sigma X =$	10	$\Sigma Y =$	78	$\Sigma XY =$	134	$\Sigma X^2 =$	30	$\Sigma Y^2 =$	1,266

$(\Sigma X)^2 = 100$ $\quad (\Sigma Y)^2 = 6{,}084$

$n = 5$

$$r = \frac{(5 \times 134) - (10 \times 78)}{\sqrt{(5 \times 30 - 100) \times (5 \times 1{,}266 - 6{,}084)}}$$

$$= \frac{670 - 780}{\sqrt{(150 - 100) \times (6,330 - 6,084)}} = \frac{-110}{\sqrt{50 \times 246}}$$

$$= \frac{-110}{\sqrt{12,300}} = \frac{-110}{110.90537} = -0.992$$

There is **partial negative correlation** between the year of sale and units sold. The value of r is close to –1, therefore a **high degree of correlation exists**, although it is not quite perfect correlation. This means that there is a **clear downward trend** in sales.

The coefficient of determination, r^2

2.8 Unless the correlation coefficient r is exactly or very nearly +1, –1 or 0, its meaning or significance is a little unclear. For example, if the correlation coefficient for two variables is +0.8, this would tell us that the variables are positively correlated, but the correlation is not perfect. It would not really tell us much else. A more meaningful analysis is available from **the square of the correlation coefficient, r**, which is called the **coefficient of determination**, r^2

KEY TERM

The **coefficient of determination**, r^2 (alternatively R^2) measures the proportion of the total variation in the value of one variable that can be explained by variations in the value of the other variable.

2.9 In Question 1 above, r = –0.992, therefore r^2 = 0.984. This means that over 98% of variations in sales can be explained by the passage of time, leaving 0.016 (less than 2%) of variations to be explained by other factors.

2.10 Similarly, if the correlation coefficient between a company's output volume and maintenance costs was 0.9, r^2 would be 0.81, meaning that 81% of variations in maintenance costs could be explained by variations in output volume, leaving only 19% of variations to be explained by other factors (such as the age of the equipment).

2.11 Note, however, that if r^2 = 0.81, we would say that 81% of **the variations in y can be explained by variations in x**. We do not necessarily conclude that 81% of variations in y are *caused* by the variations in x. We must beware of reading too much significance into our statistical analysis.

Correlation and causation

2.12 If two variables are well correlated, either positively or negatively, this may be due to **pure chance** or there may be a **reason** for it. The larger the number of pairs of data collected, the less likely it is that the correlation is due to chance, though that possibility should never be ignored entirely.

2.13 If there is a reason, it may not be causal. For example, monthly net income is well correlated with monthly credit to a person's bank account, for the logical (rather than causal) reason that for most people the one equals the other.

2.14 Even if there is a causal explanation for a correlation, it does not follow that variations in the value of one variable cause variations in the value of the other. For example, sales of ice cream and of sunglasses are well correlated, not because of a direct causal link but because the weather influences both variables.

3 LINES OF BEST FIT

3.1 **Correlation enables us to determine the strength of any relationship between two variables but it does not offer us any method of forecasting values for one variable, Y, given values of another variable, X.**

3.2 If we assume that there is a **linear relationship** between the two variables, however, and we determine the **equation of a straight line (Y = a + bX)** which is a good fit for the available data plotted on a scattergraph, we can use the equation for forecasting: we can substitute values for X into the equation and derive values for Y. If you need reminding about linear equations and graphs, refer to your Basic Maths supplement.

3.3 There are a number of techniques for estimating the equation of a line of best fit. We will be looking at the **scattergraph method** and **simple linear regression analysis**. Both provide a technique for estimating values for a and b in the equation

Y = a + bX

where X and Y are the related variables and
a and b are estimated using pairs of data for X and Y.

4 THE SCATTERGRAPH METHOD

KEY TERM

The **scattergraph method** is to plot pairs of data for two related variables on a graph, to produce a scattergraph, and then to **use judgement** to draw what seems to be a line of best fit through the data.

4.1 EXAMPLE: THE SCATTERGRAPH METHOD

Suppose we have the following pairs of data about output and costs.

Month	*Output*	*Costs*
	'000 units	£'000
1	20	82
2	16	70
3	24	90
4	22	85
5	18	73

(a) These pairs of data can be plotted on a **scattergraph** (the **horizontal** axis representing the **independent** variable and the **vertical** axis the **dependent**) and a line of best fit might be judged as the one shown below. It is drawn to pass through the middle of the data points, thereby having as many data points below the line as above it.

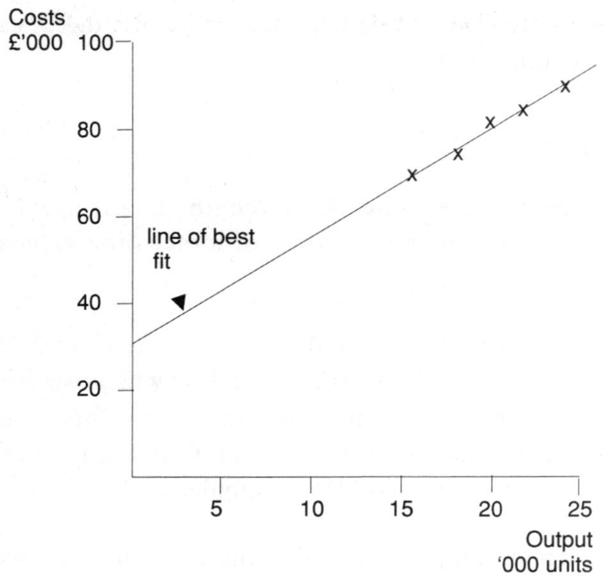

(b) A **formula for the line of best fit** can be found. In our example, suppose that we read the following data from the graph.

(i) When X = 0, Y = 22,000. This must be the value of a in the formula Y = a + bX.

(ii) When X = 20,000, Y = 81,000. Since Y = a + bX, and a = 22,000, this gives us a value for b of

$$\frac{81{,}000 - 22{,}000}{20{,}000} = 2.95$$

(c) In this example the estimated equation from the scattergraph is Y = 22,000 + 2.95X.

Forecasting and scattergraphs

4.2 If the company to which the data in Paragraph 4.1 relates wanted to predict costs at a certain level of output (say 13,000 units), the value of 13,000 could be substituted into the equation Y = 22,000 + 2.95X and an estimate of costs made.

If X = 13, Y = 22,000 + (2.95 × 13,000)

∴ Y = £60,350

4.3 Of course, predictions can be made directly from the scattergraph shown below.

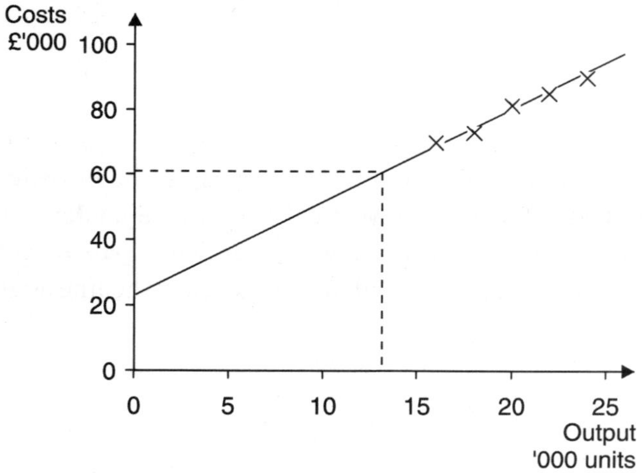

The prediction of the cost of producing 13,000 units from the scattergraph is £61,000.

5 LEAST SQUARES METHOD OF LINEAR REGRESSION ANALYSIS

EXAM FORMULA

The **least squares method of linear regression analysis** involves using the following formulae for a and b in Y = a + bX.

$$b = \frac{n\Sigma XY - \Sigma X\Sigma Y}{n\Sigma X^2 - (\Sigma X)^2}$$

$$a = \frac{\Sigma Y}{n} - b\frac{\Sigma X}{n}$$

where n is the number of pairs of data

5.1 The line of best fit that is derived represents the **regression of Y upon X**.

A different line of best fit could be obtained by interchanging X and Y in the formulae. This would then represent the regression of X upon Y (X = a + bY) and it would have a slightly different slope. For examination purposes, always use the regression of Y upon X, where X is the independent variable, and Y is the dependent variable whose value we wish to forecast for given values of X. In a time series, X will represent time.

5.2 EXAMPLE: THE LEAST SQUARES METHOD

(a) Given that there is a fairly high degree of correlation between the output and the costs detailed in Paragraph 4.1 (so that a linear relationship can be assumed), calculate an equation to determine the expected level of costs, for any given volume of output, using the least squares method.

(b) Prepare a budget for total costs if output is 22,000 units.

(c) Confirm that the degree of correlation between output and costs is high by calculating the correlation coefficient.

5.3 SOLUTION

(a) *Workings*

	X		*Y*		*XY*		X^2		Y^2
	20		82		1,640		400		6,724
	16		70		1,120		256		4,900
	24		90		2,160		576		8,100
	22		85		1,870		484		7,225
	18		73		1,314		324		5,329
$\Sigma X =$	100	$\Sigma Y =$	400	$\Sigma XY =$	8,104	$\Sigma X^2 =$	2,040	$\Sigma Y^2 =$	32,278

n = 5 (There are five pairs of data for x and y values)

$$b = \frac{n\Sigma XY - \Sigma X\Sigma Y}{n\Sigma X^2 - (\Sigma X)^2} = \frac{(5 \times 8{,}104) - (100 \times 400)}{(5 \times 2{,}040) - 100^2}$$

$$= \frac{40{,}520 - 40{,}000}{10{,}200 - 10{,}000} = \frac{520}{200} = 2.6$$

$$a = \frac{\Sigma Y}{n} - b\frac{\Sigma X}{n} = \frac{400}{5} - 2.6 \times \left(\frac{100}{5}\right) = 28$$

$$Y = 28 + 2.6X$$

where Y = total cost, in thousands of pounds
X = output, in thousands of units.

Note that the fixed costs are £28,000 (when X = 0 costs are £28,000) and the variable cost per unit is £2.60.

(b) If the output is 22,000 units, we would expect costs to be

$28 + 2.6 \times 22 = 85.2 = £85,200.$

(c) $r = \frac{520}{\sqrt{200 \times (5 \times 32,278 - 400^2)}} = \frac{520}{\sqrt{200 \times 1,390}} = \frac{520}{527.3} = +0.99$

Regression lines and time series

5.4 The same technique can be applied to calculate a **regression line** (a **trend line**) for a time series. This is particularly useful for purposes of forecasting. As with correlation, years can be numbered from 0 upwards.

Question 2

Using the data in Question 1, calculate the trend line of sales and forecast sales in 20Y2 and 20Y3.

Answer

Using workings from Question 1:

$$b = \frac{(5 \times 134) - (10 \times 78)}{(5 \times 30) - (10)^2} = \frac{670 - 780}{150 - 100} = -2.2$$

$$a = \frac{\Sigma Y}{n} - b\frac{\Sigma X}{n} = \frac{78}{5} - \frac{(-2.2 \times 10)}{5} = 20$$

∴ Y = 20 – 2.2X where X = 0 in 20X7, X = 1 in 20X8 and so on.

Using the trend line, predicted sales in 20Y2 (year 5) would be:

20 – (2.2 × 5) = 9 ie 9,000 units

and predicated sales in 20Y3 (year 6) would be:

20 – (2.2 × 6) = 6.8 ie 6,800 units.

5.5 In some instances you may have to adjust your regression line forecasts by **seasonal variations.**

Exam focus point

There was a ten mark question in the paper-based examination pilot paper for **Financial Information for Management** which required candidates to use regression analysis to calculate a total cost equation and then to use the equation to forecast total costs at given levels of activity.

Question 3

Regression analysis was used to find the equation Y = 300 – 4.7X, where X is time (in quarters) and Y is sales level in thousands of units. Given that X = 0 represents 20X0 quarter 1 what are the forecast sales levels for 20X5 quarter 4?

Answer

X = 0 corresponds to 20X0 quarter 1

Therefore X = 23 corresponds to 20X5 quarter 4

Forecast sales = 300 – (4.7 × 23)

= 191.9 = 191,900 units

Question 4

Over a 36 month period sales have been found to have an underlying regression line of Y = 14.224 + 7.898X where Y is the number of items sold and X represents the month.

What are the forecast number of items to be sold in month 37?

Answer

Y = 14.224 + 7.898X

Y = 14.224 + (7.898 × 37)

= 306.45 = 306 units

---

6 THE RELIABILITY OF REGRESSION ANALYSIS FORECASTS

6.1 As with all forecasting techniques, the results from regression analysis will not be wholly reliable. There are a number of factors which affect the reliability of forecasts made using regression analysis.

(a) **It assumes a linear relationship exists between the two variables** (since linear regression analysis produces an equation in the linear format) whereas a non-linear relationship might exist.

(b) It **assumes that the value of one variable, Y, can be predicted or estimated from the value of one other variable, X**. In reality the value of Y might depend on several other variables, not just X.

(c) When it is used for forecasting, **it assumes that what has happened in the past will provide a reliable guide to the future.**

(d) When calculating a line of best fit, there will be a range of values for X. In the example in Paragraph 5.2 and 5.3, the line Y = 28 + 2.6X was predicted from data with output values ranging from X = 16 to X = 24. Depending on the degree of correlation between X and Y, we might safely use the estimated line of best fit to predict values for Y in the future, provided that the value of X remains within the range 16 to 24. We would be on less safe ground if we used the formula to predict a value for Y when X = 10, or 30, or any other value outside the range 16 to 24, because we would have to **assume that the trend line applies outside the range of X values used to establish the line in the first place.**

(i) **Interpolation** means using a line of best fit to predict a value within the two extreme points of the observed range.

(ii) **Extrapolation** means using a line of best fit to predict a value outside the two extreme points.

When linear regression analysis is used for forecasting a time series (when the X values represent time) it **assumes that the trend line can be extrapolated into the future.** This might not necessarily be a good assumption to make.

(e) As with any forecasting process, **the amount of data available is very important.** Even if correlation is high, if we have fewer than about ten pairs of values, we must regard any forecast as being somewhat unreliable. (It is likely to provide more reliable forecasts than the scattergraph method, however, since it uses all of the available data.)

(f) **The reliability of a forecast will depend on the reliability of the data collected to determine the regression analysis equation.** If the data is not collected accurately or if data used is false, forecasts are unlikely to be acceptable.

6.2 A check on the reliability of the estimated line Y= 28 + 2.6X can be made, however, by calculating the coefficient of correlation. From Paragraph 5.3, we know that r = 0.99. This is a high positive correlation, and $r^2 = 0.9801$, indicating that 98.01% of the variation in cost can be explained by the variation in volume. This would suggest that a **fairly large degree of reliance** can probably be placed on estimates .

6.3 If there is a **perfect linear relationship** between X and Y (r = ±1) then we can predict Y from any given value of X with **great confidence**.

6.4 If correlation is high (for example r = 0.9) the actual values will all lie quite close to the regression line and so predictions should not be far out. If correlation is below about 0.7, predictions will only give a very rough guide as to the likely value of Y.

Chapter roundup

- When the value of one variable is related to the value of another, they are said to be **correlated**.
- Two variables might be **perfectly correlated**, **partly correlated** or **uncorrelated**. Correlation can be **positive** or **negative**.
- The **degree of correlation** between two variables is measured by the **Pearsonian** (product moment) **correlation coefficient, r**. The nearer r is to +1 or -1, the stronger the relationship.
- The **coefficient of determination, r^2**, measures the proportion of the total variation in the value of one variable that can be explained by the variation in the value of the other variable.
- The **scattergraph method** involves the use of judgement to draw what seems to be a line of best fit through plotted data.
- **Linear regression analysis** (the **least squares method**) is one technique for estimating a line of best fit.
- Once an equation for a line of best fit has been determined, forecasts can be made.
- Like all forecasting techniques, the results obtained will not be wholly reliable. There are a number of factors which affect the reliability of forecasts made using regression analysis.

Quick quiz

1 .... means that low values of one variable are associated with low values of the other, and high values of one variable are associated with high values of the other.

2 .... means that low values of one variable are associated with high values of the other, and high values of one variable with low values of the other.

3
- Perfect positive correlation, r = ...
- Perfect negative correlation, r = ...
- No correlation, r = ...

The correlation coefficient, r, must always fall within the range .... to ....

4 If the correlation coefficient of a set of data is 0.9, what is the coefficient of determination and how is it interpreted?

5 (a) The equation of a straight line is given as Y = a + bX. Give two methods used for estimating the above equation.

(b) If Y = a + bX, it is best to use the regression of Y upon X where X is the dependent variable and Y is the independent variable.

True ☐

False ☐

6 List five factors affecting the reliability of regression analysis forecasts.

Answers to quick quiz

1 Positive correlation

2 Negative correlation

3
- r = +1
- r = –1
- r = 0

The correlation coefficient, r, must always fall within the range –1 to +1.

4 Correlation coefficient = r = 0.9

Coefficient of determination = $r^2 = 0.9^2 = 0.81$ or 81%

This tells us that over 80% of the variations in the dependent variable (Y) can be explained by variations in the independent variable, X.

5 (a)
- Scattergraph method (line of best fit)
- Simple linear regression analysis

(b) False. When using the regression of Y upon X, X is the independent variable and Y is the dependent variable (the value of Y will depend upon the value of X).

6 (a) It assumes a linear relationship exists between the two variables.

(b) It assumes that the value of one variable, Y, can be predicted or estimated from the value of another variable, X.

(c) It assumes that what happened in the past will provide a reliable guide to the future.

(d) It assumes that the trend line can be extrapolated into the future.

(e) The amount of data available.

Now try the questions below from the Exam Question Bank

Number	Level	Marks	Time
6	MCQ	n/a	n/a
7	Examination	10	18 mins

Part B

Elements of cost

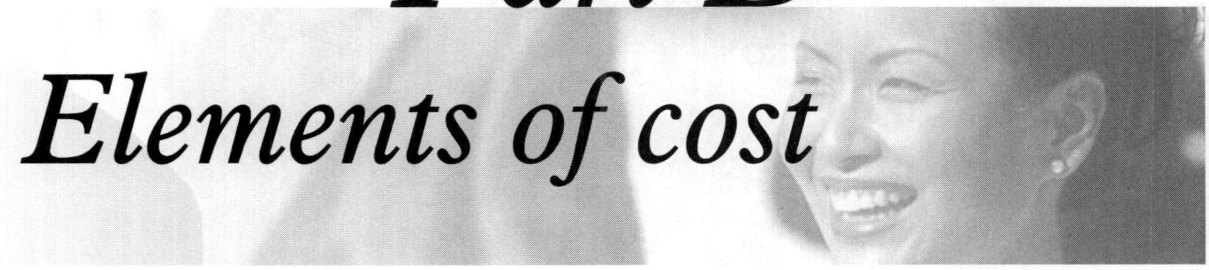

Chapter 6

MATERIAL COSTS

Introduction

The investment in stock is a very important one for most businesses, both in terms of monetary value and relationships with customers (no stock, no sale, loss of customer goodwill). It is therefore vital that management establish and maintain an **effective stock control system** and that they are aware of the major costing problem relating to materials, that of pricing materials issues and valuing stock at the end of each period.

The first half of this chapter will concentrate on a **stock control system** for materials, but similar problems and considerations apply to all forms of stock. In the second half of the chapter we will consider the methods for **pricing materials issues/valuing stock**. We will look at the various methods, their advantages and disadvantages and their impact on profitability.

Since this is a very long chapter, we recommend that you study it in two parts. Firstly, Sections 1-5 and then sections 6-10.

Study guide

Sections 8 and 9 – Material costs

- Describe the different procedures and documents necessary for ordering, receiving and issuing materials from stock
- Describe the control procedures used to monitor physical and 'book' stock and to minimise discrepancies and losses
- Calculate, explain and evaluate the value of closing stock and material issues using LIFO, FIFO and average methods (weighted and periodic)
- Prepare ledger entries to record material cost inputs and outputs
- Interpret the entries and balances in the material stock account
- Explain the reasons for holding stock
- Identify and explain the costs of having stocks

- Calculate and interpret optimal reorder quantities
- Calculate and interpret optimal reorder quantities when discounts apply
- Produce and interpret calculations to minimise stock costs when stock is gradually replenished
- Describe appropriate methods for establishing reorder levels

Exam guide

Material costs is another key area of the syllabus so look out for questions on this topic in both sections of the paper-based examination.

1 WHAT IS STOCK CONTROL?

1.1 The stocks held in any organisation can generally be classified under four main headings.

- Raw materials
- Work in progress
- Spare parts/consumables
- Finished goods

Not all organisations will have stock of all four general categories.

1.2 This chapter will concentrate on a **stock control system** for materials, but similar problems and considerations apply to all forms of stock. Controls should cover the following functions.

- The **ordering** of stock
- The **purchase** of stock
- The **receipt** of goods into store
- **Storage**
- The **issue** of stock and maintenance of stock at the most appropriate level

Qualitative aspects of stock control

1.3 We may wish to **control stock** for the following reasons.

- Holding costs of stock may be expensive.
- Production will be disrupted if we run out of raw materials.
- Unused stock with a short shelf life may incur unnecessary expenses.

1.4 If manufactured goods are made out of low quality materials, the end product will be of low quality also. It may therefore be necessary to control the quality of stock, in order to maintain a good reputation with consumers.

2 THE ORDERING, RECEIPT AND ISSUE OF RAW MATERIALS

Ordering and receiving materials

2.1 Proper records must be kept of the physical procedures for ordering and receiving a consignment of materials to ensure the following.

- That enough stock is held
- That there is no duplication of ordering
- That quality is maintained

- That there is adequate record keeping for accounts purposes

A typical series of procedures might be as follows.

(a) Current stocks run down to the level where a reorder is required. The stores department issues a **purchase requisition** which is sent to the purchasing department, authorising the department to order further stock. An example of a purchase requisition is shown below.

PURCHASE REQUISITION Req. No.

Department/job number:
Suggested Supplier:

Date

Requested by:
Latest date required:

Quantity	Code number	Description	Estimated Cost	
			Unit	£

Authorised signature:

(b) The purchasing department draws up a **purchase order** which is sent to the supplier. (The supplier may be asked to return an acknowledgement copy as confirmation of his acceptance of the order.) Copies of the purchase order must be sent to the accounts department and the storekeeper (or receiving department).

Purchase Order/Confirmation

Our Order Ref: Date

To

(Address)

Please deliver to the above address
Ordered by:
Passed and checked by:
Total Order Value £

		Subtotal		
		VAT (@ 17.5%)		
		Total		

(c) The purchasing department may have to obtain a number of quotations if either a new stock line is required, the existing supplier's costs are too high or the existing supplier no longer stocks the goods needed. Trade discounts (reduction in the price per unit given to some customers) should be negotiated where possible.

(d) The supplier delivers the consignment of materials, and the storekeeper signs a **delivery note** for the carrier. The packages must then be checked against the copy of the purchase order, to ensure that the supplier has delivered the types and quantities of materials which were ordered. (Discrepancies would be referred to the purchasing department.)

(e) If the delivery is acceptable, the storekeeper prepares a **goods received note (GRN)**, an example of which is shown below.

GOODS RECEIVED NOTE — WAREHOUSE COPY

NO 5565

DATE: TIME:

OUR ORDER NO: WAREHOUSE A

SUPPLIER AND SUPPLIER'S ADVICE NOTE NO:

QUANTITY	CAT NO	DESCRIPTION

RECEIVED IN GOOD CONDITION: (INITIALS)

(f) A copy of the **GRN** is sent to the accounts department, where it is matched with the copy of the purchase order. The supplier's invoice is checked against the purchase order and GRN, and the necessary steps are taken to pay the supplier. The invoice may contain details relating to discounts such as trade discounts, quantity discounts (order in excess of a specified amount) and settlement discounts (payment received within a specified number of days).

Question 1

What are the possible consequences of a failure of control over ordering and receipt of materials?

Answer

(a) Incorrect materials being delivered, disrupting operations
(b) Incorrect prices being paid
(c) Deliveries other than at the specified time (causing disruption)
(d) Insufficient control over quality
(e) Invoiced amounts differing from quantities of goods actually received or prices agreed

You may, of course, have thought of equally valid consequences.

Issue of materials

2.2 Materials can only be issued against a **materials/stores requisition**. This document must record not only the quantity of goods issued, but also the cost centre or the job number for which the requisition is being made. The materials requisition note may also have a column, to be filled in by the cost department, for recording the cost or value of the materials issued to the cost centre or job.

Materials requisition note			
Date required _________		Cost centre No/ Job No ___________	
Quantity	*Item code*	*Description*	£
Signature of requisitioning Manager/ Foreman ___________________________			Date ______

Materials transfers and returns

2.3 Where materials, having been issued to one job or cost centre, are later transferred to a different job or cost centre, without first being returned to stores, a **materials transfer note** should be raised. Such a note must show not only the job receiving the transfer, but also the job from which it is transferred. This enables the appropriate charges to be made to jobs or cost centres.

2.4 Material returns must also be documented on a **materials returned note**. This document is the 'reverse' of a requisition note, and must contain similar information. In fact it will often be almost identical to a requisition note. It will simply have a different title and perhaps be a distinctive colour, such as red, to highlight the fact that materials are being returned.

Impact of computerisation

2.5 Many stock control systems these days are computerised. Computerised stock control systems vary greatly, but most will have the features outlined below.

(a) **Data must be input into the system**. For example, details of goods received may simply be written on to a GRN for later entry into the computer system. Alternatively, this information may be keyed in directly to the computer: a GRN will be printed and then signed as evidence of the transaction, so that both the warehouse and the supplier can have a hard copy record in case of dispute. Some systems may incorporate the use of devices such as bar code readers.

Other types of transaction which will need to be recorded include the following.

(i) **Transfers** between different categories of stock (for example from work in progress to finished goods)

(ii) **Despatch**, resulting from a sale, of items of finished goods to customers

(iii) **Adjustments** to stock records if the amount of stock revealed in a physical stock count differs from the amount appearing on the stock records

(b) **A stock master file is maintained**. This file will contain details for every category of stock and will be updated for new stock lines. A database file may be maintained.

Question 2

What type of information do you think should be held on a stock master file?

Answer

Here are some examples.

(a) Stock code number, for reference
(b) Brief description of stock item
(c) Reorder level
(d) Reorder quantity
(e) Cost per unit
(f) Selling price per unit (if finished goods)
(g) Amount in stock
(h) Frequency of usage

The file may also hold details of stock movements over a period, but this will depend on the type of system in operation. In a **batch system**, transactions will be grouped and input in one operation and details of the movements may be held in a separate transactions file, the master file updated in total only. In an **on-line system**, transactions may be input directly to the master file, where the record of movements is thus likely to be found. Such a system will mean that the stock records are constantly up to date, which will help in monitoring and controlling stock.

The system may generate orders automatically once the amount in stock has fallen to the reorder level.

(c) **The system will generate outputs**. These may include, depending on the type of system, any of the following.

(i) **Hard copy** records, for example a printed GRN, of transactions entered into the system.

(ii) Output on a **VDU** screen in response to an enquiry (for example the current level of a particular line of stock, or details of a particular transaction).

(iii) Various **printed reports**, devised to fit in with the needs of the organisation. These may include stock movement reports, detailing over a period the movements on all stock lines, listings of GRNs, despatch notes and so forth.

2.6 A computerised stock control system is usually able to give more up to date information and more flexible reporting than a manual system but remember that both manual and computer based stock control systems need the same types of data to function properly.

3 THE STORAGE OF RAW MATERIALS

3.1 Storekeeping involves storing materials to achieve the following objectives.

- Speedy **issue** and **receipt** of materials
- Full **identification** of all materials at all times
- Correct **location** of all materials at all times
- **Protection** of materials from damage and deterioration
- Provision of **secure stores** to avoid pilferage, theft and fire
- **Efficient** use of storage space
- **Maintenance** of correct stock levels
- Keeping correct and up-to-date **records** of receipts, issues and stock levels

Recording stock levels

3.2 One of the objectives of storekeeping is to maintain accurate records of current stock levels. This involves the accurate recording of stock movements (issues from and receipts into stores). The most frequently encountered system for recording stock movements is the use of bin cards and stores ledger accounts.

Bin cards

3.3 A **bin card** shows the level of stock of an item at a particular stores location. It is kept with the actual stock and is updated by the storekeeper as stocks are received and issued. A typical bin card is shown below.

Bin card

Part code no ______________			Location ______________			
Bin number ______________			Stores ledger no ______________			
Receipts			*Issues*			Stock balance
Date	Quantity	G.R.N. No.	Date	Quantity	Req. No.	

The use of bin cards is decreasing, partly due to the difficulty in keeping them updated and partly due to the merging of stock recording and control procedures, frequently using computers.

Stores ledger accounts

3.4 A typical stores ledger account is shown below. Note that it shows the value of stock.

Stores ledger account

Material ______________							Maximum Quantity ______________				
Code ______________							Minimum Quantity ______________				
Date	Receipts				Issues				Stock		
	G.R.N No.	Quantity	Unit price £	Amount £	Stores Req. No	Quantity	Unit price £	Amount £	Quantity	Unit price £	Amount £

3.5 The above illustration shows a card for a manual system, but even when the stock records are computerised, the same type of information is normally included in the computer file. The running balance on the stores ledger account allows stock levels and valuation to be monitored.

Free stock

3.6 Managers need to know the **free stock balance** in order to obtain a full picture of the current stock position of an item. Free stock represents what is really **available for future use** and is calculated as follows.

	Materials in stock	X
+	Materials on order from suppliers	X
–	Materials requisitioned, not yet issued	(X)
	Free stock balance	X

3.7 Knowledge of the level of physical stock assists stock issuing, stocktaking and controlling maximum and minimum stock levels: knowledge of the level of free stock assists ordering.

Question 3

A wholesaler has 8,450 units outstanding for Part X100 on existing customers' orders; there are 3,925 units in stock and the calculated free stock is 5,525 units.

How many units does the wholesaler have on order with his supplier?

A 9,450 B 10,050 C 13,975 D 17,900

Answer

Free stock balance	=	units in stock + units on order – units ordered, but not yet issued
5,525	=	3,925 + units on order – 8,450
Units on order	=	10,050

The correct answer is B.

Identification of materials: stock codes (materials codes)

3.8 Materials held in stores are **coded** and **classified**. Advantages of using code numbers to identify materials are as follows.

(a) Ambiguity is avoided.

(b) Time is saved. Descriptions can be lengthy and time-consuming.

(c) Production efficiency is improved. The correct material can be accurately identified from a code number.

(d) Computerised processing is made easier.

(e) Numbered code systems can be designed to be flexible, and can be expanded to include more stock items as necessary.

The digits in a code can stand for the type of stock, supplier, department and so forth.

Stocktaking

3.9 Stocktaking involves counting the physical stock on hand at a certain date, and then checking this against the balance shown in the stock records. There are two methods of carrying out this process, **periodic stocktaking** and **continuous stocktaking**.

KEY TERMS

- **Periodic stocktaking** is a 'process whereby all stock items are physically counted and valued at a set point in time, usually at the end of an accounting period' (CIMA *Official Terminology*).
- **Continuous stocktaking** is 'the process of counting and valuing selected items at different times on a rotating basis' (CIMA *Official Terminology*). This involves a specialist team counting and checking a number of stock items each day, so that each item is checked at least once a year. Valuable items or items with a high turnover could be checked more frequently.

3.10 The **advantages of continuous stocktaking compared to periodic stocktaking** are as follows.

(a) The annual stocktaking is unnecessary and the disruption it causes is avoided.

(b) Regular skilled stocktakers can be employed, reducing likely errors.

(c) More time is available, reducing errors and allowing investigation.

(d) Deficiencies and losses are revealed sooner than they would be if stocktaking were limited to an annual check.

(e) Production hold-ups are eliminated because the stores staff are at no time so busy as to be unable to deal with material issues to production departments.

(f) Staff morale is improved and standards raised.

(g) Control over stock levels is improved, and there is less likelihood of overstocking or running out of stock.

Stock discrepancies

3.11 There will be occasions when stock checks disclose discrepancies between the physical amount of an item in stock and the amount shown in the stock records. When this occurs, the cause of the discrepancy should be investigated, and appropriate action taken to ensure that it does not happen again.

Perpetual inventory

3.12 **A perpetual inventory system involves recording every receipt and issue of stock as it occurs on bin cards and stores ledger accounts.** This means that there is a continuous record of the balance of each item of stock. The balance on the stores ledger account therefore represents the stock on hand and this balance is used in the calculation of closing stock in monthly and annual accounts. In practice, physical stocks may not agree with recorded stocks and therefore continuous stocktaking is necessary to ensure that the perpetual inventory system is functioning correctly and that minor stock discrepancies are corrected.

Obsolete, deteriorating and slow-moving stocks and wastage

3.13 **Obsolete stocks are those items which have become out-of-date and are no longer required.** Obsolete items are written off to the profit and loss account and disposed of.

3.14 Stock items may be wasted because, for example, they get broken. All **wastage** should be noted on the stock records immediately so that physical stock equals the stock balance on records and the cost of the wastage written off to the profit and loss account.

3.15 **Slow-moving stocks are stock items which are likely to take a long time to be used up**. For example, 5,000 units are in stock, and only 20 are being used each year. This is often caused by overstocking. Managers should investigate such stock items and, if it is felt that the usage rate is unlikely to increase, excess stock should be written off as for obsolete stock, leaving perhaps four or five years' supply in stock.

4 STOCK CONTROL LEVELS

Why hold stock?

4.1 The costs of purchasing stock are usually one of the largest costs faced by an organisation and, once obtained, stock has to be carefully controlled and checked.

4.2 The main reasons for holding stocks can be summarised as follows.

- To ensure sufficient goods are available to meet expected demand
- To provide a buffer between processes
- To meet any future shortages
- To take advantage of bulk purchasing discounts
- To absorb seasonal fluctuations and any variations in usage and demand
- To allow production processes to flow smoothly and efficiently
- As a necessary part of the production process (such as when maturing cheese)
- As a deliberate investment policy, especially in times of inflation or possible shortages

Holding costs

4.3 If stocks are too high, **holding costs** will be incurred unnecessarily. Such costs occur for a number of reasons.

(a) **Costs of storage and stores operations.** Larger stocks require more storage space and possibly extra staff and equipment to control and handle them.

(b) **Interest charges**. Holding stocks involves the tying up of capital (cash) on which interest must be paid.

(c) **Insurance costs**. The larger the value of stocks held, the greater insurance premiums are likely to be.

(d) **Risk of obsolescence**. The longer a stock item is held, the greater is the risk of obsolescence.

(e) **Deterioration**. When materials in store deteriorate to the extent that they are unusable, they must be thrown away with the likelihood that disposal costs would be incurred.

Costs of obtaining stock

4.4 On the other hand, if stocks are kept low, small quantities of stock will have to be ordered more frequently, thereby increasing the following **ordering or procurement costs**.

(a) **Clerical and administrative costs** associated with purchasing, accounting for and receiving goods

(b) **Transport costs**

(c) **Production run costs**, for stock which is manufactured internally rather than purchased from external sources

Stockout costs

4.5 An additional type of cost which may arise if stocks are kept too low is the type associated with running out of stock. There are a number of causes of **stockout costs**.

- Lost contribution from lost sales
- Loss of future sales due to disgruntled customers

- Loss of customer goodwill
- Cost of production stoppages
- Labour frustration over stoppages
- Extra costs of urgent, small quantity, replenishment orders

Objective of stock control

4.6 The overall objective of stock control is, therefore, to maintain stock levels so that the total of the following costs is minimised.

- Holding costs
- Ordering costs
- Stockout costs

Stock control levels

4.7 Based on an analysis of past stock usage and delivery times, a series of control levels can be calculated and used to maintain stocks at their optimum level (in other words, a level which minimises costs). These levels will determine 'when to order' and 'how many to order'.

(a) **Reorder level**. When stocks reach this level, an order should be placed to replenish stocks. The reorder level is determined by consideration of the following.

- The maximum rate of consumption
- The maximum lead time

The maximum lead time is the time between placing an order with a supplier, and the stock becoming available for use

FORMULA TO LEARN

Reorder level = maximum usage × maximum lead time

(b) **Minimum level**. This is a warning level to draw management attention to the fact that stocks are approaching a dangerously low level and that stockouts are possible.

FORMULA TO LEARN

Minimum level = reorder level – (average usage × average lead time)

(c) **Maximum level**. This also acts as a warning level to signal to management that stocks are reaching a potentially wasteful level.

FORMULA TO LEARN

Maximum level = reorder level + reorder quantity – (minimum usage × minimum lead time)

Question 4

A large retailer with multiple outlets maintains a central warehouse from which the outlets are supplied. The following information is available for Part Number SF525.

Average usage	350 per day
Minimum usage	180 per day
Maximum usage	420 per day
Lead time for replenishment	11-15 days
Re-order quantity	6,500 units
Re-order level	6,300 units

(a) Based on the data above, what is the maximum level of stock?

A 5,250 B 6,500 C 10,820 D 12,800

(b) Based on the data above, what is the approximate number of Part Number SF525 carried as buffer stock?

A 200 B 720 C 1,680 D 1,750

Answer

(a) Maximum stock level = reorder level + reorder quantity – (min usage × min lead time)
= 6,300 + 6,500 – (180 × 11)
= 10,820

The correct answer is C.

Using good MCQ technique, if you were resorting to a guess you should have eliminated option A. The maximum stock level cannot be less than the reorder quantity.

(b) Buffer stock = minimum level

Minimum level = reorder level – (average usage × average lead time)
= 6,300 – (350 × 13) = 1,750.

The correct answer is D.

Option A could again be easily eliminated. With minimum usage of 180 per day, a buffer stock of only 200 would not be much of a buffer!

(d) **Reorder quantity**. This is the quantity of stock which is to be ordered when stock reaches the reorder level. If it is set so as to minimise the total costs associated with holding and ordering stock, then it is known as the economic order quantity.

(e) **Average stock**. The formula for the average stock level assumes that stock levels fluctuate evenly between the minimum (or safety) stock level and the highest possible stock level (the amount of stock immediately after an order is received, ie safety stock + reorder quantity).

FORMULA TO LEARN

Average stock = safety stock + ½ reorder quantity

Question 5

A component has a safety stock of 500, a re-order quantity of 3,000 and a rate of demand which varies between 200 and 700 per week. The average stock is approximately

A 2,000 B 2,300 C 2,500 D 3,500

Answer

Average stock = safety stock + ½ reorder quantity
= 500 + (0.5 × 3,000)
= 2,000

The correct answer is A.

Economic order quantity (EOQ)

4.8 **Economic order theory assumes that the average stock held is equal to one half of the reorder quantity** (although as we saw in the last section, if an organisation maintains some sort of buffer or safety stock then average stock = buffer stock + half of the reorder quantity). We have seen that there are certain costs associated with holding stock. These costs tend to increase with the level of stocks, and so could be reduced by ordering smaller amounts from suppliers each time.

4.9 On the other hand, as we have seen, there are costs associated with ordering from suppliers: documentation, telephone calls, payment of invoices, receiving goods into stores and so on. These costs tend to increase if small orders are placed, because a larger number of orders would then be needed for a given annual demand.

4.10 Suppose a company purchases raw material at a cost of £16 per unit. The annual demand for the raw material is 25,000 units. The holding cost per unit is £6.40 and the cost of placing an order is £32.

4.11 We can tabulate the annual relevant costs for various order quantities as follows.

Order quantity (units)		100	200	300	400	500	600	800	1,000
Average stock (units)	(a)	50	100	150	200	250	300	400	500
Number of orders	(b)	250	125	83	63	50	42	31	25
		£	£	£	£	£	£	£	£
Annual holding cost	(c)	320	640	960	1,280	1,600	1,920	2,560	3,200
Annual order cost	(d)	8,000	4,000	2,656	2,016	1,600	1,344	992	800
Total relevant cost		8,320	4,640	3,616	3,296	3,200	3,264	3,552	4,000

Notes

(a) Average stock = Order quantity ÷ 2 (ie assuming no safety stock)
(b) Number of orders = annual demand ÷ order quantity
(c) Annual holding cost = Average stock × £6.40
(d) Annual order cost = Number of orders × £32

4.12 You will see that the economic order quantity is 500 units. At this point the total annual relevant costs are at a minimum.

4.13 We can present the information tabulated in Paragraph 4.11 in graphical form. The vertical axis represents the relevant annual costs for the investment in stocks, and the horizontal axis can be used to represent either the various order quantities or the average stock levels; two scales are actually shown on the horizontal axis so that both items can be incorporated. The graph shows that, as the average stock level and order quantity increase, the holding cost increases. On the other hand, the ordering costs decline as stock levels and order quantities increase. The total cost line represents the sum of both the holding and the ordering costs.

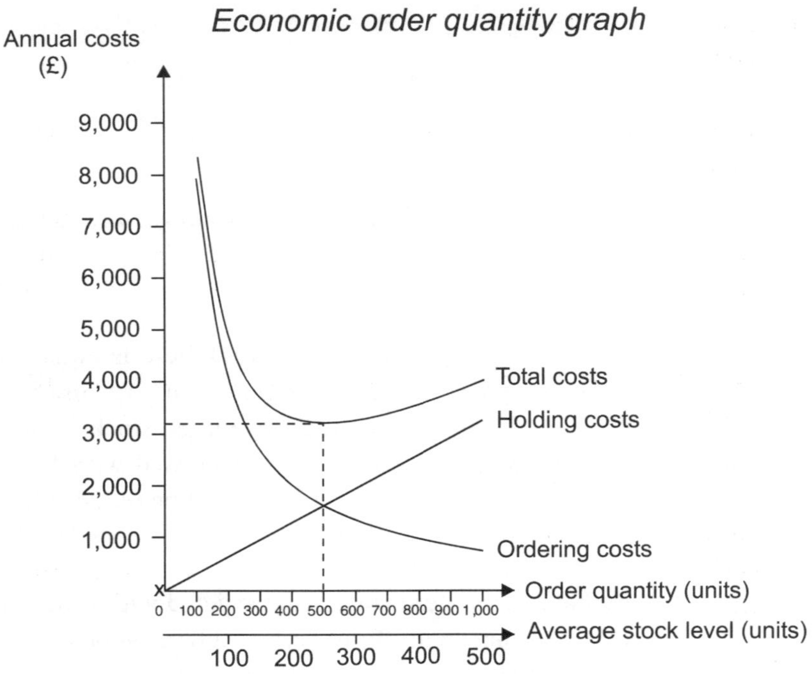

4.14 Note that the total cost line is at a minimum for an order quantity of 500 units and occurs at the point where the ordering cost curve and holding cost curve intersect. **The EOQ is therefore found at the point where holding costs equal ordering costs.**

4.15 There is also a formula for the EOQ and this will be provided in your examination.

EXAM FORMULA

$$EOQ = \sqrt{\frac{2C_0D}{C_H}}$$

where C_H = cost of holding one unit of stock for one time period
C_0 = cost of ordering a consignment from a supplier
D = demand during the time period

Question 6

Calculate the EOQ using the formula and the information in Paragraph 4.10.

Answer

$$EOQ = \sqrt{\frac{2 \times £32 \times 25,000}{£6.40}}$$

$$= \sqrt{250,000}$$

= 500 units

Economic batch quantity (EBQ)

4.16 You may come across a problem in which the **basic EOQ formula requires modification because re-supply is gradual, instead of instantaneous**. Typically, a manufacturing company might hold stocks of a finished item, which is produced in batches. Once the order for a new batch has been placed, and the production run has started, finished output might be used before the batch run has been completed.

4.17 If the daily demand for an item of stock is ten units, and the storekeeper orders 100 units in a batch. The rate of production is 50 units a day.

(a) On the first day of the batch production run, the stores will run out of its previous stocks, and re-supply will begin. 50 units will be produced during the day, and ten units will be consumed. The closing stock at the end of day 1 will be 50 – 10 = 40 units.

(b) On day 2, the final 50 units will be produced and a further ten units will be consumed. Closing stock at the end of day 2 will be (40 + 50 –10) = 80 units.

(c) In eight more days, stocks will fall to zero.

4.18 The minimum stock in this example is zero, and the maximum stock is 80 units. The maximum stock is the quantity ordered (Q = 100) minus demand during the period of the batch production run which is Q × D/R, where

D is the rate of demand
R is the rate of production
Q is the quantity ordered.

In our example, the maximum stock is $(100 - \frac{10}{50} \times 100) = 100 - 20 = 80$ units.

The maximum stock level, given gradual re-supply, is thus $Q - \frac{QD}{R} = Q(1 - D/R)$.

4.19 The position can be represented graphically as follows.

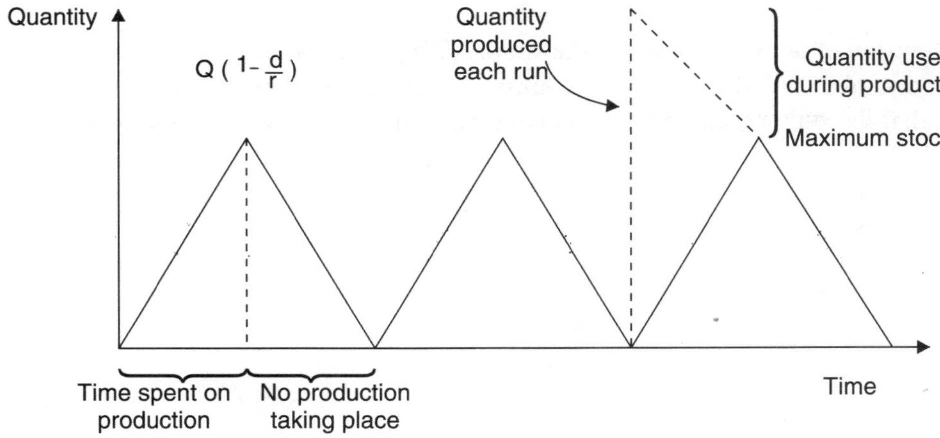

4.20 An amended EOQ (economic batch quantity, or EBQ) formula is required because average stocks are not Q/2 but Q(1 – D/R)/2.

EXAM FORMULA

The **EBQ** is $\sqrt{\dfrac{2C_oD}{C_H(1-D/R)}}$

where R = the production rate per time period (which must exceed the stock usage)
Q = the amount produced in each batch
D = the usage per time period
C_o = the set up cost per batch
C_H = the holding cost per unit of stock per time period

Question 7

A company is able to manufacture its own components for stock at the rate of 4,000 units a week. Demand for the component is at the rate of 2,000 units a week. Set up costs for each production run are £50. The cost of holding one unit of stock is £0.001 a week.

Required

Calculate the economic production run.

Answer

$$Q = \sqrt{\frac{2 \times 50 \times 2{,}000}{0.001(1-2{,}000/4{,}000)}}$$ = 20,000 units (giving a stock cycle of 10 weeks)

Bulk discounts

4.21 The solution obtained from using the simple EOQ formula may need to be modified if bulk discounts (also called quantity discounts) are available. The following graph shows the effect that discounts granted for orders of certain sizes may have on total costs.

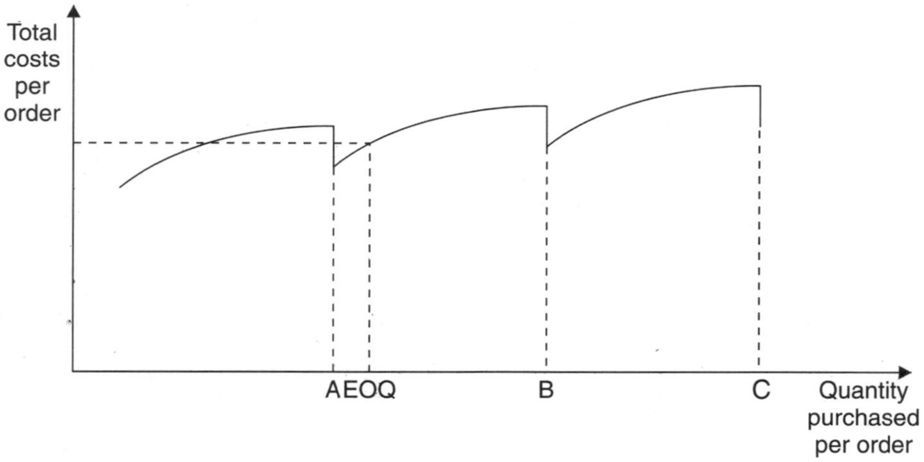

The graph above shows the following.

- Differing bulk discounts are given when the order quantity exceeds A, B and C
- The minimum total cost (ie when quantity B is ordered rather than the EOQ)

4.22 To decide mathematically whether it would be worthwhile taking a discount and ordering larger quantities, it is necessary to **minimise** the total of the following.

- Total material costs
- Ordering costs
- Stock holding costs

4.23 The **total cost** will be **minimised** at one of the following.

- At the **pre-discount EOQ level,** so that a discount is not worthwhile
- At the **minimum order size** necessary to earn the discount

4.24 EXAMPLE: BULK DISCOUNTS

The annual demand for an item of stock is 45 units. The item costs £200 a unit to purchase, the holding cost for one unit for one year is 15% of the unit cost and ordering costs are £300 an order.

The supplier offers a 3% discount for orders of 60 units or more, and a discount of 5% for orders of 90 units or more.

Required

Calculate the cost-minimising order size.

4.25 SOLUTION

(a) The EOQ ignoring discounts is $\sqrt{\dfrac{2 \times 300 \times 45}{15\% \text{of} 200}} = 30$

	£
Purchases (no discount) 45 × £200	9,000
Holding costs (W1)	450
Ordering costs (W2)	450
Total annual costs	9,900

Workings

1 **Holding costs**

Holding costs = Average stock × holding cost for one unit of stock per annum

Average stock = Order quantity ÷ 2
= 30 ÷ 2 = 15 units

Holding cost for one unit of stock per annum = 15% × £200
= £30

∴ Holding costs = 15 units × £30
= £450

2 **Ordering costs**

Ordering costs = Number of orders × ordering costs per order (£300)

Number of orders = Annual demand ÷ order quantity
= 45 ÷ 30
= 1.5 orders

∴ ordering costs = 1.5 orders × £300
= £450

(b) With a discount of 3% and an order quantity of 60, units costs are as follows.

	£
Purchases £9,000 × 97%	8,730
Holding costs (W3)	873
Ordering costs (W4)	225
Total annual costs	9,828

Workings

3 **Holding costs**

Holding costs = Average stock × holding cost for one unit of stock per annum

Average stock = Order quantity ÷ 2
= 60 ÷ 2 = 30 units

Holding cost for one unit of stock per annum = 15% × 97% × £200 = £29.10

Note. 97% = 100% – 3% discount

∴ Holding costs = 30 units × £29.10
= £873

4 **Ordering costs**

Ordering costs = Number of orders × ordering costs per order (£300)

Number of orders = Annual demand ÷ order quantity
= 45 ÷ 60
= 0.75 orders

∴ Ordering costs = 0.75 orders × £300
= £225

(c) With a discount of 5% and an order quantity of 90, units costs are as follows.

	£
Purchases £9,000 × 95%	8,550.0
Holding costs (W5)	1,282.5
Ordering costs (W6)	150.0
Total annual costs	9,982.5

Workings

5 **Holding costs**

Holding costs = Average stock × holding cost for one unit of stock per annum

Average stock = order quantity ÷ 2
= 90 ÷ 2
= 45 units

Holding cost for one unit of stock per annum = 15% × 95% × £200
= £28.50

Note. 95% = 100% – 5% discount

∴ Holding costs = 45 units × £28.50
= £1,282.50

6 **Ordering costs**

Ordering costs = Number of orders × ordering costs per order (£300)

Number of orders = Annual demand ÷ order quantity
= 45 ÷ 90
= 0.5 orders

∴ ordering costs = 0.5 orders × £300
= £150

The cheapest option is to order 60 units at a time.

4.26 Note that the value of C_H varied according to the size of the discount, because C_H was a percentage of the purchase cost. This means that **total holding costs are reduced because of a discount.** This could easily happen if, for example, most of C_H was the cost of insurance, based on the cost of stock held.

Question 8

A company uses an item of stock as follows.

Purchase price: £96 per unit
Annual demand: 4,000 units
Ordering cost: £300
Annual holding cost: 10% of purchase price
Economic order quantity: 500 units

Required

Ascertain whether the company should order 1,000 units at a time in order to secure an 8% discount.

Answer

The total annual cost at the economic order quantity of 500 units is as follows.

	£
Purchases 4,000 × £96	384,000
Ordering costs £300 × (4,000/500)	2,400
Holding costs £96 × 10% × (500/2)	2,400
	388,800

The total annual cost at an order quantity of 1,000 units would be as follows.

	£
Purchases £384,000 × 92%	353,280
Ordering costs £300 × (4,000/1,000)	1,200
Holding costs £96 × 92% × 10% × (1,000/2)	4,416
	358,896

The company should order the item 1,000 units at a time, saving £(388,800 – 358,896) = £29,904 a year.

Other systems of stores control and reordering

4.27 (a) **Under the order cycling method, quantities on hand of each stores item are reviewed periodically** (every 1, 2 or 3 months). For low-cost items, a technique called the 90-60-30 day technique can be used, so that when stocks fall to 60 days' supply, a fresh order is placed for a 30 days' supply so as to boost stocks to 90 days' supply. For high-cost items, a more stringent stores control procedure is advisable so as to keep down the costs of stock holding.

(b) **The two-bin system of stores control (or visual method of control) is one whereby each stores item is kept in two storage bins.** When the first bin is emptied, an order must be placed for re-supply; the second bin will contain sufficient quantities to last until the fresh delivery is received. This is a simple system which is not costly to operate but it is not based on any formal analysis of stock usage and may result in the holding of too much or too little stock.

(c) **Materials items may be classified as expensive, inexpensive or in a middle-cost range.** Because of the practical advantages of simplifying stores control procedures without incurring unnecessary high costs, it may be possible to segregate materials for selective stores control.

(i) Expensive and medium-cost materials are subject to careful stores control procedures to minimise cost.

(ii) Inexpensive materials can be stored in large quantities because the cost savings from careful stores control do not justify the administrative effort required to implement the control.

This selective approach to stores control is sometimes called the **ABC method** whereby materials are classified A, B or C according to their expense-group A being the expensive, group B the medium-cost and group C the inexpensive materials.

(d) A similar selective approach to stores control is the **Pareto (80/20) distribution** which is based on the finding that in many stores, 80% of the value of stores is accounted for by only 20% of the stores items, and stocks of these more expensive items should be controlled more closely.

5 STOCK VALUATION

5.1 You may be aware from your studies for Paper 1.1 **Preparing Financial Statements** that, for financial accounting purposes, stocks are valued at the **lower of cost and net realisable value**. In practice, stocks will probably be valued at cost in the stores records throughout the course of an accounting period. Only when the period ends will the value of the stock in hand be reconsidered so that items with a net realisable value below their original cost will be revalued downwards, and the stock records altered accordingly.

Charging units of stock to cost of production or cost of sales

5.2 It is important to be able to distinguish between the way in which the physical items in stock are actually issued. In practice a storekeeper may issue goods in the following way.

- The oldest goods first
- The latest goods received first
- Randomly
- Those which are easiest to reach

5.3 By comparison the cost of the goods issued must be determined on a **consistently applied basis**, and must ignore the likelihood that the materials issued will be costed at a price different to the amount paid for them.

5.4 This may seem a little confusing at first, and it may be helpful to explain the point further. Suppose that there are three units of a particular material in stock.

Units	*Date received*	*Purchase cost*
A	June 20X1	£100
B	July 20X1	£106
C	August 20X1	£109

In September, one unit is issued to production. As it happened, the physical unit actually issued was B. The accounting department must put a value or cost on the material issued, but the value would not be the cost of B, £106. The principles used to value the materials issued are not concerned with the actual unit issued, A, B, or C. Nevertheless, the accountant may choose to make one of the following assumptions.

(a) The unit issued is valued as though it were the earliest unit in stock, ie at the purchase cost of A, £100. This valuation principle is called **FIFO**, or **first in, first out**.

(b) The unit issued is valued as though it were the most recent unit received into stock, ie at the purchase cost of C, £109. This method of valuation is **LIFO**, or **last in, first out**.

(c) The unit issued is valued at an average price of A, B and C, ie £105.

5.5 In the following sections we will consider each of the pricing methods detailed above (and a few more), using the following transactions to illustrate the principles in each case.

TRANSACTIONS DURING MAY 20X3

	Quantity Units	*Unit cost* £	*Total cost* £	*Market value per unit on date of transaction* £
Opening balance, 1 May	100	2.00	200	
Receipts, 3 May	400	2.10	840	2.11
Issues, 4 May	200			2.11
Receipts, 9 May	300	2.12	636	2.15
Issues, 11 May	400			2.20
Receipts, 18 May	100	2.40	240	2.35
Issues, 20 May	100			2.35
Closing balance, 31 May	200			2.38
			1,916	

6 FIFO (FIRST IN, FIRST OUT)

6.1 **FIFO assumes that materials are issued out of stock in the order in which they were delivered into stock:** issues are priced at the cost of the earliest delivery remaining in stock.

Using **FIFO**, the cost of issues and the closing stock value in the example would be as follows.

Date of issue	*Quantity issued* Units	*Value*	£	£
4 May	200	100 o/s at £2	200	
		100 at £2.10	210	
				410
11 May	400	300 at £2.10	630	
		100 at £2.12	212	
				842
20 May	100	100 at £2.12		212
Cost of issues				1,464
Closing stock value	200	100 at £2.12	212	
		100 at £2.40	240	
				452
				1,916 *

* The cost of materials issued plus the value of closing stock equals the cost of purchases plus the value of opening stock (£1,916).

The market price of purchased materials is rising dramatically. In a period of inflation, there is a tendency with FIFO for materials to be issued at a cost lower than the current market value, although closing stocks tend to be valued at a cost approximating to current market value.

Question 9

Draw up an extract from a stores ledger account using the columns shown below. Complete the columns in as much detail as possible using the information in Paragraphs 5.5 and 6.1.

STORES LEDGER ACCOUNT

Date	Receipts				Issues				Stock		
	GRN No	Quantity	Unit price £	Amount £	Stores Req No	Quantity	Unit price £	Amount £	Quantity	Unit price £	Amount £

Answer

STORES LEDGER ACCOUNT (extract)

Date	Receipts				Issues				Stock		
	GRN No.	Quantity	Unit price £	Amount £	Stores Req. No.	Quantity	Unit price £	Amount £	Quantity	Unit price £	Amount £
1.5.X3									100	2.00	200.00
3.5.X3		400	2.10	840.00					100	2.00	200.00
									400	2.10	840.00
									500		1,040.00
4.5.X3						100	2.00	200.00			
						100	2.10	210.00	300	2.10	630.00
9.5.X3		300	2.12	636.00					300	2.10	630.00
									300	2.12	636.00
									600		1,266.00
11.5.X3						300	2.10	630.00			
						100	2.12	212.00	200	2.12	424.00
18.5.X3		100	2.40	240.00					200	2.12	424.00
									100	2.40	240.00
									300		664.00
20.5.X3						100	2.12	212.00	100	2.12	212.00
									100	2.40	240.00
31.5.X3									200		452.00

6.2 The advantages and disadvantages of the FIFO method are as follows.

Advantages	Disadvantages
It is a logical pricing method which probably represents what is physically happening: in practice the oldest stock is likely to be used first.	FIFO can be cumbersome to operate because of the need to identify each batch of material separately.
It is easy to understand and explain to managers.	Managers may find it difficult to compare costs and make decisions when they are charged with varying prices for the same materials.
The stock valuation can be near to a valuation based on replacement cost.	In a period of high inflation, stock issue prices will lag behind current market value.

7 LIFO (LAST IN, FIRST OUT)

7.1 **LIFO assumes that materials are issued out of stock in the reverse order to which they were delivered:** the most recent deliveries are issued before earlier ones, and are priced accordingly.

Using LIFO, the cost of issues and the closing stock value in the example above would be as follows.

Date of issue	*Quantity issued*	*Valuation*		
	Units		£	£
4 May	200	200 at £2.10		420
11 May	400	300 at £2.12	636	
		100 at £2.10	210	
				846
20 May	100	100 at £2.40		240
Cost of issues				1,506
Closing stock value	200	100 at £2.10	210	
		100 at £2.00	200	
				410
				1,916

Notes

(a) The cost of materials issued plus the value of closing stock equals the cost of purchases plus the value of opening stock (£1,916).

(b) In a period of inflation there is a tendency with **LIFO** for the following to occur.

  (i) Materials are issued at a price which approximates to current market value.
  (ii) Closing stocks become undervalued when compared to market value.

7.2 The advantages and disadvantages of the **LIFO** method are as follows.

Advantages	**Disadvantages**
Stocks are issued at a price which is close to current market value.	The method can be cumbersome to operate because it sometimes results in several batches being only part-used in the stock records before another batch is received.
Managers are continually aware of recent costs when making decisions, because the costs being charged to their department or products will be current costs.	LIFO is often the opposite to what is physically happening and can therefore be difficult to explain to managers.
	As with FIFO, decision making can be difficult because of the variations in prices.

8 CUMULATIVE WEIGHTED AVERAGE PRICING

8.1 The cumulative weighted average pricing method calculates a **weighted average price** for all units in stock. Issues are priced at this average cost, and the balance of stock remaining would have the same unit valuation. The average price is determined by dividing the total cost by the total number of units.

A new weighted average price is calculated whenever a new delivery of materials into store is received. This is the key feature of cumulative weighted average pricing.

8.2 In our example, issue costs and closing stock values would be as follows.

Date	*Received* Units	*Issued* Units	*Balance* Units	*Total stock value* £	*Unit cost* £	£
Opening stock			100	200	2.00	
3 May	400			840	2.10	
			* 500	1,040	2.08	
4 May		200		(416)	2.08	416
			300	624	2.08	
9 May	300			636	2.12	
			* 600	1,260	2.10	
11 May		400		(840)	2.10	840
			200	420	2.10	
18 May	100			240	2.40	
			* 300	660	2.20	
20 May		100		(220)	2.20	220
						1,476
Closing stock value			200	440	2.20	440
						1,916

* A new stock value per unit is calculated whenever a new receipt of materials occurs.

Notes

(a) The cost of materials issued plus the value of closing stock equals the cost of purchases plus the value of opening stock (£1,916).

(b) In a period of inflation, using the cumulative weighted average pricing system, the value of material issues will rise gradually, but will tend to lag a little behind the current market value at the date of issue. Closing stock values will also be a little below current market value.

8.3 The advantages and disadvantages of **cumulative weighted average pricing** are these.

Advantages	Disadvantages
Fluctuations in prices are smoothed out, making it easier to use the data for decision making.	The resulting issue price is rarely an actual price that has been paid, and can run to several decimal places.
It is easier to administer than FIFO and LIFO, because there is no need to identify each batch separately.	Prices tend to lag a little behind current market values when there is gradual inflation.

9 OTHER METHODS OF PRICING AND VALUATION

Periodic weighted average pricing

9.1 Under the periodic weighted average pricing method, a retrospective average price is calculated for *all* materials issued during the period. The average issue price is calculated for our example as follows.

$$\frac{\text{Cost of all receipts in the period} + \text{Cost of opening stock}}{\text{Number of units received in the period} + \text{Number of units of opening stock}} = \frac{£1,716 + £200}{800 + 100}$$

Issue price = £2.129 per unit

Closing stock values are a balancing figure.

9.2 The issue costs and closing stock values are calculated as follows.

Date of issue	*Quantity issued*	*Valuation*
	Units	£
4 May	200 × £2.129	426
11 May	400 × £2.129	852
20 May	100 × £2.129	213
Cost of issues		1,491
Value of opening stock plus purchases		1,916
Value of 200 units of closing stock (at £2.129)		425

9.3 The periodic weighted average pricing method is easier to calculate than the cumulative weighted average method, and therefore requires less effort, but it must be applied retrospectively since the costs of materials used cannot be calculated until the end of the period.

Standard cost pricing

9.4 **Under the standard cost pricing method, all issues are at predetermined standard price.** Such a method is used with a system of standard costing, which will be covered later in this text when we study standard costing (in Chapter 18).

Replacement cost pricing

9.5 Arguments for **replacement cost pricing** include the following.

(a) When materials are issued out of stores, they will be replaced with a new delivery; issues should therefore be priced at the current cost to the business of replacing them in stores.

(b) Closing stocks should be valued at current replacement cost in the balance sheet to show the true value of the assets of the business.

9.6 The advantages and disadvantages of **replacement costing** are as follows.

Advantages	Disadvantages
Issues are at up-to-date costs so that managers can take recent trends into account when making decisions based on their knowledge of the costs being incurred.	The price may not be an actual price paid, and a difference will then arise on issues.
It is recommended as a method of accounting for inflation.	It can be difficult to determine the replacement cost.
It is easy to operate once the replacement cost has been determined.	The method is not acceptable to the Inland Revenue or for SSAP 9, although this should not be a major consideration in internal cost accounts.

Question 10

Which pricing method can be used as a practical alternative to replacement cost pricing?

Answer

LIFO is a reasonably accurate method of accounting for inflation provided that closing stock values are periodically reviewed and revalued.

Highest in, first out (HIFO)

9.7 This method values issues at the highest price of the items in stock at the time of issue. Although prudent it is an approach which does not follow any particular chronological order.

Next in, first out (NIFO)

9.8 This method values issues at the price to be paid for the next delivery, which may or may not be the same as replacement cost. This method does value issues at the most up-to-date price but it is administratively difficult.

Specific price

9.9 This method values issues at their individual price and the stock balance is made up of individual items valued at individual prices. It is only really suitable for expensive stock lines where stock holdings and usage rates are low.

10 STOCK VALUATION AND PROFITABILITY

10.1 In the previous descriptions of FIFO, LIFO, average costing and so on, the example used raw materials as an illustration. Each method produced different figures for both the value of closing stocks and also the cost of material issues. Since raw materials costs affect the cost of production, and the cost of production works through eventually into the cost of sales, it follows that different methods of stock valuation will provide different profit figures. The following example will help to illustrate the point.

10.2 EXAMPLE: STOCK VALUATION AND PROFITABILITY

On 1 November 20X2, Delilah's Dresses Ltd held 3 pink satin dresses with orange sashes, designed by Freda Swoggs. These were valued at £120 each. During November 20X2, 12 more of the dresses were delivered as follows.

Date	*Units received*	*Purchase cost per dress*
10 November	4	£125
20 November	4	£140
25 November	4	£150

A number of the pink satin dresses with orange sashes were sold during November as follows.

Date	*Dresses sold*	*Sales price per dress*
14 November	5	£200
21 November	5	£200
28 November	1	£200

Required

Calculate the gross profit (sales – (opening stock + purchases – closing stock)) from selling the pink satin dresses with orange sashes in November 20X2, applying the following principles of stock valuation.

(a) FIFO
(b) LIFO
(c) Cumulative weighted average pricing

10.3 SOLUTION

(a) **FIFO**

Date	*Cost of sales*	*Total* £	*Closing stock* £
14 November	3 units × £120		
	+ 2 units × £125		
		610	
21 November	2 units × £125		
	+ 3 units × £140		
		670	
28 November	1 unit × £140	140	
Closing stock	4 units × £150		600
		1,420	600

(b) **LIFO**

Date	*Cost of sales*	*Total* £	*Closing stock* £
14 November	4 units × £125		
	+ 1 unit × £120		
		620	
21 November	4 units × £140		
	+ 1 unit × £120		
		680	
28 November	1 unit × £150	150	
Closing stock	3 units × £150		
	+ 1 unit × £120		
			570
		1,450	570

(c) **Cumulative weighted average pricing**

		Unit cost	Balance in stock	Cost of sales	Closing stock
		£	£	£	£
1 November	3	120.00	360		
10 November	4	125.00	500		
	7	122.86	860		
14 November	5	122.86	614	614	
	2		246		
20 November	4	140.00	560		
	6	134.33	806		
21 November	5	134.33	672	672	
	1		134		
25 November	4	150.00	600		
	5	146.80	734		
28 November	1	146.80	147	147	
30 November	4	146.80	587	1,433	587

Profitability

	FIFO	LIFO	Weighted average
	£	£	£
Opening stock	360	360	360
Purchases	1,660	1,660	1,660
	2,020	2,020	2,020
Closing stock	600	570	587
Cost of sales	1,420	1,450	1,433
Sales (11 × £200)	2,200	2,200	2,200
Gross profit	780	750	767

10.4 In the example above, **different stock valuation methods produced different costs of sale and hence different profits. As opening stock values and purchase costs are the same for each method, the different costs of sale are due to different closing stock valuations. The differences in profits therefore equal the differences in closing stock valuations.**

10.5 The profit differences are only **temporary**. In the example, the opening stock in December 20X2 will be £600, £570 or £587, depending on the stock valuation method used. Different opening stock values will affect the cost of sales and profits in December, so that in the long run, inequalities in costs of sales each month will even themselves out.

11 LEDGER ENTRIES RELATING TO MATERIALS

11.1 In cost accounting, we are concerned not only with the cost of individual items of stock, but with the total costs of all raw material stocks used, and the total costs of all finished goods sold during an accounting period. These total costs, which are the sum of all the costs on individual stores ledger records, are recorded as follows.

(a) In a **raw material stores account**, or stores ledger control account, for raw materials stocks.
(b) In a **finished goods stock (control) account**, for finished goods stocks.

The cost of stocks manufactured in the production department is recorded in the **work in progress control account**.

11.2 EXAMPLE: LEDGER ENTRIES FOR MATERIALS

At 1 July 20X6, the total value of items held in store was £50,000. During July the following transactions occurred.

	£
Materials purchased from suppliers, on credit	120,000
Materials returned to suppliers, because they were of unsatisfactory quality	3,000
Materials purchased for cash	8,000
Direct materials issued to the production department	110,000
Indirect materials issued as production overhead costs	25,000
Value of materials written off after a discrepancy was found in a stock check	1,000
Direct materials returned to store from production	4,000

Required

Draw up a stores ledger account and stock adjustment account for July 20X6.

11.3 SOLUTION

(a) The opening balance of stocks brought forward is a debit balance in the stores account.

(b) When materials are received which are bought on credit, the accounting entry is to:

DEBIT	Stores account
CREDIT	Trade creditor's (supplier's) account

(c) When materials are returned to suppliers, the reduction of items in stock and the reduction in the amounts owed to the suppliers is shown by the double entry:

CREDIT	Stores account
DEBIT	Creditor's account

(d) When materials are purchased for cash, the entry is:

DEBIT	Stores account
CREDIT	Cash (or bank) account

when the goods are received and the cash paid.

(e) When materials are issued from stores, the reduction in stocks is shown as a credit entry in the stores account. The corresponding debit entry is to work in progress account (for direct materials) or production overhead account (for indirect production materials).

CREDIT	Stores account
DEBIT	Work in progress account or production overhead account

(f) The entries are reversed when materials are returned to store unused by the department which requisitioned them.

(g) The accounting entries for stock written off ie for a loss of stocks are as follows:

CREDIT	Stores account
DEBIT	Stock adjustment account

(h) The balance on the stores account at the end of the period will be closing stocks, carried forward as opening stocks at 1 August 20X6.

In our example, the stores account for July 20X6 will be as follows.

STORES ACCOUNT

	£		£
Opening stock b/f	50,000	Returns to suppliers (creditors a/c)	3,000
Purchases (creditors a/c)	120,000		
Purchases (cash a/c)	8,000	Work in progress account - issues	110,000
Returns from WIP (WIP a/c)	4,000	Production overhead a/c -issues	25,000
		Loss of stock - adjustment a/c	1,000
		Closing stock c/f	43,000
	182,000		182,000
Opening stock b/f	43,000		

STOCK ADJUSTMENT ACCOUNT

	£		£
Stores account	1,000	Profit and loss account	1,000

Chapter roundup

- **Stock control** includes the functions of stock ordering and purchasing, receiving goods into store, storing and issuing stock and controlling the level of stocks.
- Every movement of material in a business should be documented using the following as appropriate: purchase requisition, purchase order, GRN, materials requisition note, materials transfer note and materials returned note.
- **Perpetual inventory** refers to a stock recording system whereby the records (bin cards and stores ledger accounts) are updated for each receipt and issue of stock as it occurs.
- Stocktaking can be carried out on a **continuous** or **periodic** basis.
- **Free stock balance** calculations take account of stock on order from suppliers, and of stock which has been requisitioned but not yet delivered.
- **Stock costs** include purchase costs, holding costs, ordering costs and stockout costs.
- **Stock control levels** can be calculated in order to maintain stocks at the optimum level. The three critical control levels are reorder level, minimum level and maximum level.
- The **economic order quantity** (EOQ) is the order quantity which minimises stock costs. The EOQ can be calculated using a table, graph or formula.

  $$EOQ = \sqrt{\frac{2C_oD}{C_H}}$$

- The **economic batch quantity (EBQ)** is a modification of the EOQ and is used when resupply is gradual instead of instantaneous.

  $$EBQ = \sqrt{\frac{2C_oD}{C_H(1-D/R)}}$$

- The correct pricing of issues and valuation of stock are of the utmost importance because they have a direct effect on the calculation of profit. Several different methods can be used in practice.
- **FIFO** assumes that materials are issued out of stock in the order in which they were delivered into stock: issues are priced at the cost of the earliest delivery remaining in stock. **LIFO** assumes that materials are issued out of stock in the reverse order to which they were delivered: the most recent deliveries are issued before earlier ones and issues are priced accordingly.
- There are two weighted average methods of pricing: **cumulative weighted average** and **periodic weighted average**.
- Under the **standard costing method**, all issues are at a predetermined standard price.
- Although **replacement costing** is recommended as a method of accounting for inflation, in many instances it is impractical because of the difficulty of maintaining records of replacement market values.
- The total costs of all raw materials stocks used during an accounting period are recorded in a **raw materials stores account**.
- The total costs of all finished goods sold in an accounting period are recorded in a **finished goods (stock) control account**.
- The cost of stocks manufactured in the production department is recorded in the **work in progress control account**.

Quick quiz

1 List six objectives of storekeeping.

- ....
- ....
- ....
- ....
- ....
- ....

2 Free stock represents...

3 Free stock is calculated as follows. (Delete as appropriate)

(a)	+ –	Materials in stock	X
(b)	+ –	Materials in order	X
(c)	+ –	Materials requisitioned (not yet issued)	X
		Free stock balance	X

4 How does periodic stocktaking differ from continuous stocktaking?

5 Match up the following.

Reorder level	→ ?	Maximum usage × maximum lead time
Minimum level		Safety stock + $^1/_2$ reorder level
Maximum level		Reorder level – (average usage × average lead time)
Average stock		Reorder level + reorder quantity – (minimum usage × minimum lead time)

6 $EOQ = \sqrt{\dfrac{2C_oD}{C_H}}$

Where

(a) C_H = ...

(b) C_o = ...

(c) D = ...

7 When is the economic batch quantity used?

8 Which of the following are true?

I With FIFO, the stock valuation will be very close to replacement cost.

II With LIFO, stocks are issued at a price which is close to the current market value.

III Decision making can be difficult with both FIFO and LIFO because of the variations in prices.

IV A disadvantage of the weighted average method of stock valuation is that the resulting issue price is rarely an actual price that has been paid and it may be calculated to several decimal places.

A I and II only
B I, II and III only
C I and III only
D I, II, III and IV

9 In which ledger account is the cost of stocks manufactured in the production department recorded?

Answers to quick quiz

1
- Speedy **issue** and **receipt** of materials
- Full **identification** of all materials at all times
- Correct **location** of all materials at all times
- **Protection** of materials from damage and deterioration
- Provision of **secure stores** to avoid pilferage, theft and fire
- **Efficient** use of storage space
- **Maintenance** of correct stock levels
- Keeping correct and up-to-date **records** of receipts, issues and stock levels

2 Stock that is readily available for future use.

3 (a) +
(b) +
(c) –

4 **Periodic stocktaking.** All stock items physically counted and valued, usually annually.

Continuous stocktaking. Counting and valuing selected items at different times of the year (at least once a year).

5

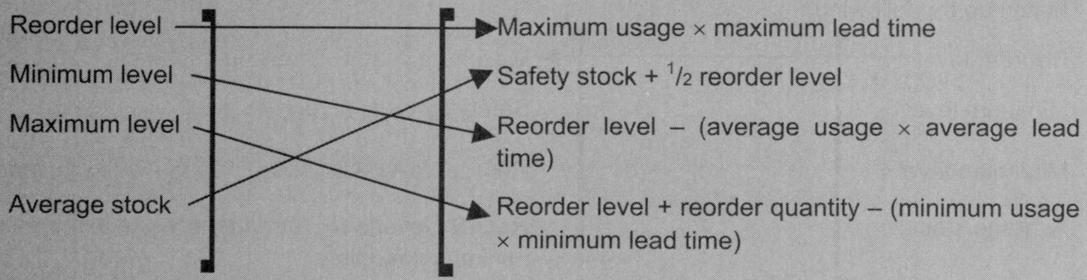

6 (a) Cost of holding one unit of stock for one time period
(b) Cost of ordering a consignment from a supplier
(c) Demand during the time period

7 When resupply of a product is gradual instead of instantaneous.

8 D

9 Work in progress control account

Now try the questions below from the Exam Question Bank

Number	Level	Marks	Time
8	MCQ	n/a	n/a
9	Examination	10	18 mins

Chapter 7

LABOUR COSTS

Introduction

Just as management need to control stocks and operate an appropriate valuation policy in an attempt to control material costs, so too must they be aware of the most suitable **remuneration policy** for their organisation. We will be looking at a number of methods of remuneration and will consider the various types of **incentive scheme** that exist. We will also examine the procedures and documents required for the accurate **recording of labour costs**. **Labour turnover** will be studied too.

Study guide

Section 10 – Labour costs

- Explain the difference between, and calculate, direct and indirect labour costs
- Explain the methods used to relate input labour costs to work done
- Prepare journal and ledger entries to record labour cost inputs and outputs
- Describe and illustrate different remuneration methods and incentive schemes
- Calculate the level, and analyse the costs and causes of, labour turnover
- Describe and illustrate measures of labour efficiency and utilisation
- Interpret the entries and balances in the labour account

Exam guide

Labour costs is a key area of the syllabus. You can expect to see questions on this topic in either Section A or Section B of the paper-based examination.

1 MEASURING LABOUR ACTIVITY

1.1 Suppose that an employee is expected to produce three units in every hour that he works. The standard rate of productivity is three units per hour, and one unit is valued at $^1/_3$ of a standard hour of output. If, during one week, the employee makes 126 units in 40 hours of work the following comments can be made.

(a) **Production** in the week is 126 units.

(b) **Productivity** is a relative measure of the hours actually taken and the hours that should have been taken to make the output.

(i)	**Either,** 126 units should take	42 hours
	But did take	40 hours
	Productivity ratio = 42/40 × 100% =	105%
(ii)	**Or alternatively**, in 40 hours, he should make (× 3)	120 units
	But did make	126 units
	Productivity ratio = 126/120 × 100% =	105%

A productivity ratio greater than 100% indicates that actual efficiency is better than the expected or 'standard' level of efficiency.

KEY TERMS

- **Production** is the quantity or volume of output produced.
- **Standard hour of production** is a concept used in standard costing, and means the number of units that can be produced by one worker working in the standard way at the standard rate for one hour.
- **Productivity** is a measure of the efficiency with which output has been produced.

1.2 Management will wish to **plan** and **control** both production levels and labour productivity.

(a) **Production levels can be raised** as follows.

- Working overtime
- Hiring extra staff
- Sub-contracting some work to an outside firm
- Managing the work force so as to achieve more output.

(b) **Production levels can be reduced as follows.**

- Cancelling overtime
- Laying off staff

(c) **Productivity,** if improved, will enable a company to achieve its production targets in fewer hours of work, and therefore at a lower cost.

Productivity and its effect on cost

1.3 **Improved productivity** is an important means of reducing total unit costs. In order to make this point clear, a simple example will be used.

1.4 Clooney Ltd has a production department in its factory consisting of a work team of just two men, Doug and George. Doug and George each work a 40 hour week and refuse to do any overtime. They are each paid £100 per week and production overheads of £400 per week are charged to their work.

(a) In week one, they produce 160 units of output between them. Productivity is measured in units of output per man hour.

Production	160 units
Productivity (80 man hours)	2 units per man hour
Total cost	£600 (labour plus overhead)
Cost per man hour	£7.50
Cost per unit	£3.75

(b) In week two, management pressure is exerted on Doug and George to increase output and they produce 200 units in normal time.

Production	200 units (up by 25%)
Productivity	2.5 units per man hour (up by 25%)
Total cost	£600
Cost per man hour	£7.50 (no change)
Cost per unit	£3.00 (a saving of 20% on the previous cost; 25% on the new cost)

(c) In week three, Doug and George agree to work a total of 20 hours of overtime for an additional £50 wages. Output is again 200 units and overhead charges are increased by £100.

Production	200 units (up 25% on week one)
Productivity (100 man hours)	2 units per hour (no change on week one)
Total cost (£600 + £50 + £100)	£750
Cost per unit	£3.75

(d) Conclusions

(i) An increase in production without an increase in productivity will not reduce unit costs (week one compared with week three).

(ii) An **increase in productivity will reduce unit costs** (week one compared with week two).

1.5 **Labour cost control** is largely concerned with **productivity**. Rising wage rates have increased automation, which in turn has improved productivity and reduced costs.

1.6 Where **automation** is introduced, productivity is often, but misleadingly, measured in terms of **output per man-hour**.

Suppose, for example, that a work-team of six men (240 hours per week) is replaced by one machine (40 hours per week) and a team of four men (160 hours per week), and as a result output is increased from 1,200 units per week to 1,600 units.

	Production	*Man hours*	*Productivity*
Before the machine	1,200 units	240	5 units per man hour
After the machine	1,600 units	160	10 units per man hour

Labour productivity has doubled because of the machine, and employees would probably expect extra pay for this success. For control purposes, however, it is likely that a new measure of productivity is required, **output per machine hour**, which may then be measured against a standard output for performance reporting.

Efficiency, capacity and production volume ratios

1.7 Other measures of labour activity include the following.

- Production volume ratio, or activity ratio
- Efficiency ratio (or productivity ratio)
- Capacity ratio

Efficiency ratio × **Capacity ratio** = **Production volume ratio**

$$\frac{\text{Expected hours to make output}}{\text{Actual hours taken}} \times \frac{\text{Actual hours worked}}{\text{Hours budgeted}} = \frac{\text{Output measured in expected or standard hours}}{\text{Hours budgeted}}$$

These ratios are usually expressed as percentages.

1.8 EXAMPLE: RATIOS

Rush and Fluster Ltd budgets to make 25,000 standard units of output (in four hours each) during a budget period of 100,000 hours.

Actual output during the period was 27,000 units which took 120,000 hours to make.

Required

Calculate the efficiency, capacity and production volume ratios.

1.9 SOLUTION

(a) Efficiency ratio $$\frac{(27{,}000 \times 4)\text{ hours}}{120{,}000} \times 100\% = 90\%$$

(b) Capacity ratio $$\frac{120{,}000\text{ hours}}{100{,}000\text{ hours}} \times 100\% = 120\%$$

(c) Production volume ratio $$\frac{(27{,}000 \times 4)\text{ hours}}{100{,}000} \times 100\% = 108\%$$

(d) The production volume ratio of 108% (more output than budgeted) is explained by the 120% capacity working, offset to a certain extent by the poor efficiency (90% × 120% = 108%).

1.10 Where efficiency standards are associated with remuneration schemes they generally allow 'normal time' (that is, time required by the average person to do the work under normal conditions) plus an allowance for rest periods and possible delays. There should therefore be a readily achievable standard of efficiency (otherwise any remuneration scheme will fail to motivate employees), but without being so lax that it makes no difference to the rate at which work is done.

2 REMUNERATION METHODS

2.1 Labour remuneration methods have an effect on the following.

- The cost of finished products and services.
- The morale and efficiency of employees.

2.2 There are three basic groups of remuneration method.

- Time work
- Piecework schemes
- Bonus/incentive schemes

Time work

FORMULA TO LEARN

The most common form of **time work** is a **day-rate system** in which wages are calculated by the following formula.

Wages = Hours worked × rate of pay per hour

2.3 If an employee works for more hours than the basic daily requirement he may be entitled to an **overtime payment**. Hours of overtime are usually paid at a **premium rate**. For instance, if the basic day-rate is £4 per hour and overtime is paid at time-and-a-quarter, eight hours of overtime would be paid the following amount.

	£
Basic pay (8 × £4)	32
Overtime premium (8 × £1)	8
Total (8 × £5)	40

2.4 The **overtime premium** is the extra rate per hour which is paid, not the whole of the payment for the overtime hours.

2.5 If employees work unsocial hours, for instance overnight, they may be entitled to a **shift premium**. The extra amount paid per hour, above the basic hourly rate, is the **shift premium**.

2.6 **Day-rate systems** may be summarised as follows.

(a) They are easy to understand.

(b) They do not lead to very complex negotiations when they are being revised.

(c) They are most appropriate when the quality of output is more important than the quantity, or where there is no basis for payment by performance.

(d) There is no incentive for employees who are paid on a day-rate basis to improve their performance.

Piecework schemes

FORMULA TO LEARN

In a **piecework scheme**, wages are calculated by the following formula.

Wages = Units produced × Rate of pay per unit

2.7 Suppose for example, an employee is paid £1 for each unit produced and works a 40 hour week. Production overhead is added at the rate of £2 per direct labour hour.

Weekly production	*Pay (40 hours)*	*Overhead*	*Conversion cost*	*Conversion cost per unit*
Units	£	£	£	£
40	40	80	120	3.00
50	50	80	130	2.60
60	60	80	140	2.33
70	70	80	150	2.14

As his output increases, his wage increases and at the same time unit costs of output are reduced.

2.8 It is normal for pieceworkers to be offered a **guaranteed minimum wage**, so that they do not suffer loss of earnings when production is low through no fault of their own.

Question 1

Penny Pincher is paid 50p for each towel she weaves, but she is guaranteed a minimum wage of £60 for a 40 hour week. In a series of four weeks, she makes 100, 120, 140 and 160 towels.

Required

Calculate her pay each week, and the conversion cost per towel if production overhead is added at the rate of £2.50 per direct labour hour.

Answer

Week	*Output*		*Pay*	*Production overhead*	*Conversion cost*	*Unit conversion cost*
	Units		£	£	£	£
1	100	(minimum)	60	100	160	1.60
2	120		60	100	160	1.33
3	140		70	100	170	1.21
4	160		80	100	180	1.13

There is no incentive to Penny Pincher to produce more output unless she can exceed 120 units in a week. The guaranteed minimum wage in this case is too high to provide an incentive.

2.9 If an employee makes several different types of product, it may not be possible to add up the units for payment purposes. Instead, a **standard time allowance** is given for each unit to arrive at a total of piecework hours for payment.

2.10 EXAMPLE: PIECEWORK

An employee is paid £5 per piecework hour produced. In a 35 hour week he produces the following output.

	Piecework time allowed per unit
3 units of product A	2.5 hours
5 units of product B	8.0 hours

Required

Calculate the employee's pay for the week.

2.11 SOLUTION

Piecework hours produced are as follows.

Product A	3 × 2.5 hours	7.5 hours
Product B	5 × 8 hours	40.0 hours
Total piecework hours		47.5 hours

Therefore employee's pay = 47.5 × £5 = £237.50 for the week.

2.12 **Differential piecework schemes** offer an incentive to employees to increase their output by paying higher rates for increased levels of production. For example:

up to 80 units per week, rate of pay per unit	=	£1.00
80 to 90 units per week, rate of pay per unit	=	£1.20
above 90 units per week, rate of pay per unit	=	£1.30

Employers should obviously be careful to make it clear whether they intend to pay the increased rate on all units produced, or on the extra output only.

2.13 **Piecework schemes** may be summarised as follows.

- They enjoy fluctuating popularity.
- They are occasionally used by employers as a means of increasing pay levels.
- They are often seen to drive employees to work too hard to earn a satisfactory wage.

Careful inspection of output is necessary to ensure that quality doesn't fall as production increases.

Bonus/incentive schemes

2.14 In general, **bonus schemes** were introduced to compensate workers paid under a time-based system for their inability to increase earnings by working more efficiently. Various types of incentive and bonus schemes have been devised which encourage greater productivity. The characteristics of such schemes are as follows.

(a) Employees are paid more for their efficiency.

(b) The profits arising from productivity improvements are shared between employer and employee.

(c) Morale of employees is likely to improve since they are seen to receive extra reward for extra effort.

2.15 A bonus scheme must satisfy certain conditions to operate successfully.

(a) Its **objectives** should be **clearly stated** and **attainable** by the employees.

(b) The **rules** and conditions of the scheme should be **easy to understand**.

(c) It must **win** the full **acceptance** of everyone concerned.

(d) It should be seen to be **fair to employees and employers**..

(e) The bonus should ideally be **paid soon after the extra effort has been made** by the employees.

(f) **Allowances** should be made for external factors outside the employees' control which reduce their productivity (machine breakdowns, material shortages).

(g) Only those employees who make the extra effort should be rewarded.

(h) The scheme must be **properly communicated** to employees.

2.16 We shall be looking at the following types of incentive schemes in detail.

- High day rate system
- Individual bonus schemes
- Group bonus schemes
- Profit sharing schemes
- Incentive schemes involving shares
- Value added incentive schemes

Some organisations employ a variety of incentive schemes. A scheme for a production labour force may not necessarily be appropriate for white-collar workers. An organisation's incentive schemes may be regularly reviewed, and altered as circumstances dictate.

High day-rate system

KEY TERM

A **high day-rate system** is a system where employees are paid a high hourly wage rate in the expectation that they will work more efficiently than similar employees on a lower hourly rate in a different company.

2.17 For example if an employee would make 100 units in a 40 hour week if he were paid £2 per hour, but 120 units if he were paid £2.50 per hour, and if production overhead is added to cost at the rate of £2 per direct labour hour, costs per unit of output would be as follows.

(a) Costs per unit of output on the low day-rate scheme would be:

$$\frac{(40 \times £4)}{100} = £1.60 \text{ per unit}$$

(b) Costs per unit of output on the high day-rate scheme would be:

$$\frac{(40 \times £4.50)}{120} = £1.50 \text{ per unit}$$

(c) Note that in this example the labour cost per unit is lower in the first scheme (80p) than in the second (83.3p), but the unit conversion cost (labour plus production overhead) is higher because overhead costs per unit are higher at 80p than with the high day-rate scheme (66.7p).

(d) In this example, the high day-rate scheme would reward both employer (a lower unit cost by 10p) and employee (an extra 50p earned per hour).

2.18 There are two **advantages** of a high day-rate scheme over other incentive schemes.

(a) It is **simple** to calculate and **easy** to understand.
(b) It **guarantees** the employee a consistently **high wage**.

2.19 The **disadvantages** of such schemes are as follows.

(a) **Employees cannot earn more than the fixed hourly rate for their extra effort.** In the previous example, if the employee makes 180 units instead of 120 units in a 40 hour week on a high day-rate pay scheme, the cost per unit would fall to £1 but his wage would be the same - 40 hours at £4.50. All the savings would go to benefit the company and none would go to the employee.

(b) **There is no guarantee that the scheme will work consistently.** The high wages may become the accepted level of pay for normal working, and supervision may be necessary to ensure that a high level of productivity is maintained. Unit costs would rise.

(c) **Employees may prefer to work at a normal rate of output**, even if this entails accepting the lower wage paid by comparable employers.

Individual bonus schemes

KEY TERM

An **individual bonus scheme** is a remuneration scheme whereby **individual** employees qualify for a bonus on top of their basic wage, with each person's bonus being calculated separately.

2.20 (a) The bonus is **unique** to the individual. It is not a share of a group bonus.

(b) The individual can earn a bonus by working at an **above-target** standard of efficiency.

(c) The individual earns a **bigger bonus the greater his efficiency**, although the bonus scheme might incorporate quality safeguards, to prevent individuals from sacrificing quality standards for the sake of speed and more pay.

2.21 To be successful, however, an **individual bonus scheme** must take account of the following factors.

(a) Each individual should be rewarded for the **work done by that individual**. This means that each person's output and time must be measured separately. Each person must therefore work without the assistance of anyone else.

(b) Work should be **fairly routine**, so that standard times can be set for jobs.

(c) The bonus should be **paid soon after the work is done**, to provide the individual with the incentive to try harder.

Group bonus schemes

KEY TERM

A **group bonus scheme** is an incentive plan which is related to the output performance of an entire group of workers, a department, or even the whole factory.

2.22 Where individual effort cannot be measured, and employees work as a team, an individual incentive scheme is impracticable but a **group bonus scheme** would be feasible.

2.23 The other **advantages** of group bonus schemes are as follows.

(a) They are **easier to administer** because they reduce the clerical effort required to measure output and calculate individual bonuses.

(b) They **increase co-operation** between fellow workers.

(c) They have been found to **reduce** accidents, spoilage, waste and absenteeism.

2.24 Serious **disadvantages** would occur in the following circumstances.

(a) The employee groups demand **low efficiency standards** as a condition of accepting the scheme.

(b) Individual employees are browbeaten by their fellow workers for working too slowly.

Profit-sharing schemes

KEY TERM

A **profit sharing scheme** is a scheme in which employees receive a certain proportion of their company's year-end profits (the size of their bonus being related to their position in the company and the length of their employment to date).

2.25 The advantage of these schemes is that the company will only pay what it can afford out of actual profits and the bonus can be paid also to non-production personnel.

The disadvantages of profit sharing are as follows.

(a) Employees must **wait until the year end** for a bonus. The company is therefore expecting a long-term commitment to greater efforts and productivity from its workers without the incentive of immediate reward.

(b) **Factors** affecting profit may be **outside the control** of employees, in spite of their greater efforts.

(c) **Too many employees** are involved in a single scheme for the scheme to have a great motivating effect on individuals.

Incentive schemes involving shares

2.26 It is becoming increasingly common for companies to use their shares, or the right to acquire them, as a form of incentive.

KEY TERMS

- A **share option scheme** is a scheme which gives its members the right to buy shares in the company for which they work at a set date in the future and at a price usually determined when the scheme is set up.
- An **employee share ownership plan (ESOP)** is a scheme which acquires shares on behalf of a number of employees, and it must distribute these shares within 20 years of acquisition.

The Government has encouraged companies to set up schemes of this nature in the hope that workers will feel they have a stake in the company which employs them. The **disadvantages** of these schemes are as follows.

(a) The benefits are not certain, as the market value of shares at a future date cannot realistically be predicted in advance.

(b) The benefits are not immediate, as a scheme must be in existence for a number of years before members can exercise their rights.

Value added incentive schemes

2.27 **Value added is an alternative to profit as a business performance measure** and it can be used as the basis of an incentive scheme. It is calculated as follows.

KEY TERM

Value added = sales – cost of bought-in materials and services

The advantage of value added over profit as the basis for an incentive scheme is that it excludes any bought-in costs, and is affected only by costs incurred internally, such as labour.

A basic value added figure would be agreed as the target for a business, and some of any excess value added earned would be paid out as a bonus. For example, it could be agreed that value added should be, say, treble the payroll costs and a proportion of any excess earned, say one third, would be paid as bonus.

Payroll costs for month	£40,000
Therefore, value added target (× 3)	£120,000
Value added achieved	£150,000
Therefore, excess value added	£30,000
Employee share to be paid as bonus	£10,000

2.28 EXAMPLE: INCENTIVE SCHEMES

Swetton Tyres Ltd manufactures a single product. Its work force consists of 10 employees, who work a 36-hour week exclusive of lunch and tea breaks. The standard time required to make one unit of the product is two hours, but the current efficiency (or productivity) ratio being achieved is 80%. No overtime is worked, and the work force is paid £4 per attendance hour.

Because of agreements with the work force about work procedures, there is some unavoidable idle time due to bottlenecks in production, and about four hours per week per person are lost in this way.

The company can sell all the output it manufactures, and makes a 'cash profit' of £20 per unit sold, deducting currently achievable costs of production but *before* deducting labour costs.

An incentive scheme is proposed whereby the work force would be paid £5 per hour in exchange for agreeing to new work procedures that would reduce idle time per employee per week to two hours and also raise the efficiency ratio to 90%.

Required

Evaluate the incentive scheme from the point of view of profitability.

2.29 SOLUTION

The current situation

Hours in attendance	10 × 36	=	360 hours
Hours spent working	10 × 32	=	320 hours
Units produced, at 80% efficiency	$\frac{320}{2} \times \frac{80}{100}$	=	128 units

	£
Cash profits before deducting labour costs (128 × £20)	2,560
Less labour costs (£4 × 360 hours)	1,440
Net profit	1,120

The incentive scheme

Hours spent working	10 × 34	=	340 hours
Units produced, at 90% efficiency	$\frac{340}{2} \times \frac{90}{100}$	=	153 units

	£
Cash profits before deducting labour costs (153 × £20)	3,060
Less labour costs (£5 × 360)	1,800
Net profit	1,260

In spite of a 25% increase in labour costs, profits would rise by £140 per week. The company and the workforce would both benefit provided, of course, that management can hold the work force to their promise of work reorganisation and improved productivity.

Question 2

The following data relate to work at a certain factory.

Normal working day	8 hours
Basic rate of pay per hour	£6
Standard time allowed to produce 1 unit	2 minutes
Premium bonus	75% of time saved at basic rate

What will be the labour cost in a day when 340 units are made?

A £48   B £51   C £63   D £68

Answer

Standard time for 340 units (× 2 minutes)	680 minutes
Actual time (8 hours per day)	480 minutes
Time saved	200 minutes

	£
Bonus = 75% × 200 minutes × £6 per hour	15
Basic pay = 8 hours × £6	48
Total labour cost	63

Therefore the correct answer is C.

Using basic MCQ technique you can eliminate option A because this is simply the basic pay without consideration of any bonus. You can also eliminate option D, which is based on the standard time allowance without considering the basic pay for the eight-hour day. Hopefully your were not forced to guess, but had you been you would have had a 50% chance of selecting the correct answer (B or C) instead of a 25% chance because you were able to eliminate two of the options straightaway.

3 RECORDING LABOUR COSTS

Organisation for controlling and measuring labour costs

3.1 Several departments and management groups are involved in the collection, recording and costing of labour. These include the following.

- Personnel
- Production planning
- Timekeeping
- Wages
- Cost accounting

Personnel department

3.2 The **personnel department** is responsible for the following.

- Engagement, transfer and discharge of employees.
- Classification and method of remuneration.

The department is headed by a **professional personnel officer** trained in personnel management, labour laws, company personnel policy and industry conditions who should have an understanding of the needs and problems of the employees.

3.3 Additional labour may be found as follows.

- Contacting recruitment agencies
- Placing advertisements in newspapers and journals (trade)
- Contacting local schools and technical colleges
- Review any CVs held on file of persons known to be available for work

All potential employees/interviewees should complete an application form.

3.4 When a person is engaged a **personnel record card** should be prepared showing full personal particulars, previous employment, medical category and wage rate. Other details to be included are National Insurance number, address, telephone number, transfers, promotions, changes in wage rates, sickness and accidents and, when an employee leaves, the reason for leaving.

3.5 Personnel departments sometimes **maintain records of overtime and shift working**. Overtime has to be sanctioned by the works manager or personnel office who advise the time-keepers who control the time booked.

3.6 The personnel department is responsible for issuing **reports to management** on normal and overtime hours worked, absenteeism and sickness, lateness, labour turnover and disciplinary action.

Production planning department

3.7 This department is responsible for the following.

- Scheduling work
- Issuing job orders to production departments
- Chasing up jobs when they run late

Timekeeping department

3.8 The **timekeeping department** is responsible for recording the attendance time and job time of the following.

- The time spent in the factory by each worker
- The time spent by each worker on each job

Such timekeeping provides basic data for statutory records, payroll preparation, labour costs of an operation or overhead distribution (where based on wages or labour hours) and statistical analysis of labour records for determining productivity and control of labour costs.

Attendance time

3.9 The bare minimum record of employees' time is a simple **attendance record** showing days absent because of holiday, sickness or other reason. A typical record of attendance is shown as follows.

NAME: A.N. OTHER *DEPT:* 072 *NI REF:* WD 4847 41C *LEAVE ENTITLEMENT:* 20

	1	2	3	4	5	6	7	8	9	10	11	12	**13**	14	15	16	17	18	19	20	21	**22**	23	24	25	26	27	28	29	30	31
JAN																															
FEB																															
MAR																															
APR																															
MAY																															
JUNE																															
JULY																															
AUG																															
SEPT																															
OCT																															
NOV																															
DEC																															

Illness: I Industrial Accident: IA Maternity: M	Leave: L Unpaid Leave: UL Special Leave: SL	Training: T Jury Service: J	*Note overleaf:* (1) The reasons for special leave (eg bereavement). (2) Ensure training is noted on personnel card.

RECORD OF ATTENDANCE

3.10 It is also necessary to have a record of the following.

- Time of arrival
- Time of breaks
- Time of departure

These may be recorded as follows.

- In a signing-in book
- By using a time recording clock which stamps the time on a clock card
- By using swipe cards (which make a computer record)

An example of a clock card is shown as follows.

No Name				Ending	
	HOURS	RATE	AMOUNT	DEDUCTIONS	
Basic O/T Others				Income Tax NI Other	
				Total deduction	
Total Less deductions Net due					
Time		Day		Basic time	Overtime
1230 T 0803 T 1700 M 1305 M 1234 M 0750 M					
Signature _ _ _ _ _ _ _ _ _ _ _					

Job time

3.11 **Continuous production**. Where **routine, repetitive** work is carried out it might not be practical to record the precise details. For example if a worker stands at a conveyor belt for seven hours his work can be measured by keeping a note of the number of units that pass through his part of the process during that time.

3.12 **Job costing**. When the work is not of a repetitive nature the records required might be one or several of the following.

(a) **Daily time sheets**. A time sheet is filled in by the employee as a record of how their time has been spent. The total time on the time sheet should correspond with time shown on the attendance record.

(b) **Weekly time sheets**. These are similar to daily time sheets but are passed to the cost office at the end of the week. An example of a weekly timesheet is shown below.

Time Sheet No. ________________

Employee Name __________ Clock Code __________ Dept ________

Date ____________________ Week No. ______________

Job No.	Start Time	Finish Time	Qty	Checker	Hrs	Rate	Extension

(c) **Job cards**. Cards are prepared for each job or batch. When an employee works on a job he or she records on the job card the time spent on that job. Job cards are therefore likely to contain entries relating to numerous employees. On completion of the job it will contain a full record of the times and quantities involved in the job or batch. A typical job card is shown as follows.

JOB CARD

Department ______________________ Job no ______________________

Date ______________________ Operation no ______________________

Time allowance ____________________ Time started ____________________

Time finished ____________________

Hours on the job ____________________

Description of job	Hours	Rate	Cost

Employee no ______________________ Certified by ______________________

Signature ______________________

A job card will be given to the employee, showing the work to be done and the expected time it should take. The employee will record the time started and time finished for each job. Breaks for tea and lunch may be noted on the card, as standard times, by the production planning department. The hours actually taken and the cost of those hours will be calculated by the accounting department.

3.13 **Piecework**. The wages of pieceworkers and the labour cost of work done by them is determined from what is known as a **piecework ticket** or an **operation card**. The card records the total number of items (or 'pieces') produced and the number of rejects. Payment is only made for 'good' production.

OPERATION CARD				
Operator's Name ______			Total Batch Quantity ______	
Clock No ______			Start Time ______	
Pay week No ______ Date ______			Stop Time ______	
Part No ______			Works Order No ______	
Operation ______			Special Instructions ______	
Quantity Produced	No Rejected	Good Production	Rate	£
Inspector ______			Operative ______	
Foreman ______			Date ______	
PRODUCTION CANNOT BE CLAIMED WITHOUT A PROPERLY SIGNED CARD				

Note that the attendance record of a pieceworker is required for calculations of holidays, sick pay and so on.

3.14 **Other types of work**. Casual workers are paid from job cards or time sheets. Time sheets are also used where outworkers are concerned.

3.15 Office work can be measured in a similar way, provided that the work can be divided into distinct jobs. Firms of accountants and advertising agencies, for example, book their staff time to individual clients and so make use of time sheets for salaried staff.

Salaried labour

3.16 Even though salaried staff are paid a flat rate monthly, they may be required to prepare timesheets. The reasons are as follows.

(a) Timesheets provide management with information (eg product costs).

(b) Timesheet information may provide a basis for billing for services provided (eg service firms where clients are billed based on the number of hours work done).

(c) Timesheets are used to record hours spent and so support claims for overtime payments by salaried staff.

3.17 An example of a timesheet (as used in the service sector) is shown as follows.

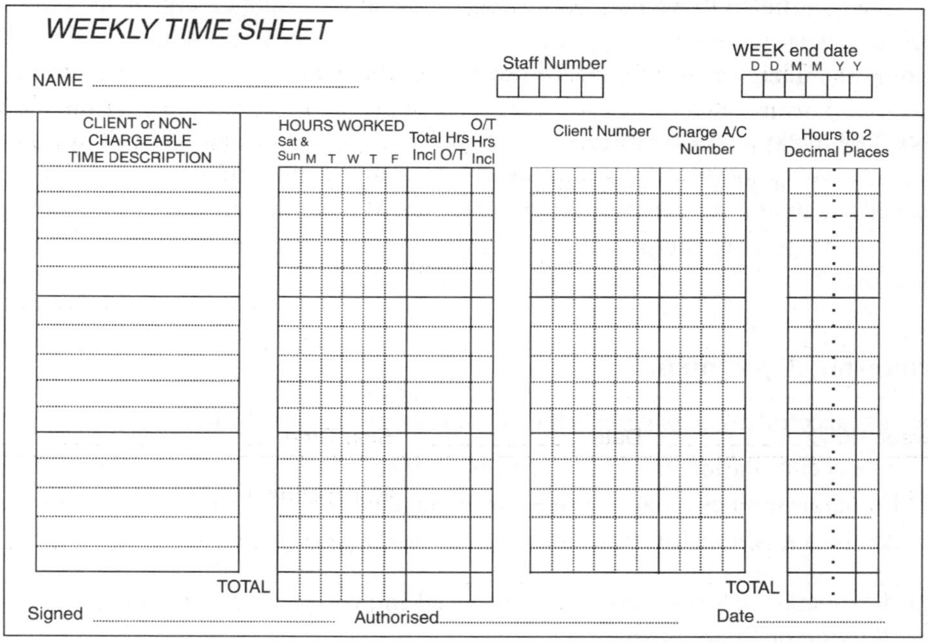

Idle time

3.18 **Idle time** occurs when employees cannot get on with their work, through no fault of their own. Examples are as follows.

- Machine breakdowns
- Shortage of work

3.19 **Idle time** has a cost because employees will still be paid their basic wage or salary for these unproductive hours and so there should be a record of idle time. This may simply comprise an entry on time sheets coded to 'idle time' generally, or separate idle time cards may be prepared. A supervisor might enter the time of a stoppage, its cause, its duration and the employees made idle on an idle time record card. Each stoppage should have a reference number which can be entered on time sheets or job cards.

Wages department

3.20 Responsibilities of the payroll department include the following.

- Preparation of the payroll and payment of wages.
- Maintenance of employee records.
- Summarising wages cost for each cost centre.
- Summarising the hours worked for each cost centre.
- Summarising other payroll information eg bonus payment, pensions etc.
- Providing an internal check for the preparation and payout of wages.

3.21 **Attendance cards** are the basis for payroll preparation. For **time workers**, the gross wage is the product of time attended and rate of pay. To this is added any overtime premium or bonus. For **piece workers**, gross wages are normally obtained by the product of the number of good units produced and the unit rate, with any premiums, bonuses and allowances for incomplete jobs added.

3.22 After calculation of net pay, a pay slip is prepared showing all details of earnings and deductions. The wage envelope or the attendance card may be used for this purpose.

3.23 When the payroll is complete, a coin and note analysis is made and a cheque drawn to cover the total amount. On receipt of the cash, the pay envelopes are made up and sealed. A receipt is usually obtained on payout (the attendance card can be used). Wages of absentees are retained until claimed by an authorised person.

3.24 **Internal checks** are necessary to prevent fraud. One method is to distribute the payroll work so that no person deals completely with any transaction. All calculations should be checked on an adding machine where possible. Makeup of envelopes should not be done by persons who prepare the payroll. The cashier should reconcile his analysis with the payroll summary.

Cost accounting department

3.25 The cost accounting department has the following responsibilities.

- The accumulation and classification of all cost data (which includes labour costs).
- Preparation of cost data reports for management.
- Analysing labour information on time cards and payroll.

3.26 In order to establish the labour cost involved in products, operations, jobs and cost centres, the following documents are used.

- Clock cards
- Job cards
- Idle time cards
- Payroll

3.27 Analyses of labour costs are used for the following.

(a) Charging wages directly attributable to production to the appropriate job or operation.

(b) Charging wages which are not directly attributable to production as follows.

(i) Idle time of production workers is charged to indirect costs as part of the overheads.

(ii) Wages costs of supervisors, or store assistants are charged to the overhead costs of the relevant department.

(c) Producing idle time reports which show a summary of the hours lost through idle time, and the cause of the idle time. Idle time may be analysed as follows.

- Controllable eg lack of materials.
- Uncontrollable eg power failure.

FORMULA TO LEARN

$$\textbf{Idle time ratio} = \frac{\text{Idle hours}}{\text{Total hours}} \times 100\%$$

3.28 The idle time ratio is useful because it shows the proportion of available hours which were lost as a result of idle time.

4 LABOUR TURNOVER

The reasons for labour turnover

4.1 Some employees will leave their job and go to work for another company or organisation. Sometimes the reasons are unavoidable.

- Illness or accidents
- A family move away from the locality
- Marriage, pregnancy or difficulties with child care provision
- Retirement or death

4.2 Other causes of labour turnover are to some extent controllable.

- Paying a lower wage rate than is available elsewhere.
- Requiring employees to work in unsafe or highly stressful conditions.
- Requiring employees to work uncongenial hours.
- Poor relationships between management and staff.
- Lack of opportunity for career enhancement.
- Requiring employees to work in inaccessible places (eg no public transport).
- Discharging employees for misconduct, bad timekeeping or unsuitability.

Measuring labour turnover

KEY TERM

Labour turnover is a measure of the number of employees leaving/being recruited in a period of time expressed as a percentage of the total labour force.

FORMULA TO LEARN

$$\textbf{Labour turnover rate} = \frac{\text{Replacements}}{\text{Average number of employees in period}} \times 100\%$$

4.3 EXAMPLE : LABOUR TURNOVER RATE

Revolving Doors plc had a staff of 2,000 at the beginning of 20X1 and, owing to a series of redundancies caused by the recession, 1,000 at the end of the year. Voluntary redundancy was taken by 1,500 staff at the end of June, 500 more than the company had anticipated, and these excess redundancies were immediately replaced by new joiners.

The labour turnover rate is calculated as follows.

$$\text{Rate} = \frac{500}{(2{,}000 + 1{,}000) \div 2} \times 100\% = 33\%$$

The costs of labour turnover

4.4 The costs of labour turnover can be large and management should attempt to keep labour turnover as low as possible so as to minimise these costs. The **cost of labour turnover** may be divided into the following.

- Preventative costs
- Replacement costs

4.5 **Replacement costs**. These are the costs incurred as a result of hiring new employees. and they include the following.

- Cost of selection and placement
- Inefficiency of new labour; productivity will be lower
- Costs of training
- Loss of output due to delay in new labour becoming available
- Increased wastage and spoilage due to lack of expertise among new staff
- The possibility of more frequent accidents at work
- Cost of tool and machine breakages

4.6 **Preventative costs** are costs incurred in order to prevent employees leaving and they include the following.

- Cost of personnel administration incurred in maintaining good relationships
- Cost of medical services including check-ups, nursing staff and so on
- Cost of welfare services, including sports facilities and canteen meals
- Pension schemes providing security to employees

The prevention of high labour turnover

4.7 Labour turnover will be reduced by the following actions.

- Paying satisfactory wages
- Offering satisfactory hours and conditions of work
- Creating a good informal relationship between members of the workforce
- Offering good training schemes and a well-understood career or promotion ladder
- Improving the content of jobs to create job satisfaction
- Proper planning so as to avoid redundancies
- Investigating the cause of an apparently high labour turnover

5 ACCOUNTING FOR LABOUR COSTS

5.1 We will use an example to briefly review the principal bookkeeping entries for wages.

5.2 EXAMPLE: THE WAGES CONTROL ACCOUNT

The following details were extracted from a weekly payroll for 750 employees at a factory.

Analysis of gross pay

	Direct workers	*Indirect workers*	*Total*
	£	£	£
Ordinary time	36,000	22,000	58,000
Overtime: basic wage	8,700	5,430	14,130
premium	4,350	2,715	7,065
Shift allowance	3,465	1,830	5,295
Sick pay	950	500	1,450
Idle time	3,200	-	3,200
	56,665	32,475	89,140
Net wages paid to employees	£45,605	£24,220	£69,825

Required

Prepare the wages control account for the week.

5.3 SOLUTION

(a) **The wages control account** acts as a sort of 'collecting place' for net wages paid and deductions made from gross pay. The gross pay is then analysed between direct and indirect wages.

(b) The first step is to determine which wage costs are **direct** and which are **indirect**. The direct wages will be debited to the work in progress account and the indirect wages will be debited to the production overhead account.

(c) There are in fact only two items of direct wages cost in this example, the ordinary time (£36,000) and the basic overtime wage (£8,700) paid to direct workers. All other payments (including the overtime premium) are indirect wages.

(d) The net wages paid are debited to the control account, and the balance then represents the deductions which have been made for income tax, national insurance, and so on.

WAGES CONTROL ACCOUNT

	£		£
Bank: net wages paid	69,825	Work in progress - direct labour	44,700
Deductions control accounts*		Production overhead control:	
(£89,140 – £69,825)	19,315	Indirect labour	27,430
		Overtime premium	7,065
		Shift allowance	5,295
		Sick pay	1,450
		Idle time	3,200
	89,140		89,140

* In practice there would be a separate deductions control account for each type of deduction made (for example, PAYE and National Insurance).

Direct and indirect labour costs

5.4 We had a brief look at direct and indirect labour costs in Chapter 3. Have a go at the following questions to remind yourself about the classification of labour costs.

Question 3

A direct labour employee's wage in week 5 consists of the following.

		£
(a)	Basic pay for normal hours worked, 36 hours at £4 per hour =	144
(b)	Pay at the basic rate for overtime, 6 hours at £4 per hour =	24
(c)	Overtime shift premium, with overtime paid at time-and-a-quarter ¼ × 6 hours × £4 per hour =	6
(d)	A bonus payment under a group bonus (or 'incentive') scheme - bonus for the month =	30
	Total gross wages in week 5 for 42 hours of work	204

Required

Establish which costs are direct costs and which are indirect costs.

Answer

Items (a) and (b) are direct labour costs of the items produced in the 42 hours worked in week 5.

Overtime premium, item (c), is usually regarded as an overhead expense, because it is 'unfair' to charge the items produced in overtime hours with the premium. Why should an item made in overtime be more costly just because, by chance, it was made after the employee normally clocks off for the day?

Group bonus scheme payments, item (d), are usually overhead costs, because they cannot normally be traced directly to individual products or jobs.

In this example, the direct labour employee costs were £168 in direct costs and £36 in indirect costs.

Question 4

Jaffa plc employs two types of labour: skilled workers, considered to be direct workers, and semi-skilled workers considered to be indirect workers. Skilled workers are paid £10 per hour and semi-skilled £5 per hour.

The skilled workers have worked 20 hours overtime this week, 12 hours on specific orders and 8 hours on general overtime. Overtime is paid at a rate of time and a quarter.

The semi-skilled workers have worked 30 hours overtime, 20 hours for a specific order at a customer's request and the rest for general purposes. Overtime again is paid at time and a quarter.

What would be the total overtime pay considered to be a direct cost for this week?

A £275
B £355
C £375
D £437.50

Answer

		Direct cost	*Indirect cost*
		£	£
Skilled workers			
Specific overtime	(12 hours × £10 × 1.25)	150	
General overtime	(8 hours × £10 × 1)	80	
	(8 hours × £10 × 0.25)		20
Semi-skilled workers			
Specific overtime	(20 hours × £5 × 1.25)	125	
General overtime	(10 hours × £5 × 1.25)		62.50
		355	82.50

The correct answer is therefore B.

If you selected option A, you forgot to include the direct cost of the general overtime of £80 for the skilled workers.

If you selected option C, you included the overtime premium for skilled workers' general overtime of £20.

If you selected option D, you calculated the total of direct cost + indirect cost instead of the direct cost.

Exam focus point

Question 4 is very similar to one of the multiple choice questions from the paper-based examination pilot paper for **Financial Information for Management**. The study guide for this paper states that candidates should be able to explain the difference between and calculate direct and indirect labour costs.

Chapter roundup

- **Labour** is a major cost in many businesses and it is therefore vital that you have understood this chapter's topics, a summary of them being set out below.
- **Production** is the quantity or volume of output produced. **Productivity** is a measure of the efficiency with which output has been produced. An increase in production without an increase in productivity will not reduce unit costs.
- There are three basic groups of **remuneration** method, **time work**, **piecework** schemes and **bonus/incentive** schemes.
- Labour attendance time is recorded on, for example, an attendance record or clock card. Job time may be recorded on daily time sheets, weekly time sheets or job cards depending on the circumstances. The manual recording of times on time sheets or job cards, is however, liable to error or even deliberate deception and may be unreliable.
- The labour cost of pieceworkers is recorded on a piecework ticket/operation card.
- **Idle time** has a cost and must, therefore, be recorded.
- **Labour turnover** is the rate at which employees leave a company and this rate should be kept as low as possible. The cost of labour turnover can be divided into **preventative** and **replacement** costs.
- The **wages control account** acts as a collecting place for wages before they are analysed to work in progress and production overhead control accounts.

Quick quiz

1 Distinguish between the terms production and productivity.

2 List five types of incentive scheme.

3 What are the requirements for a successful individual bonus scheme?

4 What is a value added incentive scheme?

5 When does idle time occur?

6 What are the responsibilities of a typical wages department?

7 Define the idle time ratio.

8 List six methods of reducing labour turnover.

Answers to quick quiz

1
- **Production** is the quantity or volume of output produced
- **Productivity** is a measure of the efficiency with which output has been produced

2
- High day rate system
- Individual bonus schemes
- Group bonus schemes
- Profit sharing schemes
- Incentive schemes involving shares
- Value added incentive schemes

3
- Each individual should be rewarded for the work done by that individual
- Work should be fairly routine, so that standard times can be set for jobs
- The bonus should be paid soon after the work is done

4 **Value added** is an alternative to profit as a business performance measure and it can be used as the basis of an incentive scheme

Value added = Sales – cost of bought-in materials and services

5 **Idle time** occurs when employees cannot get on with their work, through no fault of their own, for example when machines break down or there is a shortage of work.

6
- Preparation of the payroll and payment of wages
- Maintenance of employee records
- Summarising wages cost for each cost centre
- Summarising the hours worked for each cost centre
- Summarising other payroll information, eg bonus payment, pensions etc
- Providing an internal check for the preparation and payout of wages

7 $\text{Idle time ratio} = \frac{\text{Idle hours}}{\text{Total hours}} \times 100\%$

8
- Paying satisfactory wages
- Offering satisfactory hours and conditions of work
- Creating a good informal relationship between members of the workforce
- Offering good training schemes and a well-understood career or promotion ladder
- Improving the content of jobs to create job satisfaction
- Proper planning so as to avoid redundancies
- Investigating the cause of an apparently high labour turnover

Now try the questions below from the Exam Question Bank

Number	Level	Marks	Time
10	MCQ	n/a	n/a
11	Examination	10	18 mins

Chapter 8

OVERHEADS AND ABSORPTION COSTING

Topic list		Syllabus reference
1	Overheads	3(c)
2	Absorption costing: an introduction	3(c)
3	Overhead allocation	3(c)
4	Overhead apportionment	3(c)
5	Overhead absorption	3(c)
6	Blanket absorption rates and departmental absorption rates	3(c)
7	Normal costing	3(c)
8	Over and under absorption of overheads	3(c)
9	Ledger entries relating to overheads	3(c)
10	Non-manufacturing overheads	3(c)

Introduction

Absorption costing is a method of accounting for overheads. It is basically a method of sharing out overheads incurred amongst units produced.

This chapter begins by explaining why absorption costing might be necessary and then provides an overview of how the cost of a unit of product is built up under a system of absorption costing. A detailed analysis of this costing method is then provided, covering the three stages of absorption costing: **allocation**, **apportionment** and **absorption**. You will also see how to account for using absorption costing when it comes to preparing the profit and loss account.

Study guide

Section 11 – Overheads 1

- Explain the difference between the treatment of direct and indirect expenses
- Describe and justify the process of apportioning manufacturing overhead costs incurred to production
- Allocate and apportion factory overheads using an appropriate basis
- Reapportion service centre costs including the use of the reciprocal method
- Comment on the use of blanket, department, cost driver, actual and predetermined absorption rates
- Identify, calculate and discuss the appropriate absorption rates using relevant bases

Section 12 – Overheads 2

- Prepare journal and ledger entries for manufacturing overheads incurred and absorbed
- Calculate, explain and account for under- and over-absorbed overheads
- Describe and evaluate methods of attributing non-manufacturing overhead costs to units of output
- Describe how the cost structure of a business has changed over time and the implications of this with regard to overhead analysis

Exam guide

Overhead apportionment and absorption is one of the most important topics in your **Financial Information for Management** studies and is almost certain to appear in the exam you will be facing. Make sure that you study the contents of this chapter and work through the calculations very carefully.

1 OVERHEADS

KEY TERM

Overhead is the cost incurred in the course of making a product, providing a service or running a department, but which cannot be traced directly and in full to the product, service or department.

1.1 Overhead is actually the total of the following.

- Indirect materials
- Indirect labour
- Indirect expenses

1.2 The total of these indirect costs is usually split into the following.

- **Production** overhead
- **Administration** overhead
- **Selling and distribution** overhead

1.3 In cost accounting there are two schools of thought as to the correct method of dealing with overheads.

- Absorption costing
- Marginal costing

2 ABSORPTION COSTING: AN INTRODUCTION

2.1 **The objective of absorption costing is to include in the total cost of a product an appropriate share of the organisation's total overhead.** An appropriate share is generally taken to mean an amount which reflects the amount of time and effort that has gone into producing a unit or completing a job.

2.2 An organisation with one production department that produces identical units will divide the total overheads among the total units produced. **Absorption costing is a method for sharing overheads between different products on a fair basis.**

Is absorption costing necessary?

2.3 Suppose that a company makes and sells 100 units of a product each week. The prime cost per unit is £6 and the unit sales price is £10. Production overhead costs £200 per week and administration, selling and distribution overhead costs £150 per week. The weekly profit could be calculated as follows.

	£	£
Sales (100 units × £10)		1,000
Prime costs (100 × £6)	600	
Production overheads	200	
Administration, selling and distribution costs	150	
		950
Profit		50

2.4 **In absorption costing, overhead costs will be added to each unit of product manufactured and sold.**

	£ per unit
Prime cost per unit	6
Production overhead (£200 per week for 100 units)	2
Full factory cost	8

The weekly profit would be calculated as follows.

	£
Sales	1,000
Less factory cost of sales	800
Gross profit	200
Less administration, selling and distribution costs	150
Net profit	50

2.5 Sometimes, but not always, the overhead costs of administration, selling and distribution are also added to unit costs, to obtain a full cost of sales.

	£ per unit
Prime cost per unit	6.00
Factory overhead cost per unit	2.00
Administration etc costs per unit	1.50
Full cost of sales	9.50

The weekly profit would be calculated as follows.

	£
Sales	1,000
Less full cost of sales	950
Profit	50

2.6 It may already be apparent that the weekly profit is £50 no matter how the figures have been presented. So, how does absorption costing serve any useful purpose in accounting?

2.7 The **theoretical justification** for using absorption costing is that all production overheads are incurred in the production of the organisation's output and so each unit of the product receives some benefit from these costs. Each unit of output should therefore be charged with some of the overhead costs.

2.8 The **practical reasons** for using absorption costing are as follows.

(a) **Stock valuations**. Stock in hand must be valued for two reasons.

(i) For the closing stock figure in the balance sheet

(ii) For the cost of sales figure in the profit and loss account

The valuation of stocks will affect profitability during a period because of the way in which the cost of sales is calculated.

The cost of goods produced
\+ the value of opening stocks
– the value of closing stocks
= the cost of goods sold.

In our example, closing stocks might be valued at prime cost (£6), but in absorption costing, they would be valued at a fully absorbed factory cost, £8 per unit. (They would not be valued at £9.50, the full cost of sales, because the only costs incurred in producing goods for finished stock are factory costs.)

(b) **Pricing decisions**. Many companies attempt to fix selling prices by calculating the full cost of production or sales of each product, and then adding a margin for profit. In our example, the company might have fixed a gross profit margin at 25% on factory cost, or 20% of the sales price, in order to establish the unit sales price of £10. 'Full cost plus pricing' can be particularly useful for companies which do jobbing or contract work, where each job or contract is different, so that a standard unit sales price cannot be fixed. Without using absorption costing, a full cost is difficult to ascertain.

(c) **Establishing the profitability of different products**. This argument in favour of absorption costing is more contentious, but is worthy of mention here. If a company sells more than one product, it will be difficult to judge how profitable each individual product is, unless overhead costs are shared on a fair basis and charged to the cost of sales of each product.

Statement of standard accounting practice 9 (SSAP 9)

2.9 Of these three arguments, the problem of valuing stocks is perhaps the most significant. **Absorption costing is recommended in financial accounting** by the *Statement of standard accounting practice* on stocks and long-term contracts (SSAP 9). SSAP 9 deals with **financial accounting systems**. The cost accountant is (in theory) free to value stocks by whatever method seems best, but where companies integrate their financial accounting and cost accounting systems into a single system of accounting records, the valuation of closing stocks will be determined by SSAP 9.

2.10 SSAP 9 states that costs of all stocks should comprise those costs which have been incurred in the normal course of business in **bringing the product to its 'present location and condition'**. These costs incurred will include all related production overheads, even though these overheads may accrue on a time basis. In other words, in financial accounting, closing stocks should be valued at full factory cost, and it may therefore be convenient and appropriate to value stocks by the same method in the cost accounting system.

Costing procedures

2.11 The three stages of calculating the costs of overheads to be charged to cost units are:

- Allocation
- Apportionment
- Absorption

2.12 We shall now begin our study of absorption costing by looking at the process of **overhead allocation**.

3 OVERHEAD ALLOCATION

KEY TERM

Allocation is the process by which whole cost items are charged direct to a cost unit or cost centre.

3.1 Cost centres may be one of the following types.

(a) A **production department**, to which production overheads are charged

(b) A **production area service department**, to which production overheads are charged

(c) An **administrative department**, to which administration overheads are charged

(d) A **selling** or a **distribution department**, to which sales and distribution overheads are charged

(e) An **overhead cost centre**, to which items of expense which are shared by a number of departments, such as rent and rates, heat and light and the canteen, are charged

3.2 The following costs would therefore be charged to the following cost centres via the process of allocation.

- Direct labour will be charged to a production cost centre.
- The cost of a warehouse security guard will be charged to the warehouse cost centre.
- Paper (recording computer output) will be charged to the computer department.
- Costs such as the canteen are charged direct to various overhead cost centres.

3.3 As an example of overhead allocation, consider the following costs of a company.

Wages of the foreman of department A	£200
Wages of the foreman of department B	£150
Indirect materials consumed in department A	£50
Rent of the premises shared by departments A and B	£300

The cost accounting system might include three overhead cost centres.

Cost centre:	101	Department A
	102	Department B
	201	Rent

Overhead costs would be allocated directly to each cost centre, ie £200 + £50 to cost centre 101, £150 to cost centre 102 and £300 to cost centre 201. The rent of the factory will be subsequently shared between the two production departments, but for the purpose of day to day cost recording, the rent will first of all be charged in full to a separate cost centre.

4 OVERHEAD APPORTIONMENT

Stage 1: apportioning general overheads

4.1 **Overhead apportionment** follows on from overhead allocation. The first stage of overhead apportionment is to identify all overhead costs as production department, production service department, administration or selling and distribution overhead. The costs for heat and light, rent and rates, the canteen and so on (ie costs allocated to general overhead cost centres) must therefore be shared out between the other cost centres.

Bases of apportionment

4.2 It is considered important that overhead costs should be shared out on a **fair basis**. You will appreciate that because of the complexity of items of cost it is rarely possible to use only one method of apportioning costs to the various departments of an organisation. The bases of apportionment for the most usual cases are given below.

Overhead to which the basis applies	**Basis**
Rent, rates, heating and light, repairs and depreciation of buildings	Floor area occupied by each cost centre
Depreciation, insurance of equipment	Cost or book value of equipment
Personnel office, canteen, welfare, wages and cost offices, first aid	Number of employees, or labour hours worked in each cost centre
Heating, lighting (see above)	Volume of space occupied by each cost centre

4.3 EXAMPLE: OVERHEAD APPORTIONMENT

Burton Court plc has incurred the following overhead costs.

	£
Depreciation of factory	1,000
Factory repairs and maintenance	600
Factory office costs (treat as production overhead)	1,500
Depreciation of equipment	800
Insurance of equipment	200
Heating	390
Lighting	100
Canteen	900
	5,490

Information relating to the production and service departments in the factory is as follows.

	Department			
	Production A	*Production* B	*Service* X	*Service* Y
Floor space (square metres)	1,200	1,600	800	400
Volume (cubic metres)	3,000	6,000	2,400	1,600
Number of employees	30	30	15	15
Book value of equipment	£30,000	£20,000	£10,000	£20,000

Required

Determine how the overhead costs should be apportioned between the four departments.

4.4 SOLUTION

Item of cost	*Basis of apportionment*	*Total cost*	*To Department* A	B	X	Y
		£	£	£	£	£
Factory depreciation	(floor area)	1,000	300	400	200	100
Factory repairs	(floor area)	600	180	240	120	60
Factory office costs	(number of employees)	1,500	500	500	250	250
Equipment depreciation	(book value)	800	300	200	100	200
Equipment insurance	(book value)	200	75	50	25	50
Heating	(volume)	390	90	180	72	48
Lighting	(floor area)	100	30	40	20	10
Canteen	(number of employees)	900	300	300	150	150
Total		5,490	1,775	1,910	937	868

Stage 2: service department cost apportionment

4.5 The second stage of overhead apportionment concerns **the treatment of service cost centres.** A factory is divided into several production cost centres and also many service cost centres. Service cost centres might include the stores or the canteen

4.6 **Only the production cost centres are directly involved in the manufacture of the units.** In order to be able to add production overheads to unit costs, it is necessary to have all the overheads charged to (or located in) the production cost centres.

4.7 The next stage in absorption costing is therefore to apportion the costs of service cost centres to the production cost centres.

4.8 There are three methods by which the apportionment of service cost centre costs can be done.

(a) Apportion the costs of each service cost centre to production cost centres only (the **direct** method).

(b) Apportion the costs of each service cost centre not only to production cost centres, but also to other service cost centres which make use of its services. Eventually apportion all costs to the production cost centres alone by a gradual process of **repeated distribution** (the reciprocal method).

(c) Apportion the costs of each service cost centre, not only to production cost centres, but also to some (but not all) of the service cost centres that make use of its services. This is known as the **step-down** method.

We shall look at each of these methods in more detail below.

4.9 Whichever method is used, **the basis of apportionment must be fair**. A different apportionment basis may be applied for each service cost centre. This is demonstrated in the following table.

Service cost centre	Possible basis of apportionment
Stores	Number or cost value of material requisitions
Maintenance	Hours of maintenance work done for each cost centre
Production planning	Direct labour hours worked in each production cost centre

Direct method of apportionment

4.10 We shall start by looking at the direct method of apportionment which is best explained by means of an example.

4.11 EXAMPLE: DIRECT APPORTIONMENT

Maid Marion Ltd incurred the following overhead costs.

	Production departments		*Stores*	*Maintenance*
	P	*Q*	*department*	*department*
	£	£	£	£
Allocated costs	6,000	4,000	1,000	2,000
Apportioned costs	2,000	1,000	1,000	500
	8,000	5,000	2,000	2,500

Production department P requisitioned materials to the value of £12,000. Department Q requisitioned £8,000 of materials. The maintenance department provided 500 hours of work for department P and 750 hours for department Q. What are the total production overhead costs of Departments P and Q?

4.12 SOLUTION

Service department	*Basis of apportionment*	*Total cost*	*Dept P*	*Dept Q*
		£	£	£
Stores	Value of requisitions	2,000	1,200	800
Maintenance	Direct labour hours	2,500	1,000	1,500
		4,500	2,200	2,300
Previously allocated and apportioned costs		13,000	8,000	5,000
Total overhead		17,500	10,200	7,300

The total overhead has now been shared, on a fair basis, between the two production departments

Question 1

Sam Gittoes Ltd is preparing its production overhead budgets. Information relating to its production and service cost centres is as follows.

	Budgeted overheads	*Direct labour*	*Machine usage*	*Area*
Production departments	£	(hours)	(hours)	m^2
Machine Shop A	44,816	8,000	7,200	10,000
Machine Shop B	45,230	6,200	18,000	12,000
Assembly	26,832	20,800	-	15,000
Service departments				
Canteen	33,250	-	-	6,000
Maintenance	16,632	-	-	2,000
	166,760	35,000	25,200	45,000

Required

Using the direct method of apportionment, complete the table shown below in order to determine the overhead totals for Sam Gittoes Ltd's three production departments.

	Total	*A*	*B*	*Assembly*	*Canteen*	*Mainten-ance*	*Basis of appor-tionment*
	£	£	£	£	£	£	£
Total overheads							
Re-apportion							
Re-apportion							
Totals							

Answer

	Total	*A*	*B*	*Assembly*	*Canteen*	*Mainten-ance*	*Basis of appor-tionment*
	£	£	£	£	£	£	£
Total overheads	166,760	44,816	45,230	26,832	33,250	16,632	
Re-apportion	-	7,600	5,890	19,760	(33,250)	-	Dir labour
Re-apportion	-	4,752	11,880	-	-	(16,632)	Mac usage
Totals	166,760	57,168	63,000	46,592	-	-	

The total overhead has now been shared, on a fair basis between the three production departments.

Workings

Canteen

The canteen overheads of £33,250 are apportioned using the direct labour hour basis as follows.

Machine Shop A $\frac{8,000}{35,000} \times £33,250 = £7,600$

Machine Shop B $\frac{6,200}{35,000} \times £33,250 = £5,890$

Assembly $\frac{20,800}{35,000} \times £33,250 = £19,760$

Maintenance

The maintenance overheads of £16,632 are apportioned using the machine usage basis as follows.

Machine Shop A $\frac{7,200}{25,200} \times £16,632 = £4,752$

Machine Shop B $\frac{18,000}{25,200} \times £16,632 = £11,880$

The reciprocal (repeated distribution) method of apportionment

4.13 **Apportionment** is a procedure whereby indirect costs are spread fairly between cost centres. It could therefore be argued that a fair sharing of service cost centre costs is not possible **unless consideration is given to the work done by each service cost centre for other service cost centres.**

4.14 For example, suppose a company has two production departments and two service departments (stores and maintenance). The following information about activity in a recent costing period is available.

	Production departments *1*	*2*	*Stores department*	*Maintenance department*
Overhead costs	£10,030	£8,970	£10,000	£8,000
Value of material requisitions	£30,000	£50,000	-	£20,000
Maintenance hours used	8,000	1,000	1,000	-

The problem is that the stores department uses the maintenance department, and the maintenance department uses the stores. This is known as **reciprocal servicing.**

(a) If service department overheads were apportioned directly to production departments, ignoring the reciprocal servicing, the apportionment would be as follows.

Service department	*Basis of apportionment*	*Total cost*	*1*	*2*
		£	£	£
Stores	Material requisitions (W1)	10,000	3,750	6,250
Maintenance	Maintenance hours (W2)	8,000	7,111	889
		18,000	10,861	7,139
Overheads of departments 1 and 2		19,000	10,030	8,970
		37,000	20,891	16,109

Workings

1 **Apportionment of stores department overheads**

The overhead costs of the stores department are apportioned on the basis of the value of material requisitions.

Total value of material requisitions raised by production departments only = £30,000 (Production department 1) + £50,000 (Production department 2) = £80,000.

$\therefore$ Overheads apportioned to Production department 1 $= \frac{30,000}{80,000} \times £10,000$

$= \frac{3}{8} \times £10,000$

$= £3,750$

$\therefore$ Overheads apportioned to Production department 2 $= \frac{50,000}{80,000} \times £10,000$

$= \frac{5}{8} \times £10,000$

$= £6,250$

2 **Apportionment of maintenance department overheads**

The overhead costs of the maintenance department are apportioned on the basis of the number of maintenance hours used.

Total maintenance hours used by production departments only = 8,000 (Production department 1) + 1,000 (Production department 2) = 9,000.

$\therefore$ Overheads apportioned to production department 1 $= \frac{8,000}{9,000} \times £8,000$

$= \frac{8}{9} \times £8,000$

$= £7,111$

$\therefore$ Overheads apportioned to Production department 2 $= \frac{1,000}{9,000} \times £8,000$

$= \frac{1}{9} \times £8,000$

$= £889$

(b) If, however, recognition is made of the fact that **the stores and maintenance department do work for each other,** and the basis of apportionment remains the same, we ought to apportion service department costs as follows. The percentages are based on the value of materials requisitions and the maintenance hours.

	Production departments		*Stores*	*Maintenance*
	1	*2*	*department*	*department*
Stores (100%)	30%	50%	-	20%
Maintenance (100%)	80%	10%	10%	-

This may be done using the **reciprocal** or **repeated distribution method of apportionment** as follows.

4.15 EXAMPLE: RECIPROCAL (REPEATED DISTRIBUTION) METHOD OF APPORTIONMENT

	Production departments 1	*2*	*Stores department*	*Maintenance department*
	£	£	£	£
Overhead costs	10,030	8,970	10,000	8,000
Apportion stores (see note (a))	3,000	5,000	(10,000)	2,000
			0	10,000
Apportion maintenance	8,000	1,000	1,000	(10,000)
			1,000	0
Repeat: Apportion stores	300	500	(1,000)	200
Repeat: Apportion maintenance	160	20	20	(200)
Repeat: Apportion stores	6	10	(20)	4
Repeat: Apportion maintenance (b)	4	-	-	(4)
	21,500	15,500	0	0

Notes

(a) The first apportionment could have been the costs of maintenance, rather than stores; there is no difference to the final results. The apportionments are based on the percentages calculated in paragraph 4.14.

(b) When the repeated distributions bring service department costs down to small numbers (here £4), the final apportionment to production departments is an approximate rounding.

4.16 The total overhead of £37,000 has now been apportioned to the production departments. Have a look at the difference in the final overhead apportionments to each production department using the different apportionment methods. Unless the difference is substantial, the direct method which ignores the reciprocal servicing, might be preferred because it is **clerically simpler to use.**

Step method

4.17 The **step** method is very similar to the reciprocal method. The main difference is that the final results will depend upon which apportionment was made first.

4.18 The method works by first apportioning one of the service cost centres **to all of the other centres which make use of its services.** When the remaining service cost centre is re-apportioned, **the work done for the other service cost centre is ignored.**

4.19 EXAMPLE: STEP METHOD OF APPORTIONMENT

Using the information in the example in paragraph 4.14, apportion the overhead costs using the step method of apportionment, starting with the stores department.

	Production departments 1	*2*	*Stores department*	*Maintenance department*
	£	£	£	£
Overhead costs	10,030	8,970	10,000	8,000
Apportion stores (W1)	3,000	5,000	(10,000)	2,000
			-	10,000
Apportion maintenance (W2)	8,889	1,111	-	(10,000)
	21,919	15,081	-	-

Workings

1 **Apportion stores**

Stores department overheads are apportioned to the other departments as follows.

		Apportioned overhead
		£
Production department 1	(30/100 × £10,000)	3,000
Production department 2	(50/100 × £10,000)	5,000
Maintenance department	(20/100 × £10,000)	2,000
		10,000

2 **Apportion maintenance**

Maintenance department overheads are apportioned to the **two production departments only**. Therefore, the maintenance hours used by the stores department (10%) are excluded from the apportionment and only the maintenance hours used by the two production departments are taken into account (80% + 10% = 90%).

		Apportioned overhead
		£
Production department 1	(80/90 × £10,000)	8,889
Production department 2	(10/90 × £10,000)	1,111
		10,000

If the first apportionment had been the maintenance department, then the overheads of £8,000 would have been apportioned as follows.

	Production departments		*Stores*	*Maintenance*
	1	*2*	*department*	*department*
	£	£	£	£
Overhead costs	10,030	8,970	10,000	8,000
Apportion maintenance (W3)	6,400	800	800	(8,000)
			10,800	-
Apportion stores (W4)	4,050	6,750	(10,800)	
	20,480	16,520	-	-

3 **Apportion maintenance**

Maintenance department overheads are apportioned to the other departments as follows.

		Apportioned overhead
		£
Production department 1	(80/100 × £8,000)	6,400
Production department 2	(10/100 × £8,000)	800
Stores department	(10/100 × £8,000)	800
		8,000

4 **Apportion stores**

Stores department overheads are apportioned to the **two production departments only**. Therefore the value of the materials requisitions attributable to the maintenance department are excluded from the apportionment and only the value of the materials requisitions for the two production departments are taken into account (30% + 50% = 80%).

		Apportioned overhead
		£
Production department 1	(30/80 × £10,800)	4,050
Production department 2	(50/80 × £10,800)	6,750
		10,800

Note

Notice how the final results differ, depending upon whether stores or maintenance are apportioned first.

Using algebra

4.20 A quicker way of arriving at your results in the example in Paragraph 4.15 (repeated distribution method) is to use **algebra** and **simultaneous equations.**

4.21 Let us use the same data as the example in Paragraph 4.14.

(a) Let S be the total stores department overhead for apportionment, after it has been apportioned overhead from Maintenance.

(b) Let M be the total of maintenance department overhead after it has been apportioned overhead from Stores.

4.22 We can set up our equations as follows.

$$S = 0.1M^{\star} + £10,000 \quad (1)$$
$$M = 0.2S^{\star\star} + £8,000 \quad (2)$$

* 10% × maintenance department overhead

** 20% × stores department overhead

4.23 Multiplying (2) by 5 gives us

$$5M = S + £40,000 \quad \text{(3), which can be rearranged so that}$$
$$S = 5M - £40,000 \quad (4)$$

Subtracting (1) from (4)

$$S = 5M - £40,000 \quad (4)$$
$$S = 0.1M + £10,000 \quad (1)$$

$$0 = 4.9M - £50,000$$

$$M = \frac{£50,000}{4.9} = £10,204$$

Substituting in (1)

$$S = 0.1 \times (£10,204) + £10,000$$
$$S = £11,020$$

4.24 These overheads can be apportioned as follows, using the percentages in Paragraph 4.14(b). Note that the result is the same as that obtained when using the reciprocal (repeated distribution) method.

	Production dept A	*Production dept B*	*Stores*	*Maintenance*
	£	£	£	£
Overhead costs	10,030	8,970	10,000	8,000
Apportion stores total	3,306	5,510	(11,020)	2,204
Apportion maintenance total	8,164	1,020	1,020	(10,204)
	21,500	15,500	-	-

Exam focus point

You must never ignore the existence of reciprocal services unless a question clearly instructs you to do so. Examination questions will usually indicate clearly if you are required to use a specific method of reciprocal apportionment.

Question 2

Sandstorm Ltd is a jobbing engineering concern which has three production departments (forming, machines and assembly) and two service departments (maintenance and general).

The following analysis of overhead costs has been made for the year just ended.

	£	£
Rent and rates		8,000
Power		750
Light, heat		5,000
Repairs, maintenance:		
Forming	800	
Machines	1,800	
Assembly	300	
Maintenance	200	
General	100	
		3,200
Departmental expenses:		
Forming	1,500	
Machines	2,300	
Assembly	1,100	
Maintenance	900	
General	1,500	
		7,300
Depreciation:		
Plant		10,000
Fixtures and fittings		250
Insurance:		
Plant		2,000
Buildings		500
Indirect labour:		
Forming	3,000	
Machines	5,000	
Assembly	1,500	
Maintenance	4,000	
General	2,000	
		15,500
		52,500

Other available data are as follows.

	Floor area sq. ft	*Plant value* £	*Fixtures & fittings* £	*Effective horse-power*	*Direct cost for year* £	*Labour hours worked*	*Machine hours worked*
Forming	2,000	25,000	1,000	40	20,500	14,400	12,000
Machines	4,000	60,000	500	90	30,300	20,500	21,600
Assembly	3,000	7,500	2,000	15	24,200	20,200	2,000
Maintenance	500	7,500	1,000	5	-	-	-
General	500	-	500	-	-	-	-
	10,000	100,000	5,000	150	75,000	55,100	35,600

Service department costs are apportioned as follows.

	Maintenance	General
	%	%
Forming	20	20
Machines	50	60
Assembly	20	10
General	10	–
Maintenance	–	10
	100	100

Required

Using the data provided prepare an analysis showing the distribution of overhead costs to departments. Reapportion service cost centre costs using the reciprocal method.

Answer

Analysis of distribution of actual overhead costs

	Basis	Forming	Machines	Assembly	Machining	General	Total
		£	£	£	£	£	£
Directly allocated overheads:							
Repairs, maintenance		800	1,800	300	200	100	3,200
Departmental expenses		1,500	2,300	1,100	900	1,500	7,300
Indirect labour		3,000	5,000	1,500	4,000	2,000	15,500
Apportionment of other overheads:							
Rent, rates	1	1,600	3,200	2,400	400	400	8,000
Power	2	200	450	75	25	0	750
Light, heat	1	1,000	2,000	1,500	250	250	5,000
Dep'n of plant	3	2,500	6,000	750	750	0	10,000
Dep'n of F and F	4	50	25	100	50	25	250
Insurance of plant	3	500	1,200	150	150	0	2,000
Insurance of buildings	1	100	200	150	25	25	500
		11,250	22,175	8,025	6,750	4,300	52,500

Basis of apportionment:

1 floor area
2 effective horsepower
3 plant value
4 fixtures and fittings value

Apportionment of service department overheads to production departments, using the reciprocal method.

	Forming	Machines	Assembly	Maintenance	General	Total
	£	£	£	£	£	£
Overheads	11,250	22,175	8,025	6,750	4,300	52,500
	1,350	3,375	1,350	(6,750)	675	
					4,975	
	995	2,985	498	497	(4,975)	
	99	249	99	(497)	50	
	10	30	5	5	(50)	
	1	3	1	(5)		
	13,705	28,817	9,978	0	0	52,500

Exam focus point

There were four marks available in one of the compulsory ten-mark questions in the paper-based examination pilot paper for Paper 1.2 which required the reapportionment of service cost centre costs using the **reciprocal method**.

5 OVERHEAD ABSORPTION

KEY TERM

Overhead absorption is the process whereby overhead costs allocated and apportioned to production cost centres are added to unit, job or batch costs. Overhead absorption is sometimes called **overhead recovery.**

5.1 Having allocated and/or apportioned all overheads, the next stage in the costing treatment of overheads is to add them to, or **absorb them into, cost units.**

5.2 Overheads are usually added to cost units using a **predetermined overhead absorption rate**, which is calculated using figures from the budget.

5.3 An overhead absorption rate for the forthcoming accounting period is calculated and used as follows.

Step 1. Estimate the overhead likely to be incurred during the coming period.

Step 2. Estimate the activity level for the period. This could be total hours, units, or direct costs or whatever it is upon which the overhead absorption rates are to be based.

Step 3. Divide the estimated overhead by the budgeted activity level. This produces the overhead absorption rate.

Step 4. Absorb the overhead into the cost unit by applying the calculated absorption rate.

5.4 EXAMPLE: THE BASICS OF ABSORPTION COSTING

Athena Ltd makes two products, the Greek and the Roman. Greeks take 2 labour hours each to make and Romans take 5 labour hours. What is the overhead cost per unit for Greeks and Romans respectively if overheads are absorbed on the basis of labour hours?

5.5 SOLUTION

Step 1. Estimate the overhead likely to be incurred during the coming period

Athena Ltd estimates that the total overhead will be £50,000

Step 2. Estimate the activity level for the period

Athena Ltd estimates that a total of 100,000 direct labour hours will be worked

Step 3. Divide the estimated overhead by the budgeted activity level

$$\text{Absorption rate} = \frac{£50{,}000}{100{,}000\text{ hrs}} = £0.50 \text{ per direct labour hour}$$

Step 4. Absorb the overhead into the cost unit by applying the calculated absorption rate

	Greek	Roman
Labour hours per unit	2	5
Absorption rate per labour hour	£0.50	£0.50
Overhead absorbed per unit	£1	£2.50

5.6 It should be obvious to you that, even if a company is trying to be 'fair', there is a great lack of precision about the way an absorption base is chosen.

5.7 This arbitrariness is one of the main criticisms of absorption costing, and if absorption costing is to be used (because of its other virtues) then it is important that **the methods used are kept under regular review.** Changes in working conditions should, if necessary, lead to changes in the way in which work is accounted for.

5.8 For example, a labour intensive department may become mechanised. If a direct labour hour rate of absorption had been used previous to the mechanisation, it would probably now be more appropriate to change to the use of a machine hour rate.

Choosing the appropriate absorption base

5.9 The different **bases of absorption** (or 'overhead recovery rates') are as follows.

- A percentage of direct materials cost
- A percentage of direct labour cost
- A percentage of prime cost
- A rate per machine hour
- A rate per direct labour hour
- A rate per unit
- A percentage of factory cost (for administration overhead)
- A percentage of sales or factory cost (for selling and distribution overhead)

5.10 The choice of an absorption basis is a matter of judgement and common sense, what is required is an **absorption basis** which realistically reflects the characteristics of a given cost centre and which avoids undue anomalies.

5.11 Many factories use a **direct labour hour rate** or **machine hour rate** in preference to a rate based on a percentage of direct materials cost, wages or prime cost.

(a) A **direct labour** hour basis is most appropriate in a **labour intensive** environment.

(b) A **machine hour** rate would be used in departments where production is controlled or dictated by machines.

(c) A **rate per unit** would be effective only if all units were identical.

5.12 EXAMPLE: OVERHEAD ABSORPTION

The budgeted production overheads and other budget data of Bridge Cottage Ltd are as follows.

Budget	*Production dept A*	*Production dept B*
Overhead cost	£36,000	£5,000
Direct materials cost	£32,000	
Direct labour cost	£40,000	
Machine hours	10,000	
Direct labour hours	18,000	
Units of production		1,000

Required

Calculate the absorption rate using the various bases of apportionment.

5.13 SOLUTION

(a) Department A

(i) Percentage of direct materials cost $\frac{£36,000}{£32,000} \times 100\% = 112.5\%$

(ii) Percentage of direct labour cost $\frac{£36,000}{£40,000} \times 100\% = 90\%$

(iii) Percentage of prime cost $\frac{£36,000}{£72,000} \times 100\% = 50\%$

(iv) Rate per machine hour $\frac{£36,000}{10,000\text{hrs}} = £3.60$ per machine hour

(v) Rate per direct labour hour $\frac{£36,000}{18,000\text{hrs}} = £2$ per direct labour hour

(b) The department B absorption rate will be based on units of output.

$\frac{£5,000}{1,000\text{units}} = £5$ per unit produced

5.14 The choice of the basis of absorption is significant in determining the cost of individual units, or jobs, produced. Using the previous example, suppose that an individual product has a material cost of £80, a labour cost of £85, and requires 36 labour hours and 23 machine hours to complete. The overhead cost of the product would vary, depending on the basis of absorption used by the company for overhead recovery.

(a) As a percentage of direct material cost, the overhead cost would be 112.5% × £80 = £90.00

(b) As a percentage of direct labour cost, the overhead cost would be 90% × £85 = £76.50

(c) As a percentage of prime cost, the overhead cost would be 50% × £165 = £82.50

(d) Using a machine hour basis of absorption, the overhead cost would be 23 hrs × £3.60 = £82.80

(e) Using a labour hour basis, the overhead cost would be 36 hrs × £2 = £72.00

5.15 In theory, each basis of absorption would be possible, but the company should choose a basis for its own costs which seems to be '**fairest**'.

6 BLANKET ABSORPTION RATES AND DEPARTMENTAL ABSORPTION RATES

KEY TERM

A **blanket overhead absorption rate** is an absorption rate used throughout a factory and for all jobs and units of output irrespective of the department in which they were produced.

6.1 For example, if total overheads were £500,000 and there were 250,000 direct machine hours during the period, the **blanket overhead rate** would be £2 per direct machine hour and all jobs passing through the factory would be charged at that rate.

6.2 **Blanket overhead rates** are not appropriate in the following circumstances.

- There is more than one department.
- Jobs do not spend an equal amount of time in each department.

6.3 If a single factory overhead absorption rate is used, some products will receive a higher overhead charge than they ought 'fairly' to bear, whereas other products will be under-charged.

6.4 If a **separate absorption rate** is used for each department, charging of overheads will be fair and the full cost of production of items will represent the amount of the effort and resources put into making them.

6.5 EXAMPLE: SEPARATE ABSORPTION RATES

The Old Grammar School Ltd has two production departments, for which the following budgeted information is available.

	Department A	*Department B*	*Total*
Budgeted overheads	£360,000	£200,000	£560,000
Budgeted direct labour hours	200,000 hrs	40,000 hrs	240,000 hrs

If a single factory overhead absorption rate is applied, the rate of overhead recovery would be:

$$\frac{\text{£}560{,}000}{240{,}000 \text{ hours}} = \text{£}2.33 \text{ per direct labour hour}$$

If separate departmental rates are applied, these would be:

$$\textit{Department A} = \frac{\text{£}360{,}000}{200{,}000 \text{ hours}} = \text{£}1.80 \text{ per direct labour hour}$$

$$\textit{Department B} = \frac{\text{£}200{,}000}{40{,}000 \text{ hours}} = \text{£}5 \text{ per direct labour hour}$$

Department B has a higher overhead rate of cost per hour worked than department A.

Now let us consider two separate jobs.

Job X has a prime cost of £100, takes 30 hours in department B and does not involve any work in department A.

Job Y has a prime cost of £100, takes 28 hours in department A and 2 hours in department B.

What would be the factory cost of each job, using the following rates of overhead recovery?

(a) A single factory rate of overhead recovery
(b) Separate departmental rates of overhead recovery

6.6 SOLUTION

				Job X		*Job Y*
(a)	**Single factory rate**			£		£
	Prime cost			100		100
	Factory overhead (30 × £2.33)			70		70
	Factory cost			170		170
(b)	**Separate departmental rates**			£		£
	Prime cost			100		100.00
	Factory overhead:	department A		0	(28 × £1.80)	50.40
		department B	(30 × £5)	150	(2 × £5)	10.00
	Factory cost			250		160.40

6.7 Using a single factory overhead absorption rate, both jobs would cost the same. However, since job X is done entirely within department B where overhead costs are relatively higher, whereas job Y is done mostly within department A, where overhead costs are relatively lower, it is arguable that job X should cost more than job Y. This will occur if separate departmental overhead recovery rates are used to reflect the work done on each job in each department separately.

6.8 If all jobs do not spend approximately the same time in each department then, to ensure that all jobs are charged with their fair share of overheads, it is necessary to establish **separate overhead rates for each department.**

Question 3

The following data relate to one year in department A.

Budgeted machine hours	25,000
Actual machine hours	21,875
Budgeted overheads	£350,000
Actual overheads	£350,000

Based on the data above, what is the machine hour absorption rate as conventionally calculated?

A £12 B £14 C £16 D £18

Answer

Don't forget, if your calculations produce a solution which does not correspond with any of the options available, then eliminate the unlikely options and make a guess from the remainder. Never leave out a multiple choice question.

A common pitfall is to think 'we haven't had answer A for a while, so I'll guess that'. The examiner is *not* required to produce an even spread of A, B, C and D answers in the examination. There is no reason why the answer to *every* question cannot be D!

The correct answer in this case is B.

$$\text{Overhead absorption rate} = \frac{\text{Budgeted overheads}}{\text{Budgeted machine hours}} = \frac{£350{,}000}{25{,}000} = £14 \text{ per machine hour}$$

7 NORMAL COSTING

7.1 We know that the **overhead absorption rate is predetermined** using figures from the **annual budget**. If overheads are to be absorbed on the basis of direct labour hours, the overhead absorption rate will be calculated using the total overheads and the number of direct labour hours included in the annual budget.

7.2 Using the predetermined absorption rate, the *actual* cost of production can be established as follows.

	Direct materials
plus:	direct labour
plus:	direct expenses
plus:	overheads (based on the predetermined recovery rate)
equals:	actual cost of production

This is known as **normal costing**.

7.3 Many students become seriously confused about what can appear a very unusual method of costing. The following example should help clarify this costing method.

7.4 EXAMPLE: NORMAL COSTING

Normal Ltd budgeted to make 100 units of product Z at a cost of £3 per unit in direct materials and £4 per unit in direct labour. The sales price would be £12 per unit, and production overheads were budgeted to amount to £200. A unit basis of overhead recovery is in operation. During the period 120 units were actually produced and sold (for £12 each) and the actual cost of direct materials was £380 and of direct labour, £450. Overheads incurred came to £210.

Required

Determine the cost of sales of product Z, and the profit. Ignore administration, selling and distribution overheads.

7.5 SOLUTION

In normal costing, the cost of production and sales is the actual direct cost plus the cost of overheads, absorbed at a predetermined rate as established in the budget.

Overhead recovery rate would be £2 per unit produced (£200 ÷100 units).

The actual cost of sales is calculated as follows.

	£
Direct materials (actual)	380
Direct labour (actual)	450
Overheads absorbed (120 units × £2)	240
Full cost of sales, product Z	1,070
Sales of product Z (120 units × £12)	1,440
Profit, product Z	370

The actual overheads **incurred**, £210, are not the same as the overheads **absorbed** into the cost of production, £240. In normal absorption costing £240 is the 'correct' cost. The difference between actual overheads incurred and the overheads absorbed, is an inevitable feature of normal costing and can only be reconciled at the end of an accounting period.

This difference is known as the '**under absorption**' or '**over absorption**' of overhead.

8 OVER AND UNDER ABSORPTION OF OVERHEADS

8.1 **The rate of overhead absorption is based on estimates** (of both numerator and denominator) and it is quite likely that either one or both of the estimates will not agree with what actually occurs.

(a) **Over absorption** means that the overheads charged to the cost of sales are greater then the overheads actually incurred.

(b) **Under absorption** means that insufficient overheads have been included in the cost of sales.

It is almost inevitable that at the end of the accounting year there will have been an over absorption or under absorption of the overhead actually incurred.

8.2 Suppose that the budgeted overhead in a production department is £80,000 and the budgeted activity is 40,000 direct labour hours. The overhead recovery rate (using a direct labour hour basis) would be £2 per direct labour hour.

Actual overheads in the period are, say £84,000 and 45,000 direct labour hours are worked.

	£
Overhead incurred (actual)	84,000
Overhead absorbed (45,000 × £2)	90,000
Over absorption of overhead	6,000

In this example, the cost of produced units or jobs has been charged with £6,000 more than was actually spent. An adjustment to reconcile the overheads charged to the actual overhead is necessary and the over-absorbed overhead will be credited to the profit and loss account at the end of the accounting period.

The reasons for under-/over-absorbed overhead

8.3 **The overhead absorption rate is predetermined from budget estimates of overhead cost and the expected volume of activity**. Under- or over-recovery of overhead will occur in the following circumstances.

- Actual overhead costs are different from budgeted overheads
- The actual activity level is different from the budgeted activity level
- Actual overhead costs *and* actual activity level differ from the budgeted costs and level

8.4 EXAMPLE: REASONS FOR UNDER-/OVER-ABSORBED OVERHEAD

Pembridge Ltd has a budgeted production overhead of £50,000 and a budgeted activity of 25,000 direct labour hours and therefore a recovery rate of £2 per direct labour hour.

Required

Calculate the under-/over-absorbed overhead, and the reasons for the under-/over-absorption, in the following circumstances.

(a) Actual overheads cost £47,000 and 25,000 direct labour hours are worked.
(b) Actual overheads cost £50,000 and 21,500 direct labour hours are worked.
(c) Actual overheads cost £47,000 and 21,500 direct labour hours are worked.

8.5 SOLUTION

(a)

	£
Actual overhead	47,000
Absorbed overhead (25,000 × £2)	50,000
Over-absorbed overhead	3,000

The reason for the over absorption is that although the actual and budgeted direct labour hours are the same, actual overheads cost less than expected.

(b)

	£
Actual overhead	50,000
Absorbed overhead (21,500 × £2)	43,000
Under-absorbed overhead	7,000

The reason for the under absorption is that although budgeted and actual overhead costs were the same, fewer direct labour hours were worked than expected.

(c)

	£
Actual overhead	47,000
Absorbed overhead (21,500 × £2)	43,000
Under-absorbed overhead	4,000

The reason for the under absorption is a combination of the reasons in (a) and (b).

8.6 The distinction between **overheads incurred** (actual overheads) and **overheads absorbed** is an important one which you must learn and understand. The difference between them is known as under- or over-absorbed overheads.

Question 4

The budgeted and actual data for River Arrow Products Ltd for the year to 31 March 20X5 are as follows.

	Budgeted	*Actual*
Direct labour hours	9,000	9,900
Direct wages	£34,000	£35,500
Machine hours	10,100	9,750
Direct materials	£55,000	£53,900
Units produced	120,000	122,970
Overheads	£63,000	£61,500

The cost accountant of River Arrow Products Ltd has decided that overheads should be absorbed on the basis of labour hours.

Required

Calculate the amount of under- or over-absorbed overheads for River Arrow Products Ltd for the year to 31 March 20X5.

Answer

Overhead absorption rate $= \dfrac{£63,000}{9,000} = £7$ per hour

Overheads absorbed by production $= 9,900 \times £7 = £69,300$

	£
Actual overheads	61,500
Overheads absorbed	69,300
Over-absorbed overheads	7,800

Exam focus point

You can always work out whether overheads are under- or over-absorbed by using the following rule.

- If Actual overhead incurred – Absorbed overhead = NEGATIVE (N), then overheads are over-absorbed (O) (NO)
- If Actual overhead incurred – Absorbed overhead = POSITIVE (P), then overheads are under-absorbed (U) (PU)

So, remember the NOPU rule when you go into your examination and you won't have any trouble in deciding whether overheads are under- or over-absorbed!

Question 5

A management consultancy recovers overheads on chargeable consulting hours. Budgeted overheads were £615,000 and actual consulting hours were 32,150. Overheads were under-recovered by £35,000.

If actual overheads were £694,075 what was the budgeted overhead absorption rate per hour?

A £19.13 B £20.50 C £21.59 D £22.68

Answer

	£
Actual overheads	694,075
Under-recoverable overheads	35,000
Overheads recovered for 32,150 hours at budgeted overhead absorption rate (x)	659,075

$$32{,}150\ x = 659{,}075$$

$$x = \frac{659{,}075}{32{,}150} = £20.50$$

The correct option is B.

---

9 LEDGER ENTRIES RELATING TO OVERHEADS

9.1 The bookkeeping entries for overheads are not as straightforward as those for materials and labour. We shall now consider the way in which overheads are dealt with in a cost accounting system.

9.2 When an absorption costing system is in use we now know that the amount of overhead included in the cost of an item is absorbed at a predetermined rate. The entries made in the cash book and the nominal ledger, however, are the actual amounts.

9.3 You will remember that it is highly unlikely that the actual amount and the predetermined amount will be the same. The difference is called **under- or over-absorbed overhead**. To deal with this in the cost accounting books, therefore, we need to have an account to collect under- or over-absorbed amounts for each type of overhead.

9.4 EXAMPLE: THE UNDER-/OVER-ABSORBED OVERHEAD ACCOUNT

Mariott's Motorcycles absorbs production overheads at the rate of £0.50 per operating hour and administration overheads at 20% of the production cost of sales. Actual data for one month was as follows.

Administration overheads	£32,000
Production overheads	£46,500
Operating hours	90,000
Production cost of sales	£180,000

What entries need to be made for overheads in the ledgers?

9.5 SOLUTION

PRODUCTION OVERHEADS

	DR		CR
	£		£
Cash	46,500	Absorbed into WIP (90,000 × £0.50)	45,000
		Under absorbed overhead	1,500
	46,500		46,500

ADMINISTRATION OVERHEADS

	DR		CR
	£		£
Cash	32,000	To cost of sales (180,000 × 0.2)	36,000
Over-absorbed overhead	4,000		
	36,000		36,000

UNDER-/OVER-ABSORBED OVERHEADS

	DR		CR
	£		£
Production overhead	1,500	Administration overhead	4,000
Balance to profit and loss account	2,500		
	4,000		4,000

Less production overhead has been absorbed than has been spent so there is **under-absorbed overhead** of £1,500. More administration overhead has been absorbed (into cost of sales, note, not into WIP) and so there is **over-absorbed overhead** of £4,000. The net over-absorbed overhead of £2,500 is a credit in the profit and loss account.

10 NON-MANUFACTURING OVERHEADS

10.1 For **external reporting** (eg statutory accounts) it is not necessary to allocate non-manufacturing overheads to products. This is because many of the overheads are non-manufacturing, and are regarded as **period costs.**

10.2 For **internal reporting** purposes and for a number of industries which base the selling price of their product on estimates of **total** cost or even actual cost, a **total cost per unit of output** may be required.

10.3 Builders, law firms and garages often charge for their services by adding a **percentage profit margin** to actual cost. For product pricing purposes and for internal management reports it may therefore be appropriate to allocate non-manufacturing overheads to units of output.

Bases for apportioning non-manufacturing overheads

10.4 A number of non-manufacturing overheads such as delivery costs or salespersons' salaries are clearly identified with particular products and can therefore be classified as direct costs. The majority of non-manufacturing overheads, however cannot be directly allocated to particular units of output. Two possible methods of allocating such non-manufacturing overheads are as follows.

10.5 **Method 1: Choose a basis for the overhead absorption rate** which most closely matches the non-manufacturing overhead such as direct labour hours, direct machine hours and so on. The problem with such a method is that most non-manufacturing overheads are unaffected in the short term by changes in the level of output and tend to be fixed costs.

10.6 **Method 2 : Allocate non-manufacturing overheads on the ability of the products to bear such costs.** One possible approach is to use the manufacturing cost as the basis for allocating non-manufacturing costs to products.

FORMULA TO LEARN

The **overhead absorption rate** is calculated as follows.

$$\text{Overhead absorption rate} = \frac{\text{Estimated non-manufacturing overheads}}{\text{Estimated manufacturing costs}}$$

10.7 If, for example, budgeted distribution overheads are £200,000 and budgeted manufacturing costs are £800,000, the predetermined distribution overhead absorption rate will be 25% of manufacturing cost. Other bases for absorbing overheads are as follows.

Type of overhead	Possible absorption base
Selling and marketing	Sales value
Research and development	Consumer cost (= production cost minus cost of direct materials) or added value (= sales value of product minus cost of bought in materials and services)
Distribution	Sales values
Administration	Consumer cost or added value

Administration overheads

10.8 The administration overhead usually consists of the following.

- Executive salaries
- Office rent and rates
- Lighting
- Heating and cleaning the offices

In cost accounting, administration overheads are regarded as periodic charges which are charged against the gross costing profit for the year (as in financial accounting).

Selling and distribution overheads

10.9 **Selling and distribution overheads** are often considered collectively as one type of overhead but they are actually quite different forms of expense.

(a) **Selling costs** are incurred in order to obtain sales

(b) **Distribution costs** begin as soon as the finished goods are put into the warehouse and continue until the goods are despatched or delivered to the customer

10.10 **Selling overhead** is therefore often absorbed on the basis of sales value so that the more profitable product lines take a large proportion of overhead. The normal cost accounting entry for selling overhead is as follows.

DR	Cost of goods sold
CR	Selling overhead control account

10.11 **Distribution overhead** is more closely linked to production than sales and from one point of view could be regarded as an extra cost of production. It is, however, more usual to regard production cost as ending on the factory floor and to deal with distribution overhead separately. It is generally absorbed on a percentage of production cost but special circumstances, such as size and weight of products affecting the delivery charges, may cause a different basis of absorption to be used. The cost accounting entry is as follows.

DR	Cost of goods sold
CR	Distribution overhead control account

Chapter roundup

- **Overhead** is the cost incurred in the course of making a product, providing a service or running a department, but which cannot be traced directly and in full to the product, service or department.
- The **objective of absorption costing** is to include in the total cost of a product an appropriate share of the organisation's total overhead.
- The main reasons for using absorption costing are for **stock valuations, pricing decisions** and **establishing the profitability of different products.**
- The three stages of absorption costing are:
  - Allocation
  - Apportionment
  - Absorption
- **Allocation** is the process by which whole cost items are charged direct to a cost unit or cost centre.
- **Apportionment** is a procedure whereby indirect costs are spread fairly between cost centres. Service cost centre costs may be apportioned to production cost centres by using one of the following methods of apportionment.
  - Direct method
  - Reciprocal method
  - Step method
- The results of the reciprocal method of apportionment may also be obtained by using **algebra** and **simultaneous equations**.
- **Overhead absorption** is the process whereby costs of cost centres are added to unit, job or batch costs. Overhead absorption is sometimes called **overhead recovery**.
- **Predetermined overhead absorption rates** are calculated using budgeted figures.
- A **blanket overhead absorption rate** is an absorption rate used throughout a factory and for all jobs and units of output irrespective of the department in which they were produced.
- If an organisation has estimated fixed and variable production overheads, it may calculate a **separate absorption rate** for each.
- **Normal costing** involves using the predetermined absorption rate in order to establish the actual cost of production.
- **Over** and **under absorption of overheads** occurs because the predetermined overhead absorption rates are based on estimates.
- **Non-manufacturing overheads** may be allocated by choosing a basis for the overhead absorption rate which most closely matches the non-production overhead, or on the basis of a product's ability to bear the costs.

Quick quiz

1 What is allocation?

2 Name the three stages in charging overheads to units of output.

3 Match the following overheads with the most appropriate basis of apportionment.

Overhead	Basis of apportionment
(a) Depreciation of equipment	(1) Direct machine hours
(b) Heat and light costs	(2) Number of employees
(c) Canteen	(3) Book value of equipment
(d) Insurance of equipment	(4) Floor area

4 A direct labour hour basis is most appropriate in which of the following environments?

A Machine-intensive
B Labour-intensive
C When all units produced are identical
D None of the above

5 What is the problem with using a single factory overhead absorption rate?

6 How is under-/over-absorbed overhead accounted for?

7 Why does under- or over-absorbed overhead occur?

Answers to quick quiz

1 The process whereby whole cost items are charged direct to a cost unit or cost centre.

2
- Allocation
- Apportionment
- Absorption

3 (a) (3)
(b) (4)
(c) (2)
(d) (3)

4 B

5 Because some products will receive a higher overhead charge than they ought 'fairly' to bear and other products will be undercharged.

6 Under-/over-absorbed overhead is written as an adjustment to the profit and loss account at the end of an accounting period.

- Over-absorbed overhead → credit in profit and loss account
- Under-absorbed overhead → debit in profit and loss account

7
- Actual overhead costs are different from budgeted overheads
- The actual activity level is different from the budgeted activity level
- Actual overhead costs *and* actual activity level differ from the budgeted costs and level

Now try the questions below from the Exam Question Bank

Number	Level	Marks	Time
12	MCQ	n/a	n/a
13	Examination	10	18 mins

Chapter 9

MARGINAL AND ABSORPTION COSTING

Introduction

This chapter defines **marginal costing** and compares it with absorption costing. Whereas absorption costing recognises fixed costs (usually fixed production costs) as part of the cost of a unit of output and hence as product costs, marginal costing treats all fixed costs as period costs. Two such different costing methods obviously each have their supporters and so we will be looking at the arguments both in favour of and against each method. Each costing method, because of the different stock valuation used, produces a different profit figure and we will be looking at this particular point in detail.

Study guide

Section 14 – Marginal and absorption costing

- Explain the concept of contribution
- Demonstrate and discuss the impact of absorption and marginal costing on stock valuation and profit measurement
- Produce profit and loss accounts using absorption and marginal costing
- Reconcile the profits reported under the two methods
- Discuss the advantages and disadvantages of absorption and marginal costing

Exam guide

Look out for questions in your examination which require you to produce profit and loss accounts using absorption and marginal costing and then to reconcile the profits reported under the two methods.

1 MARGINAL COST AND MARGINAL COSTING

KEY TERMS

- **Marginal costing** is an alternative method of costing to absorption costing. In marginal costing, only variable costs are charged as a cost of sale and a contribution is calculated (sales revenue minus variable cost of sales). Closing stocks of work in progress or finished goods are valued at marginal (variable) production cost. Fixed costs are treated as a period cost, and are charged in full to the profit and loss account of the accounting period in which they are incurred.
- **Marginal cost** is the cost of a unit of a product or service which would be avoided if that unit were not produced or provided.

1.1 The **marginal production cost** per unit of an item usually consists of the following.

- Direct materials
- Direct labour
- Variable production overheads

1.2 Direct labour costs might be excluded from marginal costs when the work force is a given number of employees on a fixed wage or salary. Even so, it is not uncommon for direct labour to be treated as a variable cost, even when employees are paid a basic wage for a fixed working week. If in doubt, you should treat direct labour as a variable cost unless given clear indications to the contrary. Direct labour is often a step cost, with sufficiently short steps to make labour costs act in a variable fashion.

1.3 The **marginal cost of sales** usually consists of the marginal cost of production adjusted for stock movements plus the variable selling costs, which would include items such as sales commission, and possibly some variable distribution costs.

Contribution

KEY TERM

Contribution is the difference between sales value and the marginal cost of sales.

1.4 **Contribution** is of fundamental importance in marginal costing, and the term 'contribution' is really short for 'contribution towards covering fixed overheads and making a profit'.

2 THE PRINCIPLES OF MARGINAL COSTING

2.1 The principles of marginal costing are as follows.

(a) **Period fixed costs are the same, for any volume of sales and production** (provided that the level of activity is within the 'relevant range'). Therefore, by selling an extra item of product or service the following will happen.

- Revenue will increase by the sales value of the item sold.
- Costs will increase by the variable cost per unit.
- Profit will increase by the amount of contribution earned from the extra item.

(b) Similarly, if the volume of sales falls by one item, the profit will fall by the amount of contribution earned from the item.

(c) **Profit measurement should therefore be based on an analysis of total contribution.** Since fixed costs relate to a period of time, and do not change with increases or decreases in sales volume, it is misleading to charge units of sale with a share of fixed costs. Absorption costing is therefore misleading, and it is more appropriate to deduct fixed costs from total contribution for the period to derive a profit figure.

(d) When a unit of product is made, the extra costs incurred in its manufacture are the **variable production costs**. Fixed costs are unaffected, and no extra fixed costs are incurred when output is increased. It is therefore argued that **the valuation of closing stocks should be at variable production cost** (direct materials, direct labour, direct expenses (if any) and variable production overhead) because these are the only costs properly attributable to the product.

2.2 EXAMPLE: MARGINAL COSTING PRINCIPLES

Rain Until September Ltd makes a product, the Splash, which has a variable production cost of £6 per unit and a sales price of £10 per unit. At the beginning of September 20X0, there were no opening stocks and production during the month was 20,000 units. Fixed costs for the month were £45,000 (production, administration, sales and distribution). There were no variable marketing costs.

Required

Calculate the contribution and profit for September 20X0, using marginal costing principles, if sales were as follows.

(a) 10,000 Splashes
(b) 15,000 Splashes
(c) 20,000 Splashes

2.3 SOLUTION

The stages in the profit calculation are as follows.

- To **identify the variable cost of sales, and then the contribution.**
- Deduct fixed costs from the total contribution to derive the profit.
- Value all closing stocks at marginal production cost (£6 per unit).

	10,000 Splashes		*15,000 Splashes*		*20,000 Splashes*	
	£	£	£	£	£	£
Sales (at £10)		100,000		150,000		200,000
Opening stock	0		0		0	
Variable production cost	120,000		120,000		120,000	
	120,000		120,000		120,000	
Less value of closing stock (at marginal cost)	60,000		30,000		-	
Variable cost of sales		60,000		90,000		120,000
Contribution		40,000		60,000		80,000
Less fixed costs		45,000		45,000		45,000
Profit/(loss)		(5,000)		15,000		35,000
Profit (loss) per unit		£(0.50)		£1		£1.75
Contribution per unit		£4		£4		£4

2.4 The conclusions which may be drawn from this example are as follows.

(a) The **profit per unit varies** at differing levels of sales, because the average fixed overhead cost per unit changes with the volume of output and sales.

(b) The **contribution per unit is constant** at all levels of output and sales. Total contribution, which is the contribution per unit multiplied by the number of units sold, increases in direct proportion to the volume of sales.

(c) Since the **contribution per unit does not change**, the most effective way of calculating the expected profit at any level of output and sales would be as follows.

- First calculate the total contribution.
- Then deduct fixed costs as a period charge in order to find the profit.

(d) In our example the expected profit from the sale of 17,000 Splashes would be as follows.

	£
Total contribution (17,000 × £4)	68,000
Less fixed costs	45,000
Profit	23,000

2.5
- If total contribution **exceeds fixed costs,** a profit is made
- If total contribution **exactly equals fixed costs,** no profit or loss is made
- If total contribution is **less than fixed costs,** there will be a loss

Question 1

Mill Stream Ltd makes two products, the Mill and the Stream. Information relating to each of these products for April 20X1 is as follows.

	Mill	*Stream*
Opening stock	nil	nil
Production (units)	15,000	6,000
Sales (units)	10,000	5,000
Sales price per unit	£20	£30
Unit costs	£	£
Direct materials	8	14
Direct labour	4	2
Variable production overhead	2	1
Variable sales overhead	2	3

Fixed costs for the month

	£
Production costs	40,000
Administration costs	15,000
Sales and distribution costs	25,000

Required

(a) Using marginal costing principles and the method in 2.4(d) above, calculate the profit in April 20X1.

(b) Calculate the profit if sales had been 15,000 units of Mill and 6,000 units of Stream.

Answer

(a)

	£
Contribution from Mills (unit contribution = £20 – £16 = £4 × 10,000)	40,000
Contribution from Streams (unit contribution = £30 – £20 = £10 × 5,000)	50,000
Total contribution	90,000
Fixed costs for the period	80,000
Profit	10,000

(b) At a higher volume of sales, profit would be as follows.

	£
Contribution from sales of 15,000 Mills (× £4)	60,000
Contribution from sales of 6,000 Streams (× £10)	60,000
Total contribution	120,000
Less fixed costs	80,000
Profit	40,000

Profit or contribution information

2.6 The main advantage of **contribution information** (rather than profit information) is that it allows an easy calculation of profit if sales increase or decrease from a certain level. By comparing total contribution with fixed overheads, it is possible to determine whether profits or losses will be made at certain sales levels. **Profit information**, on the other hand, does not lend itself to easy manipulation but note how easy it was to calculate profits using contribution information in Question 1. **Contribution information** is more useful for **decision making** than profit information, as we shall see when we go on to study decision making in Section D of this Study Text.

3 MARGINAL COSTING AND ABSORPTION COSTING AND THE CALCULATION OF PROFIT

3.1 **Marginal costing** as a cost accounting system is significantly different from absorption costing. It is an **alternative method** of accounting for costs and profit, which rejects the principles of absorbing fixed overheads into unit costs.

Marginal costing	Absorption costing
Closing stocks are valued at marginal production cost.	Closing stocks are valued at full production cost.
Fixed costs are period costs.	Fixed costs are absorbed into unit costs.
Cost of sales does not include a share of fixed overheads.	Cost of sales does include a share of fixed overheads (see note below).

Note. The share of fixed overheads included in cost of sales are from the previous period (in opening stock values). Some of the fixed overheads from the current period will be excluded by being carried forward in closing stock values.

3.2 In **marginal costing**, it is necessary to identify the following.

- Variable costs
- Contribution
- Fixed costs

In **absorption costing** (sometimes known as **full costing**), it is not necessary to distinguish variable costs from fixed costs.

3.3 EXAMPLE: MARGINAL AND ABSORPTION COSTING COMPARED

Look back at the information contained in Question 1. Suppose that the budgeted production for April 20X1 was 15,000 units of Mill and 6,000 units of Stream, and production overhead is absorbed on the basis of budgeted direct labour costs.

Required

Calculate the profit if production was as budgeted, and sales were as follows.

(a) 10,000 units of Mill and 5,000 units of Stream
(b) 15,000 units of Mill and 6,000 units of Stream

Administration, sales and distribution costs should be charged as a period cost.

3.4 SOLUTION

Budgeted production overhead is calculated as follows.

		£
Fixed		40,000
Variable:	Mills (15,000 × £2)	30,000
	Streams (6,000 × £1)	6,000
Total		76,000

The **production overhead absorption rate** would be calculated as follows.

$$\frac{\text{Budgeted production overhead}}{\text{Budgeted direct labour cost}} = \frac{£76{,}000}{(15{,}000 \times £4) + (6{,}000 \times £2)} \times 100\%$$

$$= 105.56\% \text{ of direct labour cost}$$

(a) If sales are 10,000 units of Mill and 5,000 units of Stream, profit would be as follows.

	Absorption costing		
	Mills	*Streams*	*Total*
	£	£	£
Costs of production			
Direct materials	120,000	84,000	204,000
Direct labour	60,000	12,000	72,000
Overhead (105.56% of labour)	63,333	12,667	76,000
	243,333	108,667	352,000
Less closing stocks (W1)	81,111	18,111	99,222
Production cost of sales	162,222	90,556	252,778
Administration costs			15,000
Sales and distribution costs			
Variable (W2)			35,000
Fixed			25,000
Total cost of sales			327,778
Sales	200,000	150,000	350,000
Profit			22,222

Note. There is no under-/over-absorption of overhead, since actual production is the same as budgeted production.

The profit derived using absorption costing techniques is different from the profit (£10,000) using marginal costing techniques at this volume of sales (see earlier question).

(b) If production and sales are exactly the same, (15,000 units of Mill and 6,000 units of Stream) profit would be £40,000.

	£
Sales (300,000 + 180,000)	480,000
Cost of sales (W3)	440,000
Profit	40,000

* No closing stock if sales and production are equal.

Workings

1 **Closing stocks**

(a) If 15,000 units of Mills are produced and only 10,000 units are sold, there will be closing stocks of 5,000 units (15,000 – 10,000).

Therefore, of the production costs of £243,333, 5,000 units of the 15,000 units produced (5,000/15,000 = $^1/_3$) will be carried forward in closing stock ie $^1/_3$ × £243,333 = £81,111.

(b) Similarly, if 6,000 units of Streams are produced and only 5,000 units are sold there will be closing stocks of 1,000 units (6,000– 5,000).

Therefore, of the production cost of £108,667, 1,000 units of the 6,000 units produced (1,000/6,000 = $^1/_6$) will be carried forward in closing stock ie $^1/_6$ × £108,667 = £8,111.

2 **Variable sales and distribution costs**

Mills

Variable sales and distribution costs = £2 (from Question 1) × 10,000 units
= £20,000

Streams

Variable sales and distribution costs = £3 (from Question 1) × 5,000 units
= £15,000

∴ Total sales and distribution costs = £20,000 + £15,000
= £35,000

3 **Cost of sales**

	£	£
Costs of production (from part (a))		352,000
Administration costs (from Question 1)		15,000
Fixed sales and distribution costs (from Question 1)		25,000
Variable sales overhead		
Mills (15,000 × £2)	30,000	
Streams (6,000 × £3)	18,000	
		48,000
		440,000

This is the same as the profit calculated by marginal costing techniques in the earlier question.

3.5 We can draw a number of conclusions from this example.

(a) Marginal costing and absorption costing are different techniques for assessing profit in a period.

(b) If there are **changes in stocks during a period,** so that opening stock or closing stock values are different, **marginal costing and absorption costing give different results** for profit obtained.

(c) **If the opening and closing stock volumes and values are the same, marginal costing and absorption costing will give the same profit figure**. This is because the total cost of sales during the period would be the same, no matter how calculated.

The long-run effect on profit

3.6 **In the long run, total profit for a company will be the same whether marginal costing or absorption costing is used.** Different accounting conventions merely affect the profit of individual accounting periods.

3.7 EXAMPLE: COMPARISON OF TOTAL PROFITS

To illustrate this point, let us suppose that a company makes and sells a single product. At the beginning of period 1, there are no opening stocks of the product, for which the variable production cost is £4 and the sales price £6 per unit. Fixed costs are £2,000 per period, of which £1,500 are fixed production costs.

	Period 1	*Period 2*
Sales	1,200 units	1,800 units
Production	1,500 units	1,500 units

Required

Determine the profit in each period using the following methods of costing.

(a) Absorption costing. Assume normal output is 1,500 units per period.
(b) Marginal costing.

3.8 SOLUTION

(a) **Absorption costing**: the absorption rate for fixed production overhead is

$$\frac{£1,500}{1,500\text{units}} = £1 \text{ per unit}$$

	Period 1		*Period 2*		*Total*	
	£	£	£	£	£	£
Sales		7,200		10,800		18,000
Production costs						
Variable	6,000		6,000		12,000	
Fixed	1,500		1,500		3,000	
	7,500		7,500		15,000	
Add opening stock b/f	-		1,500			
	7,500		9,000			
Less closing stock c/f (W1)	1,500		-		-	
Production cost of sales	6,000		9,000		15,000	
Other costs	500		500		1,000	
Total cost of sales		6,500		9,500		16,000
Unadjusted profit		700		1,300		2,000
(Under-)/over-absorbed overhead		-		-		-
Profit		700		1,300		2,000

(b) **Marginal costing**

	Period 1		*Period 2*		*Total*	
	£	£	£	£	£	£
Sales		7,200		10,800		18,000
Variable production cost	6,000		6,000		12,000	
Add opening stock b/f	-		1,200			
	6,000		7,200			
Less closing stock c/f (W2)	1,200		-		-	
Variable production cost of sales		4,800		7,200		12,000
Contribution		2,400		3,600		6,000
Fixed costs		2,000		2,000		4,000
Profit		400		1,600		2,000

Workings

1 **Closing stock – absorption costing**

If 1,500 units are produced in period 1 and only 1,200 units are sold, there will be 300 units left in stock.

Each unit of the product has a total production cost of £5 per unit using absorption costing.

	£
Variable production cost	4
Fixed production overhead	1
Total production cost	5

∴Closing stock valuation = 300 units × £5
= £1,500

2 **Closing stock – marginal costing**

From (W1) above, there are 300 units of closing stock.

Each unit of the product has a variable production cost of £4 per unit using marginal costing (there is no fixed production overhead included as there is under the absorption costing method).

∴Closing stock valuation = 300 units × £4
= £1,200

Notes

(a) **The total profit over the two periods is the same for each method of costing, but the profit in each period is different.**

(b) In absorption costing, fixed production overhead of £300 is carried forward from period 1 into period 2 in stock values, and becomes a charge to profit in period 2. In marginal costing all fixed costs are charged in the period they are incurred, therefore the profit in period 1 is £300 lower and in period 2 is £300 higher than the absorption costing profit.

Question 2

The overhead absorption rate for product X is £10 per machine hour. Each unit of product X requires five machine hours. Stock of product X on 1.1.X1 was 150 units and on 31.12.X1 it was 100 units. What is the difference in profit between results reported using absorption costing and results reported using marginal costing?

A The absorption costing profit would be £2,500 less
B The absorption costing profit would be £2,500 greater
C The absorption costing profit would be £5,000 less
D The absorption costing profit would be £5,000 greater

Answer

Difference in profit = **change** in stock levels × fixed overhead absorption per unit = (150 – 100) × £10 × 5 = £2,500 **lower** profit, because stock levels **decreased**. The correct answer is therefore option A.

The key is the change in the volume of stock. Stock levels have **decreased** therefore absorption costing will report a **lower** profit. This eliminates options B and D.

Option C is incorrect because it is based on the closing stock only (100 units × £10 × 5 hours).

4 RECONCILING PROFITS

4.1 **The difference in profits reported under the two costing systems is due to the different stock valuation methods used.**

4.2 **If stock levels increase between the beginning and end of a period, absorption costing will report the higher profit**. This is because some of the fixed production overhead incurred during the period will be carried forward in closing stock (which reduces cost of sales) to be set against sales revenue in the following period instead of being written off in full against profit in the period concerned.

4.3 **If stock levels decrease, absorption costing will report the lower profit** because as well as the fixed overhead incurred, fixed production overhead which had been carried forward in opening stock is released and is also included in cost of sales.

4.4 EXAMPLE: RECONCILING PROFITS

The profits reported under absorption costing and marginal costing for period 1 in the example in Paragraph 3.7 would be reconciled as follows.

	£
Marginal costing profit	400
Adjust for fixed overhead in stock:	
Stock increase of 300 units × £1 per unit	300
Absorption costing profit	700

Question 3

When opening stocks were 8,500 litres and closing stocks 6,750 litres, a firm had a profit of £62,100 using marginal costing.

Assuming that the fixed overhead absorption rate was £3 per litre, what would be the profit using absorption costing?

A £41,850 B £56,850 C £67,350 D £82,350

Answer

Difference in profit = (8,500 – 6,750) × £3 = £5,250

Absorption costing profit = £62,100 – £5,250 = £56,850

The correct answer is B.

Since stock levels reduced, the absorption costing profit will be lower than the marginal costing profit. You can therefore eliminate options C and D.

Exam focus point

The effect on profit of using the two different costing methods can be confusing. You *must* get it straight in your mind before the examination. Remember that if opening stock values are greater than closing stock values, marginal costing shows the greater profit.

5 MARGINAL COSTING VERSUS ABSORPTION COSTING

5.1 The following diagram summarises the arguments in favour of both marginal and absorption costing.

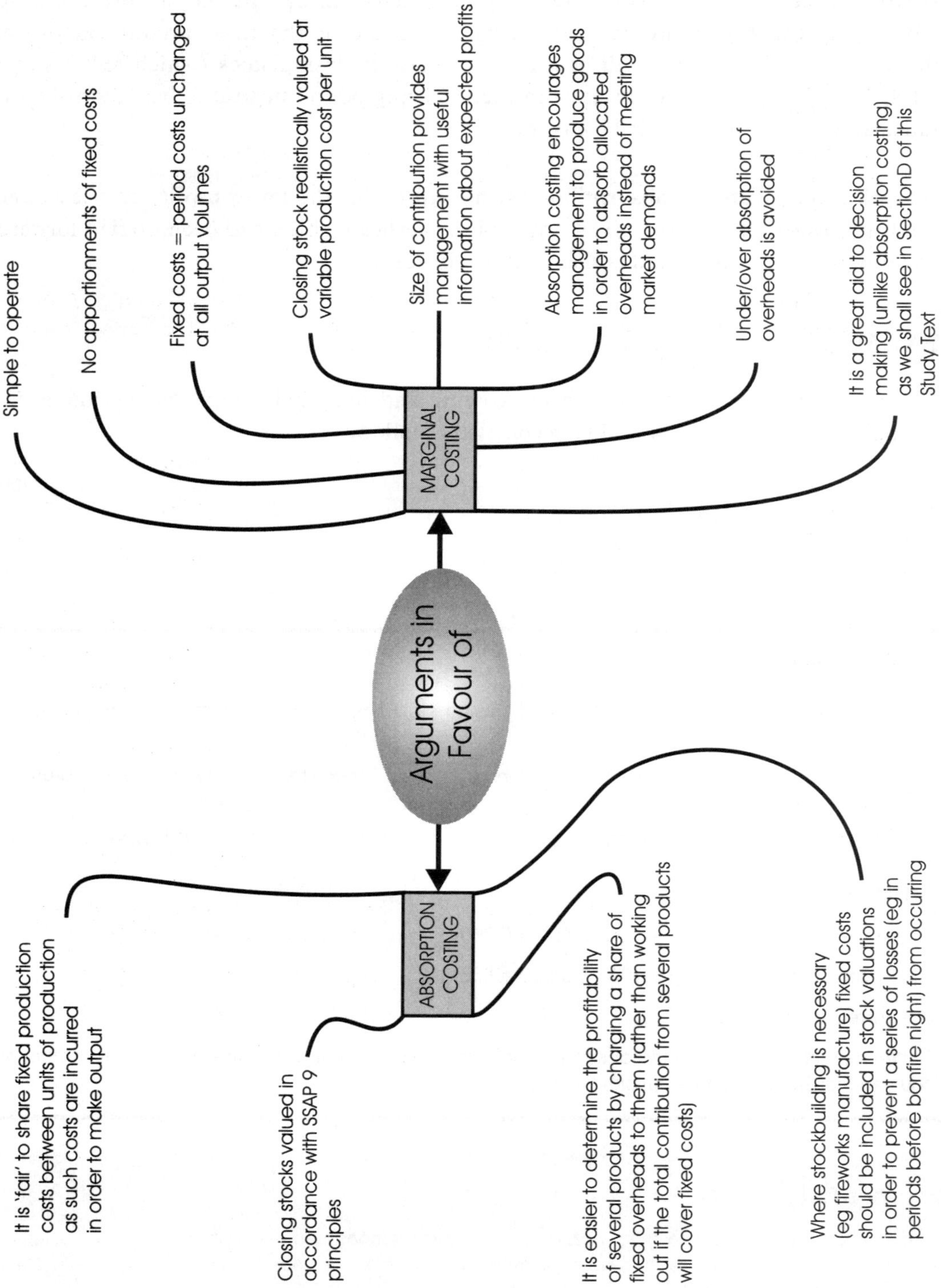
Arguments in Favour of
MARGINAL COSTING
Simple to operate
No apportionments of fixed costs
Fixed costs = period costs unchanged at all output volumes
Closing stock realistically valued at variable production cost per unit
Size of contribution provides management with useful information about expected profits
Absorption costing encourages management to produce goods in order to absorb allocated overheads instead of meeting market demands
Under/over absorption of overheads is avoided
It is a great aid to decision making (unlike absorption costing) as we shall see in SectionD of this Study Text
ABSORPTION COSTING
It is 'fair' to share fixed production costs between units of production as such costs are incurred in order to make output
Closing stocks valued in accordance with SSAP 9 principles
It is easier to determine the profitability of several products by charging a share of fixed overheads to them (rather than working out if the total contribution from several products will cover fixed costs)
Where stockbuilding is necessary (eg fireworks manufacture) fixed costs should be included in stock valuations in order to prevent a series of losses (eg in periods before bonfire night) from occurring

Chapter roundup

- In your examination you may be asked to calculate the profit for an accounting period using either of the two methods of accounting. **Absorption costing** is most often used for routine profit reporting and must be used for financial accounting purposes. **Marginal costing** provides better management information for planning and decision making.
- **Marginal cost** is the variable cost of one unit of product or service.
- **Contribution** is an important measure in marginal costing, and it is calculated as the difference between sales value and marginal or variable cost.
- In **marginal costing**, fixed production costs are treated as **period costs** and are written off as they are incurred. In **absorption costing**, fixed production costs are absorbed into the cost of units and are carried forward in stock to be charged against sales for the next period. Stock values using absorption costing are therefore greater than those calculated using marginal costing.
- **Reported profit figures using marginal costing or absorption costing will differ if there is any change in the level of stocks in the period.** If production is equal to sales, there will be no difference in calculated profits using these costing methods.
- **SSAP 9** recommends the use of absorption costing for the valuation of stocks in financial accounts.
- There are a number of arguments both for and against each of the costing systems.
- The distinction between marginal costing and absorption costing is very important and it is vital that you now understand the contrast between the two systems.

Quick quiz

1 What is marginal costing?

2 What is a period cost in marginal costing?

3 Sales value – marginal cost of sales = ...

4 What is a breakeven point?

5 Marginal costing and absorption costing are different techniques for assessing profit in a period. If there are changes in stock during a period, marginal costing and absorption costing give different results for profit obtained.

Which of the following statements are true?

I If stock levels increase, marginal costing will report the higher profit.

II If stock levels decrease, marginal costing will report the lower profit.

III If stock levels decrease, marginal costing will report the higher profit.

IV If the opening and closing stock volumes are the same, marginal costing and absorption costing will give the same profit figure.

A All of the above
B I, II and IV
C I and IV
D III and IV

6 Which of the following are arguments in favour of marginal costing?

(a) Closing stock is valued in accordance with SSAP 9.
(b) It is simple to operate.
(c) There is no under or over absorption of overheads.
(d) Fixed costs are the same regardless of activity levels.
(e) The information from this costing method may be used for decision making.

Answers to quick quiz

1 Marginal costing is an alternative method of costing to absorption costing. In marginal costing, only variable costs are charged as a cost of sale and a contribution is calculated (sales revenue – variable cost of sales).

2 A fixed cost

3 Contribution

4 The point at which total contribution exactly equals fixed costs (no profit or loss is made)

5 D

6 (b), (c), (d), (e)

Now try the questions below from the Exam Question Bank

Number	Level	Marks	Time
14	MCQ	n/a	n/a
15	Examination	10	18 mins

Part C

Costing systems

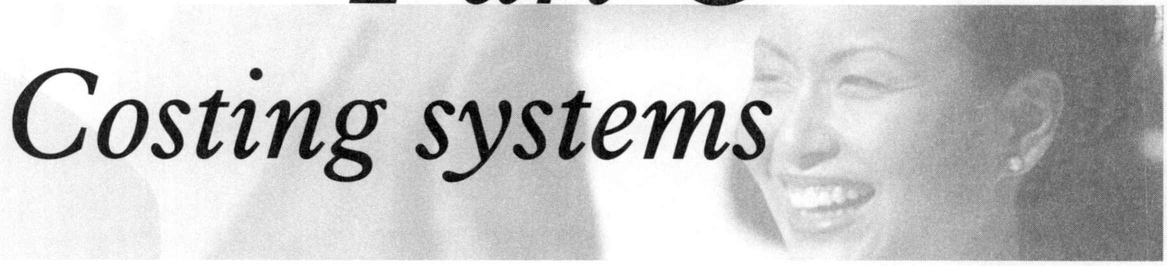

Chapter 10

JOB AND BATCH COSTING

Topic list		Syllabus reference
1	Costing methods	4(a)
2	Job costing	4(a)
3	Batch costing	4(a)

Introduction

The first costing method that we shall be looking at is **job costing**. We will see the circumstances in which job costing should be used and how the costs of jobs are calculated. We will look at how the **costing of individual jobs** fits in with the recording of total costs in control accounts and then we will move on to **batch costing**, the procedure for which is similar to job costing.

Study guide

Section 5 – Cost classification

- Describe briefly the different methods of costing final outputs and their appropriateness to different types of business organisation/situation

Section 15 – Job and batch costing

- Describe the characteristics of job and batch costing
- Describe the situations where the use of job and batch costing would be appropriate
- Discuss, and illustrate, the treatment of direct, indirect and abnormal costs
- Complete cost records and accounts in job and batch cost accounting situations
- Estimate job costs from given information

Exam guide

Job and batch costing are not included in the list of key areas of the syllabus. Make sure that you are able to deal with basic calculations which may be tested in the examination you will be facing.

1 COSTING METHODS

1.1 **A costing method is designed to suit the way goods are processed or manufactured or the way services are provided.** Each organisation's costing method will therefore have unique features but costing methods of firms in the same line of business will more than likely have common aspects. Organisations involved in completely different activities, such as hospitals and car part manufacturers, will use very different methods.

1.2 We will be considering two important costing methods in this chapter.

- Job
- Batch

1.3 The third costing method that we will be studying, **process costing**, will be covered in detail in the next chapter.

2 JOB COSTING

KEY TERMS

- A **job** is a cost unit which consists of a single order or contract.
- **Job costing** is a costing method applied where work is undertaken to customers' special requirements and each order is of comparatively short duration.

2.1 The work relating to a job moves through processes and operations as a **continuously identifiable unit**. Job costing is most commonly applied within a factory or workshop, but may also be applied to property repairs and internal capital expenditure.

Procedure for the performance of jobs

2.2 The normal procedure in jobbing concerns involves:

(a) The prospective customer approaches the supplier and indicates the **requirements** of the job.

(b) A representative sees the prospective customer and agrees with him the **precise details** of the items to be supplied. For example the quantity, quality, size and colour of the goods, the date of delivery and any special requirements.

(c) The estimating department of the organisation then **prepares an estimate for the job**. This will be based on the cost of the materials to be used, the labour expense expected, the cost overheads, the cost of any additional equipment needed specially for the job, and finally the supplier's **profit margin**. The total of these items will represent the **quoted selling price**.

(d) If the estimate is accepted the job can be **scheduled**. All materials, labour and equipment required will be 'booked' for the job. In an efficient organisation, the start of the job will be timed to ensure that while it will be ready for the customer by the promised date of delivery it will not be loaded too early, otherwise storage space will have to be found for the product until the date it is required by (and was promised to) the customer.

Job cost sheets/cards

2.3 With other methods of costing, it is usual to produce for stock; this means that management must decide in advance how many units of each type, size, colour, quality and so on will be produced during the coming year, regardless of the identity of the customers who will eventually buy the product. In job costing, because production is usually carried out in accordance with the **special requirements of each customer**, it is **usual for each job to differ in one or more respects from another job.**

2.4 A separate record must therefore be maintained to show the details of individual jobs. Such records are often known as **job cost sheets** or **job cost cards**. An example is shown on the next page.

2.5 Either the **detail of relatively small jobs** or a **summary** of direct materials, direct labour and so on **for larger jobs** will be shown on a job cost sheet.

Job cost information

2.6 Information for the direct and indirect costs will be gathered as follows.

(a) **Direct material cost**

(i) The estimated cost will be calculated by valuing all items on the **bill of materials**. Materials that have to be specially purchased for the job in question will need to be priced by the purchasing department.

(ii) The actual cost of materials used will be calculated by valuing materials issues notes for those issues from store for the job and/or from invoices for materials specially purchased. All documentation should indicate the job number to which it relates.

(b) **Direct labour cost**

(i) The estimated **labour time requirement** will be calculated from past experience of similar types of work or work study engineers may prepare estimates following detailed specifications. Labour rates will need to take account of any increases, overtime and bonuses.

(ii) The actual labour hours will be available from either time sheets or job tickets/cards, using job numbers where appropriate to indicate the time spent on each job. The actual labour cost will be calculated using the hours information and current labour rates (plus bonuses, overtime payments and so on).

(c) **Direct expenses**

(i) The estimated cost of **any expenses likely** to be incurred can be obtained from a supplier.

(ii) The details of actual direct expenses incurred can be taken from invoices.

(d) **Production overheads**

(i) The **estimated production overheads** to be included in the job cost will be calculated from **overhead absorption rates** in operation and the estimate of the basis of the absorption rate (for example, direct labour hours). This assumes the job estimate is to include overheads (in a competitive environment management may feel that if overheads are to be incurred irrespective of whether or not the job is taken on, the minimum estimated quotation price should be based on variable costs only).

(ii) The actual production overhead to be included in the job cost will be calculated from the overhead absorption rate and the actual results (such as labour hours coded to the job in question). **Inaccurate overhead absorption rates can seriously harm an organisation**; if jobs are over priced, customers will go elsewhere and if jobs are under priced revenue will fail to cover costs.

(e) **Administration, selling and distribution overheads**

The organisation may absorb **non-production overheads** using any one of a variety of methods (percentage on full production cost, for example) and estimates of these costs and the actual costs should be included in the estimated and actual job cost.

JOB COST CARD		Job No. B641
Customer Mr J White	Customer's Order No.	Vehicle make Peugot 205 GTE
Job Description Repair damage to offside front door		Vehicle reg. no. G 614 SOX
Estimate Ref. 2599	Invoice No.	
Quoted price £338.68	Invoice price £355.05	Date to collect 14.6.00

Material						Labour								Overheads			
Date	Req. No.	Qty.	Price	Cost £	Cost p	Date	Employee	Cost Ctre	Hrs.	Rate	Bonus	Cost £	Cost p	Hrs	OAR	Cost £	Cost p
12.6	36815	1	75.49	75	49	12.6	018	B	1.98	6.50	-	12	87	7.9	2.50	19	75
12.6	36816	1	33.19	33	19	13.6	018	B	5.92	6.50	-	38	48				
12.6	36842	5	6.01	30	05						13.65	13	65				
13.6	36881	5	3.99	19	95												
Total C/F				158	68	Total C/F						65	00	Total C/F		19	75

Expenses					Job Cost Summary	Actual £	Actual p	Estimate £	Estimate p
Date	Ref.	Description	Cost £	Cost p	Direct Materials B/F	158	68	158	68
					Direct Expenses B/F	50	00		
					Direct Labour B/F	65	00	180	00
12.6	-	N. Jolley Panel-beating	50	-	Direct Cost	273	68		
					Overheads B/F	19	75		
						293	43		
					Admin overhead (add 10%)	29	34		
					= Total Cost	322	77	338	68
					Invoice Price	355	05		
Total C/F			50	-	Job Profit/Loss	32	28		

Comments

Job Cost Card Completed by ....

Rectification costs

2.7 If the finished output is found to be sub-standard, it may be possible to rectify the fault. The sub-standard output will then be returned to the department or cost centre where the fault arose.

2.8 **Rectification costs** can be treated in two ways.

(a) If rectification work is not a frequent occurrence, but arises on occasions with specific jobs to which it can be traced directly, then the rectification costs should be **charged as a direct cost to the jobs concerned.**

(b) If rectification is regarded as a normal part of the work carried out generally in the department, then the rectification costs should be **treated as production overheads**. This means that they would be included in the total of production overheads for the department and absorbed into the cost of all jobs for the period, using the overhead absorption rate.

Work in progress

2.9 At the year end, the **value of work in progress** is simply the **sum of the costs incurred on incomplete jobs** (provided that the costs are lower than the net realisable value of the customer order).

Pricing the job

2.10 The usual method of fixing prices in a jobbing concern is **cost plus pricing**, which means that a desired profit margin is added to total costs to arrive at the selling price.

2.11 The estimated profit will depend on the particular circumstance of the job and organisation in question. In competitive situations the profit may be small but if the organisation is sure of securing the job the margin may be greater. In general terms, the profit earned on each job should **conform to the requirements of the organisation's overall business plan.**

2.12 The final price quoted will, of course, be affected by what competitors charge and what the customer will be willing to pay.

Exam focus point

An exam question about job costing may ask you to accumulate costs to arrive at a job cost, and then to determine a job price by adding a certain amount of profit. To do this, you need to remember the following crucial formula.

	%
Cost of job	100
+ profit	25
= price	125

Profit may be expressed either as a percentage of job cost (such as 25% 25/100 mark up) or as a percentage of price (such as 20% (25/125) margin).

Job costing and computerisation

2.13 Job cost sheets exist in manual systems, but it is **increasingly likely** that in large organisations the **job costing system will be computerised**, using accounting software specifically designed to deal with job costing requirements. A computerised job accounting system is likely to contain the following features.

(a) Every job will be given a **job code number**, which will determine how the data relating to the job is stored.

(b) A separate set of **codes will be given for the type of costs** that any job is likely to incur. Thus, 'direct wages', say, will have the same code whichever job they are allocated to.

(c) In a sophisticated system, **costs can be analysed both by job** (for example all costs related to Job 456), **but also by type** (for example direct wages incurred on all jobs). It is thus easy to perform control analysis and to make comparisons between jobs.

(d) A job costing system might have facilities built into it which incorporate other factors relating to the performance of the job. In complex jobs, sophisticated planning techniques might be employed to ensure that the job is performed in the minimum time possible: time management features may be incorporated into job costing software.

2.14 EXAMPLE: JOB COSTING

Fateful Morn Ltd is a jobbing company. On 1 June 20X2, there was one uncompleted job in the factory. The job card for this work is summarised as follows.

Job Card, Job No 6832

Costs to date	£
Direct materials	630
Direct labour (120 hours)	350
Factory overhead (£2 per direct labour hour)	240
Factory cost to date	1,220

During June, three new jobs were started in the factory, and costs of production were as follows.

Direct materials		£
Issued to:	Job 6832	2,390
	Job 6833	1,680
	Job 6834	3,950
	Job 6835	4,420
Damaged stock written off from stores		2,300

Material transfers	£
Job 6834 to Job 6833	250
Job 6832 to 6834	620

Materials returned to store	£
From Job 6832	870
From Job 6835	170

Direct labour hours recorded	
Job 6832	430 hrs
Job 6833	650 hrs
Job 6834	280 hrs
Job 6835	410 hrs

The cost of labour hours during June 20X2 was £3 per hour, and production overhead is absorbed at the rate of £2 per direct labour hour. Production overheads incurred during the month amounted to £3,800. Completed jobs were delivered to customers as soon as they were completed, and the invoiced amounts were as follows.

Job 6832	£5,500
Job 6834	£8,000
Job 6835	£7,500

Administration and marketing overheads are added to the cost of sales at the rate of 20% of factory cost. Actual costs incurred during June 20X2 amounted to £3,200.

Required

(a) Prepare the job accounts for each individual job during June 20X2; (the accounts should only show the cost of production, and not the full cost of sale).

(b) Prepare the summarised job cost cards for each job, and calculate the profit on each completed job.

2.15 SOLUTION

(a) Job accounts

JOB 6832

	£		£
Balance b/f	1,220	Job 6834 a/c	620
Materials (stores a/c)	2,390	(materials transfer)	
Labour (wages a/c)	1,290	Stores a/c (materials returned)	870
Production overhead (o'hd a/c)	860	Cost of sales a/c (balance)	4,270
	5,760		5,760

JOB 6833

	£		£
Materials (stores a/c)	1,680	Balance c/f	5,180
Labour (wages a/c)	1,950		
Production overhead (o'hd a/c)	1,300		
Job 6834 a/c (materials transfer)	250		
	5,180		5,180

JOB 6834

	£		£
Materials (stores a/c)	3,950	Job 6833 a/c (materials transfer)	250
Labour (wages a/c)	840		
Production overhead (o'hd a/c)	560	Cost of sales a/c (balance)	5,720
Job 6832 a/c (materials transfer)	620		
	5,970		5,970

JOB 6835

	£		£
Materials (stores a/c)	4,420	Stores a/c (materials returned)	170
Labour (wages a/c)	1,230		
Production overhead (o'hd a/c)	820	Cost of sales a/c (balance)	6,300
	6,470		6,470

(b) Job cards, summarised

	Job 6832	*Job 6833*	*Job 6834*	*Job 6835*
	£	£	£	
Materials	1,530*	1,930	4,320**	4,250
Labour	1,640	1,950	840	1,230
Production overhead	1,100	1,300	560	820
Factory cost	4,270	5,180 (c/f)	5,720	6,300
Admin & marketing o'hd (20%)	854		1,144	1,260
Cost of sale	5,124		6,864	7,560
Invoice value	5,500		8,000	7,500
Profit/(loss) on job	376		1,136	(60)

*£(630 + 2,390 – 620 – 870) **£(3,950 + 620 – 250)

Question 1

The following information relates to job 388886, which is being carried out by Biddy Ltd to meet a customer's order.

	Department V	*Department Q*
Direct materials used	£5,000	£3,000
Direct labour hours	400 hours	200 hours
Direct labour rate per hour	£4	£5
Production overhead per direct labour hour	£4	£4
Administration and other overhead	20% of full production cost	
Profit margin	25% of sales price	

Required

Calculate the selling price of job 388886.

Answer

	Department V	*Department Q*	*Total*
	£	£	£
Direct materials	5,000	3,000	8,000
Direct labour	1,600	1,000	2,600
Production overhead	1,600	800	2,400
Full production cost			13,000
Other overheads			2,600
Cost of the job			15,600
Profit (25% of sales=33 $^{1}/_{3}$ % of cost)			5,200
Sales price			20,800

Job costing for internal services

2.16 It is possible to use a job costing system **to control the costs of an internal service department,** such as the maintenance department or the printing department. If a job costing system is used it is possible to **charge the user departments for the cost of specific jobs carried out, rather than apportioning the total costs of these service departments** to the user departments using an arbitrarily determined apportionment basis.

2.17 An internal job costing system for service departments will have the following advantages.

Advantages	Comment
Realistic apportionment	The identification of expenses with jobs and the subsequent charging of these to the department(s) responsible means that costs are borne by those who incurred them.
Increased responsibility and awareness	User departments will be aware that they are charged for the specific services used and may be more careful to use the facility more efficiently. They will also appreciate the true cost of the facilities that they are using and can take decisions accordingly.
Control of service department costs	The service department may be restricted to charging a standard cost to user departments for specific jobs carried out or time spent. It will then be possible to measure the efficiency or inefficiency of the service department by recording the difference between the standard charges and the actual expenditure.
Planning information	This information will ease the planning process, as the purpose and cost of service department expenditure can be separately identified.

Question 2

A furniture-making business manufactures quality furniture to customers' orders. It has three production departments (A, B and C) which have overhead absorption rates (per direct labour hour) of £12.86, £12.40 and £14.03 respectively.

Two pieces of furniture are to be manufactured for customers. Direct costs are as follows.

	Job XYZ	*Job MNO*
Direct material	£154	£108
Direct labour	20 hours dept A	16 hours dept A
	12 hours dept B	10 hours dept B
	10 hours dept C	14 hours dept C

Labour rates are as follows: £3.80(A); £3.50 (B); £3.40 (C)

The firm quotes prices to customers that reflect a required profit of 25% on selling price. Calculate the total cost and selling price of each job.

Answer

		Job XYZ		*Job MNO*
		£		£
Direct material		154.00		108.00
Direct labour: dept A	(20 × 3.80)	76.00	(16 × 3.80)	60.80
dept B	(12 × 3.50)	42.00	(10 × 3.50)	35.00
dept C	(10 × 3.40)	34.00	(14 × 3.40)	47.60
Total direct cost		306.00		251.40
Overhead: dept A	(20 × 12.86)	257.20	(16 × 12.86)	205.76
dept B	(12 × 12.40)	148.80	(10 × 12.40)	124.00
dept C	(10 × 14.03)	140.30	(14 × 14.03)	196.42
Total cost		852.30		777.58
Profit (note)		284.10		259.19
Quoted selling price		1,136.40		1,036.77

(*Note.* If profit is 25% on selling price, this is the same as $33^1/_3$% (25/75) on cost.)

Question 3

A firm uses job costing and recovers overheads on direct labour.

Three jobs were worked on during a period, the details of which are as follows.

	Job 1	*Job 2*	*Job 3*
	£	£	£
Opening work in progress	8,500	0	46,000
Material in period	17,150	29,025	0
Labour for period	12,500	23,000	4,500

The overheads for the period were exactly as budgeted, £140,000.

Jobs 1 and 2 were the only incomplete jobs.

What was the value of closing work in progress?

A £81,900 B £90,175 C £140,675 D £214,425

Answer

Total labour cost = £12,500 + £23,000 + £4,500 = £40,000

$$\text{Overhead absorption rate} = \frac{£140,000}{£40,000} \times 100\% = 350\% \text{ of direct labour cost}$$

Closing work in progress valuation

		Job 1		*Job 2*	*Total*
		£		£	£
Costs given in question		38,150		52,025	90,175
Overhead absorbed	(12,500 × 350%)	43,750	(23,000 × 350%)	80,500	124,250
					214,425

Option D is correct.

We can eliminate option B because £90,175 is simply the total of the costs allocated to Jobs 1 and 2, with no absorption of overheads. Option A is an even lower cost figure, therefore it can also be eliminated.

Option C is wrong because it is a simple total of all allocated costs, including Job 3 which is not incomplete.

3 BATCH COSTING

KEY TERM

A **batch** is a group of similar articles which maintains its identity during one or more stages of production and is treated as a cost unit.

3.1 In general, the **procedures for costing batches are very similar to those for costing jobs**.

(a) The **batch is treated as a job during production** and the costs are collected in the manner already described in this chapter.

(b) Once the batch has been completed, the **cost per unit can be calculated as the total batch cost divided into the number of units in the batch.**

3.2 EXAMPLE: BATCH COSTING

Rio Ltd manufactures Brazils to order and has the following budgeted overheads for the year, based on normal activity levels.

Production departments	*Budgeted Overheads*	*Budgeted activity*
	£	
Welding	12,000	3,000 labour hours
Assembly	20,000	2,000 labour hours

Selling and administrative overheads are 25% of factory cost. An order for 500 Brazils, made as Batch 38, incurred the following costs.

Materials	£24,000
Labour	200 hours in the Welding Department at £5 per hour
	400 hours in the Assembly Department at £10 per hour

£1,000 was paid for the hire of x-ray equipment for testing the accuracy of the welds.

Required

Calculate the cost per unit for Batch 38.

3.3 SOLUTION

The first step is to calculate the overhead absorption rate for the production departments.

$$\text{Welding} = \frac{£12{,}000}{3{,}000} = £4 \text{ per labour hour}$$

$$\text{Assembly} = \frac{£20{,}000}{2{,}000} = £10 \text{ per labour hour}$$

Total cost - Batch 38

		£	£
Direct material			24,000
Direct expense			1,000
Direct labour	200 × £5 =	1,000	
	400 × £10 =	4,000	
			5,000
Prime cost			30,000
Overheads	200 × £4 =	800	
	400 × £10 =	4,000	
			4,800
Factory cost			34,800
Selling and administrative cost (25% of factory cost)			8,700
Total cost			43,500

$$\text{Cost per unit} = \frac{£43{,}500}{500} = £87$$

Chapter roundup

- **Job costing** is the costing method used where each cost unit is separately identifiable.
- Costs for each job are collected on a **job cost sheet** or **job card.**
- Material costs for each job are determined from **material requisition notes**.
- Labour times on each job are recorded on a **job ticket**, which is then costed and recorded on the job cost sheet. Some labour costs, such as overtime premium or the cost of rectifying sub-standard output, might be charged either directly to a job or else as an overhead cost, depending on the circumstances in which the costs have arisen.
- **Overhead** is absorbed into the cost of jobs using the predetermined overhead absorption rates.
- The usual method of fixing prices within a jobbing concern is **cost plus pricing**.
- **Batch costing** is similar to job costing in that each batch of similar articles is separately identifiable. The **cost per unit** manufactured in a batch is the total batch cost divided by the number of units in the batch.

Quick quiz

1 How are the material costs for each job determined?

2 Which of the following are not characteristics of job costing?

I Customer driven production
II Complete production possible within a single accounting period
III Homogeneous products

A I and II only
B I and III only
C II and III only
D III only

3 The cost of a job is £100,000

(a) If profit is 25% of the job cost, the price of the job = £.................
(b) If there is a 25% margin, the price of the job = £....................

4 What is a batch?

5 How would you calculate the cost per unit of a completed batch?

Answers to quick quiz

1 From materials requisition notes, or from suppliers' invoices if materials are purchased specifically for a particular job.

2 D

3 (a) £100,000 + (25% × £100,000) = £100,000 + £25,000 = £125,000

(b) Let price of job = x

$$\begin{aligned} \therefore \text{Profit} &= 25\% \times x \text{ (selling price)} \\ \text{If profit} &= 0.25x \\ x - 0.25x &= \text{cost of job} \\ 0.75x &= £100{,}000 \\ x &= \frac{£100{,}000}{0.75} \\ &= £133{,}333 \end{aligned}$$

4 A group of similar articles which maintains its identity during one or more stages of production and is treated as a cost unit.

5 $\dfrac{\text{Total batch cost}}{\text{Number of units in the batch}}$

Now try the questions below from the Exam Question Bank

Number	Level	Marks	Time
16	MCQ	n/a	n/a
17	Examination	10	18 mins

Chapter 11

PROCESS COSTING

Topic list		Syllabus reference
1	Introduction to process costing	4(a)
2	The basics of process costing	4(a)
3	Losses in process costing	4(a)
4	Accounting for scrap	4(a)
5	Losses with a disposal cost	4(a)
6	Valuing closing work in progress	4(a)
7	Valuing opening work in progress: FIFO method	4(a)
8	Valuing opening work in progress: weighted average cost method	4(a)

Introduction

We have already looked at two costing methods, **job costing and batch costing**. In this chapter we will consider a thrid, **process costing**. The chapter will consider the topic from basics, looking at how to account for the most simple of processes. We then move on to how to account for any **losses** which might occur, as well as what to do with any **scrapped units** which are sold. We also consider how to deal with any **closing work in progress** and then look at two methods of valuing **opening work in progress**. Valuation of both opening and closing work in progress hinges on the concept of **equivalent units**, which will be explained in detail.

Study guide

Section 5 – Cost classification

- Describe briefly the different methods of costing final outputs and their appropriateness to different types of business organisation/situation

Section 12 – Overheads 2

- Perform process cost accounting transactions for selling, distribution and administration overhead in a given business context

Section 16 – Process costing 1

- Describe the characteristics of process costing
- Describe situations where the use of process costing is appropriate
- Describe the key areas of complexity in process costing
- Define 'normal' losses and 'abnormal' gains and losses
- State and justify the treatment of normal losses and abnormal gains and losses in process accounts
- Account for process scrap
- Calculate the cost per unit of process outputs, and prepare simple process accounts, in absorption and marginal costing systems

Section 17 – Process costing 2

- Calculate and explain the concept of equivalent units
- Allocate process costs between work remaining in process and transfers out of a process using the weighted average cost and FIFO methods
- Prepare process accounts in situations where work remains incomplete
- Prepare process accounts in situations where losses and gains are identified at different stages of the process

Exam guide

Process costing is one of the key areas of the syllabus and a common examination question might require you to prepare a process account for a period. Make sure that you can deal with losses, gains, scrap and work in progress.

1 INTRODUCTION TO PROCESS COSTING

KEY TERM

Process costing is a costing method used where it is not possible to identify separate units of production, or jobs, usually because of the continuous nature of the production processes involved.

1.1 It is common to identify process costing with **continuous production** such as the following.

- Oil refining
- Paper
- Foods and drinks
- Chemicals

Process costing may also be associated with the continuous production of large volumes of low-cost items, such as **cans** or **tins**.

1.2 The following are features of process costing which make it different from job or batch costing.

(a) The **output** of one process becomes the **input** to the next until the finished product is made in the final process.

(b) The continuous nature of production in many processes means that there will usually be **closing work in progress which must be valued**. In process costing it is not possible to build up cost records of the cost per unit of output or the cost per unit of closing stock because production in progress is an **indistinguishable homogeneous mass**.

(c) There is often a **loss in process** due to spoilage, wastage, evaporation and so on.

(d) Output from production may be a single product, but there may also be a **by-product** (or by-products) and/or **joint products.**

1.3 The aim of this chapter is to describe how cost accountants keep a set of accounts to record the costs of production in a processing industry. The aim of the set of accounts is to derive a cost, or valuation, for output and closing stock.

2 THE BASICS OF PROCESS COSTING

2.1 Where a series of separate processes is required to manufacture the finished product, the output of one process becomes the input to the next until the final output is made in the final process. If two processes are required the accounts would look like this.

PROCESS 1 ACCOUNT

	Units	£		Units	£
Direct materials	1,000	50,000	Output to process 2	1,000	90,000
Direct labour		20,000			
Production overhead		20,000			
	1,000	90,000		1,000	90,000

PROCESS 2 ACCOUNT

	Units	£		Units	£
Materials from process 1	1,000	90,000	Output to finished goods	1,000	150,000
Added materials		30,000			
Direct labour		15,000			
Production overhead		15,000			
	1,000	150,000		1,000	150,000

2.2 Note that direct labour and production overhead may be treated together in an examination question as **conversion cost**.

2.3 **Added** materials, labour and overhead in process 2 are added gradually throughout the process. Materials from process 1, in contrast, will often be introduced in full at the start of process 2.

2.4 The 'units' columns in the process accounts are for **memorandum purposes** only and help you to ensure that you do not miss out any entries.

Framework for dealing with process costing

2.5 Process costing is centred around **four key steps**. The exact work done at each step will depend on whether there are normal losses, scrap, opening and closing work in progress and so on.

Step 1. **Determine output and losses.** This step involves the following.

- Determining expected output
- Calculating normal loss and abnormal loss and gain
- Calculating equivalent units if there is closing or opening work in progress

Step 2. **Calculate cost per unit of output, losses and WIP**. This step involves calculating cost per unit or cost per equivalent unit.

Step 3. **Calculate total cost of output, losses and WIP**. In some examples this will be straightforward; however in cases where there is closing and/or opening work-in-progress a **statement of evaluation** will have to be prepared.

Step 4. **Complete accounts**. This step involves the following.

- Completing the process account
- Writing up the other accounts required by the question

Exam focus point

It always saves time in an exam if you don't have to think too long about how to approach a question before you begin. This four-step approach can be applied to any process costing question so it would be a good idea to memorise it now.

3 LOSSES IN PROCESS COSTING

3.1 During a production process, a loss may occur due to wastage, spoilage, evaporation, and so on.

KEY TERMS

- **Normal loss** is the loss expected during a process. It is not given a cost.
- **Abnormal loss** is the extra loss resulting when actual loss is greater than normal or expected loss, and it is given a cost.
- **Abnormal gain** is the gain resulting when actual loss is less than the normal or expected loss, and it is given a 'negative cost'.

3.2 Since normal loss is not given a cost, the cost of producing these units is borne by the 'good' units of output.

3.3 Abnormal loss and gain units are valued at the same unit rate as 'good' units. Abnormal events do not therefore affect the cost of good production. Their costs are **analysed separately** in an **abnormal loss or abnormal gain account**.

3.4 EXAMPLE: ABNORMAL LOSSES AND GAINS

Suppose that input to a process is 1,000 units at a cost of £4,500. Normal loss is 10% and there are no opening or closing stocks. Determine the accounting entries for the cost of output and the cost of the loss if actual output were as follows.

(a) 860 units (so that actual loss is 140 units)
(b) 920 units (so that actual loss is 80 units)

3.5 SOLUTION

Before we demonstrate the use of the 'four-step framework' we will summarise the way that the losses are dealt with.

(a) Normal loss is given no share of cost.

(b) The cost of output is therefore based on the **expected** units of output, which in our example amount to 90% of 1,000 = 900 units.

(c) Abnormal loss is given a cost, which is written off to the profit and loss account via an abnormal loss/gain account.

(d) Abnormal gain is treated in the same way, except that being a gain rather than a loss, it appears as a **debit** entry in the process account (whereas a loss appears as a **credit** entry in this account).

(a) **Output is 860 units**

Step 1. **Determine output and losses**

If actual output is 860 units and the actual loss is 140 units:

	Units
Actual loss	140
Normal loss (10% of 1,000)	100
Abnormal loss	40

Step 2. **Calculate cost per unit of output and losses**

The cost per unit of output and the cost per unit of abnormal loss are based on expected output.

$$\frac{\text{Costs incurred}}{\text{Expected output}} = \frac{£4,500}{900 \text{ units}} = £5 \text{ per unit}$$

Step 3. **Calculate total cost of output and losses**

Normal loss is not assigned any cost.

	£
Cost of output (860 × £5)	4,300
Normal loss	0
Abnormal loss (40 × £5)	200
	4,500

Step 4. **Complete accounts**

PROCESS ACCOUNT

	Units	£		Units		£
Cost incurred	1,000	4,500	Normal loss	100		0
			Output (finished goods a/c)	860	(× £5)	4,300
			Abnormal loss	40	(× £5)	200
	1,000	4,500		1,000		4,500

ABNORMAL LOSS ACCOUNT

	Units	£		Units	£
Process a/c	40	200	Profit and loss a/c	40	200

(b) **Output is 920 units**

Step 1. **Determine output and losses**

If actual output is 920 units and the actual loss is 80 units:

	Units
Actual loss	80
Normal loss (10% of 1,000)	100
Abnormal gain	20

Step 2. **Calculate cost per unit of output and losses**

The cost per unit of output and the cost per unit of abnormal gain are based on **expected** output.

$$\frac{\text{Costs incurred}}{\text{Expected output}} = \frac{£4,500}{900 \text{ units}} = £5 \text{ per unit}$$

(Whether there is abnormal loss or gain does not affect the valuation of units of output. The figure of £5 per unit is exactly the same as in the previous paragraph, when there were 40 units of abnormal loss.)

Step 3. **Calculate total cost of output and losses**

	£
Cost of output (920 × £5)	4,600
Normal loss	0
Abnormal gain (20 × £5)	(100)
	4,500

Step 4. **Complete accounts**

PROCESS ACCOUNT

	Units	£		Units	£
Cost incurred	1,000	4,500	Normal loss	100	0
Abnormal gain a/c	20	(× £5) 100	Output (finished goods a/c)	920	(× £5) 4,600
	1,020	4,600		1,020	4,600

ABNORMAL GAIN

	Units	£		Units	£
Profit and loss a/c	20	100	Process a/c	20	100

3.6 EXAMPLE: ABNORMAL LOSSES AND GAINS AGAIN

During a four-week period, period 3, costs of input to a process were £29,070. Input was 1,000 units, output was 850 units and normal loss is 10%.

During the next period, period 4, costs of input were again £29,070. Input was again 1,000 units, but output was 950 units.

There were no units of opening or closing stock.

Required

Prepare the process account and abnormal loss or gain account for each period.

3.7 SOLUTION

Step 1. **Determine output and losses**

Period 3

	Units
Actual output	850
Normal loss (10% × 1,000)	100
Abnormal loss	50
Input	1,000

Period 4

	Units
Actual output	950
Normal loss (10% × 1,000)	100
Abnormal gain	(50)
Input	1,000

Step 2. **Calculate cost per unit of output and losses**

For each period the cost per unit is based on expected output.

$$\frac{\text{Cost of input}}{\text{Expected units of output}} = \frac{£29,070}{900} = £32.30 \text{ per unit}$$

Step 3. Calculate total cost of output and losses

Period 3

	£
Cost of output (850 × £32.30)	27,455
Normal loss	0
Abnormal loss (50 × £32.30)	1,615
	29,070

Period 4

	£
Cost of output (950 × £32.30)	30,685
Normal loss	0
Abnormal gain (50 × £32.30)	1,615
	29,070

Step 4. Complete accounts

PROCESS ACCOUNT

	Units	£		Units	£
Period 3					
Cost of input	1,000	29,070	Normal loss	100	0
			Finished goods a/c (× £32.30)	850	27,455
			Abnormal loss a/c (× £32.30)	50	1,615
	1,000	29,070		1,000	29,070
Period 4					
Cost of input	1,000	29,070	Normal loss	100	0
Abnormal gain a/c (× £32.30)	50	1,615	Finished goods a/c (× £32.30)	950	30,685
	1,050	30,685		1,050	30,685

ABNORMAL LOSS OR GAIN ACCOUNT

	£		£
Period 3		*Period 4*	
Abnormal loss in process a/c	1,615	Abnormal gain in process a/c	1,615

A nil balance on this account will be carried forward into period 5.

3.8 If there is a closing balance in the abnormal loss or gain account when the profit for the period is calculated, this balance is taken to the profit and loss account: an abnormal gain will be a credit to profit and loss and an abnormal loss will be a debit to profit and loss.

Question 1

3,000 units of material are input to a process. Process costs are as follows.

Material	£11,700
Conversion costs	£6,300

Output is 2,000 units. Normal loss is 20% of input.

Required

Prepare a process account and the appropriate abnormal loss/gain account.

Answer

Step 1. **Determine output and losses**

We are told that output is 2,000 units.

Normal loss = 20% × 3,000 = 600 units

Abnormal loss = (3,000 – 600) – 2,000 = 400 units

Step 2. **Calculate cost per unit of output and losses**

$$\text{Cost per unit} = \frac{£(11{,}700 + 6{,}300)}{2{,}400} = £7.50$$

Step 3. **Calculate total cost of output and losses**

		£
Output	(2,000 × £7.50)	15,000
Normal loss		0
Abnormal loss	(400 × £7.50)	3,000
		18,000

Step 4. **Complete accounts**

PROCESS ACCOUNT

	Units	£		Units	£
Material	3,000	11,700	Output	2,000	15,000
Conversion costs		6,300	Normal loss	600	
			Abnormal loss	400	3,000
	3,000	18,000		3,000	18,000

ABNORMAL LOSS ACCOUNT

	£		£
Process a/c	3,000	P&L account	3,000

Question 2

Charlton Ltd manufactures a product in a single process operation. Normal loss is 10% of input. Loss occurs at the end of the process. Data for June are as follows.

Opening and closing stocks of work in progress	Nil
Cost of input materials (3,300 units)	£59,100
Direct labour and production overhead	£30,000
Output to finished goods	2,750 units

The full cost of finished output in June was

A £74,250 B £81,000 C £82,500 D £89,100

Answer

Step 1. **Determine output and losses**

	Units
Actual output	2,750
Normal loss (10% × 3,300)	330
Abnormal loss	220
	3,300

Step 2. **Calculate cost per unit of output and losses**

$$\frac{\text{Cost of input}}{\text{Expected units of output}} = \frac{£89{,}100}{3{,}300 - 330} = £30 \text{ per unit}$$

Step 3. **Calculate total cost of output and losses**

	£
Cost of output (2,750 × £30)	82,500 **(The correct answer is C)**
Normal loss	0
Abnormal loss (220 × £30)	6,600
	89,100

If you were reduced to making a calculated guess, you could have eliminated option D. This is simply the total input cost, with no attempt to apportion some of the cost to the abnormal loss.

Option A is incorrect because it results from allocating a full unit cost to the normal loss: remember that normal loss does not carry any of the process cost.

Option B is incorrect because it results from calculating a 10% normal loss based on *output* of 2,750 units (275 units normal loss), rather than on *input* of 3,300 units.

4 ACCOUNTING FOR SCRAP

4.1 **Loss may have a scrap value**. The following basic rules are applied in accounting for this value in the process accounts.

(a) **Revenue from scrap** is treated, not as an addition to sales revenue, but as a **reduction in costs.**

(b) The scrap value of **normal loss** is therefore used to reduce the material costs of the process.

DEBIT Scrap account
CREDIT Process account

with the scrap value of the normal loss.

(c) The scrap value of **abnormal loss** is used to reduce the cost of abnormal loss.

DEBIT Scrap account
CREDIT Abnormal loss account

with the scrap value of abnormal loss, which therefore reduces the write-off of cost to the profit and loss account.

(d) The scrap value of **abnormal gain** arises because the actual units sold as scrap will be less than the scrap value of normal loss. Because there are fewer units of scrap than expected, there will be less revenue from scrap as a direct consequence of the abnormal gain. The abnormal gain account should therefore be debited with the scrap value.

DEBIT Abnormal gain account
CREDIT Scrap account

with the scrap value of abnormal gain.

(e) The **scrap account** is completed by recording the **actual cash received** from the sale of scrap.

DEBIT Cash received
CREDIT Scrap account

with the cash received from the sale of the actual scrap.

4.2 The same basic principle therefore applies that only **normal losses** should affect the cost of the good output. The scrap value of **normal loss only** is credited to the process account. The scrap values of abnormal losses and gains are analysed separately in the abnormal loss or gain account.

4.3 EXAMPLE: SCRAP AND NORMAL LOSS

Suppose that input to a process costs £1,370, normal loss is 10% and units scrapped sell for £2 each. 100 units are input and 90 units output.

Required

Show the process account and the scrap account.

4.4 SOLUTION

Step 1. **Determine output and losses**

Normal loss is 10% of 100 units, ie 10 units. Normal output is therefore 90 units (100 – 10). There is therefore no abnormal loss or gain.

Step 2. **Calculate costs of output and losses**

The total value of scrap is 10 × £2 = £20. The scrap value of normal loss is deducted from the materials cost, in order to calculate the output cost per unit, before it is credited to the process account as a value for normal loss.

The cost per unit of output would be calculated as follows.

	£	
Cost of input	1,370	
Less scrap value of normal loss (10 units × £2)	(20)	
	1,350	
Expected units of output	90	units
Cost per unit (£1,350 ÷ 90)	£15	per unit

Step 3. **Calculate total costs of output and losses**

	£
Output (90 × £15)	1,350
Normal loss (100 × £0)	-
	1,350

Step 4. **Complete accounts**

The accounting entries would be as follows.

PROCESS ACCOUNT

	Units	£		Units	£
Input costs	100	1,370	Normal loss ** (scrap a/c)	10	20
			Output (finished goods a/c)	90	1,350
	100	1,370		100	1,370

SCRAP ACCOUNT

	£		£
Scrap value of normal loss in process **	20	Cash a/c or financial ledger control = actual cash received for scrap	20
	20		20

4.5 If there is abnormal loss or abnormal gain, the scrap value of actual loss will differ from the normal loss scrap value. This discrepancy is ignored in the process account and is dealt with instead in the abnormal loss or gain account and the scrap account.

Question 3

Nan Ltd has a factory which operates two production processes. Normal spoilage in each process is 10%, and scrapped units out of process 1 sell for 50p per unit whereas scrapped units out of process 2 sell for £3. Output from process 1 is transferred to process 2: output from process 2 is finished output ready for sale.

Relevant information about costs for period 5 are as follows.

	Process 1		Process 2	
	Units	£	Units	£
Input materials	2,000	£8,100		
Transferred to process 2	1,750			
Materials from process 1			1,750	
Added materials			1,250	£1,900
Labour and overheads		£10,000		£22,000
Output to finished goods			2,800	

Required

Prepare the following cost accounts.

(a) Process 1
(b) Process 2
(c) Abnormal loss
(d) Abnormal gain
(e) Scrap

Answer

(a) *Process 1*

Step 1. **Determine output and losses**

The normal loss is 10% of 2000 units = 200 units, and the actual loss is (2000 - 1750) = 250 units. This means that there is abnormal loss of 50 units.

Actual output	1,750 units
Abnormal loss	50 units
Expected output (90% of 2,000)	1,800 units

Step 2. **Calculate cost per unit of output and losses**

(i) The total value of scrap is 250 units at 50p per unit = £125. We must split this between the scrap value of normal loss and the scrap value of abnormal loss.

	£
Normal loss	100
Abnormal loss	25
Total scrap (250 units × 50p)	125

(ii) The scrap value of normal loss is first deducted from the materials cost in the process, in order to calculate the output cost per unit and then credited to the process account as a 'value' for normal loss. The cost per unit in process 1 is calculated as follows.

	Total cost		*Cost per expected unit of output*
	£		£
Materials	8,100		
Less normal loss scrap value *	100		
	8,000	(÷ 1,800)	4.44
Labour and overhead	10,000	(÷ 1,800)	5.56
Total	18,000	(÷ 1,800)	10.00

* It is usual to set this scrap value of normal loss against the cost of materials.

Step 3. **Calculate total cost of output and losses**

		£
Output	(1,750 units × £10.00)	17,500
Normal loss	(200 units × £0.50)	100
Abnormal loss	(50 units × £10.00)	500
		18,100

Step 4. **Complete accounts**

Now we can put the process 1 account together.

PROCESS 1 ACCOUNT

	Units	£		Units	£
Materials	2,000	8,100	Output to process 2*	1,750	17,500
Labour and overhead		10,000	Normal loss (scrap a/c)	200	100
			Abnormal loss a/c*	50	500
	2,000	18,100		2,000	18,100

* At £10 per unit.

(b) *Process 2*

Step 1. **Determine output and losses**

The normal loss is 10% of the units processed = 10% of (1,750 (from process 1) + 1,250) = 300 units. The actual loss is (3,000 - 2,800) = 200 units, so that there is abnormal gain of 100 units. These are *deducted* from actual output in arriving at the number of expected units (normal output) in the period.

Expected units of output

	Units
Actual output	2,800
Abnormal gain	(100)
Expected output (90% of 3,000)	2,700

Step 2. **Calculate cost per unit of output and losses**

(i) The total value of scrap is 200 units at £3 per unit = £600. We must split this between the scrap value of normal loss and the scrap value of abnormal gain. Abnormal gain's scrap value is 'negative'.

		£
Normal loss scrap value	300 units × £3	900
Abnormal gain scrap value	100 units × £3	(300)
Scrap value of actual loss	200 units × £3	600

(ii) The scrap value of normal loss is first deducted from the cost of materials in the process, in order to calculate a cost per unit of output, and then credited to the process account as a 'value' for normal loss. The cost per unit in process 2 is calculated as follows.

	Total cost £		*Cost per expected unit of output* £
Materials:			
Transferred from process 1	17,500		
Added in process 2	1,900		
	19,400		
Less scrap value of normal loss	900		
	18,500	(÷ 2,700)	6.85
Labour and overhead	22,000	(÷ 2,700)	8.15
	40,500	(÷ 2,700)	15.00

Step 3. **Calculate total cost of output and losses**

		£
Output	(2,800 × £15.00)	42,000
Normal loss	(300 units × £3.00)	900
		42,900
Abnormal gain	(100 units × £15.00)	(1,500)
		41,400

Step 4. **Complete accounts**

PROCESS 2 ACCOUNT

	Units	£		Units	£
From process 1	1,750	17,500	Finished output	2,800	42,000
Added materials	1,250	1,900			
Labour and overhead		22,000	Normal loss (scrap a/c)	300	900
	3,000	41,400			
Abnormal gain a/c	100	1,500			
	3,100	42,900		3,100	42,900

(c) and (d)

Abnormal loss and abnormal gain accounts

For each process, one or the other of these accounts will record three items.

(i) The cost/value of the abnormal loss/gain. This is the corresponding entry to the entry in the process account.

(ii) The scrap value of the abnormal loss or gain, to set off against it.

(iii) A balancing figure, which is written to the P&L account as an adjustment to the profit figure.

ABNORMAL LOSS ACCOUNT

	£		£
Process 1	500	Scrap a/c (scrap value of abnormal loss)	25
		Profit and Loss a/c (balance)	475
	500		500

ABNORMAL GAIN ACCOUNT

	£		£
Scrap a/c (scrap value of abnormal gain units)	300	Process 2	1,500
Profit & Loss a/c (balance)	1,200		
	1,500		1,500

(e) *Scrap account*

This is credited with the cash value of actual units scrapped. The other entries in the account should all be identifiable as corresponding entries to those in the process accounts, and abnormal loss and abnormal gain accounts.

SCRAP ACCOUNT

	£		£
Normal loss:		Cash: sale of	
Process 1 (200 × 50p)	100	process 1 scrap (250 × 50p)	125
Process 2 (300 × £3)	900	Cash: sale of	
Abnormal loss a/c	25	process 2 scrap (200 × £3)	600
		Abnormal gain a/c	300
	1,025		1,025

Question 4

Look back at Question 1. Suppose the units of loss could be sold for £1 each. Prepare appropriate accounts.

Answer

Step 1. **Determine output and losses**

Actual output	2,000 units
Abnormal loss	400 units
Expected output	2,400 units

Step 2. **Calculate cost per unit of output and losses**

	£
Scrap value of normal loss	600
Scrap value of abnormal loss	400
Total scrap (1,000 units × £1)	1,000

Step 3. **Calculate total cost of output and losses**

		£
Output	(2,000 × £7.25)	14,500
Normal loss	(600 × £1.00)	600
Abnormal loss	(400 × £7.25)	2,900
		18,000

$$\text{Cost per expected unit} = \frac{£((11{,}700 - 600) + 6{,}300)}{2{,}400} = £7.25$$

Step 4. **Complete accounts**

PROCESS ACCOUNT

	Units	£		Units	£
Material	3,000	11,700	Output	2,000	14,500
Conversion costs		6,300	Normal loss	600	600
			Abnormal loss	400	2,900
	3,000	18,000		3,000	18,000

ABNORMAL LOSS ACCOUNT

	£		£
Process a/c	2,900	Scrap a/c	400
		P&L a/c	2,500
	2,900		2,900

SCRAP ACCOUNT

	£		£
Normal loss	600	Cash	1,000
Abnormal loss	400		
	1,000		1,000

5 LOSSES WITH A DISPOSAL COST

5.1 As well as being able to deal with questions in which scrap or loss units are **worthless** or have a **scrap value,** you must also be able to deal with losses which have a **disposal cost**.

5.2 The basic calculations required in such circumstances are as follows.

(a) Increase the process costs by the cost of disposing of the units of normal loss and use the resulting cost per unit to value good output and abnormal loss/gain.

(b) The normal loss is given no value in the process account.

(c) Include the disposal costs of normal loss on the debit side of the process account.

(d) Include the disposal costs of abnormal loss in the abnormal loss account and hence in the transfer of the cost of abnormal loss to the profit and loss account.

5.3 Suppose that input to a process was 1,000 units at a cost of £4,500. Normal loss is 10% and there are no opening and closing stocks. Actual output was 860 units and loss units had to be disposed of at a cost of £0.90 per unit.

Normal loss = 10% × 1,000 = 100 units. ∴ Abnormal loss = 900 – 860 = 40 units

$$\text{Cost per unit} = \frac{£4{,}500 + (100 \times £0.90)}{900} = £5.10$$

5.4 The relevant accounts would be as follows.

PROCESS ACCOUNT

	Units	£		Units	£
Cost of input	1,000	4,500	Output	860	4,386
Disposal cost of			Normal loss	100	-
normal loss		90	Abnormal loss	40	204
	1,000	4,590		1,000	4,590

ABNORMAL LOSS ACCOUNT

	£		£
Process a/c	204	Profit and loss a/c	240
Disposal cost (40 × £0.90)	36		
	240		240

6 VALUING CLOSING WORK IN PROGRESS

6.1 In the examples we have looked at so far we have assumed that opening and closing stocks of work in process have been nil. We must now look at more realistic examples and consider how to allocate the costs incurred in a period between completed output (that is, finished units) and partly completed closing stock.

6.2 Some examples will help to illustrate the problem, and the techniques used to share out (apportion) costs between finished output and closing stocks.

6.3 Suppose that we have the following account for Process 2 for period 9.

PROCESS ACCOUNT

	Units	£			£
Materials	1,000	6,200	Finished goods	800	?
Labour and overhead		2,850	Closing WIP	200	?
	1,000	9,050		1,000	9,050

How do we value the finished goods and closing work in process?

6.4 With any form of process costing involving closing WIP, we have to apportion costs between output and closing WIP. To apportion costs 'fairly' we make use of the concept of **equivalent units of production**.

Equivalent units

KEY TERM

Equivalent units are notional whole units which represent incomplete work, and which are used to apportion costs between work in process and completed output.

6.5 We will assume that in the example above the degree of completion is as follows.

(a) **Direct materials**. These are added in full at the start of processing, and so any closing WIP will have 100% of their direct material content. (This is not always the case in practice. Materials might be added gradually throughout the process, in which case closing stock will only be a certain percentage complete as to material content. We will look at this later in the chapter.)

(b) **Direct labour and production overhead.** These are usually assumed to be incurred at an even rate through the production process, so that when we refer to a unit that is 50% complete, we mean that it is half complete for labour and overhead, although it might be 100% complete for materials.

6.6 Let us also assume that the closing WIP is 100% complete for materials and 25% complete for labour and overhead.

6.7 How would we now put a value to the finished output and the closing WIP?

In **Step 1** of our framework, we have been told what output and losses are. However we also need to calculate **equivalent units**.

STATEMENT OF EQUIVALENT UNITS

		Materials		*Labour and overhead*	
	Total units	*Degree of completion*	*Equivalent units*	*Degree of completion*	*Equivalent units*
Finished output	800	100%	800	100%	800
Closing WIP	200	100%	200	25%	50
	1,000		1,000		850

6.8 In **Step 2** the important figure is **average cost per equivalent unit**. This can be calculated as follows.

STATEMENT OF COSTS PER EQUIVALENT UNIT

	Materials	*Labour and overhead*
Costs incurred in the period	£6,200	£2,850
Equivalent units of work done	1,000	850
Cost per equivalent unit (approx)	£6.20	£3.3529

6.9 To calculate total costs for **Step 3**, we prepare a statement of evaluation to show how the costs should be apportioned between finished output and closing WIP.

STATEMENT OF EVALUATION

	Materials			*Labour and overheads*			
Item	*Equivalent units*	*Cost per equivalent units*	*Cost*	*Equivalent units*	*Cost per equivalent units*	*Cost*	*Total cost*
		£	£		£	£	£
Finished output	800	6.20	4,960	800	3.3529	2,682	7,642
Closing WIP	200	6.20	1,240	50	3.3529	168	1,408
	1,000		6,200	850		2,850	9,050

6.10 The process account (work in progress, or work in process account) would be shown as follows.

PROCESS ACCOUNT

	Units	£		Units	£
Materials	1,000	6,200	Finished goods	800	7,642
Labour overhead		2,850	Closing WIP	200	1,408
	1,000	9,050		1,000	9,050

Different rates of input

6.11 In many industries, materials, labour and overhead may be **added at different rates** during the course of production.

(a) Output from a previous process (for example the output from process 1 to process 2) may be introduced into the subsequent process all at once, so that closing stock is 100% complete in respect of these materials.

(b) Further materials may be added gradually during the process, so that closing stock is only partially complete in respect of these added materials.

(c) Labour and overhead may be 'added' at yet another different rate. When production overhead is absorbed on a labour hour basis, however, we should expect the degree of completion on overhead to be the same as the degree of completion on labour.

When this situation occurs, **equivalent units**, and a **cost per equivalent unit**, should be calculated separately for each type of material, and also for conversion costs.

6.12 EXAMPLE: EQUIVALENT UNITS AND DIFFERENT DEGREES OF COMPLETION

Suppose that Columbine Ltd is a manufacturer of processed goods, and that results in process 2 for April 20X3 were as follows.

Opening stock	nil
Material input from process 1	4,000 units
Costs of input:	£
material from process 1	6,000
added materials in process 2	1,080
conversion costs	1,720

Output is transferred into the next process, process 3.

Closing work in process amounted to 800 units, complete as to:

process 1 material	100%
added materials	50%
conversion costs	30%

Required

Prepare the account for process 2 for April 20X3.

6.13 SOLUTION

(a) STATEMENT OF EQUIVALENT UNITS (OF PRODUCTION IN THE PERIOD)

			Equivalent units of production					
			Process 1		*Added*		*Labour and*	
Input	*Output*	*Total*	*material*		*materials*		*overhead*	
Units		Units	Units	%	Units	%	Units	%
4,000	Completed production	3,200	3,200	100	3,200	100	3,200	100
	Closing stock	800	800	100	400	50	240	30
4,000		4,000	4,000		3,600		3,440	

(b) STATEMENT OF COST (PER EQUIVALENT UNIT)

Input	*Cost*	*Equivalent production in units*	*Cost per unit*
	£		£
Process 1 material	6,000	4,000	1.50
Added materials	1,080	3,600	0.30
Labour and overhead	1,720	3,440	0.50
	8,800		2.30

(c) STATEMENT OF EVALUATION (OF FINISHED WORK AND CLOSING STOCKS)

Production	*Cost element*	*Number of equivalent units*	*Cost per equivalent unit*	*Total*	*Cost*
			£	£	£
Completed production		3,200	2.30		7,360
Closing stock:	process 1 material	800	1.50	1,200	
	added material	400	0.30	120	
	labour and overhead	240	0.50	120	
					1,440
					8,800

(d) PROCESS ACCOUNT

	Units	£		Units	£
Process 1 material	4,000	6,000	Process 3 a/c	3,200	7,360
Added material		1,080			
Conversion costs		1,720	Closing stock c/f	800	1,440
	4,000	8,800		4,000	8,800

7 VALUING OPENING WORK IN PROGRESS: FIFO METHOD

7.1 Opening work in progress is partly complete at the beginning of a period and is valued at the cost incurred to date. In the example in Paragraph 6.12, closing work in progress of 800 units at the end of April 20X3 would be carried forward as opening stock, value £1,440, at the beginning of May 20X3.

7.2 It therefore follows that the work required to complete units of opening stock is 100% minus the work in progress done in the previous period. For example, if 100 units of opening stock are 70% complete at the beginning of June 20X2, the equivalent units of production would be as follows.

Equivalent units in previous period	(May 20X2) (70%)	=	70
Equivalent units to complete work in current period	(June 20X2) (30%)	=	30
Total work done			100

7.3 **The FIFO method of valuation** deals with production on a first in, first out basis. The assumption is that the first units completed in any period are the units of opening stock that were held at the beginning of the period.

7.4 EXAMPLE: WIP AND FIFO

Suppose that information relating to process 1 of a two-stage production process is as follows, for August 20X2.

Opening stock 500 units: degree of completion	60%
Cost to date	£2,800
Costs incurred in August 20X2	£
Direct materials (2,500 units introduced)	13,200
Direct labour	6,600
Production overhead	6,600
	26,400
Closing stock 300 units: degree of completion	80%

There was no loss in the process.

Required

Prepare the process 1 account for August 20X2.

7.5 SOLUTION

As the term implies, first in, first out means that in August 20X2 the first units completed were the units of opening stock.

Opening stocks:	work done to date =	60%
	plus work done in August 20X2 =	40%

The cost of the work done up to 1 August 20X2 is known to be £2,800, so that the cost of the units completed will be £2,800 plus the cost of completing the final 40% of the work on the units in August 20X2.

Once the opening stock has been completed, all other finished output in August 20X2 will be work started as well as finished in the month.

	Units
Total output in August 20X2 *	2,700
Less opening stock, completed first	500
Work started and finished in August 20X2	2,200

(* Opening stock plus units introduced minus closing stock = 500 + 2,500 – 300)

What we are doing here is taking the total output of 2,700 units, and saying that we must divide it into two parts as follows.

(a) The opening stock, which was first in and so must be first out.
(b) The rest of the units, which were 100% worked in the period.

Dividing finished output into two parts in this way is a necessary feature of the FIFO valuation method.

Continuing the example, closing stock of 300 units will be started in August 20X2, but not yet completed.

The total cost of output to process 2 during 20X2 will be as follows.

		£	
Opening stock	cost brought forward	2,800	(60%)
	plus cost incurred during August 20X2, to complete	x	(40%)
		2,800 + x	
Fully worked 2,200 units		y	
Total cost of output to process 2, FIFO basis		2,800 + x + y	

Equivalent units will again be used as the basis for apportioning **costs incurred during August 20X2**. Be sure that you understand the treatment of 'opening stock units completed', and can relate the calculations to the principles of FIFO valuation.

Step 1. **Determine output and losses**

STATEMENT OF EQUIVALENT UNITS

	Total units		*Equivalent units of production in August 20X2*
Opening stock units completed	500	(40%)	200
Fully worked units	2,200	(100%)	2,200
Output to process 2	2,700		2,400
Closing stock	300	(80%)	240
	3,000		2,640

Step 2. **Calculate cost per unit of output and losses**

The cost per equivalent unit in August 20X2 can now be calculated.

STATEMENT OF COST PER EQUIVALENT UNIT

$$\frac{\text{Cost incurred}}{\text{Equivalent units}} = \frac{£26,400}{2,640}$$

Cost per equivalent unit= £10

Step 3. **Calculate total costs of output, losses and WIP**

STATEMENT OF EVALUATION

	Equivalent units	*Valuation* £
Opening stock, work done in August 20X2	200	2,000
Fully worked units	2,200	22,000
Closing stock	240	2,400
	2,640	26,400

The total value of the completed opening stock will be £2,800 (brought forward) plus £2,000 added in August before completion = £4,800.

Step 4. **Complete accounts**

PROCESS 1 ACCOUNT

	Units	£		Units	£
Opening stock	500	2,800	Output to process 2:		
Direct materials	2,500	13,200	Opening stock completed	500	4,800
Direct labour		6,600	Fully worked units	2,200	22,000
Production o'hd		6,600		2,700	26,800
			Closing stock	300	2,400
	3,000	29,200		3,000	29,200

We now know that the value of x is £(4,800 – 2,800) = £2,000 and the value of y is £22,000.

Question 5

The following information relates to process 3 of a three-stage production process for the month of January 20X4.

Opening stock

		£
300 units complete as to:		
materials from process 2	100%	4,400
added materials	90%	1,150
labour	80%	540
production overhead	80%	810
		6,900

In January 20X4, a further 1,800 units were transferred from process 2 at a valuation of £27,000. Added materials amounted to £6,600 and direct labour to £3,270. Production overhead is absorbed at the rate of 150% of direct labour cost. Closing stock at 31 January 20X4 amounted to 450 units, complete as to:

process 2 materials	100%
added materials	60%
labour and overhead	50%

Required

Prepare the process 3 account for January 20X4 using FIFO valuation principles.

Answer

Step 1. **STATEMENT OF EQUIVALENT UNITS**

	Total units	Process 2 materials		Added materials		Conversion costs
Opening stock	300	0	(10%)	30	(20%)	60
Fully worked units *	1,350	1,350		1,350		1,350
Output to finished goods	1,650	1,350		1,380		1,410
Closing stock	450	450	(60%)	270	(50%)	225
	2,100	1,800		1,650		1,635

* Transfers from process 2, minus closing stock.

Step 2. **STATEMENT OF COSTS PER EQUIVALENT UNIT**

	Total cost £	Equivalent units	Cost per equivalent unit £
Process 2 materials	27,000	1,800	15.00
Added materials	6,600	1,650	4.00
Direct labour	3,270	1,635	2.00
Production overhead (150% of £3,270)	4,905	1,635	3.00
			24.00

Step 3. **STATEMENT OF EVALUATION**

	Process 2 materials £		Additional materials £		Labour £		Overhead £	Total £
Opening stock								
cost b/f	4,400		1,150		540		810	6,900
Added in Jan 20X4	-	(30x£4)	120	(60x£2)	120	(60x£3)	180	420
	4,400		1,270		660		990	7,320
Fully worked units	20,250		5,400		2,700		4,050	32,400
Output to finished								
Goods	24,650		6,670		3,360		5,040	39,720
Closing stock								
(450x£15)	6,750	(270x£4)	1,080	(225x£2)	450	(225x£3)	675	8,955
	31,400		7,750		3,810		5,715	48,675

Step 4. **COMPLETE ACCOUNTS**

PROCESS 3 ACCOUNT

	Units	£		Units	£
Opening stock b/f	300	6,900	Finished goods a/c	1,650	39,720
Process 2 a/c	1,800	27,000			
Stores a/c		6,600			
Wages a/c		3,270			
Production o'hd a/c		4,905	Closing stock c/f	450	8,955
	2,100	48,675		2,100	48,675

8 VALUING OPENING WORK IN PROGRESS: WEIGHTED AVERAGE COST METHOD

8.1 An alternative to FIFO is the **weighted average cost method of stock valuation** which calculates a weighted average cost of units produced from both opening stock and units introduced in the current period.

By this method **no distinction is made between units of opening stock and new units introduced** to the process during the accounting period. The cost of opening stock is added to costs incurred during the period, and completed units of opening stock are each given a value of one full equivalent unit of production.

8.2 EXAMPLE: WEIGHTED AVERAGE COST METHOD

Magpie Ltd produces an item which is manufactured in two consecutive processes. Information relating to process 2 during September 20X3 is as follows.

Opening stock 800 units		
Degree of completion:		£
process 1 materials	100%	4,700
added materials	40%	600
conversion costs	30%	1,000
		6,300

During September 20X3, 3,000 units were transferred from process 1 at a valuation of £18,100. Added materials cost £9,600 and conversion costs were £11,800.

Closing stock at 30 September 20X3 amounted to 1,000 units which were 100% complete with respect to process 1 materials and 60% complete with respect to added materials. Conversion cost work was 40% complete.

Magpie Ltd uses a weighted average cost system for the valuation of output and closing stock.

Required

Prepare the process 2 account for September 20X3.

8.3 SOLUTION

Step 1. Opening stock units count as a full equivalent unit of production when the weighted average cost system is applied. Closing stock equivalent units are assessed in the usual way.

STATEMENT OF EQUIVALENT UNITS

	Total units		Process 1 material	Equivalent units: Added material		Conversion costs
Opening stock	800	(100%)	800	800		800
Fully worked units*	2,000	(100%)	2,000	2,000		2,000
Output to finished goods	2,800		2,800	2,800		2,800
Closing stock	1,000	(100%)	1,000	(60%) 600	(40%)	400
	3,800		3,800	3,400		3,200

(*3,000 units from process 1 minus closing stock of 1,000 units)

Step 2. The cost of opening stock is added to costs incurred in September 20X3, and a cost per equivalent unit is then calculated.

STATEMENT OF COSTS PER EQUIVALENT UNIT

	Process 1 material £	*Added materials* £	*Conversion costs* £
Opening stock	4,700	600	1,000
Added in September 20X3	18,100	9,600	11,800
Total cost	22,800	10,200	12,800
Equivalent units	3,800 units	3,400 units	3,200 units
Cost per equivalent unit	£6	£3	£4

Step 3. STATEMENT OF EVALUATION

	Process 1 material £	*Added materials* £	*Conversion costs* £	*Total cost* £
Output to finished goods (2,800 units)	16,800	8,400	11,200	36,400
Closing stock	6,000	1,800	1,600	9,400
				45,800

Step 4. PROCESS 2 ACCOUNT

	Units	£		Units	£
Opening stock b/f	800	6,300	Finished goods a/c	2,800	36,400
Process 1 a/c	3,000	18,100			
Added materials		9,600			
Conversion costs		11,800	Closing stock c/f	1,000	9,400
	3,800	45,800		3,800	45,800

Which method should be used?

8.4 **FIFO stock valuation is more common than the weighted average method, and should be used unless an indication is given to the contrary.** You may find that you are presented with limited information about the opening stock, which forces you to use either the FIFO or the weighted average method. The rules are as follows.

(a) If you are told the degree of completion of each element in opening stock, but not the value of each cost element, then you must use the **FIFO method.**

(b) If you are not given the degree of completion of each cost element in opening stock, but you are given the value of each cost element, then you must use the **weighted average method.**

8.5 Question 6 involves the following process costing situations.

- Normal loss (with and without sale of scrap)
- Abnormal loss
- Abnormal gain
- Opening work in progress
- Closing work in progress

Take time to work through this question carefully and to check your workings against the answer given below. This is an excellent question which should help you to consolidate all of the process costing knowledge that you have acquired whilst studying this chapter.

Question 6

Watkins Ltd has a financial year which ends on 30 April. It operates in a processing industry in which a single product is produced by passing inputs through two sequential processes. A normal loss of 10% of input is expected in each process.

The following account balances have been extracted from its ledger at 31 March 20X0.

	Debit	*Credit*
	£	£
Process 1 (Materials £4,400; Conversion costs £3,744)	8,144	
Process 2 (Process 1 £4,431; Conversion costs £5,250)	9,681	
Abnormal loss	1,400	
Abnormal gain		300
Overhead control account		250
Sales		585,000
Cost of sales	442,500	
Finished goods stock	65,000	

Watkins Ltd uses the weighted average method of accounting for work in process.

During April 20X0 the following transactions occurred.

Process 1	Materials input	4,000 kg costing	£22,000
	Labour cost		£12,000
	Transfer to process 2	2,400 kg	
Process 2	Transfer from process 1	2,400 kg	
	Labour cost		£15,000
	Transfer to finished goods	2,500 kg	

Overhead costs incurred amounted to	£54,000
Sales to customers were	£52,000

Overhead costs are absorbed into process costs on the basis of 150% of labour cost.

The losses which arise in process 1 have no scrap value: those arising in process 2 can be sold for £2 per kg.

Details of opening and closing work in process for the month of April 20X0 are as follows.

	Opening	*Closing*
Process 1	3,000 kg	3,400 kg
Process 2	2,250 kg	2,600 kg

In both processes closing work in process is fully complete as to material cost and 40% complete as to conversion cost.

Stocks of finished goods at 30 April 20X0 were valued at cost of £60,000.

Required

Prepare the Process 1 and Process 2 accounts for April 20X0 for Watkins Ltd.

Answer

(a) **Process 1**

STATEMENT OF EQUIVALENT UNITS

		Equivalent units	
	Total units	*Material costs*	*Conversion costs*
Transfers to process 2	2,400	2,400	2,400
Closing WIP	3,400	(100%) 3,400	(40%) 1,360
Normal loss (10% × 4,000)	400	0	0
Abnormal loss	800	800	800
	7,000	6,600	4,560

STATEMENT OF COSTS PER EQUIVALENT UNIT

$$\frac{\text{Costs incurred}}{\text{Equivalent units}} = \text{Cost per equivalent unit}$$

$$\therefore \text{Materials cost per equivalent unit} = \frac{£4,400 + £22,000}{6,600}$$

$$= \frac{£26,400}{6,600} = £4$$

$$\therefore \text{Conversion costs per equivalent unit} = \frac{£3,744 + £12,000 + £18,000}{4,560}$$

$$= \frac{£33,744}{4,560} = £7.40$$

STATEMENT OF EVALUATION

	Materials	*Conversion costs*	*Total*
	£	£	£
Transfers to process 2	9,600	17,760	27,360
Abnormal loss	3,200	5,920	9,120
Closing WIP	13,600	10,064	23,664
	26,400	33,744	60,144

PROCESS 1 ACCOUNT

	Kg	£		Kg	£
WIP materials	3,000	4,400	Process 2	2,400	27,360
WIP conversion costs	-	3,744	Normal loss	400	-
Materials	4,000	22,000	Abnormal loss	800	9,120
Labour	-	12,000	WIP materials	3,400	13,600
Overhead	-	18,000	WIP conversion costs	-	10,064
	7,000	60,144		7,000	60,144

(b) **Process 2**

STATEMENT OF EQUIVALENT UNITS

	Total units	*Process 1*	*Conversion costs*
Finished goods	2,500	2,500	2,500
Normal loss	240	0	0
Abnormal gain	(690)	(690)	(690)
Closing WIP	2,600*	2,600	1,040**
	4,650	4,410	2,850

*Total input units = opening WIP + input = 2,250 + 2,400 = 4,650
Total output units = finished goods + closing WIP + normal loss – abnormal gain
= 2,500 + 2,600 + 240 – 690
= 4,650

**2,600 × 40% = 1,040

STATEMENT OF COSTS PER EQUIVALENT UNIT

Process 1 = $\dfrac{£4{,}431 + £27{,}360 - 480}{4{,}410}$ = £7.10

Conversion costs = $\dfrac{£5{,}250 + £15{,}000 + £22{,}500}{2{,}850}$ = £15.00

STATEMENT OF EVALUATION

	Process 1	*Conversion costs*	*Total*
Finished goods	17,750	37,500	55,250
Abnormal gain	4,899	10,350	15,249
Closing WIP	18,460	15,600	34,060
	41,109	63,450	104,559

PROCESS 2 ACCOUNT

	Kg	£		Kg	£
WIP Process 1	2,250	4,431	Finished goods	2,500	55,250
WIP conversion costs	-	5,250	Normal loss	240	480
Process 1	2,400	27,360	WIP Process 1	2,600	18,460
Labour	-	15,000	WIP conversion costs	-	15,600
Overhead	-	22,500			
Abnormal gain	690	15,249			
	5,340	89,790		5,340	89,790

8.6 The diagram shown on the next page summarises all of the main points about process costing that we have covered in this chapter.

Chapter roundup

- Many students find process costing daunting. It shouldn't be. Use our suggested four-step approach to dealing with questions and you should find the topic quite straightforward.

  Step 1. Determine output and losses
  Step 2. Calculate cost per unit of output, losses and WIP
  Step 3. Calculate total cost of output, losses and WIP
  Step 4. Complete accounts

- **Process costing** is used where there is a continuous flow of identical units.
- Losses may occur in process. If a certain level of loss is expected, this is known as **normal loss**. If losses are greater than expected, the extra loss is **abnormal loss**. If losses are less than expected, the difference is known as **abnormal gain**.
- It is conventional for the **scrap value** of normal loss to be deducted from the cost of materials before a cost per equivalent unit is calculated.
- Abnormal losses and gains never affect the cost of good units of production. The scrap value of abnormal losses is not credited to the process account, and abnormal loss and gain units carry the same full cost as a good unit of production.
- When units are partly completed at the end of a period (and hence there is closing work in progress), it is necessary to calculate the **equivalent units of production** in order to determine the cost of a completed unit.
- Account can be taken of opening work in progress using either the **FIFO** method or the **weighted average cost method.**

SUMMARY DIAGRAM

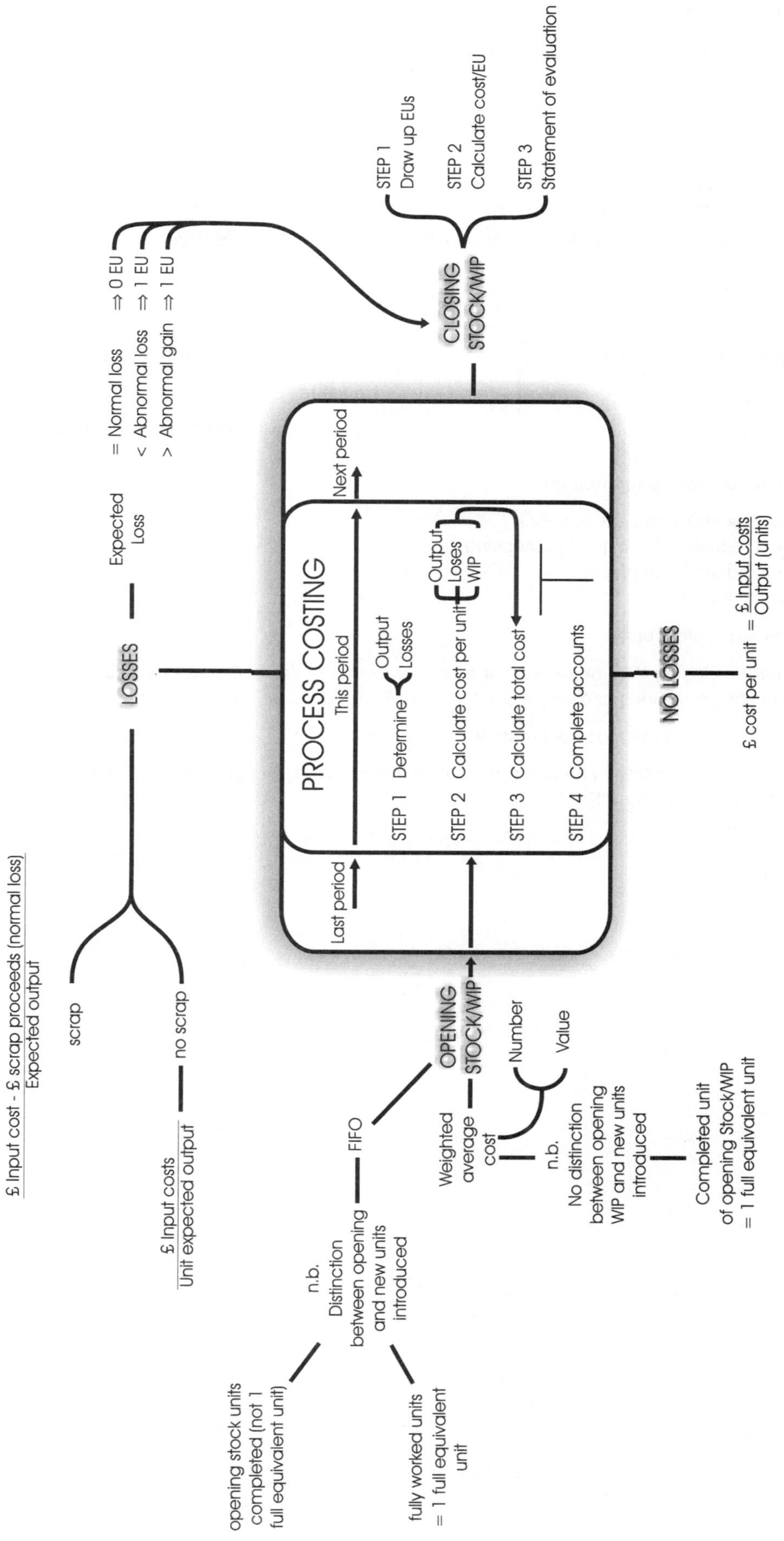

Quick quiz

1 Define process costing.

2 Process costing is centred around four key steps.

Step 1. ....

Step 2. ....

Step 3. ....

Step 4. ....

3 Abnormal gains result when actual loss is less than normal or expected loss.

True ☐

False ☐

4

Normal loss (no scrap value)		Same value as good output (positive cost)
Abnormal loss	?	No value
Abnormal gain		Same value as good output (negative cost)

5 How is revenue from scrap treated?

A As an addition to sales revenue
B As a reduction in costs of processing
C As a bonus to employees
D Any of the above

6 What is an equivalent unit?

7 When there is closing WIP at the end of a process, what is the first step in the four-step approach to process costing questions and why must it be done?

8 What is the weighted average cost method of stock valuation?

9 Unless given an indication to the contrary, the weighted average cost method of stock valuation should be used to value opening WIP.

True ☐

False ☐

Answers to quick quiz

1 **Process costing** is a costing method used where it is not possible to identify separate units of production, or jobs, usually because of the continuous nature of the production processes involved.

2 ***Step 1.*** Determine output and losses
Step 2. Calculate cost per unit of output, losses and WIP
Step 3. Calculate total cost of output, losses and WIP
Step 4. Complete accounts

3 True

4 Normal loss (no scrap value) → No value
Abnormal loss → Same value as good output (positive cost)
Abnormal gain → Same value as good output (negative cost)

5 B

6 An **equivalent unit** is a notional whole unit which represents incomplete work, and which is used to apportion costs between work in process and completed output.

7 ***Step 1.*** It is necessary to calculate the equivalent units of production (by drawing up a statement of equivalent units). Equivalent units of production are notional whole units which represent incomplete work and which are used to apportion costs between work in progress and completed output.

8 A method where no distinction is made between units of opening stock and new units introduced to the process during the current period.

9 False. FIFO stock valuation is more common than the weighted average method and should be used unless an indication is given to the contrary.

Now try the questions below from the Exam Question Bank

Number	Level	Marks	Time
18	MCQ	n/a	n/a
19	Examination	10	18 mins

Chapter 12

PROCESS COSTING, JOINT PRODUCTS AND BY-PRODUCTS

Topic list		Syllabus reference
1	Contrasting joint products and by-products	4(a)
2	Problems in accounting for joint products	4(a)
3	Dealing with common costs	4(a)
4	Joint products in process accounts	4(a)
5	Accounting for by-products	4(a)

Introduction

You should now be aware of the most simple and the more complex areas of process costing. In this chapter we are going to turn our attention to the methods of accounting for **joint products** and **by-products** which arise as a result of a **continuous process**.

Study guide

Section 17 – Process costing 2

- Distinguish between by-products and joint products
- Value by-products and joint products at the point of separation
- Prepare process accounts in situations where by-products and/or joint products occur

Exam guide

Even though this is part of the topic **process costing**, which is a key area of the syllabus, you are unlikely to be examined on **joint products** and **by-products** in Section B of the paper-based examination. Be prepared to answer multiple choice questions, however, on the contents of this chapter.

1 CONTRASTING JOINT PRODUCTS AND BY-PRODUCTS

KEY TERMS

- **Joint products** are two or more products which are output from the same processing operation, but which are indistinguishable from each other up to their point of separation.
- A **by-product** is a supplementary or secondary product (arising as the result of a process) whose value is small relative to that of the principal product.

1.1 (a) Joint products have a **substantial sales value**. Often they require further processing before they are ready for sale. Joint products arise, for example, in the oil refining industry where diesel fuel, petrol, paraffin and lubricants are all produced from the same process.

(b) The distinguishing feature of a by-product is its **relatively low sales value** in comparison to the main product. In the timber industry, for example, by-products include sawdust, small offcuts and bark.

1.2 **What exactly separates a joint product from a by-product?**

(a) A **joint product** is regarded as an important saleable item, and so it should be **separately costed**. The profitability of each joint product should be assessed in the cost accounts.

(b) A **by-product** is not important as a saleable item, and whatever revenue it earns is a 'bonus' for the organisation. Because of their relative insignificance, by-products are **not separately costed**.

Exam focus point

The study guide for Paper 1.2 states that you must be able to 'distinguish between by-products and joint products'.

2 PROBLEMS IN ACCOUNTING FOR JOINT PRODUCTS

2.1 Joint products are not separately identifiable until a certain stage is reached in the processing operations. This stage is the '**split-off point**', sometimes referred to as the **separation point**. Costs incurred prior to this point of separation are **common** or **joint costs**, and these need to be allocated (apportioned) in some manner to each of the joint products. In the following sketched example, there are two different split-off points.

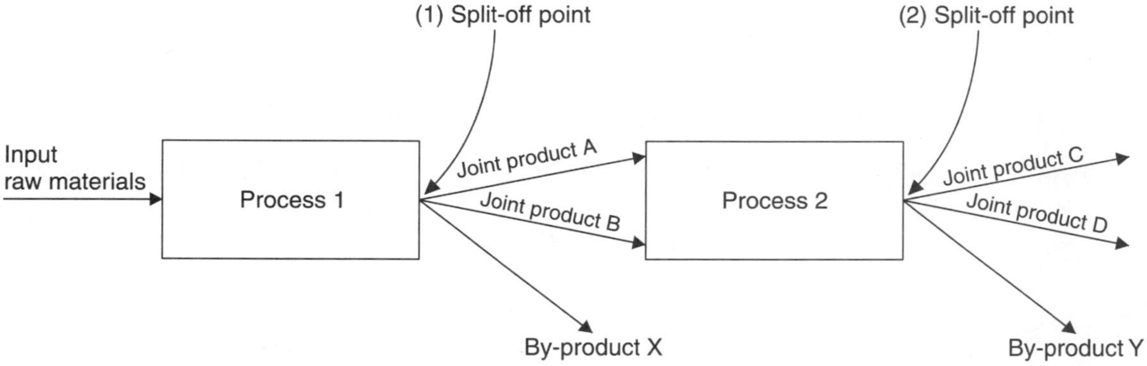

2.2 The **problems in accounting for joint products** are basically of two different sorts.

(a) How common costs should be apportioned between products, in order to put a value to closing stocks and to the cost of sale (and profit) for each product.

(b) Whether it is more profitable to sell a joint product at one stage of processing, or to process the product further and sell it at a later stage.

3 DEALING WITH COMMON COSTS

3.1 The problem of costing for joint products concerns **common costs**, that is those common processing costs shared between the units of eventual output up to their 'split-off point'.

Some method needs to be devised for sharing the common costs between the individual joint products for the following reasons.

(a) To put a value to closing stocks of each joint product.
(b) To record the costs and therefore the profit from each joint product.
(c) Perhaps to assist in pricing decisions.

3.2 Here are some examples of the common costs problem.

(a) How to spread the common costs of oil refining between the joint products made (petrol, naphtha, kerosene and so on).

(b) How to spread the common costs of running the telephone network between telephone calls in peak and cheap rate times, or between local and long distance calls.

3.3 Various methods that might be used to establish a basis for apportioning or allocating common costs to each product are as follows.

- Physical measurement
- Relative sales value apportionment method; sales value at split-off point

Dealing with common costs: physical measurement

3.4 With physical measurement, **the common cost is apportioned to the joint products on the basis of the proportion that the output of each product bears by weight or volume to the total output.** An example of this would be the case where two products, product 1 and product 2, incur common costs to the point of separation of £3,000 and the output of each product is 600 tons and 1,200 tons respectively.

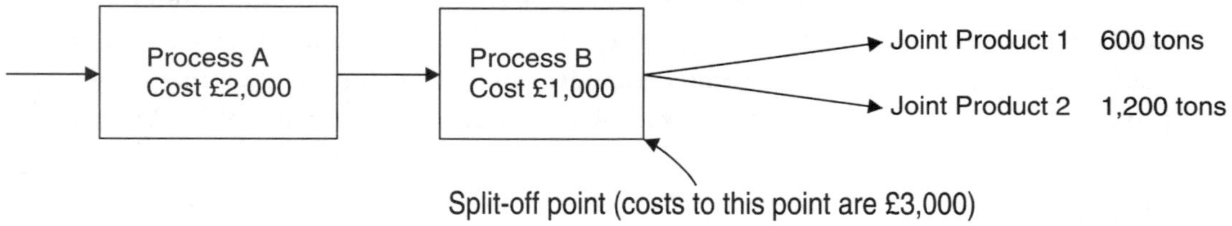

Product 1 sells for £4 per ton and product 2 for £2 per ton.

The division of the common costs (£3,000) between product 1 and product 2 could be based on the tonnage of output.

	Product 1		*Product 2*	*Total*
Output	600 tons	+	1,200 tons	1,800 tons
Proportion of common cost	$\frac{600}{1,800}$	+	$\frac{1,200}{1,800}$	
	£		£	£
Apportioned cost	1,000		2,000	3,000
Sales	2,400		2,400	4,800
Profit	1,400		400	1,800
Profit/sales ratio	58.3%		16.7%	37.5%

3.5 Physical measurement has the following limitations.

(a) Where the products separate during the processes into different states, for example where one product is a gas and another is a liquid, this method is unsuitable.

(b) This method does not take into account the relative income-earning potentials of the individual products, with the result that one product might appear very profitable and another appear to be incurring losses.

Dealing with common costs: sales value at split-off point

3.6 With relative sales value apportionment of common costs, **the cost is allocated according to the product's ability to produce income**. This method is most widely used because the assumption that some profit margin should be attained for all products under normal marketing conditions is satisfied. The common cost is apportioned to each product in the proportion that the sales (market) value of that product bears to the sales value of the total output from the particular processes concerned. Using the previous example where the sales price per unit is £4 for product 1 and £2 for product 2.

(a) Common costs of processes to split-off point	£3,000
(b) Sales value of product 1 at £4 per ton	£2,400
(c) Sales value of product 2 at £2 per ton	£2,400

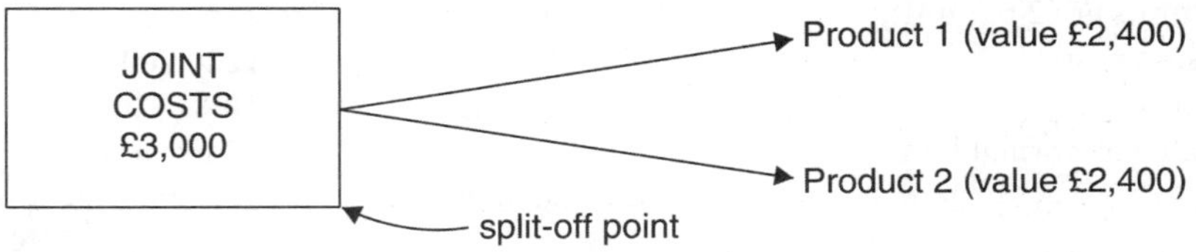

	Product 1	*Product 2*	*Total*
Sales	£2,400	£2,400	£4,800
Proportion of common cost apportioned	2,400 / 4,800	2,400 / 4,800	
	£	£	£
Apportioned cost	1,500	1,500	3,000
Sales	2,400	2,400	4,800
Profit	900	900	1,800
Profit/sales ratio	37.5%	37.5%	37.5%

3.7 A comparison of the gross profit margin resulting from the application of the above methods for allocating common costs will illustrate the greater acceptability of the relative sales value apportionment method. Physical measurement gives a higher profit margin to product 1, not necessarily because product 1 is highly profitable, but because it has been given a smaller share of common costs.

Question 1

In process costing, a joint product is

A A product which is produced simultaneously with other products but which is of lesser value than at least one of the other products

B A product which is produced simultaneously with other products and is of similar value to at least one of the other products

C A product which is produced simultaneously with other products but which is of greater value than any of the other products

D A product produced jointly with another organisation

Answer

The correct answer is B, a product which is of similar value to at least one of the other products.

4 JOINT PRODUCTS IN PROCESS ACCOUNTS

4.1 This example illustrates how joint products are incorporated into process accounts.

EXAMPLE: JOINT PRODUCTS AND PROCESS ACCOUNTS

Three joint products are manufactured in a common process, which consists of two consecutive stages. Output from process 1 is transferred to process 2, and output from process 2 consists of the three joint products, Hans, Nils and Bumpsydaisies. All joint products are sold as soon as they are produced.

Data for period 2 of 20X6 are as follows.

	Process 1	*Process 2*
Opening and closing stock	None	None
Direct material		
(30,000 units at £2 per unit)	£60,000	-
Conversion costs	£76,500	£226,200
Normal loss	10% of input	10% of input
Scrap value of normal loss	£0.50 per unit	£2 per unit
Output	26,000 units	10,000 units of Han
		7,000 units of Nil
		6,000 units of Bumpsydaisy

Selling prices are £18 per unit of Han, £20 per unit of Nil and £30 per unit of Bumpsydaisy.

Required

(a) Prepare the Process 1 account.
(b) Prepare the Process 2 account using the sales value method of apportionment.
(c) Prepare a profit statement for the joint products.

4.2 SOLUTION

(a) **Process 1 equivalent units**

	Total units	*Equivalent units*
Output to process 2	26,000	26,000
Normal loss	3,000	0
Abnormal loss (balance)	1,000	1,000
	30,000	27,000

Costs of process 1

	£
Direct materials	60,000
Conversion costs	76,500
	136,500
Less scrap value of normal loss (3,000 × £0.50)	1,500
	135,000

$$\text{Cost per equivalent unit} = \frac{£135{,}000}{27{,}000} = £5$$

PROCESS 1 ACCOUNT

	£		£
Direct materials	60,000	Output to process 2	
Conversion costs	76,500	(26,000 × £5)	130,000
		Normal loss (scrap value)	1,500
		Abnormal loss a/c	
		(1,000 × £5)	5,000
	136,500		136,500

(b) **Process 2 equivalent units**

	Total units	*Equivalent units*
Units of Hans produced	10,000	10,000
Units of Nils produced	7,000	7,000
Units of Bumpsydaisies produced	6,000	6,000
Normal loss (10% of 26,000)	2,600	0
Abnormal loss (balance)	400	400
	26,000	23,400

Costs of process 2

	£
Material costs - from process 1	130,000
Conversion costs	226,200
	356,200
Less scrap value of normal loss (2,600 × £2)	5,200
	351,000

Cost per equivalent unit $\frac{£351,000}{23,400} = £15$

Cost of good output (10,000 + 7,000 + 6,000) = 23,000 units × £15 = £345,000

The sales value of joint products, and the apportionment of the output costs of £345,000, is as follows.

	Sales value £	%	*Costs (process 2)* £
Hans (10,000 × £18)	180,000	36	124,200
Nils (7,000 × £20)	140,000	28	96,600
Bumpsydaisy (6,000 × £30)	180,000	36	124,200
	500,000	100	345,000

PROCESS 2 ACCOUNT

	£		£
Process 1 materials	130,000	Finished goods accounts	
Conversion costs	226,200	- Hans	124,200
		- Nils	96,600
		- Bumpsydaisies	124,200
		Normal loss (scrap value)	5,200
		Abnormal loss a/c	6,000
	356,200		356,200

(c) PROFIT STATEMENT

	Hans £'000	*Nils* £'000	*Bumpsydaisies* £'000
Sales	180.0	140.0	180.0
Costs	124.2	96.6	124.2
Profit	55.8	43.4	55.8
Profit/ sales ratio	31%	31%	31%

Question 2

Prepare the Process 2 account and a profit statement for the joint products in the above example using the units basis of apportionment.

Answer

PROCESS 2 ACCOUNT

	£		£
Process 1 materials	130,000	Finished goods accounts	
Conversion costs	226,200	- Hans (10,000 × £15)	150,000
		- Nils (7,000 × £15)	105,000
		- Bumpsydaisies (6,000 × £15)	90,000
		Normal loss (scrap value)	5,200
		Abnormal loss a/c (400 × £15)	6,000
	356,200		356,200

PROFIT STATEMENT

	Hans	*Nils*	*Bumpsydaisies*
	£'000	£'000	£'000
Sales	180	140	180
Costs	150	105	90
Profit	30	35	90
Profit/ sales ratio	16.7%	25%	50%

5 ACCOUNTING FOR BY-PRODUCTS

5.1 A by-product has some commercial value and any income generated from it may be treated as follows.

(a) Income (minus any post-separation further processing or selling costs) from the sale of the by-product may be **added to sales of the main product**, thereby increasing sales turnover for the period.

(b) The sales of the by-product may be **treated as a separate, incidental source of income** against which are set only post-separation costs (if any) of the by-product. The revenue would be recorded in the profit and loss account as 'other income'.

(c) The sales income of the by-product may be **deducted from the cost of production** or cost of sales of the main product.

(d) The **net realisable value of the by-product may be deducted from the cost of production of the main product**. The net realisable value is the final saleable value of the by-product minus any post-separation costs. Any closing stock valuation of the main product or joint products would therefore be reduced.

The choice of method (a), (b), (c) or (d) will be influenced by the circumstances of production and ease of calculation, as much as by conceptual correctness. The method you are most likely to come across in examinations is method (d). An example will help to clarify the distinction between the different methods.

5.2 EXAMPLE: METHODS OF ACCOUNTING FOR BY-PRODUCTS

During November 20X3, Splatter Ltd recorded the following results.

Opening stock	main product P, nil by-product Z, nil
Cost of production	£120,000

Sales of the main product amounted to 90% of output during the period, and 10% of production was held as closing stock at 30 November.

Sales revenue from the main product during November 20X2 was £150,000.

A by-product Z is produced, and output had a net sales value of £1,000. Of this output, £700 was sold during the month, and £300 was still in stock at 30 November.

Required

Calculate the profit for November using the four methods of accounting for by-products.

5.3 SOLUTION

The four methods of accounting for by-products are shown below.

(a) **Income from by-product added to sales of the main product**

	£	£
Sales of main product (£150,000 + £700)		150,700
Opening stock	0	
Cost of production	120,000	
	120,000	
Less closing stock (10%)	12,000	
Cost of sales		108,000
Profit, main product		42,700

The closing stock of the by-product has no recorded value in the cost accounts.

(b) **By-product income treated as a separate source of income**

	£	£
Sales, main product		150,000
Opening stock	0	
Cost of production	120,000	
	120,000	
Closing stock (10%)	12,000	
Cost of sales, main product		108,000
Profit, main product		42,000
Other income		700
Total profit		42,700

The closing stock of the by-product again has no value in the cost accounts.

(c) **Sales income of the by-product deducted from the cost of production in the period**

	£	£
Sales, main product		150,000
Opening stock	0	
Cost of production (120,000 – 700)	119,300	
	119,300	
Less closing stock (10%)	11,930	
Cost of sales		107,370
Profit, main product		42,630

Although the profit is different from the figure in (a) and (b), the by-product closing stock again has no value.

(d) **Net realisable value of the by-product deducted from the cost of production in the period**

	£	£
Sales, main product		150,000
Opening stock	0	
Cost of production (120,000 – 1,000)	119,000	
	119,000	
Less closing stock (10%)	11,900	
Cost of sales		107,100
Profit, main product		42,900

As with the other three methods, closing stock of the by-product has no value in the books of accounting, but the value of the closing stock (£300) has been used to reduce the cost of production, and in this respect it has been allowed for in deriving the cost of sales and the profit for the period.

Question 3

Randolph Ltd manufactures two joint products, J and K, in a common process. A by-product X is also produced. Data for the month of December 20X2 were as follows.

Opening stocks	nil	
Costs of processing	direct materials	£25,500
	direct labour	£10,000

Production overheads are absorbed at the rate of 300% of direct labour costs.

		Production	*Sales*
		Units	Units
Output and sales consisted of:	product J	8,000	7,000
	product K	8,000	6,000
	by-product X	1,000	1,000

The sales value per unit of J, K and X is £4, £6 and £0.50 respectively. The saleable value of the by-product is deducted from process costs before apportioning costs to each joint product. Costs of the common processing are apportioned between product J and product K on the basis of sales value of production.

The individual profits for December 20X2 are:

	Product J	*Product K*
	£	£
A	5,250	6,750
B	6,750	5,250
C	22,750	29,250
D	29,250	22,750

Answer

The sales value of production was £80,000.

	£	
Product J (8,000 × £4)	32,000	(40%)
Product K (8,000 × £6)	48,000	(60%)
	80,000	

	£
The costs of production were as follows.	
Direct materials	25,500
Direct labour	10,000
Overhead (300% of £10,000)	30,000
	65,500
Less sales value of by-product (1,000 × 50p)	500
Net production costs	65,000

The profit statement would appear as follows (nil opening stocks).

		Product J		Product K	Total
		£		£	£
Production costs	(40%)	26,000	(60%)	39,000	65,000
Less closing stock	(1,000 units)	3,250	(2,000 units)	9,750	13,000
Cost of sales		22,750		29,250	52,000
Sales	(7,000 units)	28,000	(6,000 units)	36,000	64,000
Profit		5,250		6,750	12,000

The correct answer is therefore A.

If you selected option B, you got the profits for each product mixed up.

If you selected option C or D, you calculated the cost of sales instead of the profit.

Chapter roundup

- **Joint products** are two or more products separated in a process, each of which has a **significant value** compared to the other. A **by-product** is an incidental product from a process which has an **insignificant value** compared to the main product.
- The point at which joint and by-products become separately identifiable is known as the **split-off point** or **separation point**. Costs incurred up to this point are called common costs or joint costs.
- The main methods of apportioning joint costs, each of which can produce significantly different results are as follows.
  - Physical measurement
  - Relative sales value apportionment method; sales value at split-off point
- The **relative sales value method** is most widely used because (ignoring the effect of further processing costs) it assumes that all products achieve the same profit margin.
- The most common method of accounting for by-products is to deduct the **net realisable value** of the by-product from the cost of the main products.

Quick quiz

1 What is the difference between a joint product and a by-product?

2 What is meant by the term 'split-off' point?

3 Name two methods of apportioning common costs to joint products.

4 Describe the four methods of accounting for by-products.

Answers to quick quiz

1 A **joint product** is regarded as an important saleable item whereas a **by-product** is not.

2 The **split-off point** (or the **separation point**) is the point at which joint products become separately identifiable in a processing operation.

3 Physical measurement and sales value at split-off point.

4 See paragraph 5.1.

Now try the questions below from the Exam Question Bank

Number	Level	Marks	Time
20	OT	n/a	n/a
21	Examination	10	18 mins

Chapter 13

SERVICE COSTING

Topic list		Syllabus reference
1	What is service costing?	4(b)
2	Unit cost measures	4(b)
3	Service cost analysis	4(b)
4	Service cost analysis in internal service situations	4(b)
5	The usefulness of costing services that do not earn revenue	4(b)
6	Service cost analysis in service industry situations	4(b)

Introduction

Having covered job, batch, contract and process costing, we will now turn our attention to **service costing**, the service being a **specialist service** provided to third parties or an **internal service** provided within an organisation. The chapter looks at the calculation of a cost per unit of service and at methods of cost accounting in both types of situation.

Study guide

Section 18 – Operation/service costing

- Describe situations where the use of operation/service costing is appropriate
- Illustrate suitable unit cost measures that may be used in a variety of different operations and services
- Carry out service cost analysis in internal service situations
- Carry out service cost analysis in service industry situations

Exam guide

Service costing is not one of the key areas of the syllabus and is most likely to be examined in the form of multiple choice questions.

1 WHAT IS SERVICE COSTING?

KEY TERM

Service costing (or **function costing**) is a costing method concerned with establishing the costs, not of items of production, but of services rendered.

1.1 Service costing is used in the following circumstances.

(a) A company operating in a service industry will cost its services, for which sales revenue will be earned; examples are electricians, car hire services, road, rail or air transport services and hotels.

(b) A company may wish to establish the cost of services carried out by some of its departments; for example the costs of the vans or lorries used in distribution, the costs of the computer department, or the staff canteen.

1.2 Service costing differs from product costing (such as job or process costing) in the following ways.

(a) With many services, the cost of direct materials consumed will be relatively small compared to the labour, direct expenses and overheads cost. In product costing the direct materials are often a greater proportion of the total cost.

(b) Although many services are revenue-earning, others are not (such as the distribution facility or the staff canteen). This means that the purpose of service costing may not be to establish a profit or loss (nor to value closing stocks for the balance sheet) but may rather be to provide management information about the comparative costs or efficiency of the services, with a view to helping managers to budget for their costs using historical data as a basis for estimating costs in the future and to control the costs in the service departments.

(c) The procedures for recording material costs, labour hours and other expenses will vary according to the nature of the service.

1.3 Specific characteristics of services are **intangibility, simultaneity, perishability** and **heterogeneity.** Consider the service of providing a haircut.

(a) A haircut is **intangible** in itself, and the performance of the service comprises many other intangible factors, like the music in the salon, the personality of the hairdresser, the quality of the coffee.

(b) The production and consumption of a haircut are **simultaneous,** and therefore it cannot be inspected for quality in advance, nor can it be returned if it is not what was required.

(c) Haircuts are **perishable,** that is, they cannot be stored. You cannot buy them in bulk, and the hairdresser cannot do them in advance and keep them stocked away in case of heavy demand. The incidence of work in progress in service organisations is less frequent than in other types of organisation.

(d) A haircut is **heterogeneous** and so the exact service received will vary each time: not only will two hairdressers cut hair differently, but a hairdresser will not consistently deliver the same standard of haircut.

2 UNIT COST MEASURES

2.1 One particular problem with service costing is the **difficulty in defining a realistic cost unit** that represents a suitable measure of the service provided. Frequently, a composite cost unit may be deemed more appropriate. Hotels, for example, may use the 'occupied bed-night' as an appropriate unit for cost ascertainment and control.

2.2 Typical cost units used by companies operating in a service industry are shown below.

Service	Cost unit
Road, rail and air transport services	Passenger/mile or kilometre, ton/mile, tonne/ kilometre
Hotels	Occupied bed-night
Education	Full-time student
Hospitals	Patient
Catering establishment	Meal served

Question 1

Can you think of examples of cost units for internal services such as canteens, distribution and maintenance?

Answer

Service	*Cost unit*
Canteen	Meal served
Vans and lorries used in distribution	Mile or kilometre, ton/mile, tonne/kilometre
Maintenance	Man hour

2.3 Each organisation will need to ascertain the **cost unit** most appropriate to its activities. If a number of organisations within an industry use a common cost unit, then valuable comparisons can be made between similar establishments. This is particularly applicable to hospitals, educational establishments and local authorities. Whatever cost unit is decided upon, the calculation of a cost per unit is as follows.

FORMULA TO LEARN

$$\textbf{Cost per service unit} = \frac{\text{Total costs for period}}{\text{Number of service units in the period}}$$

3 SERVICE COST ANALYSIS

3.1 **Service cost analysis** should be performed in a manner which ensures that the following objectives are attained.

(a) Planned costs should be compared with actual costs.

Differences should be investigated and corrective action taken as necessary.

(b) A cost per unit of service should be calculated.

If each service has a number of variations (such as maintenance services provided by plumbers, electricians and carpenters) then the calculation of a cost per unit of each service may be necessary.

(c) The cost per unit of service should be used as part of the control function.

For example, costs per unit of service can be compared, month by month, period by period, year by year and so on and any unusual trends can be investigated.

(d) Prices should be calculated for services being sold to third parties.

The procedure is similar to job costing. A mark-up is added to the cost per unit of service to arrive at a selling price.

(e) Costs should be analysed into fixed, variable and semi-variable costs to help assist management with planning, control and decision making.

4 SERVICE COST ANALYSIS IN INTERNAL SERVICE SITUATIONS

Exam focus point

The study guide for Paper 1.2 specifically mentions that candidates must be able to 'carry out service cost analysis in **internal service** situations'.

Transport costs

4.1 '**Transport costs**' is a term used here to refer to the costs of the transport services used by a company, rather than the costs of a transport organisation, such as British Rail.

4.2 If a company has a fleet of lorries or vans which it uses to distribute its goods, it is useful to know how much the department is costing for a number of reasons.

(a) Management should be able to budget for expected costs, and to control actual expenditure on transport by comparing actual costs with budgeted costs.

(b) The company may charge customers for delivery or 'carriage outwards' costs, and a charge based on the cost of the transport service might be appropriate.

(c) If management knows how much its own transport is costing, a comparison can be made with alternative forms of transport (independent transport companies, British Rail) to decide whether a cheaper or better method of delivery can be found.

(d) Similarly, if a company uses, say, a fleet of lorries, knowledge of how much transport by lorry costs should help management to decide whether another type of vehicle, say vans, would be cheaper to use.

4.3 Transport costs may be analysed to provide the cost of operating one van or lorry each year, but it is more informative to analyse costs as follows.

(a) The cost per mile or kilometre travelled.

(b) The cost per ton/mile or tonne/kilometre (the cost of carrying one tonne of goods for one kilometre distance) or the cost per kilogram/metre.

4.4 For example, suppose that a company lorry makes five deliveries in a week.

Delivery	*Tonnes carried*	*Distance (one way)* Kilometres	*Tonne/kilometres carried*
1	0.4	180	72
2	0.3	360	108
3	1.2	100	120
4	0.8	250	200
5	1.0	60	60
			560

If the costs of operating the lorry during the week are known to be £840, the cost per tonne/kilometre would be:

$$\frac{\text{£}840}{560\text{tonne/kilometre}} = \text{£}1.50 \text{ per tonne/kilometre}$$

4.5 Transport costs might be collected under five broad headings.

(a) **Running costs** such as petrol, oil, drivers' wages
(b) **Loading costs** (the labour costs of loading the lorries with goods for delivery)
(c) **Servicing, repairs**, spare parts and tyre usage
(d) **Annual direct expenses** such as road tax, insurance and depreciation
(e) **Indirect costs of the distribution department** such as the wages of managers

4.6 The role of the cost accountant is to provide a system for **recording and analysing costs**. Just as production costs are recorded by means of material requisition notes, labour time sheets and so on, so too must transport costs be recorded by means of log sheets or time sheets, and material supply notes.

The purpose of a lorry driver's log sheet is to record distance travelled, or the number of tonne/kilometres and the drivers' time.

Canteen costs

4.7 Another example of service costing is the cost of a company's **canteen services**. A feature of canteen costing is that some revenue is earned when employees pay for their meals, but the prices paid will be insufficient to cover the costs of the canteen service. The company will subsidise the canteen and a major purpose of canteen costing is to establish the size of the subsidy.

4.8 If the costs of the canteen service are recorded by a system of service cost accounting, the likely headings of expense would be as follows.

(a) **Food and drink**: separate canteen stores records may be kept, and the consumption of food and drink recorded by means of 'materials issues' notes.

(b) **Labour costs of the canteen staff**: hourly paid staff will record their time at work on a time card or time sheet. Salaried staff will be a 'fixed' cost each month.

(c) **Consumable stores** such as crockery, cutlery, glassware, table linen and cleaning materials will also be recorded in some form of stock control system.

(d) **The cost of gas and electricity** may be separately metered; otherwise an apportionment of the total cost of such utilities for the building as a whole will be made to the canteen department.

(e) Asset records will be kept and **depreciation charges** made for major items of equipment like ovens and furniture.

(f) An apportionment of other **overhead costs** of the building (rent and rates, building insurance and maintenance and so on) may be charged against the canteen.

Cash income from canteen sales will also be recorded.

4.9 Suppose that a canteen recorded the following costs and revenue during the month.

	£
Food and drink	11,250
Labour	11,250
Heating and lighting	1,875
Repairs and consumable stores	1,125
Financing costs	1,000
Depreciation	750
Other apportioned costs	875
Revenue	22,500

The canteen served 37,500 meals in the month.

The size of the subsidy could be easily identified as follows:

	£
The total costs of the canteen	28,125
Revenue	22,500
Loss, to be covered by the company	5,625

The cost per meal averages 75p and the revenue per meal 60p. If the company decided that the canteen should pay its own way, without a subsidy, the average price of a meal would have to be raised by 15 pence.

5 THE USEFULNESS OF COSTING SERVICES THAT DO NOT EARN REVENUE

5.1 The techniques for costing services are similar to the techniques for costing products, but why should we want to establish a cost for 'internal' services, services that are provided by one department for another, rather than sold externally to customers? In other words, what is the purpose of service costing for non-revenue-earning services?

5.2 Service costing has two basic purposes.

(a) **To control the costs in the service department**. If we establish a distribution cost per tonne kilometre, a canteen cost per employee, or job costs of repairs, we can establish control measures in the following ways.

(i) Comparing actual costs against a target or standard
(ii) Comparing current actual costs against actual costs in previous periods

(b) **To control the costs of the user departments**, and prevent the unnecessary use of services. If the costs of services are charged to the user departments in such a way that the charges reflect the use actually made by each department of the service department's services then the following will occur.

(i) The overhead costs of user departments will be established more accurately; indeed some service department variable costs might be identified as directly attributable costs of the user department.

(ii) If the service department's charges for a user department are high, the user department might be encouraged to consider whether it is making an excessively costly and wasteful use of the service department's service.

(iii) The user department might decide that it can obtain a similar service at a lower cost from an external service company.

5.3 EXAMPLE: COSTING INTERNAL SERVICES

(a) If maintenance costs in a factory are costed as jobs (that is, if each bit of repair work is given a job number and costed accordingly) repair costs can be charged to the departments on the basis of repair jobs actually undertaken, instead of on a more generalised basis, such as apportionment according to machine hour capacity in each department. Departments with high repair costs could then consider their high incidence of repairs, the age and reliability of their machines, or the skills of the machine operatives.

(b) If mainframe computer costs are charged to a user department on the basis of a cost per hour, the user department would assess whether it was getting good value from its use of the mainframe computer and whether it might be better to hire the service of a computer bureau, or perhaps install a stand-alone microcomputer system in the department.

6 SERVICE COST ANALYSIS IN SERVICE INDUSTRY SITUATIONS

Exam focus point

The study guide for Paper 1.2 specifically mentions that candidates must be able to 'carry out service cost analysis in **service industry** situations'.

Distribution costs

6.1 EXAMPLE: SERVICE COST ANALYSIS IN THE SERVICE INDUSTRY

This example shows how a rate per tonne/kilometre can be calculated for a distribution service.

Rick Shaw Ltd operates a small fleet of delivery vehicles. Standard costs have been established as follows.

Loading	1 hour per tonne loaded
Loading costs:	
Labour (casual)	£2 per hour
Equipment depreciation	£80 per week
Supervision	£80 per week
Drivers' wages (fixed)	£100 per man per week
Petrol	10p per kilometre
Repairs	5p per kilometre
Depreciation	£80 per week per vehicle
Supervision	£120 per week
Other general expenses (fixed)	£200 per week

There are two drivers and two vehicles in the fleet.

During a slack week, only six journeys were made.

Journey	*Tonnes carried (one way)*	*One-way distance of journey* Kilometres
1	5	100
2	8	20
3	2	60
4	4	50
5	6	200
6	5	300

Required

Calculate the expected average full cost per tonne/kilometre for the week.

6.2 SOLUTION

Variable costs	*Journey*	*1*	*2*	*3*	*4*	*5*	*6*
		£	£	£	£	£	£
Loading labour		10	16	4	8	12	10
Petrol (both ways)		20	4	12	10	40	60
Repairs (both ways)		10	2	6	5	20	30
		40	22	22	23	72	100

Total costs

	£
Variable costs (total for journeys 1 to 6)	279
Loading equipment depreciation	80
Loading supervision	80
Drivers' wages	200
Vehicles depreciation	160
Drivers' supervision	120
Other costs	200
	1,119

Journey	Tonnes	*One way distance* Kilometres	Tonne/kilometres
1	5	100	500
2	8	20	160
3	2	60	120
4	4	50	200
5	6	200	1,200
6	5	300	1,500
			3,680

Cost per tonne/kilometre $\frac{£1,119}{3,680} = £0.304$

Note that the large element of fixed costs may distort this measure but that a variable cost per tonne/kilometre of £279/3,680 = £0.076 may be useful for budgetary control.

Education

6.3 The techniques described in the preceding paragraphs can be applied, in general, to any service industry situation. Attempt the following question about education.

Question 2

A university with annual running costs of £3 million has the following students.

Classification	*Number*	*Attendance weeks per annum*	*Hours per week*
3 year	2,700	30	28
4 year	1,500	30	25
Sandwich	1,900	35	20

Required

Calculate a cost per suitable cost unit for the university to the nearest penny.

Answer

We need to begin by establishing a cost unit for the university. Since there are three different categories of students we cannot use 'a student' as the cost unit. Attendance hours would seem to be the most appropriate cost unit. The next step is to calculate the number of units.

Number of students		*Weeks*		*Hours*		*Total hours per annum*
2,700	×	30	×	28	=	2,268,000
1,500	×	30	×	25	=	1,125,000
1,900	×	35	×	20	=	1,330,000
						4,723,000

The cost per unit is calculated as follows.

$$\text{Cost per unit} = \frac{\text{Total cost}}{\text{Number of units}} = £\left(\frac{3,000,000}{4,723,000}\right) = \underline{\underline{£0.64}}$$

Question 3

State which of the following are characteristics of service costing.

(i) High levels of indirect costs as a proportion of total costs
(ii) Use of composite cost units
(iii) Use of equivalent units

A (i) only
B (i) and (ii) only
C (ii) only
D (ii) and (iii) only

Answer

B In service costing it is difficult to identify many attributable direct costs. Many costs must be shared over several cost units, therefore characteristic (i) does apply. Composite cost units such as tonne-mile or room-night are often used, therefore characteristic (ii) does apply. Equivalent units are more often used in costing for tangible products, therefore characteristic (iii) does not apply. The correct answer is therefore B.

Chapter roundup

- **Service costing** can be used by companies operating in a **service industry** or by companies wishing to establish the **cost of services carried out by some of their departments**.
- Service organisations do not make or sell tangible goods.
- **Specific characteristics of services**
  - Intangibility
  - Simultaneity
  - Perishability
  - Heterogeneity
- One main problem with service costing is being able to define a realistic **cost unit** that represents a suitable measure of the service provided. If the service is a function of two activity variables, a **composite cost unit** may be more appropriate.
- **Cost per service unit** = $\frac{\text{Total costs for period}}{\text{Number of service units in the period}}$
- Service department costing is also used to establish a specific cost for an **internal service** which is a service provided by one department for another, rather than sold externally to customers eg canteen, maintenance.

Quick quiz

1 Define service costing

2 Match up the following services with their typical cost units

Service		Cost unit
Hotels		Patient-day
Education	?	Meal served
Hospitals		Full-time student
Catering organisations		Occupied bed-night

3 What is the advantage of organisations within an industry using a common cost unit?

4 Cost per service unit = ____________________

5 Service department costing is used to establish a specific cost for an 'internal service' which is a service provided by one department for another.

True ☐

False ☐

Answers to quick quiz

1 Cost accounting for services or functions eg canteens, maintenance, personnel (service centres/functions).

2 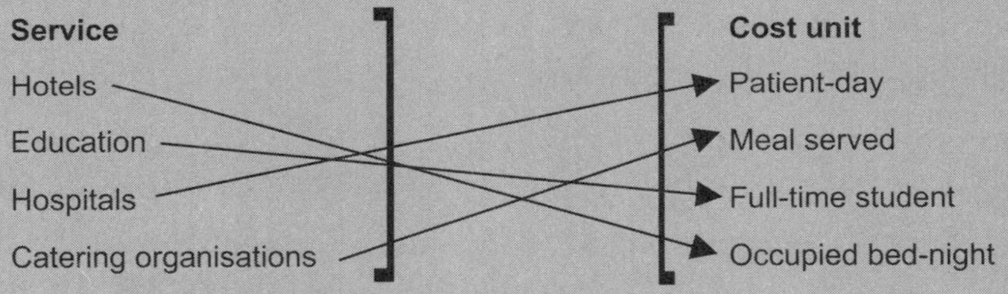

3 It is easier to make comparisons.

4 Cost per service unit = $\frac{\text{Total costs for period}}{\text{Number of service units in the period}}$

5 True

Now try the questions below from the Exam Question Bank

Number	Level	Marks	Time
22	MCQ	n/a	n/a
23	Examination	10	18 mins

Part D
Decision making

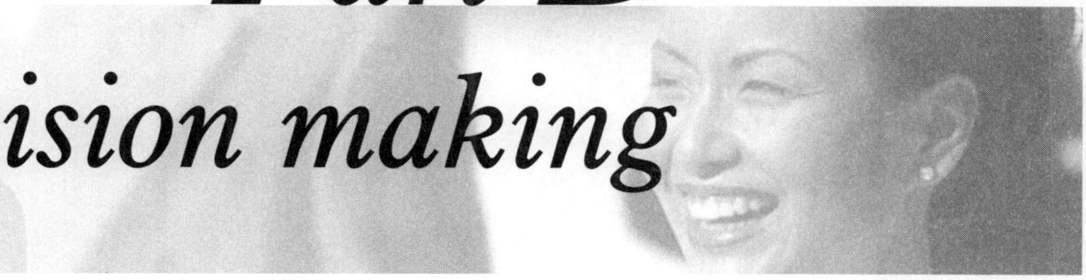

Chapter 14

COST-VOLUME-PROFIT (CVP) ANALYSIS

Introduction

You should by now realise that the cost accountant needs estimates of **fixed** and **variable costs**, and **revenues**, at various output levels. The cost accountant, must also be fully aware of **cost behaviour** because, to be able to estimate costs, he must know what a particular cost will do given particular conditions.

An understanding of cost behaviour is not all that you may need to know, however. The application of **cost-volume-profit analysis**, which is based on the cost behaviour principles and marginal costing ideas, is sometimes necessary so that the appropriate decision-making information can be provided. As you may have guessed, this chapter is going to look at that very topic, **cost-volume-profit analysis** or **breakeven analysis.**

Study guide

Section 19 – Cost-volume-profit (CVP) analysis –1

- Explain the objective of CVP analysis
- Explain the concept of breakeven
- Calculate and explain the break-even point and revenue, target profit, profit/volume ratio and margin of safety

Section 20 – Cost-volume-profit (CVP) analysis –2

- Construct breakeven, contribution and profit/volume charts from given data
- Apply the CVP model in multi-product situations

Exam guide

CVP analysis is one of the key areas of the syllabus. Most examination questions will require that you can recall the formulae included in this chapter – make sure that you learn them so that you can apply them when you need to.

1 CVP ANALYSIS AND BREAKEVEN POINT

KEY TERM

Cost-volume-profit (CVP)/breakeven analysis is the study of the interrelationships between costs, volume and profit at various levels of activity

1.1 The management of an organisation usually wishes to know the profit likely to be made if the aimed-for production and sales for the year are achieved. Management may also be interested to know the following.

(a) The **breakeven** point which is the activity level at which there is neither profit nor loss.

(b) The **amount** by which actual **sales can fall** below anticipated sales, **without** a **loss** being incurred.

1.2 The breakeven point (BEP) can be calculated arithmetically.

FORMULA TO LEARN

Breakeven point $= \dfrac{\text{Total fixed costs}}{\text{Contribution per unit}} = \dfrac{\text{Contribution required to break even}}{\text{Contribution per unit}}$

= Number of units of sale required to break even.

1.3 EXAMPLE: BREAKEVEN POINT

Expected sales	10,000 units at £8 = £80,000
Variable cost	£5 per unit
Fixed costs	£21,000

Required

Compute the breakeven point.

1.4 SOLUTION

The contribution per unit is £(8–5)	=	£3
Contribution required to break even	=	fixed costs = £21,000
Breakeven point (BEP)	=	21,000 ÷ 3
	=	7,000 units
In revenue, BEP	=	(7,000 × £8) = £56,000

Sales above £56,000 will result in profit of £3 per unit of additional sales and sales below £56,000 will mean a loss of £3 per unit for each unit by which sales fall short of 7,000 units. In other words, profit will improve or worsen by the amount of contribution per unit.

	7,000 units		7,001 units
	£		£
Revenue	56,000		56,008
Less variable costs	35,000		35,005
Contribution	21,000		21,003
Less fixed costs	21,000		21,000
Profit	0	(= breakeven)	3

2 THE PROFIT/VOLUME (P/V) RATIO

2.1 An alternative way of calculating the breakeven point to give an answer in terms of sales revenue is as follows.

FORMULA TO LEARN

$$\frac{\text{Required contribution} = \text{Fixed costs}}{\text{P/V ratio}} = \textbf{Sales revenue at breakeven point}$$

(The **profit/volume** or **P/V ratio** is also sometimes called a C/S (contribution/sales) ratio).

2.2 In the example in Paragraph 1.3 the P/V ratio is $\frac{£3}{£8} = 37.5\%$

Breakeven is where sales revenue equals $\frac{£21{,}000}{37.5\%} = £56{,}000$

At a price of £8 per unit, this represents 7,000 units of sales.

The P/V ratio is a measure of how much contribution is earned from each £1 of sales. The P/V ratio of 37.5% in the above example means that for every £1 of sales, a contribution of 37.5p is earned. Thus, in order to earn a total contribution of £21,000 and if contribution increases by 37.5p per £1 of sales, sales must be:

$$\frac{£1}{37.5\text{p}} \times £21{,}000 = £56{,}000$$

Question 1

The P/V ratio of product W is 20%. IB Ltd, the manufacturer of product W, wishes to make a contribution of £50,000 towards fixed costs. How many units of product W must be sold if the selling price is £10 per unit?

Answer

$$\frac{\text{Required contribution}}{\text{P/V ratio}} = \frac{£\ 50{,}000}{20\%} = £250{,}000$$

∴ Number of units = £250,000 ÷ £10 = 25,000.

3 THE MARGIN OF SAFETY

KEY TERM

The **margin of safety** is the difference in units between the budgeted sales volume and the breakeven sales volume and it is sometimes expressed as a percentage of the budgeted sales volume.

3.1 The margin of safety may also be expressed as the difference between the budgeted sales revenue and breakeven sales revenue, expressed as a percentage of the budgeted sales revenue.

3.2 EXAMPLE: MARGIN OF SAFETY

Mal de Mer Ltd makes and sells a product which has a variable cost of £30 and which sells for £40. Budgeted fixed costs are £70,000 and budgeted sales are 8,000 units.

Required

Calculate the breakeven point and the margin of safety.

3.3 SOLUTION

(a) Breakeven point $= \dfrac{\text{Total fixed costs}}{\text{Contribution per unit}} = \dfrac{£70{,}000}{£(40-30)}$

$= 7{,}000$ units

(b) Margin of safety $= 8{,}000 - 7{,}000$ units $= 1{,}000$ units

which may be expressed as $\dfrac{1{,}000 \text{ units}}{8{,}000 \text{ units}} \times 100\% \times 100\% = 12\tfrac{1}{2}\%$ of budget

(c) The margin of safety indicates to management that actual sales can fall short of budget by 1,000 units or 12½% before the breakeven point is reached and no profit at all is made.

4 BREAKEVEN ARITHMETIC AND PROFIT TARGETS

FORMULA TO LEARN

At the **breakeven point**, sales revenue equals total costs and there is no profit.

$S = V + F$

where S = Sales revenue
V = Total variable costs
F = Total fixed costs

Subtracting V from each side of the equation, we get:

S – V = F, that is, **total contribution = fixed costs**

4.1 EXAMPLE: BREAKEVEN ARITHMETIC

Butterfingers Ltd makes a product which has a variable cost of £7 per unit.

Required

If fixed costs are £63,000 per annum, calculate the selling price per unit if the company wishes to break even with a sales volume of 12,000 units.

4.2 SOLUTION

Contribution required to break even (= Fixed costs)	=	£63,000	
Volume of sales	=	12,000 units	
			£
Required contribution per unit (S – V)	=	£63,000 ÷ 12,000 =	5.25
Variable cost per unit (V)	=		7.00
Required sales price per unit (S)	=		12.25

Target profits

4.3 A similar formula may be applied where a company wishes to achieve a certain profit during a period. To achieve this profit, sales must cover all costs and leave the required profit.

FORMULA TO LEARN

The **target profit** is achieved when: S = V + F + P,
where P = required profit

Subtracting V from each side of the equation, we get:

S – V = F + P, so
Total contribution required = F + P

4.4 EXAMPLE: TARGET PROFITS

Riding Breeches Ltd makes and sells a single product, for which variable costs are as follows.

	£
Direct materials	10
Direct labour	8
Variable production overhead	6
	24

The sales price is £30 per unit, and fixed costs per annum are £68,000. The company wishes to make a profit of £16,000 per annum.

Required

Determine the sales required to achieve this profit.

4.5 SOLUTION

Required contribution = fixed costs + profit = £68,000 + £16,000 = £84,000

Required sales can be calculated in one of two ways.

(a) $\frac{\text{Required contribution}}{\text{Contribution per unit}} = \frac{£84,000}{£(30-24)}$ = 14,000 units, or £420,000 in revenue

(b) $\dfrac{\text{Required contribution}}{\text{P/V ratio}} = \dfrac{£84{,}000}{20\%\star} = £420{,}000$ of revenue, or 14,000 units.

$\star$ P/V ratio $= \dfrac{£30-£24}{£30} = \dfrac{£6}{£30} = 0.2 = 20\%.$

Question 2

Seven League Boots Ltd wishes to sell 14,000 units of its product, which has a variable cost of £15 to make and sell. Fixed costs are £47,000 and the required profit is £23,000.

Required

Calculate the sales price per unit.

Answer

Required contribution	=	fixed costs plus profit
	=	£47,000 + £23,000
	=	£70,000
Required sales		14,000 units

	£
Required contribution per unit sold	5
Variable cost per unit	15
Required sales price per unit	20

Decisions to change sales price or costs

4.6 You may come across a problem in which you will be expected to offer advice as to the effect of altering the selling price, variable cost per unit or fixed cost. Such problems are slight variations on basic breakeven arithmetic.

4.7 EXAMPLE: CHANGE IN SELLING PRICE

Stomer Cakes Ltd bake and sell a single type of cake. The variable cost of production is 15p and the current sales price is 25p. Fixed costs are £2,600 per month, and the annual profit for the company at current sales volume is £36,000. The volume of sales demand is constant throughout the year.

The sales manager, Ian Digestion, wishes to raise the sales price to 29p per cake, but considers that a price rise will result in some loss of sales.

Required

Ascertain the minimum volume of sales required each month to raise the price to 29p.

4.8 SOLUTION

The minimum volume of demand which would justify a price of 29p is one which would leave total profit at least the same as before, ie £3,000 per month. Required profit should be converted into required contribution, as follows.

	£
Monthly fixed costs	2,600
Monthly profit, minimum required	3,000
Current monthly contribution	5,600
Contribution per unit (25p – 15p)	10p
Current monthly sales	56,000 cakes

The minimum volume of sales required after the price rise will be an amount which earns a contribution of £5,600 per month, no worse than at the moment. The contribution per cake at a sales price of 29p would be 14p.

$$\text{Required sales} = \frac{\text{required contribution}}{\text{contribution per unit}} = \frac{£5{,}600}{14\text{p}} = 40{,}000 \text{ cakes per month.}$$

4.9 EXAMPLE: CHANGE IN PRODUCTION COSTS

Close Brickett Ltd makes a product which has a variable production cost of £8 and a variable sales cost of £2 per unit. Fixed costs are £40,000 per annum, the sales price per unit is £18, and the current volume of output and sales is 6,000 units.

The company is considering whether to have an improved machine for production. Annual hire costs would be £10,000 and it is expected that the variable cost of production would fall to £6 per unit.

Required

(a) Determine the number of units that must be produced and sold to achieve the same profit as is currently earned, if the machine is hired.

(b) Calculate the annual profit with the machine if output and sales remain at 6,000 units per annum.

4.10 SOLUTION

The current unit contribution is £(18 – (8+2)) = £8

(a)

	£
Current contribution (6,000 × £8)	48,000
Less current fixed costs	40,000
Current profit	8,000

With the new machine fixed costs will go up by £10,000 to £50,000 per annum. The variable cost per unit will fall to £(6 + 2) = £8, and the contribution per unit will be £10.

	£
Required profit (as currently earned)	8,000
Fixed costs	50,000
Required contribution	58,000
Contribution per unit	£10
Sales required to earn £8,000 profit	5,800 units

(b) **If sales are 6,000 units**

	£	£
Sales (6,000 × £18)		108,000
Variable costs: production (6,000 × £6)	36,000	
sales (6,000 × £2)	12,000	
		48,000
Contribution (6,000 × £10)		60,000
Less fixed costs		50,000
Profit		10,000

Alternative calculation	£
Profit at 5,800 units of sale (see (a))	8,000
Contribution from sale of extra 200 units (× £10)	2,000
Profit at 6,000 units of sale	10,000

Sales price and sales volume

4.11 It may be clear by now that, given no change in fixed costs, **total profit is maximised when the total contribution is at its maximum**. Total contribution in turn depends on the unit contribution and on the sales volume.

4.12 An increase in the sales price will increase unit contribution, but sales volume is likely to fall because fewer customers will be prepared to pay the higher price. A decrease in sales price will reduce the unit contribution, but sales volume may increase because the goods on offer are now cheaper. The **optimum combination** of sales price and sales volume is arguably the one which **maximises total contribution.**

4.13 EXAMPLE: PROFIT MAXIMISATION

C Ltd has developed a new product which is about to be launched on to the market. The variable cost of selling the product is £12 per unit. The marketing department has estimated that at a sales price of £20, annual demand would be 10,000 units.

However, if the sales price is set above £20, sales demand would fall by 500 units for each 50p increase above £20. Similarly, if the price is set below £20, demand would increase by 500 units for each 50p stepped reduction in price below £20.

Required

Determine the price which would maximise C Ltd's profit in the next year.

4.14 SOLUTION

At a price of £20 per unit, the unit contribution would be £(20 – 12) = £8. Each 50p increase (or decrease) in price would raise (or lower) the unit contribution by 50p. The total contribution is calculated at each sales price by multiplying the unit contribution by the expected sales volume.

Unit price	*Unit contribution*	*Sales volume*	*Total contribution*
£	£	Units	£
20.00	8.00	10,000	80,000
(a) **Reduce price**			
19.50	7.50	10,500	78,750
19.00	7.00	11,000	77,000
(b) **Increase price**			
20.50	8.50	9,500	80,750
21.00	9.00	9,000	81,000
21.50	9.50	8,500	80,750
22.00	10.00	8,000	80,000
22.50	10.50	7,500	78,750

The total contribution would be maximised, and therefore profit maximised, at a sales price of £21 per unit, and sales demand of 9,000 units.

Question 3

Betty Battle Ltd manufactures a product which has a selling price of £20 and a variable cost of £10 per unit. The company incurs annual fixed costs of £29,000. Annual sales demand is 9,000 units.

New production methods are under consideration, which would cause a £1,000 increase in fixed costs and a reduction in variable cost to £9 per unit. The new production methods would result in a superior product and would enable sales to be increased to 9,750 units per annum at a price of £21 each.

If the change in production methods were to take place, the breakeven output level would be:

A 400 units higher
B 400 units lower
C 100 units higher
D 100 units lower

Answer

	Current	*Revised*	*Difference*
	£	£	
Selling price	20	21	
Variable costs	10	9	
Contribution per unit	10	12	
Fixed costs	£29,000	£30,000	
Breakeven point (units)	2,900	2,500	**400 lower**

Breakeven point = $\frac{\text{Total fixed costs}}{\text{Contribution per unit}}$

Current BEP = $\frac{£29{,}000}{£10}$ = 2,900 units

Revised BEP = $\frac{£30{,}000}{£12}$ = 2,500 units

The correct answer is therefore B.

5 BREAKEVEN CHARTS, CONTRIBUTION CHARTS AND PROFIT/VOLUME CHARTS

Exam focus point

Remember that you can pick up easy marks in the paper-based examination for drawing graphs neatly and accurately. Always use a ruler, label your axes and use an appropriate scale.

Breakeven charts

5.1 **The breakeven point can also be determined graphically using a breakeven chart.** This is a chart which shows approximate levels of profit or loss at different sales volume levels within a limited range.

5.2 A breakeven chart has the following axes.

- A **horizontal** axis showing the **sales/output** (in value or units)
- A **vertical axis** showing £ for **sales revenues** and **costs**

5.3 The following lines are drawn on the breakeven chart.

(a) The **sales line**

- Starts at the origin
- Ends at the point signifying expected sales

(b) The **fixed costs line**

- Runs parallel to the horizontal axis
- Meets the vertical axis at a point which represents total fixed costs

(c) The **total costs line**

- Starts where the fixed costs line meets the vertical axis
- Ends at the point which represents anticipated sales on the horizontal axis and total costs of anticipated sales on the vertical axis

5.4 The **breakeven point** is the **intersection** of the **sales line** and the **total costs line.**

5.5 The distance between the **breakeven point** and the **expected (or budgeted) sales,** in units, indicates the **margin of safety**.

5.6 EXAMPLE: A BREAKEVEN CHART

The budgeted annual output of a factory is 120,000 units. The fixed overheads amount to £40,000 and the variable costs are 50p per unit. The sales price is £1 per unit.

Required

Construct a breakeven chart showing the current breakeven point and profit earned up to the present maximum capacity.

5.7 SOLUTION

We begin by calculating the profit at the budgeted annual output.

	£
Sales (120,000 units)	120,000
Variable costs	60,000
Contribution	60,000
Fixed costs	40,000
Profit	20,000

Breakeven chart (1) is shown on the following page.

The chart is drawn as follows.

(a) The **vertical axis** represents **money** (costs and revenue) and the **horizontal axis** represents the **level of activity** (production and sales).

(b) The fixed costs are represented by a **straight line parallel to the horizontal axis** (in our example, at £40,000).

(c) The **variable costs** are added 'on top of' fixed costs, to give **total costs.** It is assumed that fixed costs are the same in total and variable costs are the same per unit at all levels of output.

The line of costs is therefore a straight line and only two points need to be plotted and joined up. Perhaps the two most convenient points to plot are total costs at zero output, and total costs at the budgeted output and sales.

- At zero output, costs are equal to the amount of fixed costs only, £40,000, since there are no variable costs.

- At the budgeted output of 120,000 units, costs are £100,000.

	£
Fixed costs	40,000
Variable costs 120,000 × 50p	60,000
Total costs	100,000

(d) The sales line is also drawn by plotting two points and joining them up.

- At zero sales, revenue is nil.
- At the budgeted output and sales of 120,000 units, revenue is £120,000.

Breakeven chart (1)

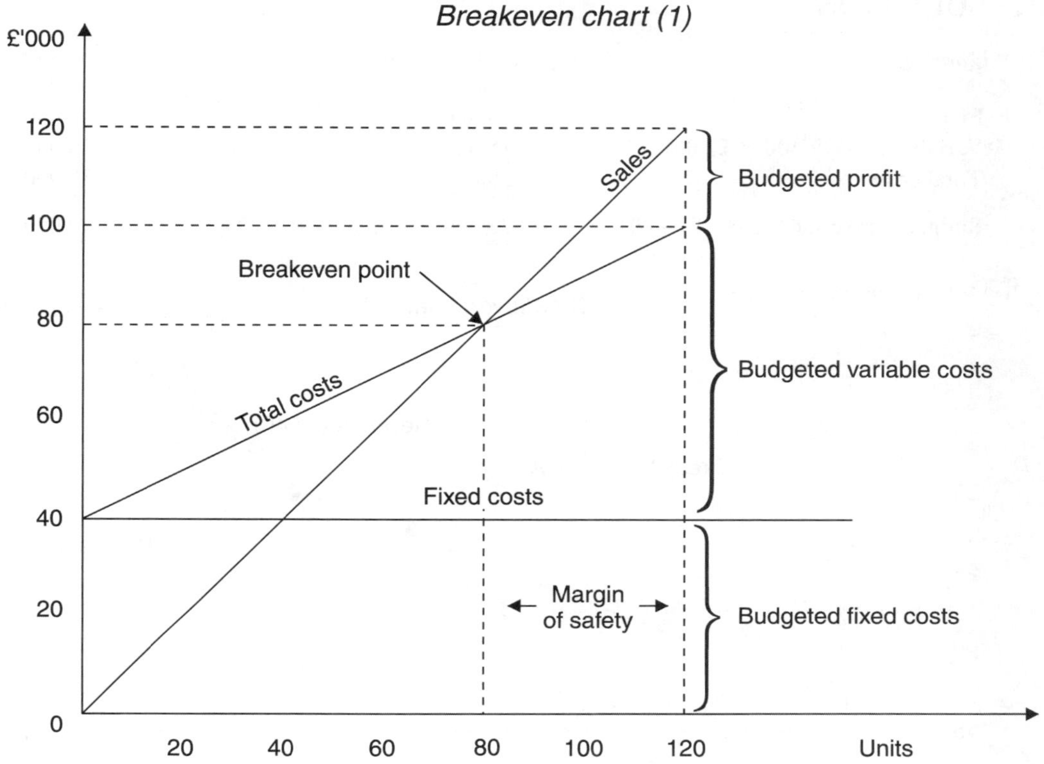

5.8 **The breakeven point is where total costs are matched exactly by total revenue.** From the chart, this can be seen to occur at output and sales of 80,000 units, when revenue and costs are both £80,000. This breakeven point can be proved mathematically as:

$$\frac{\text{Required contribution (=fixed costs)}}{\text{Contribution per unit}} = \frac{£40,000}{\text{50p per unit}} = 80,000 \text{ units}$$

5.9 The margin of safety can be seen on the chart as the difference between the budgeted level of activity and the breakeven level.

The value of breakeven charts

5.10 Breakeven charts are used as follows.

- To **plan** the production of a company's products
- To **market** a company's products
- To give a **visual display** of breakeven arithmetic

5.11 EXAMPLE: VARIATIONS IN THE USE OF BREAKEVEN CHARTS

Breakeven charts can be used to **show variations** in the possible **sales price, variable costs** or **fixed costs**. Suppose that a company sells a product which has a variable cost of £2 per unit. Fixed costs are £15,000. It has been estimated that if the sales price is set at £4.40 per unit, the expected sales volume would be 7,500 units; whereas if the sales price is lower, at £4 per unit, the expected sales volume would be 10,000 units.

Required

Draw a breakeven chart to show the budgeted profit, the breakeven point and the margin of safety at each of the possible sales prices.

5.12 SOLUTION

Workings	*Sales price £4.40 per unit*		*Sales price £4 per unit*
	£		£
Fixed costs	15,000		15,000
Variable costs (7,500 × £2.00)	15,000	(10,000 × £2.00)	20,000
Total costs	30,000		35,000
Budgeted revenue (7,500 × £4.40)	33,000	(10,000 × £4.00)	40,000

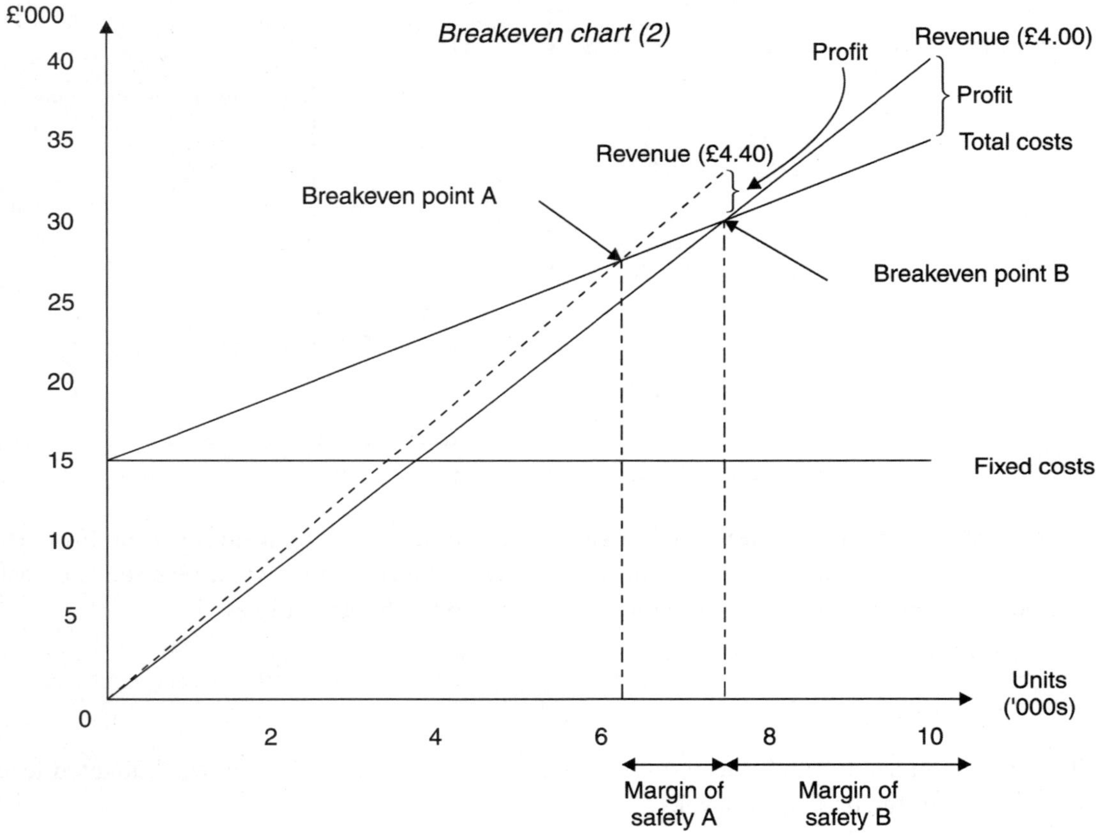

(a) **Breakeven point A** is the breakeven point at a sales price of £4.40 per unit, which is 6,250 units or £27,500 in costs and revenues.

(check: $\dfrac{\text{Required contribution to breakeven}}{\text{Contribution per unit}}$ $\dfrac{\text{£15,000}}{\text{£2.40 per unit}}$ = 6,250 units)

The margin of safety (A) is 7,500 units – 6,250 units = 1,250 units or 16.7% of expected sales.

(b) **Breakeven point B** is the breakeven point at a sales price of £4 per unit which is 7,500 units or £30,000 in costs and revenues.

(check: $\dfrac{\text{Required contribution to breakeven}}{\text{Contribution per unit}}$ $\dfrac{\text{£15,000}}{\text{£2 per unit}}$ = 7,500 units)

The margin of safety (B) = 10,000 units – 7,500 units = 2,500 units or 25% of expected sales.

5.13 Since a price of £4 per unit gives a higher expected profit and a wider margin of safety, this price will probably be preferred even though the breakeven point is higher than at a sales price of £4.40 per unit.

Contribution (or contribution breakeven) charts

5.14 As an alternative to drawing the fixed cost line first, it is possible to start with that for variable costs. This is known as a **contribution chart**. An example is shown below using the example in Paragraphs 5.6 and 5.7.

Contribution chart

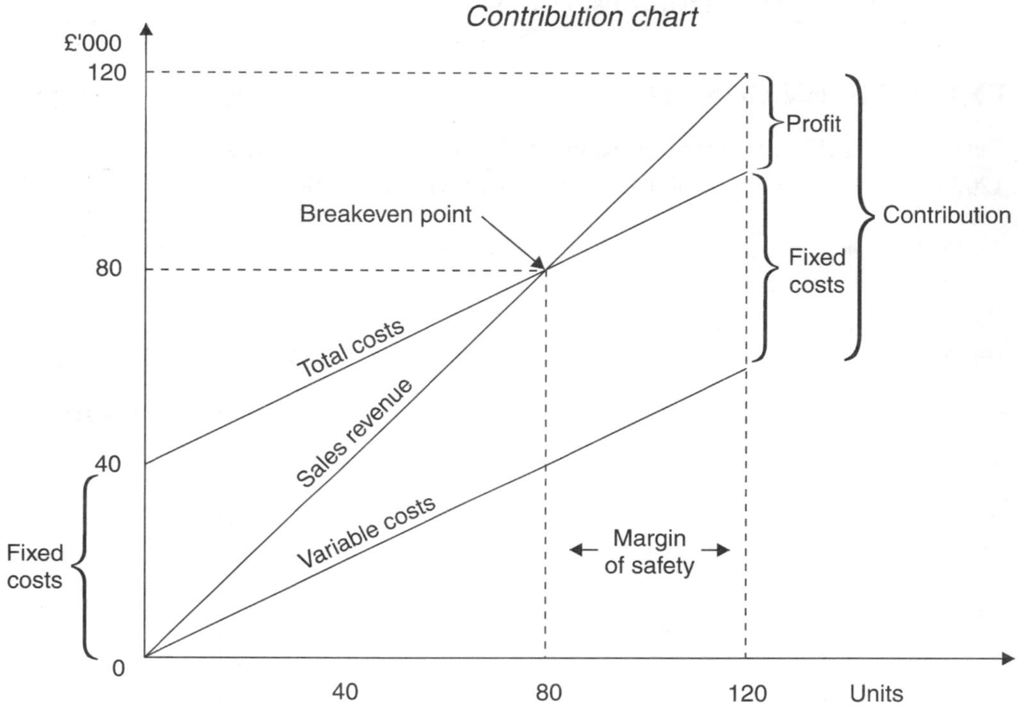

5.15 One of the **advantages** of the contribution chart is that is shows clearly the **contribution** for **different levels of production** (indicated here at 120,000 units, the budgeted level of output) as the 'wedge' shape between the sales revenue line and the variable costs line. At the **breakeven point**, the **contribution equals fixed costs** exactly. At levels of output **above** the **breakeven** point, the **contribution** is **larger**, and not only covers fixed costs, but also leaves a profit. **Below** the **breakeven** point, the **loss** is the amount by which contribution fails to cover fixed costs.

The Profit/Volume (P/V) chart

KEY TERM

The **profit/volume (P/V) chart** is a variation of the breakeven chart which illustrates the relationship of costs and profit to sales, and the margin of safety.

5.16 A P/V chart is constructed as follows (look at the chart in the example that follows as you read the explanation).

(a) 'P' is on the y axis and actually comprises not only 'profit' but contribution to profit (in monetary value), extending above and below the x axis with a zero point at the intersection of the two axes, and the negative section below the x axis representing fixed costs. This means that at zero production, the firm is incurring a loss equal to the fixed costs.

(b) 'V' is on the x axis and comprises either volume of sales or value of sales (revenue).

(c) The profit-volume line is a straight line drawn with its starting point (at zero production) at the intercept on the y axis representing the level of fixed costs, and with a gradient of contribution/unit (or the P/V ratio if sales value is used rather than units). The P/V line will cut the x axis at the breakeven point of sales volume. Any point on the P/V line above the x axis represents the profit to the firm (as measured on the vertical axis) for that particular level of sales.

5.17 EXAMPLE: P/V CHART

Let us draw a P/V chart for our example. At sales of 120,000 units, total contribution will be 120,000 × £(1 – 0.5) = £60,000 and total profit will be £20,000.

P/V chart (1)

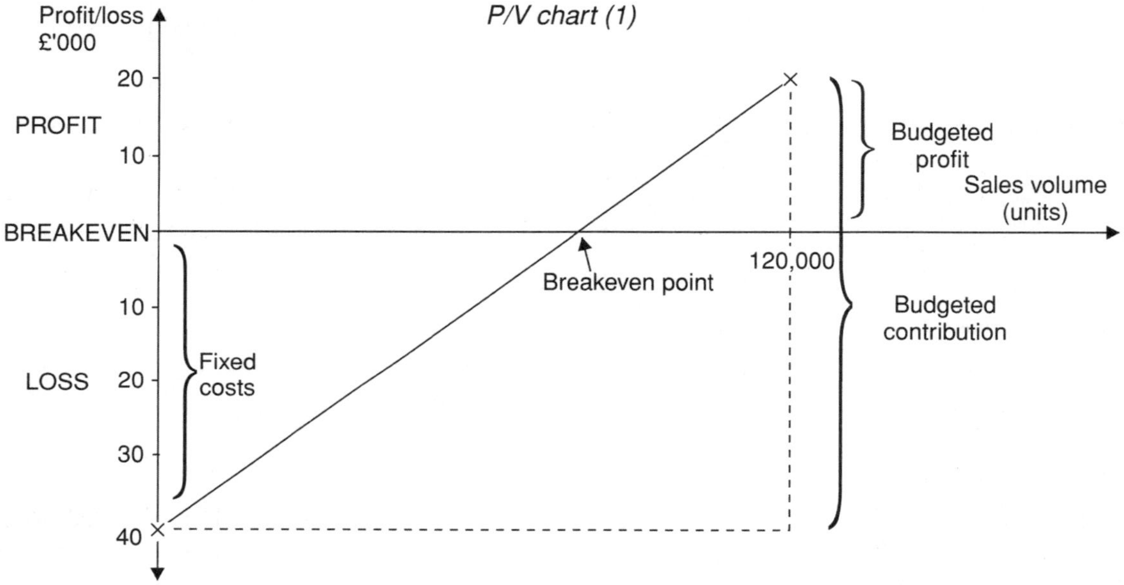

The advantage of the P/V chart

5.18 **The P/V chart shows clearly the effect on profit and breakeven point of any changes in selling price, variable cost, fixed cost and/or sales demand.** If the budgeted selling price of the product in our example is increased to £1.20, with the result that demand drops to 105,000 units despite additional fixed costs of £10,000 being spent on advertising, we could add a line representing this situation to our P/V chart.

5.19 At sales of 105,000 units, contribution will be 105,000 × £(1.20 – 0.50) = £73,500 and total profit will be £23,500 (fixed costs being £50,000).

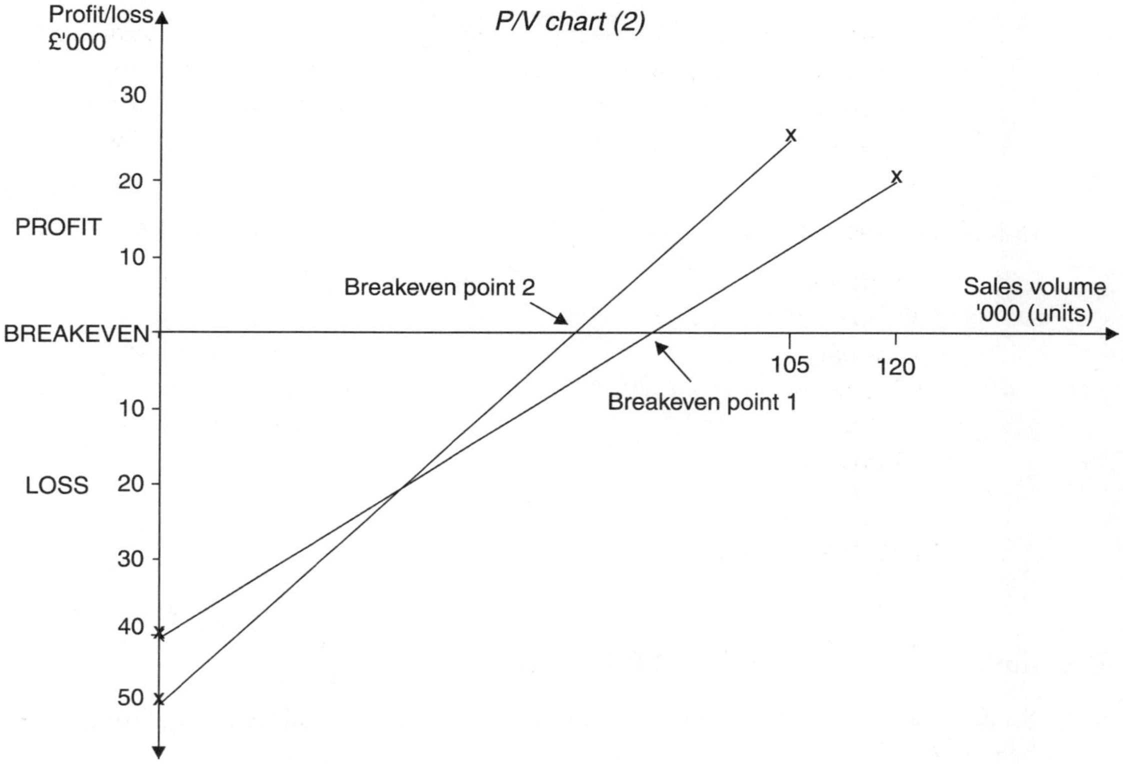

5.20 The diagram shows that if the selling price is increased, the breakeven point occurs at a lower level of sales revenue (71,429 units instead of 80,000 units), although this is not a particularly large increase when viewed in the context of the projected sales volume. It is also possible to see that for sales above 50,000 units, the profit achieved will be higher (and the loss achieved lower) if the price is £1.20. For sales volumes below 50,000 units the first option will yield lower losses.

5.21 The P/V chart is the clearest way of presenting such information; two conventional breakeven charts on one set of axes would be very confusing.

5.22 Changes in the variable cost per unit or in fixed costs at certain activity levels can also be easily incorporated into a P/V chart. The profit or loss at each point where the cost structure changes should be calculated and plotted on the graph so that the profit/volume line becomes a series of straight lines.

5.23 For example, suppose that in our example, at sales levels in excess of 120,000 units the variable cost per unit increases to £0.60 (perhaps because of overtime premiums that are incurred when production exceeds a certain level). At sales of 130,000 units, contribution would therefore be 130,000 × £(1 - 0.60) = £52,000 and total profit would be £12,000.

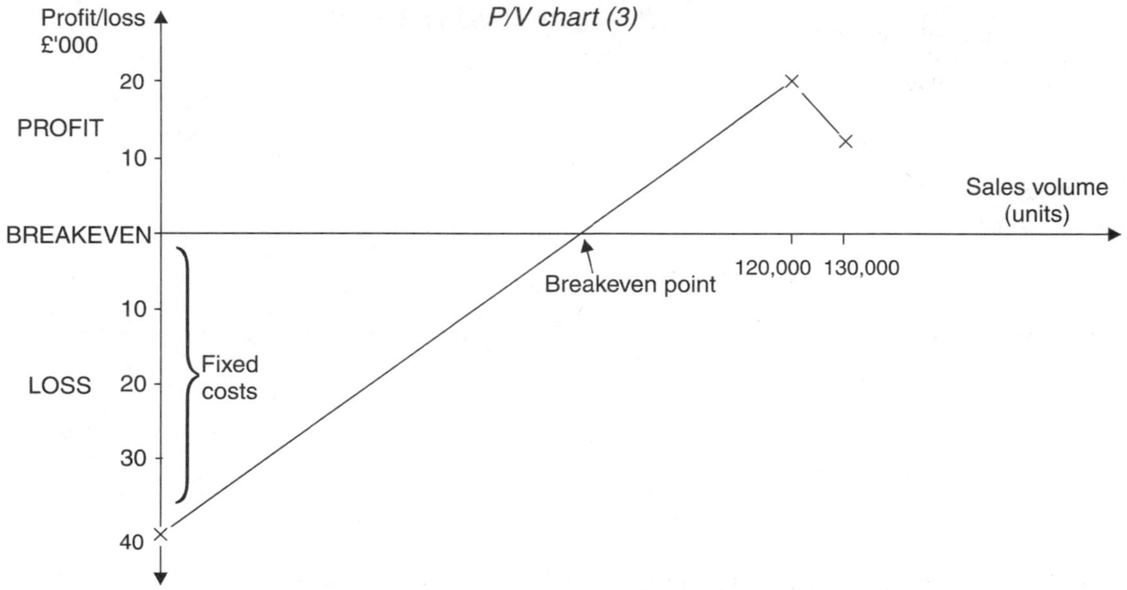

The multi-product breakeven and P/V chart

5.24 Since most companies sell more than one product, a multi-product chart of some type might be required.

5.25 **A very serious limitation of breakeven charts is that they can show the costs, revenues, profits and margins of safety for a single product only**, or for a single 'sales mix' of products.

5.26 For example suppose that Farmyard Ltd sells three products, X, Y and Z, which have variable unit costs of £3, £4 and £5 respectively. The sales price of X is £8, the price of Y is £6 and the price of Z is £6. Fixed costs per annum are £10,000.

5.27 A breakeven chart cannot be drawn, because we do not know the proportions of X, Y and Z in the sales mix. (If you are not sure about this point, you should try to draw a breakeven chart with the information given. It should not be possible.)

5.28 If, however, we now assume that budgeted sales are as follows:

X	2,000 units
Y	4,000 units
Z	3,000 units

a breakeven chart can be drawn. The chart would make the assumption that output and sales of X, Y and Z are in the proportions 2,000 : 4,000 : 3,000 at all levels of activity, in other words that the sales mix is 'fixed' in these proportions.

(a) *Workings*

Budgeted costs		*Costs*	*Budgeted revenue*	*Revenue*
		£		£
Variable costs of X	(2,000 × £3)	6,000	X (2,000 × £8)	16,000
Variable costs of Y	(4,000 × £4)	16,000	Y (4,000 × £6)	24,000
Variable costs of Z	(3,000 × £5)	15,000	Z (3,000 × £6)	18,000
Total variable costs		37,000		58,000
Fixed costs		10,000		
Total budgeted costs		47,000		

(b) The breakeven chart can now be drawn.

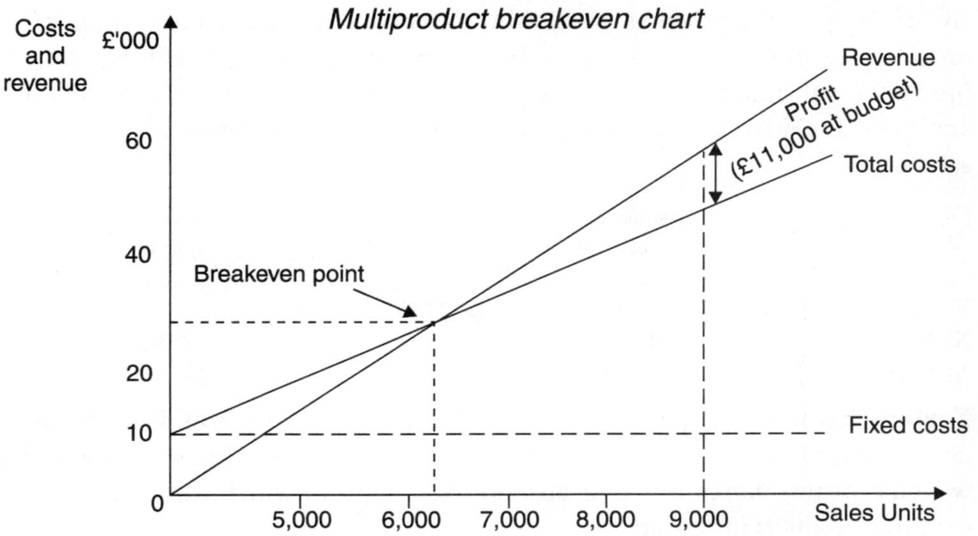

5.29 The same information could be shown on a P/V chart, as follows.

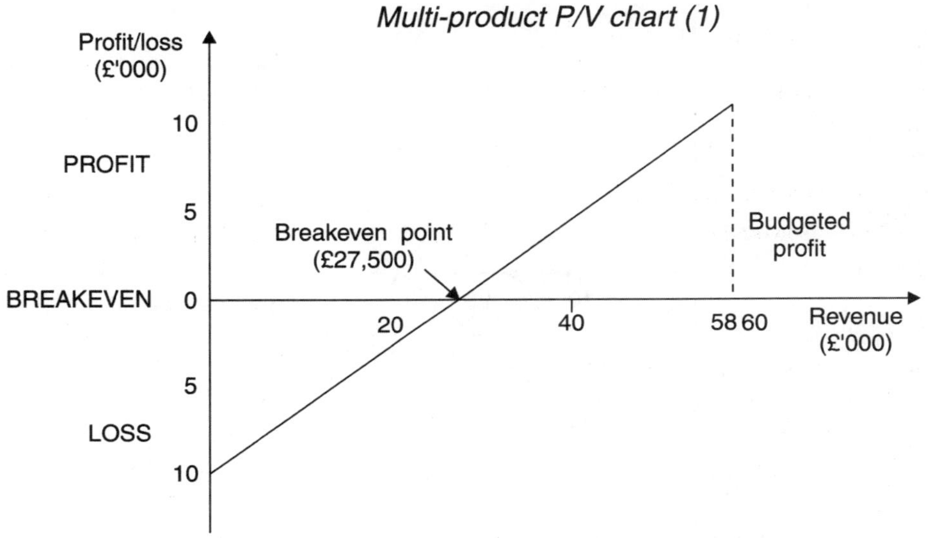

5.30 The breakeven point is approximately £27,500. This may either be read from the breakeven chart or computed mathematically. The budgeted P/V ratio for all three products together is

$$\frac{\text{contribution}}{\text{sales}} = \frac{£(58{,}000 - 37{,}000)}{£58{,}000} = 36.21\%$$

The required contribution to break even is £10,000, the amount of fixed costs. The breakeven point is

$$\frac{£10{,}000}{36.21\%} = £27{,}500 \text{ (approx) in sales revenue}$$

5.31 An addition to the P/V chart would now be made to show further information about the contribution earned by each product individually, so that their performance and profitability can be compared.

	Contribution	*Sales*	*C/S ratio*
	£	£	%
Product X	10,000	16,000	62.50
Product Y	8,000	24,000	33.33
Product Z	3,000	18,000	16.67
Total	21,000	58,000	36.21

5.32 By convention, the products are shown individually on a P/V chart from left to right, in order of the size of their P/V ratio. In this example, product X will be plotted first, then product Y and finally product Z. A dotted line is used to show the cumulative profit/loss and the cumulative sales as each product's sales and contribution in turn are added to the sales mix.

Product	*Cumulative sales* £		*Cumulative profit* £
X	16,000	(£10,000 – £10,000)	-
X and Y	40,000		8,000
X, Y and Z	58,000		11,000

You will see on the graph which follows that these three pairs of data are used to plot the dotted line, to indicate the contribution from each product. The solid line which joins the two ends of this dotted line indicates the average profit which will be earned from sales of the three products in this mix.

Multiproduct P/V chart(2)

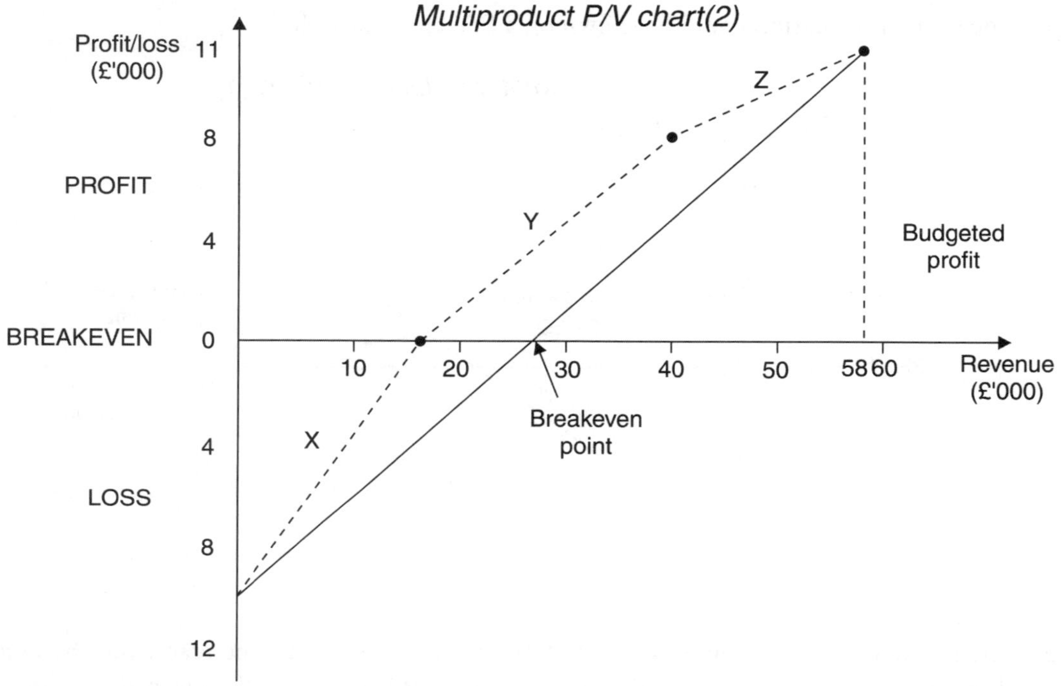

5.33 From this diagram, it may be apparent that since X is the most profitable in terms of P/V ratio, it might be worth considering an increase in the sales of X, even if there is a consequent fall in the sales of Z. Alternatively, the pricing structure of the products should be reviewed and a decision made as to whether the price of product Z should be raised so as to increase its P/V ratio (although an increase is likely to result in some fall in sales volume).

5.34 The **multi-product P/V chart** is therefore **helpful** in identifying the following.

(a) The overall company breakeven point.

(b) Which products should be expanded in output and which should be discontinued.

(c) How changes in selling price/sales volume will effect the company's breakeven point/profit.

6 LIMITATIONS OF CVP ANALYSIS

6.1 Breakeven analysis is a useful technique for managers. Breakeven arithmetic can provide **simple** and **quick** estimates. **Breakeven charts** provide a **graphical representation** of breakeven arithmetic. Breakeven analysis has a number of limitations.

- It **can only apply to a single product** or a single mix of a group of products.
- A breakeven chart may be **time-consuming** to prepare.
- It **assumes** fixed costs are constant at all levels of output.
- It **assumes** that **variable costs** are the **same** per unit at all levels of output.
- It **assumes** that **sales prices** are **constant** at all levels of output.
- It assumes **production** and **sales** are the **same** (stock levels are ignored).
- It **ignores** the **uncertainty** in the estimates of fixed costs and variable cost per unit.

Chapter roundup

- **Cost-volume- profit (CVP)/breakeven analysis** is the study of the interrelationships between costs, volume and profits at various levels of activity.
- **Breakeven point** = **Number of units of sale** required to breakeven

$$= \frac{\text{Fixed costs}}{\text{Contribution per unit}}$$

$$= \frac{\text{Contribution required to break even}}{\text{Contribution per unit}}$$

- **Breakeven point** = **Sales revenue** required to break even

$$= \frac{\text{Contribution required to break even}}{\text{P/V ratio}}$$

$$= \frac{\text{Fixed costs}}{\text{P/V ratio}}$$

- The **P/V ratio** (or **C/S ratio**) is a measure of how much contribution is earned from each £1 of sales.
- The **margin of safety** is the difference in units between the **budgeted sales volume** and the **breakeven sales volume.** It is sometimes expressed as a percentage of the budgeted sales volume.
- Alternatively, the **margin of safety** can be expressed as the difference between the **budgeted sales revenue** and the **breakeven sales revenue** expressed as a percentage of the budgeted sales revenue.
- At the **breakeven point**, sales revenue = total costs and there is no profit. At the breakeven point **total contribution = fixed costs.**
- The **target profit** is achieved when S = V + F + P. Therefore the **total contribution required** for a target profit = **fixed costs + required profit.**
- The breakeven point can also be determined graphically using a **breakeven chart** or a **contribution breakeven chart**.
- The **profit/volume (PV) chart** is a variation of the breakeven chart which illustrates the relationship of costs and profits to sales and the margin of safety.
- The **P/V chart** shows clearly the effect on profit and breakeven point of any changes in selling price, variable cost, fixed cost and/or sales demand.
- Since most companies sell more than one product, a **multi-product breakeven** or **P/V chart** might be useful in determining the breakeven point.
- **Breakeven analysis** is a useful technique for managers as it can provide simple and quick estimates. **Breakeven charts** provide a graphical representation of breakeven arithmetic. Breakeven analysis does, however, have a number of **limitations.**

Quick quiz

1 What does CVP analysis study?

2 The **breakeven point** is the .... or.. ....

3 Use the following to make up three formulae which can be used to calculate the breakeven point.

Contribution per unit
Contribution per unit
Fixed costs
Fixed costs
Contribution required to breakeven
Contribution required to breakeven
P/V ratio
P/V ratio

(a) Breakeven point (sales units) = $\frac{\qquad}{\qquad}$

or $\frac{\qquad}{\qquad}$

(b) Breakeven point (sales revenue) = $\frac{\qquad}{\qquad}$

or $\frac{\qquad}{\qquad}$

4 The P/V ratio is a measure of how much profit is earned from each £1 of sales.

True ☐

False ☐

5 The **margin of safety** is the difference in units between the budgeted sales volume and the breakeven sales volume. How is it sometimes expressed?

6 Profits are maximised at the breakeven point.

True ☐

False ☐

7 At the breakeven point, total contribution = ...

8 The total contribution required for a **target profit** = ...

9 Give three uses of breakeven charts.

10 Breakeven charts show approximate levels of profit or loss at different sales volume levels within a limited range. Which of the following are true?

I The sales line starts at the origin
II The fixed costs line runs parallel to the vertical axis
III Breakeven charts have a horizontal axis showing the sales/output (in value or units)
IV Breakeven charts have a vertical axis showing £ for revenues and costs
V The breakeven point is the intersection of the sales line and the fixed cost line

A I and II
B I and III
C I, III and IV
D I, III, IV, and V

11 On a breakeven chart, the distance between the breakeven point and the expected (or budgeted) sales, in units, indicates the ....

12 Give seven limitations of CVP analysis.

- ....
- ....
- ....
- ....
- ....
- ....
- ....

Answers to quick quiz

1 The interrelations between **costs, volume** and **profits** of a product at various activity levels.

2 The **breakeven point** is the number of units of sale required to breakeven or the sales revenue required to breakeven.

3 (a) Breakeven point (sales units) $= \dfrac{\text{Fixed costs}}{\text{Contribution per unit}}$

or $\dfrac{\text{Contribution required to break even}}{\text{Contribution per unit}}$

(b) Breakeven point (sales revenue) $= \dfrac{\text{Fixed costs}}{\text{P/V ratio}}$

or $\dfrac{\text{Contribution required to break even}}{\text{P/V ratio}}$

4 False. The P/V ratio is a measure of how much **contribution** is earned from each £1 of sales.

5 As a **percentage** of the budgeted sales volume.

6 False. At the breakeven point there is no profit.

7 At the breakeven point, total contribution = fixed costs

8 Fixed costs + required profit

9
- To plan the production of a company's products
- To market a company's products
- To give a visual display of breakeven arithmetic

10 C

11 Margin of safety

12
- It **can only apply to a single product** or a single mix of a group of products.
- A breakeven chart may be **time-consuming** to prepare.
- It **assumes** fixed costs are constant at all levels of output.
- It **assumes** that **variable costs** are the **same** per unit at all levels of output.
- It **assumes** that **sales prices** are **constant** at all levels of output.
- It assumes **production** and **sales** are the **same** (stock levels are ignored).
- It **ignores** the **uncertainty** in the estimates of fixed costs and variable cost per unit.

Now try the questions below from the Exam Question Bank

Number	Level	Marks	Time
24	MCQ	n/a	n/a
25	Examination	10	18 mins

Chapter 15

RELEVANT COSTING AND DECISION MAKING

Topic list		Syllabus reference
1	Relevant costs	6(d)
2	Choice of product (product mix) decisions	6(d)
3	Make or buy decisions	6(d)
4	Shut down decisions	6(d)
5	One-off contracts	6(d)

Introduction

Management at all levels within an organisation take decisions. The overriding requirement of the information that should be supplied by the cost accountant to aid decision making is that of **relevance.** This chapter therefore begins by looking at the costing technique required in decision-making situations, that of **relevant costing**, and explains how to decide which costs need taking into account when a decision is being made and which costs do not.

We then go on to see how to apply relevant costing to some specific decision-making scenarios.

Study guide

Section 21 – Limiting factors

- Identify, formulate and determine the optimal solution when there is a single limiting factor.

Section 23 – Relevant costing – 1

- Explain the concept of relevant costing
- Explain the relevance of such terms as opportunity and sunk costs, avoidable and unavoidable costs, fixed and variable costs, historical and replacement costs, controllable and uncontrollable costs, to decision making

Section 24 – Relevant costing – 2

- Calculate the relevant costs for materials and labour
- Calculate and explain the deprival value of an asset
- Construct a relevant cost statement and explain the results for such situations as make or buy decisions, shut down decisions and one-off contracts

Exam guide

Relevant costing is not one of the key syllabus topics for Paper 1.2. However, make sure that you can calculate relevant costs for materials and labour and the deprival value of an asset. Multiple choice questions are a good way of testing your understanding of this subject.

1 RELEVANT COSTS

Relevant costs

> **KEY TERM**
>
> A **relevant cost** is a future cash flow arising as a direct consequence of a decision.

1.1 Decision making should be based on relevant costs.

(a) **Relevant costs are future costs.** A decision is about the future and it cannot alter what has been done already. Costs that have been incurred in the past are totally irrelevant to any decision that is being made 'now'. Such costs are **past costs** or **sunk costs.**

Costs that have been incurred include not only costs that have already been paid, but also costs that have been **committed.** A **committed cost** is a future cash flow that will be incurred anyway, regardless of the decision taken now.

(b) **Relevant costs are cash flows.** Only cash flow information is required. This means that costs or charges which do not reflect **additional cash spending** (such as depreciation and notional costs) should be ignored for the purpose of decision making.

(c) **Relevant costs are incremental costs.** For example, if an employee is expected to have no other work to do during the next week, but will be paid his basic wage (of, say, £100 per week) for attending work and doing nothing, his manager might decide to give him a job which earns the organisation £40. The net gain is £40 and the £100 is irrelevant to the decision because although it is a future cash flow, it will be incurred anyway whether the employee is given work or not.

1.2 Other terms are sometimes used to describe relevant costs.

> **KEY TERM**
>
> **Avoidable costs** are costs which would not be incurred if the activity to which they relate did not exist.

1.3 One of the situations in which it is necessary to identify the avoidable costs is in deciding whether or not to **discontinue a product.** The only costs which would be saved are the **avoidable costs** which are usually the variable costs and sometimes some specific costs. Costs which would be incurred whether or not the product is discontinued are known as **unavoidable costs.**

> **KEY TERM**
>
> **Differential cost** is 'the difference in total cost between alternatives.'
>
> CIMA *Official Terminology*

1.4 For example, if decision option A costs £300 and decision option B costs £360, the differential cost is £60.

KEY TERM

An **opportunity cost** is 'The value of the benefit sacrificed when one course of action is chosen, in preference to an alternative'.

CIMA *Official Terminology*

1.5 Suppose for example that there are three options, A, B and C, only one of which can be chosen. The net profit from each would be £80, £100 and £70 respectively.

Since only one option can be selected option B would be chosen because it offers the biggest benefit.

	£
Profit from option B	100
Less opportunity cost (ie the benefit from the most profitable alternative, A)	80
Differential benefit of option B	20

The decision to choose option B would not be taken simply because it offers a profit of £100, but because it offers a differential profit of £20 in excess of the next best alternative.

Controllable and uncontrollable costs

1.6 We came across the term **controllable costs** at the beginning of this study text. **Controllable costs** are items of expenditure which can be directly influenced by a given manager within a given time span.

1.7 As a general rule, **committed fixed costs** such as those costs arising from the possession of plant, equipment and buildings (giving rise to depreciation and rent) are largely **uncontrollable** in the short term because they have been committed by longer-term decisions.

1.8 **Discretionary fixed costs**, for example, advertising and research and development costs can be thought of as being **controllable** because they are incurred as a result of decisions made by management and can be raised or lowered at fairly short notice.

Sunk costs

KEY TERM

A **sunk cost** is a past cost which is not directly relevant in decision making.

1.9 **The principle underlying decision accounting is that management decisions can only affect the future.** In decision making, managers therefore require information about **future costs and revenues** which would be affected by the decision under review. They must not be misled by events, costs and revenues in the past, about which they can do nothing.

1.10 **Sunk costs**, which have been charged already as a cost of sales in a previous accounting period or will be charged in a future accounting period although the expenditure has already been incurred, are irrelevant to decision making.

1.11 An example of a sunk cost is development costs which have already been incurred. Suppose that a company has spent £250,000 in developing a new service for customers, but the marketing department's most recent findings are that the service might not gain customer acceptance and could be a commercial failure. The decision whether or not to abandon the development of the new service would have to be taken, but the £250,000 spent so far should be ignored by the decision makers because it is a **sunk cost**.

Fixed and variable costs

Exam focus point

Unless you are given an indication to the contrary, you should assume the following.

- Variable costs will be relevant costs.
- Fixed costs are irrelevant to a decision.

This need not be the case, however, and you should analyse variable and fixed cost data carefully. Do not forget that 'fixed' costs may only be fixed in the short term.

Non-relevant variable costs

1.12 There might be occasions when a variable cost is in fact a sunk cost (and therefore a **non-relevant variable cost**). For example, suppose that a company has some units of raw material in stock. They have been paid for already, and originally cost £2,000. They are now obsolete and are no longer used in regular production, and they have no scrap value. However, they could be used in a special job which the company is trying to decide whether to undertake. The special job is a 'one-off' customer order, and would use up all these materials in stock.

(a) In deciding whether the job should be undertaken, the relevant cost of the materials to the special job is nil. Their original cost of £2,000 is a **sunk cost**, and should be ignored in the decision.

(b) However, if the materials did have a scrap value of, say, £300, then their relevant cost to the job would be the **opportunity cost** of being unable to sell them for scrap, ie £300.

Attributable fixed costs

1.13 There might be occasions when a fixed cost is a relevant cost, and you must be aware of the distinction between '**specific**' or '**directly attributable**' **fixed costs**, and general fixed overheads.

1.14 **Directly attributable fixed costs** are those costs which, although fixed within a relevant range of activity level are relevant to a decision for either of the following reasons.

(a) They could increase if certain extra activities were undertaken. For example, it may be necessary to employ an extra supervisor if a particular order is accepted. The extra salary would be an **attributable fixed cost**.

(b) They would decrease or be eliminated entirely if a decision were taken either to reduce the scale of operations or shut down entirely.

1.15 **General fixed overheads** are those fixed overheads which will be unaffected by decisions to increase or decrease the scale of operations, perhaps because they are an apportioned share of the fixed costs of items which would be completely unaffected by the decisions. General fixed overheads are not relevant in decision making.

Absorbed overhead

1.16 **Absorbed overhead** is a **notional** accounting cost and hence should be ignored for decision-making purposes. **It is overhead incurred which may be relevant to a decision.**

The relevant cost of materials

1.17 The relevant cost of raw materials is generally their **current replacement cost,** *unless* the materials have already been purchased and would not be replaced once used. In this case the relevant cost of using them is the **higher** of the following.

- Their current resale value
- The value they would obtain if they were put to an alternative use

If the materials have no resale value and no other possible use, then the relevant cost of using them for the opportunity under consideration would be nil.

Question 1

O'Reilly Ltd has been approached by a customer who would like a special job to be done for him, and who is willing to pay £22,000 for it. The job would require the following materials.

Material	*Total units required*	*Units already in stock*	*Book value of units in stock*	*Realisable value*	*Replacement cost*
			£/unit	£/unit	£/unit
A	1,000	0	-	-	6
B	1,000	600	2	2.50	5
C	1,000	700	3	2.50	4
D	200	200	4	6.00	9

Material B is used regularly by O'Reilly Ltd, and if units of B are required for this job, they would need to be replaced to meet other production demand.

Materials C and D are in stock as the result of previous over-buying, and they have a restricted use. No other use could be found for material C, but the units of material D could be used in another job as substitute for 300 units of material E, which currently costs £5 per unit (of which the company has no units in stock at the moment).

Required

Calculate the relevant costs of material for deciding whether or not to accept the contract.

Answer

(a) **Material A** is not yet owned. It would have to be bought in full at the replacement cost of £6 per unit.

(b) **Material B** is used regularly by the company. There are existing stocks (600 units) but if these are used on the contract under review a further 600 units would be bought to replace them. Relevant costs are therefore 1,000 units at the replacement cost of £5 per unit.

(c) 1,000 units of **material C** are needed and 700 are already in stock. If used for the contract, a further 300 units must be bought at £4 each. The existing stocks of 700 will not be replaced. If they are used for the contract, they could not be sold at £2.50 each. The realisable value of these 700 units is an opportunity cost of sales revenue forgone.

(d) The required units of **material D** are already in stock and will not be replaced. There is an opportunity cost of using D in the contract because there are alternative opportunities either to sell the existing stocks for £6 per unit (£1,200 in total) or avoid other purchases (of material E), which would cost 300 x £5 = £1,500. Since substitution for E is more beneficial, £1,500 is the opportunity cost.

(e) **Summary of relevant costs**

	£
Material A (1,000 × £6)	6,000
Material B (1,000 × £5)	5,000
Material C (300 × £4) plus (700 × £2.50)	2,950
Material D	1,500
Total	15,450

The relevant cost of labour

1.18 The relevant cost of labour, in different situations, is best explained by means of an example.

1.19 EXAMPLE: RELEVANT COST OF LABOUR

LW plc is currently deciding whether to undertake a new contract. 15 hours of labour will be required for the contract. LW plc currently produces product L, the standard cost details of which are shown below.

STANDARD COST CARD
PRODUCT L

	£/unit
Direct materials (10kg @ £2)	20
Direct labour (5 hrs @ £6)	30
	50
Selling price	72
Contribution	22

(a) What is the relevant cost of labour if the labour must be hired from outside the organisation?

(b) What is the relevant cost of labour if LW plc expects to have 5 hours spare capacity?

(c) What is the relevant cost of labour if labour is in short supply?

1.20 SOLUTION

(a) Where labour must be hired from outside the organisation, the relevant cost of labour will be the variable costs incurred.

Relevant cost of labour on new contract = 15 hours @ £6 = £90

(b) It is assumed that the 5 hours spare capacity will be paid anyway, and so if these 5 hours are used on another contract, there is no additional cost to LW plc.

Relevant cost of labour on new contract

	£
Direct labour (10 hours @ £6)	60
Spare capacity (5 hours @ £0)	0
	60

(c) Contribution earned per unit of Product L produced = £22

If it requires 5 hours of labour to make one unit of product L, the contribution earned per labour hour = £22/5 = £4.40.

Relevant cost of labour on new contract

	£
Direct labour (15 hours @ £6)	90
Contribution lost by not making product L (£4.40 × 15 hours)	66
	156

1.21 It is important that you should be able to identify the relevant costs which are appropriate to a decision. In many cases, this is a fairly straightforward problem, but there are cases where great care should be taken. Attempt the following question.

Question 2

A company has been making a machine to order for a customer, but the customer has since gone into liquidation, and there is no prospect that any money will be obtained from the winding up of the company.

Costs incurred to date in manufacturing the machine are £50,000 and progress payments of £15,000 had been received from the customer prior to the liquidation.

The sales department has found another company willing to buy the machine for £34,000 once it has been completed.

To complete the work, the following costs would be incurred.

(a) Materials: these have been bought at a cost of £6,000. They have no other use, and if the machine is not finished, they would be sold for scrap for £2,000.

(b) Further labour costs would be £8,000. Labour is in short supply, and if the machine is not finished, the work force would be switched to another job, which would earn £30,000 in revenue, and incur direct costs of £12,000 and absorbed (fixed) overhead of £8,000.

(c) Consultancy fees £4,000. If the work is not completed, the consultant's contract would be cancelled at a cost of £1,500.

(d) General overheads of £8,000 would be added to the cost of the additional work.

Required

Assess whether the new customer's offer should be accepted.

Answer

(a) Costs incurred in the past, or revenue received in the past are not relevant because they cannot affect a decision about what is best for the future. Costs incurred to date of £50,000 and revenue received of £15,000 are 'water under the bridge' and should be ignored.

(b) Similarly, the price paid in the past for the materials is **irrelevant**. The only relevant cost of materials affecting the decision is the opportunity cost of the revenue from scrap which would be forgone - £2,000.

(c) **Labour costs**

	£
Labour costs required to complete work	8,000
Opportunity costs: contribution forgone by losing other work £(30,000 – 12,000)	18,000
Relevant cost of labour	26,000

(d) The **incremental cost** of consultancy from completing the work is £2,500.

	£
Cost of completing work	4,000
Cost of cancelling contract	1,500
Incremental cost of completing work	2,500

(e) **Absorbed overhead is a notional accounting cost** and should be ignored. Actual overhead incurred is the only overhead cost to consider. General overhead costs (and the absorbed overhead of the alternative work for the labour force) should be ignored.

(f) **Relevant costs may be summarised as follows.**

		£	£
Revenue from completing work			34,000
Relevant costs			
Materials:	opportunity cost	2,000	
Labour:	basic pay	8,000	
	opportunity cost	18,000	
Incremental cost of consultant		2,500	
			30,500
Extra profit to be earned by accepting the order			3,500

The deprival value of an asset

Exam focus point

The study guide for Paper 1.2 states that candidates must be able to 'calculate and explain the deprival value of an asset'.

1.22 In simple terms, the deprival value of an asset represents the amount of money that a company would have to receive if it were deprived of an asset in order to be no worse off than it already is. The deprival value of an asset is best demonstrated by means of an example.

1.23 EXAMPLE: DEPRIVAL VALUE OF AN ASSET

A machine cost £14,000 ten years ago. It is expected that the machine will generate future revenues of £10,000. Alternatively, the machine could be scrapped for £8,000. An equivalent machine in the same condition would cost £9,000 to buy now. What is the deprival value of the machine?

1.24 SOLUTION

Firstly, let us think about the relevance of the costs given to us in the question.

Cost of machine = £14,000 = past/sunk cost
Future revenues = £10,000 = revenue expected to be generated
Net realisable value = £8,000 = scrap proceeds
Replacement cost = £9,000

When calculating the deprival value of an asset, use the following diagram.

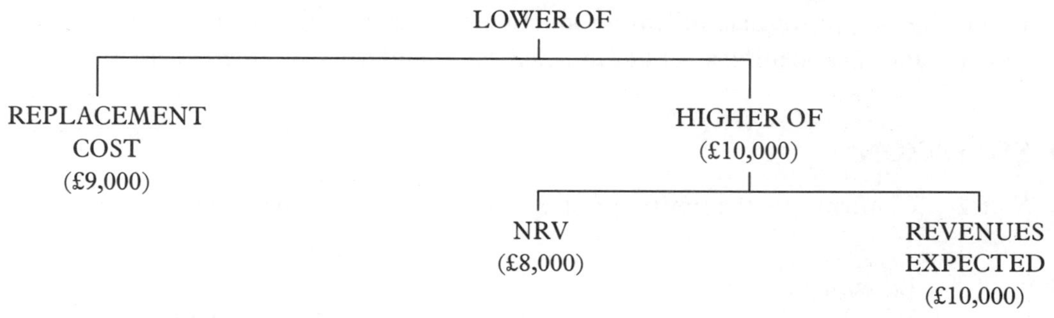

Therefore, the deprival value of the machine is the lower of the replacement cost and £10,000. The deprival value is therefore £9,000.

2 CHOICE OF PRODUCT (PRODUCT MIX) DECISIONS

2.1 One of the more common decision-making problems is a situation where there are not enough resources to meet the potential sales demand, and so a decision has to be made about what mix of products to produce, using what resources there are as effectively as possible.

KEY TERM

A **limiting factor** is a factor which limits the organisation's activities.

2.2 A **limiting factor** could be sales if there is a limit to sales demand but any one of the organisation's resources (labour, materials and so on) may be insufficient to meet the level of production demanded.

2.3 It is assumed in limiting factor accounting that management wishes to maximise profit and that **profit will be maximised when contribution is maximised** (given no change in fixed cost expenditure incurred). In other words, **marginal costing ideas are applied.**

2.4 **Contribution will be maximised by earning the biggest possible contribution from each unit of limiting factor.** For example if grade A labour is the limiting factor, contribution will be maximised by earning the biggest contribution from each hour of grade A labour worked.

2.5 **The limiting factor decision therefore involves the determination of the contribution earned by each different product from each unit of the limiting factor.**

2.6 EXAMPLE: LIMITING FACTOR

AB Ltd makes two products, the Ay and the Be. Unit variable costs are as follows.

	Ay	*Be*
	£	£
Direct materials	1	3
Direct labour (£3 per hour)	6	3
Variable overhead	1	1
	8	7

The sales price per unit is £14 per Ay and £11 per Be. During July 20X2 the available direct labour is limited to 8,000 hours. Sales demand in July is expected to be 3,000 units for Ays and 5,000 units for Bes.

Required

Determine the profit-maximising production mix, assuming that monthly fixed costs are £20,000, and that opening stocks of finished goods and work in progress are nil.

2.7 SOLUTION

Step 1. Confirm that the limiting factor is something other than sales demand.

	Ays	*Bes*	*Total*
Labour hours per unit	2 hrs	1 hr	
Sales demand	3,000 units	5,000 units	
Labour hours needed	6,000 hrs	5,000 hrs	11,000 hrs
Labour hours available			8,000 hrs
Shortfall			3,000 hrs

Labour is the limiting factor on production.

Step 2. Identify the contribution earned by each product per unit of limiting factor, that is per labour hour worked.

	Ays	*Bes*
	£	£
Sales price	14	11
Variable cost	8	7
Unit contribution	6	4
Labour hours per unit	2 hrs	1 hr
Contribution per labour hour (= unit of limiting factor)	£3	£4

Although Ays have a higher unit contribution than Bes, two Bes can be made in the time it takes to make one Ay. Because labour is in short supply it is more profitable to make Bes than Ays.

Step 3. Determine the **optimum production plan**. Sufficient Bes will be made to meet the full sales demand, and the remaining labour hours available will then be used to make Ays.

(a)

Product	*Demand*	*Hours required*	*Hours available*	*Priority of manufacture*
Bes	5,000	5,000	5,000	1st
Ays	3,000	6,000	3,000 (bal)	2nd
		11,000	8,000	

(b)

Product	*Units*	*Hours needed*	*Contribution per unit*	*Total*
			£	£
Bes	5,000	5,000	4	20,000
Ays	1,500	3,000	6	9,000
		8,000		29,000
Less fixed costs				20,000
Profit				9,000

2.8 In conclusion

(a) Unit contribution is **not** the correct way to decide priorities.

(b) Labour hours are the scarce resource, and therefore contribution **per labour hour** is the correct way to decide priorities.

(c) The Be earns £4 contribution per labour hour, and the Ay earns £3 contribution per labour hour. Bes therefore make more profitable use of the scarce resource, and should be manufactured first.

Exam focus point

If an examination question asks you to determine the optimum production plan, follow the five-step approach shown below.

Step 1. Identify the limiting factor
Step 2. Calculate contribution per unit for each product
Step 3. Calculate contribution per unit of limiting factor
Step 4. Rank products (make product with highest contribution per unit of limiting factor first)
Step 5. Make products in rank order until scare resource is used up **(optimal production plan)**

3 MAKE OR BUY DECISIONS

3.1 A **make or buy problem** involves a decision by an organisation about whether it should make a product/carry out an activity with its own internal resources, or whether it should pay another organisation to make the product/carry out the activity. Examples of make or buy decisions would be as follows.

(a) Whether a company should manufacture its own components, or buy the components from an outside supplier.

(b) Whether a construction company should do some work with its own employees, or whether it should subcontract the work to another company.

3.2 If an organisation has the freedom of choice about whether to make internally or buy externally and has no scarce resources that put a restriction on what it can do itself, the relevant costs for the decision will be the **differential costs** between the two options.

3.3 EXAMPLE: MAKE OR BUY

Buster Ltd makes four components, W, X, Y and Z, for which costs in the forthcoming year are expected to be as follows.

	W	*X*	*Y*	*Z*
Production (units)	1,000	2,000	4,000	3,000
Unit marginal costs	£	£	£	£
Direct materials	4	5	2	4
Direct labour	8	9	4	6
Variable production overheads	2	3	1	2
	14	17	7	12

Directly attributable fixed costs per annum and committed fixed costs are as follows.

	£
Incurred as a direct consequence of making W	1,000
Incurred as a direct consequence of making X	5,000
Incurred as a direct consequence of making Y	6,000
Incurred as a direct consequence of making Z	8,000
Other fixed costs (committed)	30,000
	50,000

A subcontractor has offered to supply units of W, X, Y and Z for £12, £21, £10 and £14 respectively.

Required

Decide whether Buster Ltd should make or buy the components.

3.4 SOLUTION

(a) **The relevant costs are the differential costs between making and buying,** and they consist of differences in unit variable costs plus differences in directly attributable fixed costs. Subcontracting will result in some fixed cost savings.

	W	*X*	*Y*	*Z*
	£	£	£	£
Unit variable cost of making	14	17	7	12
Unit variable cost of buying	12	21	10	14
	(2)	4	3	2

	W	*X*	*Y*	*Z*
Annual requirements (units)	1,000	2,000	4,000	3,000
	£	£	£	£
Extra variable cost of buying (per annum)	(2,000)	8,000	12,000	6,000
Fixed costs saved by buying	(1,000)	(5,000)	(6,000)	(8,000)
Extra total cost of buying	(3,000)	3,000	6,000	(2,000)

(b) The company would save £3,000 pa by subcontracting component W (where the purchase cost would be less than the marginal cost per unit to make internally) and would save £2,000 pa by subcontracting component Z (because of the saving in fixed costs of £8,000).

(c) In this example, relevant costs are the variable costs of in-house manufacture, the variable costs of subcontracted units, and the saving in fixed costs.

3.5 Other factors to consider in the make or buy decision

(a) If components W and Z are subcontracted, how will the company most profitably use the spare capacity? Would the company's workforce resent the loss of work to an outside subcontractor?

(b) Would the subcontractor be reliable with delivery times, and would he supply components of the same quality as those manufactured internally?

(c) Does the company wish to be flexible and maintain better control over operations by making everything itself?

(d) Are the estimates of fixed cost savings reliable? In the case of Product W, buying is clearly cheaper than making in-house. In the case of product Z, the decision to buy rather than make would only be financially beneficial if the fixed cost savings of £8,000 could really be 'delivered' by management.

Question 3

BB Limited makes three components - S, T and W. The following costs have been recorded.

	Component S *Unit cost*	*Component T* *Unit cost*	*Component W* *Unit cost*
	£	£	£
Variable cost	2.50	8.00	5.00
Fixed cost	2.00	8.30	3.75
Total cost	4.50	16.30	8.75

Another company has offered to supply the components to BB Limited at the following prices.

	Component S	*Component T*	*Component W*
Price each	£4	£7	£5.50

Which component(s), if any, should BB Limited consider buying in?

A Buy in all three components
B Do not buy any
C Buy in S and W
D Buy in T only

Answer

BB Ltd should buy the component if the variable cost of making the component is more than the variable cost of buying the component.

	Component S	*Component T*	*Component W*
	£	£	£
Variable cost of making	2.50	8.00	5.00
Variable cost of buying	4.00	7.00	5.50
	(1.50)	1.00	(0.50)

The variable cost of making component T is greater than the variable cost of buying it.

∴ BB Ltd should consider buying in component T only.

The correct answer is D.

Make or buy decisions and limiting factors

3.6 In a situation where a company must subcontract work to make up a shortfall in its own production capability, its total costs are minimised if those components/products subcontracted are those with the lowest extra variable cost of buying per unit of limiting factor saved by buying.

3.7 EXAMPLE: MAKE OR BUY AND LIMITING FACTORS

Green Ltd manufactures two components, the Alpha and the Beta, using the same machines for each. The budget for the next year calls for the production and assembly of 4,000 of each component. The variable production cost per unit of the final product, the gamma, is as follows.

	Machine hours	*Variable cost*
		£
1 unit of Alpha	3	20
1 unit of Beta	2	36
Assembly		20
		76

Only 16,000 hours of machine time will be available during the year, and a sub-contractor has quoted the following unit prices for supplying components: Alpha £29; Beta £40. Advise Green Ltd.

3.8 SOLUTION

(a) There is a shortfall in machine hours available, and some products must be sub-contracted.

Product	*Units*		*Machine hours*
Alpha	4,000		12,000
Beta	4,000		8,000
		Required	20,000
		Available	16,000
		Shortfall	4,000

(b) **The assembly costs are not relevant costs because they are unaffected by the make or buy decision.** The units subcontracted should be those which will add least to the costs of Green Ltd. Since 4,000 hours of work must be sub-contracted, the cheapest policy is to subcontract work which adds the least extra costs (the least extra variable costs) per hour of own-time saved.

(c)

	Alpha	Beta
	£	£
Variable cost of making	20	36
Variable cost of buying	29	40
Extra variable cost of buying	9	4
Machine hours saved by buying	3 hrs	2 hrs
Extra variable cost of buying, per hour saved	£3	£2

It is cheaper to buy Betas than to buy Alphas and so the priority for making the components in-house will be in the reverse order to the preference for buying them from a subcontractor.

(d)

Component	Hrs per unit to make in-house	Hrs required in total	Cumulative hours
Alpha	3 hrs	12,000	12,000
Beta	2 hrs	8,000	20,000
		20,000	
Hours available		16,000	
Shortfall		4,000	

There are enough machine hours to make all 4,000 units of Alpha and 2,000 units of Beta. 4,000 hours production of Beta must be sub-contracted. This will be the cheapest production policy available

(e)

Component	Machine hours	Number of units	Unit variable cost	Total variable cost
Make			£	£
Alpha	12,000	4,000	20	80,000
Beta (balance)	4,000	2,000	36	72,000
	16,000			152,000
Buy	*Hours saved*			
Beta (balance)	4,000	2,000	40	80,000
		Total variable costs of components		232,000
		Assembly costs (4,000 × £20)		80,000
		Total variable costs		312,000

4 SHUT DOWN DECISIONS

4.1 **Shut down decisions** involve the following.

(a) Whether or not to shut down a factory, department, or product line either because it is making a loss or it is too expensive to run.

(b) If the decision is to shut down, whether the closure should be permanent or temporary.

4.2 EXAMPLE: SHUT DOWN DECISIONS

Suppose that a company manufactures three products, Corfus, Cretes and Zantes. The present net profit from these is as follows.

	Corfus	Cretes	Zantes	Total
	£	£	£	£
Sales	50,000	40,000	60,000	150,000
Variable costs	30,000	25,000	35,000	90,000
Contribution	20,000	15,000	25,000	60,000
Fixed costs	17,000	18,000	20,000	55,000
Profit/loss	3,000	(3,000)	5,000	5,000

The company is concerned about its poor profit performance, and is considering whether or not to cease selling Cretes. It is felt that selling prices cannot be raised or lowered without adversely affecting net income. £5,000 of the fixed costs of Cretes are attributable fixed costs which would be saved if production ceased. All other fixed costs would remain the same.

4.3 SOLUTION

(a) By stopping production of Cretes, the consequences would be a £10,000 fall in profits.

	£
Loss of contribution	(15,000)
Savings in fixed costs	5,000
Incremental loss	(10,000)

(b) Suppose, however, it were possible to use the resources realised by stopping production of Cretes and switch to producing a new item, Rhodes, which would sell for £50,000 and incur variable costs of £30,000 and extra direct fixed costs of £6,000. A new decision is now required.

	Cretes	*Rhodes*
	£	£
Sales	40,000	50,000
Less variable costs	25,000	30,000
Contribution	15,000	20,000
Less direct fixed costs	5,000	6,000
Contribution to shared fixed costs and profit	10,000	14,000

It would be more profitable to shut down production of Cretes and switch resources to making Rhodes, in order to boost profits to £9,000.

5 ONE-OFF CONTRACTS

5.1 This type of decision-making situation will concern a contract which would utilise an organisation's spare capacity but which would have to be accepted at a price lower than that normally required by the organisation. In general you can assume that a contract will probably be **accepted if it increases contribution** and hence profit, and **rejected if it reduces contribution (and hence profit)**. Let us consider an example.

5.2 EXAMPLE: ONE-OFF CONTRACTS

Belt and Braces Ltd makes a single product which sells for £20. It has a full cost of £15 which is made up as follows.

	£
Direct material	4
Direct labour (2 hours)	6
Variable overhead	2
General fixed overhead	3
	15

The labour force is currently working at 90% of capacity and so there is a spare capacity for 2,000 units. A customer has approached the company with a request for the manufacture of a special order of 2,000 units for which he is willing to pay £25,000. Assess whether the contract should be accepted.

5.3 SOLUTION

	£	£
Value of order		25,000
Cost of order		
Direct materials (£4 × 2,000)	8,000	
Direct labour (£6 × 2,000)	12,000	
Variable overhead (£2 × 2,000)	4,000	
Relevant cost of order		24,000
Profit from order acceptance		1,000

Fixed costs will be incurred regardless of whether the contract is accepted and so are not relevant to the decision. The contract should be accepted since it increases contribution to profit by £1,000.

5.4 **Other factors to consider in the one-off contract decision**

(a) The acceptance of the contract at a lower price may lead other customers to demand lower prices as well.

(b) There may be more profitable ways of using the spare capacity.

(c) Accepting the contract may lock up capacity that could be used for future full-price business.

(d) Fixed costs may, in fact, alter if the contract is accepted.

Chapter roundup

- **Relevant costs** are future cash flows arising as a direct consequence of a decision.
    - Relevant costs are **future costs**
    - Relevant costs are **cashflows**
    - Relevant costs are **incremental costs**
- Relevant costs are also **differential costs** and **opportunity costs.**
    - **Differential cost** is the difference in total cost between alternatives.
    - An **opportunity cost** is the value of the benefit sacrificed when one course of action is chosen in preference to an alternative.
- A **sunk cost** is a past cost which is not directly relevant in decision making.
- The principle underlying decision accounting is that management decisions can only affect the **future**. Management therefore require information about **future costs and revenues.**
- **In general**, variable costs will be relevant costs and fixed costs will be irrelevant to a decision.
- The **deprival value** of an asset represents the amount of money that a company would have to receive if it were deprived of an asset in order to be no worse off than it already is.
- A **limiting factor** is a factor which limits the organisation's activities.
- In a **limiting factor situation,** contribution will be maximised by earning the biggest possible contribution per unit of limiting factor.
- In a **make or buy** situation with no limiting factors, the relevant costs for the decision are the **differential costs** between the two options.
- **Shutdown decisions** involve deciding whether or not to shut down a factory, department or product line.
- The decision to accept or reject a contract should be made on the basis of whether or not the contract **increases contribution and profit**.

Quick quiz

1 Relevant costs are:

(a)
(b)
(c)
(d)
(e)

2 Sunk costs are directly relevant in decision making.

True ☐

False ☐

3 The following information relates to machine Z.

Purchase price = £7,000
Expected future revenues = £5,000
Scrap value = £4,000
Replacement cost = £4,500

Complete the following diagram in order to calculate the deprival value of machine Z.

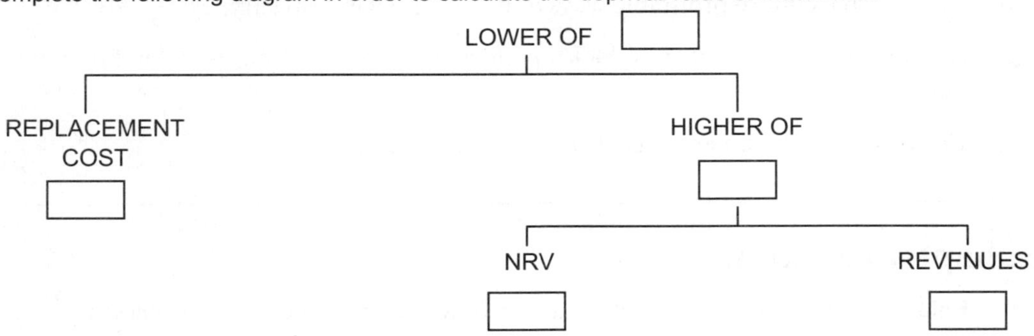

The deprival value of machine Z is ....

4 A limiting factor is a factor which ....

5 When determining the optimum production plan, what five steps are involved?

Step 1. ....
Step 2. ....
Step 3. ....
Step 4. ....
Step 5. ....

6 A sunk cost is:

A a cost committed to be spent in the current period
B a cost which is irrelevant for decision making
C a cost connected with oil exploration in the North Sea
D a cost unaffected by fluctuations in the level of activity

Answers to quick quiz

1 (a) Future costs
(b) Cash flows
(c) Incremental costs
(d) Differential costs
(e) Opportunity costs

2 False

3

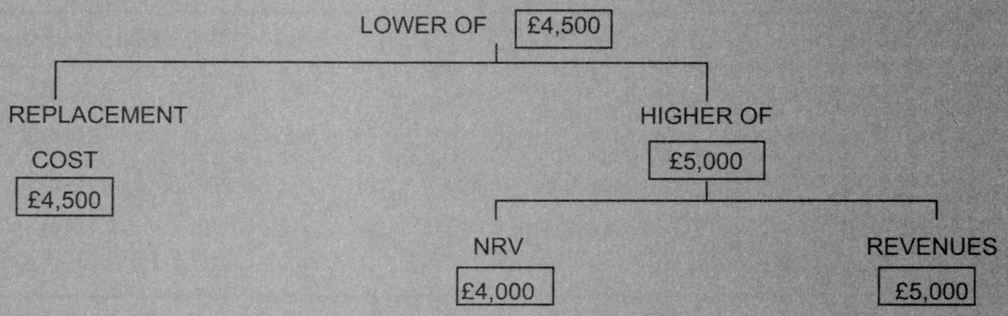

The deprival value of machine Z is **£4,500**.

4 Limits the organisation's activities.

5 ***Step 1.*** Identify the limiting factor
Step 2. Calculate contribution per unit for each product
Step 3. Calculate contribution per unit of limiting factor
Step 4. Rank products (make product with highest contribution per unit of limiting factor first)
Step 5. Make products in rank order until scare resource is used up **(optimal production plan)**

6 B

Now try the questions below from the Exam Question Bank

Number	Level	Marks	Time
26	MCQ	n/a	n/a
27	Examination	10	18 mins

Chapter 16

LINEAR PROGRAMMING

Introduction

We are now going to look at a decision-making technique which involves **allocating resources in order to achieve the best results**. The name '**linear programming**' sounds rather formidable and the technique *can* get very complicated. Don't worry though: you are only expected to be able to analyse the simplest examples, using a graphical technique (ie draw lines!) and using equations. Get a ruler and sharpen your pencil!

Study guide

Section 21 – Limiting factors

- Explain and recognise what causes optimisation problems

Section 22 – Linear programming

- Formulate a linear programming problem involving two variables
- Determine the optimal solution to a linear programming problem using a graph
- Determine the optimal solution to a linear programming problem using equations
- Explain the methods available for dealing with optimisation problems with more than two variables
- Formulate, but do not solve, a linear programming problem involving more than two variables
- Explain shadow prices (calculations not examinable)

Exam guide

The contents of this chapter are not one of the key areas of the syllabus. However, there was a compulsory ten-mark question in the pilot paper for the paper-based examination.

1 THE PROBLEM

Exam focus point

The study guide for Paper 1.2 states that candidates should be able to 'explain and recognise what causes **optimisation** problems'.

1.1 A typical business problem is to decide how a company should **divide up its production among the various types of product** it manufactures in order to obtain the **maximum possible profit**. A business cannot simply aim to produce as much as possible because there will be **limitations** or **constraints** within which the production must operate. Such constraints could be one or more of the following.

- Limited quantities of raw materials available
- A fixed number of man-hours per week for each type of worker
- Limited machine hours

1.2 Moreover, since the profits generated by different products vary, it may be better not to produce any of a less profitable line, but to concentrate all resources on producing the more profitable ones. On the other hand limitations in market demand could mean that some of the products produced may not be sold.

KEY TERM

Linear programming is a technique for solving problems of profit maximisation or cost minimisation and resource allocation. 'Programming' has nothing to do with computers: the word is simply used to denote a series of events.

2 FORMULATING THE PROBLEM

2.1 Let us imagine that B Ltd makes just two models, the Super and the Deluxe, and that the **only constraint** faced by the company is that **monthly machine capacity is restricted to 400 hours**. The Super requires 5 hours of machine time per unit and the Deluxe 1.5 hours. Government restrictions mean that the maximum number of units that can be sold each month is 150, that number being made up of any combination of the Super and the Deluxe.

2.2 Let us now work through the steps involved in setting up a linear programming model.

Step 1. **Define variables**

What are the quantities that the company can vary? Obviously not the number of machine hours or the maximum sales, which are fixed by external circumstances beyond the company's control. The only things which it can determine are the number of each type of unit to manufacture. It is these numbers which have to be determined in such a way as to get the maximum possible profit. Our variables will therefore be as follows.

Let x = the number of units of the Super manufactured.
Let y = the number of units of the Deluxe manufactured.

Step 2. **Establish constraints**

Having defined these two variables we can now translate the two constraints into inequalities involving the variables.

Let us first consider the machine hours constraint. Each Super requires 5 hours of machine time. Producing five Supers therefore requires $5 \times 5 = 25$ hours of machine time and, more generally, producing x Supers will require 5x hours. Likewise producing y Deluxes will require 1.5y hours. The total machine hours needed to make x Supers and y Deluxes is 5x + 1.5y. We know that this cannot be greater than 400 hours so we arrive at the following inequality.

$5x + 1.5y \leq 400$

We can obtain the other inequality more easily. The total number of Supers and Deluxes made each month is x + y but this has to be less than 150 due to government restrictions. The sales order constraint is therefore as follows.

$x + y \leq 150$

Non-negativity

The variables in linear programming models should usually be non-negative in value. In this example, for instance, you cannot make a negative number of units and so we need the following constraints.

$x \geq 0; y \geq 0$

Do not forget these non-negativity constraints when formulating a linear programming model.

Step 3. **Establish objective function**

We have yet to introduce the question of profits. Let us assume that the profit on each model is as follows.

	£
Super	100
Deluxe	200

The **objective** of B Ltd is to **maximise profit** and so the **function** to be maximised is as follows.

Profit (P) = 100x + 200y

The problem has now been reduced to the following four inequalities and one equation.

$$
\begin{aligned}
5x + 1.5y &\leq 400 \\
x + y &\leq 150 \\
x &\geq 0 \\
y &\geq 0 \\
P = 100x + 200y
\end{aligned}
$$

Have you noticed that **the inequalities are all linear expressions**? If plotted on a graph, they would all give **straight lines.** This explains why the technique is called **linear programming** and also gives a hint as to how we should proceed with trying to find the solution to the problem.

Question 1

Patel plc manufactures two products, X and Y, in quantities x and y units per week respectively. The contribution is £60 per X and £70 per Y. For practical reasons, no more than 100 Xs can be produced per week. If Patel plc uses linear programming to determine a profit-maximising production policy and on the basis of this information, which one of the following constraints is correct?

A $x \leq 60$
B $y \leq 100$
C $x \leq 100$
D $60x + 70y \leq 100$

Answer

The correct answer is C because the question states that the number of Xs produced cannot exceed 100 and so $x \leq 100$.

Option A has no immediate bearing on the number of units of X produced which must be ≤ 100. (£60 represents the contribution per unit of X).

We have no information on the production volume of Product Y and option B is therefore incorrect.

The contribution earned per week is given by 60x + 70y but we have no reason to suppose that this must be less than or equal to 100. Option D is therefore incorrect.

Exam focus point

Students often have problems with constraints of the style 'the quantity of one type must not exceed twice that of the other'. This can be interpreted as follows: the quantity of one type (say X) must not exceed (must be less than or equal to) twice that of the other (2Y) (ie $X \leq 2Y$).

3 GRAPHING THE MODEL

3.1 We have looked at how to **formulate a problem** and in this section we will look at solving a problem using graphs.

3.2 **A graphical solution is only possible when there are two variables in the problem. One variable is represented by the x axis and one by the y axis of the graph. Since non-negative values are not usually allowed, the graph shows only zero and positive values of x and y.**

3.3 A linear equation with one or two variables is shown as a straight line on a graph. Thus y = 6 would be shown as follows.

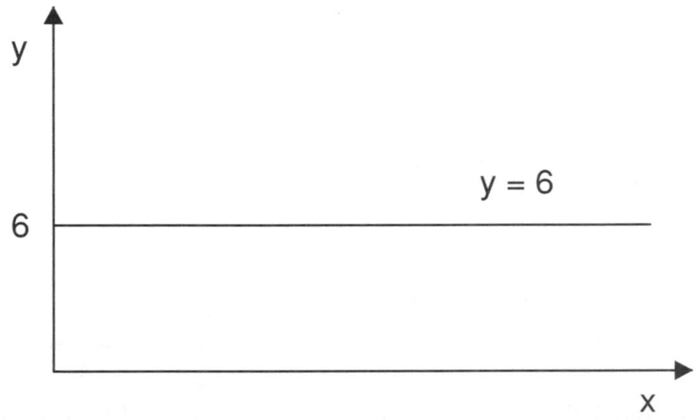

If the problem included a constraint that y could not exceed 6, the **inequality** $y \leq 6$ would be represented by the shaded area of the graph below.

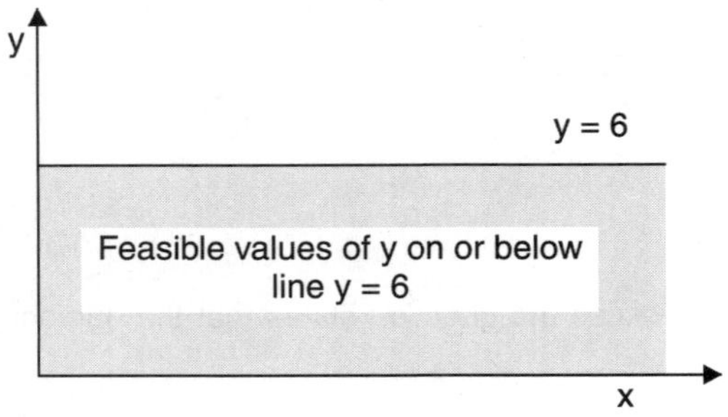

3.4 The equation 4x + 3y = 24 is also a straight line on a graph. To draw any straight line, we need only to plot two points and join them up. The easiest points to plot are the following.

(a) x = 0 (in this example, if x = 0, 3y = 24, y = 8)
(b) y = 0 (in this example, if y = 0, 4x = 24, x = 6)

By plotting the points, (0, 8) and (6, 0) on a graph, and joining them up, we have the line for 4x + 3y = 24.

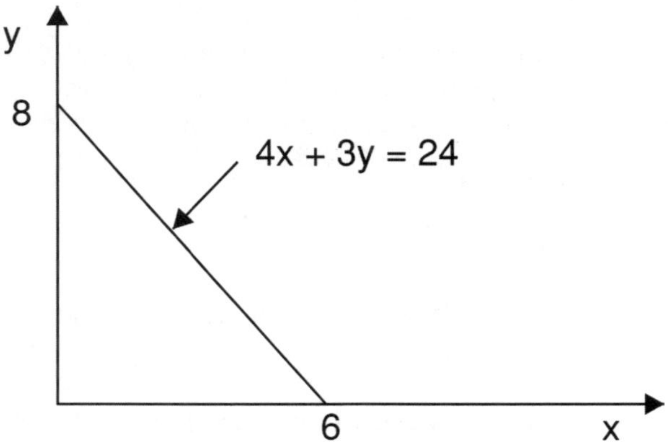

3.5 If we had a constraint 4x + 3y ≤ 24, any combined value of x and y within the shaded area below (on or below the line) would satisfy the constraint.

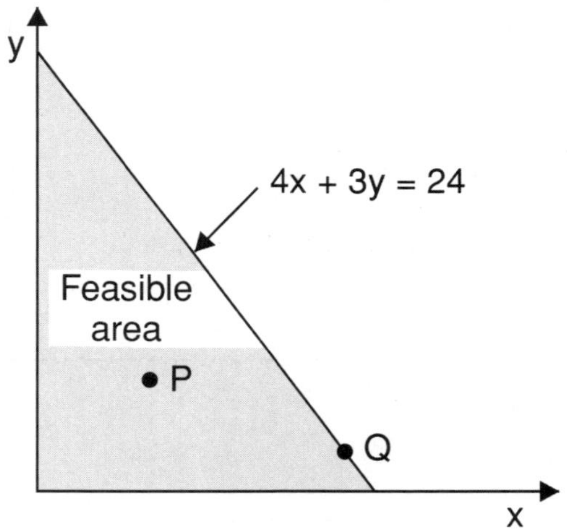

For example, at point P where (x = 2, y = 2) 4x + 3y = 14 which is less than 24; and at point Q where x = 5.5, y = 2/3, 4x + 3y = 24. Both P and Q lie within the **feasible area** (the area where the inequality is satisfied, also called the feasible region). A **feasible area** enclosed on all sides may also be called a **feasible polygon**.

3.6 The inequalities y ≥ 6, x ≥ 6 and 4x + 3y ≥ 24, would be shown graphically as follows.

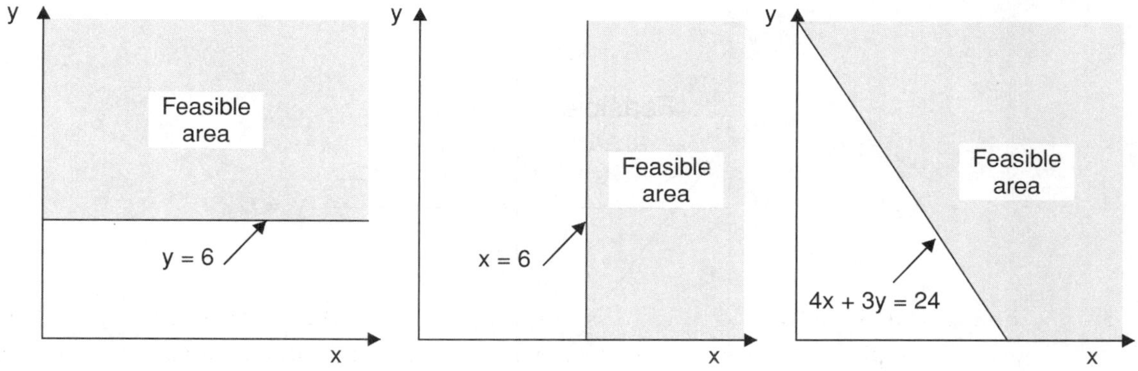

3.7 **When there are several constraints, the feasible area of combinations of values of x and y must be an area where all the inequalities are satisfied.**

Thus, if $y \leq 6$ *and* $4x + 3y \leq 24$ the feasible area would be the shaded area in the graph following

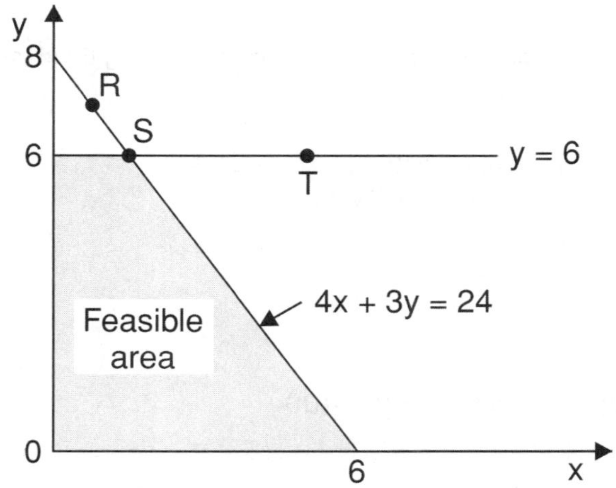

(a) Point R ($x = 0.75$, $y = 7$) is not in the feasible area because although it satisfies the inequality $4x + 3y \leq 24$, it does not satisfy $y \leq 6$.

(b) Point T ($x = 5$, $y = 6$) is not in the feasible area, because although it satisfies the inequality $y \leq 6$, it does not satisfy $4x + 3y \leq 24$.

(c) Point S ($x = 1.5$, $y = 6$) satisfies both inequalities and lies just on the boundary of the feasible area since $y = 6$ exactly, and $4x + 3y = 24$. Point S is thus at the intersection of the two equation lines.

3.8 Similarly, if $y \geq 6$ and $4x + 3y \geq 24$ but $x \leq 6$, the feasible area would be the shaded area in the graph below.

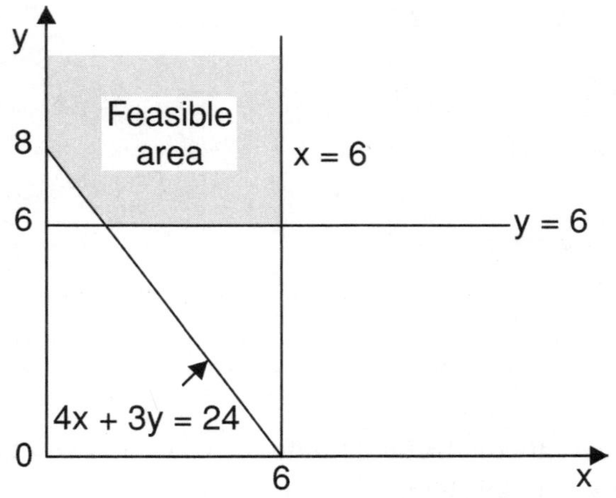

Question 2

Draw the feasible region which arises from the constraints facing B Ltd (see paragraph 2.2).

Answer

If 5x + 1.5y = 400, then if x = 0, y = 267 and if y = 0, x = 80.
If x + y = 150, then if x = 0, y = 150 and if y = 0, x = 150

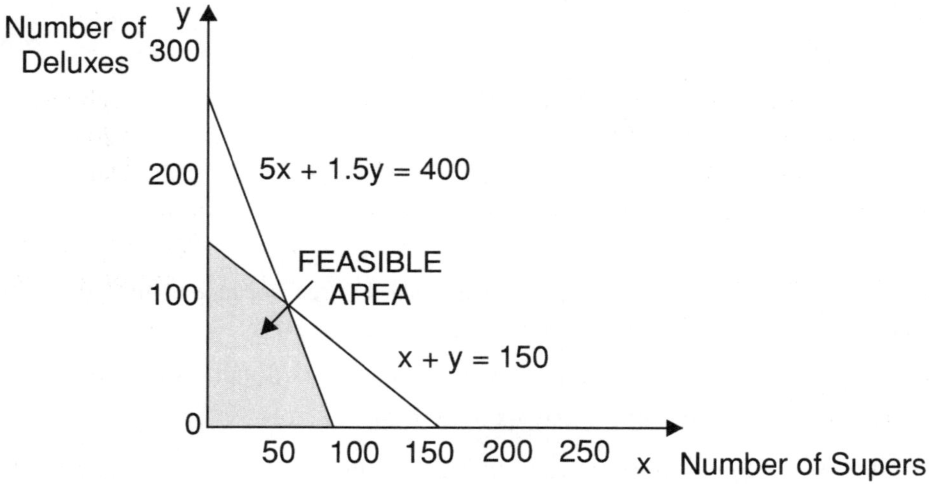

Question 3

In a linear programming problem, one of the constraints is given by 2x ≤ 3y. Which of the following statements about the graphical presentation of this constraint is correct?

I The constraint line passes through the point x = 2, y = 3.
II The constraint line passes through the origin.
III The constraint line passes through the point x = 3, y = 2.
IV The region below the constraint line is part of the feasible area.

A I and II only
B I and III only
C II and III only
D II, III and IV only

Answer

When x = 0 then y must also equal 0, therefore statement II is correct.

When x = 3, 6 = 3y and hence y = 2, therefore statement III is correct.

Statements II and III are correct and therefore option C is the right answer.

Statement I is incorrect since when x = 2, 4 = 3y and y = 1.33 and y does not equal 3 when x = 2.

Statement IV is incorrect since 3y is greater than 2x above the line, not below it.

4 FINDING THE BEST SOLUTION

4.1 Having found the **feasible region** (which includes all the possible solutions to the problem) we need to find which of these possible solutions is **'best'** in the sense that it yields the **maximum possible profit**. We could do this by finding out what profit each of the possible solutions would give, and then choosing as our 'best' combination the one for which the profit is greatest.

4.2 Consider, however, the feasible region of the problem faced by B Ltd (see the solution to Question 2). Even in such a simple problem as this, there are a great many possible solution points within the feasible area. Even to write them all down would be a time consuming process and also an unnecessary one, as we shall see.

4.3 Let us look again at the graph of B Ltd's problem.

Consider, for example, the point A at which 40 Supers and 80 Deluxes are being manufactured. This will yield a profit of ((40 × 100) + (80 × 200)) = £20,000. We would clearly get more profit at point B, where the same number of Deluxes are being manufactured but where the number of Supers being manufactured has increased by five, or from point C where the same number of Supers but 10 more Deluxes are manufactured. This argument suggests that **the 'best' solution is going to be a point on the edge of the feasible area rather than in the middle of it.**

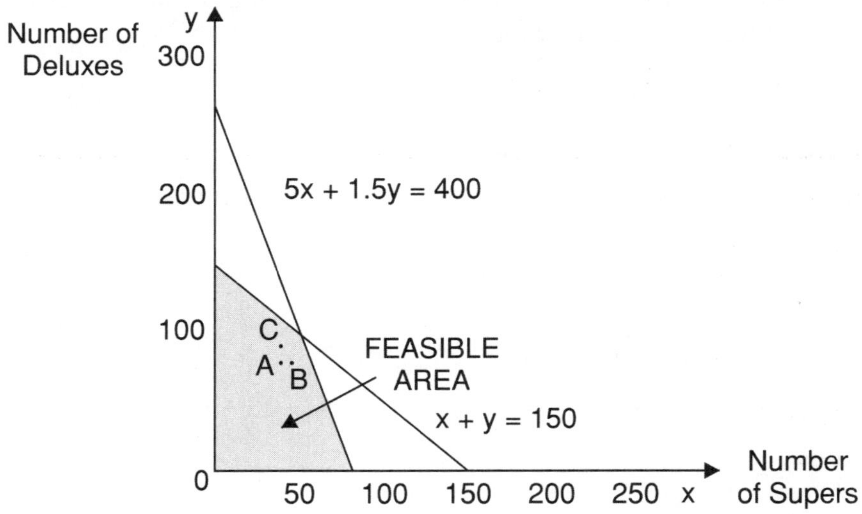

4.4 This still leaves us with quite a few points to look at but there is a way we can narrow down the candidates for the best solution still further. Suppose that B Ltd wish to make a profit of £10,000. The company could sell the following combinations of Supers and Deluxes.

(a) 100 Super, no Deluxe

(b) No Super, 50 Deluxe

(c) A proportionate mix of Super and Deluxe, such as 80 Super and 10 Deluxe or 50 Super and 25 Deluxe

4.5 The possible combinations of Supers and Deluxes required to earn a profit of £10,000 could be shown by the straight line 100x + 200y = 10,000.

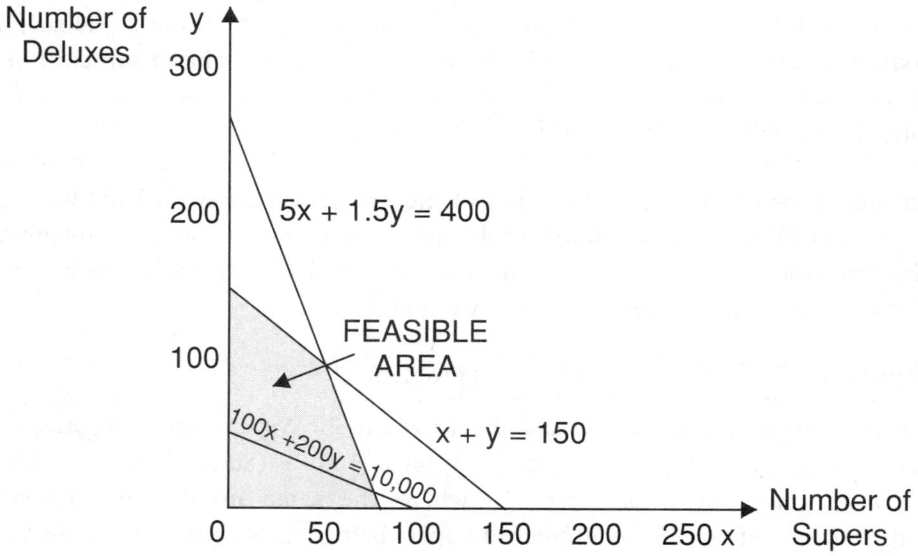

4.6 For a total profit of £15,000, a similar line 100x + 200y = 15,000 could be drawn to show the various combinations of Supers and Deluxes which would achieve the total of £15,000.

Similarly a line 100x + 200y = 8,000 would show the various combinations of Supers and Deluxes which would earn a total profit of £8,000.

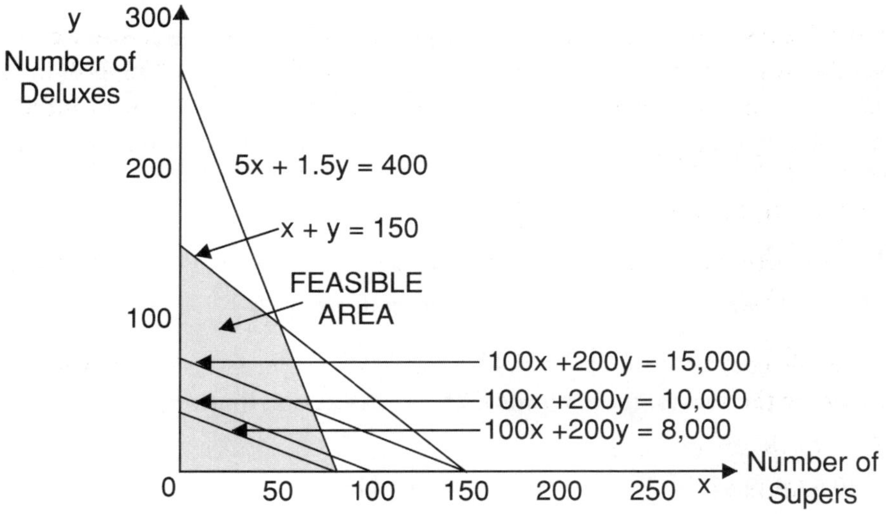

4.7 **These profit lines are all parallel.** (They are called **iso-profit lines,** 'iso' meaning equal.) A similar line drawn for any other total profit would also be parallel to the three lines shown here. This means that if we wish to know the slope or gradient of the profit line, for any value of total profit, we can simply draw one line for any convenient value of profit, and we will know that all the other lines will be parallel to the one drawn: they will have the same slope.

4.8 **Bigger profits are shown by lines further from the origin** (100x + 200y = 15,000), **smaller profits by lines closer to the origin** (100x + 200y = 8,000). As B Ltd try to **increase possible profit** we need to **slide the profit line outwards from the origin**, while always keeping it **parallel** to the other profit lines.

4.9 As we do this there will come a point at which, if we were to move the profit line out any further, it would cease to lie in the feasible region and therefore larger profits could not be achieved in practice because of the constraints. In our example concerning B Ltd this will happen, as you should test for yourself, where the profit line is just passing through the intersection of x + y = 150 with the y axis (at (0, 150)). The point (0, 150) will therefore give us the best production combination of the Super and the Deluxe, that is, to produce 150 Deluxe models and no Super models.

4.10 EXAMPLE: A MAXIMISATION PROBLEM

Brunel Ltd manufactures plastic-covered steel fencing in two qualities, standard and heavy gauge. Both products pass through the same processes, involving steel-forming and plastic bonding.

Standard gauge fencing sells at £18 a roll and heavy gauge fencing at £24 a roll. Variable costs per roll are £16 and £21 respectively. There is an unlimited market for the standard gauge, but demand for the heavy gauge is limited to 1,300 rolls a year. Factory operations are limited to 2,400 hours a year in each of the two production processes.

	Processing hours per roll	
Gauge	*Steel-forming*	*Plastic-bonding*
Standard	0.6	0.4
Heavy	0.8	1.2

What is the production mix which will maximise total contribution and what would be the total contribution?

4.11 SOLUTION

(a) Let S be the number of standard gauge rolls per year.

Let H be the number of heavy gauge rolls per year.

The objective is to maximise 2S + 3H (contribution) subject to the following constraints.

$0.6S + 0.8H \leq 2,400$ (steel-forming hours)
$0.4S + 1.2H \leq 2,400$ (plastic-bonding hours)
$H \leq 1,300$ (sales demand)
$S, H \geq 0$

Note that **the constraints are inequalities,** and are not equations. There is no requirement to use up the total hours available in each process, nor to satisfy all the demand for heavy gauge rolls.

(b) If we take the production constraint of 2,400 hours in the steel-forming process

$0.6S + 0.8H \leq 2,400$

it means that since there are only 2,400 hours available in the process, output must be limited to a maximum of:

(i) $\frac{2,400}{0.6} = 4,000$ rolls of standard gauge;

(ii) $\frac{2,400}{0.8} = 3,000$ rolls of heavy gauge; or

(iii) a proportionate combination of each.

This maximum output represents the boundary line of the constraint, where the inequality becomes the equation

$0.6S + 0.8H = 2,400.$

(c) The line for this equation may be drawn on a graph by joining up two points on the line (such as S = 0, H = 3,000; H = 0, S = 4,000).

(d) The other constraints may be drawn in a similar way with lines for the following equations.

$0.4S + 1.2H = 2,400$ (plastic-bonding)
$H = 1,300$ (sales demand)

(e)

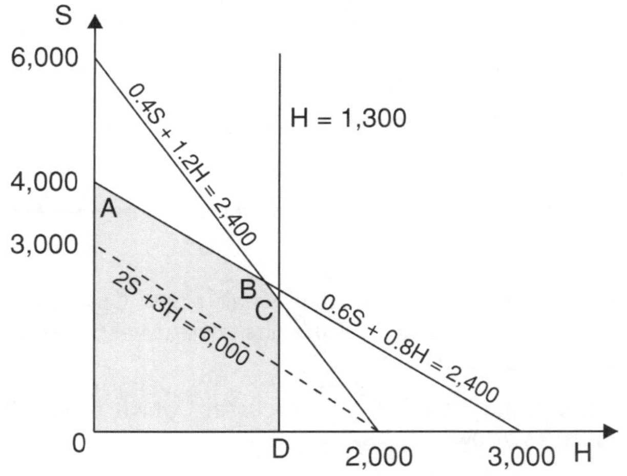

To satisfy all the constraints simultaneously, the values of S and H must lie on or below each constraint line. The outer limits of the **feasible polygon** are the lines, but all combined values of S and H within the shaded area are **feasible solutions.**

(f) The next step is to find the **optimal solution**, which **maximises the objective function**. Since the objective is to **maximise contribution**, the solution to the problem must involve relatively high values (within the feasible polygon) for S, or H or a combination of both.

If, as is likely, there is only one combination of S and H which provides the optimal solution, this combination will be one of the **outer corners of the feasible polygon.** There are four such corners, A, B, C and D. However, it is possible that any combination of values for S and H on the boundary line between two of these corners might provide solutions with the same total contribution.

(g) To solve the problem we establish **the slope of the iso-contribution lines,** by drawing a line for any one level of contribution. In our solution, a line 2S + 3H = 6,000 has been drawn. (6,000 was chosen as a convenient multiple of 2 and 3). **This line has no significance except to indicate the slope, or gradient, of every iso-contribution line for 2S + 3H.**

Using a ruler to judge at which corner of the feasible polygon we can draw an **iso-contribution line** which is as far to the right as possible, (away from the origin) but which still touches the **feasible polygon.**

(h) This occurs at corner B where the constraint line 0.4S + 1.2H = 2,400 crosses with the constraint line 0.6S + 0.8H = 2,400. At this point, there are simultaneous equations, from which the exact values of S and H may be calculated.

0.4S +	1.2H	=	2,400	(1)
0.6S +	0.8H	=	2,400	(2)
1.2S +	3.6H	=	7,200	(3) ((1) × 3)
1.2S +	1.6H	=	4,800	(4) ((2) × 2)
	2H	=	2,400	(5) ((3) - (4))
	H	=	1,200	(6)

Substituting 1,200 for H in either equation, we can calculate that S = 2,400.

The contribution is maximised where H = 1,200, and S = 2,400.

	Units	Contribution per unit	Total contribution
		£	£
Standard gauge	2,400	2	4,800
Heavy gauge	1,200	3	3,600
			8,400

Question 4

The Dervish Chemical Company operates a small plant. Operating the plant requires two raw materials, A and B, which cost £5 and £8 per litre respectively. The maximum available supply per week is 2,700 litres of A and 2,000 litres of B.

The plant can operate using either of two processes, which have differing contributions and raw materials requirements, as follows.

Process	*Raw materials consumed (litres per processing hour)* A	B	*Contribution per hour* £
1	20	10	70
2	30	20	60

The plant can run for 120 hours a week in total, but for safety reasons, process 2 cannot be operated for more than 80 hours a week.

Formulate a linear programming model, and then solve it, to determine how many hours process 1 should be operated each week and how many hours process 2 should be operated each week.

Answer

The decision variables are processing hours in each process. If we let the processing hours per week for process 1 be P_1 and the processing hours per week for process 2 be P_2 we can formulate an objective and constraints as follows.

The objective is to maximise $70P_1 + 60P_2$, subject to the following constraints.

$20P_1 + 30P_2$	$\leq$	2,700	(material A supply)
$10P_1 + 20P_2$	$\leq$	2,000	(material B supply)
P_2	$\leq$	80	(maximum time for P_2)
$P_1 + P_2$	$\leq$	120	(total maximum time)
P_1, P_2	$\geq$	0	(non-negativity)

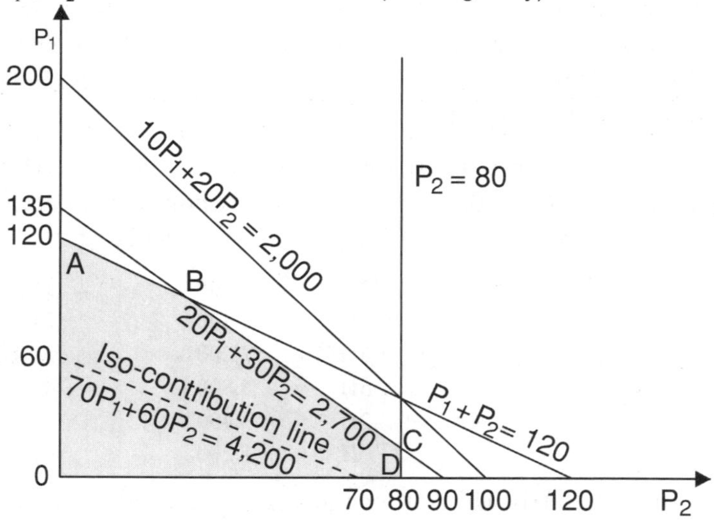

The feasible area is ABCDO. The optimal solution, found by moving the iso-contribution line outwards, is at point A, where $P_1 = 120$ and $P_2 = 0$. Total contribution would be 120×70 = £8,400 a week.

Multiple solutions

4.12 **It is possible that the optimum position might lie, not at a particular corner, but all along the length of one of the sides of the feasibility polygon. This will occur if the iso-contribution line is exactly parallel to one of the constraint lines.**

4.13 If this happens then there is no one optimum solution but a **range of optimum solutions**. All of these will maximise the objective function at the same level. However, *any* value of the decision variables that happens to satisfy the constraint between the points where the constraint line forms part of the feasibility region would produce this optimum level of contribution.

Minimisation problems in linear programming

4.14 Although decision problems with limiting factors usually involve the maximisation of contribution, there may be a requirement to **minimise costs**. A graphical solution, involving two variables, is very similar to that for a maximisation problem, with the exception that instead of finding a contribution line touching the feasible area as far away from the origin as possible, we look for a **total cost line touching the feasible area as close to the origin as possible**.

4.15 EXAMPLE: A MINIMISATION PROBLEM

Claire Speke Ltd has undertaken a contract to supply a customer with at least 260 units in total of two products, X and Y, during the next month. At least 50% of the total output must be units of X. The products are each made by two grades of labour, as follows.

	X	*Y*
	Hours	*Hours*
Grade A labour	4	6
Grade B labour	4	2
Total	8	8

Although additional labour can be made available at short notice, the company wishes to make use of 1,200 hours of Grade A labour and 800 hours of Grade B labour which has already been assigned to working on the contract next month. The total variable cost per unit is £120 for X and £100 for Y.

Claire Speke Ltd wishes to minimise expenditure on the contract next month. How much of X and Y should be supplied in order to meet the terms of the contract?

4.16 SOLUTION

(a) Let the number of units of X supplied be x, and the number of units of Y supplied be y.

The objective is to minimise 120x + 100y (costs), subject to the following constraints.

$x + y$	$\geq$	260	(supply total)
x	$\geq$	$0.5\,(x + y)$	(proportion of x in total)
$4x + 6y$	$\geq$	1,200	(Grade A labour)
$4x + 2y$	$\geq$	800	(Grade B labour)
x, y	$\geq$	0	

The constraint $x \geq 0.5\,(x + y)$ needs simplifying further.

x	$\geq 0.5\ (x + y)$
2x	$\geq\ x + y$
x	$\geq\ y$

In a graphical solution, the line will be x = y. Check this carefully in the following diagram.

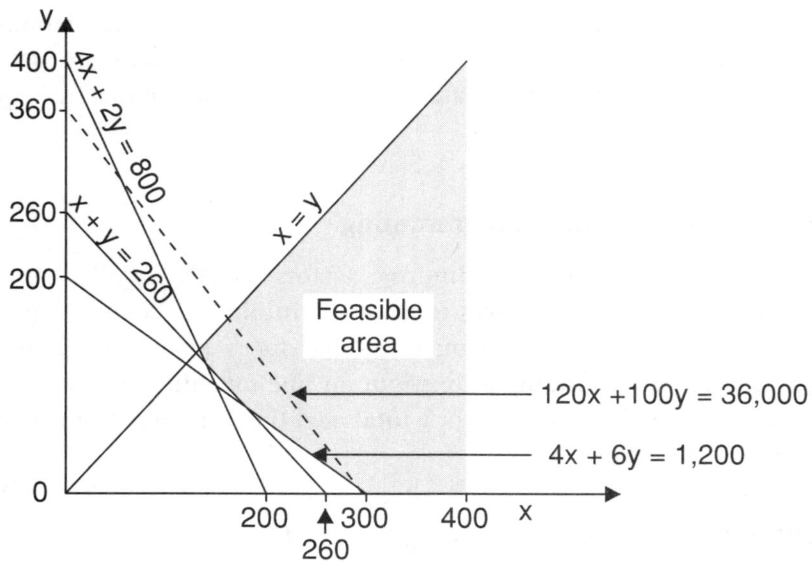

(b) The cost line 120x + 100y = 36,000 has been drawn to show the slope of every cost line 120x + 100 y. **Costs are minimised where a cost line touches the feasible area as close as possible to the origin of the graph.** This occurs where the constraint line 4x + 2y = 800 crosses the constraint line x + y = 260. This point is found as follows.

x + y	=	260	(1)
4x + 2y	=	800	(2)
2x + y	=	400	(3) ((2) ÷ 2)
x	=	140	(4) ((3) - (1))
y	=	120	(5)

(c) Costs will be minimised by supplying the following.

	Unit cost	*Total cost*
	£	£
140 units of X	120	16,800
120 units of Y	100	12,000
		28,800

The proportion of units of X in the total would exceed 50%, and demand for Grade A labour would exceed the 1,200 hours minimum.

The use of simultaneous equations

4.17 You might think that a lot of time could be saved if we started by solving the simultaneous equations in a linear programming problem and did not bother to draw the graph.

Certainly, this procedure may give the right answer, but in general, it is *not* recommended until you have shown graphically which constraints are effective in determining the optimal solution. (In particular, if a question requires 'the graphical method', you *must* draw a graph). To illustrate this point, consider the following graph.

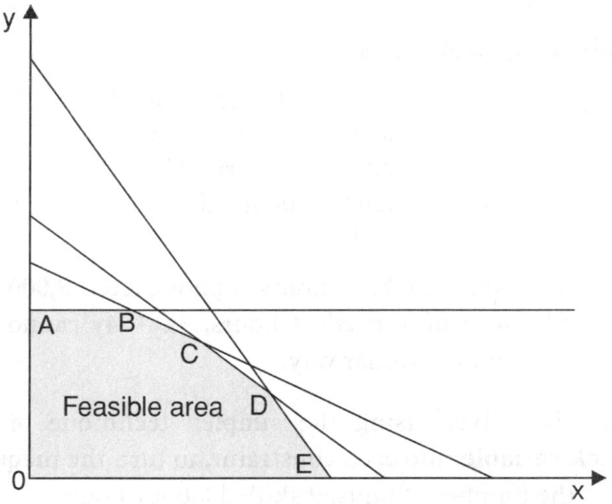

4.18 No figures have been given on the graph but the feasible area is OABCDE. When solving this problem, we would know that the optimum solution would be at one of the corners of the feasible area. We need to work out the profit at each of the corners of the feasible area and pick the one where the profit is greatest.

Once the optimum point has been determined graphically, simultaneous equations can be applied to find the exact values of x and y at this point.

5 TWO-PLUS VARIABLE MODELS

5.1 **The graphical method cannot be used when there are more than two decision variables. A method called the simplex method is available in these circumstances**, but in practice it is much easier to use a computer. You need to have a **basic understanding** of how to formulate the equations for two-plus variable problems. You will not, however, be required to interpret computer output.

5.2 TDS Ltd manufactures two products, X and Y, which earn a contribution of £8 and £14 per unit respectively. At current selling prices, there is no limit to sales demand for Y, but maximum demand for X would be 1,200 units. The company aims to maximise its annual profits, and fixed costs are £15,000 per annum. In the year to 30 June 20X2, the company expects to have a limited availability of resources and estimates of availability are:

Skilled labour	maximum 9,000	hours
Machine time	maximum 4,000	hours
Material M	maximum 1,000	tonnes

The usage of these resources per unit of product are:

	X	*Y*
Skilled labour time	3 hours	4 hours
Machine time	1 hour	2 hours
Material M	½ tonne	¼ tonne

5.3 The linear programming problem would now be formulated as follows:

Let x and y be the number of units made and sold of product X and product Y respectively.

Objective function

Maximise contribution = 8x + 14y

Subject to the following constraints

$3x + 4y$	$\leq$	9,000	(skilled labour)*
$x + 2y$	$\leq$	4,000	(machine time)
$0.5x + 0.25y$	$\leq$	1,000	(material M)
x	$\leq$	1,200	(demand for X)
x, y	$\geq$	0	

* This constraint is that skilled labour hours cannot exceed 9,000 hours, and since a unit of X needs 3 hours and a unit of Y needs 4 hours, 3x + 4y cannot exceed 9,000. The other constraints are formulated in a similar way.

5.4 The problem can be solved using the simplex technique of linear programming by introducing a **slack variable** into each constraint, to turn the inequality into an equation.

Let	a	=	the number of unused skilled labour hours
	b	=	the number of unused machine hours
	c	=	the number of unused tonnes of material M
	d	=	the amount by which demand for X falls short of 1,200 units.

Then

$3x + 4y + a$	=	9,000	(labour hours)
$x + 2y + b$	=	4,000	(machine hours)
$0.5x + 0.25y + c$	=	1,000	(tonnes of M)
$x + d$	=	1,200	(demand for X)

5.5 The **simplex technique** uses the decision variables (here x and y) and the slack variables to test a number of feasible solutions to the problem until the **optimal solution** is found (here, until the combination of values for x, y, a, b, c and d is found that maximises total contribution).

The technique is a repetitive step-by-step process (and therefore an ideal computer application), that tests a number of **feasible solutions** in turn. If the manual process is used this is done in the form of a tableau (or 'table' or 'matrix') of figures. This is best illustrated by giving the final tableau to the problem here, which shows the **contribution-maximising** solution.

Variables in the solution	*x*	*y*	*a*	*b*	*c*	*d*	*Solution column*
x	1	0	1	-2	0	0	1,000
y	0	1	-0.5	1.5	0	0	1,500
c	0	0	-0.375	0.625	1	0	125
d	0	0	-1	2	0	1	200
Solution row	0	0	1	5	0	0	29,000

5.6 The value of the **objective function** - here, the **total contribution** - is in both the solution row and the solution column. Here it is £29,000.

Shadow prices

5.7 The **shadow price** (or **dual price**) of a resource is the amount by which the value of the objective function (contribution) will go up (or down) if one unit more (or less) of the resource were made available. Here, the shadow prices are:

a £1 per labour hour

b £5 per machine hour

The **solution row** gives the shadow prices of each variable.

5.8 This means that if more labour hours could be made available **at their normal variable cost per hour** total contribution could be increased by £1 per extra labour hour. Similarly, if more machine time could be made available, **at its normal variable cost**, total contribution could be increased by £5 per extra machine hour.

5.9 **The shadow or dual price is the opportunity cost of the scarce resources, which is the amount of benefit forgone by not having the availability of the extra resources.**

Chapter roundup

- **Linear programming**, at least at this fairly simple level, is a technique that can be carried out in a fairly 'handle-turning' manner once you have got the basic ideas sorted out. The steps involved are as follows.

  ① Define variables → ② Establish constraints → ③ Construct objective function

  ⑥ Add iso-profit/contribution line ← ⑤ Establish feasible region ← ④ Graph constraints

  → Determine optimal solution

- The **graphical method** can only cope with two variables. If there are more than two decision variables a computer software package is likely to be used.

Quick quiz

1 What are the three main steps involved in setting up a linear programming model?

Step 1. ....

Step 2. ....

Step 3. ....

2 Draw the inequality $4x + 3y \leq 24$ on the graph below.

3 A feasible area enclosed on all sides may also be called a ....

4 How does the graphical solution of minimisation problems differ from that of maximisation problems?

5 The graphical method cannot be used when there are more than two decision variables.

True ☐

False ☐

6 When there are more than two decision variables a method called the .... method is available in these circumstances.

7 What is a shadow price?

Answers to quick quiz

1 ***Step 1.*** Define variables
Step 2. Establish constraints
Step 3. Establish objective function

2

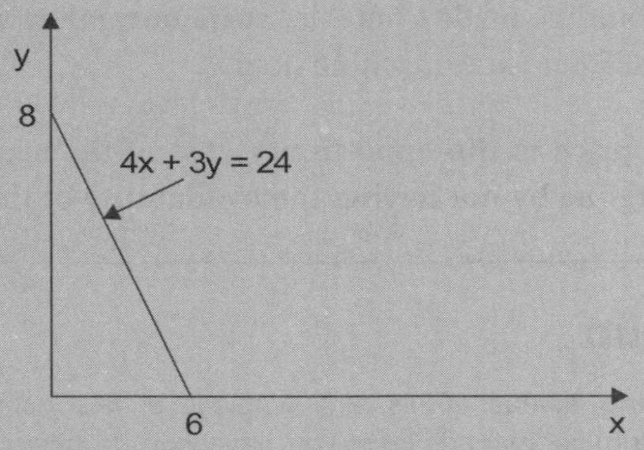

3 Feasible polygon.

4 Instead of finding a contribution line touching the feasible area as far away from the origin as possible, we look for a total cost line touching the feasible area **as close to the origin as possible**.

5 True

6 Simplex

7 The **shadow price** of a resource is the amount by which the value of the objective function (contribution) will go up (or down) if one unit more (or less) of the resource were made available. The shadow price is also known as the **dual price.**

Now try the questions below from the Exam Question Bank

Number	Level	Marks	Time
28	MCQ	n/a	n/a
29	Examination	10	18 mins

Chapter 17

PRICING

Topic list		Syllabus reference
1	Factors influencing the price of a product	6(e), (f)
2	Full cost-plus pricing	6(e), (f)
3	Marginal cost-plus pricing	6(e), (f)
4	Other pricing policies	6(e), (f)
5	The optimum price/output level	6(e), (f)

Introduction

In this chapter we will begin by looking at the factors which influence the price of a product. Perhaps the most important of these is the level of **demand** for an organisation's product and how that demand changes as the price of the product changes (its **elasticity of demand**). We will then turn our attention to specific approaches to pricing with a look at two **cost-based approaches: full cost-plus pricing** and **marginal cost-plus pricing**. The next section of the chapter will discuss the **pricing policies** to adopt in particular circumstances, such as when a new product is launched.

We will end the chapter by looking at the **optimum price/output level**. This is the point at which a business can maximise its profits.

Study guide

Section 25 - Pricing

- Explain the factors that influence the price of a product
- Establish the price/demand relationship of a product
- Establish the optimum price/output level when considering profit maximisation and maximisation of revenue
- Calculate prices using full cost and marginal cost as the pricing base
- Discuss the advantages and disadvantages of these pricing bases
- Discuss pricing policy in the context of price skimming, penetration pricing, premium pricing and price discrimination

Exam guide

Pricing methods is one of the key areas of the syllabus for Paper 1.2.

1 FACTORS INFLUENCING THE PRICE OF A PRODUCT

1.1 In this first section of the chapter you will be learning about the many factors which influence the price which can be charged for a product or service. We will begin by looking at the basic economic analysis of demand.

The economic analysis of demand

1.2 There are two extremes in the relationship between price and demand. A supplier can either **sell a certain quantity, Q, at any price** (as in graph (a)). Demand is totally unresponsive to changes in price and is said to be **completely inelastic**. Alternatively, **demand might be limitless at a certain price** P (as in graph (b)), but there would be no demand above price P and there would be little point in dropping the price below P. In such circumstances demand is said to be **completely elastic**.

(a)

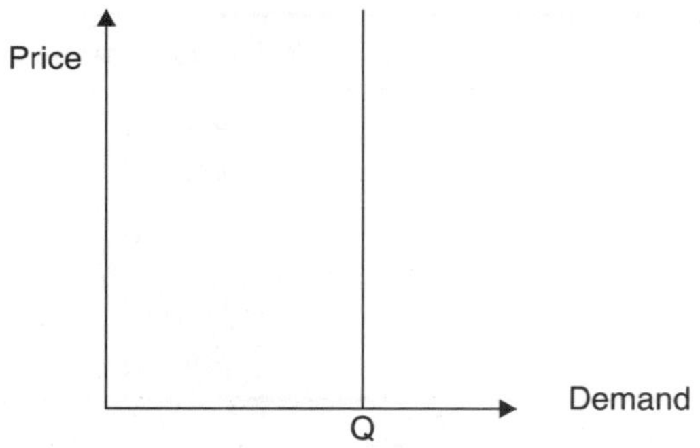

(b)

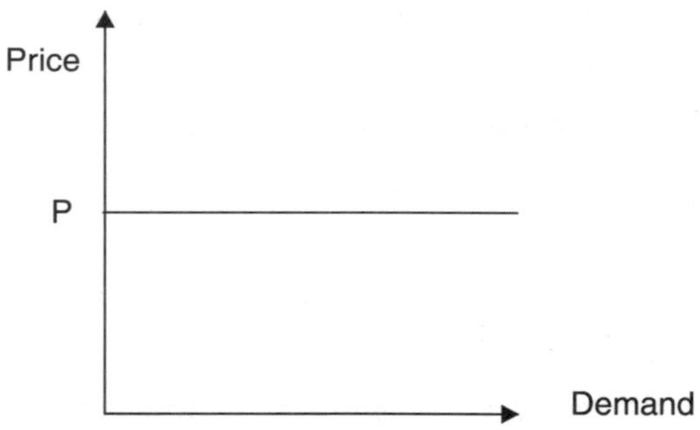

1.3 A more **normal situation** is shown below. The **downward-sloping** demand curve shows that demand will increase as prices are lowered. Demand is therefore **elastic**.

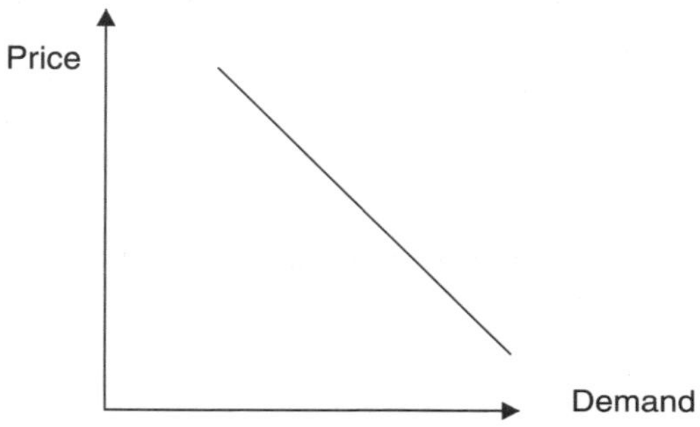

Price elasticity of demand (η)

KEY TERM

Price elasticity of demand (η) is a measure of the extent of change in market demand for a good in response to a change in its price. It is measured as:

$$\frac{\text{The change in quantity demanded, as a \% of demand}}{\text{The change in price, as a \% of the price}}$$

1.4 Since the demand goes up when the price falls, and goes down when the price rises, the elasticity has a negative value, but it is usual to ignore the minus sign.

1.5 EXAMPLE: PRICE ELASTICITY OF DEMAND

The price of a good is £1.20 per unit and annual demand is 800,000 units. Market research indicates that an increase in price of 10 pence per unit will result in a fall in annual demand of 75,000 units. What is the price elasticity of demand?

1.6 SOLUTION

Annual demand at £1.20 per unit is 800,000 units.
Annual demand at £1.30 per unit is 725,000 units.

% change in demand = (75,000/800,000) × 100% = 9.375%
% change in price = (10p/120p) × 100% = 8.333%
Price elasticity of demand = (–9.375/8.333) = –1.125
Ignoring the minus sign, price elasticity is 1.125.

The demand for this good, at a price of £1.20 per unit, would be referred to as **elastic** because the **price elasticity of demand is greater than 1**.

Elastic and inelastic demand

1.7 The value of demand elasticity may be anything from zero to infinity.

KEY TERM

Demand is referred to as **inelastic** if the absolute value is less than 1 and **elastic** if the absolute value is greater than 1.

1.8 (a) Where demand is inelastic, the quantity demanded falls by a smaller percentage than the percentage increase in price.

(b) Where demand is **elastic, demand falls** by a **larger percentage than the percentage rise in price**.

Question 1

If the price elasticity of demand is zero, which of the following is/are true?

I Demand is 'perfectly inelastic'
II There is no change in price regardless of the quantity demanded
III The demand curve is a vertical straight line
IV There is no change in the quantity demanded, regardless of any change in price

A I and III only
B I and IV only
C I, II and III only
D I, III and IV only

Answer

Demand is perfectly inelastic when price changes have no impact on demand. The price elasticity of demand will equal zero only if demand remains unchanged. Statement I is therefore correct.

The price elasticity of demand will equal zero only if demand remains unchanged. If the price remains unchanged, the denominator of the price elasticity of demand equation will have an infinite value. Statement II is therefore incorrect.

If the price elasticity of demand is zero it means that demand never changes and so the graph is a vertical straight line. Statement III is therefore correct.

The price elasticity of demand will equal zero only when demand remains unchanged. Statement IV is therefore correct.

The correct answer is therefore D since statements I, III and IV are correct.

Elasticity and the pricing decision

1.9 In practice, organisations will have only a rough idea of the shape of their demand curve. Data about quantities sold at certain prices over a period of time will be limited and there may be other factors that might have an effect on the demand for a product.

1.10 Despite this limitation, an awareness of the concept of elasticity can assist management with pricing decisions.

(a) In circumstances of **inelastic demand, prices should be increased** because revenues will increase and total costs will reduce (because quantities sold will reduce).

(b) In circumstances of **elastic demand,** increases in prices will bring decreases in revenue and decreases in price will bring increases in revenue. Management therefore have to **decide** whether the **increase/decrease in costs will be less than/greater than the increases/decreases in revenue.**

(c) In situations of **very elastic demand,** overpricing can lead to a massive drop in quantity sold and hence a massive drop in profits. Similarly, underpricing might led to demand outstripping supply (stockouts) and therefore a drop in profits. **Elasticity must therefore be reduced by creating a customer preference which is unrelated to price** (through advertising and promotional activities).

(d) In situations of **very inelastic demand,** customers are **not sensitive to price. Quality, service, product mix and location** are therefore **more important** to a firm's pricing strategy.

1.11 Factors that determine the degree of elasticity are as follows.

(a) **The price of the good.**

(b) **The price of other goods.** For some goods the market demand is interconnected.

(i) **Substitutes.** An increase in demand for one version of a good is likely to cause a decrease in demand for others. Common examples are rival brands of the same commodity (such as *Coca-Cola* and *Pepsi-Cola*).

(ii) **Complements.** An increase in demand for one is likely to cause an increase in demand for the other, for examples, cups and saucers.

(c) **Income.** A rise in income gives households more to spend and they will want to buy more goods. Different goods are affected in different ways.

(i) **Normal goods** are those for which a **rise in income increases the demand.**

(ii) **Inferior goods** are those for which **demand falls as income rises** (eg cheap wine).

(iii) For some goods **demand rises up to a certain point and then remains unchanged,** because there is a limit to which consumers can or want to consume. Examples are basic foodstuffs such as salt and bread.

(d) **Tastes and fashions.** A change in fashion will alter the demand for a good, or a particular variety of a good. Changes in taste may stem from psychological, social or economic causes. There is an argument that tastes and fashions are created by the producers of products and services. There is undeniably some truth in this, but the modern focus on responding to customers' needs and wants suggests otherwise.

(e) **Expectations.** Where consumers believe that prices will rise or that shortages will occur they will attempt to stock up on the product, thereby creating excess demand in the short term.

(f) **Obsolescence**. Many products and services have to be replaced periodically.

(i) **Physical goods** are literally 'consumed'. Carpets become threadbare, glasses get broken, foodstuffs get eaten, children grow out of clothes.

(ii) **Technological developments** render some goods **obsolete**. Manual office equipment has been largely replaced by electronic equipment, because it does a better job, more quickly, quietly, efficiently and effectively.

Demand and the market

1.12 Economic theory suggests that the volume of **demand** for a good in **the market as a whole** is influenced by a variety of variables.

- The price of the good
- The price of other goods
- The size and distribution of household income
- Expectations
- Obsolescence
- The perceived quality of the product
- Tastes and fashion

Demand and the individual firm

1.13 The **volume of demand for one organisation's goods rather than another's** is influenced by three principal factors:

- Product life cycle
- Quality
- Marketing

Product life cycle

KEY TERM

Product life cycle is 'The period which begins with the initial product specification, and ends with the withdrawal from the market of both the product and its support. It is characterised by defined stages including research, development, introduction, maturity, decline and abandonment.' (CIMA *Official Terminology*)

1.14 Most products pass through the following phases.

Phase	Description
Introduction	The product is introduced to the market. Heavy capital expenditure will be incurred on product development and perhaps also on the purchase of new fixed assets and building up stocks for sale. On its introduction to the market, the product will begin to earn some revenue, but initially demand is likely to be small. Potential customers will be unaware of the product or service, and the organisation may have to spend further on advertising to bring the product or service to the attention of the market.
Growth	The product gains a bigger market as demand builds up. Sales revenues increase and the product begins to make a profit. The initial costs of the investment in the new product are gradually recovered.

Phase	Description
Maturity	Eventually, the growth in demand for the product will slow down and it will enter a period of relative maturity. It will continue to be profitable. The product may be modified or improved, as a means of sustaining its demand.
Saturation and decline	At some stage, the market will have bought enough of the product and it will therefore reach 'saturation point'. Demand will start to fall. For a while, the product will still be profitable in spite of declining sales, but eventually it will become a loss-maker and this is the time when the organisation should decide to stop selling the product or service, and so the product's life cycle should reach its end.

1.15 **The life expectancy of a product will influence the pricing decision. Short-life products** must be quite **highly priced** so as to give the manufacturer a chance to **recover his investment** and **make a worthwhile** return. This is why fashion goods and new high technology goods, for example, tend to have high prices.

1.16 We have already mentioned that the current tendency is towards **shorter product life cycles**. The **life cycles** of different products may **vary in terms of length of phases, overall length and shape**.

(a) Fashion products and high technology products have a very short life because they become rapidly out-dated by new fashions and new technological developments.

(b) **Different versions of the same product may have different life cycles**, and consumers are often aware of this. For example, the prospective buyer of a new car is more likely to purchase a recently introduced Ford than a Vauxhall that has been on the market for several years, even if there is nothing to choose in terms of quality and price.

Quality

1.17 One firm's product may be perceived to be better quality than another's, and may in some cases actually be so, if it uses sturdier materials, goes faster or does whatever it is meant to do in a 'better' way. Generally, **the better quality good will be more in demand** than other versions.

Marketing

1.18 You may be familiar with the 'four Ps' of the marketing mix, all of which influence demand for a firm's goods.

- Price
- Product
- Place (where the goods can be purchased)
- Promotion (means of drawing attention to goods)

1.19 Some larger organisations go to considerable effort to estimate the demand for their products or services at differing price levels by producing estimated demand curves. A **knowledge of demand curves can be very useful**: for example, a large transport company such as *Stagecoach* might be considering an increase in bus fares or underground fares. The effect on total revenues and profit of the fares increase could be estimated from a knowledge of the demand for transport services at different price levels. If an increase in the price per ticket caused a large fall in demand (that is, if demand were price-elastic) total revenues and profits would fall; whereas a fares increase when demand is price-inelastic would boost total revenue and since a transport authority's costs are largely fixed, would probably boost total profits too.

Markets

1.20 The price that an organisation can charge for its products will be determined to a greater or lesser degree by the market in which it operates.

KEY TERMS

- **Perfect competition**: many buyers and many sellers all dealing in an identical product. Neither producer nor user has any market power and both must accept the prevailing market price.
- **Monopoly**: one seller who dominates many buyers. The monopolist can use his market power to set a profit-maximising price.
- **Monopolistic competition**: a large number of suppliers offer similar, but not identical, products. The similarities ensure elastic demand whereas the slight differences give some monopolistic power to the supplier.
- **Oligopoly**: where relatively few competitive companies dominate the market. Whilst each large firm has the ability to influence market prices the unpredictable reaction from the other giants makes the final industry price indeterminate. Cartels are often formed.

Other factors influencing the price of a product

1.21

Influence	Explanation/example
Price sensitivity	This will vary amongst purchasers. Those that can pass on the cost of purchases will be the least sensitive and will therefore respond more to other elements of perceived value. For example, the business traveller will be more concerned about the level of service and quality of food in looking for an hotel than price, provided that it fits the corporate budget. In contrast, the family on holiday are likely to be very price sensitive when choosing an overnight stay.
Price perception	This is the way customers react to prices. For example, customers may react to a price increase by buying more. This could be because they expect further price increases to follow (they are 'stocking up').
Compatibility with other products	A typical example is operating systems on computers, for which a user would like to have a wide range of compatible software available. For these types of product there is usually a **cumulative effect on demand**. The more people who buy one of the formats, the more choice there is likely to be of software for that format. This in turn is likely to influence future purchasers. The owner of the rights to the preferred format will eventually find little competition and will be able to charge a premium price for the product.

Influence	Explanation/example
Competitors	An organisation, in setting prices, sends out signals. Competitors are likely to react to these signals in some way. In some industries (such as petrol retailing) pricing moves in unison; in others, price changes by one supplier may initiate a price war, with each supplier undercutting the others. Competition is discussed in more detail below.
Competition from substitute products	These are products which could be transformed for the same use or which might become desirable to customers at particular price levels. For example, train travel comes under competition as the quality, speed and comfort of coach travel rises. Similarly, if the price of train travel rises it comes under competition from cheaper coach travel and more expensive air travel.
Suppliers	If an organisation's suppliers notice a price rise for the organisation's products, they may seek a rise in the price for their supplies to the organisation on the grounds that it is now able to pay a higher price.
Inflation	In periods of inflation the organisation may need to change prices to reflect increases in the prices of supplies and so on. Such changes may be needed to keep relative (real) prices unchanged.
Quality	In the absence of other information, customers tend to judge quality by price. Thus a price change may send signals to customers concerning the quality of the product. A price rise may indicate improvements in quality, a price reduction may signal reduced quality, for example through the use of inferior components.
Incomes	In times of rising incomes, price may become a less important marketing variable compared with product quality and convenience of access (distribution). When income levels are falling and/or unemployment levels rising, price will become a much more important marketing variable.
Ethics	Ethical considerations are a further factor, for example whether or not to exploit short-term shortages through higher prices.

Competition

1.22 In established industries dominated by a few major firms, it is generally accepted that a price initiative by one firm will be countered by a price reaction by competitors. In these circumstances, prices tend to be fairly **stable**, unless pushed upwards by inflation or strong growth in demand.

1.23 If a rival cuts its prices in the expectation of increasing its market share, a firm has several options.

(a) It will **maintain its existing prices** if the expectation is that only a small market share would be lost, so that it is more profitable to keep prices at their existing level. Eventually, the rival firm may drop out of the market or be forced to raise its prices.

(b) It may **maintain its prices but respond with a non-price counter-attack**. This is a more positive response, because the firm will be securing or justifying its current prices with a product change, advertising, or better back-up services.

(c) It may **reduce its prices**. This should protect the firm's market share so that the main beneficiary from the price reduction will be the consumer.

(d) It may **raise its prices and respond with a non-price counter-attack**. The extra revenue from the higher prices might be used to finance an advertising campaign or product design changes. A price increase would be based on a campaign to emphasise the quality difference between the firm's own product and the rival's product.

2 FULL COST-PLUS PRICING

2.1 **In practice cost is one of the most important influences on price**. Many firms base price on simple **cost-plus rules** (costs are estimated and then a profit margin is added in order to set the price). We had a brief look at cost-plus pricing when we studied job costing in Chapter 10.

KEY TERM

Full cost-plus pricing is a method of determining the sales price by calculating the full cost of the product and adding a percentage mark-up for profit.

2.2 The 'full cost' may be a fully absorbed production cost only, or it may include some absorbed administration, selling and distribution overhead.

2.3 A business might have an idea of the percentage profit margin it would like to earn, and so might **decide on an average profit mark-up** as a general guideline for pricing decisions.

2.4 Businesses that carry out a large amount of **contract work or jobbing work**, for which individual job or contract prices must be quoted regularly would find this a useful method to adopt. The percentage profit **mark-up**, however, **does not have to be rigid and fixed**, but can be varied to suit different circumstances.

2.5 EXAMPLE: FULL COST-PLUS PRICING

Markup Ltd has begun to produce a new product, Product X, for which the following cost estimates have been made.

	£
Direct materials	27
Direct labour: 4 hrs at £5 per hour	20
Variable production overheads: machining, ½ hr at £6 per hour	3
	50

Production fixed overheads are budgeted at £300,000 per month and because of the shortage of available machining capacity, the company will be restricted to 10,000 hours of machine time per month. The absorption rate will be a direct labour rate, however, and budgeted direct labour hours are 25,000 per month. It is estimated that the company could obtain a minimum contribution of £10 per machine hour on producing items other than product X.

The direct cost estimates are not certain as to material usage rates and direct labour productivity, and it is recognised that the estimates of direct materials and direct labour costs may be subject to an error of ± 15%. Machine time estimates are similarly subject to an error of ± 10%.

The company wishes to make a profit of 20% on full production cost from product X.

Required

Ascertain the full cost-plus based price.

2.6 SOLUTION

Even for a relatively 'simple' cost-plus pricing estimate, some problems can arise, and certain assumptions must be made and stated. In this example, we can identify two problems.

- Should the opportunity cost of machine time be included in cost or not?
- What allowance, if any, should be made for the possible errors in cost estimates?

Different assumptions could be made.

(a) **Exclude machine time opportunity costs: ignore possible costing errors**

	£
Direct materials	27.00
Direct labour (4 hours)	20.00
Variable production overheads	3.00
Fixed production overheads	
(at $\frac{£300{,}000}{25{,}000}$ = £12 per direct labour hour)	48.00
Full production cost	98.00
Profit mark-up (20%)	19.60
Selling price per unit of product X	117.60

(b) **Include machine time opportunity costs: ignore possible costing errors**

	£
Full production cost as in (a)	98.00
Opportunity cost of machine time:	
contribution forgone (½ hr × £10)	5.00
Adjusted full cost	103.00
Profit mark-up (20%)	20.60
Selling price per unit of product X	123.60

(c) **Exclude machine time opportunity costs but make full allowance for possible under-estimates of cost**

	£	£
Direct materials	27.00	
Direct labour	20.00	
	47.00	
Possible error (15%)	7.05	
		54.05
Variable production overheads	3.00	
Possible error (10%)	0.30	
		3.30
Fixed production overheads (4 hrs × £12)	48.00	
Possible error (labour time) (15%)	7.20	
		55.20
Potential full production cost		112.55
Profit mark-up (20%)		22.51
Selling price per unit of product X		135.06

(d) **Include machine time opportunity costs and make a full allowance for possible under-estimates of cost**

	£
Potential full production cost as in (c)	112.55
Opportunity cost of machine time:	
potential contribution forgone (½ hr × £10 × 110%)	5.50
Adjusted potential full cost	118.05
Profit mark-up (20%)	23.61
Selling price per unit of product X	141.66

Using different assumptions, we could arrive at any of four different unit prices in the range £117.60 to £141.66.

Disadvantages of full cost-plus pricing

2.7 (a) It fails to recognise that since demand may be determining price, there will be a profit-maximising combination of price and demand.

(b) There may be a need to **adjust prices to market and demand conditions.**

(c) **Budgeted output volume** needs to be established. Output volume is a key factor in the overhead absorption rate.

(d) A **suitable basis for overhead absorption** must be selected, especially where a business produces more than one product.

Advantages of full cost-plus pricing

2.8 (a) It is a **quick, simple and cheap** method of pricing which can be delegated to junior managers.

(b) Since the size of the profit margin can be varied, a decision based on a price in excess of full cost should ensure that a company working at normal capacity will **cover all of its fixed costs and make a profit.**

Question 2

A company budgets to make 20,000 units which have a variable cost of production of £4 per unit. Fixed production costs are £60,000 per annum. If price is to be 40% higher than full cost, what is the price of the product using the full cost-plus method?

A £9.80
B £2.80
C £7.00
D £5.60

Answer

Full cost per unit = variable cost + fixed cost

Variable cost = £4 per unit

Fixed cost = $\frac{£60,000}{20,000}$ = £3 per unit

Full cost per unit = £(4 + 3) = £7

$\therefore$ Price using full cost-plus pricing method $= £7.00 \times \frac{140\%}{100}$

$= £9.80$

Option A is therefore correct.

If you selected option B, you have calculated the profit (40% × £7.00) instead of the full cost plus the profit (£7.00 + £2.80 = £9.80).

If you selected option C, you forgot to add the profit to the full cost.

If you selected option D, you have increased the variable cost by 40% only and have not included fixed costs at all.

---

3 MARGINAL COST-PLUS PRICING

KEY TERM

Marginal cost plus pricing/mark-up pricing is a method of determining the sales price by adding a profit margin on to either marginal cost of production or marginal cost of sales.

3.1 Whereas a full cost-plus approach to pricing draws attention to net profit and the net profit margin, a variable cost-plus approach to pricing **draws attention to gross profit** and the **gross profit margin,** or **contribution**.

Question 3

A product has the following costs.

	£
Direct materials	5
Direct labour	3
Variable overheads	7

Fixed overheads are £10,000 per month. Budgeted sales per month are 400 units to allow the product to break even.

Required

Determine the profit margin which needs to be added to *marginal* cost to allow the product to break even.

Answer

Breakeven point is when total contribution equals fixed costs.

At breakeven point, £10,000 = 400 (price – £15)
∴ £25 = price – £15
∴ £40 = price
∴ Profit margin = 40 – 15/15 × 100% = $166^2/_3$%

Advantages of marginal cost-plus pricing

3.2 (a) It is a **simple and easy** method to use.

(b) The **mark-up percentage can be varied,** and so mark-up pricing can be adjusted to reflect demand conditions.

(c) It **draws management attention to contribution,** and the effects of higher or lower sales volumes on profit. For example, if a product costs £10 per unit and a mark-up of 150% (£15) is added to reach a price of £25 per unit, management should be clearly aware that every additional £1 of sales revenue would add 60 pence to contribution and profit (£15 ÷ £25 = £0.60).

(d) In practice, mark-up pricing is **used** in businesses **where there is a readily-identifiable basic variable cost**. Retail industries are the most obvious example, and it is quite common for the prices of goods in shops to be fixed by adding a mark-up (20% or 33.3%, say) to the purchase cost.

Disadvantages of marginal cost-plus pricing

3.3 (a) Although the size of the mark-up can be varied in accordance with demand conditions, it does not ensure that sufficient attention is paid to demand conditions, competitors' prices and profit maximisation.

(b) It **ignores fixed overheads** in the pricing decision, but the sales price must be sufficiently high to ensure that a profit is made after covering fixed costs.

> **Exam focus point**
>
> The 12/01 paper-based exam required candidates to calculate two different cost-plus prices (from standard cost information) using two different bases and to explain an advantage and disadvantage of each method. There were six marks available.

4 OTHER PRICING POLICIES

Special orders

4.1 A special order is a **one-off revenue earning opportunity**. These may arise in the following situations.

(a) When a business has a regular source of income but also has some **spare capacity** allowing it to take on extra work if demanded. For example a brewery might have a capacity of 500,000 barrels per month but only be producing and selling 300,000 barrels per month. It could therefore consider special orders to use up some of its spare capacity.

(b) When a business has **no regular source of income** and relies exclusively on its ability to respond to demand. A building firm is a typical example as are many types of sub-contractors. In the service sector consultants often work on this basis.

4.2 The **basic approach** in both situations is to determine the **price at which the firm would break even** if it undertook the work, that is, the **minimum price** that it could afford to charge. It would have to cover the incremental costs of producing and selling the item and the opportunity costs of the resources consumed.

4.3 In today's competitive markets it is very much the **modern trend to tailor products or services to customer demand** rather than producing for stock. This suggests that **'special' orders may become the norm** for most businesses.

New products

4.4 Suppose that Novo plc is about to launch a new product with a variable cost of £10 per unit. The company has carried out market research (at a cost of £15,000) to determine the potential demand for the product at various selling prices.

Selling price	*Demand*
£	Units
30	20,000
25	30,000
20	40,000

Its current capacity is for 20,000 units but additional capacity can be made available by using the resources of another product line. If this is done the lost contribution from the other product will be £35,000 for each additional 10,000 units of capacity.

How could we **analyse this information** for senior management in a way that helps them to **decide on the product's launch price**?

4.5 **Tabulation** is the approach to use with a problem of this type.

Selling price	*Demand*	*Variable costs*	*Opportunity costs*	*Total costs*	*Sales revenue*	*Contribution*
£	Units ('000)	£'000	£'000	£'000	£ '000	£'000
30	20	200	-	200	600	400
25	30	300	35	335	750	415
20	40	400	70	470	800	330

4.6 The **optimum price to maximise short-term profits is £25**. However, it is quite possible that the aim will **not** be to maximise short-term profits, and a number of other strategies may be adopted, as discussed below.

4.7 The main **objections** to the approach described above are that it only **considers a limited range of prices** (what about charging £27.50?) and it **takes no account of the uncertainty of forecast demand.**

4.8 A new product pricing strategy will depend largely on whether a company's product or service is the first of its kind on the market.

(a) If the **product is the first of its kind**, there will be **no competition** yet, and the company, for a time at least, will be a **monopolist**. Monopolists have more influence over price and are able to set a price at which they think they can maximise their profits. A monopolist's price is likely to be higher, and his profits bigger, than those of a company operating in a competitive market.

(b) If the new product being launched by a company is **following a competitor's product** onto the market, the pricing strategy will be **constrained by what the competitor** is already doing. The new product could be given a higher price if its quality is better, or it could be given a price which matches the competition. Undercutting the competitor's price might result in a price war and a fall of the general price level in the market.

Market penetration pricing

KEY TERM

Market penetration pricing is a policy of low prices when the product is first launched in order to obtain sufficient penetration into the market.

4.9 **Circumstances in which a penetration policy may be appropriate**

- If the firm wishes to **discourage new entrants** into the market
- If the firm wishes to **shorten the initial period of the product's life cycle** in order to enter the growth and maturity stages as quickly as possible
- If there are **significant economies of scale** to be achieved **from a high volume of output**, so that quick penetration into the market is desirable in order to gain unit cost reductions
- If **demand is highly elastic** and so would respond well to low prices.

4.10 Penetration prices are prices which aim to **secure a substantial share in a substantial total market**. A firm might therefore **deliberately build excess production capacity** and set its prices very low. As demand builds up the spare capacity will be used up gradually and unit costs will fall and the firm might even reduce prices further as unit costs fall. In this way, early losses will enable the firm to dominate the market and have the lowest costs.

Market skimming pricing

KEY TERM

Market skimming pricing involves charging high prices when a product is first launched and spending heavily on advertising and sales promotion to obtain sales.

4.11 As the product moves into the later stages of its life cycle, **progressively lower prices will be charged** and so the profitable 'cream' is skimmed off in stages until sales can only be sustained at lower prices.

4.12 The aim of market skimming is to **gain high unit profits early in the product's life**. High unit prices make it **more likely that competitors will enter the market** than if lower prices were to be charged.

4.13 **Circumstances in which such a policy may be appropriate**

(a) Where the product is **new and different**, so that customers are prepared to pay high prices so as to be one up on other people who do not own it.

(b) Where the **strength** of demand and the **sensitivity of demand** to price are **unknown**. It is better from the point of view of marketing to start by charging high prices and then reduce them if the demand for the product turns out to be price elastic than to start by charging low prices and then attempt to raise them substantially if demand appears to be insensitive to higher prices.

(c) Where **high prices** in the early stages of a product's life might **generate high initial cash flows**. A firm with liquidity problems may prefer market-skimming for this reason.

(d) Where the firm **can identify different market segments** for the product, each prepared to pay progressively lower prices. If **product differentiation** can be introduced, it may be possible to continue to sell at higher prices to some market segments when lower prices are charged in others. This is discussed further below.

(e) Where products may have a **short life cycle**, and so need to recover their development costs and make a profit relatively quickly.

Premium pricing

4.14 This involves making a product **appear 'different'** through **product differentiation** so as **to justify a premium price**. The product may be different in terms of, for example, quality, reliability, durability, after sales service or extended warranties. Heavy advertising can establish brand loyalty which can help to sustain a premium and premium prices will always be paid by those customers who blindly equate high price with high quality.

Price discrimination

KEY TERM

Price discrimination is the practice of charging different prices for the same product to different groups of buyers when these prices are not reflective of cost differences.

4.15 In certain circumstances the **same product** can be sold at different prices to **different customers**. There are a number of bases on which such discriminating prices can be set.

Basis	Detail
By market segment	A cross-channel ferry company would market its services at different prices in England and France, for example. Services such as cinemas and hairdressers are often available at lower prices to old age pensioners and/or juveniles.
By product version	Many car models have **optional extras** which enable one brand to appeal to a wider cross-section of customers. The final price need not reflect the cost price of the optional extras directly: usually the top of the range model would carry a price much in excess of the cost of provision of the extras, as a prestige appeal.
By place	Theatre seats are usually sold according to their location so that patrons pay different prices for the same performance according to the seat type they occupy.
By time	This is perhaps the most popular type of price discrimination. Off-peak travel bargains, hotel prices and telephone charges are all attempts to increase sales revenue by covering variable but not necessarily average cost of provision. Railway companies are successful price discriminators, charging more to rush hour rail commuters whose demand is inelastic at certain times of the day.

Conditions required for effective price discrimination

4.16 (a) The market must be **segmentable** in price terms, and different sectors must show different levels of demand. Each of the sectors must be identifiable, distinct and separate from the others.

(b) There must be little or **no** chance of a **black market** developing (this would allow those in the lower priced segment to resell to those in the higher priced segment).

(c) There must be little or **no** chance that **competitors** can undercut the firm's prices in the higher priced market segments.

(d) The cost of segmenting and **administering** the arrangements should not exceed the extra revenue derived from the price discrimination strategy.

5 THE OPTIMUM PRICE/OUTPUT LEVEL

Demand curves

5.1 We had a brief look at demand curves at the beginning of this chapter. We shall now look at how to derive an equation for such curves when demand is linear.

5.2 Some businesses enjoy a **monopoly position** in their market even in a competitive market. This is because they develop a **unique marketing mix**, for example a **unique combination of price and quality**, or a **monopoly in a localised area**. The significance of a monopoly situation is as follows.

5.3 Monopoly situations are significant for the following reasons.

(a) **The business does not have to 'follow the market' on price**. It is not a 'price taker', but has more choice and flexibility in the prices it sets. Because the business has this freedom of choice in pricing, it will find that at higher prices demand for its products or services will be less. Conversely, at lower prices, demand for its products or services will be higher.

(b) **There will be an optimum price/output level at which the business can maximise its profits**. This is the price level at which the marginal cost of making an extra unit of output is equal to the marginal revenue obtained from selling it (**MC = MR**).

Deriving the demand curve

FORMULA TO LEARN

When demand is linear the equation for the **demand curve** is

$$P = a - \frac{bQ}{\Delta Q}$$

where P = the price
Q = the quantity demanded
a = the price at which demand would be nil
b = the amount by which the price falls for each stepped change in demand
ΔQ = the stepped change in demand

The constant a is calculated as follows.

$$a = £(\text{current price}) + \frac{\text{Current quantity at current price}}{\text{Change in quantity when price is changed by £b}} \times £b$$

When demand is linear, an alternative equation for the **demand curve** (**linear demand function**) is

$$P = a + bQ$$

$$\text{where } b = \frac{\Delta P}{\Delta Q} = \frac{\text{change in price}}{\text{change in quantity}}$$

5.4 EXAMPLE: DERIVING THE DEMAND CURVE

(a) Suppose the current price of a product is £12. At this price the company sells 60 items a month. One month the company decides to raise the price to £14, but only 45 items are sold at this price. Clearly, if the company decided to go on raising its price, eventually it would sell no items at all.

(b) Assuming demand is linear, each increase of £2 in the price would result in a fall in demand of 15 units. Therefore, for demand to be nil, the price needs to rise from its current level by as many times as there are 15 units in 60 units: 60/15 = 4.

(c) The price needs to rise by £2 four times from its current level of £12 before no items at all are sold.

£12 + (4 × £2) = £20

Using the expression above, this can be shown as

$$a = £12 + \frac{60}{15} \times £2 \quad = £20$$

(d) The **demand equation** can now be determined: we have all the information we need.

$$P \quad = \quad a - \frac{bQ}{\Delta Q}$$

$$P \quad = \quad 20 - \frac{2Q}{15}$$

(e) We can check this by substituting £12 and £14 for P

$$12 = 20 - 2 \times \frac{60}{15} = 20 - 8 = 12$$

$$14 = 20 - \frac{2 \times 45}{15} = 20 - 6 = 14$$

(f) The equation can also be re-arranged for Q.

$$Q = \frac{(a \times \Delta Q) - (\Delta Q \times P)}{b}$$

Alternative approach

$P_1 = £12, Q_1 = 60$

$P_2 = £14, Q_2 = 45$

$$b = \frac{\Delta P}{\Delta Q} = \frac{12 - 14}{60 - 45} = \frac{-2}{15}$$

$a = P - bQ$

$$a = 12 - (\frac{-2}{15} \times 60)$$

$a = 12 - (-8)$

$a = 20$

∴ The linear demand function is $P = 20 - \frac{2Q}{15}$ (as calculated above).

5.5 Attempt the following question about finding an expression for a demand curve.

Question 4

Lynn has set up her own market stall selling terracotta pots for gardens. As an experiment she has tried two different prices, each for one week. At a price of £3 she sold 400 pots and at a price of £4 she sold 340 pots. Assuming that demand is linear, find the linear demand function for Lynn's stall.

Answer

If $P = a - \frac{bQ}{\Delta Q}$

$$a = £4 + \left(\frac{340 \times 1}{60}\right)$$

$$= £(4 + 5.67) = £9.67$$

$$\therefore P = 9.67 - \frac{1 \times Q}{60}$$

Alternative approach

If $P = a + bQ$

$P_1 = £3$, $P_2 = £4$

$Q_1 = 400$, $Q_2 = 340$

$$\therefore b = \frac{\Delta P}{\Delta Q} = \frac{+1}{-60} = \frac{-1}{60}$$

$$a = P - bQ$$

$$a = 3 - (\frac{-1 \times 400}{60})$$

$$= 3 + 6.67$$

$$= 9.67$$

$\therefore$ The linear demand function is $P = 9.67 - \frac{Q}{60}$

Exam focus point

Remember to show all of your workings when performing mathematical calculations in the paper-based exam – it shows the examiner that you know exactly what you are doing even if your final answer isn't correct because you have made a simple error.

Optimum pricing in practice

5.6 Disadvantages of the optimum price/output level approach to pricing

- It assumes that the demand curve and total costs can be identified with certainty. This is extremely unlikely to be so.
- It ignores the market research costs associated with acquiring knowledge of demand.
- It assumes the firm has no production constraints which could mean that the equilibrium point between supply and demand cannot be reached.
- It assumes that the organisation wishes to maximise profits. In fact it may have other objectives.
- It assumes that price is the only influence on quantity demanded. This is not always the case.

Profit maximisation

5.7 **Profit maximisation** is assumed to be the goal of the firm in most economic and accounting textbooks. This is usually the case of small owner-managed companies or partnerships.

5.8 We can define **profits** as **total revenue minus total costs** at any level of output. Profits are at a maximum where the (vertical) distance between the total revenue (TR) and total cost (TC) curves is greatest.

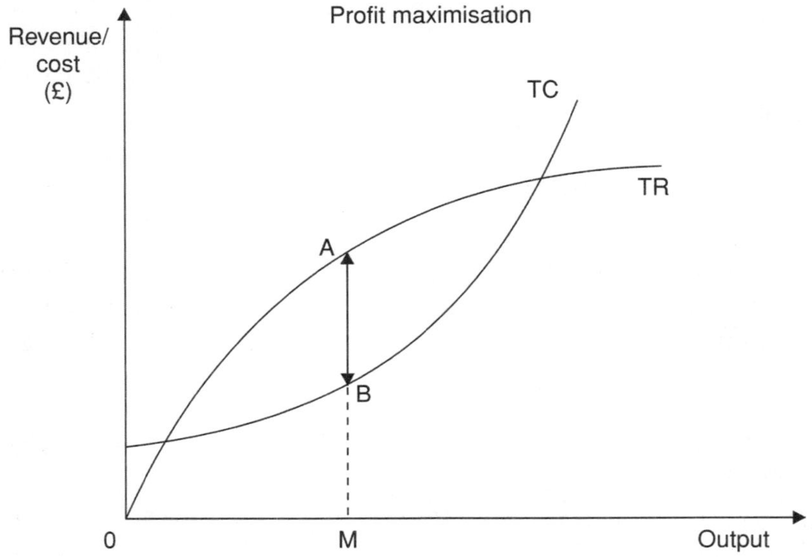

- Profits are at a maximum along line AB
- Point M indicates the output at which profits will be maximised

Total revenue, average revenue and marginal revenue

5.9 **Total revenue (TR)** is the total income obtained from selling a given quantity of output. We can think of this as quantity sold multiplied by the price per unit.

5.10 **Average revenue (AR)** we can think of as the price per unit sold.

5.11 **Marginal revenue (MR)** is the addition to total revenue earned from the sale of one extra unit of output.

5.12 If a firm can sell all its extra output at the same price, the AR 'curve' will be a **straight line** on a graph, **horizontal** to the x axis. The marginal revenue per unit from selling extra units at a fixed price must be the same as the average price.

5.13 In general, though, the AR falls as more units are sold, so the MR must be less than the AR. If the price per unit must be lowered to sell more units, then the marginal revenue per unit obtained from selling the extra units will be less than the previous price per unit.

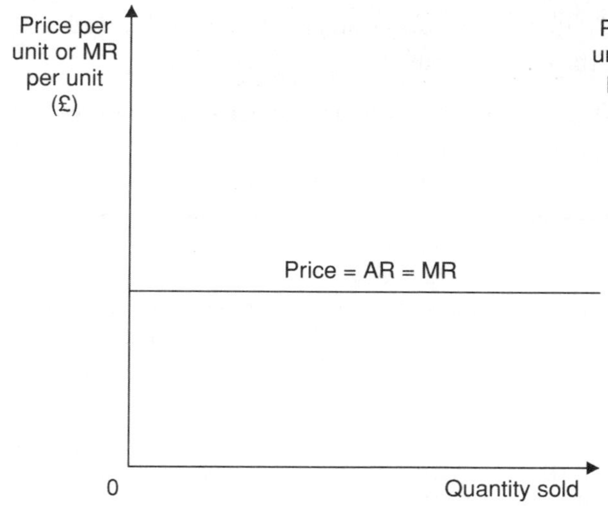

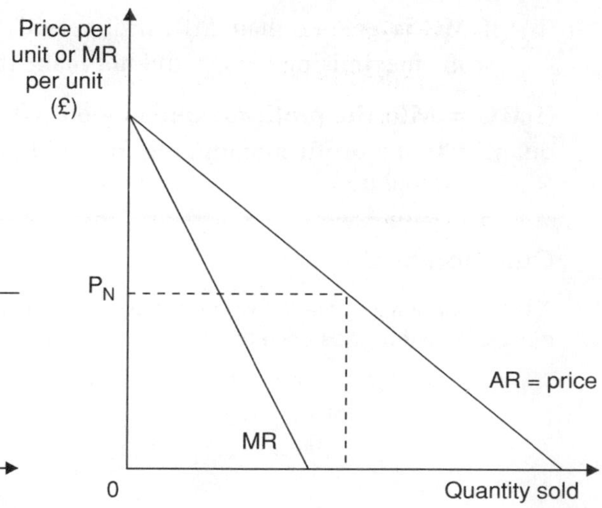

5.14 Note that all units are sold at the same price. The firm has to reduce its price to sell more, but the price must be reduced for **all** units sold, not just for the extra units. This is because we are assuming that all output is produced for a single market, where a single price will prevail.

5.15 When the price per unit has to be reduced in order to increase the firm's sales the marginal revenue can become **negative**. This happens at price P_N when a reduction in price does not increase output sufficiently to earn the same total revenue as before. In this situation, the **price elasticity of demand** would be **inelastic**.

5.16 **Revenue is maximised when MR = O** ie when the marginal revenue line shown in the graph in paragraph 5.12 cuts the x-axis. When MR = O additional units sold do not create any additional revenue, and revenue is therefore **maximised** at this point.

Profit maximisation: MC = MR

5.17 As a firm produces and sells more units, its total costs will increase and its total revenues will also increase (unless the price elasticity of demand is inelastic and the firm faces a downward sloping AR curve).

(a) Provided that the extra cost of making an extra unit is **less than** the extra revenue obtained from selling it, the firm will increase its profits by making and selling the extra unit.

(b) If the extra cost of making an extra unit of output **exceeds** the extra revenue obtainable from selling it, the firm's profits would be reduced by making and selling the extra unit.

(c) If the extra cost of making an extra unit of output is **exactly equal** to the extra revenue obtainable from selling it, bearing in mind that economic cost includes an amount for normal profit, it will be worth the firm's while to make and sell the extra unit. And since the extra cost of yet another unit would be higher (the law of diminishing returns applies) whereas extra revenue per unit from selling extra units is never higher, the **profit-maximising output** is reached at this point where **MC = MR**.

5.18 In other words, given the **objective of profit maximisation**:

(a) if MC is less than MR, profits will be increased by making and selling more;

(b) if MC is greater than MR, profits will fall if more units are made and sold, and a profit-maximising firm would not make the extra output.

If MC = MR, the profit-maximising output has been reached, and so this is the output quantity that a profit-maximising firm will decide to supply.

Question 5

A firm operates in a market where there is imperfect competition, so that to sell more units of output, it must reduce the sales price of all the units it sells. The following data is available for prices and costs.

Total output	*Sales price per unit (AR)*	*Average cost of output (AC)*
Units	£	£ per unit
0	-	-
1	504	720
2	471	402
3	439	288
4	407	231
5	377	201
6	346	189
7	317	182
8	288	180
9	259	186
10	232	198

The total cost of zero output is £600.

At what output level and price would the firm maximise its profits, assuming that fractions of units cannot be made?

Answer

Units	*Price*	*Total revenue*	*Marginal revenue*	*Total cost*	*Marginal cost*	*Profit*
	£	£	£	£	£	£
0	0	0	0	600	-	(600)
1	504	504	504	720	120	(216)
2	471	942	438	804	84	138
3	439	1,317	375	864	60	453
4	407	1,628	311	924	60	704
5	377	1,885	257	1,005	81	880
6	346	2,076	191	1,134	129	942
7*	317	2,219	143	1,274	140	945
8	288	2,304	85	1,440	166	864
9	259	2,331	27	1,674	234	657
10	232	2,320	-11	1,980	306	340

* Profit is maximised at 7 units of output where MR is most nearly equal to MC.

Chapter roundup

- **Price elasticity** is a measure of the extent of change in market demand for a good in response to a change in its price. If **demand is elastic** a reduction in price would lead to a rise in total sales revenue. If **demand is inelastic** a reduction in price would lead to a fall in total sales revenue.
- In **full cost-plus pricing** the sales price is determined by calculating the full cost of the product and then adding a percentage mark-up for profit. **Marginal cost-plus pricing** involves adding a profit margin to the marginal cost of production/sales. The most important criticism of full cost-plus pricing is that it fails to recognise that since sales demand may be determined by the sales price, there will be a profit-maximising combination of price and demand. A marginal costing approach is more likely to help with identifying a profit-maximising price.
- The basic approach to pricing **special orders** is **minimum pricing**.
- Three alternative pricing strategies for **new** products are **market penetration pricing, market skimming pricing** and **premium pricing**.
- **Price discrimination** may be used to make products appear to be different and segment markets so that premium prices can be justified in some markets.
- Some organisations produce estimated **demand curves** in order to ascertain how price increases will affect total revenues and profits.
- When demand is linear, the **equation for the demand curve** is as follows.

  $P = a - \frac{bQ}{\Delta Q}$ or $P = a + bQ$
- The **optimum price/output level** at which a business can maximise its profits is when **MC = MR** (marginal cost = marginal revenue).
- **Revenue is maximised** when **MR = 0**, ie when additional units sold do not create any additional revenue.

Quick quiz

1 The price elasticity of demand for a particular good at the current price is 1.2. Demand for this good at this price is (1) **elastic/inelastic**. If the price of the good is reduced, total sales revenue will (2) **rise/fall/stay the same.**

2 Name the five stages of the product life cycle.

3 Name one advantage, and one disadvantage of full cost-plus pricing.

4 A company knows that demand for its new product will be highly elastic. The most appropriate pricing strategy for the new product will be

Market penetration pricing	☐
Market skimming pricing	☐

5 If demand is linear, and the linear demand function is P = a + bQ

P = ...

Q = ...

b = $\frac{\text{........................}}{\text{........................}}$

a = ...

6 Profits are maximised when marginal cost is equal to marginal revenue.

True	☐
False	☐

7 When are revenues maximised?

Answers to quick quiz

1 (1) elastic, (2) rise

2 Introduction, growth, maturity, saturation and decline

3 Advantage = pricing rule can be delegated
Disadvantage = takes no account of market and demand conditions

4 Market penetration pricing

5 P = price

Q = quantity

$$b = \frac{\Delta P}{\Delta Q} = \frac{\text{change in price}}{\text{change in quantity}}$$

a = constant

6 True. Profits are maximised when MC = MR.

7 Revenues are maximised when MR = 0.

Now try the questions below from the Exam Question Bank

Number	Level	Marks	Time
30	MCQ	n/a	n/a
31	Examination	10	18 mins

Part E
Standard costing and variance analysis

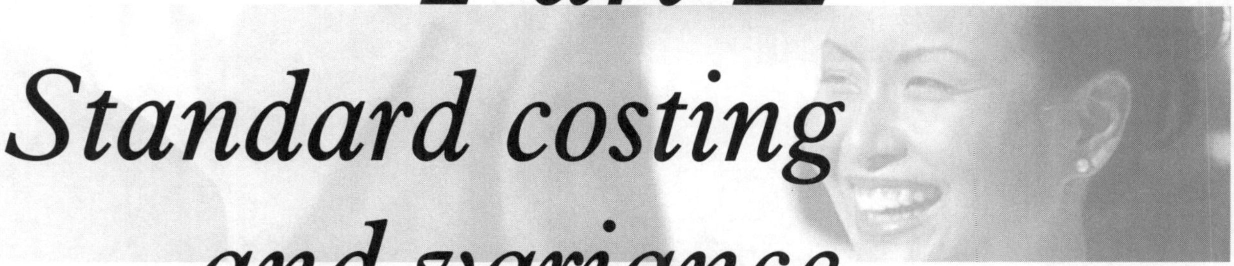

Chapter 18

STANDARD COSTING

Topic list		Syllabus reference
1	What is standard costing?	5(a), 3(c)
2	Setting standards	5(a), 3(c)

Introduction

Just as there are **standards** for most things in our daily lives (cleanliness in hamburger restaurants, educational achievement of nine year olds, number of trains running on time), there are standards for the costs of products and services. Moreover, just as the standards in our daily lives are not always met, the standards for the costs of products and services are not always met. We will not, however, be considering the standards of cleanliness of hamburger restaurants in this chapter but we will be looking at standards for **costs**, what they are used for and how they are set.

In the next chapter we will see how **standard costing** forms the basis of a process called **variance analysis**, a vital management control tool.

Study guide

Section 8 – Material costs 1

- Calculate the standard cost of stocks from given information

Section 14 – Marginal and absorption costing

- Establish the standard cost per unit from given data under absorption and marginal costing

Section 26 – Standard costing –1

- Explain the purpose of standard costing
- Establish the standard cost per unit from given data under absorption and marginal costing

1 WHAT IS STANDARD COSTING?

1.1 The building blocks of standard costing are standard costs and so before we look at standard costing in any detail you really need to know what a standard cost is.

Standard cost

1.2 The standard cost of product 1234 is set out below.

STANDARD COST CARD - PRODUCT 1234

	£	£
Direct materials		
Material X – 3 kg at £4 per kg	12	
Material Y – 9 litres at £2 per litre	18	
		30
Direct labour		
Grade A – 6 hours at £1.50 per hour	9	
Grade B – 8 hours at £2 per hour	16	
		25
Standard direct cost		55
Variable production overhead – 14 hours at £0.50 per hour		7
Standard variable cost of production		62
Fixed production overhead – 14 hours at £4.50 per hour		63
Standard full production cost		125
Administration and marketing overhead		15
Standard cost of sale		140
Standard profit		20
Standard sales price		160

KEY TERM

A **standard cost** is a planned unit cost.

1.3 Notice how the total standard cost is built up from standards for each cost element: standard quantities of materials at standard prices, standard quantities of labour time at standard rates and so on. It is therefore determined by management's estimates of the following.

- The expected prices of materials, labour and expenses
- Efficiency levels in the use of materials and labour
- Budgeted overhead costs and budgeted volumes of activity

We will see how management arrives at these estimates in Section 2.

1.4 But why should management want to prepare standard costs? Obviously to assist with standard costing, but what is the point of standard costing?

The uses of standard costing

1.5 **Standard costing** has a variety of uses but its two principal ones are as follows.

(a) To **value stocks** and **cost production** for cost accounting purposes. It is an alternative method of valuation to methods like FIFO and LIFO which we looked at in Chapter 6.

(b) To act as a **control device** by establishing standards (planned costs), highlighting (via **variance analysis** which we will cover in the next chapter) activities that are not conforming to plan and thus **alerting management** to areas which may be out of control and in need of corrective action.

Question 1

Bloggs Ltd makes one product, the joe. Two types of labour are involved in the preparation of a joe, skilled and semi-skilled. Skilled labour is paid £10 per hour and semi-skilled £5 per hour. Twice as many skilled labour hours as semi-skilled labour hours are needed to produce a joe, four semi-skilled labour hours being needed.

A joe is made up of three different direct materials. Seven kilograms of direct material A, four litres of direct material B and three metres of direct material C are needed. Direct material A costs £1 per kilogram, direct material B £2 per litre and direct material C £3 per metre.

Variable production overheads are incurred at Bloggs Ltd at the rate of £2.50 per direct labour (skilled) hour.

A system of absorption costing is in operation at Bloggs Ltd. The basis of absorption is direct labour (skilled) hours. For the forthcoming accounting period, budgeted fixed production overheads are £250,000 and budgeted production of the joe is 5,000 units.

Administration, selling and distribution overheads are added to products at the rate of £10 per unit.

A mark-up of 25% is made on the joe.

Required

Using the above information draw up a standard cost card for the joe.

Answer

STANDARD COST CARD - PRODUCT JOE

Direct materials	£	£
A - 7 kgs × £1	7	
B - 4 litres × £2	8	
C - 3 m × £3	9	
		24
Direct labour		
Skilled - 8 × £10	80	
Semi-skilled - 4 × £5	20	
		100
Standard direct cost		124
Variable production overhead - 8 × £2.50		20
Standard variable cost of production		144
Fixed production overhead - 8 × £6.25 (W)		50
Standard full production cost		194
Administration, selling and distribution overhead		10
Standard cost of sale		204
Standard profit (25% × 204)		51
Standard sales price		255

Working

$$\text{Overhead absorption rate} = \frac{£250,000}{5,000 \times 8} = £6.25 \text{ per skilled labour hour}$$

1.6 Although the use of standard costs to simplify the keeping of cost accounting records should not be overlooked, we will be concentrating on the **control** and **variance analysis** aspect of standard costing.

KEY TERM

Standard costing is 'A control technique which compares standard costs and revenues with actual results to obtain variances which are used to stimulate improved performance'.

CIMA *Official Terminology*

1.7 Notice that the above definition highlights the control aspects of standard costing.

Standard costing as a control technique

1.8 **Standard costing** therefore involves the following.

- The establishment of predetermined estimates of the costs of products or services
- The collection of actual costs
- The comparison of the actual costs with the predetermined estimates.

1.9 The predetermined costs are known as **standard costs** and the difference between standard and actual cost is known as a **variance**. The process by which the total difference between standard and actual results is analysed is known as **variance analysis**.

1.10 Although standard costing can be used in a variety of costing situations (batch and mass production, process manufacture, jobbing manufacture (where there is standardisation of parts) and service industries (if a realistic cost unit can be established)), the greatest benefit from its use can be gained if there is a **degree of repetition** in the production process. It is therefore most suited to **mass production** and **repetitive assembly work**.

2 SETTING STANDARDS

2.1 Standard costs may be used in both absorption costing and in marginal costing systems. We shall, however, confine our description to standard costs in absorption costing systems.

2.2 As we noted earlier, the standard cost of a product (or service) is made up of a number of different standards, one for each cost element, each of which has to be set by management. We have divided this section into two: the first part looks at setting the monetary part of each standard, whereas the second part looks at setting the resources requirement part of each standard.

Direct material prices

2.3 **Direct material prices** will be estimated by the purchasing department from their knowledge of the following.

- Purchase contracts already agreed
- Pricing discussions with regular suppliers
- The forecast movement of prices in the market
- The availability of bulk purchase discounts

2.4 Price inflation can cause difficulties in setting realistic standard prices. Suppose that a material costs £10 per kilogram at the moment and during the course of the next twelve months it is expected to go up in price by 20% to £12 per kilogram. What standard price should be selected?

- The current price of £10 per kilogram
- The average expected price for the year, say £11 per kilogram

2.5 Either would be possible, but neither would be entirely satisfactory.

(a) If the **current price** were used in the standard, the reported price variance will become adverse as soon as prices go up, which might be very early in the year. If prices go up gradually rather than in one big jump, it would be difficult to select an appropriate time for revising the standard.

(b) If an **estimated mid-year price** were used, price variances should be favourable in the first half of the year and adverse in the second half of the year, again assuming that prices go up gradually throughout the year. Management could only really check that in any month, the price variance did not become excessively adverse (or favourable) and that the price variance switched from being favourable to adverse around month six or seven and not sooner.

Direct labour rates

2.6 **Direct labour rates per hour** will be set by discussion with the personnel department and by reference to the payroll and to any agreements on pay rises with trade union representatives of the employees.

(a) A separate hourly rate or weekly wage will be set for each different labour grade/type of employee.

(b) An average hourly rate will be applied for each grade (even though individual rates of pay may vary according to age and experience).

2.7 Similar problems when dealing with inflation to those described for material prices can be met when setting labour standards.

Overhead absorption rates

2.8 When standard costs are fully absorbed costs, the **absorption rate** of fixed production overheads will be **predetermined,** usually each year when the budget is prepared, and based in the usual manner on budgeted fixed production overhead expenditure and budgeted production.

For selling and distribution costs, standard costs might be absorbed as a percentage of the standard selling price.

2.9 Standard costs under marginal costing will, of course, not include any element of absorbed overheads.

Standard resource requirements

2.10 To estimate the materials required to make each product (**material usage**) and also the labour hours required (**labour efficiency**), **technical specifications** must be prepared for each product by production experts (either in the production department or the work study department).

(a) The '**standard product specification**' for materials must list the quantities required per unit of each material in the product. These standard input quantities must be made known to the operators in the production department so that control action by management to deal with **excess material wastage** will be understood by them.

(b) The '**standard operation sheet**' for labour will specify the expected hours required by each grade of labour in each department to make one unit of product. These standard times must be carefully set (for example by work study) and must be understood by the labour force. Where necessary, **standard procedures** or **operating methods** should be stated.

Performance standards

2.11 The quantity of material and labour time required will depend on the level of performance required by management. There are two types of **performance standard** which might be used. Standards may be set at '**attainable levels** which assume efficient levels of operation, but which include **allowances** for normal loss, waste and machine downtime, or at **ideal levels**, which make **no allowance** for the above losses, and are only attainable under the most favourable conditions' (CIMA *Official Terminology*).

2.12 **Ideal standards** are sometimes thought to have a negative motivational impact, because employees will often feel that the goals are unattainable and not work so hard. When setting standards, managers must be aware of two requirements.

- The need to establish a useful control measure
- The need to set a standard which will have the desired motivational effect.

These two requirements are often conflicting, so that the final standard cost might be a compromise between the two.

Taking account of wastage, losses etc

2.13 If, during processing, the quantity of material input to the process is likely to reduce (due to wastage, evaporation and so on), the quantity input must be greater than the quantity in the finished product and a material standard must take account of this.

2.14 Suppose that the fresh raspberry juice content of a litre of Purple Pop is 100ml and that there is a 10% loss of raspberry juice during process due to evaporation. The standard material usage of raspberry juice per litre of Purple Pop will be:

$$100\text{ml} \times \frac{100\%}{(100-10)\%} = 100\text{ml} \times \frac{100\%}{90\%} = 111.11\text{ml}$$

Exam focus point

Make sure that you understand how to account for wastage and losses etc when calculating standard costs. Examination questions could well ask you to calculate the standard cost of a product given that there is loss due to evaporation or idle time and so on. Have a go at question 2 below.

Question 2

A unit of product X requires 24 active labour hours for completion. It is anticipated that there will be 20% idle time which is to be incorporated into the standard times for all products. If the wage rate is £10 per hour, what is the standard labour cost of one unit of product X?

A £192 B £240 C £288 D £300

Answer

The basic labour cost for 24 hours is £240. However with idle time it will be necessary to pay for more than 24 hours in order to achieve 24 hours of actual work Therefore options A and B are incorrect.

$$\text{Standard labour cost} = \text{active hours for completion} \times \frac{100}{80} \times £10$$

$$= 24 \times 1.25 \times £10 = \underline{\underline{£300}}$$

Option D is correct.

Option C is incorrect because it results from simply adding an extra 20 per cent to the labour hours. However the idle hours are 20 per cent of the *total* hours worked, therefore we need to add 25 per cent to the required active hours, as shown in the working.

2.15 **Problems in setting standards**

(a) Deciding how to incorporate **inflation** into planned unit costs

(b) Agreeing on a **performance standard** (attainable or ideal)

(c) Deciding on the **quality** of materials to be used (a better quality of material will cost more, but perhaps reduce material wastage)

(d) Estimating materials **prices** where seasonal price variations or bulk purchase discounts may be significant

(e) Finding sufficient **time** to construct accurate standards as standard setting can be a **time-consuming process**

(f) Incurring the **cost of setting up and maintaining a system** for establishing standards

(g) Dealing with possible **behavioural problems,** managers responsible for the achievement of standards possibly resisting the use of a standard costing control system for fear of being blamed for any adverse variances

2.16 **The advantages of standard costing**

(a) Carefully planned standards are an **aid to more accurate budgeting.**

(b) Standard costs provide a **yardstick** against which actual costs can be measured.

(c) The **setting of standards** involves determining the best materials and methods which may lead to **economies.**

(d) A **target of efficiency** is set for employees to reach and **cost consciousness** is stimulated.

(e) Variances can be calculated which enable the principle of '**management by exception**' to be operated. Only the variances which exceed acceptable tolerance limits need to be investigated by management with a view to control action.

(f) Standard costs **simplify the process of bookkeeping** in cost accounting, because they are easier to use than LIFO, FIFO and weighted average costs.

(g) Standard times **simplify the process of production scheduling.**

(h) Standard performance levels might provide an **incentive for individuals** to achieve targets for themselves at work.

Chapter roundup

- A **standard cost** is a **predetermined estimated unit cost**, used for stock valuation and control.
- A **standard cost card** shows full details of the standard cost of each product.
- Differences between actual and standard cost are called **variances**.
- **Performance standards** are used to set efficiency targets. There are basically two types: **attainable and ideal**.
- A standard cost is an **average** expected unit cost. The actual cost of individual items may fluctuate around this average.
- There are a number of advantages and disadvantages associated with standard costing.

Quick quiz

1 A standard cost is ....

2 What are two main uses of standard costing?

3 A control technique which compares standard costs and revenues with actual results to obtain variances which are used to stimulate improved performance is known as:

A Standard costing
B Variance analysis
C Budgetary control
D Budgeting

4 Standard costs may only be used in absorption costing.

True ☐

False ☐

5 Two types of performance standard are

(a) ....
(b) ....

6 List three problems in setting standards.

7 List three advantages of using standard costing.

Answers to quick quiz

1 A planned unit cost.

2 (a) To value stocks and cost production for cost accounting purposes.

(b) To act as a control device by establishing standards and highlighting activities that are not conforming to plan and bringing these to the attention of management.

3 A

4 False. They may be used in a marginal costing system as well.

5 (a) Attainable
(b) Ideal

6 See Paragraph 2.15.

7 See Paragraph 2.16.

Now try the questions below from the Exam Question Bank

Number	Level	Marks	Time
32	MCQ	n/a	n/a
33	Examination	10	18 mins

Chapter 19

BASIC VARIANCE ANALYSIS

Introduction

The actual results achieved by an organisation during a reporting period (week, month, quarter, year) will, more than likely, be different from the expected results (the expected results being the standard costs and revenues which we looked at in the previous chapter). Such differences may occur between individual items, such as the cost of labour and the volume of sales, and between the total expected profit/contribution and the total actual profit/contribution.

Management will have spent considerable time and trouble setting standards. Actual results have differed from the standards. The wise manager will consider the differences that have occurred and use the results of these considerations to assist in attempts to attain the standards. The wise manager will use **variance analysis** as a method of **control**.

This chapter examines **variance analysis** and sets out the method of calculating the variances stated below in the Study Guide.

We will then go on to look at the reasons for and significance of cost variances.

Chapter 20 of this **Financial Information for Management** Study Text will build on the basics set down in this chapter by introducing **sales variances** and **operating statements.**

Study guide

Section 5 – Cost classification

- Describe the nature of control achieved through the comparison of actual costs against plan

Section 12 Overheads – 2

- Calculate and explain fixed overhead expenditure, volume and, where appropriate, efficiency and capacity variances

Section 26 – Standard costing – 1

- Explain the purpose of the following variances:

  - materials price and usage
  - labour rate, idle time and efficiency
  - variable overhead expenditure and efficiency
  - fixed overhead expenditure, volume and where appropriate, efficiency and capacity

Section 27 – Standard costing – 2

- Calculate and interpret the above variances using the appropriate costing method

Exam guide

Variance calculation is a very important part of your **Financial Information for Management** studies and it is vital that you are able to calculate all of the different types of variance included in the syllabus.

1 VARIANCES

KEY TERM

A **variance** is 'The difference between a planned, budgeted, or standard cost and the actual cost incurred. The same comparisons may be made for revenues.'

CIMA *Official Terminology*

1.1 The process by which the **total** difference between standard and actual results is analysed is known as **variance analysis**.

KEY TERM

Variance analysis is defined as 'The evaluation of performance by means of variances, whose timely reporting should maximise the opportunity for managerial action'.

CIMA *Official Terminology*

1.2 When actual results are better than expected results, we have a **favourable variance** (F). If, on the other hand, actual results are worse than expected results, we have an **adverse variance** (A).

1.3 Variances can be divided into three main groups.

- Variable cost variances
- Sales variances
- Fixed production overhead variances.

In the remainder of this chapter we will consider, in detail, variable cost variances and fixed production overhead variances.

2 DIRECT MATERIAL COST VARIANCES

KEY TERM

The **direct material total variance** is the difference between what the output actually cost and what it should have cost, in terms of material.

2.1 The **direct material total variance** can be divided into two sub-variances.

KEY TERMS

- The **direct material price variance.** This is the **difference between the standard cost and the actual cost for the actual quantity of material used or purchased.** In other words, it is the difference between what the material did cost and what it should have cost.
- The **direct material usage variance.** This is the **difference between the standard quantity of materials that should have been used for the number of units actually produced, and the actual quantity of materials used, valued at the standard cost per unit of material.** In other words, it is the difference between how much material should have been used and how much material was used, valued at standard cost.

2.2 EXAMPLE: DIRECT MATERIAL VARIANCES

Product X has a standard direct material cost as follows.

10 kilograms of material Y at £10 per kilogram = £100 per unit of X.

During period 4, 1,000 units of X were manufactured, using 11,700 kilograms of material Y which cost £98,600.

Required

Calculate the following variances.

(a) The direct material total variance
(b) The direct material price variance
(c) The direct material usage variance

2.3 SOLUTION

(a) **The direct material total variance**

This is the difference between what 1,000 units should have cost and what they did cost.

	£
1,000 units should have cost (× £100)	100,000
but did cost	98,600
Direct material total variance	1,400 (F)

The variance is **favourable** because the units cost less than they should have cost.

Now we can break down the direct material total variance into its two constituent parts: the direct material **price** variance and the direct material **usage** variance.

(b) **The direct material price variance**

This is the difference between what 11,700 kgs should have cost and what 11,700 kgs did cost.

	£
11,700 kgs of Y should have cost (× £10)	117,000
but did cost	98,600
Material Y price variance	18,400 (F)

The variance is **favourable** because the material cost less than it should have.

(c) **The direct material usage variance**

This is the difference between how many kilograms of Y should have been used to produce 1,000 units of X and how many kilograms were used, valued at the standard cost per kilogram.

1,000 units should have used (× 10 kgs)	10,000 kgs
but did use	11,700 kgs
Usage variance in kgs	1,700 kgs (A)
× standard cost per kilogram	× £10
Usage variance in £	£17,000 (A)

The variance is **adverse** because more material than should have been used was used.

(d) **Summary**

	£
Price variance	18,400 (F)
Usage variance	17,000 (A)
Total variance	1,400 (F)

Materials variances and opening and closing stock

2.4 Suppose that a company uses raw material P in production, and that this raw material has a standard price of £3 per metre. During one month 6,000 metres are bought for £18,600, and 5,000 metres are used in production. At the end of the month, stock will have been increased by 1,000 metres. In variance analysis, the problem is to decide the **material price variance**. Should it be calculated on the basis of **materials purchased** (6,000 metres) or on the basis of **materials used** (5,000 metres)?

2.5 The answer to this problem depends on how **closing stocks** of the raw materials will be valued.

(a) If they are valued at **standard cost,** (1,000 units at £3 per unit) the price variance is calculated on material **purchases** in the period.

(b) If they are valued at **actual cost** (FIFO) (1,000 units at £3.10 per unit) the price variance is calculated on materials **used in production** in the period.

2.6 A **full standard costing system** is usually in operation and therefore the price variance is usually calculated on **purchases** in the period. The variance on the full 6,000 metres will be written off to the costing profit and loss account, even though only 5,000 metres are included in the cost of production.

2.7 There are two main advantages in extracting the material price variance at the time of **receipt.**

(a) If variances are extracted at the time of receipt they will be **brought to the attention of managers earlier** than if they are extracted as the material is used. If it is necessary to correct any variances then management action can be more timely.

(b) Since variances are extracted at the time of receipt, **all stocks will be valued at standard price.** This is administratively easier and it means that all issues from stocks can be made at standard price. If stocks are held at actual cost it is necessary to calculate a separate price variance on each batch as it is issued. Since issues are usually made in a number of small batches this can be a time-consuming task, especially with a manual system.

2.8 The price variance would be calculated as follows.

	£
6,000 metres of material P purchased should cost (× £3)	18,000
but did cost	18,600
Price variance	600 (A)

3 DIRECT LABOUR COST VARIANCES

3.1 The calculation of **direct labour variances** is very similar to the calculation of direct material variances.

KEY TERMS

- The **direct labour total variance** (the difference between what the output should have cost and what it did cost, in terms of labour) can be divided into two sub-variances.
- **The direct labour rate variance**. This is similar to the direct material price variance. It is the **difference between the standard cost and the actual cost for the actual number of hours paid for.**

  In other words, it is the difference between what the labour did cost and what it should have cost.
- **The direct labour efficiency variance**. This is similar to the direct material usage variance. It is the **difference between the hours that should have been worked for the number of units actually produced, and the actual number of hours worked, valued at the standard rate per hour.**

  In other words, it is the difference between how many hours should have been worked and how many hours were worked, valued at the standard rate per hour.

3.2 EXAMPLE: DIRECT LABOUR VARIANCES

The standard direct labour cost of product X is as follows.

2 hours of grade Z labour at £5 per hour = £10 per unit of product X.

During period 4, 1,000 units of product X were made, and the direct labour cost of grade Z labour was £8,900 for 2,300 hours of work.

Required

Calculate the following variances.

(a) The direct labour total variance
(b) The direct labour rate variance
(c) The direct labour efficiency (productivity) variance

3.3 SOLUTION

(a) **The direct labour total variance**

This is the difference between what 1,000 units should have cost and what they did cost.

	£
1,000 units should have cost (× £10)	10,000
but did cost	8,900
Direct labour total variance	1,100 (F)

The variance is **favourable** because the units cost less than they should have done.

Again we can analyse this total variance into its two constituent parts.

(b) **The direct labour rate variance**

This is the difference between what 2,300 hours should have cost and what 2,300 hours did cost.

	£
2,300 hours of work should have cost (× £5 per hr)	11,500
but did cost	8,900
Direct labour rate variance	2,600 (F)

The variance is **favourable** because the labour cost less than it should have cost.

(c) **The direct labour efficiency variance**

1,000 units of X should have taken (× 2 hrs)	2,000 hrs
but did take	2,300 hrs
Efficiency variance in hours	300 hrs (A)
× standard rate per hour	× £5
Efficiency variance in £	£1,500 (A)

The variance is **adverse** because more hours were worked than should have been worked.

(d) **Summary**

	£
Rate variance	2,600 (F)
Efficiency variance	1,500 (A)
Total variance	1,100 (F)

Idle time variance

3.4 A company may operate a costing system in which any **idle time** is recorded. Idle time may be caused by machine breakdowns or not having work to give to employees, perhaps because of bottlenecks in production or a shortage of orders from customers. When idle time occurs, the labour force is still paid wages for time at work, but no actual work is done. Time paid for without any work being done is unproductive and therefore inefficient. In variance analysis, **idle time is always an adverse efficiency variance**.

3.5 When idle time is recorded separately, it is helpful to provide control information which identifies the cost of idle time separately, and in variance analysis, there will be an idle time variance **as a separate part of the total labour efficiency variance**. The remaining efficiency variance will then relate only to the productivity of the labour force during the hours spent **actively working**.

3.6 EXAMPLE: LABOUR VARIANCES WITH IDLE TIME

Refer to the standard cost data in Paragraph 3.2. During period 5, 1,500 units of product X were made and the cost of grade Z labour was £17,500 for 3,080 hours. During the period, however, there is a shortage of customer orders and 100 hours were recorded as idle time.

Required

Calculate the following variances.

(a) The direct labour total variance
(b) The direct labour rate variance
(c) The idle time variance
(d) The direct labour efficiency variance

3.7 SOLUTION

(a) **The direct labour total variance**

	£
1,500 units of product X should have cost (× £10)	15,000
but did cost	17,500
Direct labour total variance	2,500 (A)

Actual cost is greater than standard cost. The variance is therefore **adverse.**

(b) **The direct labour rate variance**

The rate variance is a comparison of what the hours paid should have cost and what they did cost.

	£
3,080 hours of grade Z labour should have cost (× £5)	15,400
but did cost	17,500
Direct labour rate variance	2,100 (A)

Actual cost is greater than standard cost. The variance is therefore **adverse**.

(c) **The idle time variance**

The idle time variance is the hours of idle time, valued at the standard rate per hour.

Idle time variance = 100 hours (A) × £5 = £500 (A)

Idle time is **always** an adverse variance.

(d) **The direct labour efficiency variance**

The efficiency variance considers the hours actively worked (the difference between hours paid for and idle time hours). In our example, there were (3,080 – 100) = 2,980 hours when the labour force was not idle. The variance is calculated by taking the amount of output produced (1,500 units of product X) and comparing the time it should have taken to make them, with the actual time spent **actively** making them (2,980 hours). Once again, the variance in hours is valued at the **standard rate per labour hour.**

1,500 units of product X should take (× 2hrs)	3,000 hrs
but did take (3,080 – 100)	2,980 hrs
Direct labour efficiency variance in hours	20 hrs (F)
× standard rate per hour	× £5
Direct labour efficiency variance in £	£100 (F)

(e) **Summary**

	£
Direct labour rate variance	2,100 (A)
Idle time variance	500 (A)
Direct labour efficiency variance	100 (F)
Direct labour total variance	2,500 (A)

3.8 Remember that, if idle time is recorded, the actual hours used in the efficiency variance calculation are the **hours worked and not the hours paid for.**

Question 1

Growler Ltd is planning to make 100,000 units per period of product AA. Each unit of AA should require 2 hours to produce, with labour being paid £11 per hour. Attainable work hours are less than clock hours, so 250,000 hours have been budgeted in the period.

Actual data for the period was:

Units produced	120,000
Direct labour cost	£3,200,000
Clock hours	280,000

Required

Calculate the following variances.

(a) Labour rate variance
(b) Labour efficiency variance
(c) Idle time variance

Answer

The information means that clock hours have to be multiplied by $\frac{200,000}{250,000}$ (80%) in order to arrive at a realistic efficiency variance.

(a) **Labour rate variance**

	£'000	
280,000 hours should have cost (× £11)	3,080	
but did cost	3,200	
Labour rate variance	120	(A)

(b) **Labour efficiency variance**

120,000 units should have taken (× 2 hours)	240,000	Hrs
but did take (280,000 × 80%)	224,000	Hrs
	16,000	hrs (F)
	× £11	
Labour efficiency variance	£176,000	(F)

(c) **Idle time variance**

280,000 × 20%	56,000	hrs
	× £11	
	£616,000	(A)

4 VARIABLE PRODUCTION OVERHEAD VARIANCES

4.1 Suppose that the variable production overhead cost of product X is as follows.

2 hours at £1.50 = £3 per unit

During period 6, 400 units of product X were made. The labour force worked 820 hours, of which 60 hours were recorded as idle time. The variable overhead cost was £1,230.

Calculate the following variances.

(a) The variable overhead total variance
(b) The variable production overhead expenditure variance
(c) The variable production overhead efficiency variance

4.2 Since this example relates to variable production costs, the total variance is based on actual units of production. (If the overhead had been a variable selling cost, the variance would be based on sales volumes.)

	£	
400 units of product X should cost (× £3)	1,200	
but did cost	1,230	
Variable production overhead total variance	30	(A)

4.3 In many variance reporting systems, the variance analysis goes no further, and expenditure and efficiency variances are not calculated. However, the adverse variance of £30 may be explained as the sum of two factors.

(a) The hourly rate of spending on variable production overheads was higher than it should have been, that is there is an **expenditure variance**.

(b) The labour force worked inefficiently, and took longer to make the output than it should have done. This means that spending on variable production overhead was higher than it should have been, in other words there is an **efficiency (productivity) variance**. The variable production overhead efficiency variance is exactly the same, in hours, as the direct labour efficiency variance, and occurs for the same reasons.

4.4 It is usually assumed that **variable overheads are incurred during active working hours**, but are not incurred during idle time (for example the machines are not running, therefore power is not being consumed, and no indirect materials are being used). This means in our example that although the labour force was paid for 820 hours, they were actively working for only 760 of those hours and so variable production overhead spending occurred during 760 hours.

KEY TERM

The **variable production overhead expenditure variance** is the difference between the amount of variable production overhead that should have been incurred in the actual hours actively worked, and the actual amount of variable production overhead incurred.

4.5 (a)

	£
760 hours of variable production overhead should cost (× £1.50)	1,140
but did cost	1,230
Variable production overhead expenditure variance	90 (A)

KEY TERM

The **variable production overhead efficiency variance**. If you already know the direct labour efficiency variance, the variable production overhead efficiency variance is exactly the same in hours, but priced at the variable production overhead rate per hour.

(b) In our example, the efficiency variance would be as follows.

400 units of product X should take (× 2hrs)	800 hrs
but did take (active hours)	760 hrs
Variable production overhead efficiency variance in hours	40 hrs (F)
× standard rate per hour	× £1.50
Variable production overhead efficiency variance in £	£60 (F)

(c) **Summary**

	£
Variable production overhead expenditure variance	90 (A)
Variable production overhead efficiency variance	60 (F)
Variable production overhead total variance	30 (A)

5 FIXED PRODUCTION OVERHEAD VARIANCES

5.1 You may have noticed that the method of calculating cost variances for variable cost items is essentially the same for labour, materials and variable overheads. Fixed production overhead variances are very different. In an **absorption costing system**, they are an attempt to explain the **under- or over-absorption of fixed production overheads** in production costs. We looked at under/over absorption of fixed overheads in Chapter 8.

5.2 The fixed production overhead total variance (ie the under- or over-absorbed fixed production overhead) may be broken down into two parts as usual.

- An **expenditure** variance
- A **volume** variance. This in turn may be split into two parts
  - **A volume efficiency variance**
  - **A volume capacity variance**

5.3 You will find it easier to calculate and understand **fixed overhead variances**, if you keep in mind the whole time that you are trying to 'explain' (put a name and value to) any under- or over-absorbed overhead.

Remember that the **absorption rate** is calculated as follows.

$$\textbf{Overhead absorption rate} = \frac{\text{Budgeted fixed overhead}}{\text{Budgeted activity level}}$$

Remember that the budgeted fixed overhead is the **planned** or **expected** fixed overhead and the budgeted activity level is the **planned** or **expected** activity level.

If either of the following are incorrect, then we will have an under- or over-absorption of overhead.

- The numerator (number on top) = Budgeted fixed overhead
- The denominator (number on bottom) = Budgeted activity level

The fixed overhead expenditure variance

5.4 The fixed overhead expenditure variance occurs if the numerator is incorrect. It measures the under- or over-absorbed overhead caused by the **actual total overhead** being different from the budgeted total overhead.

5.5 Therefore, fixed overhead expenditure variance = **Budgeted (planned) expenditure – Actual Expenditure.**

The fixed overhead volume variance

5.6 As we have already stated, the fixed overhead volume variance is made up of the following sub-variances.

- Fixed overhead efficiency variance
- Fixed overhead capacity variance

These variances arise if the denominator (ie the budgeted activity level) is incorrect.

5.7 The fixed overhead efficiency and capacity variances measure the under- or over-absorbed overhead caused by the **actual activity level** being different from the budgeted activity level used in calculating the absorption rate.

5.8 There are two reasons why the **actual activity** level may be different from the **budgeted activity level** used in calculating the absorption rate.

(a) The workforce may have worked more or less efficiently than the standard set. This deviation is measured by the **fixed overhead efficiency variance.**

(b) The hours worked by the workforce could have been different to the budgeted hours (regardless of the level of efficiency of the workforce) because of overtime and strikes etc. This deviation from the standard is measured by the **fixed overhead capacity variance.**

How to calculate the variances

5.9 In order to clarify the overhead variances which we have encountered in this section, consider the following definitions which are expressed in terms of how each overhead variance should be calculated.

KEY TERMS

- **Fixed overhead total variance** is the difference between fixed overhead incurred and fixed overhead absorbed. In other words, it is the under- or over-absorbed fixed overhead.
- **Fixed overhead expenditure variance** is the difference between the budgeted fixed overhead expenditure and actual fixed overhead expenditure.
- **Fixed overhead volume variance** is the difference between actual and budgeted (planned) volume multiplied by the standard absorption rate per *unit*.
- **Fixed overhead volume efficiency variance** is the difference between the number of hours that actual production should have taken, and the number of hours actually taken (that is, worked) multiplied by the standard absorption rate per *hour*.
- **Fixed overhead volume capacity variance** is the difference between budgeted (planned) hours of work and the actual hours worked, multiplied by the standard absorption rate per *hour*.

5.10 You should now be ready to work through an example to demonstrate all of the fixed overhead variances.

5.11 EXAMPLE: FIXED OVERHEAD VARIANCES

Suppose that a company plans to produce 1,000 units of product E during August 20X3. The expected time to produce a unit of E is five hours, and the budgeted fixed overhead is £20,000. The standard fixed overhead cost per unit of product E will therefore be as follows.

5 hours at £4 per hour = £20 per unit

Actual fixed overhead expenditure in August 20X3 turns out to be £20,450. The labour force manages to produce 1,100 units of product E in 5,400 hours of work.

Task

Calculate the following variances.

(a) The fixed overhead total variance
(b) The fixed overhead expenditure variance
(c) The fixed overhead volume variance
(d) The fixed overhead volume efficiency variance
(e) The fixed overhead volume capacity variance

5.12 SOLUTION

All of the variances help to assess the under- or over-absorption of fixed overheads, some in greater detail than others.

(a) **Fixed overhead total variance**

	£
Fixed overhead incurred	20,450
Fixed overhead absorbed (1,100 units × £20 per unit)	22,000
Fixed overhead total variance	1,550 (F)
(= under-/over-absorbed overhead)	

The variance is favourable because more overheads were absorbed than budgeted.

(b) **Fixed overhead expenditure variance**

	£
Budgeted fixed overhead expenditure	20,000
Actual fixed overhead expenditure	20,450
Fixed overhead expenditure variance	450 (A)

The variance is adverse because actual expenditure was greater than budgeted expenditure.

(c) **Fixed overhead volume variance**

The production volume achieved was greater than expected. The fixed overhead volume variance measures the difference at the standard rate.

	£
Actual production at standard rate (1,100 × £20 per unit)	22,000
Budgeted production at standard rate (1,000 × £20 per unit)	20,000
Fixed overhead volume variance	2,000 (F)

The variance is **favourable** because output was greater than expected.

(i) The labour force may have worked efficiently, and produced output at a faster rate than expected. Since overheads are absorbed at the rate of £20 per unit, more will be absorbed if units are produced more quickly. This **efficiency variance** is exactly the same in hours as the direct labour efficiency variance, but is valued in £ at the standard absorption rate for fixed overhead.

(ii) The labour force may have worked longer hours than budgeted, and therefore produced more output, so there may be a **capacity variance**.

(d) **Fixed overhead volume efficiency variance**

The volume efficiency variance is calculated in the same way as the labour efficiency variance.

1,100 units of product E should take (× 5 hrs)	5,500 hrs
but did take	5,400 hrs
Fixed overhead volume efficiency variance in hours	100 hrs (F)
× standard fixed overhead absorption rate per hour	× £4
Fixed overhead volume efficiency variance in £	£400 (F)

The labour force has produced 5,500 standard hours of work in 5,400 actual hours and so output is 100 standard hours (or 20 units of product E) higher than budgeted for this reason and the variance is **favourable**.

(e) **Fixed overhead volume capacity variance**

The volume capacity variance is the difference between the budgeted hours of work and the actual active hours of work (excluding any idle time).

Budgeted hours of work	5,000 hrs
Actual hours of work	5,400 hrs
Fixed overhead volume capacity variance	400 hrs (F)
× standard fixed overhead absorption rate per hour	× £4
Fixed overhead volume capacity variance in £	£1,600 (F)

Since the labour force worked 400 hours longer than planned, we should expect output to be 400 standard hours (or 80 units of product E) higher than budgeted and hence the variance is **favourable**.

The variances may be summarised as follows.

	£
Expenditure variance	450 (A)
Efficiency variance	400 (F)
Capacity variance	1,600 (F)
Over-absorbed overhead (total variance)	£1,550 (F)

Exam focus point

In general, a favourable cost variance will arise if actual results are less than expected results. Be aware, however, of the **fixed overhead volume variance** and the **fixed overhead volume capacity variance** which give rise to favourable and adverse variances in the following situations.

- A favourable fixed overhead volume variance occurs when actual production is **greater than** budgeted (planned) production
- An adverse fixed overhead volume variance occurs when actual production is **less than budgeted** (planned) production
- A favourable fixed overhead volume capacity variance occurs when actual hours of work are **greater than** budgeted (planned) hours of work
- An adverse fixed overhead volume capacity variance occurs when actual hours of work are **less than** budgeted (planned) hours of work

5.13 Do not worry if you find fixed production overhead variances more difficult to grasp than the other variances we have covered. Most students do. Read over this section again and then try the following practice questions.

The following information relates to questions 2, 3 and 4

Barbados Ltd has prepared the following standard cost information for one unit of Product Zeta.

Direct materials	4kg @ £10/kg	£40.00
Direct labour	2 hours @ £4/hour	£8.00
Fixed overheads	3 hours @ £2.50	£7.50

The fixed overheads are based on a budgeted expenditure of £75,000 and budgeted activity of 30,000 hours.

Actual results for the period were recorded as follows.

Production	9,000 units
Materials – 33,600 kg	£336,000
Labour – 16,500 hours	£68,500
Fixed overheads	£70,000

Question 2

The direct material price and usage variances are:

	Material price	*Material usage*
	£	£
A	-	24,000 (F)
B	-	24,000 (A)
C	24,000 (F)	-
D	24,000 (A)	-

Answer

Material price variance

	£
33,600 kg should have cost (× £10/kg)	336,000
and did cost	336,000
	-

Material usage variance

9,000 units should have used (× 4kg)	36,000 kg
but did use	33,600 kg
	2,400 kg (F)
× standard cost per kg	× £10
	24,000 (F)

The correct answer is therefore A.

Question 3

The direct labour rate and efficiency variances are:

	Labour rate	*Labour efficiency*
	£	£
A	6,000 (F)	2,500 (A)
B	6,000 (A)	2,500 (F)
C	2,500 (A)	6,000 (F)
D	2,500 (F)	6,000 (A)

Answer

Direct labour rate variance

	£
16,500 hrs should have cost (× £4)	66,000
but did cost	68,500
	2,500 (A)

Direct labour efficiency variance

9,000 units should have taken (× 2 hrs)	18,000 hrs
but did take	16,500 hrs
	1,500 (F)
× standard rate per hour (× £4)	× £4
	6,000 (F)

The correct answer is therefore C.

Question 4

The total fixed production overhead variance is:

A £5,000 (A)
B £5,000 (F)
C £2,500 (A)
D £2,500 (F)

Answer

	£
Fixed production overhead absorbed (£7.50 × 9,000)	67,500
Fixed production overhead incurred	70,000
	2,500 (A)

The correct answer is therefore C.

6 THE REASONS FOR COST VARIANCES

6.1 There are many possible reasons for cost variances arising, as you will see from the following list of possible causes.

Exam focus point

This is not an exhaustive list and in an examination question you should review the information given and use your imagination and common sense to suggest possible reasons for variances.

Variance	Favourable	Adverse
(a) Material price	Unforeseen discounts received More care taken in purchasing Change in material standard	Price increase Careless purchasing Change in material standard
(b) Material usage	Material used of higher quality than standard More effective use made of material Errors in allocating material to jobs	Defective material Excessive waste Theft Stricter quality control Errors in allocating material to jobs
(c) Labour rate	Use of apprentices or other workers at a rate of pay lower than standard	Wage rate increase Use of higher grade labour
(d) Idle time	**The idle time variance is always adverse**	Machine breakdown Non-availability of material Illness or injury to worker
(e) Labour efficiency	Output produced more quickly than expected because of work motivation, better quality of equipment or materials, or better methods. Errors in allocating time to jobs	Lost time in excess of standard allowed Output lower than standard set because of deliberate restriction, lack of training, or sub-standard material used Errors in allocating time to jobs
(f) Overhead expenditure	Savings in costs incurred More economical use of services	Increase in cost of services used Excessive use of services Change in type of services used
(g) Overhead volume efficiency	Labour force working more efficiently (favourable labour efficiency variance)	Labour force working less efficiently (adverse labour efficiency variance)
(h) Overhead volume capacity	Labour force working overtime	Machine breakdown, strikes, labour shortages

7 THE SIGNIFICANCE OF COST VARIANCES

7.1 Once variances have been calculated, management have to decide whether or not to investigate their causes. It would be extremely time consuming and expensive to investigate every variance therefore managers have to decide which variances are worthy of investigation.

7.2 There are a number of factors which can be taken into account when deciding whether or not a variance should be investigated.

(a) **Materiality.** A standard cost is really only an **average** expected cost and is not a rigid specification. Small variations either side of this average are therefore bound to occur. The problem is to decide whether a variation from standard should be considered **significant** and worthy of investigation. **Tolerance limits** can be set and only variances which exceed such limits would require investigating.

(b) **Controllability.** Some types of variance may not be controllable even once their cause is discovered. For example, if there is a general worldwide increase in the price of a raw material there is nothing that can be done internally to control the effect of this. If a central decision is made to award all employees a 10% increase in salary, staff costs in division A will increase by this amount and the variance is not controllable by division A's manager. Uncontrollable variances call for a change in the plan, not an investigation into the past.

(c) **The type of standard being used.**

(i) The efficiency variance reported in any control period, whether for materials or labour, will depend on the **efficiency level** set. If, for example, an **ideal standard** is used, variances will always be **adverse**.

(ii) A similar problem arises if **average price levels** are used as standards. If inflation exists, favourable price variances are likely to be reported at the beginning of a period, to be offset by adverse price variances later in the period as inflation pushes prices up.

(d) **Interdependence between variances** . Quite possibly, individual variances should not be looked at in isolation. One variance might be inter-related with another, and much of it might have occurred only because the other, inter-related, variance occurred too. We will investigate this issue further in a moment.

(e) **Costs of investigation.** The costs of an investigation should be weighed against the benefits of correcting the cause of a variance.

Interdependence between variances

7.3 **When two variances are interdependent (interrelated) one will usually be adverse and the other one favourable.**

Interdependence – materials price and usage variances

7.4 It may be decided to purchase cheaper materials for a job in order to obtain a favourable **price variance**. This may lead to higher materials wastage than expected and therefore, **adverse usage variances occur**. If the cheaper materials are more difficult to handle, there might be some **adverse labour efficiency variance** too.

If a decision is made to purchase more expensive materials, which perhaps have a longer service life, the price variance will be adverse but the usage variance might be favourable.

Interdependence – labour rate and efficiency variances

7.5 If employees in a workforce are paid higher rates for experience and skill, using a highly skilled team should incur an **adverse rate variance** at the same time as a **favourable efficiency variance**. In contrast, a **favourable rate variance** might indicate a high proportion of inexperienced workers in the workforce, which could result in an **adverse labour efficiency variance** and possibly an **adverse materials usage variance** (due to high rates of rejects).

Chapter roundup

- **Variances** measure the difference between **actual results** and **expected results**.
- The direct material total variance can be subdivided into the **direct material price** variance and the **direct material usage** variance.
- Direct material price variances are usually extracted at the time of **receipt** of the materials, rather than at the time of usage.
- The direct labour total variance can be subdivided into the **direct labour rate** variance and the **direct labour efficiency** variance.
- If **idle time** arises, it is usual to calculate a separate idle time variance, and to base the calculation of the efficiency variance on **active hours** (when labour actually worked) only. It is always an **adverse** variance.
- The variable production overhead total variance can be subdivided into the variable production overhead **expenditure** variance and the variable production overhead **efficiency** variance **(based on active hours).**
- The fixed production overhead total variance can be subdivided into an **expenditure** variance and a **volume** variance. The fixed production overhead volume variance can be further subdivided into an **efficiency** and a **capacity** variance.
- Ensure that you can provide possible **reasons** for cost variances.
- Materiality, controllability, the type of standard being used, the interdependence of variances and the cost of an investigation should be taken into account when deciding whether to investigate reported variances.

Quick quiz

1 Subdivide the following variances.

(a) Direct materials cost variance

(b) Direct labour cost variance

(c) Variable production overhead variance

2 What are the two main advantages in calculating the material price variance at the time of receipt of materials?

3 Idle time variances are always adverse.

True ☐

False ☐

4 Adverse material usage variances might occur for the following reasons.

I Defective material
II Excessive waste
III Theft
IV Unforeseen discounts received

A I
B I and II
C I, II and III
D I, II, III and IV

5 List the factors which should be taken into account when deciding whether or not a variance should be investigated.

Answers to quick quiz

1 (a) → Price / → Usage

(b) → Rate / → Efficiency

(c) → Expenditure / → Efficiency

2 (a) The earlier variances are extracted, the sooner they will be brought to the attention of managers.

(b) All stocks will be valued at standard price which requires less administration effort.

3 True

4 C

5
- Materiality
- Controllability
- Type of standard being used
- Interdependence between variances
- Costs of investigation

Now try the questions below from the Exam Question Bank

Number	Level	Marks	Time
34	MCQ	n/a	n/a
35	Examination	10	18 mins

Chapter 20

FURTHER VARIANCE ANALYSIS

Introduction

The objective of cost variance analysis, which we looked at in the previous chapter, is to assist management in the **control of costs**. Costs are, however, only one factor which contribute to the achievement of planned profit. **Sales** are another important factor and sales variances can be calculated to aid management's control of their business. We will therefore begin this chapter by examining **sales variances**.

Having discussed the variances you need to know about, we will be looking in Section 2 at the **ways in which variances should be presented to management** to aid their control of the organisation.

We then consider in Section 3 how **marginal cost variances** differ from absorption cost variances and how marginal costing information should be presented.

Finally we will consider **how actual data can be derived from standard cost details and variances**.

Study guide

Section 5 – Cost classification

- Describe the nature of control achieved through the comparison of actual costs against plan

Section 26 – Standard costing – 1

- Explain the purpose of sales volume and price variances

Section 27 – Standard costing – 2

- Calculate and interpret sales volume and price variances using the appropriate costing method
- Prepare operating statements to reconcile budgeted to actual profit
- Discuss the implications of the results of variance analysis for management

Exam guide

Variance analysis is traditionally a very popular exam topic. Make sure that you are able to prepare operating statements and explain why calculated variances have occurred.

1 SALES VARIANCES

Selling price variance

KEY TERM

The **selling price variance** is a measure of the effect on expected profit of a different selling price to standard selling price. It is calculated as the **difference between what the sales revenue should have been for the actual quantity sold, and what it was.**

1.1 Suppose that the standard selling price of product X is £15. Actual sales in 20X3 were 2,000 units at £15.30 per unit. The selling price variance is calculated as follows.

	£
Sales revenue from 2,000 units should have been (× £15)	30,000
but was (× £15.30)	30,600
Selling price variance	600 (F)

1.2 The variance calculated in paragraph 1.1 is **favourable** because the price was higher than expected.

Sales volume profit variance

KEY TERM

The **sales volume profit variance** is the difference between the actual units sold and the budgeted (planned) quantity, valued at the standard profit per unit. In other words, it measures **the increase or decrease in standard profit as a result of the sales volume being higher or lower than budgeted (planned).**

1.3 Suppose that a company budgets to sell 8,000 units of product J for £12 per unit. The standard full cost per unit is £7. Actual sales were 7,700 units, at £12.50 per unit.

The **sales volume profit variance** is calculated as follows.

Budgeted sales volume	8,000 units
Actual sales volume	7,700 units
Sales volume variance in units	300 units (A)
× standard profit per unit (£(12–7))	× £5
Sales volume variance	£1,500 (A)

1.4 The variance calculated in paragraph 1.3 is **adverse** because actual sales were less than budgeted (planned).

Question 1

Jasper Ltd has the following budget and actual figures for 20X4.

	Budget	*Actual*
Sales units	600	620
Selling price per unit	£30	£29

Standard full cost of production = £28 per unit.

Required

Calculate the selling price variance and the sales volume profit variance.

Answer

Sales revenue for 620 units should have been (× £30)	18,600	
but was (× £29)	17,980	
Selling price variance	620	(A)
Budgeted sales volume	600 units	
Actual sales volume	620 units	
Sales volume variance in units	20 units	(F)
× standard profit per unit (£(30 – 28))	× £2	
Sales volume profit variance	£40	(F)

The significance of sales variances

1.5 The possible **interdependence** between sales price and sales volume variances should be obvious to you. A reduction in the sales price might stimulate bigger sales demand, so that an adverse sales price variance might be counterbalanced by a favourable sales volume variance. Similarly, a price rise would give a favourable price variance, but possibly at the cost of a fall in demand and an adverse sales volume variance.

1.6 It is therefore important in analysing an unfavourable sales variance that the overall consequence should be considered, that is, has there been a counterbalancing favourable variance as a direct result of the unfavourable one?

2 OPERATING STATEMENTS

2.1 So far, we have considered how variances are calculated without considering how they combine to reconcile the difference between budgeted profit and actual profit during a period. This reconciliation is usually presented as a report to senior management at the end of each control period. The report is called an **operating statement** or **statement of variances**.

KEY TERM

An **operating statement** is 'A regular report for management of actual costs, and revenues, as appropriate. Usually compares actual with budget and shows variances'.

CIMA *Official Terminology*

2.2 An extensive example will now be introduced, both to revise the variance calculations already described, and also to show how to combine them into an operating statement.

2.3 EXAMPLE: VARIANCES AND OPERATING STATEMENTS

Sydney Ltd manufactures one product, and the entire product is sold as soon as it is produced. There are no opening or closing stocks and work in progress is negligible. The company operates a standard costing system and analysis of variances is made every month. The standard cost card for the product, a boomerang, is as follows.

STANDARD COST CARD - BOOMERANG

		£
Direct materials	0.5 kilos at £4 per kilo	2.00
Direct wages	2 hours at £2.00 per hour	4.00
Variable overheads	2 hours at £0.30 per hour	0.60
Fixed overhead	2 hours at £3.70 per hour	7.40
Standard cost		14.00
Standard profit		6.00
Standing selling price		20.00

Selling and administration expenses are not included in the standard cost, and are deducted from profit as a period charge.

Budgeted (planned) output for the month of June 20X7 was 5,100 units. Actual results for June 20X7 were as follows.

Production of 4,850 units was sold for £95,600.
Materials consumed in production amounted to 2,300 kgs at a total cost of £9,800.
Labour hours paid for amounted to 8,500 hours at a cost of £16,800.
Actual operating hours amounted to 8,000 hours.
Variable overheads amounted to £2,600.
Fixed overheads amounted to £42,300.
Selling and administration expenses amounted to £18,000.

Required

Calculate all variances and prepare an operating statement for the month ended 30 June 20X7.

2.4 SOLUTION

(a)

	£
2,300 kg of material should cost (× £4)	9,200
but did cost	9,800
Material price variance	600 (A)

(b)

4,850 boomerangs should use (× 0.5 kgs)	2,425 kg
but did use	2,300 kg
Material usage variance in kgs	125 kg (F)
× standard cost per kg	× £4
Material usage variance in £	£ 500 (F)

(c)

	£
8,500 hours of labour should cost (× £2)	17,000
but did cost	16,800
Labour rate variance	200 (F)

(d)

4,850 boomerangs should take (× 2 hrs)	9,700 hrs
but did take (active hours)	8,000 hrs
Labour efficiency variance in hours	1,700 hrs (F)
× standard cost per hour	× £2
Labour efficiency variance in £	£3,400 (F)

(e) Idle time variance 500 hours (A) × £2 — £1,000 (A)

(f)

	£
8,000 hours incurring variable o/hd expenditure should cost (× £0.30)	2,400
but did cost	2,600
Variable overhead expenditure variance	200 (A)

(g) Variable overhead efficiency variance in hours is the same as the labour efficiency variance:

1,700 hours (F) × £0.30 per hour	£ 510 (F)

(h)

	£
Budgeted fixed overhead (5,100 units × 2 hrs × £3.70)	37,740
Actual fixed overhead	42,300
Fixed overhead expenditure variance	4,560 (A)

(i)

	£
4,850 boomerangs should take (× 2 hrs)	9,700 hrs
but did take (active hours)	8,000 hrs
Fixed overhead volume efficiency variance in hrs	1,700 hrs (F)
× standard fixed overhead absorption rate per hour	× £3.70
Fixed overhead volume efficiency variance in £	6,290 (F)

(j)

	£
Budgeted hours of work (5,100 × 2 hrs)	10,200 hrs
Actual hours of work	8,000 hrs
Fixed overhead volume capacity variance in hrs	2,200 hrs (A)
× standard fixed overhead absorption rate per hour	× £3.70
Fixed overhead volume capacity variance in £	8,140 (A)

(k)

	£
Revenue from 4,850 boomerangs should be (× £20)	97,000
but was	95,600
Selling price variance	1,400 (A)

(l)

Budgeted sales volume	5,100 units
Actual sales volume	4,850 units
Sales volume profit variance in units	250 units
× standard profit per unit	× £6 (A)
Sales volume profit variance in £	£1,500 (A)

2.5 There are several ways in which an operating statement may be presented. Perhaps the most common format is one which **reconciles budgeted profit to actual profit**. In this example, sales and administration costs will be introduced at the end of the statement, so that we shall begin with 'budgeted profit before sales and administration costs'.

2.6 Sales variances are reported first, and the total of the budgeted profit and the two sales variances results in a figure for 'actual sales minus the standard cost of sales'. The cost variances are then reported, and an actual profit (before sales and administration costs) calculated. Sales and administration costs are then deducted to reach the actual profit for June 20X7.

SYDNEY LTD - OPERATING STATEMENT JUNE 20X7

		£	£
Budgeted (planned) profit before sales and administration costs			30,600
Sales variances: price		1,400 (A)	
volume		1,500 (A)	
			2,900 (A)
Actual sales minus the standard cost of sales			27,700
Cost variances	(F)	(A)	
	£	£	
Material price		600	
Material usage	500		
Labour rate	200		
Labour efficiency	3,400		
Labour idle time		1,000	
Variable overhead expenditure		200	
Variable overhead efficiency	510		
Fixed overhead expenditure		4,560	
Fixed overhead volume efficiency	6,290		
Fixed overhead volume capacity		8,140	
	10,900	14,500	3,600 (A)
Actual profit before sales and administration costs			24,100
Sales and administration costs			18,000
Actual profit, June 20X7			6,100

Check	£	£
Sales		95,600
Materials	9,800	
Labour	16,800	
Variable overhead	2,600	
Fixed overhead	42,300	
Sales and administration	18,000	
		89,500
Actual profit		6,100

3 VARIANCES IN A STANDARD MARGINAL COSTING SYSTEM

3.1 In all of the examples we have worked through so far, a system of standard absorption costing has been in operation. If an organisation uses **standard marginal costing** instead of standard absorption costing, there will be two differences in the way the variances are calculated.

(a) In marginal costing, fixed costs are not absorbed into product costs and so there are no fixed cost variances to explain any under or over absorption of overheads. There will, therefore, be **no fixed overhead volume variance**. There will be a fixed overhead expenditure variance which is calculated in exactly the same way as for absorption costing systems.

(b) The **sales volume variance** will be valued at **standard contribution margin** (sales price per unit minus variable costs of sale per unit), **not** standard **profit** margin.

Preparing a marginal costing operating statement

3.2 Returning once again to the example of Sydney Ltd, the variances in a system of standard marginal costing would be as follows.

(a) There is **no fixed overhead volume variance** (and therefore no fixed overhead volume efficiency and volume capacity variances).

(b) The standard contribution per unit of boomerang is £(20 – 6.60) = £13.40, therefore the **sales volume contribution variance** of 250 units (A) is valued at (× £13.40) = £3,350 (A).

3.3 The other variances are unchanged. However, this operating statement differs from an absorption costing operating statement in the following ways.

(a) It begins with the budgeted **contribution** (£30,600 + budgeted fixed production costs £37,740 = £68,340).

(b) The subtotal before the analysis of cost variances is actual sales (£95,600) less the standard **variable** cost of sales (£4,850 × £6.60) = £63,590.

(c) **Actual contribution** is highlighted in the statement.

(d) Budgeted (planned) fixed production overhead is adjusted by the fixed overhead expenditure variance to show the **actual** fixed production overhead expenditure.

3.4 Therefore a marginal costing operating statement might look like this.

SYDNEY LTD - OPERATING STATEMENT JUNE 20X7

	£	£	£
Budgeted (planned) contribution			68,340
Sales variances: volume		3,350 (A)	
price		1,400 (A)	
			4,750 (A)
Actual sales minus the standard variable cost of sales			63,590
	(F)	(A)	
	£	£	
Variable cost variances			
Material price		600	
Material usage	500		
Labour rate	200		
Labour efficiency	3,400		
Labour idle time		1,000	
Variable overhead expenditure		200	
Variable overhead efficiency	510		
	4,610	1,800	
			2,810 (F)
Actual contribution			66,400
Budgeted (planned) fixed production overhead		37,740	
Expenditure variance		4,560 (A)	
Actual fixed production overhead			42,300
Actual profit before sales and administration costs			24,100
Sales and administration costs			18,000
Actual profit			6,100

3.5 Notice that the actual profit is the same as the profit calculated by standard absorption costing because there were no changes in stock levels. Absorption costing and marginal costing do not always produce an identical profit figure.

Question 2

Piglet Ltd, a manufacturing firm, operates a standard marginal costing system. It makes a single product, PIG, using a single raw material LET.

Standard costs relating to PIG have been calculated as follows.

Standard cost schedule – PIG	*Per unit*
	£
Direct material, LET, 100 kg at £5 per kg	500
Direct labour, 10 hours at £8 per hour	80
Variable production overhead, 10 hours at £2 per hour	20
	600

The standard selling price of a PIG is £900 and Piglet Ltd produce 1,020 units a month.

During December 20X0, 1,000 units of PIG were produced. Relevant details of this production are as follows.

Direct material LET

90,000 kgs costing £720,000 were bought and used.

Direct labour

8,200 hours were worked during the month and total wages were £63,000.

Variable production overhead

The actual cost for the month was £25,000.

Stocks of the direct material LET are valued at the standard price of £5 per kg.

Each PIG was sold for £975.

Required

Calculate the following for the month of December 20X0.

(a) Variable production cost variance
(b) Direct labour cost variance, analysed into rate and efficiency variances
(c) Direct material cost variance, analysed into price and usage variances
(d) Variable production overhead variance, analysed into expenditure and efficiency variances
(e) Selling price variance
(f) Sales volume contribution variance

Answer

(a) This is simply a 'total' variance.

	£
1,000 units should have cost (× £600)	600,000
but did cost (see working)	808,000
Variable production cost variance	208,000 (A)

(b) **Direct labour cost variances**

	£
8,200 hours should cost (× £8)	65,600
but did cost	63,000
Direct labour rate variance	2,600 (F)

1,000 units should take (× 10 hours)	10,000 hrs
but did take	8,200 hrs
Direct labour efficiency variance in hrs	1,800 hrs (F)
× standard rate per hour	× £8
Direct labour efficiency variance in £	£14,400 (F)

Summary	£
Rate	2,600 (F)
Efficiency	14,400 (F)
Total	17,000 (F)

(c) **Direct material cost variances**

	£
90,000 kg should cost (× £5)	450,000
but did cost	720,000
Direct material price variance	270,000 (A)
1,000 units should use (× 100 kg)	100,000 kg
but did use	90,000 kg
Direct material usage variance in kgs	10,000 kg (F)
× standard cost per kg	× £5
Direct material usage variance in £	£50,000 (F)

Summary

	£
Price	270,000 (A)
Usage	50,000 (F)
Total	220,000 (A)

(d) **Variable production overhead variances**

	£
8,200 hours incurring o/hd should cost (× £2)	16,400
but did cost	25,000
Variable production overhead expenditure variance	8,600 (A)
Efficiency variance in hrs (from (b))	1,800 hrs (F)
× standard rate per hour	× £2
Variable production overhead efficiency variance	£3,600 (F)

Summary

	£
Expenditure	8,600 (A)
Efficiency	3,600 (F)
Total	5,000 (A)

(e) **Selling price variance**

	£
Revenue from 1,000 units should have been (× £900)	900,000
but was (× £975)	975,000
Selling price variance	75,000 (F)

(f) **Sales volume contribution variance**

Budgeted sales	1,020 units
Actual sales	1,000 units
Sales volume variance in units	20 units (A)
× standard contribution margin (£(900 – 600))	× £300
Sales volume contribution variance in £	£6,000 (A)

Workings

	£
Direct material	720,000
Total wages	63,000
Variable production overhead	25,000
	808,000

3.6 The summary diagram on the next page summarises how the different variances are calculated and how they interrelate with each other.

SUMMARY DIAGRAM

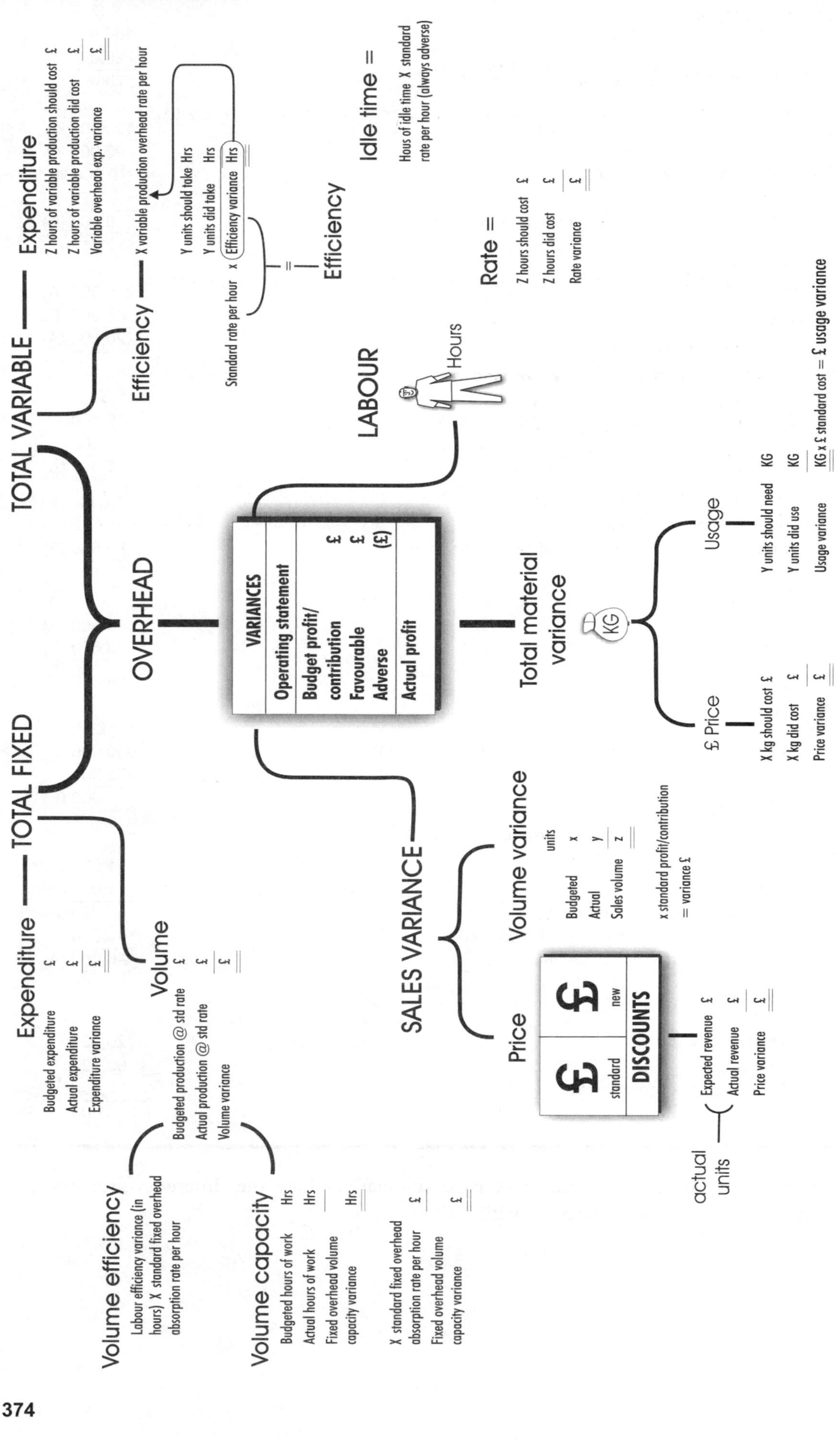

4 DERIVING ACTUAL DATA FROM STANDARD COST DETAILS AND VARIANCES

4.1 EXAMPLE: WORKING BACKWARDS

The standard cost card for the trough, one of the products made by Pig Ltd, is as follows.

	£
Direct material 16 kgs × £6 per kg	96
Direct labour 6 hours × £12 per hour	72
Fixed production overhead 6 hours × £14 per hour	84
	252

Pig Ltd reported the following variances in control period 13 in relation to the trough.

Direct material price: £18,840 favourable
Direct material usage: £480 adverse
Direct labour rate: £10,598 adverse
Direct labour efficiency: £8,478 favourable
Fixed production overhead expenditure: £14,192 adverse
Fixed production overhead volume: £11,592 favourable

Actual fixed production overhead cost £200,000 and direct wages, £171,320. Pig Ltd paid £5.50 for each kg of direct material. There was no opening or closing stocks of the material.

Required

Calculate the following.

(a) Budgeted output
(b) Actual output
(c) Actual hours worked
(d) Average actual wage rate per hour
(e) Actual number of kilograms purchased and used

4.2 SOLUTION

(a) Let budgeted output = q

Fixed production overhead expenditure variance = budgeted overhead – actual overhead = £(84q – 200,000) = £14,192 (A)

$\therefore$ 84q – 200,000 = –14,192
84q = –14,192 + 200,000
q = 185,808 ÷ 84
$\therefore$ q = 2,212 units

(b)

	£
Total direct wages cost	171,320
Adjust for variances:	
labour rate	(10,598)
labour efficiency	8,478
Standard direct wages cost	169,200

$\therefore$ Actual output = Total standard cost ÷ unit standard cost
= £169,200 ÷ £72
= 2,350 units

(c)

	£
Total direct wages cost	171,320.0
Less rate variance	(10,598.0)
Standard rate for actual hours	160,722.0
÷ standard rate per hour	÷ £12.0
Actual hours worked	13,393.5 hrs

(d) Average actual wage rate per hour = actual wages/actual hours = £171,320/13,393.5 = £12.79 per hour.

(e) Number of kgs purchased and used = x

	£
x kgs should have cost (× £6)	6.0x
but did cost (× £5.50)	5.5x
Direct material price variance	0.5x

$\therefore$ £0.5x = £18,840

$\therefore$ x = 37,680 kgs

Question 3

XYZ Ltd uses standard costing. The following data relates to labour grade II.

Actual hours worked	10,400 hours
Standard allowance for actual production	8,320 hours
Standard rate per hour	£5
Rate variance (adverse)	£416

What was the actual rate of pay per hour?

A £4.95
B £4.96
C £5.04
D £5.05

Answer

Rate variance per hour worked = $\frac{£416}{10,400}$ = £0.04 (A)

Actual rate per hour = £(5.00 + 0.04) = £5.04.

The correct answer is C.

You should have been able to eliminate options A and B because they are both below the standard rate per hour. If the rate variance is adverse then the actual rate must be above standard.

Option D is incorrect because it results from basing the calculations on standard hours rather than actual hours.

Question 4

The standard material content of one unit of product A is 10kgs of material X which should cost £10 per kilogram. In June 20X4, 5,750 units of product A were produced and there was an adverse material usage variance of £1,500.

Required

Calculate the quantity of material X used in June 20X4.

Answer

Let the quantity of material X used = Y

5,750 units should have used (× 10kgs)	57,500 kgs
but did use	Y kgs
Usage variance in kgs	(Y – 57,500) kgs
× standard price per kg	× £10
Usage variance in £	£1,500 (A)

$\therefore$ 10(Y – 57,500) = 1,500
Y – 57,500 = 150
$\therefore$ Y = 57,650 kgs

Exam focus point

One way that the examiner can test your understanding of variance analysis is to provide information about variances from which you have to 'work backwards' to determine the actual results.

Make sure that you understand the examples and questions covering this technique that we have provided in this section. This type of question **really** tests your understanding of the subject. If you simply memorise variance formulae you will have difficulty in answering such questions.

Chapter roundup

- The **selling price variance** measures the effect on profit of a different selling price to standard selling price.
- The **sales volume profit variance** measures the effect on profit of sales volume being different to budgeted (planned) volume.
- **Operating statements** show how the combination of variances reconcile budgeted profit and actual profit.
- There are two main differences between the variances calculated in an absorption costing system and the variances calculated in a marginal costing system.
  - In a marginal costing system **the only fixed overhead variance is an expenditure variance.**
  - The sales volume variance is **valued at standard contribution margin**, not standard profit margin.
- Variances can be used to derive actual data from standard cost details.

Quick quiz

1 What is the sales volume profit variance?

2 A regular report for management of actual cost, and revenue, and usually comparing actual results with budgeted (planned) results (and showing variances) is known as

A Bank statement
B Variance statement
C Budget statement
D Operating statement

3 If an organisation uses standard marginal costing instead of standard absorption costing, which two variances are calculated differently?

Answers to quick quiz

1. It is a measure of the increase or decrease in standard profit as a result of the sales volume being higher or lower than budgeted (planned).
2. D
3. (a) In marginal costing there is no fixed overhead volume variance (because fixed costs are not absorbed into product costs).

   (b) In marginal costing, the sales volume variance will be valued at standard contribution margin and not standard profit margin.

Now try the questions below from the Exam Question Bank

Number	Level	Marks	Time
36	MCQ	n/a	n/a

Appendix: Basic Maths

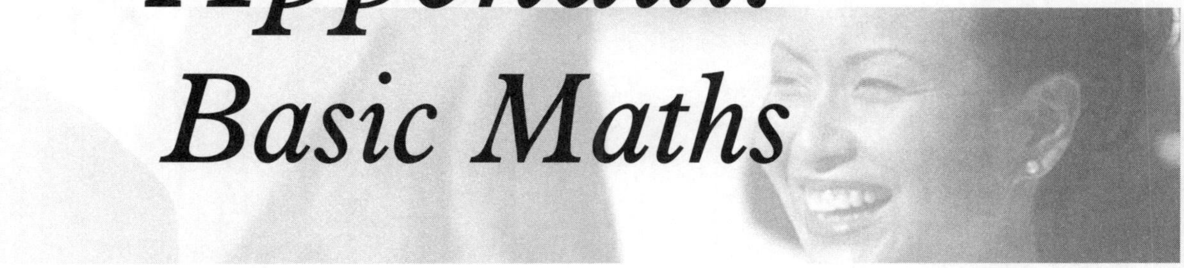

Appendix

BASIC MATHS

Topic list

1 USING THIS APPENDIX

1.1 The **Financial Information for Management** syllabus assumes that you have some basic knowledge of basic mathematics and statistics. The purpose of this appendix is to provide the knowledge required in this area if you haven't studied it before, or to provide a means of reminding you of basic maths and statistics if you are feeling a little rusty in one or two areas!

1.2 Accordingly, this appendix sets out from first principles a good deal of the knowledge that you are assumed to possess in the main body of the Study Text. You may wish to work right through it now. You may prefer to dip into it as and when you need to. You may just like to try a few questions to sharpen up your knowledge. Don't feel obliged to learn everything in the following pages: they are intended as an extra resource to be used in whatever way best suits you.

2 INTEGERS, FRACTIONS AND DECIMALS

2.1 An **integer** is a whole number and can be either positive or negative. The integers are therefore as follows.

$$....., -5, -4, -3, -2, -1, 0, 1, 2, 3, 4, 5.....$$

2.2 **Fractions** (such as $^1/_2$, $^1/_4$, $^{19}/_{35}$, $^{101}/_{377}$, ...) and **decimals** (0.1, 0.25, 0.3135 .....) are both ways of showing parts of a whole. Fractions can be turned into decimals by dividing the numerator by the denominator (in other words, the top line by the bottom line). To turn decimals into fractions, all you have to do is remember that places after the decimal point stand for tenths, hundredths, thousandths and so on.

Significant digits

2.3 Sometimes a decimal number has too many digits in it for practical use. This problem can be overcome by rounding the decimal number to a specific number of **significant digits** by discarding digits using the following rule.

If the first digit to be discarded is greater than or equal to five then add one to the previous digit. Otherwise the previous digit is unchanged.

2.4 EXAMPLE: SIGNIFICANT DIGITS

(a) 187.392 correct to five significant digits is 187.39

Discarding a 2 causes nothing to be added to the 9.

(b) 187.392 correct to four significant digits is 187.4

Discarding the 9 causes one to be added to the 3.

(c) 187.392 correct to three significant digits is 187

Discarding a 3 causes nothing to be added to the 7.

Question 1

What is 17.385 correct to four significant digits?

Answer

17.39

---

3 MATHEMATICAL NOTATION

Brackets

3.1 **Brackets** are commonly used to indicate which parts of a mathematical expression should be grouped together, and calculated before other parts. In other words, brackets can indicate a priority, or an order in which calculations should be made. The rule is as follows.

(a) Do things in brackets before doing things outside them.

(b) Subject to rule (a), do things in this order.

  (i) Powers and roots
  (ii) Multiplications and divisions, working from left to right
  (iii) Additions and subtractions, working from left to right

3.2 Thus brackets are used for the sake of **clarity**. Here are some examples.

(a) $3 + 6 \times 8 = 51$. This is the same as writing $3 + (6 \times 8) = 51$.

(b) $(3 + 6) \times 8 = 72$. The brackets indicate that we wish to multiply the sum of 3 and 6 by 8.

(c) $12 - 4 \div 2 = 10$. This is the same as writing $12 - (4 \div 2) = 10$ or $12 - (4/2) = 10$.

(d) $(12 - 4) \div 2 = 4$. The brackets tell us to do the subtraction first.

3.3 A figure outside a bracket may be multiplied by two or more figures inside a bracket, linked by addition or subtraction signs. Here is an example.

$5(6 + 8) = 5 \times (6 + 8) = 5 \times 6 + 5 \times 8 = 70$

This is the same as $5(14) = 5 \times 14 = 70$

The multiplication sign after the 5 can be omitted, as shown here ($5(6 + 8)$), but there is no harm in putting it in ($5 \times (6 + 8)$) if you want to.

Similarly:

$5(8 - 6) = 5(2) = 10$; or
$5 \times 8 - 5 \times 6 = 10$

3.4 When two sets of figures linked by addition or subtraction signs within brackets are multiplied together, each figure in one bracket is multiplied in turn by every figure in the second bracket. Thus:

$(8 + 4)(7 + 2) = (12)(9) = 108$ or
$8 \times 7 + 8 \times 2 + 4 \times 7 + 4 \times 2 =$
$56 + 16 + 28 + 8 = 108$

Negative numbers

3.5 When a negative number (-p) is added to another number (q), the net effect is to subtract p from q.

(a) $10 + (-6) = 10 - 6 = 4$
(b) $-10 + (-6) = -10 - 6 = -16$

3.6 When a negative number (-p) is subtracted from another number (q), the net effect is to add p to q.

(a) $12 - (-8) = 12 + 8 = 20$
(b) $-12 - (-8) = -12 + 8 = -4$

3.7 When a negative number is multiplied or divided by another negative number, the result is a positive number.

$-8 \times (-4) = +32$
$-18/(-3) = +6$

3.8 If there is only one negative number in a multiplication or division, the result is negative.

$-8 \times 4 = -32$
$3 \times (-2) = -6$
$12/(-4) = -3$
$-20/5 = -4$

Question 2

Work out the following.

(a) $(72 - 8) - (-3 + 1)$

(b) $\frac{88 + 8}{12} + \frac{(29 - 11)}{-2}$

(c) 8(2 - 5) - (4 - (-8))

(d) $\frac{-36}{9-3} - \frac{84}{3-10} - \frac{-81}{3}$

Answer

(a) 64 - (-2) = 64 + 2 = 66

(b) 8 + (-9) = -1

(c) -24 - (12) = -36

(d) -6 - (-12) - (-27) = -6 + 12 + 27 = 33

Reciprocals

3.9 The **reciprocal** of a number is just 1 divided by that number. For example, the reciprocal of 2 is 1 divided by 2, ie ½.

Extra symbols

3.10 You will come across several mathematical signs in this book and there are five which you should learn right away.

(a) $>$ means 'greater than'. So $46 > 29$ is true, but $40 > 86$ is false.
(b) $\geq$ means 'is greater than or equal to'. So $4 \geq 3$ and $4 \geq 4$.
(c) $<$ means ' is less than'. So $29 < 46$ is true, but $86 < 40$ is false.
(d) $\leq$ means ' is less than or equal to'. So $7 \leq 8$ and $7 \leq 7$.
(e) $\neq$ means 'is not equal to'. So we could write $100.004 \neq 100$.

4 PERCENTAGES AND RATIOS

4.1 Percentages are used to indicate the **relative size** or **proportion** of items, rather than their absolute size. For example, if one office employs ten accountants, six secretaries and four supervisors, the **absolute** values of staff numbers and the *percentage* of the total work force in each type would be as follows.

	Accountants	*Secretaries*	*Supervisors*	*Total*
Absolute numbers	10	6	4	20
Percentages	50%	30%	20%	100%

4.2 The idea of percentages is that the whole of something can be thought of as 100%. The whole of a cake, for example, is 100%. If you share it out equally with a friend, you will get half each, or $^{100\%}/_2$ = 50% each.

4.3 To turn a percentage into a fraction or decimal you divide by 100. To turn a fraction or decimal back into a percentage you multiply by 100%. Consider the following.

(a) $0.16 = 0.16 \times 100\% = 16\%$
(b) $^4/_5 = {^4/_5} \times 100\% = {^{400}/_5}\% = 80\%$
(c) $40\% = {^{40}/_{100}} = {^2/_5} = 0.4$

4.4 There are two main types of situations involving percentages.

(a) You may be required to calculate a percentage of a figure, having been given the percentage.

Question: What is 40% of £64?

Answer: 40% of £64 = 0.4 × £64 = £25.60.

(b) You may be required to state what percentage one figure is of another, so that you have to work out the percentage yourself.

Question: What is £16 as a percentage of £64?

Answer: £16 as a percentage of £64 = $\frac{16}{64} \times 100\% = \frac{1}{4} \times 100\% = 25\%$

In other words, put the £16 as a fraction of the £64, and then multiply by 100%.

Proportions

4.5 A **proportion** means writing a percentage as a proportion of 1 (that is, as a decimal).

100% can be thought of as the whole, or 1. 50% is half of that, or 0.5. Consider the following.

Question: There are 14 women in an audience of 70. What proportion of the audience are men?

Answer: Number of men = 70 - 14 = 56

Proportion of men = $\frac{56}{70} = \frac{8}{10} = 80\% = 0.8$

(a) $^8/_{10}$ or $^4/_5$ is the **fraction** of the audience made up by men.
(b) 80% is the **percentage** of the audience made up by men.
(c) 0.8 is the **proportion** of the audience made up by men.

Ratios

4.6 Suppose Tom has £12 and Dick has £8. The **ratio** of Tom's cash to Dick's cash is 12:8. This can be cancelled down, just like a fraction, to 3:2.

4.7 Usually an examination question will pose the problem the other way around: Tom and Dick wish to share £20 out in the ratio 3:2. How much will each receive?

4.8 Because 3 + 2 = 5, we must divide the whole up into five equal parts, then give Tom three parts and Dick two parts.

(a) £20 ÷ 5 = £4 (so each part is £4)

(b) Tom's share = 3 × £4 = £12

(c) Dick's share = 2 × £4 = £8

(d) **Check:** £12 + £8 = £20 (adding up the two shares in the answer gets us back to the £20 in the question).

4.9 This method of calculating ratios as amounts works no matter how many ratios are involved. Here is another example.

Question: A, B, C and D wish to share £600 in the ratio 6:1:2:3. How much will each receive?

Answer: (a) Number of parts = 6 + 1 + 2 + 3 = 12.

(b) Value of each part = £600 ÷ 12 = £50

(c) A: $6 \times £50 = £300$
B: $1 \times £50 = £50$
C: $2 \times £50 = £100$
D $3 \times £50 = £150$

(d) *Check:* $£300 + £50 + £100 + £150 = £600$.

Question 3

(a) Peter and Paul wish to share £60 in the ratio 7 : 5. How much will each receive?

(b) Bill and Ben own 300 and 180 flower pots respectively. What is the ratio of Ben's pots: Bill's pots?

(c) Tom, Dick and Harry wish to share out £800. Calculate how much each would receive if the ratio used was:

(i) 3 : 2 : 5;
(ii) 5 : 3 : 2;
(iii) 3 : 1 : 1.

(d) Lynn and Laura share out a certain sum of money in the ratio 4 : 5, and Laura ends up with £6.

(i) How much was shared out in the first place?

(ii) How much would have been shared out if Laura had got £6 and the ratio had been 5 : 4 instead of 4 : 5?

Answer

(a) There are 7 + 5 = 12 parts
Each part is worth £60 ÷ 12 = £5
Peter receives 7 × £5 = £35
Paul receives 5 × £5 = £25

(b) Ben's pots: Bill's pots = 180 : 300 = 3 : 5

(c) (i) Total parts = 10
Each part is worth £800 ÷ 10 = £80
Tom gets 3 × £80 = £240
Dick gets 2 × £80 = £160
Harry gets 5 × £80 = £400

(ii) Same parts as (i) but in a different order.
Tom gets £400
Dick gets £240
Harry gets £160

(iii) Total parts = 5
Each part is worth £800 ÷ 5 = £160
Therefore Tom gets £480
Dick and Harry each get £160

(d) (i) Laura's share = £6 = 5 parts
Therefore one part is worth £6 ÷ 5 = £1.20
Total of 9 parts shared out originally
Therefore total was 9 × £1.20 = = £10.80

(ii) Laura's share = £6 = 4 parts
Therefore one part is worth £6 ÷ 4 = £1.50
Therefore original total was 9 × £1.50 = £13.50

---

5 ROOTS AND POWERS

5.1 The square root of a number is a value which, when multiplied by itself, equals the original number.

$\sqrt{9} = 3$, since $3 \times 3 = 9$

5.2 Similarly, the cube root of a number is the value which, when multiplied by itself twice, equals the original number.

$\sqrt[3]{64} = 4$, since $4 \times 4 \times 4 = 64$

5.3 The nth root of a number is a value which, when multiplied by itself (n - 1) times, equals the original number.

5.4 Powers work the other way round.
Thus the 6th power of $2 = 2^6 = 2 \times 2 \times 2 \times 2 \times 2 \times 2 = 64$.

Similarly, $3^4 = 3 \times 3 \times 3 \times 3 = 81$.

Since $\sqrt{9} = 3$, it also follows that $3^2 = 9$, and since $\sqrt[3]{64} = 4$, $4^3 = 64$.

5.5 When a number with an index (a 'to the power of' value) is multiplied by the *same* number with the same or a different index, the result is that number to the power of the sum of the indices.

(a) $5^2 \times 5 = 5^2 \times 5^1 = 5^{(2+1)} = 5^3 = 125$
(b) $4^3 \times 4^3 = 4^{(3+3)} = 4^6 = 4{,}096$

5.6 Similarly, when a number with an index is divided by the *same* number with the same or a different index, the result is that number to the power of the first index minus the second index.

(a) $6^4 \div 6^3 = 6^{(4-3)} = 6^1 = 6$
(b) $7^8 \div 7^6 = 7^{(8-6)} = 7^2 = 49$

5.7 Any figure to the power of zero equals one. $1^0 = 1$, $2^0 = 1$, $3^0 = 1$, $4^0 = 1$ and so on.

Similarly, $8^2 \div 8^2 = 8^{(2-2)} = 8^0 = 1$

5.8 An index can be a fraction, as in $16^{\frac{1}{2}}$. What $16^{\frac{1}{2}}$ means is the square root of 16 ($\sqrt{16}$ or 4). If we multiply $16^{\frac{1}{2}}$ by $16^{\frac{1}{2}}$ we get $16^{(\frac{1}{2}+\frac{1}{2})}$ which equals 16^1 and thus 16.

Similarly, $216^{\frac{1}{3}}$ is the cube root of 216 (which is 6) because $216^{\frac{1}{3}} \times 216^{\frac{1}{3}} \times 216^{\frac{1}{3}} =$
$216^{(\frac{1}{3}+\frac{1}{3}+\frac{1}{3})}$
$= 216^1 = 216$.

5.9 An index can be a negative value. The negative sign represents a reciprocal. Thus 2^{-1} is the reciprocal of, or one over, 2^1

$$= \frac{1}{2^1} = \frac{1}{2}$$

Here are some more examples.

(a) $2^{-2} = \frac{1}{2^2} = \frac{1}{4}$ and $2^{-3} = \frac{1}{2^3} = \frac{1}{8}$

(b) $5^{-6} = \frac{1}{5^6} = \frac{1}{15{,}625}$

(c) $4^5 \times 4^{-2} = 4^5 \times \frac{1}{4^2} = 4^{5-2} = 4^3 = 64$

5.10 When we multiply or divide by a number with a negative index, the rules previously stated still apply.

(a) $9^2 \times 9^{-2} = 9^{(2+(-2))} = 9^0 = 1$ (That is, $9^2 \times \frac{1}{9^2} = 1$)

(b) $4^5 \div 4^{-2} = 4^{(5-(-2))} = 4^7 = 16{,}384$

(c) $3^8 \times 3^{-5} = 3^{(8-5)} = 3^3 = 27$

(d) $3^{-5} \div 3^{-2} = 3^{-5-(-2)} = 3^{-3} = \frac{1}{3^3} = \frac{1}{27}$. (This could be re-expressed as $\frac{1}{3^5} \div \frac{1}{3^2} = \frac{1}{3^5} \times 3^2 = \frac{1}{3^3}$.)

Question 4

Work out the following, using your calculator as necessary.

(a) $(18.6)^{2.6}$
(b) $(18.6)^{-2.6}$
(c) $\sqrt[2.6]{18.6}$
(d) $(14.2)^4 \times (14.2)^{\frac{1}{4}}$
(e) $(14.2)^4 + (14.2)^{\frac{1}{4}}$

Answer

(a) $(18.6)^{2.6} = 1{,}998.64$

(b) $(18.6)^{-2.6} = (\frac{1}{18.6})^{2.6} = 0.0005$

(c) $\sqrt[2.6]{18.6} = 3.078$

(d) $(14.2)^4 \times (14.2)^{\frac{1}{4}} = (14.2)^{4.25} = 78{,}926.98$

(e) $(14.2)^4 + (14.2)^{\frac{1}{4}} = 40{,}658.69 + 1.9412 = 40{,}660.6312$

---

6 EQUATIONS

6.1 So far all our problems have been formulated entirely in terms of specific numbers. However, think back to when you were calculating powers with your calculator earlier in this chapter. You probably used the x^y key on your calculator. x and y stood for whichever numbers we happened to have in our problem, for example, 3 and 4 if we wanted to work out 3^4. When we use letters like this to stand for any numbers we call them **variables**. Today when we work out 3^4, x stands for 3. Tomorrow, when we work out 7^2, x will stand for 7: its value can vary.

6.2 The use of variables enables us to state general truths about mathematics.

For example:

$x = x$
$x^2 = x \times x$

If y = 0.5 × x, then x = 2 × y

These will be true **whatever** values x and y have. For example, let y = 0.5 × x

If y = 3, x = 2 × y = 6
If y = 7, x = 2 × y = 14
If y = 1, x = 2 × y = 2, and so on for any other choice of a value for y.

6.3 We can use variables to build up useful **formulae**. We can then put in values for the variables, and get out a value for something we are interested in.

6.4 Let us consider an example. For a business, profit = revenue - costs. Since revenue = selling price × units sold, we can say that

profit = selling price × units sold - costs.

'Selling price × units sold - costs' is a **formula** for profit.

We can then use single letters to make the formula quicker to write.

Let	x	=	profit
	p	=	selling price
	u	=	units sold
	c	=	cost

Then x = p × u - c.

If we are then told that in a particular month, p = £5, u = 30 and c = £118, we can find out the month's profit.

Profit = x = p × u - c = £5 × 30 - £118
= £150 - £118 = £32.

6.5 It is usual when writing formulae to leave out multiplication signs between letters. Thus p × u - c can be written as pu - c. We will also write (for example) 2x instead of 2 × x.

Equations

6.6 In the above example, pu - c was a formula for profit. If we write x = pu - c, we have written an equation. It says that one thing (profit, x) is equal to another (pu - c).

6.7 Sometimes, we are given an equation with numbers filled in for all but one of the variables. The problem is then to find the number which should be filled in for the last variable. This is called **solving** the equation.

6.8 (a) Returning to x = pu - c, we could be told that for a particular month p = £4, u = 60 and c = £208. We would then have the **equation** x = £4 × 60 - £208. We can solve this easily by working out £4 × 60 - £208 = £240 - £208 = £32. Thus x = £32.

(b) On the other hand, we might have been told that in a month when profits were £172, 50 units were sold and the selling price was £7. The thing we have not been told is the month's costs, c. We can work out c by writing out the equation.

£172 = £7 × 50 - c

£172 = £350 - c

We need c to be such that when it is taken away from £350 we have £172 left. With a bit of trial and error, we can get to c = £178.

6.9 Trial and error takes far too long in more complicated cases, however, and we will now go on to look at a rule for solving equations, which will take us directly to the answers we want.

The rule for solving equations

6.10 To solve an equation, we need to get it into the form:

Unknown variable = something with just numbers in it, which we can work out.

We therefore want to get the unknown variable on one side of the = sign, and everything else on the other side.

6.11 The rule is that you can do what you like to one side of an equation, so long as you do the same thing to the other side straightaway. The two sides are equal, and they will stay equal so long as you treat them in the same way.

6.12 For example, you can do any of the following.

Add 37 to both sides.
Subtract 3x from both sides.
Multiply both sides by -4.329.
Divide both sides by (x + 2).
Take the reciprocal of both sides.
Square both sides.
Take the cube root of both sides.

6.13 We can do any of these things to an equation either before or after filling in numbers for the variables for which we have values.

6.14 (a) In Paragraph 6.8, we had

$$£172 = £350 - c.$$

We can then get

$£172 + c = £350$	(add c to each side)
$c = £350 - £172$	(subtract £172 from each side)
$c = £178$	(work out the right hand side).

(b)

$450 = 3x + 72$	(initial equation: x unknown)
$450 - 72 = 3x$	(subtract 72 from each side)
$\frac{450 - 72}{3} = x$	(divide each side by 3)
$126 = x$	(work out the left hand side).

(c)

$3y + 2 = 5y - 7$	(initial equation: y unknown)
$3y + 9 = 5y$	(add 7 to each side)
$9 = 2y$	(subtract 3y from each side)
$4.5 = y$	(divide each side by 2).

(d)

$\frac{\sqrt{3x^2 + x}}{2\sqrt{x}} = 7$	(initial equation: x unknown)
$\frac{3x^2 + x}{4x} = 49$	(square each side)

$(3x+1)/4 = 49$ (cancel x in the numerator and the denominator of the left hand side: this does not affect the value of the left hand side, so we do not need to change the right hand side)

$3x + 1 = 196$ (multiply each side by 4)

$3x = 195$ (subtract 1 from each side)

$x = 65$ (divide each side by 3).

(e) Our example in Paragraph 6.6 was x = pu - c. We could change this, so as to give a formula for p.

$x = pu - c$

$x + c = pu$ (add c to each side)

$\frac{x+c}{u} = p$ (divide each side by u)

$p = \frac{x+c}{u}$ (swap the sides for ease of reading).

Given values for x, c and u we can now find p. We have *re-arrange*d the equation to give p *in terms of* x, c and u.

(f) Given that $y = \sqrt{3x+7}$, we can get an equation giving x in terms of y.

$y = \sqrt{3x+7}$

$y^2 = 3x + 7$ (square each side)

$y^2 - 7 = 3x$ (subtract 7 from each side)

$x = \frac{y^2-7}{3}$ (divide each side by 3, and swap the sides for ease of reading).

(g) Given that $7 + g = \frac{5}{3\sqrt{h}}$, we can get an equation giving h in terms of g.

$7 + g = \frac{5}{3\sqrt{h}}$

$\frac{1}{7+g} = \frac{3\sqrt{h}}{5}$ (take the reciprocal of each side)

$\frac{5}{7+g} = 3\sqrt{h}$ (multiply each side by 5)

$\frac{5}{3(7+g)} = \sqrt{h}$ (divide each side by 3)

$h = \frac{25}{9(7+g)^2}$ (square each side, and swap the sides for ease of reading).

6.15 In equations, you may come across expressions like 3(x + 4y - 2) (that is, 3 × (x + 4y - 2)). These can be re-written in separate bits without the brackets, simply by multiplying the number outside the brackets by each item inside them. Thus 3(x + 4y - 2) = 3x + 12y - 6.

Question 5

Find the value of x in each of the following equations.

(a) $47x + 256 = 52x$

(b) $4\sqrt{x} + 32 = 40.6718$

(c) $\frac{1}{3x+4} = \frac{5}{2.7x-2}$

(d) $x^3 = 4.913$

(e) $34x - 7.6 = (17x - 3.8) \times (x + 12.5)$

Answer

(a)
$47x + 256 = 52x$
$256 = 5x$ (subtract 47x from each side)
$51.2 = x$ (divide each side by 5).

(b)
$4\sqrt{x} + 32 = 40.6718$
$4\sqrt{x} = 8.6718$ (subtract 32 from each side)
$\sqrt{x} = 2.16795$ (divide each side by 4)
$x = 4.7$ (square each side).

(c)
$\frac{1}{3x+4} = \frac{5}{2.7x-2}$

$3x + 4 = \frac{2.7x-2}{5}$ (take the reciprocal of each side)

$15x + 20 = 2.7x - 2$ (multiply each side by 5)
$12.3x = -22$ (subtract 20 and subtract 2.7x from each side)
$x = -1.789$ (divide each side by 12.3).

(d)
$x^3 = 4.913$
$x = 1.7$ (take the cube root of each side).

(e) $34x - 7.6 = (17x - 3.8) \times (x + 12.5)$

This one is easy if you realise that $17 \times 2 = 34$ and $3.8 \times 2 = 7.6$, so

$2 \times (17x - 3.8) = 34x - 7.6$.

We can then divide each side by $17x - 3.8$ to get

$2 = x + 12.5$
$-10.5 = x$ (subtract 12.5 from each side).

Question 6

(a) Re-arrange $x = (3y - 20)^2$ to get an expression for y in terms of x.

(b) Re-arrange $2(y - 4) - 4(x^2 + 3) = 0$ to get an expression for x in terms of y.

Answer

(a) $x = (3y - 20)^2$

$\sqrt{x} = 3y - 20$ (take the square root of each side)
$20 + \sqrt{x} = 3y$ (add 20 to each side)

$y = \frac{20 + \sqrt{x}}{3}$ (divide each side by 3, and swap the sides for ease of reading).

(b) $2(y - 4) - 4(x^2 + 3) = 0$
$2(y - 4) = 4(x^2 + 3)$ (add $4(x^2 + 3)$ to each side)

$0.5(y - 4) = x^2 + 3$ (divide each side by 4)

$0.5(y - 4) - 3 = x^2$ (subtract 3 from each side)

$x = \sqrt{0.5(y-4)-3}$ (take the square root of each side, and swap the sides for ease of reading)

$x = \sqrt{0.5y-5}$ (simplify 0.5(y-4) - 3: this is an optional last step).

7 LINEAR EQUATIONS

7.1 A linear equation has the general form y = a + bx

where y is the dependent variable whose value depends upon the value of x;

x is the independent variable whose value helps to determine the corresponding value of y;

a is a constant, that is, a fixed amount;

b is also a constant, being the coefficient of x (that is, the number by which the value of x should be multiplied to derive the value of y).

7.2 Let us establish some basic linear equations. Suppose that it takes Joe Bloggs 15 minutes to walk one mile. How long does it take Joe to walk two miles? Obviously it takes him 30 minutes. How did you calculate the time? You probably thought that if the distance is doubled then the time must be doubled. How do you explain (in words) the relationships between the distance walked and the time taken? One explanation would be that every mile walked takes 15 minutes.

7.3 That is an explanation in words. Can you explain the relationship with an equation?

7.4 First you must decide which is the dependent variable and which is the independent variable. In other words, does the time taken depend on the number of miles walked or does the number of miles walked depend on the time it takes to walk a mile? Obviously the time depends on the distance. We can therefore let y be the dependent variable (time taken in minutes) and x be the independent variable (distance walked in miles).

7.5 We now need to determine the constants a and b. There is no fixed amount so a = 0. To ascertain b, we need to establish the number of times by which the value of x should be multiplied to derive the value of y. Obviously y = 15x where y is in minutes. If y were in hours then $y = x/4$.

7.6 EXAMPLE: DERIVING A LINEAR EQUATION

A salesman's weekly wage is made up of a basic weekly wage of £100 and commission of £5 for every item he sells. Derive an equation which describes this scenario.

7.7 SOLUTION

x	=	number of items sold
y	=	weekly wage
a	=	£100
b	=	£5
∴ y	=	5x + 100

7.8 Note that the letters used in an equation do not have to be x and y. It may be sensible to use other letters, for example we could use p and q if we are describing the relationship between the price of an item and the quantity demanded.

8 LINEAR EQUATIONS AND GRAPHS

8.1 One of the clearest ways of presenting the relationship between two variables is by plotting a linear equation as a straight line on a graph.

The rules for drawing graphs

8.2 A graph has a horizontal axis, the x axis and a vertical axis, the y axis. The x axis is used to represent the independent variable and the y axis is used to represent the dependent variable.

8.3 If calendar time is one variable, it is always treated as the independent variable. When time is represented on the x axis of a graph, we have a time series.

8.4 (a) If the data to be plotted are derived from calculations, rather than given in the question, make sure that there is a neat table in your working papers.

(b) The scales on each axis should be selected so as to use as much of the graph paper as possible. Do not cramp a graph into one corner.

(c) In some cases it is best not to start a scale at zero so as to avoid having a large area of wasted paper. This is perfectly acceptable as long as the scale adopted is clearly shown on the axis. One way of avoiding confusion is to break the axis concerned, as follows.

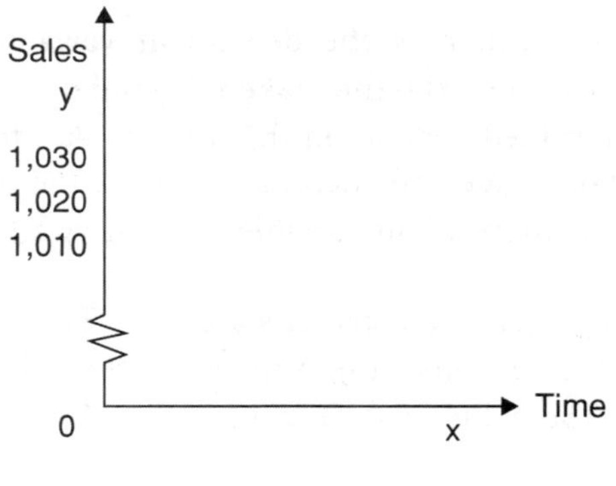

(d) The scales on the x axis and the y axis should be marked. For example, if the y axis relates to amounts of money, the axis should be marked at every £1, or £100 or £1,000 interval or at whatever other interval is appropriate. The axes must be marked with values to give the reader an idea of how big the values on the graph are.

(e) A graph should not be overcrowded with too many lines. Graphs should always give a clear, neat impression.

(f) A graph must always be given a title, and where appropriate, a reference should be made to the source of data.

8.5 EXAMPLE: DRAWING GRAPHS

Plot the graphs for the following relationships.

(a) $y = 4x + 5$
(b) $y = 10 - x$

In each case consider the range of values from x = 0 to x = 10

8.6 SOLUTION

The first step is to draw up a table for each equation. Although the problem mentions x = 0 to x = 10, it is not necessary to calculate values of y for x = 1, 2, 3 etc. A graph of a linear equation can actually be drawn from just two (x, y) values but it is always best to calculate a number of values in case you make an arithmetical error. We have calculated six values. You could settle for three or four.

(a)		(b)	
x	*y*	*x*	*y*
0	5	0	10
2	13	2	8
4	21	4	6
6	29	6	4
8	37	8	2
10	45	10	0

(a)

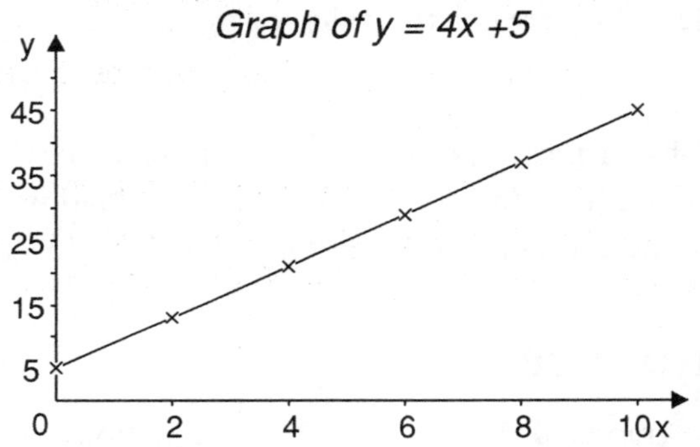

(b)

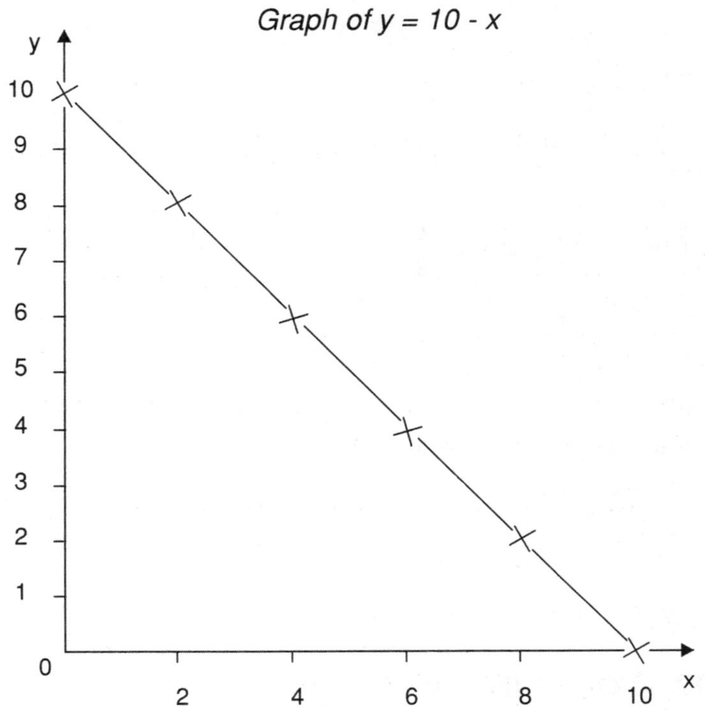

The intercept and the slope

8.7 The graph of a linear equation is determined by two things, the gradient (or slope) of the straight line and the point at which the straight line crosses the y axis.

8.8 The point at which the straight line crosses the y axis is known as the intercept. Look back at Paragraph 8.6. The intercept of y = 4x + 5 is (0, 5) and the intercept of y = 10 – x is (0, 10). It is no coincidence that the intercept is the same as the constant represented by a in the general form of the equation y = a + bx. a is the value y takes when x = 0, in other words a constant, and so is represented on a graph by the point (0, a).

8.9 The gradient of the graph of a linear equation is $(y_2 - y_1)/(x_2 - x_1)$ where (x_1, y_1) and (x_1, x_2) are two points on the straight line.

The slope of y = 4x + 5 = (21 – 13)/(4–2) = 8/2 = 4 where (x_1, y_1) = (2, 13) and (x_2, y_2) = (4,21)

The slope of y = 10 – x = (6–8)/(4–2) = – 2/2 = –1.

8.10 Note that the gradient of y = 4x + 5 is positive whereas the gradient of y = 10 – x is negative. A positive gradient slopes upwards from left to right whereas a negative gradient slopes downwards from right to left. The greater the value of the gradient, the steeper the slope.

8.11 Just as the intercept can be found by inspection of the linear equation, so can the gradient. It is represented by the coefficient of x (b in the general form of the equation). The slope of the graph y = 7x – 3 in therefore 7 and the slope of the graph y = 3,597 – 263 x is -263.

8.12 EXAMPLE: INTERCEPT AND SLOPE

Find the intercept and slope of the graphs of the following linear equations.

(a) $y = \frac{x}{10} - \frac{1}{3}$

(b) $4y = 16x - 12$

8.13 SOLUTION

(a) Intercept $= a = -\frac{1}{3}$ ie $(0, -\frac{1}{3})$

Slope $= b = \frac{1}{10}$

(b) 4y = 16x – 12
Equation must be form y = a + bx

$y = -\frac{12}{4} + \frac{16}{4}x = -3 + 4x$
Intercept = a = –3 ie (0, –3)
Slope = 4

9 SIMULTANEOUS LINEAR EQUATIONS

9.1 Simultaneous equations are two or more equations which are satisfied by the same variable values. For example, we might have the following two linear equations.

$$y = 3x + 16$$

$$2y = x + 72$$

9.2 There are two unknown values, x and y, and there are two different equations which both involve x and y. There are as many equations as there are unknowns and so we can find the values of x and y.

Graphical solution

9.3 One way of finding a solution is by a graph. If both equations are satisfied together, the values of x and y must be those where the straight line graphs of the two equations intersect.

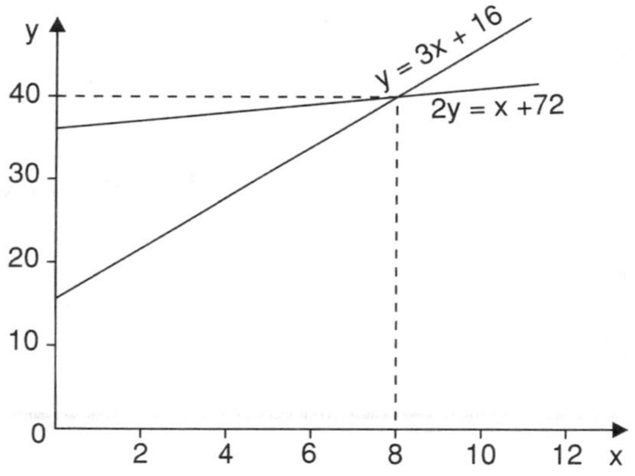

Since both equations are satisfied, the values of x and y must lie on both the lines. Since this happens only once, at the intersection of the lines, the value of x must be 8, and of y 40.

Algebraic solution

9.4 A more common method of solving simultaneous equations is by algebra.

(a) Returning to the original equations, we have:

$$y = 3x + 16 \quad (1)$$
$$2y = x + 72 \quad (2)$$

(b) Rearranging these, we have:

$$y - 3x = 16 \quad (3)$$
$$2y - x = 72 \quad (4)$$

(c) If we now multiply equation (4) by 3, so that the coefficient for x becomes the same as in equation (3) we get:

$$6y - 3x = 216 \quad (5)$$
$$y - 3x = 16 \quad (3)$$

(d) Subtracting (3) from (5) means that we lose x and we get:

$$5y = 200$$
$$y = 40$$

(e) Substituting 40 for y in any equation, we can derive a value for x. Thus substituting in equation (4) we get:

$$2(40) - x = 72$$
$$80 - 72 = x$$
$$8 = x$$

(f) The solution is y = 40, x = 8.

9.5 EXAMPLE: SIMULTANEOUS EQUATIONS

Solve the following simultaneous equations using algebra.

$$5x + 2y = 34$$
$$x + 3y = 25$$

9.6 SOLUTION

5x + 2y	=	34	(1)	
x + 3y	=	25	(2)	
5x + 15y	=	125	(3)	5 × (2)
13y	=	91	(4)	(3) - (1)
y	=	7		
x + 21	=	25		Substitute into (2)
x	=	25 - 21		
x	=	4		

The solution is x = 4, y = 7.

Question 7

Solve the following simultaneous equations to derive values for x and y.

4x + 3y = 23 (1)
5x - 4y = -10 (2)

Answer

(a) If we multiply equation (1) by 4 and equation (2) by 3, we will obtain coefficients of +12 and -12 for y in our two products.

16x + 12y = 92 (3)
15x - 12y = -30 (4)

(b) Add (3) and (4).

31x = 62
x = 2

(c) Substitute x = 2 into (1)

4(2) + 3y	=	23
3y	=	23 - 8 = 15
y	=	5

(d) The solution is x = 2, y = 5.

Appendix: Mathematical Tables

Regression analysis

$$a = \frac{\sum y}{n} - \frac{b\sum x}{n}$$

$$b = \frac{n\sum xy - \sum x\sum y}{n\sum x^2 - (\sum x)^2}$$

$$r = \frac{n\Sigma xy - \Sigma x\Sigma y}{\sqrt{[n\Sigma x^2 - (\Sigma x)^2][n\Sigma y^2 - (\Sigma y)^2]}}$$

$$\text{Economic order quantity} = \sqrt{\frac{2C_0D}{C_h}}$$

$$\text{Economic batch quantity} = \sqrt{\frac{2C_0D}{C_h\,(1 - \frac{D}{R})}}$$

PRESENT VALUE TABLE

Present value of 1 ie $(1+r)^{-n}$

where r = discount rate

n = number of periods until payment

Periods (n)	Discount rates (r) 1%	2%	3%	4%	5%	6%	7%	8%	9%	10%
1	0.990	0.980	0.971	0.962	0.952	0.943	0.935	0.926	0.917	0.909
2	0.980	0.961	0.943	0.925	0.907	0.890	0.873	0.857	0.842	0.826
3	0.971	0.942	0.915	0.889	0.864	0.840	0.816	0.794	0.772	0.751
4	0.961	0.924	0.888	0.855	0.823	0.792	0.763	0.735	0.708	0.683
5	0.951	0.906	0.863	0.822	0.784	0.747	0.713	0.681	0.650	0.621
6	0.942	0.888	0.837	0.790	0.746	0.705	0.666	0.630	0.596	0.564
7	0.933	0.871	0.813	0.760	0.711	0.665	0.623	0.583	0.547	0.513
8	0.923	0.853	0.789	0.731	0.677	0.627	0.582	0.540	0.502	0.467
9	0.914	0.837	0.766	0.703	0.645	0.592	0.544	0.500	0.460	0.424
10	0.905	0.820	0.744	0.676	0.614	0.558	0.508	0.463	0.422	0.386
11	0.896	0.804	0.722	0.650	0.585	0.527	0.475	0.429	0.388	0.350
12	0.887	0.788	0.701	0.625	0.557	0.497	0.444	0.397	0.356	0.319
13	0.879	0.773	0.681	0.601	0.530	0.469	0.415	0.368	0.326	0.290
14	0.870	0.758	0.661	0.577	0.505	0.442	0.388	0.340	0.299	0.263
15	0.861	0.743	0.642	0.555	0.481	0.417	0.362	0.315	0.275	0.239

Periods (n)	11%	12%	13%	14%	15%	16%	17%	18%	19%	20%
1	0.901	0.893	0.885	0.877	0.870	0.862	0.855	0.847	0.840	0.833
2	0.812	0.797	0.783	0.769	0.756	0.743	0.731	0.718	0.706	0.694
3	0.731	0.712	0.693	0.675	0.658	0.641	0.624	0.609	0.593	0.579
4	0.659	0.636	0.613	0.592	0.572	0.552	0.534	0.516	0.499	0.482
5	0.593	0.567	0.543	0.519	0.497	0.476	0.456	0.437	0.419	0.402
6	0.535	0.507	0.480	0.456	0.432	0.410	0.390	0.370	0.352	0.335
7	0.482	0.452	0.425	0.400	0.376	0.354	0.333	0.314	0.296	0.279
8	0.434	0.404	0.376	0.351	0.327	0.305	0.285	0.266	0.249	0.233
9	0.391	0.361	0.333	0.308	0.284	0.263	0.243	0.225	0.209	0.194
10	0.352	0.322	0.295	0.270	0.247	0.227	0.208	0.191	0.176	0.162
11	0.317	0.287	0.261	0.237	0.215	0.195	0.178	0.162	0.148	0.135
12	0.286	0.257	0.231	0.208	0.187	0.168	0.152	0.137	0.124	0.112
13	0.258	0.229	0.204	0.182	0.163	0.145	0.130	0.116	0.104	0.093
14	0.232	0.205	0.181	0.160	0.141	0.125	0.111	0.099	0.088	0.078
15	0.209	0.183	0.160	0.140	0.123	0.108	0.095	0.084	0.074	0.065

ANNUITY TABLE

Present value of annuity of 1, ie $\frac{1-(1+r)^{-n}}{r}$

where r = discount rate

n = number of periods.

Periods					**Discount rates (r)**					
(n)	**1%**	**2%**	**3%**	**4%**	**5%**	**6%**	**7%**	**8%**	**9%**	**10%**
1	0.990	0.980	0.971	0.962	0.952	0.943	0.935	0.926	0.917	0.909
2	1.970	1.942	1.913	1.886	1.859	1.833	1.808	1.783	1.759	1.736
3	2.941	2.884	2.829	2.775	2.723	2.673	2.624	2.577	2.531	2.487
4	3.902	3.808	3.717	3.630	3.546	3.465	3.387	3.312	3.240	3.170
5	4.853	4.713	4.580	4.452	4.329	4.212	4.100	3.993	3.890	3.791
6	5.795	5.601	5.417	5.242	5.076	4.917	4.767	4.623	4.486	4.355
7	6.728	6.472	6.230	6.002	5.786	5.582	5.389	5.206	5.033	4.868
8	7.652	7.325	7.020	6.733	6.463	6.210	5.971	5.747	5.535	5.335
9	8.566	8.162	7.786	7.435	7.108	6.802	6.515	6.247	5.995	5.759
10	9.471	8.983	8.530	8.111	7.722	7.360	7.024	6.710	6.418	6.145
11	10.368	9.787	9.253	8.760	8.306	7.887	7.499	7.139	6.805	6.495
12	11.255	10.575	9.954	9.385	8.863	8.384	7.943	7.536	7.161	6.814
13	12.134	11.348	10.635	9.986	9.394	8.853	8.358	7.904	7.487	7.103
14	13.004	12.106	11.296	10.563	9.899	9.295	8.745	8.244	7.786	7.367
15	13.865	12.849	11.938	11.118	10.380	9.712	9.108	8.559	8.061	7.606

Periods										
(n)	**11%**	**12%**	**13%**	**14%**	**15%**	**16%**	**17%**	**18%**	**19%**	**20%**
1	0.901	0.893	0.885	0.877	0.870	0.862	0.855	0.847	0.840	0.833
2	1.713	1.690	1.668	1.647	1.626	1.605	1.585	1.566	1.547	1.528
3	2.444	2.402	2.361	2.322	2.283	2.246	2.210	2.174	2.140	2.106
4	3.102	3.037	2.974	2.914	2.855	2.798	2.743	2.690	2.639	2.589
5	3.696	3.605	3.517	3.433	3.352	3.274	3.199	3.127	3.058	2.991
6	4.231	4.111	3.998	3.889	3.784	3.685	3.589	3.498	3.410	3.326
7	4.712	4.564	4.423	4.288	4.160	4.039	3.922	3.812	3.706	3.605
8	5.146	4.968	4.799	4.639	4.487	4.344	4.207	4.078	3.954	3.837
9	5.537	5.328	5.132	4.946	4.772	4.607	4.451	4.303	4.163	4.031
10	5.889	5.650	5.426	5.216	5.019	4.833	4.659	4.494	4.339	4.192
11	6.207	5.938	5.687	5.453	5.234	5.029	4.836	4.656	4.486	4.327
12	6.492	6.194	5.918	5.660	5.421	5.197	4.988	4.793	4.611	4.439
13	6.750	6.424	6.122	5.842	5.583	5.342	5.118	4.910	4.715	4.533
14	6.982	6.628	6.302	6.002	5.724	5.468	5.229	5.008	4.802	4.611
15	7.191	6.811	6.462	6.142	5.847	5.575	5.324	5.092	4.876	4.675

Exam question bank

1 INFORMATION FOR MANAGEMENT MCQs

(a) Which of the following statements is/are true?

I Information is the raw material for data processing

II External sources of information include an organisation's financial accounting records

III The main objective of a non-profit making organisation is usually to provide goods and services

A I and III only
B I, II and III
C II and III only
D III only

(b) Which of the following statements is **not** true?

A Management accounts detail the performance of an organisation over a defined period and the state of affairs at the end of that period

B There is no legal requirement to prepare management accounts

C The format of management accounts is entirely at management discretion

D Management accounts are both an historical record and a future planning tool

(c) Which of the following could higher level management carry out?

(i) taking long-term decisions
(ii) taking short-term decisions
(iii) defining the objectives of an organisation

A (i) and (ii) only
B (i) and (iii) only
C (ii) and (iii) only
D (i), (ii) and (iii)

(d) Which of the following statements is **not** correct?

A Financial accounting information can be used for internal reporting purposes

B Routine information can be used to make decisions regarding both the long term and the short term

C Management accounting provides information relevant to decision making, planning, control and evaluation of performances

D Cost accounting can be used to provide stock valuations for internal reporting only

2 THE ROLE OF INFORMATION TECHNOLOGY IN MANAGEMENT INFORMATION MCQs

(a) Which of the following is an output device?

A Screen
B Keyboard
C CPU
D Disk

(b) A method of input which involves a machine that is able to read characters by using lasers to detect the shape of those characters is known as

A MICR
B OCR
C OMR
D CPU

3 COST CLASSIFICATION MCQs

(a) Which of the following items might be a suitable cost unit within the accounts payable department of a company?

(i) Postage cost
(ii) Invoice processed
(iii) Supplier account

A Item (i) only
B Item (ii) only
C Item (iii) only
D Items (ii) and (iii) only

(b) Which of the following are direct expenses?

(i) The cost of special designs, drawing or layouts
(ii) The hire of tools or equipment for a particular job
(iii) Salesman's wages
(iv) Rent, rates and insurance of a factory

A (i) and (ii)
B (i) and (iii)
C (i) and (iv)
D (iii) and (iv)

4 COST BEHAVIOUR MCQs

(a) Variable costs are conventionally deemed to

A be constant per unit of output
B vary per unit of output as production volume changes
C be constant in total when production volume changes
D vary, in total, from period to period when production is constant

(b) The following is a graph of total cost against level of activity.

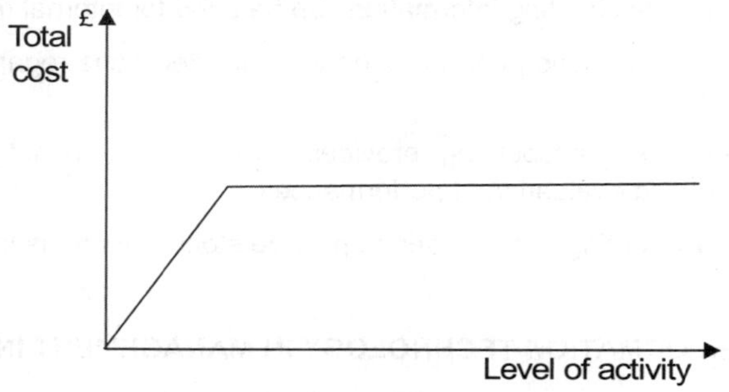

To which one of the following costs does the graph correspond?

A Photocopier rental costs, where a fixed rental is payable up to a certain number of copies each period. If the number of copies exceeds this amount, a constant charge per copy is made for all subsequent copies during that period.

B Vehicle hire costs, where a constant rate is charged per mile travelled, up to a maximum monthly payment regardless of the miles travelled.

C Supervisor salary costs, where one supervisor is needed for every five employees added to the staff.

D The cost of direct materials, where the unit rate per kg purchased reduces when the level of purchases reaches a certain amount.

5 COST BEHAVIOUR AND PRODUCTION LEVEL *18 mins*

Fixed and variable cost analysis enables management to decide whether an incentive scheme would be attractive to both employers and employees.

Suppose that Given Hann Hoffa Ltd is a company which manufactures a single product which sells for £20. The costs of production have been estimated to be as follows.

Fixed costs per month	£1,000
Variable costs	£12 per unit

The variable costs have been analysed further.

(a) Labour costs (2 hours at £2 per hour) = £4
(b) Material and other costs = £8

Demand for the product varies from 400 units to 800 units per month. The maximum output which can be achieved is currently only 600 units per month, because the available labour hours are restricted to 1,200 hours per month. The nature of the product is such that stocks of work-in-progress or finished goods cannot be stored.

An incentive scheme has been proposed whereby the payment to employees will be increased from £2 to £3 per hour, provided that the time taken to produce each unit is reduced from 2 hours to 1½ hours.

Required

(a) Ascertain the effect of the incentive scheme on employees' wages and company profits at the following output levels.

(i) At the minimum level of output per month
(ii) At the current maximum level of output per month **(5 marks)**

(b) Show by how much the company would profit if output and sales were increased to the new maximum level. **(3 marks)**

(c) Draw conclusions from these figures about the effects of the incentive scheme. **(2 marks)**

(10 marks)

6 CORRELATION AND REGRESSION MCQs

(a) A company's weekly costs (£C) were plotted against production level (P) for the last 50 weeks and a regression line calculated to be C = 1,000 + 250P. Which statement about the breakdown of weekly costs is true?

A Fixed costs are £1,000. Variable costs per unit are £5.
B Fixed costs are £250. Variable costs per unit are £4.
C Fixed costs are £250. Variable costs per unit are £1,000.
D Fixed costs are £1,000. Variable costs per unit are £250.

(b) The value of the correlation coefficient between x and y is 0.9. Which of the following is correct?

A There is a weak relationship between x and y

B x is 90% of y

C If the values of x and y were plotted on a graph, the line relating them would have a slope of 0.9

D There is a very strong relationship between x and y

7 SOUTH (PILOT PAPER) *18 mins*

South has reported the following costs for the past four months:

Month	*Activity level (units)*	*Total cost*
1	300	£3,800
2	400	£4,000
3	150	£3,000
4	260	£3,500

Required:

(a) Using regression analysis calculate the total cost equation. **(6 marks)**

(b) Calculate the total cost of the following activity levels:

(i) 200 units
(ii) 500 units

and comment on the usefulness of your equation with regard to these estimates. **(4 marks)**

(10 marks)

8 MATERIAL COSTS MCQs

(a) In a period of continual price inflation for material purchases

A the LIFO method will produce lower profits than the FIFO method, and lower closing stock values

B the LIFO method will produce lower profits than the FIFO method, and higher closing stock values

C the FIFO method will produce lower profits than the LIFO method, and lower closing stock values

D the FIFO method will produce lower profits than the LIFO method, and higher closing stock values

(b) The following data relates to an item of raw material

Unit cost of raw material	£20
Usage per week	250 units
Cost of ordering material, per order	£400
Annual cost of holding stock, as a % of cost	10%
Number of weeks in a year	48

What is the economic order quantity, to the nearest unit?

A 316 units
B 693 units
C 1,549 units
D 2,191 units

(c) The following data relates to the stores ledger control account of Duckboard Limited, a manufacturing company, for the month of October.

	£
Opening stock	18,500
Closing stock	16,100
Deliveries from suppliers	142,000
Returns to suppliers	2,300
Cost of indirect materials issued	25,200

The issue of direct materials would have been recorded in the cost accounts as follows.

			£	£
A	*Debit*	Stores ledger control account	119,200	
	Credit	Work in progress control account		119,200
B	*Debit*	Work in progress control account	119,200	
	Credit	Stores ledger control account		119,200
C	*Debit*	Stores ledger control account	116,900	
	Credit	Work in progress control account		116,900
D	*Debit*	Work in progress control account	116,900	
	Credit	Stores ledger control account		116,900

9 WIVELSFIELD (PILOT PAPER) *18 mins*

Wivelsfield currently uses the economic order quantity (EOQ) to establish the optimal reorder levels for their main raw material. The company has been approached by an alternative supplier who would be willing to offer the following discounts.

Order level	*Discount*
0 - 199 units	1%
200 - 499 units	3%
500 - 699 units	5%
700 units or more	7%

Information regarding current stock costs are as follows:

Holding cost per unit per annum = 10% of purchase price
Order costs = £2 per order
Annual demand = 15,000 units
Purchase price = £15

Current EOQ = 200 units

Required:

(a) Calculate the new optimal reorder level. **(6 marks)**
(b) Explain your approach with regard to each discount band. **(4 marks)**

(10 marks)

10 LABOUR COSTS MCQs

(a) Gross wages incurred in department 1 in June were £54,000. The wages analysis shows the following summary breakdown of the gross pay.

		Paid to direct labour	*Paid to indirect labour*
		£	£
Ordinary time		25,185	11,900
Overtime:	basic pay	5,440	3,500
	premium	1,360	875
Shift allowance		2,700	1,360
Sick pay		1,380	300
		36,065	17,935

What is the direct wages cost for department 1 in June?

A £25,185
B £30,625
C £34,685
D £36,065

(b) The wages control account for A Limited for February is shown below.

WAGES CONTROL ACCOUNT

	£		£
Bank	128,400	Work in progress control	79,400
Balance c/d	12,000	Production overhead control	61,000
	140,400		140,400
		Balance b/d	12,000

Which of the following statements about wages for February is *not* correct?

A Wages paid during February amounted to £128,400
B Wages for February were prepaid by £12,000
C Direct wages cost incurred during February amounted to £79,400
D Indirect wages cost incurred during February amounted to £61,000

11 REMUNERATION SCHEMES *18 mins*

The following information is available.

Normal working day	8 hours
Guaranteed rate of pay (on time basis)	£5.50 per hour
Standard time allowed to produce one unit	3 minutes
Piecework price	£0.10 per standard minute
Premium bonus	75% of time saved, in addition to hourly pay

Required:

(a) For daily production levels of 80, 120 and 210 units, calculate earnings based on the following remuneration methods.

(i) Piecework, where earnings are guaranteed at 80% of time-based pay
(ii) Premium bonus system **(7 marks)**

(b) What is idle time and how is it measured? **(3 marks)**

(10 marks)

12 OVERHEADS AND ABSORPTION COSTING MCQs

A company absorbs overheads based on labour hours. Data for the latest period are as follows.

Budgeted labour hours	8,500
Budgeted overheads	£148,750
Actual labour hours	7,928
Actual overheads	£146,200

(a) Based on the data given above, what is the labour hour overhead absorption rate?

A £17.20 per hour
B £17.50 per hour
C £18.44 per hour
D £18.76 per hour

(b) Based on the data given above, what is the amount of under-/over-absorbed overhead?

A £2,550 under-absorbed overhead
B £2,550 over-absorbed overhead
C £7,460 over-absorbed overhead
D £7,460 under-absorbed overhead

13 WARNINGLID (PILOT PAPER) *18 mins*

Warninglid has two production centres and two service centres to which the following applies:

	Production departments		*Service centres*		
	1	*2*	*Stores*	*Maintenance*	*Total*
Floor area (m^2)	5,900	1,400	400	300	8,000
Cubic capacity (m^3)	18,000	5,000	1,000	1,000	25,000
Number of employees	14	6	3	2	25
Direct labour hours	2,400	1,040			
Machine hours	1,500	4,570			

The following overheads were recorded for the month just ended:

	£'000
Rent	12
Heat and light	6
Welfare costs	2
Supervisors	
Department 1	1.5
Department 2	1

The service centres work for the other centres as follows:

	1	*2*	*Stores*	*Maintenance*
Work done by:				
Stores	50%	40%	-	10%
Maintenance	45%	50%	5%	-

Required:

(a) What would be the overheads allocated and apportioned to each department? **(3 marks)**

(b) Calculate the total overheads included in the production departments after reapportionment using the reciprocal method. **(4 marks)**

(c) Calculate the overhead absorption rate for each production department. Justify the basis that you have used. **(3 marks)**

(10 marks)

14 MARGINAL AND ABSORPTION COSTING MCQ

(a) The overhead absorption rate for product Y is £2.50 per direct labour hour. Each unit of Y requires 3 direct labour hours. Stock of product Y at the beginning of the month was 200 units and at the end of the month was 250 units. What is the difference in the profits reported for the month using absorption costing compared with marginal costing?

A The absorption costing profit would be £375 less
B The absorption costing profit would be £125 greater
C The absorption costing profit would be £375 greater
D The absorption costing profit would be £1,875 greater

15 PROFIT DIFFERENCES *18 mins*

The following data have been extracted from the budgets and standard costs of ABC Limited, a company which manufactures and sells a single product.

	£ per unit
Selling price	45.00
Direct materials cost	10.00
Direct wages cost	4.00
Variable overhead cost	2.50

Fixed production overhead costs are budgeted at £400,000 per annum. Normal production levels are thought to be 320,000 units per annum.

Budgeted selling and distribution costs are as follows.

Variable	£1.50 per unit sold
Fixed	£80,000 per annum

Budgeted administration costs are £120,000 per annum.

The following patterns of sales and production are expected during the first six months of 20X3.

	January - March	*April - June*
Sales (units)	60,000	90,000
Production (units)	70,000	100,000

There is no stock on 1 January 20X3.

Required:

Prepare profit statements for each of the two quarters, in a columnar format, using the following

(a) Marginal costing. **(4 marks)**
(b) Absorption costing. **(6 marks)**

(10 marks)

16 JOB AND BATCH COSTING MCQ

Ali Pali Ltd is a small jobbing company. Budgeted direct labour hours for the current year were 45,000 hours and budgeted direct wages costs were £180,000.

Job number 34679, a rush job for which overtime had to be worked by skilled employees, had the following production costs.

	£	£
Direct materials		2,000
Direct wages		
Normal rate (400 hrs)	2,000	
Overtime premium	500	
		2,500
Production overhead		4,000
		8,500

Production overhead is based on a direct labour hour rate

If production overhead had been based on a percentage of direct wages costs instead, the production cost of job number 34679 would have been:

A £5,500
B £9,000
C £10,250
D £10,750

17 INDRICAR LIMITED *18 mins*

Indricar Limited manufactures carpets for the hotel trade. They do not carry any stock of finished goods as they only manufacture specifically to customers' orders. They do however hold a range of raw materials in their storeroom.

At 30 November 20X8 they had two incomplete jobs in progress. The details of this work and the costs incurred up to and including the 30 November 20X8 were as follows:

	Job X123		*Job X124*	
Direct material	£1,250		£722	
Direct labour	£820	(164 hours)	£600	(120 hours)
Factory overhead	£1,640		£1,200	

For the period from 1 December 20X8 to 31 December 20X8 the company accepted three more jobs, X125, X126 and X127 and incurred additional costs as follows:

	Job X123	*Job X124*	*Job X125*	*Job X126*	*Job X127*
Direct material issued from stores	£420	£698	£1,900	£1,221	£516
Direct material returned to stores	(£120)	Nil	(£70)	(£217)	Nil
Direct material transfers	(£100)	Nil	£100	Nil	Nil
Direct labour hours	52	78	312	151	58

Direct labour is paid at a rate of £5.00 per hour and factory production overhead is absorbed at the rate of 200% of labour cost.

During the month of December Jobs X123, X124 and X125 were completed, but Jobs X126 and X127 would not be completed until January 20X9. On completion of a job the company adds 20% to the total factory production in order to recover its selling, distribution and administration costs. The amounts invoiced to customers during December for the completed jobs were:

Job X123	*Job X124*	*Job X125*
£6,250	£6,000	£7,900

Required:

(a) Calculate the total production cost for Jobs X123, X124, X125, X126 and X127 taking into account the recovery of selling, distribution and administration overhead as appropriate. **(8 marks)**

(b) Calculate the profit or loss arising on those Jobs completed and invoiced to customers during December 20X8. **(2 marks)**

(10 marks)

18 PROCESS COSTING MCQs

The following data relates to questions (a) and (b)

A chemical is manufactured in two processes, X and Y. Data for process Y for last month are as follows.

Material transferred from process X	2,000 litres @ £4 per litre
Conversion costs incurred	£12,250
Output transferred to finished goods	1,600 litres
Closing work in progress	100 litres

Normal loss is 10% of input. All losses are fully processed and have a scrap value of £4 per litre.

Closing work in progress is fully complete for material, but is only 50 per cent processed.

(a) What is the value of the completed output (to the nearest £)?

A £15,808
B £17,289
C £17,244
D £17,600

(b) What is the value of the closing work in progress (to the nearest £)?

A £674
B £728
C £750
D £1,100

19 PRODUCT XK

18 mins

A chemical producer manufactures Product XK by means of two successive processes, Process 1 and Process 2. The information provided below relates to the most recent accounting period, period 10.

	Process 1	*Process 2*
Opening work in progress	Nil	Nil
Material input during period	2,400 units - cost £5,280	2,200 units (from Process 1)
Added material		£9,460
Direct labour	£2,260	£10,560
Factory overhead	100% of labour cost	2/3 of labour cost
Transfer to Process 2	2,200 units	
Transfer to finished goods		2,200 units
Closing work in progress	200 units 100% complete with respect to materials and 30% complete with respect to labour and production overhead.	Nil

Required:

(a) Calculate the value of the goods transferred from Process 1 to Process 2 during period 10. **(4 marks)**

(b) Calculate the value of the closing work in progress left in Process 1 at the end of period 10. **(3 marks)**

(c) Calculate the value of the goods transferred from Process 2, to finished goods, during period 10, and the value of one unit of production. **(3 marks)**

(10 marks)

20 JOINT PRODUCTS AND BY-PRODUCTS MCQs

(a) SH Ltd manufactures three joint products and one by-product from a single process.

Data for May are as follows.

Opening and closing stocks	Nil
Raw materials input	£90,000
Conversion costs	£70,000

Output

		Units	*Sales price* £ per unit
Joint product	J	2,500	36
	K	3,500	40
	L	2,000	35
By-product M		4,000	1

By-product sales revenue is credited to the process account. Joint costs are apportioned on a physical units basis.

What were the full production costs of product K in May?

A £45,500
B £46,667
C £68,250
D £70,000

(b) Samakand Preparations operates a continuous process producing three products and one by-product. Output from the process for one month was as follows.

	Selling price per unit	**Output**
Joint product	£	Units
A	36	20,000
B	50	44,000
C	40	35,000
By-product		
D	4	20,000

Total output costs were £4,040,000.

Using the sales revenue basis for allocating joint costs, the unit valuation for joint product B was (to 2 decimal places):

A £45.00
B £45.91
C £50.00
D £100.00

21 CHEMICALS X, Y AND Z *18 mins*

Chemicals X, Y and Z are produced from a single joint process. The information below relates to the month of November 20X8:

Input into process:	Direct materials 3,200 litres, cost £24,000 Direct labour £48,000 Factory overheads are absorbed at 120% of prime cost
Output from process:	Scrap normally accounts for 10% of input and can be sold for £16.20 per litre. Actual scrap in November 20X8 was 10% of input. Proceeds from the sale of scrap is credited to the process account. Chemical X - 1,440 litres Chemical Y - 864 litres Chemical Z - 576 litres

The selling price of the three chemicals are	Chemical X - £100 per litre Chemical Y - £80 per litre Chemical Z - £60 per litre

Required:

Calculate the total cost of each of Chemicals X, Y and Z using the following methods for splitting joint costs.

(a) Relative sales value **(5 marks)**
(b) Volume **(5 marks)**

All workings should be to the nearest £. **(10 marks)**

22 SERVICE COSTING MCQ

Which of the following would be appropriate cost units for a transport business?

(i) Cost per tonne-kilometre
(ii) Fixed cost per kilometre
(iii) Maintenance cost of each vehicle per kilometre

A (i) only
B (i) and (ii) only
C (i) and (iii) only
D All of them

23 HAPPY RETURNS LTD *18 mins*

Happy Returns Ltd operates a haulage business with three vehicles. The following estimated cost and performance data are available:

Petrol	£0.50 per kilometre on average
Repairs	£0.30 per kilometre
Depreciation	£1.00 per kilometre, plus £50 per week per vehicle
Drivers' wages	£300.00 per week per vehicle
Supervision and general expenses	£550.00 per week
Loading costs	£6.00 per tonne

During week 26 it is expected that all three vehicles will be used, 280 tonnes will be loaded and a total of 3,950 kilometres travelled (including return journeys when empty) as shown in the following table:

Journey	*Tonnes carried (one way)*	*Kilometres (one way)*
1	34	180
2	28	265
3	40	390
4	32	115
5	26	220
6	40	480
7	29	90
8	26	100
9	25	135
	280	1,975

Required:

(a) Calculate the number of tonne-kilometres relevant to week 26. **(2 marks)**
(b) Calculate the total variable costs incurred during week 26. **(4 marks)**
(c) Calculate the total fixed costs incurred during week 26. **(2 marks)**
(d) Calculate the average cost per tonne - kilometre for week 26. **(2 marks)**

(10 marks)

24 BREAKEVEN ANALYSIS MCQs

(a) A company manufactures a single product for which cost and selling price data are as follows.

Selling price per unit	£12
Variable cost per unit	£8
Fixed costs per month	£96,000
Budgeted monthly sales	30,000 units

The margin of safety, expressed as a percentage of budgeted monthly sales, is (to the nearest whole number):

A 20%
B 25%
C 73%
D 125%

(b)

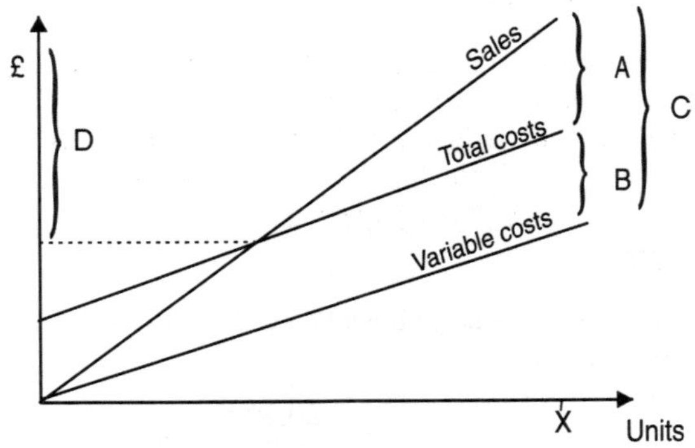

In the above breakeven chart, the contribution at level of activity x can be read as:

A distance A
B distance B
C distance C
D distance D

25 BUILDING COMPANY *18 mins*

A building company constructs a standard unit which sells for £30,000. The company's costs can be readily identifiable between fixed and variable costs.

Budgeted data for the coming six months includes the following.

	Sales	*Profit*
	Units	£
January	18	70,000
February	20	100,000
March	30	250,000
April	22	130,000
May	24	160,000
June	16	40,000

You are told that the fixed costs for the six months have been spread evenly over the period under review to arrive at the monthly profit projections.

Required:

(a) Calculate the total fixed costs for the period using the high-low method. **(3 marks)**

(b) Calculate the breakeven point in terms of both units and sales revenue. **(3 marks)**

(c) Prepare a breakeven chart for the six months under review. Make sure that your graph shows the following.

- Total sales
- Costs (fixed, variable and total)
- Output
- Breakeven point

- Margin of safety
- Total budgeted sales

(4 marks)

(10 marks)

26 RELEVANT COSTING AND DECISION MAKING MCQs

(a) Sue is considering starting a new business and she has already spent £5,000 on market research and intends to spend a further £2,000.

In the assessment of the relevant costs of the decision to set up the business, market research costs are:

A a sunk cost of £7,000
B a sunk cost of £5,000 and an incremental cost of £2,000
C a sunk cost of £2,000 and an incremental cost of £5,000
D an opportunity cost of £7,000

(b) ABC Ltd is in the process of deciding whether or not to accept a special order. The order will require 100 litres of liquid X. ABC Ltd has 85 litres of liquid X in stock but no longer produces the product which required liquid X. It could therefore sell the 85 litres for £2 per litre if it rejected the special order. The liquid was purchased three years ago at a price of £8 per litre but its replacement cost is £10 per litre. What is the relevant cost of liquid X to include in the decision-making process?

A £200
B £320
C £800
D £1,000

27 ABC LTD

18 mins

ABC Ltd makes three products, all of which use the same machine which is available for 50,000 hours per period.

The standard costs of the products per unit are as follows.

	Product A	*Product B*	*Product C*
	£	£	£
Direct materials	70	40	80
Direct labour:			
Machinists (£8 per hour)	48	32	56
Assemblers (£6 per hour)	36	40	42
Total variable cost	154	112	178
Selling price per unit	£200	£158	£224
Maximum demand (units)	3,000	2,500	5,000

Fixed costs are £300,000 per period.

ABC Ltd could buy in similar quality products at the following unit prices.

A	£175
B	£140
C	£200

Required:

(a) Calculate the deficiency in machine hours for the next period. **(3 marks)**
(b) Determine the priority ranking for internal manufacture. **(4 marks)**
(c) Determine which product(s) and quantities (if any) should be bought externally. **(3 marks)**

(10 marks)

28 LINEAR PROGRAMMING MCQs

(a) A company produces two types of orange juice, ordinary (X cartons per year) and premium (Y cartons per year). Which of the following inequalities represents the fact that the amount of ordinary orange juice produced must be no more than twice the amount of premium orange juice produced.

A $X \geq 2Y$
B $2X \geq Y$
C $2X \leq Y$
D $X \leq 2Y$

(b) In a linear programming problem, the constraints are $X \leq 41$ and $Y \geq 19$. Describe the feasible region, assuming where appropriate that the axes also constitute boundaries.

A A rectangle to the left of X = 41 and below Y = 19
B An infinite rectangle to the right of X = 41 and below Y = 19
C An infinite region above Y = 19 and to the right of X = 41
D An infinite rectangle to the left of X = 41 and above Y = 19

29 CUCKFIELD (PILOT PAPER) *18 mins*

Cuckfield manufactures two products, the D and the H, which have the following standard costs per unit:

	D	*H*
	£	£
Materials		
A (at £3/kg)	9	6
N (at £7/litre)	3.50	14
Labour		
Skilled (at £10/hour)	10	14
Semi skilled (at £6/hour)	9	9
Overheads		
(at 60% of direct material cost)	5.70	13.80
	37.20	56.80
Selling price	40.00	70.00
Profit	2.80	13.20

Unfortunately there is a problem obtaining some of the raw materials for production. Only 3,000 kg of material A is available and only 1,000 litres of material N can be found for the week.

There are 45 semi-skilled workers who can only work a 40 hour week as there has been an overtime ban. Skilled workers are guaranteed a 35 hour week. There are 20 of these workers and there is no overtime ban for these employees.

The company's objective is to maximise contribution.

Required:

(a) Formulate the constraint equations for this problem excluding the non-negativity constraint. **(4 marks)**

(b) Plot the constraints on a graph and suggest possible points for the optimal solution. (Note: calculations for the optimal solution are NOT required). **(6 marks)**

(10 marks)

30 PRICING MCQs

(a) S Limited manufactures product G, for which cost data are as follows.

	£ per unit
Direct material and labour	7
Variable overhead	2
Total variable cost	9

The following revenue functions have been established for product G.

Price = 25 – (0.2 × quantity)

Marginal revenue = 25 – (0.4 × quantity)

At what selling price per unit would profits from product G be maximised?

A £13.50
B £16.00
C £17.00
D £23.72

(b) The price of a good is £1.50 per unit and annual demand is 600,000 units. If an increase in price of 10p per unit results in a fall in demand of 65,000 units per year, what is the price elasticity of demand (to 3 dp)?

A 1.625
B 0.615
C 1.944
D 1.612

(c) The current price of a product is £30 and the producers sell 100 items a week at this price. One week the price is dropped by £3 as a special offer and the producers sell 150 items.

On deriving a demand curve where

P = price and Q = quantity sold

	P	**Q**
A	36 + 3Q/50	(1,800 – 50P)/3
B	36 – 3Q/50	(1,800 + 50P)/3
C	36 + 3Q/50	(1,800 + 50P)/3
D	36 – 3Q/50	(1,800 – 50P)/3

(d) Gerard plc has recently spent time researching and developing a new product. Gerard plc uses cost plus 25% to set selling prices.

The standard cost per unit has been estimated as follows.

	£
Direct materials	34
Direct labour	26
Fixed overheads	14
	74

Using the marginal cost-plus and the full-cost plus approaches, the relevant selling prices will be:

	Marginal cost-plus selling price	*Full-cost plus selling price*
	£	£
A	92.50	75.00
B	75.00	92.50
C	88.80	72.00
D	72.00	88.80

31 DEMAND, PRICE, REVENUE AND COSTS *18 mins*

When the price of a product X is £48, seventy units are demanded each week. When the price is £78, only 40 units are demanded each week. The manufacturer's fixed costs are £1,710 a week and variable costs are £9 per unit.

Required:

(a) Calculate the equation of the demand function linking price (P) to quantity demanded (X). **(5 marks)**

(b) Calculate the equation of the revenue function linking revenue to price (P) and quantity sold (X). **(3 marks)**

(c) Determine the equation of the total cost function. **(2 marks)**

(10 marks)

32 STANDARD COSTING MCQs

(a) Which of the following would *not* be used to estimate standard direct material prices?

A The availability of bulk purchase discounts
B Purchase contracts already agreed
C The forecast movement of prices in the market
D Performance standards in operation

(b) JC Limited operates a bottling plant. The liquid content of a filled bottle of product T is 2 litres. During the filling process there is a 30% loss of liquid input due to spillage and evaporation. The standard price of the liquid is £1.20 per litre. The standard cost of the liquid per bottle of product T, to the nearest penny, is

A £2.40
B £2.86
C £3.12
D £3.43

33 DOODLE LTD *18 mins*

Doodle Ltd manufactures and sells a range of products, one of which is the squiggle.

The following data relates to the expected costs of production and sale of the squiggle.

Budgeted production for the year	11,400 units
Standard details for one unit:	
direct materials	30 metres at £6.10 per metre
direct wages	
Department P	40 hours at £2.20 per hour
Department Q	36 hours at £2.50 per hour
Budgeted costs and hours per annum	
Variable production overhead (factory total)	
Department P	£525,000 : 700,000 hours
Department Q	£300,000 : 600,000 hours

Fixed overheads to be absorbed by the squiggle

Production	£1,083,000 (absorbed on a direct labour hour basis)
Administration	£125,400 (absorbed on a unit basis)
Marketing	£285,000 (absorbed on a unit basis)

Required:

(a) Prepare a standard cost sheet for the squiggle, to include the following.

(i) Standard total direct cost **(2 marks)**
(ii) Standard variable production cost **(2 marks)**
(iii) Standard production cost **(2 marks)**
(iv) Standard full cost of sale **(2 marks)**

(b) Calculate the standard sales price per unit which allows for a standard profit of 10% on the sales price. **(2 marks)**

(10 marks)

34 BASIC VARIANCE ANALYSIS MCQs

(a) The standard cost information for SC Limited's single product shows the standard direct material content to be 4 litres at £3 per litre.

Actual results for May were:

Production	1,270 units
Material used	5,000 litres at a cost of £16,000

All of the materials were purchased and used during the period. The direct material price and usage variances for May are:

	Material price	*Material usage*
A	£1,000 (F)	£240 (F)
B	£1,000 (A)	£240 (F)
C	£1,000 (F)	£240 (A)
D	£1,000 (A)	£256 (F)

The following information relates to questions (b) and (c)

The standard variable production overhead cost of product B is as follows.

4 hours at £1.70 per hour = £6.80 per unit

During period 3 the production of B amounted to 400 units. The labour force worked 1,690 hours, of which 30 hours were recorded as idle time. The variable overhead cost incurred was £2,950.

(b) The variable production overhead expenditure variance for period 3 was

A £77 adverse
B £128 adverse
C £128 favourable
D £230 adverse

(c) The variable production overhead efficiency variance for period 3 was

A £102 favourable
B £102 adverse
C £105 adverse
D £153 adverse

35 BRAIN LTD *18 mins*

Brain Ltd produces and sells one product only, the Blob, the standard cost for one unit being as follows.

	£
Direct material A - 10 kilograms at £20 per kg	200
Direct material B - 5 litres at £6 per litre	30
Direct wages - 5 hours at £6 per hour	30
Fixed production overhead	50
Total standard cost	315

The fixed overhead included in the standard cost is based on an expected monthly output of 900 units. Fixed production overhead is absorbed on the basis of direct labour hours.

During April 20X3 the actual results were as follows.

Production	800 units
Material A	7,800 kg used, costing £159,900
Material B	4,300 litres used, costing £23,650
Direct wages	4,200 hours worked for £24,150
Fixed production overhead	£47,000

Required:

(a) Calculate price and usage variances for each material. **(4 marks)**

(b) Calculate labour rate and efficiency variances. **(2 marks)**

(c) Calculate fixed production overhead expenditure and volume variances and then subdivide the volume variance. **(4 marks)**

(10 marks)

36 FURTHER VARIANCE ANALYSIS MCQs

(a) W Ltd uses a standard absorption costing system. The following data relate to one of its products.

	£ per unit	£ per unit
Selling price		27.00
Variable costs	12.00	
Fixed costs	9.00	
		21.00
Profit		6.00

Budgeted sales for control period 7 were 2,400 units, but actual sales were 2,550 units. The revenue earned from these sales was £67,320.

Profit reconciliation statements are drawn up using absorption costing principles. What sales variances would be included in such a statement for period 7?

	Price	*Volume*
A	£1,530 (F)	£900 (F)
B	£1,530 (A)	£900 (F)
C	£1,530 (F)	£900 (A)
D	£1,530 (A)	£900 (A)

(b) A standard marginal costing system:

(i) calculates fixed overhead variances using the budgeted absorption rate per unit
(ii) calculates sales volume variances using the standard contribution per unit
(iii) values finished goods stock at the standard variable cost of production

Which of the above statements is/are correct?

A (i), (ii) and (iii)
B (i) and (ii) only
C (ii) and (iii) only
D (i) and (iii) only

Exam answer bank

1 INFORMATION FOR MANAGEMENT MCQs

(a) D **Data** is the raw material for data processing. **Information** is data that has been processed in such a way as to be meaningful to the person who receives it. Statement I is therefore incorrect.

An organisation's financial accounting records are an example of an **internal** source of information. Statement II is therefore incorrect.

The main objective of a non-profit making organisation is usually to provide goods and services. Statement III is therefore correct.

(b) A **Financial accounts** (not management accounts) detail the performance of an organisation over a defined period and the state of affairs at the end of that period. **Management accounts** are used to aid management record, plan and control the organisation's activities and to help the decision-making process.

(c) D Higher level management are likely to be involved with taking decisions at all levels within an organisation.

(d) D Cost accounting can be used to provide stock valuations for external reporting **also**.

2 THE ROLE OF INFORMATION TECHNOLOGY IN MANAGEMENT INFORMATION MCQs

(a) A A **screen** is an output device.

A **keyboard** is an input device.

The **CPU** performs the processing function.

A **disk** is a storage device.

(b) B **MICR** is the recognition of characters by a machine that reads special formatted characters printed in magnetic ink.

OMR involves marking a pre-printed source document which is then read by a device which translates the marks on the document into machine code.

CPU is the central processing unit.

Option B is therefore correct.

3 COST CLASSIFICATION MCQs

(a) D It would be appropriate to use the cost per invoice processed and the cost per supplier account for control purposes. Therefore items (ii) and (iii) are suitable cost units and the correct answer is D.

Postage cost, item (i), is an expense of the department, therefore option A is not a suitable cost unit.

If you selected option B or option C you were probably rushing ahead and not taking care to read all the options. Items (ii) and (iii) *are* suitable cost units, but neither of them are the *only* suitable suggestions.

(b) A Special designs, and the hire of tools etc for a particular job can be traced to a specific cost unit. Therefore they are direct expenses and the correct answer is A.

Item (iii) is a selling and distribution overhead and item (iv) describes production overheads.

4 COST BEHAVIOUR MCQs

(a) A Variable costs are conveniently deemed to increase or decrease in direct proportion to changes in output. Therefore the correct answer is A. Descriptions B and D imply a changing unit rate, which does not comply with this convention. Description C relates to a fixed cost.

(b) B The cost depicted begins as a linear variable cost, increasing at a constant rate in line with activity. At a certain point the cost becomes fixed regardless of the level of activity. The vehicle hire costs follow this pattern.

Graphs for the other options would look like this.

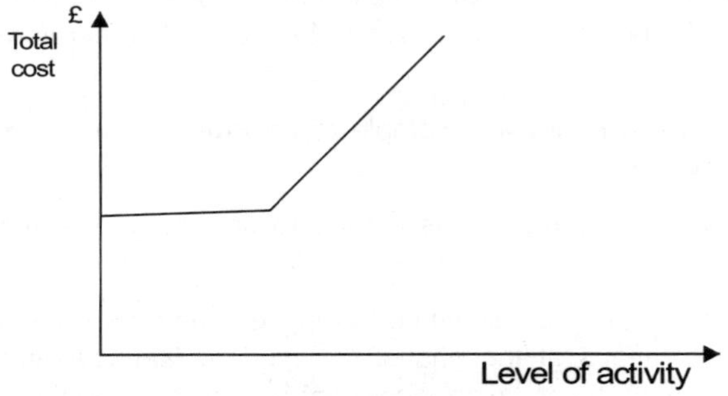

Option A

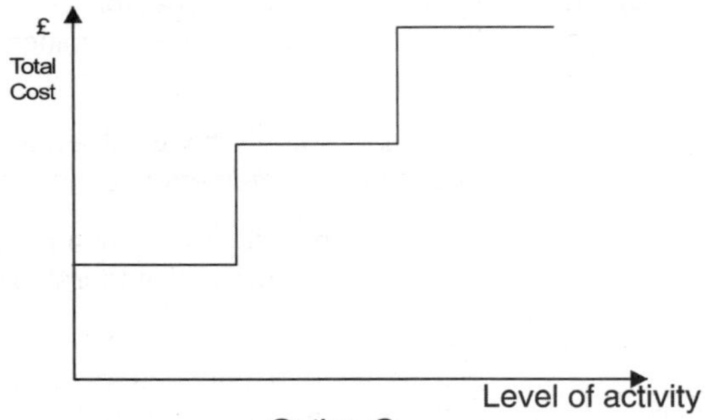

Option C

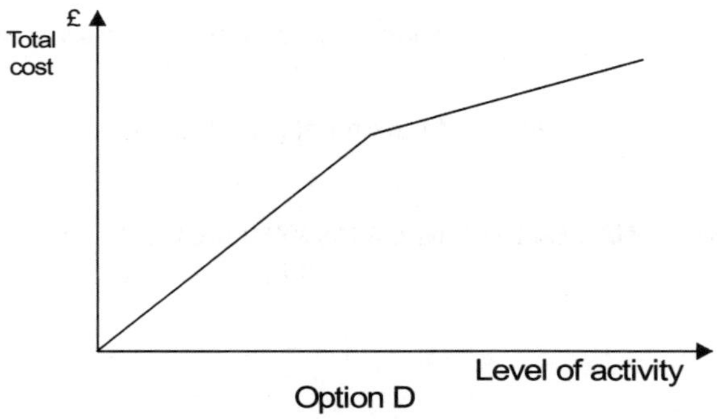

Option D

5 COST BEHAVIOUR AND PRODUCTION LEVEL

(a) (i) **400 units per month**

		With the incentive scheme		*Without the incentive scheme*
	£	£	£	£
Sales (400 × £20)		8,000		8,000
Materials etc costs (400 × £8)	3,200		3,200	
Labour costs (400 × £3 × 1½ hrs)	1,800		(400 × £2 × 2hrs) 1,600	
Total variable costs		5,000		4,800
Contribution		3,000		3,200
Fixed costs		1,000		1,000
Profit		2,000		2,200

The labour force would work fewer hours (600 instead of 800) but would receive £200 more in pay. Company profits would fall by £200 if the scheme is introduced and demand is 400 units.

(ii) **600 units per month**

		With the incentive scheme		*Without the incentive scheme*
	£	£	£	£
Sales (600 × £20)		12,000		12,000
Materials etc costs (600 × £8)	4,800		4,800	
Labour costs (600 × £3 × 1½ hrs)	2,700		(600 × £2 × 2hrs) 2,400	
Total variable costs		7,500		7,200
		4,500		4,800
Fixed costs		1,000		1,000
Profit		3,500		3,800

The labour force would again work fewer hours (900 instead of 1,200) but would receive £300 more in pay. With the introduction of the scheme, company profits would be £300 lower if demand is only 600 units.

(b) Maximum output = 1,200 hrs ÷ 1½ hrs per unit
= 800 units per month

This is also the maximum demand per month.

	With the incentive scheme	£	£
Sales	(800 × £20)		16,000
Materials etc costs	(800 × £8)	6,400	
Labour costs	(800 × 1½ hrs × £3)	3,600	
Total variable costs			10,000
			6,000
Fixed costs			1,000
Profit			5,000

Employees would receive higher wages, and company profits would be capable of reaching £5,000 per month if maximum demand is achieved.

(c) The particular incentive scheme under review does not benefit the company unless actual output and sales exceed the current maximum levels, that is unless the improved productivity results in improved sales volumes.

6 CORRELATION AND REGRESSION MCQs

(a) D If C = 1,000 + 250P, then fixed costs are £1,000 and variable costs are £250 per unit.

(b) D The correlation coefficient of 0.9 is very close to 1 and so there is a very strong relationship between x and y.

7 SOUTH

(a) Let x = monthly activity level
y = total cost (in £'000)

x	*y*	*xy*	x^2
units	£'000		
300	3.8	1,140	90,000
400	4.0	1,600	160,000
150	3.0	450	22,500
260	3.5	910	67,600
1,110	14.3	4,100	340,100

n = 4

The total cost equation can be calculated using the following equation which is provided in your examination.

$$\text{If } y = a + bx,\quad b = \frac{n\Sigma xy - \Sigma x\Sigma y}{n\Sigma x^2 - (\Sigma x)^2}$$

$$\text{and} \quad a = \frac{\Sigma y}{n} - b\frac{\Sigma x}{n}$$

$$b = \frac{(4 \times 4{,}100) - (1{,}110 \times 14.3)}{(4 \times 340{,}100) - (1{,}110)^2}$$

$$= \frac{16{,}400 - 15{,}873}{1{,}360{,}400 - 1{,}232{,}100}$$

$$= \frac{527}{128{,}300} = 0.0041$$

$$a = \frac{14.3}{4} - 0.0041 \times \frac{1{,}110}{4}$$

$= 3.575 - 1.13775$
$= 2.43725$, say 2.437 (to 3 dp)

Therefore, total cost equation (in £'000) = y

$y = 2.437 + 0.0041x$

where x = the monthly activity level

(Alternatively, total cost equation (in £'000), y, is

$y = 2.437 + 4.1x$.)

(b) (i) Using y (in £'000) = 2.437 + 0.0041x

where x = 200

$y = 2.437 + (200 \times 0.0041)$
$= 2.437 + 0.82$
$= 3.257$

Therefore, at an activity level of 200 units, total cost = £3,257

Since 200 units lies within the range of data used to calculate the total cost equation (150 – 400 units) a fair degree of reliance can be placed on this estimated cost.

(ii) Using y (in £'000) = 2.437 + 0.0041x

where x = 500

$y = 2.437 + (500 \times 0.0041)$
$= 2.437 + 2.05$
$= 4.487$

Therefore, at an activity level of 500 units, total cost = £4,487.

Since 500 units lies outside the range of data used to calculate the total cost equation (150 – 400 units) the total cost calculated is probably not a very reliable estimation.

8 MATERIAL COSTS MCQs

(a) A With LIFO, if newer stocks cost more to buy from suppliers than older stocks, the costs of material issued and used will be higher. It follows that the cost of sales will be higher and the profit lower.

Closing stocks with LIFO will be priced at the purchase price of earlier items that were received into stock. In a period of rising prices, this means that closing stocks will be valued at old, out-of-date and low prices. Therefore the correct answer is A.

If you chose option B you were correct about the profits but your reasoning concerning the stock values was wrong.

(b) D $\text{EOQ} = \sqrt{\dfrac{2 \times £400 \times (250 \times 48)}{£20 \times 10\%}} = 2{,}191$

Therefore the correct answer is D.

If you selected option A you used **weekly** usage in the calculations instead of the annual usage.

If you selected option B you did not take ten per cent of the material cost as the annual stockholding cost.

If you selected option C you omitted the 2.

(c) D The easiest way to solve this question is to draw up a stores ledger control account.

STORES LEDGER CONTROL ACCOUNT

	£		£
Opening stock b/f	18,500	Creditors (returns)	2,300
Creditors/cash (deliveries)	142,000	Overhead account (indirect materials)	25,200
		WIP (balancing figure)	116,900
		Closing stock c/f	16,100
	160,500		160,500

If you selected option C you determined the correct value of the direct materials issued but you **reversed the entries.**

If you selected options A or B you placed the figure for returns on the **wrong side of your account**, and in option A you **reversed the entries** for the issue of direct materials from stores.

9 WIVELSFIELD

(a) New EOQ can be calculated using the following equation which is provided in your examination.

$$EOQ = \sqrt{\frac{2CoD}{CH}}$$

Where Co = £2
D = 15,000 units
CH = 10% × £15 = £1.50 × 0.97 = £1.455

At an order quantity of 200, there is a 3% discount, so CH will be adjusted to equal 97% × £1.50 = £1.455.

$$EOQ = \sqrt{\frac{2 \times £2 \times 15{,}000}{1.455}}$$

= 203 units

Order quantity Q	*Purchase cost* £	*Order costs* £	*Holding costs* £	*Total* £
203 (W1)	218,250	148	148	218,546
500 (W2)	213,750	60	356	214,166
700 (W3)	209,250	44	488	209,782

An order quantity of 700 units gives rise to the lowest total cost and therefore 700 units is the optimal order quantity.

Workings

(1) **Purchase costs** = £15 × 0.97 × 15,000 = £218,250

Order costs = Number of orders × £2

Number of orders = $\frac{15{,}000}{203}$ = 73.89, say 74

∴ order costs = 74 × £2 = £148

Holding costs = Costs of holding average stock

Average stock = $\frac{Q}{2} = \frac{203}{2}$ = 102

∴ Holding costs = 102 × 10% × £15 × 0.97
= £148

(2) **Purchase costs** = £15 × 0.95 × 15,000 = £213,750

Order costs = Number of orders × £2

Number of orders = $\frac{15{,}000}{500}$ = 30

∴ Order costs = 30 × £2 = £60

Holding costs = costs of holding average stock

Average stock = $\frac{Q}{2} = \frac{500}{2}$ = 250

Cost of holding one unit of stock = £15 × 0.95 × 0.1
= £1.425

∴ Holding costs = 250 × £1.425
= £356

(3) **Purchase costs** = £15 × 0.93 × 15,000 = £209,250

Order costs = Number of orders × £2

Number of orders = $\frac{15,000}{700}$ = 21.43, say 22

∴ order costs = 22 × £2 = £44

Holding costs = cost of holding average stock

Average stock = $\frac{Q}{2} = \frac{700}{2}$ = 350

∴ Holding costs = 350 × 93% × £15 × 0.1
= £488

(b) The first discount band of 0-199 units has been excluded because this band is below the current EOQ. The new EOQ of 203 units is subject to a 3% discount and so the total costs of 203,500 and 700 units being ordered were calculated taking into account the discounts that were available at each order level.

10 LABOUR COSTS MCQs

(a) B The only direct costs are the wages paid to direct workers for ordinary time, plus the basic pay for overtime.

£25,185 + £5,440 = £30,625.

If you selected option A you forgot to include the basic pay for overtime of direct workers, which is always classified as a direct labour cost.

If you selected option C you have included overtime premium and shift allowances, which are usually treated as indirect costs. However, if overtime and shiftwork are incurred specifically for a particular cost unit, then they are classified as direct costs of that cost unit. There is no mention of such a situation here.

Option D includes sick pay, which is classified as an indirect labour cost.

(b) B The credit balance on the wages control account indicates that the amount of wages incurred and analysed between direct wages and indirect wages was **higher** than the wages paid through the bank. Therefore there was a £12,000 balance of **wages owing** at the end of February and statement B is not correct. Therefore the correct option is B.

Statement A is correct. £128,400 of wages was paid from the bank account.

Statement C is correct. £79,400 of direct wages was transferred to the work in progress control account.

Statement D is correct. £61,000 of indirect wages was transferred to the production overhead control account.

11 REMUNERATION SCHEMES

(a) (i) **Piecework scheme**

Level of output (units)		80	120	210
Standard minutes produced (× 3)		240	360	630
∴ Piecework value (× £0.1)		£24	£36	£63
∴ Earnings	(note)	£35.20	£36	£63

(*Note*. Earnings are guaranteed at 80% of time-based pay = 80% × 8 hours × £5.5 = £35.20. Since this is greater than the piecework earnings, it will be the amount paid.)

(ii) **Premium bonus system**

Level of output (units)	80	120	210
Standard hours allowed (× 3/60)	4	6	10.5
Actual hours taken	8	8	8
∴ Time saved - hours	-	-	2.5
Premium bonus - 75% of time saved	-	-	1.875
∴ Hours to be paid	8	8	9.875
at £5.5 per hour = earnings	£44	£44	£54.31

(b) **Idle time** occurs when employees cannot get on with their own work, though this is through no fault of their own. Idle time occurs when machines break down and when there is a shortage of work.

Idle time can be measured by calculating an **idle time ratio.**

$$\text{Idle time ratio} = \frac{\text{Idle hours}}{\text{Total hours}} \times 100\%$$

12 OVERHEADS AND ABSORPTION COSTING MCQs

(a) B

$$\text{Overhead absorption rate} = \frac{\text{budgeted overheads}}{\text{budgeted labour hours}} = \frac{£148{,}750}{8{,}500} = £17.50 \text{ per hr}$$

If you selected option A you divided the actual overheads by the budgeted labour hours. Option C is based on the actual overheads and actual labour hours. If you selected option D you divided the budgeted overheads by the actual hours.

(b) D

	£
Overhead absorbed = £17.50 × 7,928 =	138,740
Overhead incurred =	146,200
Under-absorbed overhead =	7,460

If you selected options A or B you calculated the difference between the budgeted and actual overheads and interpreted it as an under or over absorption. If you selected option C you performed the calculations correctly but misinterpreted the result as an over absorption.

13 WARNINGLID

(a)

	Production departments		*Service centres*		
	1	*2*	*Stores*	*Maintenance*	*Total*
	£	£	£	£	£
Rent (W1)	8,850	2,100	600	450	12,000
Heat and light (W2)	4,320	1,200	240	240	6,000
Welfare costs (W3)	1,120	480	240	160	2,000
Supervisors	1,500	1,000	-	-	2,500
	15,790	4,780	1,080	850	22,500

Workings

(1) **Rent**

Rent is allocated on the basis of floor area. Total floor area = 8,000 m^2.

Production department 1 $\frac{5{,}900}{8{,}000} \times £12{,}000 = £8{,}850$

Production department 2 $\frac{1{,}400}{8{,}000} \times £12{,}000 = £2{,}100$

Stores centre $\frac{400}{8{,}000} \times £12{,}000 = £600$

Maintenance centre $\frac{300}{8,000} \times £12,000 = £450$

(2) **Heat and light**

Heat and light costs are allocated on the basis of cubic capacity (total = 25,000 m^3).

Production department 1 $\frac{18,000}{25,000} \times £6,000 = £4,320$

Production department 2 $\frac{5,000}{25,000} \times £6,000 = £1,200$

Stores centre $\frac{1,000}{25,000} \times £6,000 = £240$

Maintenance centre $\frac{1,000}{25,000} \times £6,000 = £240$

(3) **Welfare costs**

Welfare costs are allocated on the basis of number of employees (total = 25).

Production department 1 $\frac{14}{25} \times £2,000 = £1,120$

Production department 2 $\frac{6}{25} \times £2,000 = £480$

Stores centre $\frac{3}{25} \times £2,000 = £240$

Maintenance centre $\frac{2}{25} \times £2,000 = £160$

(b) Reapportionment of overheads using the reciprocal method can be calculated by using algebra.

Let S = total stores service centre overhead for apportionment after it has been apportioned overhead from maintenance centre

M = total of maintenance service centre overhead after it has been apportioned overhead from stores centre

S = 1,080 + 0.05M
M = 850 + 0.1S

∴ S = 1,080 + 0.05 (850 + 0.1S)
= 1,080 + 42.5 + 0.005S
= 1,122.5 + 0.005S

0.995S = 1,122.5

$S = \frac{1,122.5}{0.995}$

S = 1,128

If S = 1,128

M = 850 + (0.1 × 1,128)
= 850 + 112.8
= 962.8
= 963

	Production departments		*Service centres*		
	1	*2*	*Stores*	*Maintenance*	*Total*
	£	£	£	£	£
Overhead costs	15,790	4,780	1,080	850	22,500
Apportion stores total	564	451	(1,128)	113	-
Apportion maintenance total	433	482	48	(963)	-
	16,787	5,713	-	-	22,500

(c) Production department 1 is **labour intensive** and so an overhead rate per labour hour should be calculated.

$$\text{Overhead absorption rate per labour hour} = \frac{\text{Total overheads}}{\text{Total labour hours}}$$

$$= \frac{£16{,}787}{2{,}400}$$

$$= £7$$

Production department 2 is **machine intensive** and so an overhead rate per machine hour should be calculated.

$$\text{Overhead absorption rate per machine hour} = \frac{\text{Total overheads}}{\text{Total machine hours}}$$

$$= \frac{£5{,}713}{4{,}572}$$

$$= £1.25$$

14 MARGINAL AND ABSORPTION COSTING MCQs

(a) C Difference in profit = change in stock level × fixed overhead per unit
= (200 – 250) × (£2.50 × 3)
= £375

The absorption costing profit will be greater because stocks have increased.

If you selected option A you calculated the correct profit difference but the absorption costing profit would be greater because fixed overheads are carried forward in the increasing stock levels.

If you selected option B you multiplied the stock difference by the direct labour-hour rate instead of by the total overhead cost per **unit**, which takes three hours.

If you selected option D you based the profit difference on the closing stock only (250 units × £2.50 × 3).

15 PROFIT DIFFERENCES

(a) **Marginal costing profit statement**

	January - March		*April - June*	
	£'000	£'000	£'000	£'000
Sales (W1)		2,700		4,050
Opening stock (W4)	-		165	
Variable production costs (W2)	1,155		1,650	
Closing stock (W4)	(165)		(330)	
Cost of sales		(990)		(1,485)
		1,710		2,565
Variable selling costs (W5)		(90)		(135)
Contribution		1,620		2,430
Fixed production overhead (per quarter)		(100)		(100)
Fixed selling costs (per quarter)		(20)		(20)
Administration costs (per quarter)		(30)		(30)
Budgeted profit		1,470		2,280

(b) **Absorption costing profit statement**

	January - March		April - June	
	£'000	£'000	£'000	£'000
Sales		2,700.0		4,050.0
Opening stock (W4)		-	177.5	
Production costs (W2)	1,242.5		1,775.0	
Closing stock (W4)	(177.5)		(355.0)	
Cost of sales		1,065.0		1,597.5
		1,635.0		2,452.5
(Under-)/over-absorbed overheads (W6)		(12.5)		25.0
		1,622.5		2,477.5
Variable selling costs (W5)		(90.0)		(135.0)
Fixed selling costs (per quarter)		(20.0)		(20.0)
Administration costs (per quarter)		(30.0)		(30.0)
Budgeted profit		1,482.5		2,292.5

Workings

1 Sales are 60,000 or 90,000 × £45

2 Production costs are calculated as follows.

	Per unit	*70,000 units*	*100,000 units*
	£	£'000	£'000
Direct materials	10.00		
Direct wages	4.00		
Variable overhead	2.50		
Variable production cost	16.50	1,155.00	1,650
Variable production cost	16.50	1,155.00	1,650
Fixed production overhead (W3)	1.25	87.50	125
Total production cost	17.75	1,242.50	1,775

3 Fixed production overhead per unit

$$\frac{\text{Total cost}}{\text{Total absorption basis}} \quad \frac{£400{,}000}{320{,}000 \text{ units}} = £1.25$$

Fixed production overheads are absorbed on a per unit basis in the absence of alternative instructions.

4 Closing stock

January - March	Units	*Marginal costing* £'000	*Absorption costing* £'000
Opening stock	-	-	-
Production (Jan-March)	70,000		
Sales	60,000		
Closing stock - March (W2)	10,000	165	177.5
Production (April-June)	100,000		
	110,000		
Sales	90,000		
Closing stock - June (W2)	20,000	330	355

5 Variable selling costs

	January - March	*April - June*
	£'000	£'000
60,000 × £1.50	90	
90,000 × £1.50		135

6 (Under-)/over-absorbed fixed production overheads

Budgeted production per quarter = 320,000 ÷ 4 = 80,000 units

		£
January - March	(70,000 – 80,000) × £1.25 (W3)	(12,500)
April - June	(100,000 – 80,000) × £1.25 (W3)	25,000

Note. If overheads are underabsorbed, too little overhead is charged to profit and vice versa. The profit statement must be adjusted accordingly. The effect of the adjustment is to make **total** production costs equal whether marginal costing or absorption costing is used.

	Marginal costing			*Absorption costing*	
	£'000	£'000		£'000	£'000
Variable cost	(1,155)	(1,650)	Production cost	(1,242.5)	(1,775.0)
Fixed cost	(100)	(100)	Under-/over-absorbed	(12.5)	25.0
	(1,255)	(1,750)		(1,255.0)	(1,750.0)

16 JOB AND BATCH COSTING MCQ

D

Hours for job 34679	= 400 hours
Production overhead cost	£4,000
∴ Overhead absorption rate (£4,000 ÷ 400)	£10 per direct labour hour
Budgeted direct labour hours	45,000
∴ Total budgeted production overheads	£450,000
Budgeted direct wages cost	£180,000
∴ Absorption rate as % of wages cost	= £450,000/£180,000 × 100%
	= 250%

Cost of job 34679

	£
Direct materials	2,000
Direct labour, including overtime premium *	2,500
Overhead (250% × £2,500)	6,250
Total production cost	10,750

* The overtime premium is a direct labour cost because the overtime was worked specifically for this job.

If you selected option A you got your calculation of the overhead absorption rate 'upside down' and derived a percentage rate of 40 per cent in error. If you selected option B you did not include the overtime premium and the corresponding overhead. If you selected option C you did not include the overtime premium in the direct labour costs.

17 INDRICAR LIMITED

(a)

		Job X123	Job X124	Job X125	Job X126	Job X127
		£	£	£	£	£
Direct material:	to 30.11.X8	1,250	722	-	-	-
	December X8	420	698	1,900	1,221	516
	returns	(120)	-	(70)	(217)	-
	transfers	(100)	-	100	-	-
		1,450	1,420	1,930	1,004	516
Direct labour:	to 30.11.X8	820	600	-	-	-
	December X8	260	390	1,560	755	290
Total direct cost		2,530	2,410	3,490	1,759	806
Factory production overhead (W1)		2,160	1,980	3,120	1,510	580
Total factory production cost		4,690	4,390	6,610	3,269	1,386
Selling, distn and admin cost (20%)		938	878	1,322		
Total cost		5,628	5,268	7,932		

Working

		Job X123	Job X124	Job X125	Job X126	Job X127
		£	£	£	£	£
1	Direct labour cost	1,080	990	1,560	755	290
	Factory production overhead (200%)	2,160	1,980	3,120	1,510	580

(b) **Tutor's hint.** Profits or losses arising on jobs = Amounts invoiced to customers – total cost of job.

	Job X123	*Job X124*	*Job X125*
	£	£	£
Amounts invoiced to customer	6,250	6,000	7,900
Total cost (from (a))	5,628	5,268	7,932
Profit/(loss) on job	622	732	(32)

18 PROCESS COSTING MCQs

(a) D ***Step 1.*** **Determine output and losses**

Input	*Output*	*Total*	*Equivalent units of production* *Process X*		Conversion costs	
Units		Units	Units	%	Units	%
2,000	Finished units	1,600	1,600	100	1,600	100
	Normal loss	200				
	Abnormal loss (balance)	100	100	100	100	100
	Closing stock	100	100	100	50	50
2,000		2,000	1,800		1,750	

Step 2**. Calculate cost per unit of output, losses and WIP**

Input	*Cost*	*Equivalent units*	*Cost per equivalent unit*
	£		£
Process X material (£8,000 – 800)	7,200	1,800	4
Conversion costs	12,250	1,750	7
			11

Step 3. **Calculate total cost of output**

Cost of completed production = £11 × 1,600 litres = £17,600

If you selected option A you included the normal loss in your equivalent units calculation, but these units do not carry any of the process costs. If you selected option B you did not allow for the fact that the work in progress units were incomplete as regards conversion costs. If you selected option C you reduced the process costs by the scrap value of all lost units, instead of the normal loss units only.

(b) C Using the unit rates from answer (a) step 2, we can proceed again to step 3.

Calculate the total cost of work in progress

	Cost element	*Number of equivalent units*	*Cost per equivalent unit*	*Total*
			£	£
Work in progress	Process X material	100	4	400
	Conversion costs	50	7	350
				750

If you selected option A you included the normal loss in your equivalent units calculation. If you selected option B you reduced the process costs by the scrap value of all lost units, instead of the normal loss units only. Option D does not allow for the fact that the work in progress (WIP) is incomplete when calculating the total cost of WIP.

19 PRODUCT XK

(a) The value of goods transferred from Process 1 to Process 2 during period 10 was £9,240.

(b) The value of closing work in progress left in Process 1 at the end of Period 10 was £560.

Workings for parts (a) and (b)

Remember that when closing WIP is partly completed, it is necessary to construct a **statement of equivalent units** in order to apportion costs fairly and proportionately.

STATEMENT OF EQUIVALENT UNITS

Input Units	Output	Total Units	Process 1 material	Labour	Overheads
2,400	Completed production (transfer to Process 2)	2,200	2,200 (100%)	2,200 (100%)	2,200
	Closing work in progress	200	200 (100%)	60 (30%)	60 (30%)
2,400		2,400	2,400	2,260	2,260

STATEMENT OF COST PER EQUIVALENT UNIT

Input	Cost £	Cost £	Equivalent units produced	Cost per unit £
Process 1 materials		5,280	2,400	2.20
Labour	2,260			
Overhead	2,260	4,520	2,260	2.00
		9,800		4.20

STATEMENT OF EVALUATION

Output	Number of equivalent units	Cost per unit	Value £	Value £
Transfers to Process 2	2,200	4.20		9,240
Closing work in progress				
Process 1 materials	200	2.20	440	
Labour and overhead	60	2.00	120	
				560
				9,800

PROCESS 1 ACCOUNT

	Units	£		Units	£
Process 1	2,400	5,280	Transfers to Process 2	2,200	9,240
Labour and overheads		4,520	Closing WIP	200	560
	2,400	9,800		2,400	9,800

(c) STATEMENT OF EQUIVALENT UNITS

Input Units	Output	Total	Materials	Labour and overhead
2,200	Transferred from Process 1	2,200	2,200 (100%)	2,200 (100%)
2,200		2,200	2,200	2,200

NB. No opening or closing WIP in Process 2.

STATEMENT OF COST PER EQUIVALENT UNIT

Input	Cost £	Cost £	Equivalent units produced	Cost per unit
Transfers from Process 1		9,240	2,200	4.20
Added materials		9,460	2,200	4.30
Labour	10,560			
Overhead	7,040	17,600	2,200	8.00
Value of one unit of production =				16.50

Value of goods transferred from Process 2 to finished goods = 2,200 units × £16.50 = £36,300.

20 JOINT PRODUCTS AND BY-PRODUCTS MCQs

(a) C **Net process costs**

	£
Raw materials	90,000
Conversion costs	70,000
Less by-product revenue	(4,000)
Net process costs	156,000

Apportionment of net process costs

		Units	£	*Apportioned costs* £
Product	J	2,500	£156,000 × (2,500/8,000)	48,750
	K	3,500	£156,000 × (3,500/8,000)	68,250
	L	2,000	£156,000 × (2,000/8,000)	39,000
		8,000		156,000

If you selected option A or B you apportioned a share of the process costs to the by-product, and with option B or D you did not deduct the by-product revenue from the process costs.

(b) A *Workings*

	Sales revenue £	
Joint product		
A	720,000	(£36 × 20,000)
B	2,200,000	(£50 × 44,000)
C	1,400,000	(£40 × 35,000)
By-product		
D	80,000	(£4 × 20,000)
Total sales revenues	4,400,000	

Joint costs to be allocated = Total output costs – sales revenue from by-product D

= £4,040,000 – £80,000
= £3,960,000

Costs allocated to joint product B = $\frac{£2,200,000}{£4,400,000}$ × £3,960,000
= £1,980,000

Unit valuation (joint product B) = $\frac{£1,980,000}{£44,000}$
= £45 (to 2 decimal places)

If you selected option B, you forgot to deduct the sales revenue (from by-product D) from the joint costs to be allocated.

If you selected option C, you excluded by-product D from your calculations completely.

If you selected option D, you divided the total sales revenue (instead of the joint costs to be allocated) by the number of units of joint product D.

21 CHEMICALS X, Y AND Z

Initial assumption: prime cost is calculated, for the purposes of absorbing overhead, before the deduction of scrap value.

Common process costs

	£
Direct materials	24,000
Direct labour	48,000
Prime cost	72,000
Factory overheads 120%	86,400
Total production cost	158,400
Less: Scrap proceeds (3,200 litres × 10% × £16.20)	(5,184)
Total common costs	153,216

(a) **Apportioning costs according to sales value**

Chemical	*Output* litres	£ per litre	*Sales value* £		*Total cost* £
X	1,440	100	144,000	(144,000/247,680 × £153,216)	89,079
Y	864	80	69,120	(69,120/247,680 × £153,216)	42,758
Z	576	60	34,560	(34,560/247,680 × £153,216)	21,379
			247,680		153,216

(b) **Apportioning costs according to volume**

Chemical	*Output* litres		*Total cost* £
X	1,440	(1,440/2,880 × £153,216)	76,608
Y	864	(864/2,880 × £153,216)	45,965
Z	576	(576/2,880 × £153,216)	30,643
	2,880		153,216

22 SERVICE COSTING MCQ

C Cost per tonne - kilometre (i) is appropriate for cost control purposes because it **combines** the distance travelled and the load carried, **both of which affect cost.**

The fixed cost per kilometre (ii) is not particularly useful for control purposes because it **varies with the number of kilometres travelled.**

The maintenance cost of each vehicle per kilometre (iii) can be useful for control purposes because it **focuses on a particular aspect** of the cost of operating each vehicle. Therefore the correct answer is C.

23 HAPPY RETURNS LTD

(a) **Calculation of tonne km**

Journey	*Tonnes*	*Km*	*Tonne km*
1	34	180	6,120
2	28	265	7,420
3	40	390	15,600
4	32	115	3,680
5	26	220	5,720
6	40	480	19,200
7	29	90	2,610
8	26	100	2,600
9	25	135	3,375
	280	1,975	66,325

(b) **Distance travelled 1,975 × 2 = 3,950 km**

Calculation of total variable costs

Variable costs	£	£
Petrol (£0.50 × 3,950)		1,975
Repairs (£0.30 × 3,950)		1,185
Deprecation (£1.00 × 3,950)		3,950
Loading costs (£6.00 × 280)		1,680
Total variable costs		8,790

(c) **Calculation of total fixed costs**

Fixed costs		
Deprecation (£50 × 3)	150	
Drivers' wages (£300 × 3)	900	
Supervision and general expenses	550	
Total fixed costs		1,600

(d) **Average cost per tonne km** = $\frac{\text{Total costs}}{\text{Total tonne - kilometres}}$

$= \frac{10,390}{66,325}$

= £0.1567 per tonne km

24 BREAKEVEN ANALYSIS MCQs

(a) A Breakeven point = $\frac{\text{Fixed costs}}{\text{Contribution per unit}} = \frac{£96,000}{£(12-8)} =$ 24,000 units

Budgeted sales	30,000 units
Margin of safety	6,000 units

Expressed % of budget = $\frac{6,000}{30,000} \times 100\% = 20\%$

If you selected option B you calculated the correct margin of safety in units, but you then expressed this as a percentage of the breakeven point. If you selected option C you divided the fixed cost by the selling price to determine the breakeven point, but the selling price also has to cover the variable cost. You should have been able to eliminate option D; the margin of safety expressed as a percentage must always be less than 100 per cent.

(b) C Contribution at level of activity x = sales value less variable costs, which is indicated by distance C. Distance A indicates the profit at activity x, B indicates the fixed costs and D indicates the margin of safety in terms of sales value.

25 BUILDING COMPANY

(a)

	Units	Profit £'000
High - March	30	250
Low - June	16	40
	14	210
Variable cost per unit (£210,000/14)		£15,000

	£'000
Taking March as an example	
Sales (30 × £30,000)	900
Profit	250
Total costs	650
Variable costs (30 × £15,000)	450
Fixed costs	200

Fixed costs for the six months = 6 × £200,000 = £1,200,000.

(b)

Per unit	£'000
Selling price	30
Variable cost	15
Contribution	15

Breakeven point is where total contribution = fixed costs. Breakeven point is therefore where £15,000N – £1,200,000, where N is the breakeven quantity of units.

N = £(1,200,000/15,000) = 80 units

Breakeven sales revenue = 80 × £30,000 = £2,400,000

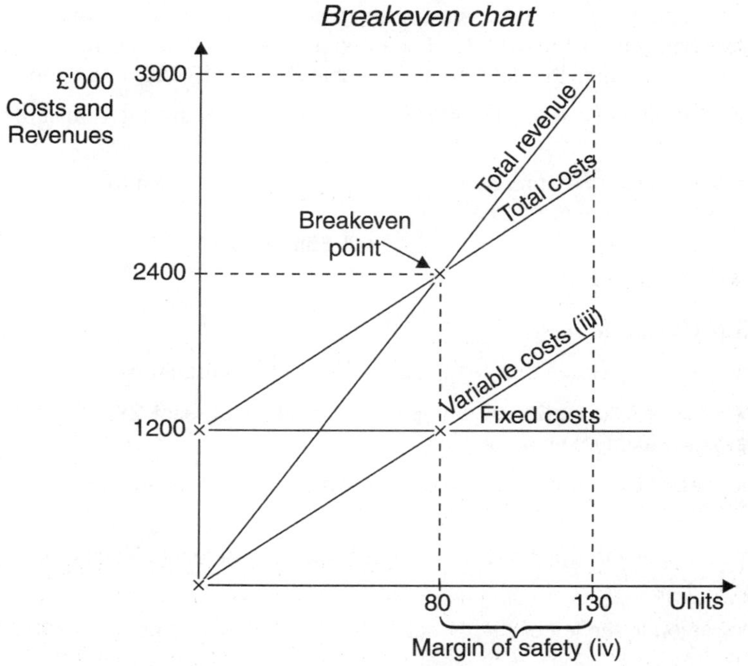

Note that at 80 units, the variable cost is 80 × £15,000 = £1,200,000.

26 RELEVANT COSTING AND DECISION MAKING MCQs

(a) B £5,000 has been spent on market research already and is therefore a **sunk cost** and irrelevant to the decision. The further £2,000 will only be spent if Sue continues with the project, therefore it is an **incremental (relevant) cost** of the decision to go ahead.

The cost is not an opportunity cost (option D) because Sue has not forgone an alternative use for the resources.

(b) B The relevant cost of the material in stock is the **opportunity cost of £2 per litre**, because the material would be sold if the order was rejected. The remainder of the required material **must be purchased at £10 per litre**.

Relevant cost is therefore (85 × £2)+ (15 × £10) = £320.

If you selected option A you valued all of the 100 litres required at £2 per litre, but this opportunity cost only applies to the 85 litres in stock. Option C values the stock items at their original cost of £8 per litre, but this is a **sunk cost** which is not relevant to decisions about the future use of the material. Option D values all the material at replacement cost, but the items in stock will not be replaced by ABC Limited.

27 ABC LTD

(a)

	Product A	*Product B*	*Product C*	*Total*
Machine hours required per unit	6	4	7	
Maximum demand (units)	3,000	2,500	5,000	
Total machine hours required	18,000	10,000	35,000	63,000
Machine hours available				50,000
Deficiency in machine hours for next period				13,000

(b)

	Product A	*Product B*	*Product C*
	£ per unit	£ per unit	£ per unit
External purchase price	175	140	200
Variable cost of internal manufacture	154	112	178
Saving through internal manufacture	21	28	22
Machine hours per unit	6	4	7
Saving per machine hour	£3.50	£7.00	£3.14
Priority ranking for internal manufacture	2	1	3

(c) Since all products can be sold for more than their bought-in cost, unsatisfied demand should be met through external purchases. Purchases should be made in the reverse order of the above ranking shown in (b), until the deficiency in machine hours (13,000) has been covered.

Some units of Product C should therefore be purchased from the external supplier.

Number of units of C to be purchased $= \dfrac{13{,}000 \text{ hours}}{7}$ (from (a))

= **1,858 units**

28 LINEAR PROGRAMMING MCQs

(a) D This inequality states that X must be at most 2Y, as required.

The inequality in **option A** states that X must be at least 2Y, whereas 2Y is meant to be the very maximum value of X.

The inequality in **option B** states that Y must be at most 2X, whereas X is meant to be at most 2Y.

The inequality in **option C** states that Y must be at least 2X, whereas X is meant to be at most 2Y.

(b) D The region to the left of X = 41 satisfies $X \leq 41$ while that above Y = 19 satisfies $Y \geq 19$.

Option A is incorrect because the region you have described is bounded by $X \leq 41$, but $Y \leq 19$ instead of $Y \geq 19$.

Option B is incorrect because the region you have described is bounded by $X \geq 41$ and $Y \leq 19$ instead of by $X \leq 41$ and $Y \geq 19$.

Option C is incorrect because the region you have described is bounded by $Y \geq 19$ but by $X \geq 41$ instead of $X \leq 41$.

29 CUCKFIELD

(a) Let the number of units of product D made be D
Let the number of units of product H made be H

The constraints are therefore as follows.

Material A	(1) $3D + 2H \leq 3{,}000$	
Material N	(2) $0.5D + 2H \leq 1{,}000$	
Semi-skilled labour	(3) $1.5D + 1.5H \leq 1{,}800$	(W1)
Skilled labour	(4) $D + 1.4H \geq 700$	(W2)

Workings

(1) Semi-skilled workers can only work a 40-hour week. There are 45 semi-skilled workers. 45 × 40 hours = 1,800 hours.

(2) Skilled labour workers are guaranteed a 35-hour week. Therefore, the number of skilled hours worked must be **greater than or equal to** 700 (20 × 35 hours).

(b)

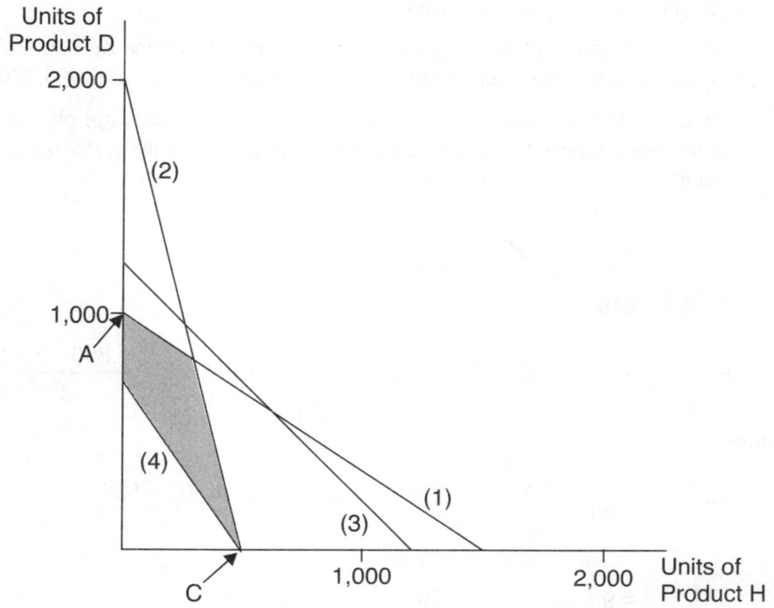

The optimal solution will be either A, B or C as shown on the graph above.

Workings

(1) $3D + 2H \leq 3{,}000$

If D = 0, H = 1,500	(3,000/2)
If H = 0, D = 1,000	(3,000/3)

(2) $0.5D + 2H \leq 1{,}000$

If D = 0, H = 500	(1,000/2)
If H = 0, D = 2,000	(1,000/0.5)

(3) $1.5D + 1.5H \leq 1{,}800$

If D = 0, H = 1,200	(1,800/1.5)
If H = 0, D = 1,200	(1,800/1.5)

(4) $D + 1.4H \geq 700$

If D = 0, H = 500	(700/1.4)
If H = 0, D = 700	(700/1)

30 PRICING MCQs

(a) C Profit is maximised when

$$\begin{aligned} \text{marginal cost} &= \text{marginal revenue} \\ 9 &= 25 - (0.4 \times \text{quantity}) \\ (0.4 \times \text{quantity}) &= 16 \\ \text{quantity} &= 40 \end{aligned}$$

Substituting in the equation for price:

$$\begin{aligned} \text{price} &= 25 - (0.2 \times 40) \\ &= £17.00 \end{aligned}$$

If you selected option A or B you used only the variable overhead and the direct cost respectively as the marginal cost per unit.

(b) A

$$\% \text{ change in demand} = \frac{65}{600} \times 100\% = 10.8333\%$$

$$\% \text{ change in price} = \frac{10}{150} \times 100\% = 6.6667\%$$

$$\text{Price elasticity of demand} = \frac{10.8333}{6.6667} = 1.625 \text{ (to 3dp)}$$

Option A is therefore correct.

If you chose option B, you mixed up the denominator and the numerator in the price elasticity of demand equation.

If you selected option C, you based the changes in price and demand on the final values of £1.60 and 535,000 instead of the initial values of £1.50 and 600,000.

If you selected option D, you have rounded the percentage changes to one decimal place only (and cannot therefore calculate the price elasticity of demand correct to three decimal places).

(c) D $a = £30 + \frac{100}{50} \times £3$

$= £36$

$P = 36 - \frac{3Q}{50}$ or $Q = \frac{1{,}800 - 50P}{3}$

Check

$27 = 36 - \frac{3Q}{50}$ $150 = \frac{1{,}800 - 50P}{3}$

$\frac{3Q}{50} = 9$ $50P = 1{,}800 - 450$

$Q = 150$ $P = 27$

Alternative approach

$P_1 = £30,\ Q_1 = 100$

$P_2 = £27,\ Q_2 = 150$

$b = \frac{\Delta P}{\Delta Q} = \frac{30 - 27}{100 - 150} = \frac{3}{-50}$

$a = P - bQ$

$a = 30 - (\frac{-3 \times 100}{50})$

$a = 30 + 6$

$a = 36$

∴ An expression for the demand curve is $P = 36 - \frac{3Q}{50}$ or $Q = \frac{1{,}800 - 50P}{3}$

(d) B

Marginal cost-plus selling price = 125% × (£34 + £26)
= 125% × £60
= £75

Full cost-plus selling price = 125% × £74
= £92.50

If you selected option A you confused the two different pricing methods. If you selected options C or D you used a mark up of 20% instead of 25%.

31 DEMAND, PRICE, REVENUE AND COSTS

(a) $P = a - \frac{bQ}{\Delta Q}$

$a = £48 + \frac{70}{-30} \times -£30$

$= 118$

$P = 118 - \frac{30X}{30}$

$P = 118 - X$

Alternative approach

$P = a + bQ$

where $b = \dfrac{\Delta P}{\Delta Q}$

$b = \dfrac{48-78}{70-40} = \dfrac{-30}{30} = -1$

$\therefore$ $a = P - bX$

If P = 48, b = –1 and Q = 70, then

$a = 48 - (-1 \times 70)$

$= 48 + 70$

$= 118$

$\therefore$ The demand function is $\underline{\underline{P = 118 - X}}$

(b) Revenue (R) $= \text{price} \times \text{quantity sold}$
$= PX$
$= (118 - X)X$
$= 118X - X^2$

(c) Total costs = fixed costs + variable costs
$= 1{,}710 + 9X$

32 STANDARD COSTING MCQs

(a) D Performance standards would be taken into account when estimating **material usage**, they would not have a direct effect on material price. Therefore the correct answer is D.

All of the other factors would be used to estimate standard material prices for a forthcoming period.

(b) D Required liquid input = 2 litres × $\dfrac{100}{70}$ = 2.86 litres

Standard cost of liquid input = 2.86 × £1.20 = £3.43 (to the nearest penny)

If you selected option A you made no allowance for spillage and evaporation. Option B is the figure for the quantity of material input, not its cost. If you selected option C you simply added an extra 30 per cent to the finished volume. However, the wastage is 30 per cent of the liquid **input**, not 30 per cent of output.

33 DOODLE LTD

Workings

The **budgeted (planned) direct labour hours** = 11,400 × (40 + 36) = 866,400 direct labour hours.

The **fixed production overhead absorption rate** = £1.25 per hour (£1,083,000 ÷ 866,400 hours).

The **variable production overhead rate** (both for costs incurred and absorbed) is:

department P : 75 pence per hour
department Q : 50 pence per hour

Administration overhead = £125,400 ÷ 11,400 = £11 per unit

Marketing overhead = £285,000 ÷ 11,400 = £25 per unit

STANDARD COST SHEET - THE SQUIGGLE

			£	£
		Direct materials: 30 metres at £6.10		183
		Direct wages		
		Department P: 40 hours at £2.20	88	
		Department Q: 36 hours at £2.50	90	
				178
(a)	(i)	Standard total direct cost		361
		Variable production overhead		
		Department P: 40 hours at £0.75	30	
		Department Q: 36 hours at £0.50	18	
				48
	(ii)	Standard variable production cost		409
		Fixed production overhead: 76 hours at £1.25		95
	(iii)	Standard production cost		504
		Administration overhead		11
		Marketing overhead		25
	(iv)	Standard cost of sale		540
		Standard profit (10% of sales price)		60
(b)		Standard sales price		600

34 BASIC VARIANCE ANALYSIS MCQs

(a) B

	£
Material price variance	
5,000 litres did cost	16,000
But should have cost (× £3)	15,000
	1,000 (A)
Material usage variance	
1,270 units did use	5,000 litres
But should have used (× 4 litres)	5,080 litres
Usage variance in litres	80 (F)
× standard cost per litre	£3
	240 (F)

If you selected options A or C you calculated the money values of the variances correctly but misinterpreted their direction.

If you selected option D you valued the usage variance in litres at the actual cost per litre instead of the standard cost per litre.

(b) B

	£
1,660 hours of variable production overhead should cost (× £1.70)	2,822
But did cost	2,950
	128 (A)

If you selected option A you based your expenditure allowance on all of the labour hours worked. However, it is usually assumed that **variable overheads are incurred during active working hours**, but are not incurred during idle time.

If you selected option C you calculated the correct money value of the variance but you misinterpreted its direction.

Option D is the variable production overhead total variance.

(c) B

400 units of Product B should take (× 4 hours)	1,600 hours
But did take (active hours)	1,660 hours
Efficiency variance in hours	60 hours (A)
× standard rate per hour	× £1.70
	102 (A)

If you selected option A you calculated the correct money value of the variance but you misinterpreted its direction.

If you selected option C you valued the efficiency variance in hours at the actual variable production overhead rate per hour. Option D bases the calculation on all of the hours worked, instead of only the **active hours**.

35 BRAIN LTD

(a) **Price variance - A**

	£
7,800 kgs should have cost (× £20)	156,000
but did cost	159,900
Price variance	3,900 (A)

Usage variance - A

800 units should have used (× 10 kgs)	8,000 kgs
but did use	7,800 kgs
Usage variance in kgs	200 kgs (F)
× standard cost per kilogram	× £20
Usage variance in £	£4,000 (F)

Price variance - B

	£
4,300 litres should have cost (× £6)	25,800
but did cost	23,650
Price variance	2,150 (F)

Usage variance - B

800 units should have used (× 5 l)	4,000 l
but did use	4,300 l
Usage variance in litres	300 (A)
× standard cost per litre	× £6
Usage variance in £	£1,800 (A)

(b) **Labour rate variance**

	£
4,200 hours should have cost (× £6)	25,200
but did cost	24,150
Rate variance	1,050 (F)

Labour efficiency variance

800 units should have taken (× 5 hrs)	4,000 hrs
but did take	4,200 hrs
Efficiency variance in hours	200 hrs (A)
× standard rate per hour	× £6
Efficiency variance in £	£1,200 (A)

(c) **Fixed overhead expenditure variance**

	£
Budgeted expenditure (£50 × 900)	45,000
Actual expenditure	47,000
Expenditure variance	2,000 (A)

Fixed overhead volume variance

	£
Budgeted production at standard rate (900 × £50)	45,000
Actual production at standard rate (800 × £50)	40,000
Volume variance	5,000 (A)

Fixed overhead volume efficiency variance

	£
800 units should have taken (× 5 hrs)	4,000 hrs
but did take	4,200 hrs
Volume efficiency variance in hours	200 hrs
× standard absorption rate per hour	× £10
Volume efficiency variance	£2,000 (A)

Fixed overhead volume capacity variance

Budgeted hours	4,500 hrs
Actual hours	4,200 hrs
Volume capacity variance in hours	300 hrs (A)
× standard absorption rate per hour (£50 ÷ 5)	× £10
	£3,000 (A)

36 FURTHER VARIANCE ANALYSIS MCQs

(a) B

	£
Revenue from 2,550 units should have been (× £27)	68,850
but was	67,320
Sales price variance	1,530 (A)

Actual sales	2,550 units
Budgeted sales	2,400 units
Variance in units	150 units (F)
x standard profit per unit (£(27 – 12))	× £6
Sales volume variance in £	£900 (F)

If you selected option A, C or D, you calculated the monetary values of the variances correctly, but misinterpreted their direction.

(b) C Statement (i) is not correct. Fixed overhead is not absorbed into production costs in a marginal costing system.

Statement (ii) is correct. Sales volume variances are calculated using the standard contribution per unit (and not the standard profit per unit which is used in standard absorption costing systems).

Statement (iii) is correct. As stated above, fixed overhead is not absorbed into production costs in a marginal costing system.

Index

Note: **Key Terms** and their page references are given in **bold**.

REVIEW FORM & FREE PRIZE DRAW

All original review forms from the entire BPP range, completed with genuine comments, will be entered into a draw on 31 January 2005 and 31 July 2005. The names on the first four forms picked out will be sent a cheque for £50.

Name: ______________________ **Address:** ______________________

____

How have you used this Text?
(Tick one box only)

- ☐ Home study (book only)
- ☐ On a course: college ______________
- ☐ With 'correspondence' package
- ☐ Other ______________

Why did you decide to purchase this Text?
(Tick one box only)

- ☐ Have used complementary Kit
- ☐ Have used BPP Texts in the past
- ☐ Recommendation by friend/colleague
- ☐ Recommendation by a lecturer at college
- ☐ Saw advertising
- ☐ Other ______________

During the past six months do you recall seeing/receiving any of the following?
(Tick as many boxes as are relevant)

- ☐ Our advertisement in *ACCA Student Accountant*
- ☐ Our advertisement in *Pass*
- ☐ Our advertisement in *PQ*
- ☐ Our brochure with a letter through the post

Which (if any) aspects of our advertising do you find useful?
(Tick as many boxes as are relevant)

- ☐ Prices and publication dates of new editions
- ☐ Information on Text content
- ☐ Facility to order books off-the-page
- ☐ None of the above

Which BPP products have you used?

Text	☑	**Success CD**	☐	**i-Learn**	☐
Kit	☐	**Success Tape**	☐	**i-Pass**	☐
Passcard	☐	**Big Picture Poster**	☐	**Virtual Campus**	☐

Your ratings, comments and suggestions would be appreciated on the following areas of this Text.

	Very useful	*Useful*	*Not useful*
Introductory section (Key study steps, personal study)	☐	☐	☐
Chapter introductions	☐	☐	☐
Key terms	☐	☐	☐
Quality of explanations	☐	☐	☐
Case examples and other examples	☐	☐	☐
Questions and answers in each chapter	☐	☐	☐
Chapter roundups	☐	☐	☐
Quick quizzes	☐	☐	☐
Exam focus points	☐	☐	☐
Question bank	☐	☐	☐
Answer bank	☐	☐	☐
List of key terms and index	☐	☐	☐
Icons	☐	☐	☐

	Excellent	*Good*	*Adequate*	*Poor*
Overall opinion of this Text	☐	☐	☐	☐

Do you intend to continue using BPP Products? ☐ Yes ☐ No

Please note any further comments and suggestions/errors on the reverse of this page. The BPP author of this edition can be e-mailed at: lynnwatkins@bpp.com

Please return to: Catherine Watton, ACCA Range Manager, BPP Professional Education, FREEPOST, London, W12 8BR

REVIEW FORM & FREE PRIZE DRAW (continued)

TELL US WHAT YOU THINK

Because the following specific areas of the text contain new material and cover highly examinable topics etc, your comments on their usefulness are particularly welcome.

- Absorption and marginal costing (Chapters 8 and 9)
- Process costing (Chapter 11)
- Standard costing (Chapter 18)
- Variance analysis (Chapters 19 and 20)

Please note any further comments and suggestions/errors below.

FREE PRIZE DRAW RULES

1 Closing date for 31 January 2005 draw is 31 December 2004. Closing date for 31 July 2005 draw is 30 June 2005.

2 No purchase necessary. Entry forms are available upon request from BPP Professional Education. No more than one entry per title, per person. Draw restricted to persons aged 16 and over.

3 Winners will be notified by post and receive their cheques not later than 6 weeks after the draw date.

4 The decision of the promoter in all matters is final and binding. No correspondence will be entered into.

See overleaf for information on other
BPP products and how to order

ACCA Order

To BPP Professional Education, Aldine Place, London W12 8AW
Tel: 020 8740 2211 Fax: 020 8740 1184
email: publishing@bpp.com website: www.bpp.com
Order online www.bpp.com

Mr/Mrs/Ms (Full name) ______

Daytime delivery address ______

Postcode ______

Daytime Tel ______ Date of exam (month/year) ______ Scots law variant Y / N

	6/04 Texts	1/04 Kits	1/04 Passcards	***Success CDs	Big Picture Posters	8/04 i-Learn	8/04 i-Pass	Virtual Campus
PART 1								
1.1 Preparing Financial Statements	£24.95	£10.95	£6.95	£14.95	£6.95	£34.95	£24.95	£90
1.2 Financial Information for Management	£24.95	£10.95	£6.95	£14.95	£6.95	£34.95	£24.95	£90
1.3 Managing People	£24.95	£10.95	£6.95	£14.95	£6.95	£34.95	£24.95	£90
PART 2								
2.1 Information Systems	£24.95	£10.95	£6.95	£14.95	£6.95	£34.95	£24.95	£90
2.2 Corporate and Business Law **	£24.95	£10.95	£6.95	£14.95	£6.95	£34.95	£24.95	£90
2.3 Business Taxation FA2003 (12/04 exams)	£20.95	£10.95	£6.95	£14.95	£6.95	£34.95	£24.95	£90
2.3 Business Taxation FA2004 (**8/04** for 6/05 exams)†	£24.95			£14.95	£6.95			£90
2.4 Financial Management and Control	£24.95	£10.95	£6.95	£14.95	£6.95	£34.95	£24.95	£90
2.5 Financial Reporting (7/04)	£24.95	£10.95	£6.95	£14.95	£6.95	£34.95	£24.95	£90
2.6 Audit and Internal Review (12/04 exams)	£24.95	£10.95	£6.95	£14.95	£6.95	£34.95	£24.95	£90
2.6 Audit and Internal Review (**9/04** for 6/05 exams)†	£24.95			£14.95	£6.95			£90
PART 3								
3.1 Audit and Assurance Services	£24.95	£10.95	£6.95	£14.95	£6.95		£24.95	
3.2 Advanced Taxation FA2003 (12/04 exams)	£20.95	£10.95	£6.95	£14.95	£6.95		£24.95	
3.2 Advanced Taxation FA2004 (**9/04** for 6/05 exams)†	£24.95			£14.95	£6.95			
3.3 Performance Management	£24.95	£10.95	£6.95	£14.95	£6.95		£24.95	
3.4 Business Information Management	£24.95	£10.95	£6.95	£14.95	£6.95		£24.95	
3.5 Strategic Business Planning and Development	£24.95	£10.95	£6.95	£14.95	£6.95		£24.95	
3.6 Advanced Corporate Reporting (7/04)	£24.95	£10.95	£6.95	£14.95	£6.95		£24.95	
3.7 Strategic Financial Management	£24.95	£10.95	£6.95	£14.95	£6.95		£24.95	
INTERNATIONAL STREAM								
1.1 Preparing Financial Statements	£24.95	£10.95	£6.95			£34.95	£24.95	
2.2 Corporate and Business Law	£24.95	£10.95	£6.95					
2.5 Financial Reporting	£24.95	£10.95	£6.95			£34.95	£24.95	
2.6 Audit and Internal Review	£24.95	£10.95	£6.95			£34.95	£24.95	
3.1 Audit and Assurance Services	£24.95	£10.95	£6.95					
3.6 Advanced Corporate Reporting	£24.95	£10.95	£6.95					
Success in Your Research and Analysis Project - Tutorial Text (10/04)	£24.95							
Learning to Learn (7/02)	£9.95							

SUBTOTAL £

Occasionally we may wish to email you relevant offers and information about courses and products.
Please tick to opt into this service.

POSTAGE & PACKING

Study Texts

	First	Each extra	Online	
UK	£5.00	£2.00	£2.00	£
Europe*	£6.00	£4.00	£4.00	£
Rest of world	£20.00	£10.00	£10.00	£

Kits

	First	Each extra	Online	
UK	£5.00	£2.00	£2.00	£
Europe*	£6.00	£4.00	£4.00	£
Rest of world	£20.00	£10.00	£10.00	£

Passcards/Success Tapes/CDs

	First	Each extra	Online	
UK	£2.00	£1.00	£1.00	£
Europe*	£3.00	£2.00	£2.00	£
Rest of world	£8.00	£8.00	£8.00	£

Grand Total (incl. Postage)

I enclose a cheque for £
(Cheques to *BPP Professional Education*)

Or charge to Visa/Mastercard/Switch

Card Number

Expiry date ______ Start Date ______

Issue Number (Switch Only) ______

Signature ______

We aim to deliver to all UK addresses inside 5 working days; a signature will be required. Orders to all EU addresses should be delivered within 6 working days. All other orders to overseas addresses should be delivered within 8 working days. * Europe includes the Republic of Ireland and the Channel Islands.† **For 6/05 exam, New edition Kit, Passcard, i-Learn and i-Pass available 2005 .** ** For Scots law variant students, a free **Scots Law Supplement** is available with the 2.2 Text. Please indicate in the name and address section if this applies to you. ***Alternatively, Success Tapes are available for the same papers, all £12.95.